Contents

P9-DXK-473

The 4-wheel drive Bronco II

About this manual

Its purpose

The purpose of this manual is to help you get the best value from your vehicle. It can do so in several ways. It can help you decide what work must be done, even if you choose to have it done by a dealer service department or a repair shop; it provides information and procedures for routine maintenance and servicing; and it offers diagnostic and repair procedures to follow when trouble occurs.

It is hoped that you will use the manual to tackle the work yourself. For many simpler jobs, doing it yourself may be quicker than arranging an appointment to get the vehicle into a shop and making the trips to leave it and pick it up. More importantly, a lot of money can be saved by avoiding the expense the shop must pass on to you to cover its labor and overhead costs. An added benefit is the sense of satisfaction and accomplishment that you feel after having done the job yourself.

Using the manual

The manual is divided into Chapters. Each Chapter is divided into numbered Sections, which are headed in bold type between horizontal lines. Each Section consists of consecutively numbered paragraphs.

At the beginning of each numbered section you will be referred to any illustrations which apply to the procedures in that section. The reference numbers used in illustration captions pinpoint the pertinent Section and the Step within that section. That is, illustration 3.2 means the illustration refers to Section 3 and Step (or paragraph) 2 within that Section.

Procedures, once described in the text, are not normally repeated. When it is necessary to refer to another Chapter, the reference will be given as Chapter and Section number i.e. Chapter 1/16). Cross references given without use of the word "Chapter" apply to Sections and/or paragraphs in the same Chapter. For example, "see Section 8" means in the same Chapter.

Reference to the left or right side of the vehicle is based on the assumption that one is sitting in the driver's seat, facing forward.

Even though extreme care has been taken during the preparation of this manual, neither the publisher nor the author can accept responsibility for any errors in, or omissions from, the information given.

NOTE

A **Note** provides information necessary to properly complete a procedure or information which will make the steps to be followed easier to understand.

CAUTION

A **Caution** indicates a special procedure or special steps which must be taken in the course of completing the procedure in which the **Caution** is found which are necessary to avoid damage to the assembly being worked on.

WARNING

A **Warning** indicates a special procedure or special steps which must be taken in the course of completing the procedure in which the **Warning** is found which are necessary to avoid injury to the person performing the procedure.

Introduction to the Ford Ranger and Bronco II

The Ford Ranger and Bronco II models are available in a variety of trim options.

Engine options include the 2.0L and 2.3L inline four cylinder engines and the 2.8L and 2.9L V6 engines.

Chassis layout is conventional with the engine mounted at the front and the power being transmitted through either a manual or automatic transmission to a driveshaft and solid rear axle on 4x2 models. On 4x4 models a transfer case transmits power to the front axle by way of a driveshaft. Transmissions used are a four speed manual, four speed manual with overdrive, three speed automatic and three speed automatic with overdrive.

The two wheel drive vehicles employ twin I-beam front suspension with coil springs and radius arms. The four wheel drive vehicles employ a similar independent front suspension system composed of a two-piece front drive axle assembly, coil springs and radius arms. Both types use semi-elliptical leaf springs at the rear.

All vehicles are equipped with front disc and rear drum brakes, with vacuum assistance available as an option.

The 2-wheel drive Ranger pick-up

Vehicle identification numbers

Modifications are a continuing and unpublicized process in vehicle manufacturing. Since spare parts manuals and lists are compiled on a numerical basis, the individual vehicle numbers are essential to correctly identify the component required.

Vehicle identification number (VIN)

This very important identification number is located on a plate attached to the top left corner of the dashboard of the vehicle. The VIN also appears on the Vehicle Certificate of Title and Registration. It contains valuable information such as where and when the vehicle was manufactured, the model year and the body style.

Truck Safety Compliance Certification Label

This metal plate is located on the driver's door lock pillar. Like the VIN, it contains valuable information concerning the production of the vehicle as well as information about the way in which the vehicle is equipped. This plate is especially useful for matching the color and type of paint during repair work.

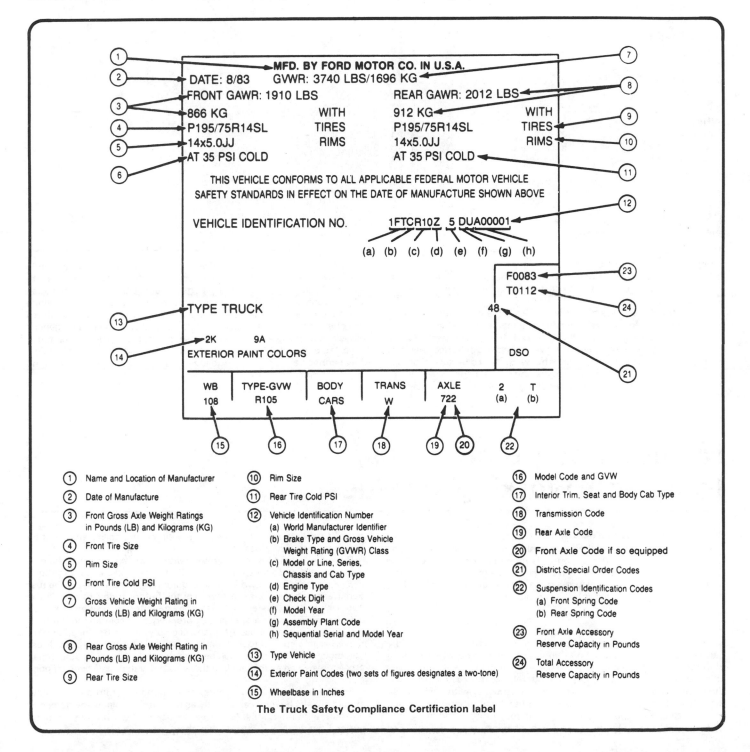

① Name and Location of Manufacturer	⑩ Rim Size
② Date of Manufacture	⑪ Rear Tire Cold PSI
③ Front Gross Axle Weight Ratings in Pounds (LB) and Kilograms (KG)	⑫ Vehicle Identification Number
④ Front Tire Size	(a) World Manufacturer Identifier
⑤ Rim Size	(b) Brake Type and Gross Vehicle Weight Rating (GVWR) Class
⑥ Front Tire Cold PSI	(c) Model or Line, Series, Chassis and Cab Type
⑦ Gross Vehicle Weight Rating in Pounds (LB) and Kilograms (KG)	(d) Engine Type
	(e) Check Digit
⑧ Rear Gross Axle Weight Rating in Pounds (LB) and Kilograms (KG)	(f) Model Year
	(g) Assembly Plant Code
⑨ Rear Tire Size	(h) Sequential Serial and Model Year

⑯ Model Code and GVW
⑰ Interior Trim, Seat and Body Cab Type
⑱ Transmission Code
⑲ Rear Axle Code
⑳ Front Axle Code if so equipped
㉑ District Special Order Codes
㉒ Suspension Identification Codes
  (a) Front Spring Code
  (b) Rear Spring Code
㉓ Front Axle Accessory Reserve Capacity in Pounds
㉔ Total Accessory Reserve Capacity in Pounds

⑬ Type Vehicle
⑭ Exterior Paint Codes (two sets of figures designates a two-tone)
⑮ Wheelbase in Inches

The Truck Safety Compliance Certification label

General dimensions

Overall length
Bronco II . . . . 158.4 in
Ranger (SWB) . . . . 175.6 in
Ranger (LW) . . . . 187.6 in

Overall width
Bronco II . . . . 68.0 in
Ranger . . . . 66.9 in

Overall height
Bronco II . . . . 69.0 in
Ranger . . . . 64.0 in

Wheelbase
Bronco II . . . . 94.0 in
Ranger (SWB) . . . . 107.9 in
Ranger (LWB) . . . . 113.9 in

Buying parts

Replacement parts are available from many sources, which generally fall into one of two categories — authorized dealer parts departments and independent retail auto parts stores. Our advice concerning these parts is as follows:

Authorized dealer parts department: This is the best source for parts which are unique to your vehicle and not generally available elsewhere such as major engine parts, transaxle parts, trim pieces, etc. It is also the only place you should buy parts if your vehicle is still under warranty, as non-factory parts may invalidate the warranty. To be sure of obtaining the correct parts, have your engine and chassis numbers available and, if possible, take the old parts along for positive identification.

Retail auto parts stores: Good auto parts stores will stock frequently needed components which wear out relatively fast such as clutch components, exhaust systems, brake parts, tune-up parts, etc. These stores often supply new or reconditioned parts on an exchange basis, which can save a considerable amount of money. Discount auto parts stores are often very good places to buy materials and parts needed for general vehicle maintenance such as oil, grease, filters, spark plugs, belts, touch up paint, bulbs, etc. They also usually sell tools and general accessories, have convenient hours, charge lower prices, and can often be found not far from your home.

Maintenance techniques, tools and working facilities

Maintenance techniques

There are a number of techniques involved in maintenance and repair that will be referred to throughout this manual. Application of these techniques will enable the home mechanic to be more efficient, better organized and capable of performing the various tasks properly, which will ensure that the repair job is thorough and complete.

Fasteners

Fasteners are nuts, bolts, studs and screws used to hold two or more parts together. There are a few things to keep in mind when working with fasteners. Almost all of them use a locking device of some type, either a lockwasher, locknut, locking tab or thread adhesive. All threaded fasteners should be clean and straight, with undamaged threads and undamaged corners on the hex head where the wrench fits. Develop the habit of replacing all damaged nuts and bolts with new ones. Special locknuts with nylon or fiber inserts can only be used

once. If they are removed, they lose their locking ability and must be replaced with new ones.

Rusted nuts and bolts should be treated with a penetrating fluid to ease removal and prevent breakage. Some mechanics use turpentine in a spout-type oil can, which works quite well. After applying the rust penetrant, let it work for a few minutes before trying to loosen the nut or bolt. Badly rusted fasteners may have to be chiseled or sawed off or removed with a special nut breaker, available at tool stores.

If a bolt or stud breaks off in an assembly, it can be drilled and removed with a special tool commonly available for this purpose. Most automotive machine shops can perform this task, as well as other repair procedures, such as the repair of threaded holes that have been stripped out.

Flat washers and lockwashers, when removed from an assembly, should always be replaced exactly as removed. Replace any damaged washers with new ones. Never use a lockwasher on any soft metal surface (such as aluminum), thin sheet metal or plastic.

Fastener sizes

For a number of reasons, automobile manufacturers are making wider and wider use of metric fasteners. Therefore, it is important to be able to tell the difference between standard (sometimes called U.S. or SAE) and metric hardware, since they cannot be interchanged.

All bolts, whether standard or metric, are sized according to diameter, thread pitch and length. For example, a standard 1/2 — 13 x 1 bolt is 1/2 inch in diameter, has 13 threads per inch and is 1 inch long. An M12 — 1.75 x 25 metric bolt is 12 mm in diameter, has a thread pitch of 1.75 mm (the distance between threads) and is 25 mm long. The two bolts are nearly identical, and easily confused, but they are not interchangeable.

In addition to the differences in diameter, thread pitch and length, metric and standard bolts can also be distinguished by examining the bolt heads. To begin with, the distance across the flats on a standard bolt head is measured in inches, while the same dimension on a metric bolt is sized in millimeters (the same is true for nuts). As a result, a standard wrench should not be used on a metric bolt and a metric wrench should not be used on a standard bolt. Also, most standard bolts have slashes radiating out from the center of the head to denote the grade or strength of the bolt, which is an indication of the amount of torque that can be applied to it. The greater the number of slashes, the greater the strength of the bolt. Grades 0 through 5 are commonly used on automobiles. Metric bolts have a property class (grade) number, rather than a slash, molded into their heads to indicate bolt strength. In this case, the higher the number, the stronger the bolt. Property class numbers 8.8, 9.8 and 10.9 are commonly used on automobiles.

Strength markings can also be used to distinguish standard hex nuts from metric hex nuts. Many standard nuts have dots stamped into one side, while metric nuts are marked with a number. The greater the number of dots, or the higher the number, the greater the strength of the nut.

Metric studs are also marked on their ends according to property class (grade). Larger studs are numbered (the same as metric bolts),

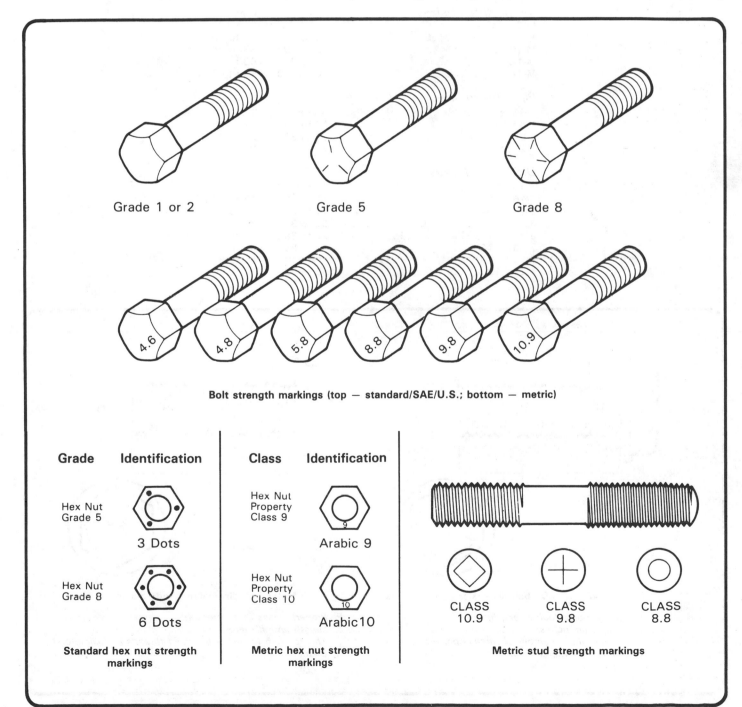

Bolt strength markings (top — standard/SAE/U.S.; bottom — metric)

Grade	Identification
Hex Nut Grade 5	3 Dots
Hex Nut Grade 8	6 Dots

Standard hex nut strength markings

Class	Identification
Hex Nut Property Class 9	Arabic 9
Hex Nut Property Class 10	Arabic 10

Metric hex nut strength markings

CLASS 10.9   CLASS 9.8   CLASS 8.8

Metric stud strength markings

while smaller studs carry a geometric code to denote grade.

It should be noted that many fasteners, especially Grades 0 through 2, have no distinguishing marks on them. When such is the case, the only way to determine whether it is standard or metric is to measure the thread pitch or compare it to a known fastener of the same size.

Standard fasteners are often referred to as SAE, as opposed to metric. However, it should be noted that SAE technically refers to a non-metric *fine thread* fastener only. Coarse thread non-metric fasteners are referred to as U.S.S. sizes.

Since fasteners of the same size (both standard and metric) may have different strength ratings, be sure to reinstall any bolts, studs or nuts removed from your vehicle in their original locations. Also, when replacing a fastener with a new one, make sure that the new one has a strength rating equal to or greater than the original.

Tightening sequences and procedures

Most threaded fasteners should be tightened to a specific torque value (torque is the twisting force applied to a threaded component such as a nut or bolt). Overtightening the fastener can weaken it and cause it to break, while undertightening can cause it to eventually come loose. Bolts, screws and studs, depending on the material they are made of and their thread diameters, have specific torque values, many of which are noted in the Specifications at the beginning of each Chapter. Be sure to follow the torque recommendations closely. For fasteners not assigned a specific torque, a general torque value chart is presented here as a guide. As was previously mentioned, the size and grade of a fastener determine the amount of torque that can safely be applied to it. The figures listed here are approximate for Grade 2 and Grade 3 fasteners. Higher grades can tolerate higher torque values.

Metric thread sizes	Ft-lb	Nm/m
M-6	6 to 9	9 to 12
M-8	14 to 21	19 to 28
M-10	28 to 40	38 to 54
M-12	50 to 71	68 to 96
M-14	80 to 140	109 to 154
Pipe thread sizes		
1/8	5 to 8	7 to 10
1/4	12 to 18	17 to 24
3/8	22 to 33	30 to 44
1/2	25 to 35	34 to 47
U.S. thread sizes		
1/4 – 20	6 to 9	9 to 12
5/16 – 18	12 to 18	17 to 24
5/16 – 24	14 to 20	19 to 27
3/8 – 16	22 to 32	30 to 43
3/8 – 24	27 to 38	37 to 51
7/16 – 14	40 to 55	55 to 74
7/16 – 20	40 to 60	55 to 81
1/2 – 13	55 to 80	75 to 108

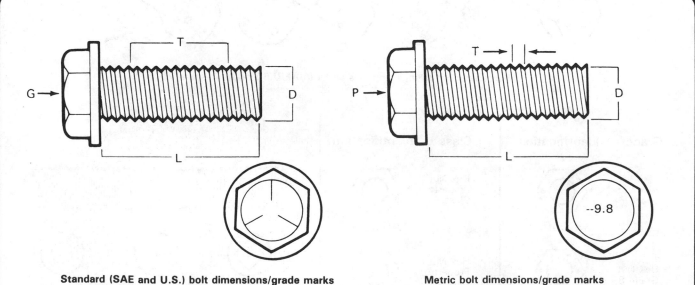

Standard (SAE and U.S.) bolt dimensions/grade marks

    G *Grade marks (bolt strength)*
    L *Length (in inches)*
    T *Thread pitch (number of threads per inch)*
    D *Nominal diameter (in inches)*

Metric bolt dimensions/grade marks

    P *Property class (bolt strength)*
    L *Length (in millimeters)*
    T *Thread pitch (distance between threads in millimeters)*
    D *Diameter*

Fasteners laid out in a pattern, such as cylinder head bolts, oil pan bolts, differential cover bolts, etc., must be loosened or tightened in sequence to avoid warping the component. This sequence will normally be shown in the appropriate Chapter. If a specific pattern is not given, the following procedures can be used to prevent warping.

Initially, the bolts or nuts should be assembled finger-tight only. Next, they should be tightened one full turn each, in a criss-cross or diagonal pattern. After each one has been tightened one full turn, return to the first one and tighten them all one-half turn, following the same pattern. Finally, tighten each of them one-quarter turn at a time until each fastener has been tightened to the proper torque. To loosen and remove the fasteners, the procedure would be reversed.

Component disassembly

Component disassembly should be done with care and purpose to help ensure that the parts go back together properly. Always keep track of the sequence in which parts are removed. Make note of special characteristics or marks on parts that can be installed more than one way, such as a grooved thrust washer on a shaft. It is a good idea to lay the disassembled parts out on a clean surface in the order that they were removed. It may also be helpful to make sketches or take instant photos of components before removal.

When removing fasteners from a component, keep track of their locations. Sometimes threading a bolt back in a part, or putting the washers and nut back on a stud, can prevent mix-ups later. If nuts and bolts cannot be returned to their original locations, they should be kept in a compartmented box or a series of small boxes. A cupcake or muffin tin is ideal for this purpose, since each cavity can hold the bolts and nuts from a particular area (i.e. oil pan bolts, valve cover bolts, engine mount bolts, etc.). A pan of this type is especially helpful when working on assemblies with very small parts, such as the carburetor, alternator, valve train or interior dash and trim pieces. The cavities can be marked with paint or tape to identify the contents.

Whenever wiring looms, harnesses or connectors are separated, it is a good idea to identify the two halves with numbered pieces of masking tape so they can be easily reconnected.

Gasket sealing surfaces

Throughout any vehicle, gaskets are used to seal the mating surfaces between two parts and keep lubricants, fluids, vacuum or pressure contained in an assembly.

Many times these gaskets are coated with a liquid or paste-type gasket sealing compound before assembly. Age, heat and pressure can sometimes cause the two parts to stick together so tightly that they are very difficult to separate. Often, the assembly can be loosened by striking it with a soft-face hammer near the mating surfaces. A regular hammer can be used if a block of wood is placed between the hammer and the part. Do not hammer on cast parts or parts that could be easily damaged. With any particularly stubborn part, always recheck to make sure that every fastener has been removed.

Avoid using a screwdriver or bar to pry apart an assembly, as they can easily mar the gasket sealing surfaces of the parts, which must remain smooth. If prying is absolutely necessary, use an old broom handle, but keep in mind that extra clean up will be necessary if the wood splinters.

After the parts are separated, the old gasket must be carefully scraped off and the gasket surfaces cleaned. Stubborn gasket material can be soaked with rust penetrant or treated with a special chemical to soften it so it can be easily scraped off. A scraper can be fashioned from a piece of copper tubing by flattening and sharpening one end. Copper is recommended because it is usually softer than the surfaces to be scraped, which reduces the chance of gouging the part. Some gaskets can be removed with a wire brush, but regardless of the method used, the mating surfaces must be left clean and smooth. If for some reason the gasket surface is gouged, then a gasket sealer thick enough to fill scratches will have to be used during reassembly of the components. For most applications, a non-drying (or semi-drying) gasket sealer should be used.

Hose removal tips

Warning: *If the vehicle is equipped with air conditioning, do not disconnect any of the A/C hoses without first having the system depressurized by a dealer service department or an air conditioning specialist.*

Hose removal precautions closely parallel gasket removal precautions. Avoid scratching or gouging the surface that the hose mates against or the connection may leak. This is especially true for radiator hoses. Because of various chemical reactions, the rubber in hoses can bond itself to the metal spigot that the hose fits over. To remove a hose, first loosen the hose clamps that secure it to the spigot. Then, with slip-joint pliers, grab the hose at the clamp and rotate it around the spigot. Work it back and forth until it is completely free, then pull it off. Silicone or other lubricants will ease removal if they can be applied between the hose and the outside of the spigot. Apply the same lubricant to the inside of the hose and the outside of the spigot to simplify installation.

As a last resort (and if the hose is to be replaced with a new one anyway), the rubber can be slit with a knife and the hose peeled from the spigot. If this must be done, be careful that the metal connection is not damaged.

If a hose clamp is broken or damaged, do not reuse it. Wire-type clamps usually weaken with age, so it is a good idea to replace them with screw-type clamps whenever a hose is removed.

Tools

A selection of good tools is a basic requirement for anyone who plans to maintain and repair his or her own vehicle. For the owner who has few tools, the initial investment might seem high, but when compared to the spiraling costs of professional auto maintenance and repair, it is a wise one.

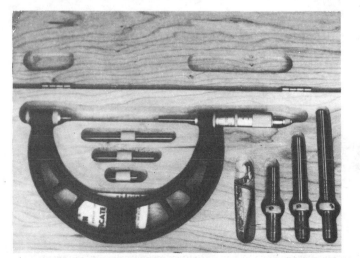

Micrometer set

Dial indicator set

Dial caliper

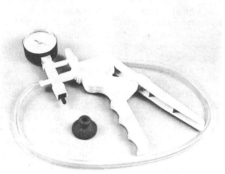

Hand-operated vacuum pump

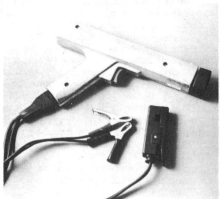

Timing light

Compression gauge with spark plug
hole adapter

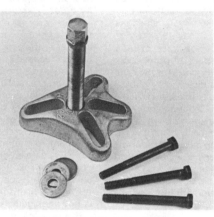

Damper/steering wheel puller

General purpose puller

Hydraulic lifter removal tool

Valve spring compressor

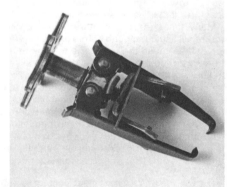

Valve spring compressor

Ridge reamer

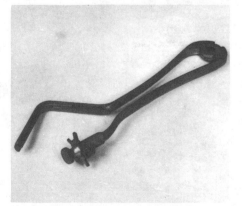

Piston ring groove cleaning tool

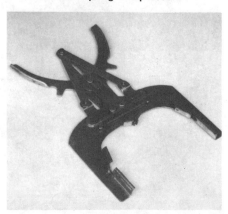

Ring removal/installation tool

Ring compressor

Cylinder hone

Brake hold-down spring tool

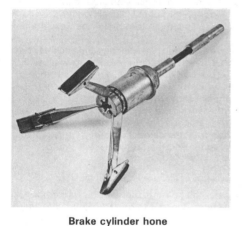

Brake cylinder hone

Clutch plate alignment tool

Tap and die set

To help the owner decide which tools are needed to perform the tasks detailed in this manual, the following tool lists are offered: *Maintenance and minor repair, Repair/overhaul* and *Special*.

The newcomer to practical mechanics should start off with the maintenance and minor repair tool kit, which is adequate for the simpler jobs performed on a vehicle. Then, as confidence and experience grow, the owner can tackle more difficult tasks, buying additional tools as they are needed. Eventually the basic kit will be expanded into the repair and overhaul tool set. Over a period of time, the experienced do-it-yourselfer will assemble a tool set complete enough for most repair and overhaul procedures and will add tools from the special category when it is felt that the expense is justified by the frequency of use.

Maintenance and minor repair tool kit

The tools in this list should be considered the minimum required for performance of routine maintenance, servicing and minor repair work. We recommend the purchase of combination wrenches (box-end and open-end combined in one wrench). While more expensive than open end wrenches, they offer the advantages of both types of wrench.

Combination wrench set (1/4-inch to 1 inch or 6 mm to 19 mm)
Adjustable wrench, 8 inch
Spark plug wrench with rubber insert
Spark plug gap adjusting tool
Feeler gauge set
Brake bleeder wrench
Standard screwdriver (5/16-inch x 6 inch)
Phillips screwdriver (No. 2 x 6 inch)
Combination pliers — 6 inch
Hacksaw and assortment of blades
Tire pressure gauge
Grease gun
Oil can
Fine emery cloth
Wire brush

Battery post and cable cleaning tool
Oil filter wrench
Funnel (medium size)
Safety goggles
Jackstands (2)
Drain pan

Note: *If basic tune-ups are going to be part of routine maintenance, it will be necessary to purchase a good quality stroboscopic timing light and combination tachometer/dwell meter. Although they are included in the list of special tools, it is mentioned here because they are absolutely necessary for tuning most vehicles properly.*

Repair and overhaul tool set

These tools are essential for anyone who plans to perform major repairs and are in addition to those in the maintenance and minor repair tool kit. Included is a comprehensive set of sockets which, though expensive, are invaluable because of their versatility, especially when various extensions and drives are available. We recommend the 1/2-inch drive over the 3/8-inch drive. Although the larger drive is bulky and more expensive, it has the capacity of accepting a very wide range of large sockets. Ideally, however, the mechanic should have a 3/8-inch drive set and a 1/2-inch drive set.

Socket set(s)
Reversible ratchet
Extension — 10 inch
Universal joint
Torque wrench (same size drive as sockets)
Ball peen hammer — 8 ounce
Soft-face hammer (plastic/rubber)
Standard screwdriver (1/4-inch x 6 inch)
Standard screwdriver (stubby — 5/16-inch)
Phillips screwdriver (No. 3 x 8 inch)
Phillips screwdriver (stubby — No. 2)

Pliers — vise grip
Pliers — lineman's
Pliers — needle nose
Pliers — snap-ring (internal and external)
Cold chisel — 1/2-inch
Scribe
Scraper (made from flattened copper tubing)
Centerpunch
Pin punches (1/16, 1/8, 3/16-inch)
Steel rule/straightedge — 12 inch
Allen wrench set (1/8 to 3/8-inch or 4 mm to 10 mm)
A selection of files
Wire brush (large)
Jackstands (second set)
Jack (scissor or hydraulic type)

Note: *Another tool which is often useful is an electric drill motor with a chuck capacity of 3/8-inch and a set of good quality drill bits.*

Special tools

The tools in this list include those which are not used regularly, are expensive to buy, or which need to be used in accordance with their manufacturer's instructions. Unless these tools will be used frequently, it is not very economical to purchase many of them. A consideration would be to split the cost and use between yourself and a friend or friends. In addition, most of these tools can be obtained from a tool rental shop on a temporary basis.

This list primarily contains only those tools and instruments widely available to the public, and not those special tools produced by the vehicle manufacturer for distribution to dealer service departments. Occasionally, references to the manufacturer's special tools are inluded in the text of this manual. Generally, an alternative method of doing the job without the special tool is offered. However, sometimes there is no alternative to their use. Where this is the case, and the tool cannot be purchased or borrowed, the work should be turned over to the dealer service department or an automotive repair shop.

Valve spring compressor
Piston ring groove cleaning tool
Piston ring compressor
Piston ring installation tool
Cylinder compression gauge
Cylinder ridge reamer
Cylinder surfacing hone
Cylinder bore gauge
Micrometers and/or dial calipers
Hydraulic lifter removal tool
Balljoint separator
Universal-type puller
Impact screwdriver
Dial indicator set
Stroboscopic timing light (inductive pick-up)
Hand operated vacuum/pressure pump
Tachometer/dwell meter
Universal electrical multimeter
Cable hoist
Brake spring removal and installation tools
Floor jack

Buying tools

For the do-it-yourselfer who is just starting to get involved in vehicle maintenance and repair, there are a number of options available when purchasing tools. If maintenance and minor repair is the extent of the work to be done, the purchase of individual tools is satisfactory. If,

on the other hand, extensive work is planned, it would be a good idea to purchase a modest tool set from one of the large retail chain stores. A set can usually be bought at a substantial savings over the individual tool prices, and they often come with a tool box. As additional tools are needed, add-on sets, individual tools and a larger tool box can be purchased to expand the tool selection. Building a tool set gradually allows the cost of the tools to be spread over a longer period of time and gives the mechanic the freedom to choose only those tools that will actually be used.

Tool stores will often be the only source of some of the special tools that are needed, but regardless of where tools are bought, try to avoid cheap ones, especially when buying screwdrivers and sockets, because they won't last very long. The expense involved in replacing cheap tools will eventually be greater than the initial cost of quality tools.

Care and maintenance of tools

Good tools are expensive, so it makes sense to treat them with respect. Keep them clean and in usable condition and store them properly when not in use. Always wipe off any dirt, grease or metal chips before putting them away. Never leave tools lying around in the work area. Upon completion of a job, always check closely under the hood for tools that may have been left there so they won't get lost during a test drive.

Some tools, such as screwdrivers, pliers, wrenches and sockets, can be hung on a panel mounted on the garage or workshop wall, while others should be kept in a tool box or tray. Measuring instruments, gauges, meters, etc. must be carefully stored where they cannot be damaged by weather or impact from other tools.

When tools are used with care and stored properly, they will last a very long time. Even with the best of care, though, tools will wear out if used frequently. When a tool is damaged or worn out, replace it. Subsequent jobs will be safer and more enjoyable if you do.

Working facilities

Not to be overlooked when discussing tools is the workshop. If anything more than routine maintenance is to be carried out, some sort of suitable work area is essential.

It is understood, and appreciated, that many home mechanics do not have a good workshop or garage available, and end up removing an engine or doing major repairs outside. It is recommended, however, that the overhaul or repair be completed under the cover of a roof.

A clean, flat workbench or table of comfortable working height is an absolute necessity. The workbench should be equipped with a vise that has a jaw opening of at least four inches.

As mentioned previously, some clean, dry storage space is also required for tools, as well as the lubricants, fluids, cleaning solvents, etc. which will soon become necessary.

Sometimes waste oil and fluids, drained from the engine or cooling system during normal maintenance or repairs, present a disposal problem. To avoid pouring them on the ground or into a sewage system, pour the used fluids into large containers, seal them with caps and take them to an authorized disposal site or recycling center. Plastic jugs, such as old antifreeze containers, are ideal for this purpose.

Always keep a supply of old newspapers and clean rags available. Old towels are excellent for mopping up spills. Many mechanics use rolls of paper towels for most work because they are readily available and disposable. To help keep the area under the vehicle clean, a large cardboard box can be cut open and flattened to protect the garage or shop floor.

Whenever working over a painted surface, such as when leaning over a fender to service something under the hood, always cover it with an old blanket or bedspread to protect the finish. Vinyl covered pads, made especially for this purpose, are available at auto parts stores.

Jacking and Towing

Jacking

Caution: *On vehicles equipped with limited slip differentials, do not run the engine with the vehicle on a jack.*

When lifting a vehicle with either the supplied jack or a floor jack, block the wheel that is diagonally opposite to the one being lifted to prevent the vehicle from moving. **Warning:** *If equipped with an under-chassis mounted spare tire, remove the tire or tire carrier from the rack before the vehicle is raised in order to avoid sudden weight release from* *the chassis.*

Ford recommends that you position the jack under the axles, shock absorber or jacking bracket, as close to the wheel to be removed as possible. Note that on two wheel drive vehicles a special jacking pin is provided on the front axle. This pin should only be used with the factory supplied jack or a jack with a shaft and cap which fits firmly in the bracket.

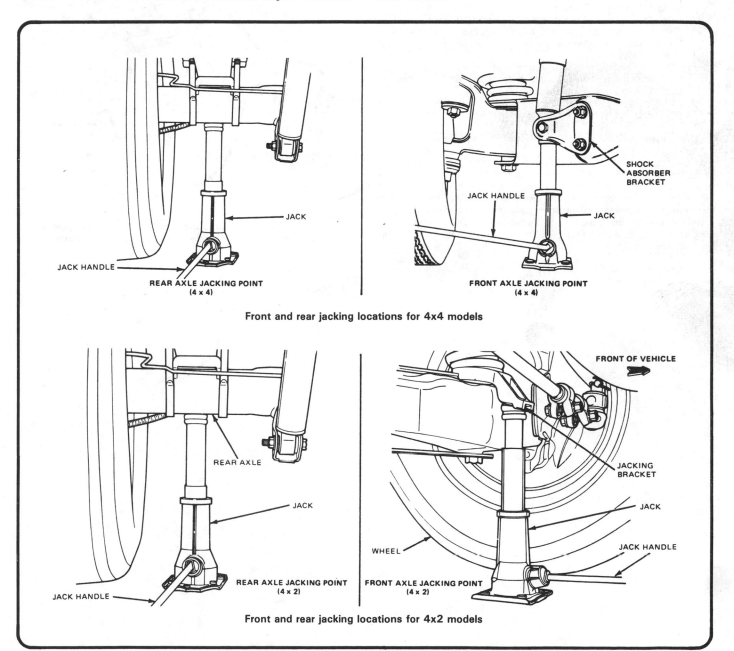

Front and rear jacking locations for 4x4 models

Front and rear jacking locations for 4x2 models

Towing

Be sure the parking brake is released and the transmission is in neutral. As a general rule, towed vehicles should be pulled with the driving wheels off the ground. If the vehicle is to be towed with the rear wheels on the ground, it is recommended that the driveshaft be removed. On four wheel drive vehicles be sure the manual locking hubs are in the free position and that the transfer case is in neutral.

If towing a vehicle by the rear, the front wheels must be clamped in the straight ahead position with a steering wheel clamp. Do not use the steering column lock for this purpose.

Two wheel drive vehicles being towed with the rear wheels or all four wheels on the ground should not be towed in excess of 35 mph or for more than 50 miles. For towing with the drive wheels raised there is no distance limit, but do not exceed 50 mph.

Towing equipment specifically designed for towing purposes should be used and should be attached to the main structural member of the vehicle — not the bumper or brackets. Safety is a major consideration when towing and all applicable state and local laws must be obeyed. A safety chain system must be used for all towing.

Booster battery (jump) starting

Certain precautions must be observed when using a booster battery to jump start a vehicle.

  a) Before connecting the booster battery, make sure that the ignition switch is in the Off position.
  b) Turn off the lights, heater and other electrical loads.
  c) The eyes should be shielded. Safety goggles are a good idea.
  d) Make sure the booster battery is the same voltage as the dead one in the vehicle.
  e) The two vehicles must not touch each other.
  f) Make sure the transmission is in Neutral (manual transmission) or Park (automatic transmission).
  g) If the booster battery is not a maintenance-free type, remove the vent caps and lay a cloth over the vent holes.

Connect the red jumper cable to the *positive* (+) terminals of each battery.

Connect one end of the black jumper cable to the *negative* (−) terminal of the booster battery. The other end of this cable should be connected to a good ground on the vehicle to be started, such as a bolt or bracket on the engine block. Use caution to insure that the cable will not come into contact with the fan, drivebelts or other moving parts of the engine.

Start the engine using the booster battery, then, with the engine running at idle speed, disconnect the jumper cables in the reverse order of connection.

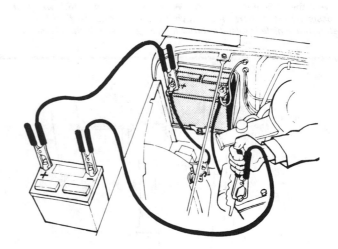

Booster cable connections (note that the negative cable is *not* attached to the negative terminal of the dead battery)

Automotive chemicals and lubricants

A number of automotive chemicals and lubricants are available for use during vehicle maintenance and repair. They include a wide variety of products ranging from cleaning solvents and degreasers to lubricants and protective sprays for rubber, plastic and vinyl.

Cleaners

Carburetor cleaner and choke cleaner is a strong solvent for gum, varnish and carbon. Most carburetor cleaners leave a dry-type lubricant film which will not harden or gum up. Because of this film it is not recommended for use on electrical components.

Brake system cleaner is used to remove grease and brake fluid from the brake system where clean surfaces are absolutely necessary. It leaves no residue and often eliminates brake squeal caused by contaminants.

Electrical cleaner removes oxidation, corrosion and carbon deposits from electrical contacts, restoring full current flow. It can also be used to clean spark plugs, carburetor jets, voltage regulators and other parts where an oil-free surface is desired.

Demoisturants remove water and moisture from electrical components such as alternators, voltage regulators, electrical connectors and fuse blocks. It is non-conductive, non-corrosive and non-flammable.

Degreasers are heavy-duty solvents used to remove grease from the outside of the engine and from chassis components. They can be sprayed or brushed on, and, depending on the type, are rinsed off either with water or solvent.

Lubricants

Motor oil is the lubricant formulated for use in engines. It normally contains a wide variety of additives to prevent corrosion and reduce foaming and wear. Motor oil comes in various weights (viscosity ratings) from 5 to 80. The recommended weight of the oil depends on the season, temperature and the demands on the engine. Light oil is used in cold climates and under light load conditions. Heavy oil is used in hot climates and where high loads are encountered. Multi-viscosity oils are designed to have characteristics of both light and heavy oils and are available in a number of weights from 5W-20 to 20W-50.

Gear oil is designed to be used in differentials, manual transaxles and other areas where high-temperature lubrication is required.

Chassis and wheel bearing grease is a heavy grease used where increased loads and friction are encountered, such as for wheel bearings, balljoints, tie rod ends and universal joints.

High temperature wheel bearing grease is designed to withstand the extreme temperatures encountered by wheel bearings in disc brake equipped vehicles. It usually contains molybdenun disulfide (moly), which is a dry-type lubricant.

White grease is a heavy grease for metal to metal applications where water is a problem. White grease stays soft under both low and high temperatures (usually from −100°F to +190°F), and will not wash off or dilute in the presence of water.

Assembly lube is a special extreme pressure lubricant, usually containing moly, used to lubricate high-load parts such as main and rod bearings and cam lobes for initial start-up of a new engine. The assembly lube lubricates the parts without being squeezed out or washed away until the engine oiling system begins to function.

Silicone lubricants are used to protect rubber, plastic, vinyl and nylon parts.

Graphite lubricants are used where oils cannot be used due to contamination problems, such as in locks. The dry graphite will lubricate metal parts while remaining uncontaminated by dirt, water, oil or acids. It is electrically conductive and will not foul electrical contacts in locks such as the ignition switch.

Moly penetrants loosen and lubricate frozen, rusted and corroded fasteners and prevent future rusting or freezing.

Heat-sink grease is a special electrically non-conductive grease that is used for mounting HEI ignition modules where it is essential that heat be transferred away from the module.

Sealants

RTV sealant is one of the most widely used gasket compounds. Made from silicone, RTV is air curing, it seals, bonds, waterproofs, fills surface irregularities, remains flexible, doesn't shrink, is relatively easy to remove, and is used as a supplementary sealer with almost all low and medium temperature gaskets.

Anaerobic sealant is much like RTV in that it can be used either to seal gaskets or to form gaskets by itself. It remains flexible, is solvent resistant and fills surface imperfections. The difference between an anaerobic sealant and an RTV-type sealant is in the curing. RTV cures when exposed to air, while an anaerobic sealant cures only in the absence of air. This means that an anaerobic sealant cures only after the assembly of parts, sealing them together.

Thread and pipe sealant is used for sealing hydraulic and pneumatic fittings and vacuum lines. It is usually made from a teflon compound, and comes in a spray, a paint-on liquid and as a wrap-around tape.

Chemicals

Anti-seize compound prevents seizing, galling, cold welding, rust and corrosion in fasteners. High temperature anti-seize, usually made with copper and graphite lubricants, is used for exhaust system and manifold bolts.

Anaerobic locking compounds are used to keep fasteners from vibrating or working loose, and cure only after installation, in the absence of air. Medium strength locking compound is used for small nuts, bolts and screws that you expect to be removing later. High strength locking compound is for large nuts, bolts and studs which you don't intend to be removing on a regular basis.

Oil additives range from viscosity index improvers to chemical treatments that claim to reduce internal engine friction. It should be noted that most oil manufacturers caution against using additives with their oils.

Gas additives perform several functions, depending on their chemical makeup. They usually contain solvents that help dissolve gum and varnish that build up on carburetor and intake parts. They also serve to break down carbon deposits that form on the inside surfaces of the combustion chambers. Some additives contain upper cylinder lubricants for valves and piston rings, and others chemicals to remove condensation from the gas tank.

Other

Brake fluid is specially formulated hydraulic fluid that can withstand the heat and pressure encountered in brake systems. Care must be taken that this fluid does not come in contact with painted surfaces or plastics. An opened container should always be resealed to prevent contamination by water or dirt.

Weatherstrip adhesive is used to bond weatherstripping around doors, windows and trunk lids. It is sometimes used to attach trim pieces.

Undercoating is a petroleum-based tar-like substance that is designed to protect metal surfaces on the underside of the vehicle from corrosion. It also acts as a sound-deadening agent by insulating the bottom of the vehicle.

Waxes and polishes are used to help protect painted and plated surfaces from the weather. Different types of paint may require the use of different types of wax and polish. Some polishes utilize a chemical or abrasive cleaner to help remove the top layer of oxidized (dull) paint on older vehicles. In recent years many non-wax polishes that contain a wide variety of chemicals such as polymers and silicones have been introduced. These non-wax polishes are usually easier to apply and last longer than conventional waxes and polishes.

Safety first!

Regardless of how enthusiastic you may be about getting on with the job at hand, take the time to ensure that your safety is not jeopardized. A moment's lack of attention can result in an accident, as can failure to observe certain simple safety precautions. The possibility of an accident will always exist, and the following points should not be considered a comprehensive list of all dangers. Rather, they are intended to make you aware of the risks and to encourage a safety conscious approach to all work you carry out on your vehicle.

Essential DOs and DON'Ts

DON'T rely on a jack when working under the vehicle. Always use approved jackstands to support the weight of the vehicle and place them under the recommended lift or support points.

DON'T attempt to loosen extremely tight fasteners (i.e. wheel lug nuts) while the vehicle is on a jack — it may fall.

DON'T start the engine without first making sure that the transmission is in Neutral (or Park where applicable) and the parking brake is set.

DON'T remove the radiator cap from a hot cooling system — let it cool or cover it with a cloth and release the pressure gradually.

DON'T attempt to drain the engine oil until you are sure it has cooled to the point that it will not burn you.

DON'T touch any part of the engine or exhaust system until it has cooled sufficiently to avoid burns.

DON'T siphon toxic liquids such as gasoline, antifreeze and brake fluid by mouth, or allow them to remain on your skin.

DON'T inhale brake lining dust — it is potentially hazardous (see *Asbestos* below)

DON'T allow spilled oil or grease to remain on the floor — wipe it up before someone slips on it.

DON'T use loose fitting wrenches or other tools which may slip and cause injury.

DON'T push on wrenches when loosening or tightening nuts or bolts. Always try to pull the wrench toward you. If the situation calls for pushing the wrench away, push with an open hand to avoid scraped knuckles if the wrench should slip.

DON'T attempt to lift a heavy component alone — get someone to help you.

DON'T rush or take unsafe shortcuts to finish a job.

DON'T allow children or animals in or around the vehicle while you are working on it.

DO wear eye protection when using power tools such as a drill, sander, bench grinder, etc. and when working under a vehicle.

DO keep loose clothing and long hair well out of the way of moving parts.

DO make sure that any hoist used has a safe working load rating adequate for the job.

DO get someone to check on you periodically when working alone on a vehicle.

DO carry out work in a logical sequence and make sure that everything is correctly assembled and tightened.

DO keep chemicals and fluids tightly capped and out of the reach of children and pets.

DO remember that your vehicle's safety affects that of yourself and others. If in doubt on any point, get professional advice.

Asbestos

Certain friction, insulating, sealing, and other products — such as brake linings, brake bands, clutch linings, torque converters, gaskets, etc. — contain asbestos. *Extreme care must be taken to avoid inhalation of dust from such products since it is hazardous to health.* If in doubt, assume that they *do* contain asbestos.

Fire

Remember at all times that gasoline is highly flammable. Never smoke or have any kind of open flame around when working on a vehicle. But the risk does not end there. A spark caused by an electrical short circuit, by two metal surfaces contacting each other, or even by static electricity built up in your body under certain conditions, can ignite gasoline vapors, which in a confined space are highly explosive. Do not, under any circumstances, use gasoline for cleaning parts. Use an approved safety solvent.

Always disconnect the battery ground (–) cable *at the battery* before working on any part of the fuel system or electrical system. Never risk spilling fuel on a hot engine or exhaust component.

It is strongly recommended that a fire extinguisher suitable for use on fuel and electrical fires be kept handy in the garage or workshop at all times. Never try to extinguish a fuel or electrical fire with water.

Fumes

Certain fumes are highly toxic and can quickly cause unconsciousness and even death if inhaled to any extent. Gasoline vapor falls into this category, as do the vapors from some cleaning solvents. Any draining or pouring of such volatile fluids should be done in a well ventilated area.

When using cleaning fluids and solvents, read the instructions on the container carefully. Never use materials from unmarked containers.

Never run the engine in an enclosed space, such as a garage. Exhaust fumes contain carbon monoxide, which is extremely poisonous. If you need to run the engine, always do so in the open air, or at least have the rear of the vehicle outside the work area.

If you are fortunate enough to have the use of an inspection pit, never drain or pour gasoline and never run the engine while the vehicle is over the pit. The fumes, being heavier than air, will concentrate in the pit with possibly lethal results.

The battery

Never create a spark or allow a bare light bulb near the battery. The battery normally gives off a certain amount of hydrogen gas, which is highly explosive.

Always disconnect the battery ground (–) cable *at the battery* before working on the fuel or electrical systems.

If possible, loosen the filler caps or cover when charging the battery from an external source. Do not charge at an excessive rate or the battery may burst.

Take care when adding water and when carrying a battery. The electrolyte, even when diluted, is very corrosive and should not be allowed to contact clothing or skin.

Always wear eye protection when cleaning the battery to prevent the caustic deposits from entering your eyes.

Household current

When using an electric power tool, inspection light, etc., which operates on household current, always make sure that the tool is correctly connected to its plug and that, where necessary, it is properly grounded. Do not use such items in damp conditions and, again, do not create a spark or apply excessive heat in the vicinity of fuel or fuel vapor.

Secondary ignition system voltage

A severe electric shock can result from touching certain parts of the ignition system (such as the spark plug wires) when the engine is running or being cranked, particularly if components are damp or the insulation is defective. In the case of an electronic ignition system, the secondary system voltage is much higher and could prove fatal.

Conversion factors

Length (distance)

Inches (in)	X	25.4	= Millimetres (mm)	X 0.0394	= Inches (in)
Feet (ft)	X	0.305	= Metres (m)	X 3.281	= Feet (ft)
Miles	X	1.609	= Kilometres (km)	X 0.621	= Miles

Volume (capacity)

Cubic inches (cu in; in³)	X	16.387	= Cubic centimetres (cc; cm³)	X 0.061	= Cubic inches (cu in; in³)
Imperial pints (Imp pt)	X	0.568	= Litres (l)	X 1.76	= Imperial pints (Imp pt)
Imperial quarts (Imp qt)	X	1.137	= Litres (l)	X 0.88	= Imperial quarts (Imp qt)
Imperial quarts (Imp qt)	X	1.201	= US quarts (US qt)	X 0.833	= Imperial quarts (Imp qt)
US quarts (US qt)	X	0.946	= Litres (l)	X 1.057	= US quarts (US qt)
Imperial gallons (Imp gal)	X	4.546	= Litres (l)	X 0.22	= Imperial gallons (Imp gal)
Imperial gallons (Imp gal)	X	1.201	= US gallons (US gal)	X 0.833	= Imperial gallons (Imp gal)
US gallons (US gal)	X	3.785	= Litres (l)	X 0.264	= US gallons (US gal)

Mass (weight)

Ounces (oz)	X	28.35	= Grams (g)	X 0.035	= Ounces (oz)
Pounds (lb)	X	0.454	= Kilograms (kg)	X 2.205	= Pounds (lb)

Force

Ounces-force (ozf; oz)	X	0.278	= Newtons (N)	X 3.6	= Ounces-force (ozf; oz)
Pounds-force (lbf; lb)	X	4.448	= Newtons (N)	X 0.225	= Pounds-force (lbf; lb)
Newtons (N)	X	0.1	= Kilograms-force (kgf; kg)	X 9.81	= Newtons (N)

Pressure

Pounds-force per square inch (psi; lbf/in²; lb/in²)	X	0.070	= Kilograms-force per square centimetre (kgf/cm²; kg/cm²)	X 14.223	= Pounds-force per square inch (psi; lbf/in²; lb/in²)
Pounds-force per square inch (psi; lbf/in²; lb/in²)	X	0.068	= Atmospheres (atm)	X 14.696	= Pounds-force per square inch (psi; lbf/in²; lb/in²)
Pounds-force per square inch (psi; lbf/in²; lb/in²)	X	0.069	= Bars	X 14.5	= Pounds-force per square inch (psi; lbf/in²; lb/in²)
Pounds-force per square inch (psi; lbf/in²; lb/in²)	X	6.895	= Kilopascals (kPa)	X 0.145	= Pounds-force per square inch (psi; lbf/in²; lb/in²)
Kilopascals (kPa)	X	0.01	= Kilograms-force per square centimetre (kgf/cm²; kg/cm²)	X 98.1	= Kilopascals (kPa)

Torque (moment of force)

Pounds-force inches (lbf in; lb in)	X	1.152	= Kilograms-force centimetre (kgf cm; kg cm)	X 0.868	= Pounds-force inches (lbf in; lb in)
Pounds-force inches (lbf in; lb in)	X	0.113	= Newton metres (Nm)	X 8.85	= Pounds-force inches (lbf in; lb in)
Pounds-force inches (lbf in; lb in)	X	0.083	= Pounds-force feet (lbf ft; lb ft)	X 12	= Pounds-force inches (lbf in; lb in)
Pounds-force feet (lbf ft; lb ft)	X	0.138	= Kilograms-force metres (kgf m; kg m)	X 7.233	= Pounds-force feet (lbf ft; lb ft)
Pounds-force feet (lbf ft; lb ft)	X	1.356	= Newton metres (Nm)	X 0.738	= Pounds-force feet (lbf ft; lb ft)
Newton metres (Nm)	X	0.102	= Kilograms-force metres (kgf m; kg m)	X 9.804	= Newton metres (Nm)

Power

Horsepower (hp)	X	745.7	= Watts (W)	X 0.0013	= Horsepower (hp)

Velocity (speed)

Miles per hour (miles/hr; mph)	X	1.609	= Kilometres per hour (km/hr; kph)	X 0.621	= Miles per hour (miles/hr; mph)

Fuel consumption*

Miles per gallon, Imperial (mpg)	X	0.354	= Kilometres per litre (km/l)	X 2.825	= Miles per gallon, Imperial (mpg)
Miles per gallon, US (mpg)	X	0.425	= Kilometres per litre (km/l)	X 2.352	= Miles per gallon, US (mpg)

Temperature

Degrees Fahrenheit = (°C x 1.8) + 32   Degrees Celsius (Degrees Centigrade; °C) = (°F - 32) x 0.56

*It is common practice to convert from miles per gallon (mpg) to litres/100 kilometres (l/100km), where mpg (Imperial) x l/100 km = 282 and mpg (US) x l/100 km = 235

Troubleshooting

Contents

This section provides an easy reference guide to the more common problems which may occur during the operation of your vehicle. These problems and possible causes are grouped under various components or systems; i.e. Engine, Cooling system, etc., and also refer to the Chapter and/or Section which deals with the problem.

Remember that successful troubleshooting is not a mysterious *black art* practiced only by professional mechanics. It's simply the result of a bit of knowledge combined with an intelligent, systematic approach to the problem. Always work by a process of elimination, starting with the simplest solution and working through to the most complex — and never overlook the obvious. Anyone can forget to fill the gas tank or leave the lights on overnight, so don't assume that you are above such oversights.

Finally, always get clear in your mind why a problem has occurred and take steps to ensure that it doesn't happen again. If the electrical system fails because of a poor connection, check all other connections in the system to make sure that they don't fail as well. If a particular fuse continues to blow, find out why — don't just go on replacing fuses. Remember, failure of a small component can often be indicative of potential failure or incorrect functioning of a more important component or system.

Engine

1 Engine will not rotate when attempting to start

1 Battery terminal connections loose or corroded. Check the cable terminals at the battery. Tighten the cable or remove corrosion as necessary.
2 Battery discharged or faulty. If the cable connections are clean and tight on the battery posts, turn the key to the On position and switch on the headlights and/or windshield wipers. If they fail to function, the battery is discharged.
3 Automatic transmission not completely engaged in Park or clutch not completely depressed.
4 Broken, loose or disconnected wiring in the starting circuit. Inspect all wiring and connectors at the battery, starter solenoid and ignition switch.
5 Starter motor pinion jammed in flywheel ring gear. If manual transmission, place transmission in gear and rock the vehicle to manually turn the engine. Remove starter and inspect pinion and flywheel at earliest convenience.
6 Starter solenoid faulty (Chapter 5).
7 Starter motor faulty (Chapter 5).
8 Ignition switch faulty (Chapter 12).

2 Engine rotates but will not start

1 Fuel tank empty.
2 Battery discharged (engine rotates slowly). Check the operation of electrical components as described in previous Section.
3 Battery terminal connections loose or corroded. See previous Section.
4 Carburetor flooded and/or fuel level in carburetor incorrect. This will usually be accompanied by a strong fuel odor from under the hood. Wait a few minutes, depress the accelerator pedal all the way to the floor and attempt to start the engine.
5 Choke control inoperative (Chapter 1).
6 Fuel not reaching carburetor or fuel injectors. With ignition switch in Off position, open hood, remove the top plate of air cleaner assembly and observe the top of the carburetor (manually move the choke plate back if necessary). Have an assistant depress the accelerator pedal and check that fuel spurts into the carburetor. If not, check the fuel filter (Chapter 1), fuel lines and fuel pump (Chapter 4).
7 Fuel injector or fuel pump faulty (fuel injected vehicles) (Chapter 4).
8 No power to fuel pump (Chapter 4).
9 Worn, faulty or incorrectly gapped spark plugs (Chapter 1).
10 Broken, loose or disconnected wiring in the starting circuit (see previous Section).
11 Distributor loose, causing ignition timing to change. Turn the distributor as necessary to start engine, then set ignition timing as soon as possible (Chapter 1).
12 Broken, loose or disconnected wires at the ignition coil or faulty coil (Chapter 5).

3 Starter motor operates without rotating engine

1 Starter pinion sticking. Remove the starter (Chapter 5) and inspect.
2 Starter pinion or flywheel teeth worn or broken. Remove the cover at the rear of the engine and inspect.

4 Engine hard to start when cold

1 Battery discharged or low. Check as described in Section 1.
2 Choke control inoperative or out of adjustment (Chapter 4).
3 Carburetor flooded (see Section 2).
4 Fuel supply not reaching the carburetor (see Section 2).
5 Carburetor/fuel injection system in need of overhaul (Chapter 4).
6 Distributor rotor carbon tracked and/or mechanical advance mechanism rusted (Chapter 5).
7 Fuel injection malfunction (Chapter 4).

5 Engine hard to start when hot

1 Air filter clogged (Chapter 1).
2 Fuel not reaching the injectors (see Section 2).
3 Corroded electrical leads at battery (Chapter 1).
4 Bad engine ground (Chapter 1).
5 Starter worn (Chapter 5).
6 Corroded electrical leads at fuel injection (Chapter 4).

6 Starter motor noisy or excessively rough in engagement

1 Pinion or flywheel gear teeth worn or broken. Remove the cover at the rear of the engine (if so equipped) and inspect.
2 Starter motor mounting bolts loose or missing.

7 Engine starts but stops immediately

1 Loose or faulty electrical connections at distributor, coil or alternator.
2 Insufficient fuel reaching the fuel injector. Disconnect the fuel line at the fuel injector and remove the filter (Chapter 1). Place a container under the disconnected fuel line. Observe the flow of fuel from the line. If little or none at all, check for blockage in the lines and/or replace the fuel pump (Chapter 4).
3 Vacuum leak at the gasket surfaces of the fuel injection unit. Make sure that all mounting bolts/nuts are tightened securely and that all vacuum hoses connected to the fuel injection unit and manifold are positioned properly and in good condition.

8 Engine lopes while idling or idles erratically

1 Vacuum leakage. Check mounting bolts/nuts at the carburetor/fuel injection unit and intake manifold for tightness. Make sure that all vacuum hoses are connected and in good condition. Use a stethoscope or a length of fuel hose held against your ear to listen for vacuum leaks while the engine is running. A hissing sound will be heard. A soapy water solution will also detect leaks. Check the carburetor/fuel injector and intake manifold gasket surfaces.
2 Leaking EGR valve or plugged PCV valve (see Chapters 1 and 6).
3 Air filter clogged (Chapter 1).
4 Fuel pump not delivering sufficient fuel to the carburetor/fuel injector (see Section 7).
5 Carburetor out of adjustment (Chapter 4).
6 Leaking head gasket. If this is suspected, take the vehicle to a repair shop or dealer where the engine can be pressure checked.
7 Timing chain and/or gears worn (Chapter 2).
8 Camshaft lobes worn (Chapter 2).

9 Engine misses at idle speed

1 Spark plugs worn or not gapped properly (Chapter 1).
2 Faulty spark plug wires (Chapter 1).
3 Choke not operating properly (Chapter 1).
4 Sticking or faulty emissions system components (Chapter 6).
5 Clogged fuel filter and/or foreign matter in fuel. Remove the fuel filter (Chapter 1) and inspect.
6 Vacuum leaks at intake or at hose connections. Check as described in Section 8.
7 Incorrect idle speed or idle mixture (Chapter 1).
8 Incorrect ignition timing (Chapter 1).
9 Uneven or low cylinder compression. Check compression as described in Chapter 1.

10 Engine misses throughout driving speed range

1 Fuel filter clogged and/or impurities in the fuel system (Chapter 1).

Also check fuel output at the carburetor/fuel injector (see Section 7).
2   Faulty or incorrectly gapped spark plugs (Chapter 1).
3   Incorrect ignition timing (Chapter 1).
4   Check for cracked distributor cap, disconnected distributor wires and damaged distributor components (Chapter 1).
5   Leaking spark plug wires (Chapter 1).
6   Faulty emissions system components (Chapter 6).
7   Low or uneven cylinder compression pressures. Remove spark plugs and test compression with gauge (Chapter 1).
8   Weak or faulty ignition system (Chapter 5).
9   Vacuum leaks at fuel injection unit or vacuum hoses (see Section 8).

11   Engine stalls

1   Idle speed incorrect (Chapter 1).
2   Fuel filter clogged and/or water and impurities in the fuel system (Chapter 1).
3   Choke improperly adjusted or sticking (Chapter 1).
4   Distributor components damp or damaged (Chapter 5).
5   Faulty emissions system components (Chapter 6).
6   Faulty or incorrectly gapped spark plugs (Chapter 1). Also check spark plug wires (Chapter 1).
7   Vacuum leak at the fuel injection unit or vacuum hoses. Check as described in Section 8.

12   Engine lacks power

1   Incorrect ignition timing (Chapter 1).
2   Excessive play in distributor shaft. At the same time, check for worn rotor, faulty distributor cap, wires, etc. (Chapters 1 and 5).
3   Faulty or incorrectly gapped spark plugs (Chapter 1).
4   Fuel injection unit not adjusted properly or excessively worn (Chapter 4).
5   Faulty coil (Chapter 5).
6   Brakes binding (Chapter 1).
7   Automatic transmission fluid level incorrect (Chapter 1).
8   Clutch slipping (Chapter 8).
9   Fuel filter clogged and/or impurities in the fuel system (Chapter 1).
10 Emissions control system not functioning properly (Chapter 6).
11 Use of substandard fuel. Fill tank with proper octane fuel.
12 Low or uneven cylinder compression pressures. Test with compression tester, which will detect leaking valves and/or blown head gasket (Chapter 1).

13   Engine backfires

1   Emissions system not functioning properly (Chapter 6).
2   Ignition timing incorrect (Chapter 1).
3   Faulty secondary ignition system (cracked spark plug insulator, faulty plug wires, distributor cap and/or rotor) (Chapters 1 and 5).
4   Fuel injection unit in need of adjustment or worn excessively (Chapter 4).
5   Vacuum leak at fuel injection unit(s) or vacuum hoses. Check as described in Section 8.
6   Valve clearances incorrectly set, and/or valves sticking (Chapter 2).
7   Crossed plug wires (Chapter 1).

14   Pinging or knocking engine sounds during acceleration or uphill

1   Incorrect grade of fuel. Fill tank with fuel of the proper octane rating.
2   Ignition timing incorrect (Chapter 1).
3   Fuel injection unit in need of adjustment (Chapter 4).
4   Improper spark plugs. Check plug type against Emissions Control Information label located in engine compartment. Also check plugs and wires for damage (Chapter 1).
5   Worn or damaged distributor components (Chapter 5).
6   Faulty emissions system (Chapter 6).
7   Vacuum leak. Check as described in Section 8.

15   Engine diesels (continues to run) after switching off

1   Idle speed too high (Chapter 1).
2   Electrical solenoid at side of carburetor not functioning properly (not all models, see Chapter 4).
3   Ignition timing incorrectly adjusted (Chapter 1).
4   Thermo-controlled air cleaner heat valve not operating properly (Chapter 6).
5   Excessive engine operating temperature. Probable causes of this are malfunctioning thermostat, clogged radiator, faulty water pump (Chapter 3).

Engine electrical system

16   Battery will not hold a charge

1   Alternator drivebelt defective or not adjusted properly (Chapter 1).
2   Electrolyte level low or battery discharged (Chapter 1).
3   Battery terminals loose or corroded (Chapter 1).
4   Alternator not charging properly (Chapter 5).
5   Loose, broken or faulty wiring in the charging circuit (Chapter 5).
6   Short in vehicle wiring causing a continual drain on battery.
7   Battery defective internally.

17   Ignition light fails to go out

1   Fault in alternator or charging circuit (Chapter 5).
2   Alternator drivebelt defective or not properly adjusted (Chapter 1).

18   Ignition light fails to come on when key is turned on

1   Warning light bulb defective (Chapter 12).
2   Alternator faulty (Chapter 5).
3   Fault in the printed circuit, dash wiring or bulb holder (Chapter 12).

Fuel system

19   Excessive fuel consumption

1   Dirty or clogged air filter element (Chapter 1).
2   Incorrectly set ignition timing (Chapter 1).
3   Choke sticking or improperly adjusted (Chapter 1).
4   Emissions system not functioning properly (not all vehicles, see Chapter 6).
5   Carburetor idle speed and/or mixture not adjusted properly (Chapter 1).
6   Carburetor/fuel injection internal parts excessively worn or damaged (Chapter 4).
7   Low tire pressure or incorrect tire size (Chapter 1).

20   Fuel leakage and/or fuel odor

1   Leak in a fuel feed or vent line (Chapter 4).
2   Tank overfilled. Fill only to automatic shut-off.
3   Emissions system filter clogged (Chapter 1).
4   Vapor leaks from system lines (Chapter 4).
5   Carburetor/fuel injection internal parts excessively worn or out of adjustment (Chapter 4).

Cooling system

21   Overheating

1   Insufficient coolant in system (Chapter 1).

2   Water pump drivebelt defective or not adjusted properly (Chapter 1).
3   Radiator core blocked or radiator grille dirty and restricted (Chapter 3).
4   Thermostat faulty (Chapter 3).
5   Fan blades broken or cracked (Chapter 3).
6   Radiator cap not maintaining proper pressure. Have cap pressure tested by gas station or repair shop.
7   Ignition timing incorrect (Chapter 1).

22   Overcooling

1   Thermostat faulty (Chapter 3).
2   Inaccurate temperature gauge (Chapter 12)

23   External coolant leakage

1   Deteriorated or damaged hoses or loose clamps. Replace hoses and/or tighten clamps at hose connections (Chapter 1).
2   Water pump seals defective. If this is the case, water will drip from the weep hole in the water pump body (Chapter 1).
3   Leakage from radiator core or header tank. This will require the radiator to be professionally repaired (see Chapter 3 for removal procedures).
4   Engine drain plugs or water jacket core plugs leaking (see Chapter 2).

24   Internal coolant leakage

Note: *Internal coolant leaks can usually be detected by examining the oil. Check the dipstick and inside of the rocker arm cover for water deposits and an oil consistency like that of a milkshake.*

1   Leaking cylinder head gasket. Have the cooling system pressure tested.
2   Cracked cylinder bore or cylinder head. Dismantle engine and inspect (Chapter 2).

25   Coolant loss

1   Too much coolant in system (Chapter 1).
2   Coolant boiling away due to overheating (see Section 16).
3   Internal or external leakage (see Sections 25 and 26).
4   Faulty radiator cap. Have the cap pressure tested.

26   Poor coolant circulation

1   Inoperative water pump. A quick test is to pinch the top radiator hose closed with your hand while the engine is idling, then let it loose. You should feel the surge of coolant if the pump is working properly (Chapter 1).
2   Restriction in cooling system. Drain, flush and refill the system (Chapter 1). If necessary, remove the radiator (Chapter 3) and have it reverse flushed.
3   Water pump drivebelt defective or not adjusted properly (Chapter 1).
4   Thermostat sticking (Chapter 3).

Clutch

27   Fails to release (pedal pressed to the floor — shift lever does not move freely in and out of Reverse)

1   Clutch hydraulic system low or has air and needs to be bled (Chapter 8).
2   Clutch fork off ball stud. Look under the vehicle, on the left side of transmission.
3   Clutch plate warped or damaged (Chapter 8).

28   Clutch slips (engine speed increases with no increase in vehicle speed)

1   Clutch plate oil soaked or lining worn. Remove clutch (Chapter 8) and inspect.
2   Clutch plate not seated. It may take 30 or 40 normal starts for a new one to seat.
3   Pressure plate worn (Chapter 8).

29   Grabbing (chattering) as clutch is engaged

1   Oil on clutch plate lining. Remove (Chapter 8) and inspect. Correct any leakage source.
2   Worn or loose engine or transmission mounts. These units move slightly when clutch is released. Inspect mounts and bolts.
3   Worn splines on clutch plate hub. Remove clutch components (Chapter 8) and inspect.
4   Warped pressure plate or flywheel. Remove clutch components and inspect.

30   Squeal or rumble with clutch fully engaged (pedal released)

1   Improper adjustment; no free play (Chapter 1).
2   Release bearing binding on transmission bearing retainer. Remove clutch components (Chapter 8) and check bearing. Remove any burrs or nicks, clean and relubricate before reinstallation.
3   Weak linkage return spring. Replace the spring.

31   Squeal or rumble with clutch fully disengaged (pedal depressed)

1   Worn, defective or broken release bearing (Chapter 8).
2   Worn or broken pressure plate springs (or diaphragm fingers) (Chapter 8).
3   Air in hydraulic line (Chapter 8).

32   Clutch pedal stays on floor when disengaged

1   Bind in linkage or release bearing. Inspect linkage or remove clutch components as necessary.
2   Linkage springs being over extended. Adjust linkage for proper free play. Make sure proper pedal stop (bumper) is installed.

Manual transmission
Note: *All the following references are to Chapter 7, unless noted.*

33   Noisy in Neutral with engine running

1   Input shaft bearing worn.
2   Damaged main drive gear bearing.
3   Worn countershaft bearings.
4   Worn or damaged countershaft end play shims.

34   Noisy in all gears

1   Any of the above causes, and/or:
2   Insufficient lubricant (see checking procedures in Chapter 1).

35   Noisy in one particular gear

1   Worn, damaged or chipped gear teeth for that particular gear.
2   Worn or damaged synchronizer for that particular gear.

36 Slips out of high gear

1   Transmission mounting bolts loose (Chapter 7).
2   Shift rods not working freely (Chapter 7).
3   Damaged mainshaft pilot bearing.
4   Dirt between transmission case and engine or misalignment of transmission (Chapter 7).
5   Damaged mainshaft pilot bearing (Chapter 7).

37 Difficulty in engaging gears

1   Clutch not releasing completely (see clutch adjustment in Chapter 8).
2   Loose, damaged or out-of-adjustment shift linkage. Make a thorough inspection, replacing parts as necessary (Chapter 7).
3   Air in hydraulic system (Chapter 8).

38 Oil leakage

1   Excessive amount of lubricant in transmission (see Chapter 1 for correct checking procedures). Drain lubricant as required.
2   Side cover loose or gasket damaged.
3   Rear oil seal or speedometer oil seal in need of replacement (Chapter 7).
4   Clutch hydraulic system leaking (Chapter 8).

Automatic transmission

Note: *Due to the complexity of the automatic transmission, it is difficult for the home mechanic to properly diagnose and service this component. For problems other than the following, the vehicle should be taken to a dealer or reputable mechanic.*

39 General shift mechanism problems

1   Chapter 7 deals with checking and adjusting the shift linkage on automatic transmissions. Common problems which may be attributed to poorly adjusted linkage are:
   Engine starting in gears other than Park or Neutral.
   Indicator on shifter pointing to a gear other than the one actually being used.
   Vehicle moves when in Park.
2   Refer to Chapter 7 to adjust the linkage.

40 Transmission will not downshift with accelerator pedal pressed to the floor

   Chapter 7 deals with adjusting the kickdown rod to enable the transmission to downshift properly.

41 Transmission slips, shifts rough, is noisy or has no drive in forward or reverse gears

1   There are many probable causes for the above problems, but the home mechanic should be concerned with only one possibility — fluid level.
2   Before taking the vehicle to a repair shop, check the level and condition of the fluid as described in Chapter 1. Correct fluid level as necessary or change the fluid and filter if needed. If the problem persists, have a professional diagnose the probable cause.

42 Fluid leakage

1   Automatic transmission fluid is a deep red color. Fluid leaks should not be confused with engine oil, which can easily be blown by air flow to the transmission.
2   To pinpoint a leak, first remove all built-up dirt and grime from around the transmission. Degreasing agents and/or steam cleaning will achieve this. With the underside clean, drive the vehicle at low speeds so air flow will not blow the leak far from its source. Raise the vehicle and determine where the leak is coming from. Common areas of leakage are:
   a) Pan: Tighten mounting bolts and/or replace pan gasket as necessary (see Chapters 1 and 7).
   b) Filler pipe: Replace the rubber seal where pipe enters transmission case.
   c) Transmission oil lines: Tighten connectors where lines enter transmission case and/or replace lines.
   d) Vent pipe: Transmission overfilled and/or water in fluid (see checking procedures, Chapter 1).
   e) Speedometer connector: Replace the O-ring where speedometer cable enters transmission case (Chapter 7).

Transfer case

43 Transfer case difficult to shift into the desired range

1   Speed may be too great to permit engagement. Stop the vehicle and shift into the desired range.
2   Shift linkage loose, bent or binding. Check the linkage for damage or wear and replace or lubricate as necessary (Chapter 7).
3   If the vehicle has been driven on a paved surface for some time, the driveline torque can make shifting difficult. Stop and shift into 2-wheel drive on paved or hard surfaces.
4   Insufficient or incorrect grade or lubricant. Drain and refill the transfer case with the specified lubricant (Chapter 1).
5   Worn or damaged internal components. Disassembly and overhaul of the transfer case may be necessary (Chapter 7).

44 Transfer case noisy in all gears

   Insufficient or incorrect grade of lubricant. Drain and refill (Chapter 1).

45 Noisy or jumps out of 4-wheel drive Low range

1   Transfer cased not fully engaged. Stop the vehicle, shift into Neutral and then engage 4L.
2   Shift linkage loose, worn or binding. Tighten, repair or lubricate linkage as necessary.
3   Shift fork cracked, inserts worn or fork binding on the rail. Disassemble and repair as necessary (Chapter 7).

46 Lubricant leaks from the vent or output shaft seals

1   Transfer case is overfilled. Drain to the proper level (Chapter 1).
2   Vent is clogged or jammed closed. Clear or replace the vent.
3   Output shaft seal incorrectly installed or damaged. Replace the seal and check contact surfaces for nicks and scoring.

Axles

47 Noise

1   Road noise. No corrective procedures available.
2   Tire noise. Inspect tires and check tire pressures (Chapter 1).
3   Rear wheel bearings loose, worn or damaged (Chapter 10).

48 Vibration

   See probable causes under Driveshaft. Proceed under the guidelines listed for the driveshaft. If the problem persists, check the rear wheel bearings by raising the rear of the vehicle and spinning the wheels by hand. Listen for evidence of rough (noisy) bearings. Remove and inspect (Chapter 8).

49   Oil leakage

1   Pinion seal damaged (Chapter 8).
2   Axle shaft oil seals damaged (Chapter 8).
3   Differential inspection cover leaking. Tighten mounting bolts or replace the gasket as required (Chapter 8).

Brakes

Note: *Before assuming that a brake problem exists, make sure that the tires are in good condition and inflated properly (see Chapter 1), that the front end alignment is correct and that the vehicle is not loaded with weight in an unequal manner.*

50   Vehicle pulls to one side during braking

1   Defective, damaged or oil contaminated disc brake pads on one side. Inspect as described in Chapter 9.
2   Excessive wear of brake pad material or disc on one side. Inspect and correct as necessary.
3   Loose or disconnected front suspension components. Inspect and tighten all bolts to the specified torque (Chapter 10).
4   Defective caliper assembly. Remove caliper and inspect for stuck piston or other damage (Chapter 9).

51   Noise (high-pitched squeal without the brakes applied)

Disc brake pads worn out. The noise comes from the wear sensor rubbing against the disc (does not apply to all vehicles). Replace pads with new ones immediately (Chapter 9).

52   Excessive brake pedal travel

1   Partial brake system failure. Inspect entire system (Chapter 9) and correct as required.
2   Insufficient fluid in master cylinder. Check (Chapter 1), add fluid and bleed system if necessary (Chapter 9).
3   Rear brakes not adjusting properly. Make a series of starts and stops while the vehicle is in Reverse. If this does not correct the situation, remove drums and inspect self-adjusters (Chapter 9).

53   Brake pedal feels spongy when depressed

1   Air in hydraulic lines. Bleed the brake system (Chapter 9).
2   Faulty flexible hoses. Inspect all system hoses and lines. Replace parts as necessary.
3   Master cylinder mounting bolts/nuts loose.
4   Master cylinder defective (Chapter 9).

54   Excessive effort required to stop vehicle

1   Power brake booster not operating properly (Chapter 9).
2   Excessively worn linings or pads. Inspect and replace if necessary (Chapter 9).
3   One or more caliper pistons or wheel cylinders seized or sticking. Inspect and rebuild as required (Chapter 9).
4   Brake linings or pads contaminated with oil or grease. Inspect and replace as required (Chapter 9).
5   New pads or shoes installed and not yet seated. It will take a while for the new material to seat against the drum (or rotor).

55   Pedal travels to the floor with little resistance

Little or no fluid in the master cylinder reservoir caused by leaking wheel cylinder(s), leaking caliper piston(s), loose, damaged or disconnected brake lines. Inspect entire system and correct as necessary.

56   Brake pedal pulsates during brake application

1   Wheel bearings not adjusted properly or in need of replacement (Chapter 1).
2   Caliper not sliding properly due to improper installation or obstructions. Remove and inspect (Chapter 9).
3   Rotor defective. Remove the rotor (Chapter 9) and check for excessive lateral runout and parallelism. Have the rotor resurfaced or replace it with a new one.

Suspension and steering systems

57   Vehicle pulls to one side

1   Tire pressures uneven (Chapter 1).
2   Defective tire (Chapter 1).
3   Excessive wear in suspension or steering components (Chapter 10).
4   Front end in need of alignment.
5   Front brakes dragging. Inspect brakes as described in Chapter 9.

58   Shimmy, shake or vibration

1   Tire or wheel out-of-balance or out-of-round. Have professionally balanced.
2   Loose, worn or out-of-adjustment wheel bearings (Chapters 1 and 8).
3   Shock absorbers and/or suspension components worn or damaged (Chapter 10).

59   Excessive pitching and/or rolling around corners or during braking

1   Defective shock absorbers. Replace as a set (Chapter 10).
2   Broken or weak springs and/or suspension components. Inspect as described in Chapter 10.

60   Excessively stiff steering

1   Lack of fluid in power steering fluid reservoir (Chapter 1).
2   Incorrect tire pressures (Chapter 1).
3   Lack of lubrication at steering joints (Chapter 1).
4   Front end out of alignment.
5   See also section titled *Lack of power assistance.*

61   Excessive play in steering

1   Loose front wheel bearings (Chapter 1).
2   Excessive wear in suspension or steering components (Chapter 10).
3   Steering gearbox out of adjustment (Chapter 10).

62   Lack of power assistance

1   Steering pump drivebelt faulty or not adjusted properly (Chapter 1).
2   Fluid level low (Chapter 1).
3   Hoses or lines restricted. Inspect and replace parts as necessary.
4   Air in power steering system. Bleed system (Chapter 10).

63   Excessive tire wear (not specific to one area)

1   Incorrect tire pressures (Chapter 1).
2   Tires out of balance. Have professionally balanced.
3   Wheels damaged. Inspect and replace as necessary.
4   Suspension or steering components excessively worn (Chapter 10).

64   Excessive tire wear on outside edge

1   Inflation pressures incorrect (Chapter 1).
2   Excessive speed in turns.
3   Front end alignment incorrect (excessive toe-in). Have professionally aligned.
4   Suspension arm bent or twisted (Chapter 10).

65   Excessive tire wear on inside edge

1   Inflation pressures incorrect (Chapter 1).
2   Front end alignment incorrect (toe-out). Have professionally aligned.
3   Loose or damaged steering components (Chapter 10).

66   Tire tread worn in one place

1   Tires out of balance.
2   Damaged or buckled wheel. Inspect and replace if necessary.
3   Defective tire (Chapter 1).

Chapter 1 Tune-up and routine maintenance

Contents

Specifications

Recommended lubricants, fluids and capacities

Engine oil type	Consult your owner's manual or local Ford dealer for recommendations on the particular service grade and viscosity oil recommended for your area
Engine oil capacity (without filter)	4 qts*

Ford recommends that 1985 and 1986 2.0L and 2.3L models must have the filter changed with every oil change.

Engine oil capacity (with filter)	
1983-1985 2.0L and 2.3L	4 qts 1 pt
2.8L and 2.9L	5 qts
Coolant type	Ethylene glycol antifreeze and water
Cooling system capacity	
2.0L and 2.3L	
standard and extra/super cooling	6.5 qts
A/C	7.2 qts
2.8L and 2.9L	
standard and super cooling without A/C	7.2 qts
standard and super cooling with A/C	7.8 qts
Brake fluid type	C6AZ-19542-A or B (ESA-M6C25-A) or equivalent DOT 3
Manual transmission oil type	D8DZ-19C547-A (ESP-M2C83-C) or equivalent
Manual transmission oil capacity	
1983-1984 all	3 pts
1985-1986 Mitsubishi	4.8 pts
1985 Mazda	3 pts
1986 Mazda	3.6 pts
Automatic transmission	
C3	
fluid type	Dexron II
refill (from dry) capacity	8 qts
C5	
fluid type	Motorcraft type H
refill (from dry) capacity	
4X2	7.5 qts
4X4	7.9 qts

Recommended lubricants, fluids and capacities

Automatic transmission (continued)
A4LD
  fluid type .... Dexron II
  refill (from dry) capacity
    4X2 .... 9.5 qts
    4X4 .... 10.3 qts
Transfer case
  fluid type .... Dexron II
  fluid capacity .... 3 pts
Front drive axle
  oil type .... hypoid gear lubricant C6AZ-19580-E (ESW-M2C105-A)
  oil capacity* .... 1 pt

*add 0.5 ounces of friction modifier C8AZ-19B546-A or equivalent

Rear axle
  oil type .... EOAZ-19580-A (ESP-52C154-A)*
  oil capacity
    1983-1984 6.75 inch ring gear .... 3.3 pts
    1983-1984 7.5 inch ring gear .... 5 pts
    1985-1986 Ranger 7.5 inch ring gear .... 5 pts
    1985-1986 Bronco II 7.5 inch ring gear .... 5.5 pts
    all with 8.8 inch ring gear .... 5.5 pts

*add 4 ounces of friction modifier EST-M2C118-A to limited slip axles

Power steering fluid type .... ATF Type F
Front wheel bearing lubricant .... Multi-Purpose NLGI No. 2 wheel bearing grease
Windshield washer solvent .... Ford Ultra-Clear or equivalent
Radiator Cap operating pressure .... 13 psi
Engine idle speed .... See emission control information label in engine compartment

Ignition system

Distributor direction of rotation .... clockwise (all)
Firing order
  2.0L and 2.3L 1-3-4-2
  2.8L and 2.9L 1-4-2-5-3-6
Spark plug type and gap .... See emission control information label
Ignition timing .... See emission control information label

Torque specifications	**Ft-lbs**
Rocker arm cover/cam cover	
2.0L and 2.3L	6 to 8
2.8L and 2.9L	3 to 5
Oil pan drain plug	
2.0L and 2.3L	15 to 25
2.8L and 2.9L	15 to 21
Spark plugs	
2.0L and 2.3L	5 to 10
2.8L	18 to 28
Carburetor/EFI mounting nuts/bolts	
YFA 1-V	13 to 14
2150 2-V	14 to 16
1983-1985 electronic fuel injection body	12 to 15
1986 2.9L electronic fuel injection body	6 to 8
Distributor hold-down bolt	
1983-1984	14 to 21
1985-1986	17 to 25
Manual transmission drain plug	
1983-1984	29 to 43
1985-1986 Mitsubishi	25 to 32
1985-1986 Mazda	29 to 43
Manual transmission filler plug	
1983-1984	18 to 29
1985-1986 Mitsubishi	22 to 25
1985-1986 Mazda	18 to 29
Transfer case drain plug	14 to 22
Automatic transmission pan bolts	
C3 and C5	12 to 16
A4LD	5 to 10
Automatic transmission filter to valve body	25 to 40 in-lbs
Rear axle filler/inspection plug	15 to 30
Front drive axle inspection plug	15 to 30
Rear axle cover bolts	25 to 35
Wheel lug nuts	
1983-1985	85 to 115
1986	100

1 Introduction and routine maintenance schedule

Refer to illustrations 1.11a and 1.11b

This Chapter is designed to help the home mechanic maintain his or her vehicle for peak performance, economy, safety and long life.

On the following pages you will find a maintenance schedule, along with sections which deal specifically with each item on the schedule. Included are visual checks, adjustments and item replacements.

Servicing your vehicle using the time/mileage maintenance schedule and the sequenced Sections will give you a planned program of maintenance. Keep in mind that it is a full plan, and maintaining only a few items at the specified intervals will not give you the same results.

You will find as you service your vehicle that many of the procedures can be grouped together. Examples of this are:

If the vehicle is fully raised for a chassis lubrication check the exhaust system, suspension, steering and fuel system.

If the tires and wheels are removed, as during a routine tire rotation, check the brakes and wheel bearings.

If you must borrow or rent a torque wrench, service the spark plugs and check the carburetor or EFI (Electronic Fuel Injection) mounting torque.

The first step of this maintenance plan is to prepare yourself before the actual work begins. Read through the appropriate Sections for all work that is to be performed before you begin. Gather together all the necessary parts and tools. If it appears that you could have a problem during a particular job, don't hesitate to seek advice from your local parts man or dealer service department.

Routine maintenance intervals

The following recommendations are given with the assumption that the vehicle owner will be doing the maintenance or service work, as opposed to having a dealer service department do the work. The following are factory maintenance recommendations. However, subject to the preference of the individual owner interested in keeping his or her vehicle in peak condition at all times, and with the vehicle's ultimate resale in mind, many of these operations may be performed more often. We encourage such owner initiative.

When the vehicle is new it should be serviced initially by a factory authorized dealer service department to protect the factory warranty. In many cases the initial maintenance check is done at no cost to the owner.

Refer to the accompanying illustrations for engine compartment component locations.

Every 250 miles or weekly, whichever comes first

Check the automatic transmission fluid level (Sec 4)
Check power steering fluid level (Sec 4)
Check and service the battery (Sec 5)
Check the engine oil level (Sec 4)
Check the engine coolant level (Sec 4)
Check the windshield washer fluid level (Sec 4)
Check the tires and tire pressures (Sec 3)

Every 7500 miles or 7.5 months, whichever comes first

Change engine oil (Sec 16)
Change engine oil filter (Sec 16)
Check wheel lug nut torque (Sec 23)
Inspect and lubricate automatic transmission linkage (bellcrank system) (Sec 10)
Lubricate driveshaft U-joints if equipped with fittings (Sec 10)
Lubricate rear driveshaft double cardan joint centering ball (Bronco II and Ranger SWB 4x4) (Sec 10)
Initial engine drivebelt check. Future checks every 30,000 miles or 30 months (Sec 6)
Initial valve clearance check (2.8L). Future checks every 30,000 miles or 30 months (Sec 22)
Check carburetor or EFI mounting bolt torque (Sec 21)

Lubricate the chassis components (Sec 10)
Check the steering and suspension components (Sec 12)
Check the rear axle oil level (Sec 4)
Check and replace (if necessary) the windshield wiper blades (Sec 9)
Check and adjust the idle speed (Sec 15)

Every 12,000 miles or 12 months, whichever comes first

Drain, flush and refill the engine cooling system (Sec 28)
Check the engine coolant condition and effectiveness (Sec 4)
Check all hoses and clamps (Sec 8)

Every 15,000 miles or 15 months, whichever comes first

Rotate the tires (Sec 23)
Check the Air Cleaner Vacuum Motor for proper operation (Sec 20)
Replace the fuel filter (Sec 18)
Change the rear axle oil (if vehicle is used to pull trailer) (Sec 27)

Every 24,000 miles or 24 months, whichever comes first

Check the EGR system (Sec 32)
Check and adjust the ignition timing (Sec 33)
Check the spark plug wires, distributor cap and rotor (Sec 35)

Every 30,000 miles or 30 months, whichever comes first

Replace the spark plugs (Sec 34)
Check the engine drivebelts (first check at 7500 miles) (Sec 6)
Replace the air filter (Sec 30)
Replace the PCV filter (Sec 30)
Clean the choke linkage (Sec 19)
Check the valve clearance (2.8L) (first check at 7500 miles) (Sec 22)
Check the master cylinder fluid level (Sec 4)
Check the clutch reservoir fluid level (Sec 4)
Inspect and lubricate the front wheel bearings (Chapter 8)
Inspect the disc brake system (Sec 13)
Inspect the drum brake system (Sec 13)
Inspect the exhaust system (Chapter 4)
Inspect the parking brake system (Sec 13)
Lubricate the throttle ball stud (Sec 19)
Lubricate the front driveaxle slip joint (4x4) (Sec 10)
Inspect the hub lock lubrication (4x4) (Chapter 8)
Replace the distributor cap and rotor (Sec 36)
Inspect the rear suspension springs and bushings (Chapter 10)

Every 60,000 miles or 60 months, whichever comes first

Inspect and clean the injector tips (Chapter 4)
Replace the PCV valve (Sec 20)
Replace the ignition wires (Sec 36)
Check the thermactor hoses and clamps (Sec 8)
Replace the EGR valve (Sec 32)
Replace the EVP sensor (if equipped) (Sec 32)
Replace the EGR vacuum solenoids (Sec 32)
Replace the EGO sensor (Chapter 6)
Change the transfer case oil (4x4) (Chapter 8)

Heavy-duty operation

Heavy-duty operation is defined as off-road operation (see below), extended idling, towing trailers, operating in dusty conditions or excessive short run use and extended periods of snow plowing. Shorter maintenance intervals are recommended in these instances.

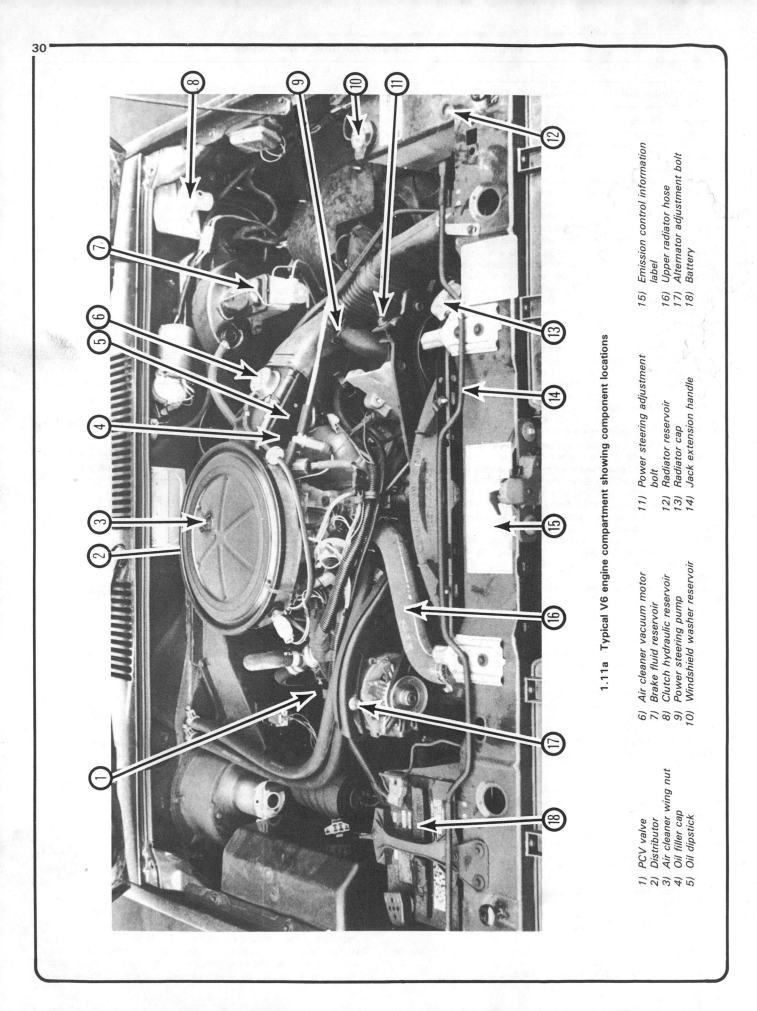

1.11a Typical V6 engine compartment showing component locations

1) PCV valve
2) Distributor
3) Air cleaner wing nut
4) Oil filler cap
5) Oil dipstick

6) Air cleaner vacuum motor
7) Brake fluid reservoir
8) Clutch hydraulic reservoir
9) Power steering pump
10) Windshield washer reservoir

11) Power steering adjustment bolt
12) Radiator reservoir
13) Radiator cap
14) Jack extension handle

15) Emission control information label
16) Upper radiator hose
17) Alternator adjustment bolt
18) Battery

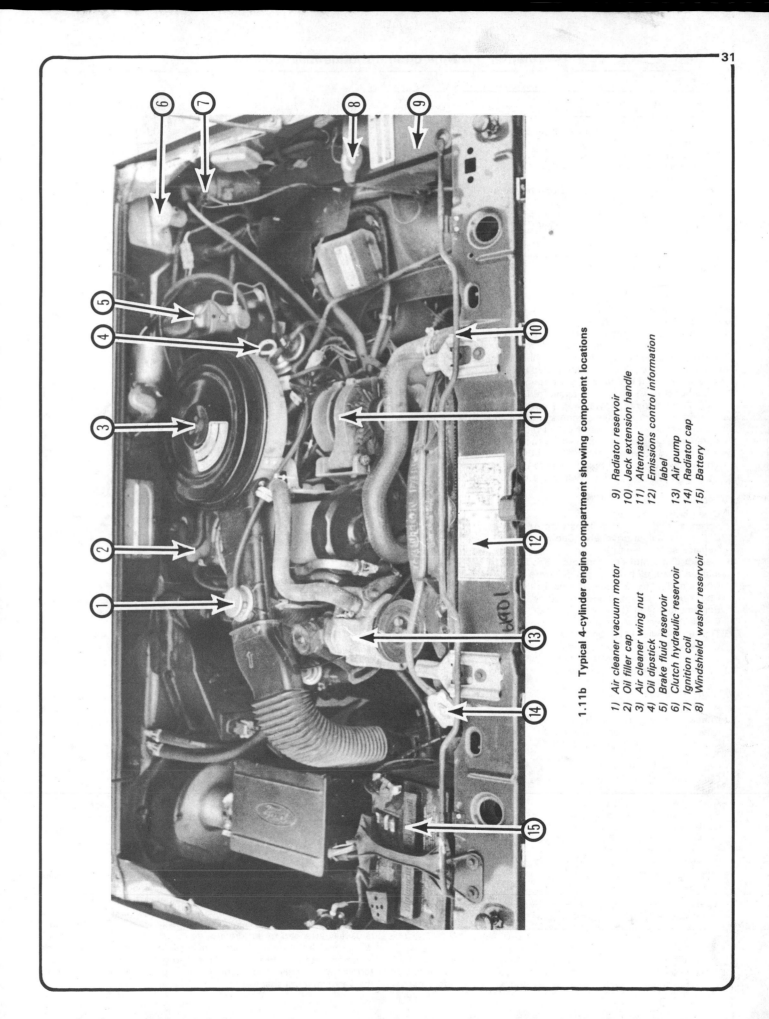

1.11b Typical 4-cylinder engine compartment showing component locations

1) Air cleaner vacuum motor
2) Oil filler cap
3) Air cleaner wing nut
4) Oil dipstick
5) Brake fluid reservoir
6) Clutch hydraulic reservoir
7) Ignition coil
8) Windshield washer reservoir
9) Radiator reservoir
10) Jack extension handle
11) Alternator
12) Emissions control information label
13) Air pump
14) Radiator cap
15) Battery

Off-road operation

After driving off road through mud, sand or water, check the following daily:
Brake discs and pads
Brake drums and shoes
Brake lines and hoses
Transmission, transfer case and differential oil
Air filter
Lubricate the steering linkage and knuckles and driveshaft universal joints daily or as soon as practical

2 Tune-up sequence

The term *Tune-up* is loosely used for any operation that puts the engine back in proper running condition. A tune-up is not a specific operation, but rather a combination of operations, such as replacing the spark plugs, adjusting the idle speed, setting the ignition timing, etc.

If, from the time the vehicle is new, the routine maintenance schedule (Section 1) is followed closely and frequent checks are made of fluid levels and high wear items, as suggested throughout this manual, the engine will be kept in relatively good running condition and the need for additional tune-ups will be minimized.

More likely than not, however, there will be times when the engine is running poorly due to lack of regular maintenance. This is even more likely if a used vehicle, which has not received regular and frequent maintenance checks, is purchased. In such cases, an engine tune-up will be needed outside of the regular routine maintenance intervals.

The following series of operations are those most often needed to bring a poor running engine back into a proper state of tune.

Minor tune-up
Clean battery (Sec 5)
Check all engine-related fluids (Sec 4)
Check and adjust drivebelts (Sec 6)
Replace spark plugs (Sec 34)
Inspect distributor cap and rotor (Sec 35)
Inspect spark plug wires and coil wire (Sec 35)
Check and adjust idle speed (Sec 15)
Check and adjust ignition timing (Sec 33)
Replace fuel filter (Sec 18)
Check PCV valve (Sec 3)
Tighten carburetor/TBI bolts (Sec 21)
Check air and PCV filters (Sec 30)
Clean and lubricate throttle linkage (Sec 19)
Check all underhood hoses (Sec 8)

Major tune-up
All of the above plus:
Check EGR system (Sec 6)
Check charging system (Chapter 5)
Check fuel pump output (Sec 17)
Test battery (Sec 5)
Check engine compression (Sec 37)
Check and adjust fuel/air mixture (see VECI label)
Check cooling system (Sec 7)
Adjust valves (Sec 22)
Replace distributor cap and rotor (Sec 35)
Replace spark plug wires and coil wire (Sec 35)
Replace air and PCV filters (Sec 30)
Check choke operation (Sec 14)
Check air cleaner vacuum motor operation (Sec 20)
Check fuel system (Sec 17)

3 Tire and tire pressure checks

Refer to illustrations 3.3 and 3.6

1   Periodically inspecting the tires may not only prevent you from being stranded with a flat tire, but can also give you clues as to possible problems with the steering and suspension systems before major

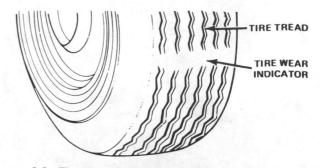

3.3   Thread wear indicator at the replacement stage

3.6   The use of an accurate tire pressure gauge is essential for long tire life

damage occurs.
2   Proper tire inflation adds miles to the life of the tires, allows the vehicle to achieve maximum miles per gallon and contributes to the overall quality of the ride.
3   When inspecting the tires, first check the wear of the tread (see illustration). Irregularities in the tread pattern (cupping, flat spots, more wear on one side than the other) are indications of front end alignment and/or balance problems. If any of these conditions are noted, take the vehicle to a repair shop to correct the problem.
4   Check the tread area for cuts and punctures. Many times a nail or tack will embed itself in the tread and yet the tire will hold air pressure for a short time. In most cases, a repair shop or gas station can repair the punctured tire.
5   It is also important to check the sidewalls of the tires. Check for deteriorated rubber, cuts and punctures. Also inspect the inboard side of the tire for signs of brake fluid leakage, indicating that a thorough brake inspection is needed immediately.
6   Incorrect tire pressure cannot be determined merely by looking at the tire. This is especially true for radial tires. A tire pressure gauge must be used (see illustration). If you do not already have a reliable gauge, it is a good idea to purchase one and keep it in the glovebox. Built-in pressure gauges at gas stations are often inaccurate.
7   Always check tire inflation when the tires are cold. Cold, in this case, means the vehicle has not been driven more than one mile after sitting for three hours or more. It is normal for the pressure to increase between four and eight pounds when the tires are hot.
8   Unscrew the valve cap and press the gauge firmly onto the valve stem. Observe the reading on the gauge and compare the figure to the recommended tire pressure listed on the tire placard. The tire placard is usually attached to the driver's door.
9   Check all tires and add air as necessary to bring them up to the recommended pressure levels. Do not forget the spare tire. Be sure to reinstall the valve caps, which will keep dirt and moisture out of the valve stem mechanism.

4.4a Remove the oil dipstick, wipe it clean, then reinsert it all the way before withdrawing it for an accurate oil check

4.4b The oil level should appear between the safe marks; do not overfill the crankcase

index finger and wipe the oil up the dipstick, looking for small dirt or metal particles. This is an indication that the oil should be replaced (Section 16).

4 Fluid level checks

Refer to illustrations 4.4a, 4.4b, 4.16, 4.20, 4.37, 4.46a, 4.46b, and 4.50.

1 There are a number of components on a vehicle which rely on the use of fluids to perform their job. During normal operation of the vehicle, these fluids are used up and must be replenished before damage occurs. See *Recommended lubricants and fluids* at the front of this Chapter for the specific fluid to be used when addition is required. When checking fluid levels, it is important to have the vehicle on a level surface.

Engine oil

2 The engine oil level is checked with a dipstick, which is located at the side of the engine block. The dipstick travels through a tube and into the oil pan.

3 The oil level should be checked before the vehicle has been driven or about 15 minutes after the engine has been shut off. If the oil is checked immediately after driving the vehicle, some of the oil will remain in the upper engine components, producing an inaccurate reading on the dipstick.

4 Pull the dipstick from the tube (see illustration) and wipe all the oil from the end with a clean rag. Insert the clean dipstick all the way back into the oil pan and pull it out again. Observe the oil at the end of the dipstick. At its highest point, the level should be between the Add and Safe marks (see illustration).

5 It takes approximately one quart of oil to raise the level from the Add mark to the Full mark on the dipstick. Do not allow the level to drop below the Add mark as engine damage due to oil starvation may occur. On the other hand, do not overfill the engine by adding oil above the Safe mark since it may result in oil-fouled spark plugs, oil leaks or oil seal failures.

6 Oil is added to the engine after removing a twist-off cap located on the rocker arm cover or through a raised tube near the front of the engine. The cap should be marked *Engine oil* or *Oil*. An oil can spout or funnel will reduce spills.

7 Checking the oil level can be an important preventative maintenance step. If you find the oil level dropping abnormally, it is an indication of oil leakage or internal engine wear which should be corrected. If there are water droplets in the oil, or if it is milky looking, component failure is indicated and the engine should be checked immediately. The condition of the oil can also be checked along with the level. With the dipstick removed from the engine, take your thumb and

Engine coolant

8 All vehicles covered by this manual are equipped with a pressurized coolant recovery system which makes coolant level checks very easy. A clear or white coolant reservoir attached to the inner fender panel is connected by a hose to the radiator cap. As the engine heats up during operation, coolant is forced from the radiator, through the connecting tube and into the reservoir. As the engine cools, the coolant is automatically drawn back into the radiator to keep the level correct.

9 The coolant level should be checked when the engine is hot by observing the level of fluid in the reservoir. If the system is completely cool, also check the level in the radiator by removing the cap.

10 **Warning:** *Under no circumstances should the radiator cap or the coolant recovery reservoir cap be removed when the system is hot, because escaping steam and scalding liquid could cause serious personal injury.* In the case of the radiator, wait until the system has cooled completely, then wrap a thick cloth around the cap and turn it to the first stop. If any steam escapes, wait until the system has cooled further, then remove the cap. The coolant recovery cap may be removed carefully after it is apparent that no further boiling is occurring in the recovery tank.

11 If only a small amount of coolant is required to bring the system up to the proper level, plain water can be used. However, to maintain the proper antifreeze/water mixture in the system, both should be mixed together to replenish a low level. Antifreeze offering protection to −20°F should be mixed with water in the proportion specified on the container. Do not allow antifreeze to come in contact with your skin or painted surfaces of the vehicle. Flush contacted areas immediately with plenty of water.

12 As the coolant level is checked, note the condition of the coolant. It should be relatively clear. If it is brown or a rust color, the system should be drained, flushed and refilled (Section 28).

13 If the cooling system requires repeated additions to maintain the proper level, have the radiator cap checked for proper sealing ability. Also check for leaks in the system (cracked hoses, loose hose connections, leaking gaskets, etc.).

Windshield washer fluid

14 Fluid for the windshield washer system is located in a plastic reservoir. The level in the reservoir should be maintained at the Full mark, except during periods when freezing temperatures are expected, at which times the fluid level should be maintained no higher than 3/4-full to allow for expansion should the fluid freeze. The use of an additive will help lower the freezing point of the fluid and will result in better cleaning of the windshield surface. Do not use antifreeze, however, since it will cause damage to the paint.

15 To help prevent icing in cold weather, warm the windshield with the defroster before using the washer.

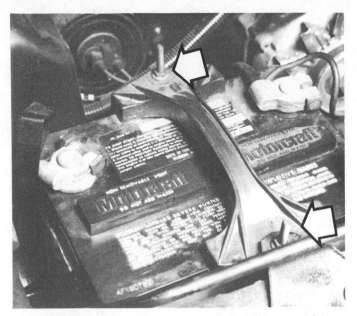

4.16   This type of battery never requires adding water, but normal maintenance should be performed. Arrows point to bolts holding battery tie down bracket

4.20   Clean dirt and grease from master cylinder cover before removing to check fluid level

Battery electrolyte

16   All vehicles with which this manual is concerned are equipped with a maintenance free battery, which is permanently sealed (except for vent holes) and has no filler caps (see illustration).

Brake fluid

17   The brake fluid reservoir is located directly above the brake master cylinder, which is attached to either the firewall at the left of the engine or to the brake vacuum booster in that same location.
18   Remove any accumulation of dirt or loose particles from the cover. If checking the brake fluid on a vehicle with water or snow on it, be sure to clean the hood and cowling completely of any liquid. Serious contamination of the brake fluid can result if even one drop of water is allowed to enter the brake fluid reservoir.
19   Snap the retaining clip to the side to release the cover from the master cylinder reservoir.
20   Remove the cover (see illustration) being very careful not to let any type of contamination enter the reservoir.
21   Observe the fluid level inside the dual chambers. Check that it is within 1/4-inch of the top of the cylinder.
22   Small amounts of fluid can be added to the system to make up for any fluid lost due to evaporation or brake component wear. If a large amount of fluid is necessary to bring the system back up to the proper level, check the system for any signs of leakage. Loss of braking capability can result from leakage in the brake hydraulic system.
23   Clean the cover carefully and replace it on the cylinder. Be careful not to allow any contaminants to fall into the reservoir.
24   Replace the retaining clip.
25   If upon checking the master cylinder fluid level you discover one or both reservoirs empty or nearly empty, the brake system should be bled (Chapter 9).

Manual transmission oil

26   Manual transmissions do not have a dipstick. The fluid level is checked with the engine cold by removing a plug in the left side of the transmission case. Locate the plug and use a rag to clean the plug and the area around it, then remove it with a wrench.
27   If oil immediately starts leaking out, thread the plug back into the transmission because the level is all right. If there is no leakage, completely remove the plug and place your little finger inside the hole. The oil level should be just at the bottom of the plug hole.
28   If the transmission needs more oil, use a syringe to squeeze the appropriate lubricant into the plug hole.
29   Thread the plug back into the transmission and tighten it securely.
30   Drive the vehicle a short distance, then check for leaks around the plug.

4.37   Follow the directions stamped on the transmission dipstick to get an accurate reading

Automatic transmission fluid

31   The level of the automatic transmission fluid should be carefully maintained. Low fluid level can lead to slipping or loss of drive, while overfilling can cause foaming and loss of fluid.
32   With the parking brake set, start the engine, then move the shift lever through all the gear ranges, ending in Park. The fluid level must be checked with the vehicle level and the engine running at idle. **Note:** *Incorrect fluid level readings will result if the vehicle has just been driven at high speeds for an extended period, in hot weather in city traffic, or if it's been pulling a trailer. If any of these conditions apply, wait until the fluid has cooled (about 30 minutes).*
33   Remove the transmission dipstick (located on the passenger side of the engine compartment).
34   Carefully touch the end of the dipstick to determine if the fluid is cool (about room temperature), warm or hot (uncomfortable to the touch).
35   Wipe the fluid from the dipstick with a clean rag and push it back into the filler tube until the cap seats.
36   Pull the dipstick out and note the fluid level.
37   If the fluid felt cool, the level should be near the add mark (see illustration).
38   If the fluid felt warm, the level should be near the full mark.
39   Add just enough of the recommended fluid to fill the transmission

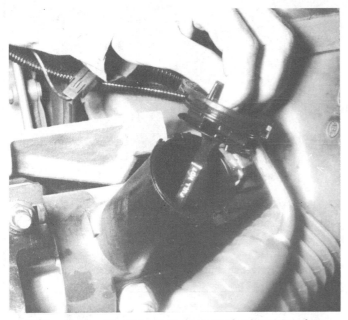

4.46a   Take extra care not to drop any foreign matter into the steering pump when checking the fluid level

4.46b   Check the power steering fluid level with engine at normal operating temperature. Fluid should not go above the Full Hot mark

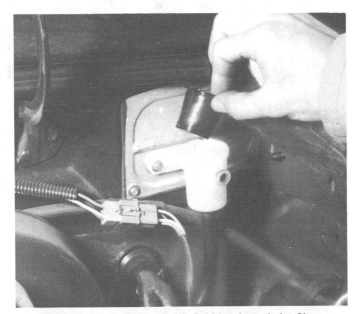

4.50   Check hydraulic clutch fluid level regularly. Clean the rubber cup before returning it to the reservoir

to the proper level. It takes about one pint to raise the level from the Add mark to the Full mark with a hot transmission, so add the fluid a little at a time and keep checking the level until it is correct.
40 The condition of the fluid should also be checked along with the level. If the fluid is a dark reddish-brown color, or if the fluid has a burned smell, the fluid should be changed. If you are in doubt about the condition of the fluid, purchase some new fluid and compare the two for color and smell.

Power steering fluid
41 Unlike manual steering, the power steering system relies on fluid which may, over a period of time, require replenishing.
42 The reservoir for the power steering pump will either be located near the front of the engine or on the engine compartment firewall.
43 For the check, the front wheels should be pointed straight ahead and the engine should be off.
44 Use a clean rag to wipe off the reservoir cap and the area around

the cap. This will help prevent any foreign matter from entering the reservoir during the check.
45 Make sure the engine is at normal operating temperature.
46 Remove the dipstick (see illustration), wipe it off with a clean rag, reinsert it, then withdraw it and read the fluid level (see illustration). The level should be at the Full Hot mark.
47 If additional fluid is required, pour the specified type directly into the reservoir, using a funnel to prevent spills.
48 If the reservoir requires frequent fluid additions, all power steering hoses, hose connections, the power steering pump and the steering assembly should be carefully checked for leaks.

Hydraulic clutch
49 The fluid cylinder for the hydraulic clutch used on manual transmission equipped models is located in the engine compartment on the left side of the firewall.
50 The clutch reservoir fluid level should be checked periodically. At the same time the rubber cap and cup should be washed in clean brake fluid (see illustration).

---

5   Battery check and maintenance

1   Tools and materials required for battery maintenance include eye and hand protection, baking soda, petroleum jelly, a battery cable puller and cable/terminal post cleaning tools.
2   A sealed maintenance-free battery is standard equipment on all vehicles with which this manual is concerned. Although this type of battery has many advantages over the older, capped cell type, and never requires the addition of water, it should nevertheless be routinely maintained according to the procedures which follow. **Warning:** *Hydrogen gas in small quantities is present in the area of the two small side vents on sealed batteries, so keep lighted tobacco and open flames or sparks away from them.*
3   The external condition of the battery should be monitored periodically for damage such as a cracked case or cover.
4   Check the tightness of the battery cable clamps to ensure good electrical connections and check the entire length of each cable for cracks and frayed conductors.
5   If corrosion is evident, remove the cables from the terminals, clean them with a battery brush and reinstall the cables. Corrosion can be kept to a minimum by applying a layer of petroleum jelly or grease to the terminals and cable clamps after they are assembled.
6   Make sure that the rubber protector (if so equipped) over the positive terminal is not torn or missing. It should completely cover the terminal.
7   Make sure that the battery carrier is in good condition and that

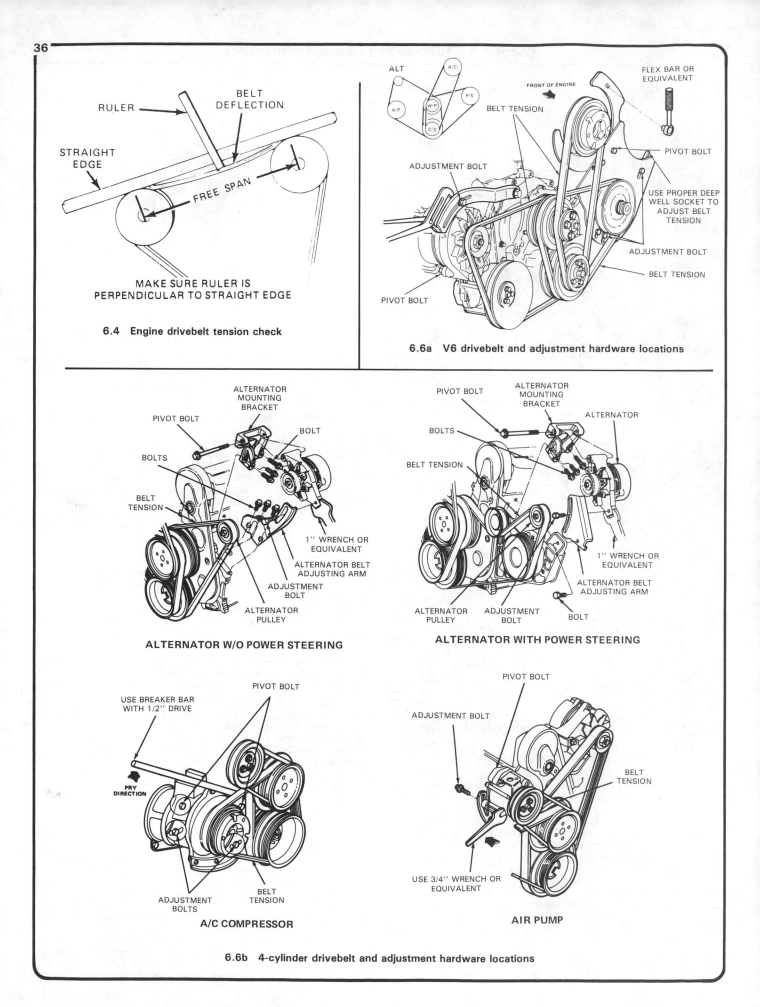

RULER

BELT
DEFLECTION

STRAIGHT
EDGE

FREE SPAN

MAKE SURE RULER IS
PERPENDICULAR TO STRAIGHT EDGE

6.4   Engine drivebelt tension check

ALT

A/C

A/P

W/P

P/S

C/S

FRONT OF ENGINE

FLEX BAR OR
EQUIVALENT

BELT TENSION

ADJUSTMENT BOLT

PIVOT BOLT

USE PROPER DEEP
WELL SOCKET TO
ADJUST BELT
TENSION

ADJUSTMENT BOLT

BELT TENSION

PIVOT BOLT

6.6a   V6 drivebelt and adjustment hardware locations

ALTERNATOR
MOUNTING
BRACKET

PIVOT BOLT

BOLT

BOLTS

BELT
TENSION

1'' WRENCH OR
EQUIVALENT

ALTERNATOR BELT
ADJUSTING ARM

ADJUSTMENT
BOLT

ALTERNATOR
PULLEY

ALTERNATOR W/O POWER STEERING

PIVOT BOLT

ALTERNATOR
MOUNTING
BRACKET

ALTERNATOR

BOLTS

BELT TENSION

1'' WRENCH OR
EQUIVALENT

ALTERNATOR BELT
ADJUSTING ARM

BOLT

ALTERNATOR
PULLEY

ADJUSTMENT
BOLT

ALTERNATOR WITH POWER STEERING

PIVOT BOLT

USE BREAKER BAR
WITH 1/2'' DRIVE

PRY
DIRECTION

ADJUSTMENT
BOLTS

BELT
TENSION

A/C COMPRESSOR

PIVOT BOLT

ADJUSTMENT BOLT

BELT
TENSION

USE 3/4'' WRENCH OR
EQUIVALENT

AIR PUMP

6.6b   4-cylinder drivebelt and adjustment hardware locations

6.8 Loosen bolt (arrow) and use a pry bar (arrow) to adjust the alternator belt

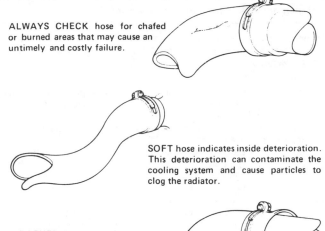

ALWAYS CHECK hose for chafed or burned areas that may cause an untimely and costly failure.

SOFT hose indicates inside deterioration. This deterioration can contaminate the cooling system and cause particles to clog the radiator.

HARDENED hose can fail at any time. Tightening hose clamps will not seal the connection or stop leaks.

SWOLLEN hose or oil soaked ends indicate danger and possible failure from oil or grease contamination. Squeeze the hose to locate cracks and breaks that cause leaks.

7.4 Check all coolant hoses periodically as shown

the hold-down clamp bolts are tight. If the battery is removed from the carrier, make sure that no parts remain in the bottom of the carrier when the battery is reinstalled. When reinstalling the hold-down clamp bolts, do not overtighten them.

8 Corrosion on the hold-down components, battery case and surrounding areas may be removed with a solution of water and baking soda. Protective gloves should be worn. Thoroughly wash all cleaned areas with plain water.

9 Any metal parts of the vehicle damaged by corrosion should be cleaned, covered with a zinc-based primer, then painted.

10 Further information on the battery, charging and jump-starting can be found in Chapter 5 and at the front of this manual.

6 Drivebelt check and adjustment

1 The drivebelts, or V-belts as they are sometimes called, are located at the front of the engine and play an important role in the overall operation of the vehicle and its components. Due to their function and material make-up, the belts are prone to failure after a period of time and should be inspected and adjusted periodically to prevent major engine damage.

2 The number of belts used on a particular vehicle depends on the accessories installed. Drivebelts are used to turn the alternator, power steering pump, water pump and air-conditioning compressor. Depending on the pulley arrangement, a single belt may be used to drive more than one of these components.

3 With the engine off, open the hood and locate the various belts at the front of the engine. Using your fingers, move along the belts checking for cracks and separation of the belt plies. Also check for fraying and glazing, which gives the belt a shiny appearance. Both sides of the belt should be inspected, which means you will have to twist the belt to check the underside.

4 The tension of each belt is checked by pushing on the belt at a distance halfway between the pulleys. Push firmly with your thumb and see how much the belt moves down (see illustration). A rule of thumb is that if the distance from pulley center-to-pulley center is between 7 and 11 inches, the belt should deflect 1/4-inch. If the belt is longer and travels between pulleys spaced 12 to 16 inches apart, the belt should deflect 1/2-inch.

5 If it is necessary to adjust the belt tension, either to make the belt tighter or looser, it is done by moving the belt-driven accessory on the bracket.

6 For each component there will be an adjustment or strap bolt and a pivot bolt (see illustrations). Both bolts must be loosened slightly to enable you to move the component.

7 After the two bolts have been loosened, move the component away from the engine (to tighten the belt) or toward the engine (to loosen the belt). Hold the accessory in position and check the belt tension. If it is correct, tighten the two bolts until just snug, then recheck the tension. If the tension is all right, tighten the bolts.

8 It will often be necessary to use some sort of pry bar to move the accessory while the belt is adjusted (see illustration). If this must be done to gain the proper leverage, be very careful not to damage the component being moved or the part being pried against.

7 Cooling system check

1 Many major engine failures can be attributed to a faulty cooling system. If the vehicle is equipped with an automatic transmission, the cooling system also plays an important role in prolonging transmission life.

2 The cooling system should be checked with the engine cold. Do this before the vehicle is driven for the day or after it has been shut off for at least three hours.

3 Remove the radiator cap and thoroughly clean the cap (inside and out) with clean water. Also clean the filler neck on the radiator. All traces of corrosion should be removed.

4 Carefully check the upper and lower radiator hoses along with the smaller diameter heater hoses. Inspect each hose along its entire length, replacing any hose which is cracked, swollen or shows signs of deterioration. Cracks may become more apparent if the hose is squeezed (see illustration).

5 Make sure that all hose connections are tight. A leak in the cooling system will usually show up as white or rust colored deposits on the areas adjoining the leak.

6 Use compressed air or a soft brush to remove bugs, leaves, etc. from the front of the radiator or air-conditioning condenser. Be careful not to damage the delicate cooling fins or cut yourself on them.

7 Have the cap and system pressure tested. If you do not have a pressure tester, most gas stations and repair shops will do this for a minimal charge.

8   Underhood hose check and replacement

Warning: *Replacement of air conditioner hoses must be left to a dealer or air conditioning specialist who can depressurize the system and perform the work safely.*

Vacuum hoses

1   High temperatures under the hood can cause the deterioration of the rubber and plastic hoses used for engine, accessory and emission systems operation.

2   Periodic inspection should be made for cracks, loose clamps, material hardening and leaks.

3   Some, but not all, vacuum hoses use clamps to secure the hoses to fittings. Where clamps are used, check to be sure they haven't lost their tension, allowing the hose to leak. Where clamps are not used, make sure the hose has not expanded and/or hardened where it slips over the fitting, allowing it to leak.

4   It is quite common for vacuum hoses, especially those in the emissions system, to be color coded or identified by colored stripes molded into the hose. Various systems require hoses with different wall thicknesses, collapse resistance and temperature resistance. When replacing hoses be sure to use the same hose material on the new hose.

5   Often the only effective way to check a hose is to remove it completely from the vehicle. Where more than one hose is removed, be sure to label the hoses and their attaching points to insure proper reattachment.

6   When checking vacuum hoses, be sure to include any plastic T-fittings in the check. Check the fittings for cracks and the hose where it fits over the fitting for enlargement, which could cause leakage.

7   A small piece of vacuum hose (1/4-inch inside diameter) can be used as a stethoscope to detect vacuum leaks. Hold one end of the hose to your ear and probe around vacuum hoses and fittings, listening for the ''hissing'' sound characteristic of a vacuum leak. **Warning:** *When probing with the vacuum hose stethoscope, be careful not to allow your body or the hose to come into contact with moving engine components such as drivebelts, the cooling fan, etc.*

Fuel hose

8   **Warning:** *There are certain precautions which must be taken when inspecting or servicing fuel system components. Work in a well ventilated area and do not allow open flames (cigarettes, appliance pilot lights, etc.) or bare light bulbs near the work area. Mop up any spills immediately and do not store fuel soaked rags where they could ignite.*

9   The fuel lines are usually under a small amount of pressure, so if any fuel lines are to be disconnected be prepared to catch fuel spillage.

10   Check all rubber fuel lines for deterioration and chafing. Check especially for cracking in areas where the hose bends and just before clamping points, such as where a hose attaches to the fuel pump, fuel filter and carburetor or fuel injection unit.

11   High quality fuel line, usually identified by the word *Fluroelastomer* printed on the hose, should be used for fuel line replacement. Under no circumstances should unreinforced vacuum line, clear plastic tubing or water hose be used for fuel line replacement.

12   Spring-type clamps are commonly used on fuel lines. These clamps often lose their tension over a period of time, and can be ''sprung'' during the removal process. Therefore it is recommended that all spring-type clamps be replaced with screw clamps whenever a hose is replaced.

Metal lines

13   Sections of metal line are often used for fuel line between the fuel pump and carburetor or fuel injection unit. Check carefully to be sure the line has not been bent and crimped and that cracks have not started in the line in the area of bends.

14   If a section of metal fuel line must be replaced, only seamless steel tubing should be used, since copper and aluminum tubing do not have the strength necessary to withstand normal engine operating vibration.

15   Check the metal brake lines where they enter the master cylinder and brake proportioning unit (if used) for cracks in the lines or loose fittings. Any sign of brake fluid leakage calls for an immediate thorough inspection of the brake system.

9   Windshield wiper blade — inspection and replacement

1   The windshield wiper and blade assembly should be inspected periodically for damage, loose components and cracked or worn blade elements.

2   Road film can build up on the wiper blades and affect their efficiency, so they should be washed regularly with a mild detergent solution.

3   The action of the wiping mechanism can loosen the bolts, nuts and fasteners. They should be checked and tightened, as necessary, at the same time the wiper blades are checked.

4   If the wiper blade elements are cracked, worn or warped, they should be replaced with new ones.

5   Remove the wiper blade by raising the wiper arm and pushing the wire clip to release the wiper blade.

6   With the blade in hand, pull the rubber element away from the end that is held with a tab, then push the element out the opposite end.

7   Install the blade by inserting the pronged end of the arm into the blade hole and pushing the blade towards the arm to lock in place.

10   Chassis lubrication

Refer to illustrations 10.2, 10.8 and 10.10.

Note: *Two wheel drive models and 1983 and later four wheel drive models have permanently lubricated front suspension and steering components which do not require periodic lubrication. If your vehicle does not have grease fittings it is of the permanently lubricated type.*

1   A grease gun and a cartridge filled with the proper grease (see *Recommended lubricants and fluids*) are usually the only equipment necessary to lubricate the chassis components. In some chassis locations, plugs may be installed rather than grease fittings, in which case grease fittings will have to be purchased and installed.

2   Refer to the accompanying illustration, which shows where the various grease fittings are located. Look under the vehicle to find these components and determine if grease fittings or solid plugs are installed. If there are plugs, remove them and buy grease fittings which will thread into the component. A Ford dealer or auto parts store will be able to supply replacement fittings. Straight, as well as angled, fittings are available.

3   For easier access under the vehicle, raise it with a jack and place jackstands under the frame. Make sure the vehicle is securely supported by the stands.

4   Before proceeding, force a little of the grease out of the nozzle to remove any dirt from the end of the gun. Wipe the nozzle clean with a rag.

5   With the grease gun, plenty of clean rags and the diagram, crawl under the vehicle and begin lubricating the components.

6   Wipe the grease fitting nipple clean and push the nozzle firmly over the fitting nipple. Squeeze the trigger on the grease gun to force grease into the component . **Note:** *The upper steering arm joints (one for each front wheel) should be lubricated until the rubber reservoir is firm to the touch. Do not pump too much grease into these fittings as it could rupture the reservoir. On the lower suspension fittings, continue pumping grease into the nipple until grease seeps out of the joint between the two components.* If the grease seeps out around the grease gun nozzle, the nipple is clogged or the nozzle is not seated on the fitting nipple.

7   Wipe the excess grease from the components and the grease fitting.

8   While you are under the vehicle, clean and lubricate the parking brake cable, along with the cable guides and levers. This can be done by smearing some of the chassis grease onto the cable and its related parts with your fingers. Use multi-purpose grease on the transmission shift linkage rods and swivels (see illustration).

9   Lower the vehicle to the ground for the remaining body lubrication steps.

10   Open the hood and smear a little chassis grease on the hood latch mechanism (see illustration). If the hood has an inside release, have an assistant pull the release knob from inside the vehicle as you lubricate the cable at the latch.

11   Lubricate all the hinges (door, hood, hatch) with a few drops of

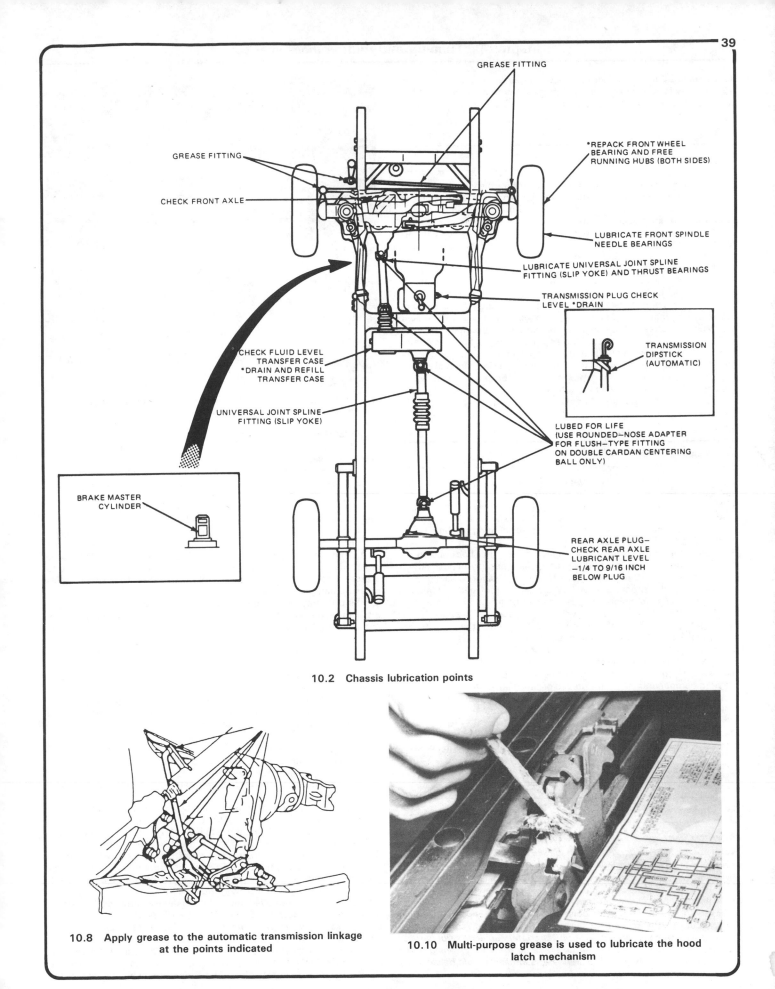

GREASE FITTING

GREASE FITTING

CHECK FRONT AXLE

*REPACK FRONT WHEEL BEARING AND FREE RUNNING HUBS (BOTH SIDES)

LUBRICATE FRONT SPINDLE NEEDLE BEARINGS

LUBRICATE UNIVERSAL JOINT SPLINE FITTING (SLIP YOKE) AND THRUST BEARINGS

TRANSMISSION PLUG CHECK LEVEL *DRAIN

TRANSMISSION DIPSTICK (AUTOMATIC)

CHECK FLUID LEVEL TRANSFER CASE *DRAIN AND REFILL TRANSFER CASE

UNIVERSAL JOINT SPLINE FITTING (SLIP YOKE)

LUBED FOR LIFE (USE ROUNDED−NOSE ADAPTER FOR FLUSH−TYPE FITTING ON DOUBLE CARDAN CENTERING BALL ONLY)

BRAKE MASTER CYLINDER

REAR AXLE PLUG− CHECK REAR AXLE LUBRICANT LEVEL −1/4 TO 9/16 INCH BELOW PLUG

10.2   Chassis lubrication points

10.8   Apply grease to the automatic transmission linkage at the points indicated

10.10   Multi-purpose grease is used to lubricate the hood latch mechanism

light engine oil to keep them in proper working order.
12 The key lock cylinders can be lubricated with spray-on graphite, which is available at auto parts stores.

11 Exhaust system check

1   With the engine cold (at least three hours after the vehicle has been driven), check the complete exhaust system from its starting point at the engine to the end of the tailpipe. This should be done on a hoist where unrestricted access is available.
2   Check the pipes and connections for signs of leakage and/or corrosion, indicating a potential failure. Make sure that all brackets and hangers are in good condition and tight.
3   Inspect the underside of the body for holes, corrosion, open seams, etc. which may allow exhaust gases to enter the passenger compartment. Seal all body openings with silicone or body putty.
4   Rattles and other noises can often be traced to the exhaust system, especially the mounts and hangers. Try to move the pipes, muffler and catalytic converter. If the components can come in contact with the body or suspension parts, secure the exhaust system with new mounts.
5   Check the running condition of the engine by inspecting inside the end of the tailpipe. The exhaust deposits here are an indication of engine state-of-tune. If the pipe is black and sooty or coated with white deposits, the engine is in need of a tune-up, including a thorough carburetor inspection and adjustment.

12 Suspension and steering check

1   Whenever the front of the vehicle is raised for service check the suspension and steering components for wear.
2   Indications of a fault in these systems are excessive play in the steering wheel before the front wheels react, excessive sway around corners, body movement over rough roads or binding at some point as the steering wheel is turned.
3   Before the vehicle is raised for inspection, test the shock absorbers by pushing down to rock the vehicle at each corner. If you push down and the vehicle does not come back to a level position within one or two bounces, the shocks are worn and must be replaced. Additional information on suspension components can be found in Chapter 10.
4   Raise the front end of the vehicle and support it securely on jackstands placed under the frame rails. Because of the work to be done, make sure the vehicle cannot fall from the stands.
5   Check the wheel bearings (see Section 29).
6   Crawl under the vehicle and check for loose bolts, broken or disconnected parts and deteriorated rubber bushings on all suspension and steering components. Look for grease or fluid leaking from around the steering box. Check the power steering hoses and connections for leaks. Check the balljoints for wear.
7   Have an assistant turn the steering wheel from side-to-side and check the steering components for free movement, chafing and binding. If the steering does not react with the movement of the steering wheel, try to determine where the slack is located.

13 Brake check

Refer to illustration 13.5.
Note: *For detailed photographs of the brake system, refer to Chapter 9.*
1   The brakes should be inspected every time the wheels are removed or whenever a defect is suspected. Indications of a potential brake system defect are: the vehicle pulls to one side when the brake pedal is depressed; noises coming from the brakes when they are applied; excessive brake pedal travel; pulsating pedal; and leakage of fluid, usually seen on the inside of the tire or wheel. **Warning:** *Dust and dirt present on brake and clutch assemblies contain asbestos fibers that are hazardous to your health when made airborne by cleaning with compressed air or dry brushing. Wheel assemblies should be cleaned using a vacuum.*

13.5 Disc pad inspection hole reveals thickness of pads (arrows)

Disc brakes

2   The front disc brakes can be visually checked without removing any parts except the wheels.
3   Raise the vehicle and place it securely on jackstands. Remove the wheels (see *Jacking and towing* at the front of the manual, if necessary).
4   The disc brake calipers, which contain the pads, are now visible. There is an outer pad and an inner pad in each caliper.
5   Check the pad thickness by looking at each end of the caliper and through the inspection hole in the caliper body (see illustration). If the lining material is 1/16-inch or less in thickness, the pads should be replaced. Keep in mind that the lining material is riveted or bonded to a metal backing shoe and the metal portion is not included in this measurement.
6   Since it may be difficult to measure the exact thickness of the remaining lining material, remove the pads for further inspection or replacement if you are in doubt as to the thickness or condition of the pad.
7   Before installing the wheels, check for leakage around the brake hose connections leading to the caliper and damage (cracking, splitting, etc.) to the brake hose. Replace the hose or fittings as necessary, referring to Chapter 9.
8   Check the condition of the rotor. Look for scoring, gouging and burned spots. If these conditions exist, the hub/rotor assembly should be removed for servicing (Chapter 9).

Drum brakes — rear

9   Using a scribe or chalk, mark the drum and hub so the drum can be reinstalled in the same position.
10 If so equipped, remove the drum retaining ring with a pair of wire cutters.
11 Pull the brake drum off the axle and brake assembly. If this proves difficult, make sure the parking brake is released, then squirt some penetrating oil around the center hub area. Allow the oil to soak in and again try to pull the drum off. Then, if the drum cannot be pulled off, the brake shoes will have to be adjusted. This is done by first removing the rubber plug in the backing plate. Pull the self-adjusting lever off the sprocket and use a small screwdriver to turn the adjuster wheel, which will move the shoes away from the drum.
12 With the drum removed, carefully brush away any accumulations of dirt and dust. **Warning:** *Do not blow the dust out with compressed air. Make an effort not to inhale the dust because it contains asbestos and is harmful to your health.*
13 Note the thickness of the lining material on both the front and rear brake shoes. If the material has worn away to within 1/16-inch of the recessed rivets or metal backing, the shoes should be replaced. If the

14.3 With the air cleaner top plate removed, the choke plate can be checked

linings look worn, but you are unable to determine their exact thickness, compare them with a new set at an auto parts store. The shoes should also be replaced if they are cracked, glazed (shiny surface) or contaminated with brake fluid.

14 Check to see that all the brake assembly springs are connected and in good condition.

15 Check the brake components for signs of fluid leakage. With your finger, carefully pry back the rubber cups on the wheel cylinder located at the top of the brake shoes. Any leakage is an indication that the wheel cylinders should be overhauled immediately (Chapter 9). Check the hoses and connections for signs of leakage.

16 Wipe the inside of the drum with a clean rag and denatured alcohol. Again, be careful not to breathe the dangerous asbestos dust.

17 Check the inside of the drum for cracks, scores, deep scratches and hard spots, which will appear as small discolored areas. If imperfections cannot be removed with fine emery cloth, the drum must be taken to a machine shop for resurfacing.

18 After the inspection process, if all parts are found to be in good condition, reinstall the brake drum (replace rubber plug in inspection/adjustment hole). Install the wheel and lower the vehicle to the ground.

Parking brake

19 The easiest way to check the operation of the parking brake is to park the vehicle on a steep hill with the parking brake set and the transmission in Neutral. If the parking brake cannot prevent the vehicle from rolling, it is in need of adjustment (see Chapter 9).

14 Carburetor choke check

Refer to illustration 14.3

1 The choke only operates when the engine is cold, so this check should be performed before the engine has been started for the day.

2 Open the hood and remove the top plate of the air cleaner assembly. It is held in place by nuts or a wing nut. If any vacuum hoses must be disconnected, make sure you tag them to ensure reinstallation in their original positions. Place the top plate and nuts aside, out of the way of moving engine components.

3 Look at the top of the carburetor at the center of the air cleaner housing. You will notice a flat plate at the carburetor opening (see illustration).

4 Have an assistant press the accelerator pedal to the floor. The plate should close completely. Start the engine while you observe the plate at the carburetor. **Warning:** *Do not position your face directly over the carburetor, because the engine could backfire and cause serious burns.*

When the engine starts, the choke plate should open slightly.

5 Allow the engine to continue running at idle speed. As the engine warms up to operating temperature, the plate should slowly open, allowing more air to enter through the carburetor.

6 After a few minutes, the choke plate should be all the way open to the vertical position.

7 If a malfunction is detected during the above checks, refer to Chapter 4 for specific information related to adjusting and servicing choke components.

15 Engine idle speed check and adjustment

1 The engine idle speed is adjustable on some models and should be checked at the scheduled maintenance interval.

2 On those vehicles with provisions for idle speed adjustment, the specifications for such adjustments are shown on the vehicle Emissions Control Information label. The adjustments must be made using calibrated test equipment, and should therefore be made by a dealer or automotive repair facility.

16 Engine oil and filter change

Refer to illustration 16.14

1 Frequent oil changes may be the best form of preventative maintenance available to the home mechanic. When engine oil ages, it becomes diluted and contaminated, which leads to premature engine wear.

2 Although some sources recommend oil filter changes every other oil change, we feel that the minimal cost of an oil filter and the relative ease with which it is installed dictate that a new filter be used whenever the oil is changed.

3 The tools necessary for a normal oil and filter change are a wrench to fit the drain plug at the bottom of the oil pan, an oil filter wrench to remove the old filter, a container with at least a six-quart capacity to drain the old oil into and a funnel or oil can spout to help pour fresh oil into the engine.

4 You should have plenty of clean rags and newspapers handy to mop up any spills. Access to the underside of the vehicle is greatly improved if the vehicle can be lifted on a hoist, driven onto ramps or supported by jackstands. **Warning:** *Do not work under a vehicle which is supported only with a bumper, hydraulic or scissor-type jack.*

5 If this is your first oil change on the vehicle, it is a good idea to crawl underneath and familiarize yourself with the locations of the oil drain plug and the oil filter. The engine and exhaust components will be warm during the actual work, so it is a good idea to figure out any potential problems before the engine and its accessories are hot.

6 Allow the engine to warm up to normal operating temperature. If the new oil or any tools are needed, use this warm-up time to gather everything necessary for the job. The correct type of oil to buy for your application can be found in *Recommended lubricants and fluids* near the front of this manual.

7 With the engine oil warm (warm engine oil will drain better and more built-up sludge will be removed with the oil), raise and support the vehicle. Make sure it is firmly supported.

8 Move all necessary tools, rags and newspapers under the vehicle. Position the drain pan under the drain plug. Keep in mind that the oil will initially flow from the pan with some force, so place the pan accordingly.

9 Being careful not to touch any of the hot exhaust pipe components, use the wrench to remove the drain plug near the bottom of the oil pan. Depending on how hot the oil has become, you may want to wear gloves while unscrewing the plug the final few turns.

10 Allow the old oil to drain into the pan. It may be necessary to move the pan farther under the engine as the oil flow slows to a trickle.

11 After all the oil has drained, wipe off the drain plug with a clean rag. Small metal particles may cling to the plug and would immediately contaminate the new oil.

12 Clean the area around the drain plug opening and reinstall the plug. Tighten the plug securely with the wrench. If a torque wrench is available, use it to tighten the plug.

13 Move the drain pan into position under the oil filter.

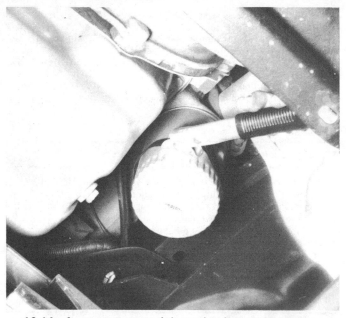

16.14   A strap-type wrench is used to loosen the oil filter

14   Use the filter wrench to loosen the oil filter (see illustration). Chain or metal band-type filter wrenches may distort the filter canister, but this is of no concern as the filter will be discarded anyway.
15   Sometimes the oil filter is on so tight it cannot be loosened, or it is positioned in an area which is inaccessible with a filter wrench. As a last resort, you can punch a metal bar or long screwdriver directly through the side of the canister and use it as a T-bar to turn the filter. If so, be prepared for oil to spurt out of the canister as it is punctured.
16   Completely unscrew the old filter. Be careful, it is full of oil. Empty the oil inside the filter into the drain pan.
17   Compare the old filter with the new one to make sure they are the same type.
18   Use a clean rag to remove all oil, dirt and sludge from the area where the oil filter mounts to the engine. Check the old filter to make sure the rubber gasket is not stuck to the engine mounting surface. If the gasket is stuck to the engine (use a flashlight if necessary), remove it.
19   Open one of the cans of new oil and fill the new filter about half-full of fresh oil. Apply a light coat of oil to the rubber gasket of the new oil filter.
20   Attach the new filter to the engine following the tightening directions printed on the filter canister or packing box. Most filter manufacturers recommend against using a filter wrench due to the possibility of overtightening and damage to the seal.
21   Remove all tools, rags, etc. from under the vehicle, being careful not to spill the oil in the drain pan, then lower the vehicle.
22   Move to the engine compartment and locate the oil filler cap on the engine. In most cases there will be a screw-off cap on the rocker arm cover or a cap at the end of a fill tube at the front of the engine. In any case, the cap will most likely be labeled *Engine Oil* or *Oil*.
23   If an oil can spout is used, push the spout into the top of the oil can and pour the fresh oil through the filler opening. A funnel may also be used.
24   Pour three quarts of fresh oil into the engine. Wait a few minutes to allow the oil to drain into the pan, then check the level on the oil dipstick (see Section 4 if necessary). If the oil level is at or near the lower Add mark, start the engine and allow the new oil to circulate.
25   Run the engine for only about a minute and then shut it off. Immediately look under the vehicle and check for leaks at the oil pan drain plug and around the oil filter. If either is leaking, tighten with a bit more force.
26   With the new oil circulated and the filter now completely full, recheck the level on the dipstick and add enough oil to bring the level to the Full mark on the dipstick.
27   During the first few trips after an oil change, make it a point to check frequently for leaks and proper oil level.
28   The old oil drained from the engine cannot be reused in its present state and should be disposed of. Oil reclamation centers, auto repair shops and gas stations will normally accept the oil, which can be refined and used again. After the oil has cooled, it can be drained into a suitable container (capped plastic jugs, topped bottles, milk cartons, etc.) for transport to one of these disposal sites.

17   Fuel system check

Warning: *There are certain precautions to take when inspecting or servicing the fuel system components. Work in a well-ventilated area and do not allow open flames (cigarettes, appliance pilot lights, etc.) to get near the work area. Mop up spills immediately and do not store fuel-soaked rags where they could ignite.*

1   If your vehicle is equipped with fuel injection, refer to the fuel injection pressure relief procedure (Chapter 4) before servicing any component of the fuel system.
2   The non-EFI fuel system is under a small amount of pressure, so if any fuel lines are disconnected for servicing, be prepared to catch the fuel as it spurts out. Fuel injection lines are under considerable pressure which must be relieved before the lines can be disconnected (see Chapter 4). Plug all disconnected fuel lines immediately after disconnection to prevent the tank from emptying itself.
3   The fuel system is most easily checked with the vehicle raised on a hoist so the components underneath the vehicle are readily visible and accessible.
4   If the smell of gasoline is noticed while driving or after the vehicle has been in the sun, the system should be thoroughly inspected immediately.
5   Remove the gas filler cap and check for damage, corrosion and an unbroken seal. Replace the cap with a new one, if necessary.
6   With the vehicle raised, inspect the gas tank and filler neck for punctures, cracks and other damage. The connection between the filler neck and the tank is especially critical. Sometimes a rubber filler neck will leak due to loose clamps or deteriorated rubber, problems a home mechanic can usually rectify. **Warning:** *Do not, under any circumstances, try to repair a fuel tank yourself (except rubber components). A welding torch or any open flame can easily cause the fuel vapors to explode if the proper precautions are not taken.*
7   Carefully check all rubber hoses and metal lines leading away from the fuel tank. Check for loose connections, deteriorated hoses, crimped lines and other damage. Follow the lines up to the front of the vehicle, carefully inspecting them all the way. Repair or replace damaged sections as necessary.

18   Fuel filter replacement

Refer to illustration 18.11

Carburetor equipped models
Removal
1   Remove the air cleaner assembly.
2   Use a end wrench on the fuel filter to prevent the filter from turning and loosen the fuel line.
3   Unscrew the filter from the carburetor.

Installation
4   Apply one drop of thread-locking compound to the external threads of the new filter. Thread the filter into the carburetor inlet port.
5   Apply a drop of light oil to the fuel supply tube nut and flare, and hand start the nut into the fuel filter inlet approximately two threads. Use a wrench to hold the filter and tighten the fuel line nut.
6   Use a wrench to hold the filter and tighten the fuel line nut.
7   Start the engine and check for leaks.
8   Install air cleaner assembly.

EFI engine
Note: *The in-line EFI reservoir type fuel filter should last the life of the car and is not part of the routine maintenance. Should you need to replace it follow these procedures.* **Caution:** *Service with the front end at or above the level of the rear of the vehicle to prevent leakage or siphoning of fuel. Relieve tank pressure by removing the fill cap. Replace the cap after the pressure is relieved.*

Removal
4x2 models
9   Remove the reservoir shield (if so equipped) by removing either

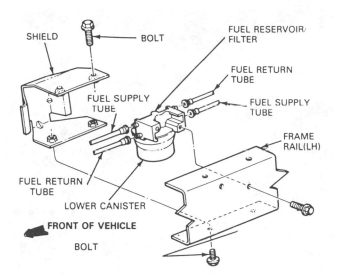

SHIELD — BOLT

FUEL RESERVOIR/FILTER

FUEL RETURN TUBE

FUEL SUPPLY TUBE

FUEL SUPPLY TUBE

FRAME RAIL(LH)

FUEL RETURN TUBE

LOWER CANISTER

FRONT OF VEHICLE

BOLT

18.10 The inline EFI fuel reservoir is located on the frame rail

20.5 With the engine cold the damper door should close off the outside air

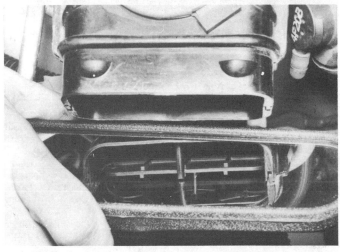

20.6 As the engine warms up the damper door should open

three or four screws (depending on vehicle).

10 Unscrew the lower canister, using a flexible strap type oil filter wrench, and slide the filter and canister out from the frame rail (see illustration). **Note:** *The filter will be full of fuel.*

11 Empty the fuel from the filter canister. Remove the filter cartridge and O-ring.

4x4 models

12 Due to the close clearance on the 4x4 model, the reservoir shield should not be completely removed from the vehicle when servicing the reservoir fuel filter. The following procedures should be used.

13 Remove the three reservoir shield attaching bolts. If the vehicle has a transfer case skid plate, it may need to be removed to provide hand access to the canister.

14 Rotate the reservoir shield counter-clockwise and slide it forward on the frame rail until access to the reservoir is attained.

15 Unscrew the reservoir canister, using a flexible strap type oil filter wrench. **Note:** *The fuel filter canister will be full of fuel.* After separating it from the upper housing, the canister can be lifted over top of the front wheel driveshaft, then down and out.

16 Empty the fuel from fuel canister. Remove the filter cartridge and O-ring.

Installation both models

17 Install the new fuel filter cartridge into the fuel filter canister.

18 Position the new O-ring so that it is seated in the O-ring groove of the canister.

19 While keeping the canister level, to keep from dislodging the O-ring, position the canister to the bottom of the reservoir housing and screw it into place. Complete the filter canister tightening by turning canister about one-sixth of a turn past initial O-ring compression, using an oil filter wrench. **Note:** *The rubber grommet on the filter will automatically seat on the piloted stud of the upper housing as the canister is tightened.*

20 Slide the reservoir shield into position and install the mounting bolts.

19 Throttle linkage check

1 The throttle linkage is a cable type and although there are no adjustments to the linkage itself, periodic maintenance is necessary to assure its proper function.

2 Remove the air cleaner (refer to Chapter 2) so the entire linkage is visible.

3 Check the entire length of the cable to make sure that it is not binding.

4 Check all the nylon bushings for wear, replacing them with new ones as necessary.

5 Lubricate the cable mechanisms with engine oil at the pivot points, but do not lubricate the cable itself.

20 Air Cleaner Air Vacuum Motor check

Refer to illustrations 20.5 and 20.6

1 All engines are equipped with a thermostatically controlled air cleaner which draws air into the carburetor from different locations, depending upon engine temperature.

2 This is a simple check which may require the use of a small mirror.

3 Open the hood and locate the damper door in the air cleaner assembly. It will be located inside the snorkel attached to the air cleaner housing.

4 If there is a flexible air duct attached to the end of the snorkel, leading to an area behind the grille, disconnect it at the snorkel. This will enable you to look through the end of the snorkel and see the damper door inside.

5 The check should be made when the engine and outside air are cold. Start the engine and look through the snorkel at the damper door, which should move to a closed position (see illustration). With the damper closed, air cannot enter through the end of the snorkel, but instead enters the air cleaner through the flexible duct attached to the exhaust manifold heat stove passage.

6 As the engine warms up to operating temperature, the damper should open (see illustration) to allow air through the snorkel end. Depending on ambient temperature, this may take 10 to 15 minutes. To speed up this check you can reconnect the snorkel air duct, drive the vehicle and then check to see if the damper is completely open.

7 See Chapter 6 for more information if the thermo-controlled air cleaner is not operating properly.

21.5   A torque check of the carburator (or fuel injection unit) mounting bolts will help eliminate vacuum leaks in the induction system

21   Carburetor/throttle body mounting torque check

Refer to illustration 21.5

1   The carburetor/EFI is attached to the top of the intake manifold by four nuts or bolts. These fasteners can sometimes work loose from vibration and temperature changes during normal engine operation, causing a vacuum leak.

2   To tighten the mounting nuts/bolts, a torque wrench is necessary. If you do not own one, they can usually be rented on a daily basis.

3   Remove the air cleaner assembly, tagging each hose to be disconnected with a piece of numbered tape to make reassembly easier.

4   Locate the mounting nuts/bolts at the base of the carburetor/throttle body. Decide what adapters will be necessary, if any, to tighten the fasteners with a socket and the torque wrench.

5   Tighten the nuts/bolts to the specified torque (see illustration). Do not overtighten them, as the threads could strip.

6   If you suspect that a vacuum leak exists at the bottom of the carburetor or throttle body, obtain a length of hose about the diameter of fuel hose. Start the engine and place one end of the hose next to your ear as you probe around the base with the other end. You will hear a hissing sound if a leak exists. **Warning:** *Make sure to keep the hose, clothing and your body away from moving or hot engine components while making this check.*

7   If, after the nuts/bolts are properly tightened, a vacuum leak still exists, the carburetor/throttle body must be removed and a new gasket installed. See Chapter 4 for more information.

8   After tightening the fasteners, reinstall the air cleaner and return all hoses to their original positions.

22   Valve clearance 2.8L V6 — adjustment

Refer to illustrations 22.14 and 22.17

Rocker arm cover — removal

1   Disconnect the negative cable from the battery.

2   Remove the air cleaner.

3   Remove the PCV valve and hose.

4   Remove the carburetor choke air deflector plate.

5   Remove the rocker arm cover attaching bolts and load distribution washers (patch pieces).

6   On vehicles equipped with automatic transmissions, remove the transmission dipstick tube and bracket, which is attached to rocker arm cover.

7   Disconnect the kickdown linkage from the carburetor (automatic

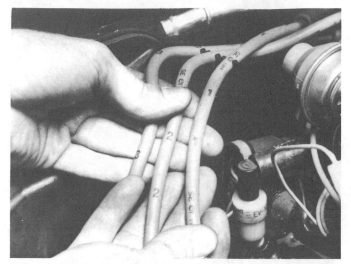

22.14   The factory spark plug wires are numbered to make proper reinstallation easier

22.17   To adjust valve clearance loosen or tighten the adjusting bolt until the feeler gauge meets slight resistance

transmission only).

8   Position the air cleaner vacuum motor hose and wiring harness away from the right rocker arm cover.

9   Disconnect the vacuum line at the canister purge solenoid and disconnect the line routed from the canister to the purge solenoid.

10   Disconnect power brake booster hose, if so equipped.

11   Using a flat screwdriver, gently pry up on the valve cover to break the seal, being careful not to bend the cover.

12   Remove the rocker covers.

Valve clearance adjustment

13   After removing the valve cover and before adjusting the valves, refer to Chapter 2 Specifications and torque the head bolts. **Note:** *The emission label located under the hood on the fan shroud will have valve lash specification printed on it.*

14   Position the number 1 piston at top dead center (TDC) on the compression stroke. To do this, first check each number on the spark plug wires (see illustration) or number them if not marked. Remove the spark plugs. Locate the number 1 spark plug wire and trace it back to the distributor. Write a number 1 on the distributor body directly below the terminal where the number 1 spark plug wire attaches to the distributor cap. Repeat this procedure for the remaining cylinders, then remove the distributor cap and wires.

15   Slip a wrench or socket over the large bolt at the front of the crankshaft and slowly turn it in a clockwise direction until the TDC mark on the pulley is aligned with the pointer. The distributor rotor

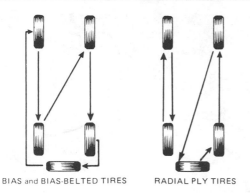

BIAS and BIAS-BELTED TIRES   RADIAL PLY TIRES

23.2 Tire rotation for bias-ply and radial tires

should be pointing at the number 1 you made on the distributor body. If it isn't, turn the crankshaft one more complete revolution (360°) in a clockwise direction. If the rotor is now pointing at the 1 on the distributor body, the number 1 piston is at TDC on the compression stroke.

16 **Note:** *When checking lash, insert the feeler gauge between rocker arm and valve tip at the side of the valve tip and move toward opposite edge with a motion that is parallel to center line of the crankshaft.* Do not insert feeler at outboard edge and move inward toward carburetor (perpendicular to the crank center line). This will produce an erroneous ''feel'' that will result in excessively tight valves.

17 If the feeler gauge will not fit between the valve stem and the rocker arm, or if it is loose, simply loosen or tighten, (as necessary) the adjusting bolt (see illustration) until the gauge is able to be inserted and withdrawn with only slight resistance to the gauge.

18 The valves in the remaining cylinders can now be checked by bringing each piston, in order (1-4-2-5-3-6), to TDC by turning the crankshaft in a clockwise direction until the distributor rotor is pointing to the appropiate cylinder number you previously marked on the distributor body.

19 Clean all old gasket material from cylinder heads and rocker arm cover gasket surfaces.

20 Install rocker arm covers, using new gaskets. **Caution:** *Failure to install a new rocker cover gasket and reinstall rocker cover reinforcement pieces will result in oil leaks.*

21 On vehicles equipped with automatic transmission, install transmission dipstick tube and bracket.

22 Connect the kickdown linkage (automatic transmission only).

23 After ensuring that all rocker arm cover load distribution washers (patch pieces) are installed in their original position, tighten the rocker arm cover bolts to the specified torque.

24 Install the spark plug wires and distributor cap.

25 Install the PCV valve and hose.

26 Install the carburetor choke air deflector plate.

27 Reposition the air cleaner vacuum motor hose and wiring harness in their original places.

28 Connect the vacuum line at the canister purge solenoid and connect the line routed from canister to purge solenoid.

29 Connect the power brake hose, if so equipped.

30 Install the air cleaner.

31 Start the engine and check for oil and vacuum leaks.

23 Tire rotation

Refer to illustration 23.2

1 The tires should be rotated at the specified intervals and whenever uneven wear is noticed. Since the vehicle will be raised and the tires removed anyway, this is a good time to check the brakes (Section 13) and the wheel bearings (Section 27). Read over these Sections if this is to be done at the same time.

2 Refer to the accompanying illustration of the bias-ply and radial-ply tire rotation patterns. Do not include *Temporary Use Only* spare tires in the rotation sequence.

3 Refer to the information in *Jacking and towing* at the front of this manual for the proper procedures to follow when raising the vehicle and changing a tire. If the brakes are to be checked, do not apply the parking brake as stated. Make sure the tires are blocked to prevent the vehicle from rolling.

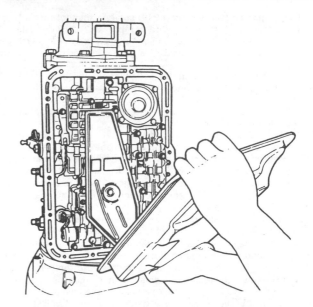

24.10 Once the pan is removed the filter/strainer is accessible

4 Preferably, the entire vehicle should be raised. This can be done on a hoist or by jacking up each corner and then lowering the vehicle onto jackstands placed under the frame rails. Always use four jackstands and make sure the vehicle is firmly supported.

5 After rotation, check and adjust the the tire pressures as necessary and be sure to check the lug nut tightness.

24 Automatic transmission fluid and filter change

Refer to illustration 24.10

Caution: *Use of fluid other than that listed in the Specifications could result in transmission malfunction and/or failure.*

1 At the specified time intervals, the transmission fluid should be changed and the filter replaced with a new one. Since there is no drain plug, the transmission oil pan must be removed from the bottom of the transmission to drain the fluid.

2 Before any draining, purchase the specified transmission fluid (see *Recommended lubricants* near the front of this Chapter) a new filter and all necessary gaskets. **Note:** *Due to the susceptibility of automatic transmissions to contamination, under no circumstances should the old filter or gaskets be reused.*

3 Other tools necessary for this job include jackstands to support the vehicle in a raised position, a wrench to remove the oil pan bolts, a standard screwdriver, a drain pan capable of holding at least 9 U.S. quarts, newspapers and clean rags.

4 The fluid should be drained immediately after the vehicle has been driven. This will remove any built-up sediment better than if the fluid is cold. Because of this, it may be wise to wear protective gloves. Fluid temperatures can exceed 350°F in a hot transmission.

5 After the vehicle has been driven to warm up the fluid, raise it and place it on jackstands for access underneath.

6 Move the necessary equipment under the vehicle, being careful not to touch any of the hot components.

7 Place the drain pan under the transmission oil pan and remove the oil pan bolts along the rear and sides of the pan. Loosen, but do not remove, the front pan bolts.

8 Carefully pry the pan down at the rear, allowing the hot fluid to drain into the drain pan. If necessary, use a screwdriver to break the gasket seal at the rear of the pan. However, do not damage the pan or transmission in the process.

9 Support the pan and remove the remaining bolts at the front of the pan. Lower the pan and drain the remaining fluid. As this is done, check the fluid for metal particles which may be an indication of transmission failure.

10 Now visible on the bottom of the transmission is the filter/strainer (see illustration). Remove the filter and gasket.

11 Thoroughly clean the oil pan with solvent. Inspect for metal particles and foreign matter. Dry with compressed air, if available.
12 It is important that all the remaining gasket material be removed from the pan mounting flange. Use a gasket scrapper or putty knife for this.
13 Clean the filter mounting surface on the valve body. Again this surface should be smooth and free of old gasket material.
14 Place the new filter into position with a new gasket between it and the transmission valve body. Install the mounting screws and tighten them to specified torque.
15 Apply a bead of gasket sealant around the oil pan mounting surface, with the sealant to the inside of the bolt holes. Press the new gasket into place on the pan, making sure all bolt holes line up.
16 Lift the pan up to the bottom of the transmission and install the mounting bolts. Tighten the bolts in a diagonal fashion, working around the pan. Using a torque wrench, tighten the bolts to the specified torque.
17 Remove the jackstands and lower the vehicle.
18 Open the hood and remove the dipstick from the its guide tube.
19 Since fluid capacities vary between the various transmission types, it is best to add a little fluid at a time, continually checking the level with the dipstick. Allow the fluid time to drain into the pan. Add fluid until the level just registers on the dipstick. In most cases, a good starting point will be 4 to 5 pints (6 to 7 pints on 4x4) added to the transmission through the filler tube (use a funnel to prevent spills).
20 With the selector lever in Park apply the brake and start the engine without depressing the accelerator (if possible). Do not race the engine. Run at a low idle only for at least two minutes.
21 Depress the brake pedal and shift the transmission through each gear. Place the selector in the Neutral position and, with the engine still idling, check the level on the dipstick. Look under the vehicle for leaks around the transmission oil pan mating surface.
22 Add more fluid through the dipstick tube until the level on the dipstick is just above the middle hole.
23 Push the dipstick back into the tube and drive the vehicle until it reaches normal operating temperature. Park on a level surface and check the fluid level with the engine idling and the transmission in Neutral. The level should now be at or just below the Don't Add mark on the dipstick. If not, add more fluid as necessary to bring the level up to this point. Do not overfill.

25 Manual transmission oil change

The Ranger 4x4 and Bronco II come equipped with a Mitsubishi five speed transmission while the 4x2 Ranger comes equipped with a Mazda 5 speed (1983 came with 4 speed) manual transmission. The following procedures explain the lubricant change procedures for all models.
1   Drive the vehicle for 15 minutes in stop-and-go traffic to warm the oil in the case. Use all of the gears during this driving cycle to ensure that the lubricant is sufficiently warm to drain completely.
2   Raise the vehicle to a level position using either a hydraulic lift or four jackstands (see *Jacking and towing* at front of this manual). Remove the drain plug from the transmission. Allow plenty of time for the lubricant to drain.
3   After all the lubricant has drained, replace the case drain plug and tighten it to specifications.
4   Using the proper grade and type of hypoid gear oil, refill the transmission case until the lubricant reaches the filler hole level.
5   Replace the filler plug and tighten the plug to the correct torque specification. Drive the vehicle for a short distance and recheck the oil level. In some cases a small amount of additional oil will have to be added.
6   After driving the vehicle, recheck the drain and filler plugs for any signs of leakage.

26 Transfer case fluid change

Refer to illustration 26.3
1   Raise the vehicle and support it securely on jackstands.
2   If so equipped, remove the skid plate attaching bolts from the frame and remove the skid plate.

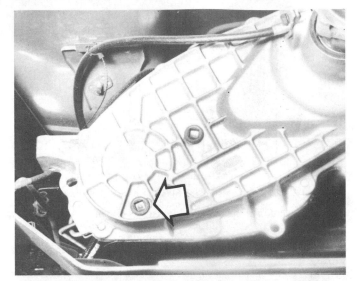

26.3   Arrow indicates the transfer case drain plug. The top plug is for filling the transfer case

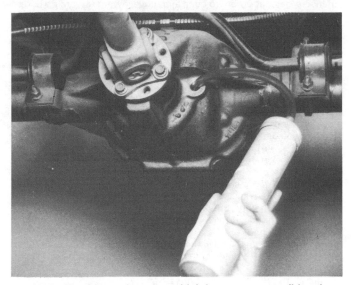

27.5   To change the rear end lubricant, use a small hand pump to remove the old oil

3   Place a drain pan under the transfer case, remove the drain plug (see illustration) and drain the fluid from the transfer case.
4   Install the drain plug and tighten it to the specified torque. Remove the filler plug and install 1.4 liters (3 U.S. pints) of Dexron II automatic transmission fluid, or equivalent.
5   Install the filler plug and tighten it to the specified torque.
6   Install the skid plate.
7   Drive the vehicle for a short period and recheck the oil level.

27 Differential lube change

Refer to illustrations 27.5 and 27.6
1   Drive the vehicle for 10 to 15 minutes at highway speeds to warm the axle lubricant to normal operating temperature.
2   Raise the vehicle, support it securely on jackstands, and place a drain pan under the axle to be drained.
3   Wire brush the filler plug area of the axle housing cover or carrier assembly to prevent the entry of rust, dirt, etc. into the axle assembly.
4   Remove the axle lubricant filler plug.
5   Using a suction-type utility pump, drain the axle lubricant (see illustration) from the axle by inserting the pump tube through the axle filler plug hole into the bottom of the housing.

27.6 Drain/fill plug (arrow) for the front drive axle

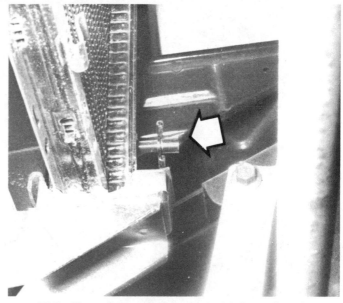

28.6 The radiator drain plug (arrow) is located on the bottom right side of the radiator

6 Fill the axle housing with the specified amount and type of lubricant as shown in the Specifications. On 7.5 inch ring gear axles, the fluid level should be 12.7mm (1/2 inch) below the bottom of the fill plug hole (see illustration).
7 Install the filler plug and tighten to the specified torque.

28 Cooling system servicing (draining, flushing and refilling)

Refer to illustration 28.6

1 Periodically the cooling system should be drained, flushed and re-filled to replenish the antifreeze mixture and prevent formation of rust and corrosion, which can impair the performance of the cooling system and ultimately cause engine damage.
2 At the same time the cooling system is serviced, all hoses and the radiator cap should be inspected and replaced if defective (see Section 7).
3 Since antifreeze is a corrosive and poisonous solution, be careful not to spill any of the coolant mixture on the vehicle's paint or your skin. If this happens, rinse immediately with plenty of clean water. Also, consult your local authorities about the dumping of antifreeze before draining the cooling system. In many areas reclamation centers have been set up to collect automobile oil and drained antifreeze/water mix-tures, rather than allowing them to be added to the sewage system.
4 With the engine cold, remove the radiator cap. On models with a separate thermostat housing and removable cap, remove cap and thermostat as well.
5 Move a large container under the radiator to catch the coolant as it is drained.
6 Drain the radiator. Most models are equipped with a drain plug at the bottom (see illustration). If this drain is corroded and cannot be turned easily, or if the radiator is not equipped with a drain, disconnect the lower radiator hose to allow the coolant to drain. Be careful that none of the solution is splashed on your skin or into your eyes.
7 If accessible, remove the engine drain plug.
8 Disconnect the hose from the coolant reservoir and remove the reservoir. Flush it out with clean water.
9 Place a garden hose in the radiator filler neck and flush the system until the water runs clear at all drain points.
10 In severe cases of contamination or clogging of the radiator, remove it (see Chapter 3) and reverse flush it. This involves inserting the hose in the bottom radiator outlet to allow the clear water to run against the normal flow, draining through the top. A radiator repair shop should be consulted if further cleaning or repair is necessary.
11 When the coolant is regularly drained and the system refilled with the correct antifreeze/water mixture, there should be no need to use chemical cleaners or descalers.
12 To refill the system, reconnect the radiator hoses and install the drain plugs securely in the engine. Special thread-sealing tape, available at auto parts stores, should be used on the drain plugs. Install the reser-voir and the overflow hose.
13 Fill the radiator to the base of the filler neck and then add more coolant to the reservoir until it reaches the mark. On models with a thermostat housing with a removable cap, install the radiator cap and fill the cooling system through the thermostat housing. Install the ther-mostat and cap.
14 Run the engine until normal operating temperature is reached and, with the engine idling, add coolant to the reservoir up to the Full Hot level.
15 Always refill the system with a mixture of high quality antifreeze and water in the proportion called for on the antifreeze container or in your owner's manual. Chapter 3 also contains information on anti-freeze mixtures.
16 Keep a close watch on the coolant level and the various cooling system hoses during the first few miles of driving. Tighten the hose clamps and/or add more coolant as necessary.

29 Front wheel bearings — servicing

Refer to illustrations 29.3, 29.9, 29.15 and 29.17
Note: *Servicing of 4x4 front wheel bearings is covered in Chapter 8.*
1 In most cases, the front wheel bearings will not need servicing until the brake pads are changed. However, these bearings should be checked whenever the front wheels are raised.
2 With the vehicle firmly supported on jackstands, spin the wheel and check for noise, rolling resistance and free play. Grab the top of the tire with one hand and the bottom with the other. Move the tire in and out on the spindle. If it moves more than 0.005 inch, the bearings should be checked, then repacked with grease or replaced if necessary.
3 To remove the bearings for replacing or repacking, begin by remov-ing the hub cap and wheel (see illustration).
4 Remove the brake caliper as described in Chapter 9.
5 Use wire to hang the caliper assembly out of the way. Be careful not to kink or damage the brake hose.
6 Pry the grease cap off the hub with a screwdriver.
7 Use needle nose pliers to straighten out the cotter pin and then pull the cotter pin out of the locking nut. Discard the cotter pin and install a new one on reassembly.
8 Remove the spindle nut cover, spindle nut and washer from the

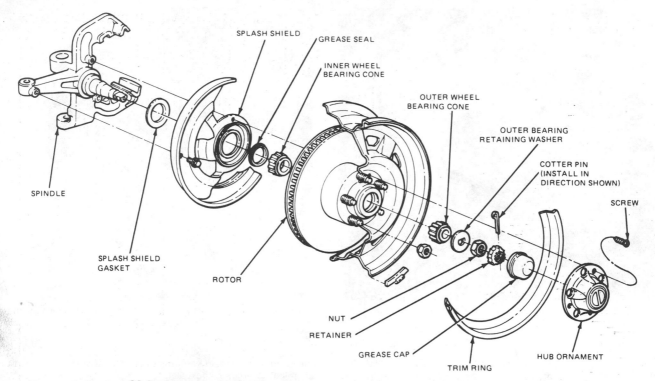

SPLASH SHIELD

GREASE SEAL

INNER WHEEL
BEARING CONE

OUTER WHEEL
BEARING CONE

OUTER BEARING
RETAINING WASHER

COTTER PIN
(INSTALL IN
DIRECTION SHOWN)

SCREW

SPINDLE

SPLASH SHIELD
GASKET

ROTOR

NUT

RETAINER

GREASE CAP

TRIM RING

HUB ORNAMENT

29.3   Front wheel assembly — exploded view for two-wheel drive model

29.9   Pull out on the rotor to loosen the outer bearing

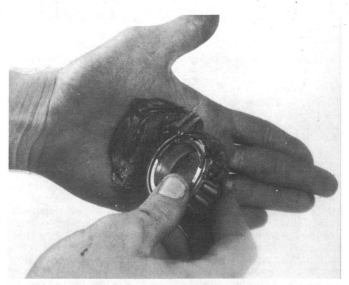

29.15   Packing the bearing with high-temperature wheel bearing grease (work it well into the rollers)

end of the spindle.

9   Pull the hub assembly out slightly and then push it back into its original position. This should force the outer bearing off the spindle enough so that it can be removed with your fingers (see illustration).

10   The hub assembly can now be pulled off the spindle.

11   Use the screwdriver to pry out the inner bearing lip seal on the rear side of the hub. As this is done, note the direction in which the seal is installed.

12   The inner bearing can now be removed from the hub, again noting how it is installed.

13   Use parts solvent to clean all traces of old grease from the bearings, hub and spindle. A small brush may prove useful. Make sure no bristles from the brush embed themselves inside the bearing rollers. Allow the parts to air dry.

14   Carefully inspect the bearings for cracks, heat discoloration, bent rollers, etc. Check the bearing races inside the hub for cracks, scoring

and uneven surfaces. If the bearing races are in need of replacement this job is best left to a repair shop which can press the new races into position.

15   Use high-temperature front wheel bearing grease to pack the bearings. Work the grease completely into the bearings, forcing it between the rollers, cone and cage (see illustration).

16   Put a small amount of grease inboard of each bearing race inside the hub. Using your finger, form a dam at these points to provide extra grease availability and to keep thinned grease from flowing out of the bearing.

17   Apply a thin layer of grease to the spindle (see illustration).

18   Place the grease packed inner bearing into the rear of the hub and put a little more grease outside of the bearing.

19   Place a new seal over the inner bearing and tap the seal with a hammer until it is flush with the hub.

20   Carefully place the hub assembly on the spindle and push the

29.17 Apply a thin coat of grease to the spindle surface

30.2 Removing the air filter element

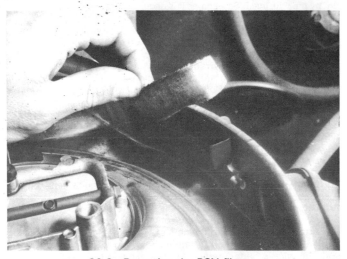

30.8 Removing the PCV filter

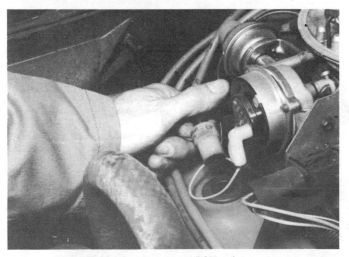

31.2 Removing the PCV valve

grease-packed outer bearing into position .

21 Install the washer and spindle nut. Tighten the spindle nut only slightly.

22 Spin the hub in a forward direction to seat the bearings and remove any grease or burrs which could cause excessive bearing play later.

23 Tighten the spindle nut securely with a wrench, spin the wheel, then loosen the spindle nut until it is just clear of the washer behind it.

24 Using your hand (not a wrench), tighten the nut until it is snug. Install a new cotter pin through the hole in the spindle and spindle nut. If the nut slit does not line up, loosen the nut slightly until it does. From the hand-tight position, the nut should not be loosened more than one-half flat to install the cotter pin.

25 Bend the ends of the new cotter pin until they are flat against the nut. Cut off any extra length which could interfere with the dust cap.

26 Install the dust cap, tapping it into place with a rubber mallet.

27 Refer to Chapter 9 for caliper installation.

28 Install the tire/wheel assembly.

29 Grab the top and bottom of the tire and check the bearings in the same manner as described in the begining of this section.

30 Lower the vehicle, tighten the lug nuts and install the hub cap.

30 Air filter and PCV filter replacement

Refer to illustrations 30.2 and 30.8

Air filter replacement

1 The air filter is located inside the air cleaner housing on the top of the carburetor. To remove the filter, unscrew the wing nut at the top of the cleaner and remove the cover. **Caution:** *While the cover is off, be careful not to drop anything into the carburetor.*

2 Carefully lift the air filter out of the housing (see illustration).

3 To check the filter, hold it up to a strong light. If you can see light coming through the paper element, the filter is all right. Check all the way around the filter.

4 Clean the inside of the air cleaner housing with a rag. Again, be careful that no dirt or debris falls down into the carburetor.

5 Place the filter back into the air cleaner housing. Make sure it seats properly in the bottom of the housing.

6 Reinstall the cover and wing nut.

PCV filter replacement

7 Remove the air cleaner top plate .

8 Lift out the small rectangular filter (attached to the air cleaner housing where the PCV hose is mounted) and install the new one (see illustration).

9 Reinstall the air cleaner top and tighten the wing nut.

31 Positive Crankcase Ventilation (PCV) — valve replacement

Refer to illustration 31.2

1 Purchase the correct replacement PCV valve at a dealer parts department or auto parts store.

2 Pull the valve and hose from the rocker arm cover or cam cover (see illustration).

3   Release the hose clamp and slide it away from the valve.
4   After noting the valve arrow direction, pull the valve from the hose.
5   Push the new valve into the hose with the arrow pointing in the original direction.
6   Secure the clamp at the end of the hose and push the valve and hose into the rocker cover or cam cover.
7   To remove the PCV hose from the air cleaner, use a pair of pliers to lift the clip inside the air cleaner housing.

32   Exhaust Gas Recirculation (EGR) valve — check

1   Connect a vacuum tester to the EGR valve.
2   Apply 5 to 6 inches Hg. of vacuum to the valve.
3   Trap the vacuum and hold it. The vacuum should not drop more than 1 inch Hg. in 30 seconds.
4   If the conditions are not met in Steps 2 and 3, service or replace the valve, O-ring, or EVP as required.

33   Ignition timing check and adjustment

Refer to illustration 33.5

Note: *Begining in 1985 all 2.8L and 2.3L engines come equipped with an integrally mounted TFI-IV ignition module and no distributor calibration is required and it is not normally necessary to adjust initial timing. If timing the engine becomes necessary refer to the Emission Control Label in the engine compartment. Ignition timing on Duraspark III (prior to 1985) ignition systems is controlled by Electronic Engine Control (EEC) and also is not adjustable. The information which follows is applicable only to vehicles equipped with the Duraspark II ignition system.*

1   Start the engine and bring it to normal operating temperature.
2   Shut the engine off and connect the stroboscopic-type timing light according to the manufacturer's instructions. At the same time, refer to the Emissions Control Information label (located inside the engine compartment on the radiator shroud) for the proper engine timing specifications. Make sure the wiring leads for the timing light are not contacting any heat source such as an exhaust manifold and that they are routed away from any moving parts such as the vehicle's cooling fan.
3   Remove and block any vacuum hoses leading to the distributor if this is dictated by the instructions on the Emission Control Information label. Use a golf tee, pencil or other similar device to block off any vacuum lines. **Warning:** *Make sure that you have no dangling articles of clothing such as ties or jewelry which can be caught in the moving components of the engine.*
4   Start the engine and make sure it is idling at the proper speed, according to the Emissions Control Information label. If not, see Chapter 4.
5   Aim the timing light at the timing marks. If the timing marks do not show up clearly, it may be necessary to stop the engine and clean the timing pointer and crankshaft pulley with a rag and cleaning agent then apply a thin coat of white paint to the mark to help it show up (see illustration).
6   Compare the position of the timing marks with the timing specifications for your vehicle. If the marks line up, the ignition timing is correct and no adjustment is necessary. If the timing is incorrect, turn off the engine.
7   Loosen the distributor hold-down bolt.
8   Restart the engine and rotate the distributor in either direction while pointing the timing light at the timing marks.
9   Be sure the timing marks are aligned correctly and turn off the engine.
10   Tighten the distributor hold-down bolt.
11   Restart the engine and check the timing to make sure it has not moved while tightening down the clamp bolt.
12   Recheck the idle speed to make sure it has not changed significantly. If the idle speed has changed, reset the idle speed and recheck the timing, as timing will vary with engine rpm.
13   Reconnect all vacuum hoses and other connections removed for checking purposes.

34   Spark plugs — replacement

Note: *The best policy to follow when replacing the spark plugs is to purchase the new spark plugs beforehand, adjust them to the proper gap (see the Emission Control Information label under hood) and replace the plugs one at a time. When buying the new plugs be sure to obtain the correct type for your specific engine.*

1   Allow the engine to cool thoroughly before attempting to remove the plugs. During this time, each of the new spark plugs can be inspected for defects and the gap can be checked.
2   The gap is checked by inserting the proper thickness gauge between the electrodes at the tip of the plug. The gap between these electrodes should be the same as that given in the Specifications. The gauge should just touch each of the electrodes as it passes between them. If the gap is incorrect, use the notched adjuster on the feeler gauge body to bend the curved side electrode slightly until the proper gap is achieved. If the side electrode is not exactly over the center one, use the notched adjuster to align the two.
3   With the engine cool, remove the spark plug wire from one spark plug. A spark plug wire puller is available from your local parts store for removing the wires. Otherwise, grab the boot at the end of the wire, not by the wire itself. Sometimes it is necessary to use a twisting motion while the boot and plug wire are pulled free.
4   Before the plug is removed use compressed air to blow any dirt or foreign material away from the spark plug area. A bicycle pump will also work.
5   Place the spark plug wrench or socket over the plug and remove it by turning it in a counterclockwise direction. **Note:** *a quick visual inspection of the old spark plug will reveal a great deal about the running condition of the engine. Compare each spark plug to the accompanying chart for diagnosis.*
6   Carefully insert one of the new plugs into the spark plug hole and tighten it by hand. **Caution:** *Be careful not to cross-thread the spark plug in the hole. If resistance is felt as you thread the spark plug in by hand, back it out and start again. Do not, under any circumstances, force the spark plug into the hole with a wrench or socket.*
7   Once you have installed the plug as far as it will go by hand, tighten it securely with the socket to the specified torque.
8   Before pushing the spark plug wire onto the end of the plug, inspect it for cracks and corrosion (see section 35).
9   Attach the plug wire to the new spark plug, again using a twisting motion on the boot until it is firmly seated on the spark plug. Make sure the wire is routed away from the exhaust manifold.
10   Follow the above procedures for the remaining spark plugs, replacing them one at a time to prevent mixing up the spark plug wires.

33.5   Paint the timing mark to make it easier to see when checking the timing

Measuring plug gap. A feeler gauge of the correct size (see ignition system specifications) should have a slight 'drag' when slid between the electrodes. Adjust gap if necessary

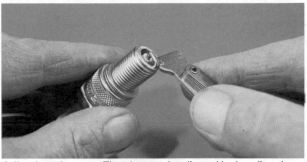

Adjusting plug gap. The plug gap is adjusted by bending the ground electrode inwards, or outwards, as necessary until the correct clearance is obtained. Note the use of the correct tool

Normal. Gray brown deposits, lightly coated core nose. Gap increasing by around 0.001 in (0.025 mm) per 1000 miles (1600 km). Plugs ideally suited to engine, and engine in good condition

Carbon fouling. Dry, black, sooty deposits. Will cause weak spark and eventually misfire. Fault: over-rich fuel mixture. Check: carburetor mixture settings, float level and jet sizes; choke operation and cleanliness of air filter. Plugs can be re-used after cleaning

Oil fouling. Wet, oily deposits. Will cause weak spark and eventually misfire. Fault: worn bores/piston rings or valve guides; sometimes occurs (temporarily) during running-in period. Plugs can be re-used after thorough cleaning

Overheating. Electrodes have glazed appearance, core nose very white – few deposits. Fault: plug overheating. Check: plug value, ignition timing, fuel octane rating (too low) and fuel mixture (too weak). Discard plugs and cure fault immediately

Electrode damage. Electrodes burned away; core nose has burned, glazed appearance. Fault: pre-ignition. Check: as for 'Overheating' but may be more severe. Discard plugs and remedy fault before piston or valve damage occurs

Split core nose (may appear initially as a crack). Damage is self-evident, but cracks will only show after cleaning. Fault: pre-ignition or wrong gap-setting technique. Check: ignition timing, cooling system, fuel octane rating (too low) and fuel mixture (too weak). Discard plugs, rectify fault immediately

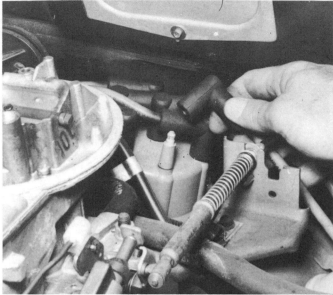

35.6   Replace the plug wires one at a time so not to mix them up

35.9   Check the distributor cap contacts for corrosion

35 Spark plug wires, distributor cap and rotor check and replacement

Refer to illustrations 35.6 and 35.9

1   The spark plug wires should be checked at the recommended intervals and whenever new spark plugs are installed in the engine.
2   The wires should be inspected one at a time to prevent mixing up the order, which is essential for proper engine operation.
3   Disconnect the plug wire from the spark plug. A removal tool can be used for this purpose or you can grab the rubber boot, twist slightly and pull the wire free. Do not pull on the wire itself, only on the rubber boot.
4   Inspect inside the boot for corrosion, which will look like a white crusty powder. Push the wire and boot back onto the end of the spark plug. It should be a tight fit on the plug. If it is not, remove the wire and use pliers to carefully crimp the metal connector inside the boot until it fits securely on the end of the spark plug.
5   Using a clean rag, wipe the entire length of the wire to remove any built-up dirt and grease. Once the wire is clean, check for burns, cracks and other damage. Do not bend the wire since the conductor inside might break.
6   Disconnect the wire from the distributor (see illustration). Again, pull only on the rubber boot. Check for corrosion and a tight fit in the same manner as the spark plug end. Replace the wire in the distributor.
7   Check the remaining spark plug wires, making sure they are securely fastened at the distributor and the spark plug when the check is complete.
8   If new spark plug wires are required, purchase a set for your specific engine model. Wire sets are available pre-cut, with the rubber boots already installed. Remove and replace the wires one at a time to avoid mix-ups in the firing order.
9   Check the distributor cap and rotor for wear (see illustration). Look for cracks, carbon tracks and worn, burned or loose contacts. Replace the cap and rotor with new parts if defective. It is common practice to install new cap and rotor whenever new spark plug wires are installed. When installing a new cap, remove the wires from the old cap one at a time and attach them to the new cap in the exact same location.

36 Compression check

Refer to illustration 36.5

1   A compression check will tell you what condition the engine is in. Specifically, it can tell you if the compression is down due to leakage

36.5   Use a compression gauge to check cylinder compression

caused by worn piston rings, defective valves and seats or a leaking head gasket. Make sure the engine oil is of the correct viscosity and that the battery is fully charged.
2   Run the engine until it reaches normal operating temperature.
3   Turn the engine off. Set the carburetor throttle plate to the wide-open position. This may be verified by removing the top plate of the air cleaner and looking down into the carburetor throat. The throttle plates should be perpendicular to the ground.
4   Remove all spark plug wires from the plugs after marking them for position. Clean the area around the spark plugs before you remove them. This will keep dirt from falling into the cylinders while performing the compression test. Remove the spark plugs.
5   Install the compression gauge into the number one cylinder spark plug hole (see illustration).
6   Crank the engine for approximately five revolutions with a remote starter or with an assistant operating the ignition switch.
7   Observe the pattern that the engine follows as it builds up to the

highest reading. The compression should build up quickly in a healthy engine. Low compression on the first stroke. followed by gradually increasing pressure on successive strokes, indicates worn piston rings. A low compression reading on the first stroke, which does not build up during successive compression strokes, indicates leaking valves or a defective head gasket. Record the highest gauge reading obtained. Repeat the procedure for the remaining cylinders and compare the readings. The compression is considered normal if the lowest cylinder reading is within 75 percent of the highest cylinder reading with a minimum reading of 100 pounds.

8   Variations exceeding 75 percent are a good indication of internal engine component problems. To further diagnose the engine using the compression gauge, select the low reading cylinder for a ''wet'' test.

9   To perform a wet compression test, pour a couple of teaspoons of engine oil (a squirt can works well) into each cylinder, through the spark plug hole, and repeat the test.

10 If the compression increases after the oil is added, the piston rings are worn. If the compression does not increase significantly the leakage is occuring at the valves or head gasket.

11 If two adjacent cylinders have equally low compression, there is a strong possibility that the head gasket between them is blown. The appearance of coolant in the combustion chambers or the crankcase would verify this condition.

12 If the compression is higher than normal, the combustion chambers are probably coated with carbon deposits. If that is the case, the cylinder head or heads should be removed and decarbonized.

13 If compression is down, or varies greatly between cylinders, it would be a good idea to have a leak down test performed by an automotive shop. The test will pinpoint exactly where the leakage is occuring.

Chapter 2 Part A   2.0L and 2.3L engines

Contents

Specifications

Camshaft
    bearing journal diameter . . . .   1.7713 to 1.7720 in
    bearing clearance . . . .   0.001 to 0.003 in
    endplay . . . .   0.001 to 0.007 in

Torque specifications	**Ft-lbs**
Camshaft sprocket bolt	50 to 71
Rear camshaft retaining plate bolt	6 to 9
Auxiliary shaft sprocket bolt	28 to 40
Auxiliary shaft thrust plate bolts	6 to 9
Timing belt outer cover bolts	6 to 9
Timing belt tensioner bolt	14 to 21
Timing belt tensioner pivot bolt	28 to 40
Cam cover bolts	6 to 8
Spark plugs	5 to 10
Cylinder head bolts	
step 1	50 to 60
step 2	80 to 90
Flywheel/driveplate bolts	56 to 64
Bellhousing bolts	28 to 38
Starter bolts	15 to 20
Thermactor pump pivot bolt	30 to 40
Thermactor pump adjusting bolt	30 to 40
Fan (water pump pulley) bolts	14 to 21
Alternator pivot bolt	45 to 61
Alternator adjustment bolt	5 to 6
Thermostat housing bolts	14 to 21
Intake manifold bolts	
step 1	5 to 7
step 2	14 to 21
Exhaust manifold bolts	
step 1	5 to 7
step 2	16 to 23
EGR line retaining bolt	9 to 11
EGR tube nut	9 to 11
Oil pan bolts	8 to 10
Oil pump bolts	14 to 21
Oil pump pick-up tube bolts	14 to 21
Oil pan drain plug	15 to 25

2.3 Detach the wiring harness clip (arrow) and move the harness forward

2.5 Removing this bolt (arrow) releases the metal heater pipes from the cam cover

The 2.0 and 2.3 liter engines described in this chapter are of inline design and constructed of cast iron. The valves are actuated by a single overhead camshaft and hydraulic valve lash adjusters.

The camshaft is driven from the crankshaft by a toothed belt, which also operates the auxiliary shaft. The auxiliary shaft drives the oil pump, distributor and fuel pump. Tension on the belt is maintained by an idler pulley which runs on the outside of the belt.

The water pump, fan and alternator are driven by separate drivebelts.

2 Cam cover — removal and installation

Refer to illustrations 2.3, 2.5 and 2.6
Note: *To remove the cam cover on 2.3L with EFI it will be necessary to remove the throttle linkage and throttle body assembly (refer to Chapter 4).*

1 Disconnect negative cable at the battery.
2 Remove the air cleaner.
3 Remove the wiring harness from the retaining clip and move it out of way (see illustration).
4 Disconnect the spark plug wires and label each plug wire for reinstallation.
5 Disconnect the metal heater lines attached to the cam cover and move them aside (see illustration).
6 Remove the cam cover retaining bolts (see illustration).
7 Lightly tap the cover with a soft face hammer or a block of wood to break the seal. Be careful not to bend the cover.
8 Remove the cover.
9 Installation is the reverse of the removal procedure.

3 Valve train components — removal and installation

Refer to illustrations 3.3 and 3.4
Note: *If the valve or valve seat has not been damaged, the valve spring damper assembly, seals and retainers may be replaced by holding the affected valve against its seat, using compressed air. Install an air hose adapter in the spark plug hole. When air pressure is supplied to the adapter, the valves will be held in place by the pressure. If the air pressure does not hold the valve shut, the valve is damaged or burned and the cylinder head must be removed and serviced (See Section 9 for removal and Chapter 2C for servicing).*

If you do not have access to compressed air bring the piston to just before top dead center (TDC) on the compression stroke. Feed a long piece of 1/4-inch cord in through the spark plug hole until it fills the

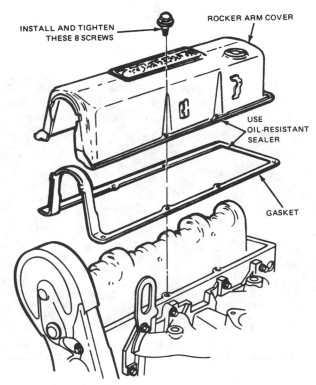

2.6 2.0L & 2.3L 4-cylinder cam cover assembly

INSTALL AND TIGHTEN THESE 8 SCREWS

ROCKER ARM COVER

USE OIL-RESISTANT SEALER

GASKET

1 General Information

The repair procedures included in this Part are based on the assumption that the engine is still installed in the vehicle. Therefore, if this information is being used during a complete overhaul, with the engine already out of the vehicle and on a stand, many of the steps included here will not apply. The last section in this Part gives the procedures on engine removal and installation.

All information concerning engine block and cylinder head servicing can be found in Part C of this Chapter. The specifications found in this Part apply only to those procedures found in this Part.

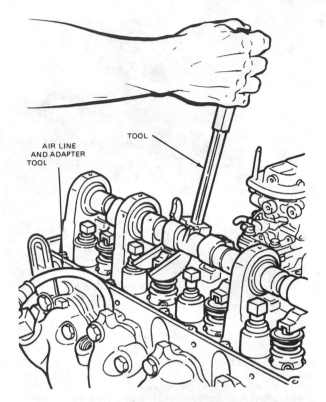

3.3   While compressed air holds the valve closed, a special compressor is used to collapse the spring so the cam follower and lash adjuster can be removed

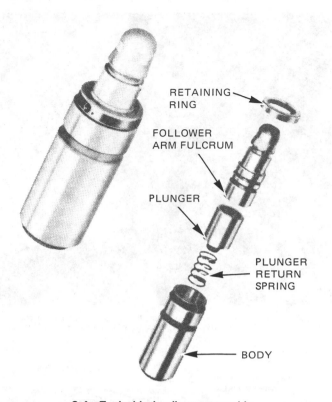

3.4   Typical lash adjuster assembly

4.2   Loosen the thermactor pump bolts (arrows) and pivot the thermactor towards the engine to remove the belt

combustion chamber. Be sure to leave the end of the cord hanging out of the spark plug hole so it can be removed easily. Rotate the crankshaft with a wrench (in the normal direction of rotation) until slight resistance is felt.

Removal

1   Refer to Section 2 and remove the cam cover.
2   Rotate the camshaft so that the camshafts lobe is at its lowest point (valve completely closed).
3   Using tool T74P-6565-A or an equivalent spring compressor, compress the valve spring (see illustration) and slide the cam follower over the lash adjuster and out.
4   Lift out the hydraulic lash adjuster (see illustration).
5   With spring compressed remove the keepers, spring retainer and valve spring. Remove and discard the stem seal.
6   **Caution:** *If air pressure has forced the piston to the bottom of the cylinder, removal of the air pressure will allow the valve to fall into the cylinder. A rubber band or tape wrapped around the end of the valve stem will prevent this.*
7   Inspect the valve stem for damage. Rotate the valve and check the stem tip for eccentric movement. Move the valve up and down through normal travel in the valve guide and check the stem for binding. If the valve has been damaged, it will be necessary to remove the cylinder head.
8   Before assembly install a new valve seal.
9   Place the plastic installation cap over end of the valve stem.
10   Start the valve stem seal carefully over cap and push the seal down until jacket touches the top of the guide.
11   Remove the plastic installation cap and use installation tool T73P-6571-A or two screwdrivers to bottom the seal on the valve guide.
12   Place the hydraulic lash adjuster in position in the bore.
13   Use tool T73P-6571-A or its equivalent and install the valve spring assembly, retainer and keepers.
14   Apply assembly lube to all contact surfaces of the cam follower.
15   Compress the valve spring, using tool T74P-6565-A or a valve spring compressor and position the cam follower over the lash adjuster and the valve stem.
16   Clean the gasket surfaces of the cam cover and cylinder head.

17   Coat the gasket surfaces of the cam cover and the *up* side of the cam cover gasket with contact adhesive or sealer and allow them to dry. Install the gasket in the cam cover, making sure the locating tabs are properly positioned in the slots in the cover.
18   Install the cam cover and tighten the bolts to the specified torque (Section 2).

---

4   Timing belt — removal and installation

Refer to illustrations 4.2, 4.4, 4.8, 4.11 and 4.30

1   Disconnect the battery ground cable at the battery.
2   Loosen the thermactor pump bolts and remove the drivebelt (see illustration).

4.4   Loosen the alternator through bolt and the adjusting
strap bolt to remove the belt

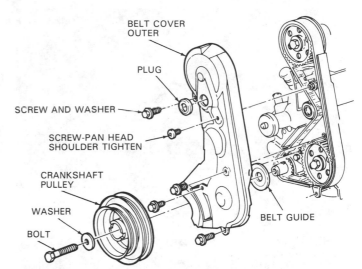

4.8   Timing belt cover assembly

3   Remove the fan and the water pump pulley (Chapter 3).
4   Loosen the alternator retaining bolts and remove the drivebelt (see illustration).
5   Drain the cooling system and remove the upper radiator hose (Chapter 3).
6   Remove the thermostat housing and gasket .
7   Remove the crankshaft drivebelt pulley and belt guide.
8   Remove the four timing belt outer cover retaining bolts and remove the timing belt cover (see illustration).
9   Turn the engine over until the number one piston is at top dead center on the compression stroke. Always turn engine in direction of normal rotation. **Caution:** *Backward rotation may cause the timing belt to jump time.*
10   Remove the distributor cap and make sure the rotor is pointing to the number one plug wire terminal.
11   Loosen the belt tensioner lock nut and position spreader tool T74P-6254-A or a breaker bar on the tension roll pin and retract the belt tensioner (see illustration). Tighten the adjustment screw to hold the tensioner in the retracted position.
12   Remove the timing belt and inspect for wear or damage. If worn replace the belt.
13   Check that the crankshaft sprocket and the camshaft sprocket both align with their respective timing marks.
14   Install the timing belt over the crankshaft sprocket and then over the auxiliary sprocket.
15   Pull the belt up (pulling slack from between the auxiliary and camshaft sprockets) and install on the camshaft sprocket in a counterclockwise direction so no slack will be between these two sprockets. Align the belt fore and aft on the sprockets.
16   Loosen the tensioner adjustment bolt to allow the tensioner to move against the belt. If the spring does not have enough tension to move the roller against the belt (the belt hangs loose), it may be necessary to insert tool T74P-6254-A or a breaker bar between the tensioner and tension roll pin and push the roller against the belt. Tighten the bolt to the specified torque. **Note:** *The spring can not be used to set belt tension. A wrench must be used on the tensioner assembly.*
17   Be sure the belt does not jump time during rotation by removing the spark plugs. Rotate the crankshaft two complete turns in the direction of normal rotation to make sure the belt is seated and to remove any slack.
18   Tighten the tensioner adjustment and pivot bolts to the specified torque. Recheck the alignment of the timing marks.
19   Install the timing belt cover and tighten the four retaining bolts to the specified torque.

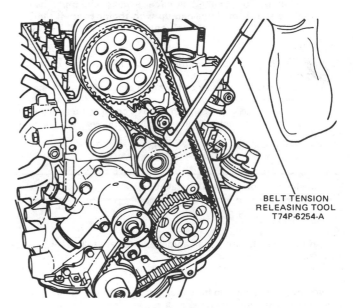

4.11   A special Ford tool can be used to release the
tension on the timing belt

20   Install the drivebelt guide and crankshaft pulley.
21   Install the thermostat housing and tighten the bolts to the specified torque.
22   Install the upper radiator hose to the radiator and fill the cooling system with a 50/50 mixture of antifreeze and water.
23   Install the alternator drivebelt, adjust the belt tension and tighten the retaining bolts to the specified torque.
24   Install the water pump pulley and fan and tighten the bolts to the specified torque.
25   Install the thermactor pump drivebelt and adjust the tension.
26   Reconnect the battery.
27   Start the engine and check for leaks.

Timing marks — checking

Note: *An access plug is provided in the timing belt cover so that camshaft timing can be checked without removal of the cover.*
28   Bring the number one piston to top dead center on the compression stroke.
29   Remove the distributor cap and check that the distributor rotor is facing the No. 1 position on the distributor cap.

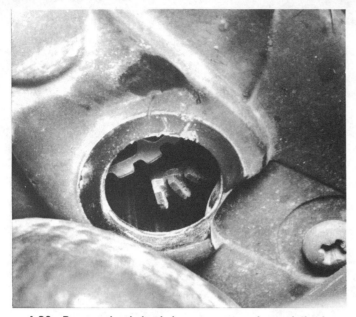

**4.30   Remove the timing belt cover access plug and check
that the timing mark is lined up with the pointer on the
inner belt cover**

30 Remove the access plug from the cam drive belt cover (see illustration).
31 Make sure the timing mark on the crank pulley aligns with the TDC mark on the belt cover.
32 Look through the access hole in the belt cover to be sure that the timing mark on the cam drive sprocket is lined up with the pointer on the inner belt cover.
33 Reinstall the belt cover access plug.

---

5   Camshaft — removal and installation

Refer to illustration 5.20

Removal
1 Before the camshaft can be removed the cam followers must be removed.
2 Remove the rocker arm cover, the timing belt cover and the timing belt.
3 Remove the spring clip from the hydraulic valve lash adjuster end of the cam followers.
4 Using special tool T74P-6565-A inserted beneath the camshaft, compress the lash adjuster of the first valve to be removed, ensuring that the cam lobe is facing away from the follower. This will permit the cam followers to be removed. Keep the cam followers in order so they can be reinstalled in their original positions. **Note:** *On some valves it may be necessary to compress the valve spring slightly to remove the cam follower.*
5 Lift out the hydraulic lash adjusters, keeping each one with its respective cam follower.
6 Using a metal bar, lock the camshaft drive sprocket. Remove the mounting bolt and washer.
7 Draw off the sprocket with a puller then remove the belt guide.
8 Remove the sprocket locating key from the end of the camshaft.
9 Remove the camshaft retaining plate from the rear bearing pedestal.
10 Using a hammer and a brass or aluminum drift, drive out the camshaft toward the front of the engine, taking the front seal with it. Be very careful not to damage the camshaft bearings and journals as it is pushed out.

Camshaft and bearings — inspection
11 After the camshaft has been removed from the engine, cleaned with solvent and dried, inspect the bearing journals for uneven wear, pitting or evidence of seizure. If the journals are damaged, the bearing inserts in the head are probably damaged as well. Both the camshaft

and bearings will have to be replaced with new ones. Measure the inside diameter of each camshaft bearing and record the results (take two measurements, 90° apart, at each bearing).
12 Measure the bearing journals with a micrometer to determine if they are excessively worn or out-of-round. If they are more than 0.005-inch out-of-round, the camshaft should be replaced with a new one. Subtract the bearing journal diameters from the corresponding bearing inside diameter measurements to obtain the clearance. If it is excessive, new bearings must be installed. **Note:** *Camshaft bearing replacement requires special tools and expertise that place it outside the scope of the do-it-yourselfer. Take the head to an automotive machine shop to ensure that the job is done correctly.*
13 Check the camshaft lobes for heat discoloration, score marks, chipped areas, pitting or uneven wear. If the lobes are in good condition the camshaft can be reused.
14 Make sure that the camshaft oil passages are clear and clean.
15 To check the thrust plate for wear, install the camshaft in the cylinder head and position the thrust plate at the rear. Using a dial indicator, check the total end play by tapping the camshaft carefully back-and-forth. If the endplay is outside the specified limit, replace the thrust plate with a new one.

Cam followers — inspection
16 The faces of the cam followers which bear on the camshaft should show no signs of pitting, scoring or other forms of wear. They should not be a loose fit on the pivot bolt.
17 Inspect the face which bears on the valve stem. If it is pitted, the cam follower must be replaced with a new one.
18 If excessive cam follower wear is evident (and possibly excessive cam lobe wear), it may be due to a malfunction of the valve drive lubrication tube. If this has occurred, replace the tube and the cam follower. If more than one cam follower is excessively worn, replace the camshaft, all the cam followers and the lubrication tube. This also applies where excessive cam lobe wear is found.
19 During any operation which requires removal of the cam cover, make sure that oil is being discharged from the lubrication tube nozzles by cranking the engine with the starter motor.

Installation
20 Liberally coat the camshaft journals and bearings with engine assembly lube, then carefully install the shaft in the cylinder head (see illustration).
21 Install the retainer plate and bolts.
22 Lubricate a new camshaft seal with engine oil and carefully tap it into position at the front of the cylinder head.
23 Install the belt guide and pin at the front end of the camshaft, then carefully tap on the sprocket.
24 Install a new sprocket bolt.
25 Coat the hydraulic lash adjusters with engine assembly lube, then install each one into its respective position.
26 Coat the surface of the camshaft lobes and cam followers with engine assembly lube.
27 Using special tool T74P-6565-B to compress each lash adjuster, position each cam follower on its respective valve end and adjuster, ensuring that the camshaft is rotated as necessary. Install the retaining spring clips. **Note:** *On some valves it may be necessary to compress the valve spring slightly when fitting the cam follower.*

---

6   Auxiliary shaft — removal, inspection and installation

1 Remove the belt cover and the camshaft timing belt according to the procedure outlined in Section 4.
2 Using a metal bar or a large screwdriver to lock the auxiliary shaft sprocket in place, remove the sprocket retaining bolt and washer.
3 Pull out the sprocket using a universal puller and remove the sprocket locking key from the shaft.
4 Remove the three bolts from the auxiliary shaft cover and remove the cover.
5 Remove the shaft retaining plate bolts and the retaining plate.
6 Withdraw the shaft. If it is tight, reinstall the bolt and washer. Use a pry bar and spacer block to pry out the shaft. Be extremely careful not to damage the bearings as you pull the shaft out of the block.
7 Examine the auxiliary shaft bearing for scoring and pitting. Replacement will have to be dealt with by a shop, for although it is easy to

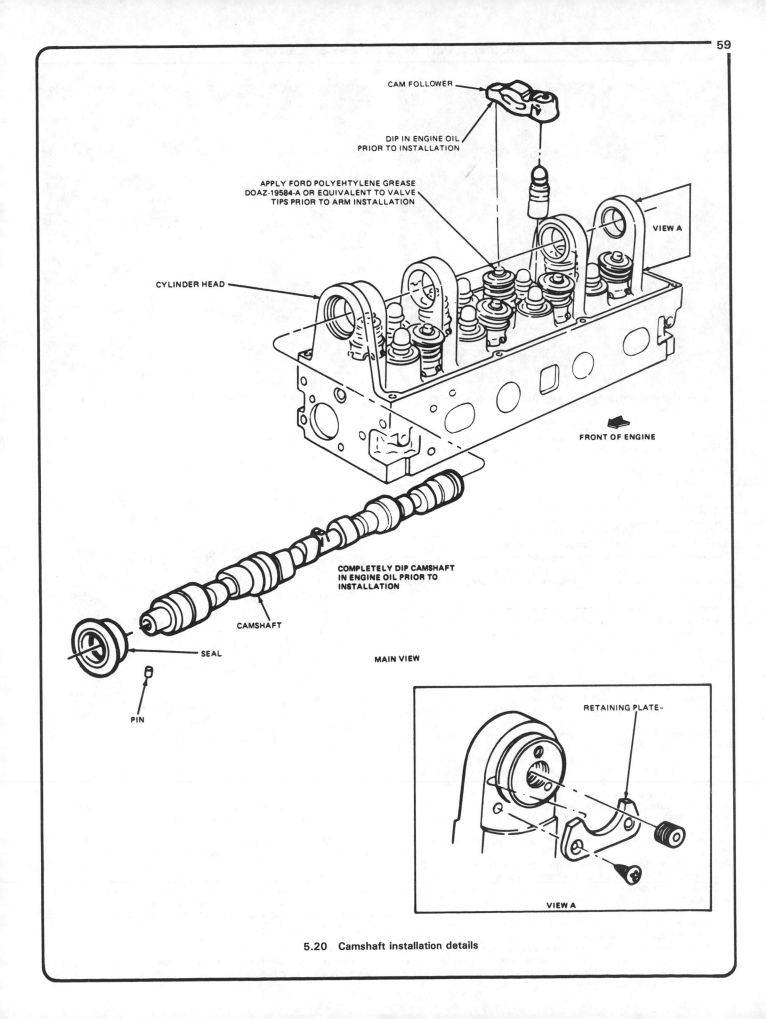

CAM FOLLOWER

DIP IN ENGINE OIL
PRIOR TO INSTALLATION

APPLY FORD POLYEHTYLENE GREASE
DOAZ-19584-A OR EQUIVALENT TO VALVE
TIPS PRIOR TO ARM INSTALLATION

VIEW A

CYLINDER HEAD

FRONT OF ENGINE

COMPLETELY DIP CAMSHAFT
IN ENGINE OIL PRIOR TO
INSTALLATION

CAMSHAFT

SEAL

MAIN VIEW

PIN

RETAINING PLATE-

VIEW A

5.20 Camshaft installation details

7.7   Remove the heat tube (arrow) from the EGR valve

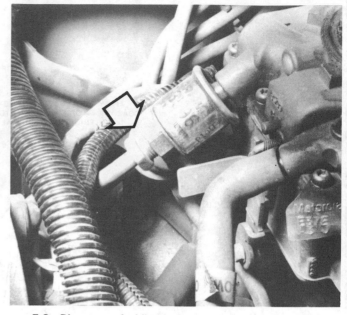

7.8   Disconnect fuel line (arrow) at carburetor fuel filter

remove the old bearing, the correct installation of the new one requires special tools. See your local Ford dealer or machine shop for this work. The auxiliary shaft may show signs of wear on the bearing journal or the eccentric. Any signs of scoring or damage to the bearing journals *cannot* be removed by grinding. If in doubt, ask your service department to check the auxiliary shaft and give advice on replacement. Examine the gear teeth for wear and damage. If either is evident, a replacement shaft must be obtained.

8   Dip the auxiliary shaft completely in engine oil before installing it into the block. Tap it in gently with a soft face hammer to ensure that it is seated. Install the retaining plate and the auxiliary shaft cover.

9   The remainder of the procedure is the reverse of removal. Make sure that the auxiliary shaft key is in place before installing the sprocket.

---

7   Intake manifold — removal and installation

Refer to illustrations 7.7, 7.8 and 7.19

Note: *For 2.3L electronic fuel injected engines refer to Chapter 4.*

1   Drain the cooling system (Chapter 3).

2   Disconnect the negative cable at the battery.

3   Remove the air cleaner assembly and air ducts.

4   Disconnect the throttle cable by lifting the cable out of its retaining bracket.

5   Disconnect the vacuum hoses from carburetor as required and label them for reinstallation.

6   Remove the water hose from the manifold cover nipple fitting.

7   Disconnect the heat tube at the EGR valve (see illustration).

8   Disconnect the fuel line at the carburetor fuel filter (see illustration).

9   Remove the dipstick tube retaining bolt attached to the intake manifold and move the dipstick tube out of the way.

10   Disconnect and remove the PCV system at the intake manifold and the engine block.

11   Remove the two distributor cap screws and remove the distributor cap.

12   Remove the plastic PCV valve from the valve cover.

13   Remove the lifting eye bracket retaining bolts.

14   Remove the intake manifold by loosening the retaining bolts two turns at a time until bolts are completely removed.

15   Remove the intake manifold.

16   Clean the intake manifold gasket surface.

17   Clean the cylinder head gasket surface.

18   Position the new intake manifold gasket on the head.

19   Position the intake manifold, along with lifting eye bracket, to the head, install the retaining bolts and tighten each in sequence to the

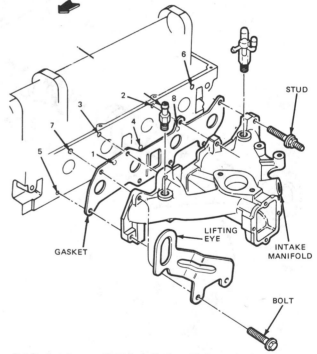

7.19   Intake manifold installation. Tighten the bolts in the sequence shown

specified torque (see illustration).

20   The remainder of the installation is the reverse of the disassembly procedures.

---

8   Exhaust manifold — removal and installation

Refer to illustrations 8.2, 8.6 and 8.8

Removal

1   Remove the air cleaner and duct assembly and label any vacuum lines as you remove them.

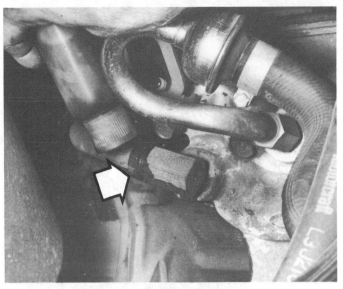

8.2   Remove EGR line (arrow) at exhaust manifold and
loosen EGR tube

8.6   Remove two exhaust pipe flange bolts

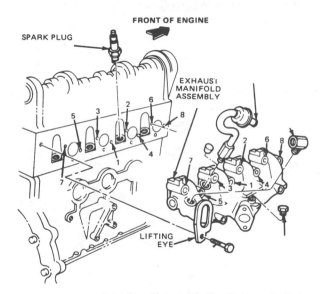

8.8   Exhaust manifold installation details. Tighten the bolts
in the sequence shown

2   Remove the EGR line retaining bolts at the exhaust manifold and
loosen at the EGR tube (Chapter 6) (see illustration).
3   Remove the check valve at the exhaust manifold and the hose at
the rear of the air bypass valve.
4   Remove the bolt attaching the heater hoses to the cam cover.
5   Remove the eight exhaust manifold bolts attaching the manifold
to the cylinder head.
6   Remove the two bolts attaching the exhaust pipe to the manifold
(see illustration).
7   Remove the exhaust manifold.

Installation
8   Install the eight exhaust manifold bolts attaching the manifold to
the cylinder head and tighten to the specified torque in the sequence
shown (see illustration).
9   Install the two exhaust pipe bolts attaching the exhaust pipe to
the exhaust manifold.
10 Position the heater hoses on the cam cover.
11 Install the check valve at the exhaust manifold.
12 Install the hose at the rear of the air bypass valve.
13 Install the EGR line at the exhaust manifold and tighten to the

specified torque. Install the EGR tube and tighten the tube nut to the
specified torque.
14 Install the air cleaner and duct assembly.

9   Cylinder head — removal and installation

Refer to illustration 9.28
Note: *Any time you remove the timing belt always begin the procedure
by putting the engine at top dead center (TDC) on the compression
stroke of the number one cylinder (Section 4).*
1   Drain the cooling system (Chapter 3).
2   Remove the air cleaner assembly and the air duct.
3   Remove the bolt retaining the heater hose to the cam cover.
4   Disconnect the distributor cap and remove from the distributor.
5   Remove the spark plug wires from the spark plugs and remove the
distributor cap and wires as an assembly. Remove the spark plugs.
6   Disconnect all necessary vacuum hoses and label them for
reinstallation.
7   Remove the dipstick tube.
8   Remove the cam cover retaining bolts and remove the cover (Section 2).
9   Remove the intake manifold bolts (Section 7).
10 Loosen the alternator retaining bolts, remove the belt from the
pulley and remove the mounting bracket bolts.
11 Disconnect the upper radiator hose at both ends and remove it from
the engine.
12 Remove the timing belt cover.
13 Check that the timing is correct (Section 4) then loosen the cam
idler retaining bolts. Position the idler in the unloaded position and
tighten the retaining bolts.
14 Remove the timing belt from the cam pulley and auxiliary pulley.
15 Remove the heat stove from the exhaust manifold.
16 Remove the exhaust manifold retaining bolts (Section 8).
17 Remove the timing belt idler and bracket bolts.
18 Remove the timing belt idler spring stop from the cylinder head.
19 Disconnect the oil sending unit lead wire.
20 Refer to Section 7 and remove the intake manifold.
21 Remove the cylinder head retaining bolts.
22 Remove the cylinder head.
23 Clean all gasket surfaces.
24 Blow all oil out of the head bolt holes in block with compressed air.
25 Position the new head gasket on the block.
26 Turn the camshaft until the pin is in the 5:30 position. **Caution:**
*This must be done to avoid damage to the valves when the head is
installed.*
27 Position the cylinder head on the block.

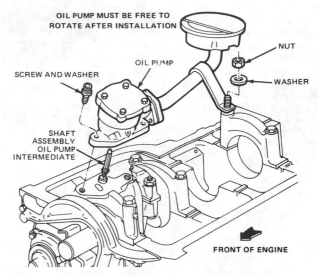

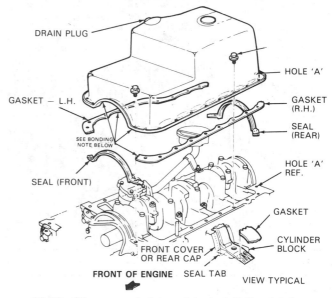

FRONT OF ENGINE

WHEN INSTALLING CYLINDER HEAD, POSITION THE CAMSHAFT AS SHOWN TO AVOID DAMAGE TO PROTRUDING VALVES.

TIGHTEN THE CYLINDER HEAD BOLTS TO SPECIFICATIONS IN TWO PROGRESSIVE STEPS IN THE SEQUENCE SHOWN.

PIN

9.28   Tighten the head bolts to specification in two progressive steps using the numbered sequence shown

OIL PUMP MUST BE FREE TO ROTATE AFTER INSTALLATION

NUT

WASHER

OIL PUMP

SCREW AND WASHER

SHAFT ASSEMBLY OIL PUMP INTERMEDIATE

FRONT OF ENGINE

10.30   Tighten the oil pan bolts in clockwise sequence from hole 'A' as noted above

DRAIN PLUG

HOLE 'A'

GASKET (R.H.)

SEAL (REAR)

HOLE 'A' REF.

GASKET

CYLINDER BLOCK

GASKET — L.H.

SEE BONDING NOTE BELOW

SEAL (FRONT)

FRONT COVER OR REAR CAP

SEAL TAB

VIEW TYPICAL

FRONT OF ENGINE

10.29   Oil pump and pick up tube installation details

28 Install the cylinder head bolts and tighten them in sequence (see illustration) to the specified torque.
29 Return the camshaft to the number one piston at top dead center position.
30 The remainder of the installation is the reverse of the removal procedures.

10   Oil pan — removal and installation

Refer to illustrations 10.29 and 10.30
Note: *Only vehicles equipped with automatic transmissions will have oil pans which can be removed out the front of the engine compartment. Those with manual transmissions must be removed out the rear.*
1 Disconnect battery negative cable at the battery.
2 Remove the air cleaner and attaching hoses as an assembly.
3 Remove the oil dipstick.
4 Remove the engine mount retaining nuts.
5 Remove the oil cooler lines at the radiator, if so equipped.
6 Remove the two bolts retaining the fan shroud to the radiator and remove the shroud on models without air conditioning. If equipped with air conditioning place the shroud over the fan.
7 Remove the radiator retaining bolts (automatic only).
8 Drain the radiator and remove the hoses. Move the radiator upward and wire it to the hood (automatic only).
9 Raise and support the vehicle on jackstands.
10 Drain the oil from crankcase and remove the oil filter.
11 Remove the starter cable from starter and remove the starter (Chapter 5).
12 Disconnect the exhaust manifold tube to the inlet pipe bracket at the thermactor check valve (Chapter 4).
13 Remove the transmission mount to crossmember retaining nuts.
14 Remove the bellcrank from converter housing (automatic).
15 Remove the oil cooler lines from retainer at the block (automatic only).
16 Remove the front crossmember (automatic only).
17 Disconnect the right front lower shock absorber mount (manual only).
18 Position a jack under engine, raise the engine and block it with

a piece of wood approximately 2-1/2 inches thick between the motor mount and the frame rail.
19 Remove the jack.
20 Position the jack under the transmission and raise it slightly (automatic only).
21 Remove the oil pan retaining bolts and lower pan to the chassis.
22 Remove the oil pump drive and pick-up tube assembly and drop the tube assembly into the oil pan.
23 Remove the oil pan (out the front on automatics — out the rear on manual).
24 Clean the oil pan.
25 Clean the oil pan gasket surface on the cylinder block.
26 Clean the oil pump exterior and oil pump pick-up tube screen.
27 To install, position the oil pan gasket and end seals to the cylinder block. Use gasket sealer to retain the gasket.
28 Place the oil pump and pick-up tube assembly inside the oil pan.
29 Position the oil pan under the engine, reach inside and install the oil pump and pick up tube assembly, tightening the bolts to the specified torque (see illustration).
30 Install the oil pan to cylinder block retaining bolts and tighten to the specified torque in the sequence shown (see illustration).
31 The remainder of the installation is the reverse of the removal procedures.

11   Flywheel and rear cover plate — removal and installation

1   Remove the engine.
2   Remove the pressure plate and the clutch disk from the rear of the flywheel as described in Chapter 8.
3   With the clutch removed, lock the flywheel using a large screwdriver in mesh with the starter ring gear and remove the six bolts securing the flywheel to the crankshaft. The bolts should be removed a quarter turn at a time in a diagonal and progressive manner.
4   Mark the mating position of the flywheel and crankshaft flange and then remove the flywheel.
5   Remove the engine rear cover plate bolts and ease the rear cover plate over the two dowel pins. Remove the cover plate.
6   If the flywheel ring gear is badly worn or has teeth missing, it should be replaced by an automotive machine shop.
7   Installation of the flywheel and clutch is the reverse of the removal procedure. Be sure to tighten all bolts to the specified torque. For further information on clutch servicing, see Chapter 8.

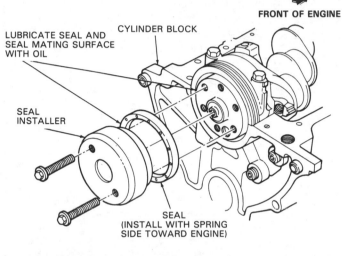

FRONT OF ENGINE

CYLINDER BLOCK

LUBRICATE SEAL AND
SEAL MATING SURFACE
WITH OIL

SEAL
INSTALLER

SEAL
(INSTALL WITH SPRING
SIDE TOWARD ENGINE)

NOTE: REAR FACE OF SEAL MUST BE WITHIN 0.127mm (0.005-INCH) OF THE REAR FACE OF THE BLOCK.

12.5   A special Ford tool is used to install the rear main oil seal

12   Rear oil seal — removal and installation

Refer to illustration 12.5

1   Remove the transmission and all other components necessary, such as the clutch, pressure plate, driveplate, starter and transfer case to get at the oil seal in the back of the engine (Chapters 7 and 8).
2   Remove the oil pan (Section 10).
3   Use a small punch to punch two holes on opposite sides of the seal and install small sheet metal screws into the seal. Pull on the screws with two large screwdrivers until seal is removed from engine. It may be necessary to place small blocks of wood against the cylinder block to provide a fulcrum point for prying. **Caution:** *Be careful not to scratch or otherwise damage the crankshaft oil seal surface.*
4   Apply sealer to the mating edges of the seal and the seal bore in the cylinder block.
5   Position the seal on seal installer tool T82L-6701-A or its equivalent, then position the tool and seal to the rear of engine (see illustration). Install the seal with the spring side toward the engine. Alternate tightening of the bolts to seat the seal properly.
6   The remainder of the installation is the reverse of the removal procedures.

13   Motor mounts — removal and installation

Front motor mounts

1   Remove the nuts from the top of motor mount brackets.

2   Raise the vehicle and support it securely on jackstands.
3   Place a jack and wooden block under the oil pan and lift the engine clear of the insulators.
4   Remove the nut attaching the insulator to the crossmember.
5   Remove the insulator.
6   Position the new insulator to the crossmember.
7   Lower the engine onto the insulators.
8   Lower the vehicle.
9   Install the attaching nuts and tighten.

Rear support

10   Raise the vehicle and support it securely on jackstands.
11   Remove the two nuts attaching the rear motor mount to engine support.
12   Place a piece of wood between the jack and oil pan and raise the engine, transmission and transfer case (if equipped).
13   Remove the two bolts attaching the motor mount to the rear of the engine.
14   Remove the motor mount.
15   Install the new mount and tighten the bolts.
16   Lower the engine and transmission.
17   Install the attaching nuts and tighten.

14   Engine — removal and installation

Removal

1   Drain the coolant from the radiator (Chapter 3).
2   Remove the air cleaner and duct assembly.
3   On the 2.3L EFI engine, disconnect the air cleaner outlet tube at the throttle body, the idle speed control hose and the heat riser tube.
4   Disconnect the battery ground cable at both the engine and battery and disconnect the battery positive cable at the battery.
5   Index with paint or scratch a line to show the location of the hood hinges and remove the hood.
6   Disconnect the upper and lower radiator hoses.
7   Remove the radiator shroud bolts.
8   Remove the radiator upper supports.
9   Loosen the alternator retaining bolt and remove the drivebelt.
10   Remove the fan, the shroud assembly and the radiator.
11   Remove the oil filler cap.
12   Disconnect the coil primary wire at the coil. Disconnect the oil pressure and the water temperature sending wires from the sending units.
13   Disconnect the alternator wires from the alternator, the starter cable from the starter and the accelerator cable from the carburetor. If so equipped, disconnect the transmission kickdown rod.
14   If so equipped, remove the air conditioner compressor from the mounting bracket and position it out of the way. **Warning:** *Before removing the compressor, the system must be evacuated by an air-conditioning technician.*
15   Disconnect the power brake vacuum hose from the booster.
16   Disconnect the chassis fuel line from the fuel pump. On the 2.3L EFI engine, disconnect the two push connect fittings at engine fuel rail (Chapter 4).
17   Disconnect the heater hoses from the engine.
18   Remove the engine mount nuts (Section 13).
19   Raise the vehicle and support on jackstands.
20   Drain the oil from crankcase.
21   Remove the starter motor (Chapter 5).
22   Disconnect the exhaust pipe at the exhaust manifold.
23   Remove the dust cover (manual transmission) or converter inspection plate (automatic transmission).
24   On vehicles with a manual transmission, remove the flywheel housing cover attaching bolts.
25   On vehicles with automatic transmissions, remove the converter-to-drivebolt bolts, then remove the converter housing lower attaching bolts.
26   Lower the vehicle.
27   Support the transmission with a jack.
28   Remove the flywheel housing or converter housing upper attaching bolts.
29   Check that all wires, vacuum lines and hoses are disconnected and the engine is ready to be removed.
30   Attach the engine lifting hooks to the lifting brackets. Carefully,

so as not to damage any components, lift the engine out of the vehicle.
31 Remove the clutch and flywheel or driveplate from the rear of the engine and install the engine on a stand.

Installation

32 Remove the engine from the work stand and install the driveplate or flywheel and clutch assembly, tightening the bolts to the specified torque.
33 Lower the engine into the engine compartment.
34 On a vehicle with an automatic transmission, start the converter pilot into the crankshaft.
35 On a vehicle with a manual transmission, start the transmission input shaft into the clutch disc. It may be necessary to adjust the position of the transmission in relation to the engine if the input shaft will not enter the clutch disc. If the engine hangs up after the shaft enters, turn the crankshaft in a clockwise direction slowly (transmission in gear), until the shaft splines mesh with the clutch disc splines.

36 Install the flywheel housing or converter housing attaching bolts. Remove the engine lifting hooks from the lifting brackets.
37 Remove the jack from under the transmission and raise the vehicle and support it securely on jackstands.
38 On a vehicle with a manual transmission, install the flywheel housing (bellhousing) lower bolts, tightening them to the specified torque.
39 On a vehicle with an automatic transmission, attach the converter to the flywheel bolts and tighten. Install the converter housing (bellhousing) bolts and tighten to the specified torque.
40 Install the dust cover (manual transmission) or converter inspection plate (automatic transmission).
41 Connect the exhaust pipe to the exhaust manifold.
42 Install the starter motor and tighten the bolts to the specified torque. Connect the starter cables (Chapter 5).
43 Remove the jackstands and lower the vehicle.
44 The remainder of the installation is the reverse of the removal procedures.

Chapter 2 Part B   2.8L and 2.9L V6 engines

Contents

Specifications

Camshaft end play	0.0008 to 0.004 in
Valve clearance	
2.8L solid lifter	
intake	0.014 in
exhaust	0.016 in
2.9L hydraulic lifter	4-1/2 turns past zero lash

Torque specifications	**Ft-lbs**
Camshaft gear bolt	
2.8L	30 to 36
2.9L	19 to 28
Camshaft thrust plate bolts	13 to 16
Crankshaft damper/pulley bolt	85 to 96
Cylinder head bolts in sequence	
2.8L	
step 1	29 to 40
step 2	40 to 51
step 3	70 to 85
2.9L	
step 1	22
step 2	51 to 55
step 3	turn an additional 90° past step 2
Exhaust manifold	20 to 30
Exhaust manifold shroud	4 to 5
Flywheel to crankshaft	47 to 52
Front cover to cylinder block	13 to 16
Intake manifold to cylinder block (bolt/nut) in sequence	
step 1	3 to 6
step 2	6 to 11
step 3	11 to 15
step 4	15 to 18
Intake manifold to cylinder block (stud)	10 to 12
EFI intake plenum	
step 1	7
step 2	15 to 18
EFI throttle body to plenum	6 to 10
EFI fuel rail to intake manifold	7 to 10
Oil pump pick-up tube to pump	6 to 10
Oil pump pick-up tube to main bearing cap	12 to 15
Oil pan drain plug	15 to 21
Oil pan to cylinder block	5 to 8
Rocker arm cover bolt	3 to 5
Rocker arm shaft support bolt	43 to 50
Water outlet connection bolt	
2.8L	12 to 15
2.9L	6 to 9
Water pump to front cover	7 to 9
Spark plug	18 to 28
Alternator mounting bracket-to-cylinder head	14 to 22
Alternator bracket-to-cylinder block	28 to 40
Alternator pivot bolt	45 to 60
Alternator adjusting arm-to-front cover	60 to 70
Alternator adjusting arm-to-alternator	24 to 40

Specifications (continued)
Torque specifications (continued)

Fan-to-water pump hub	15 to 25
Thermactor pump bracket-to-cylinder block	28 to 40
Thermactor pump bracket-to-cylinder block	18 to 25
Thermactor pump adjusting arm-to-pump	22 to 32
Thermactor pump pivot bolt	30 to 45
Front engine mount nuts	65 to 85

See Part C of this Chapter for other specifications

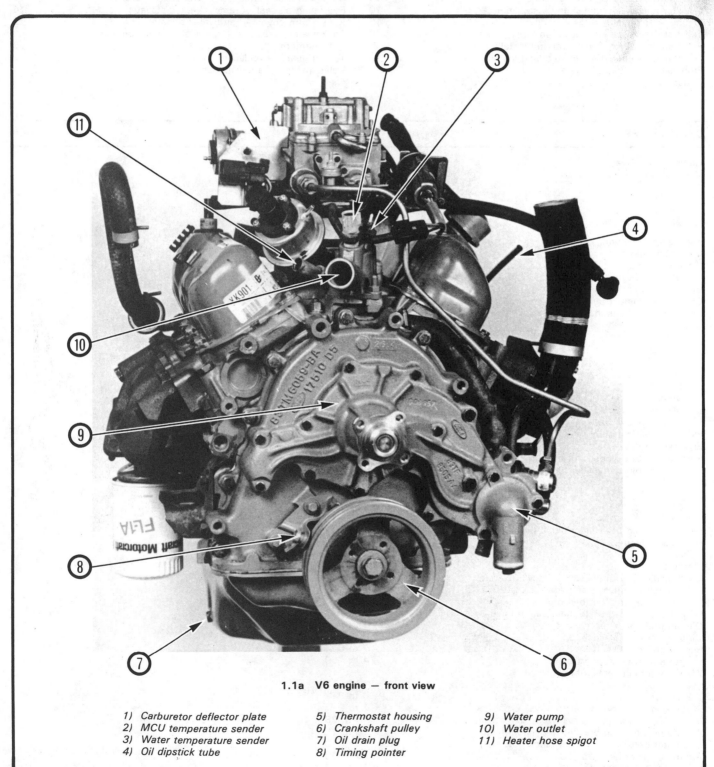

1.1a   V6 engine — front view

1) *Carburetor deflector plate*	5) *Thermostat housing*	9) *Water pump*
2) *MCU temperature sender*	6) *Crankshaft pulley*	10) *Water outlet*
3) *Water temperature sender*	7) *Oil drain plug*	11) *Heater hose spigot*
4) *Oil dipstick tube*	8) *Timing pointer*	

1   General information

Refer to illustrations 1.1a, 1.1b and 1.1c

The forward Sections in this Part of Chapter 2 are devoted to in-vehicle repair procedures. The latter Sections in this Part involve the removal and installation procedures for the 2.8 liter and 2.9 liter V6 engines. All information concerning engine block and cylinder head servicing can be found in Part C of this Chapter.

The repair procedures included in this Part are based on the assump-tion that the engine is still installed in the vehicle. Therefore, if this information is being used during a complete engine overhaul — with the engine already out of the vehicle and on a stand — many of the steps included here will not apply.

The specifications included in this Part of Chapter 2 apply only to the engine and procedures found here. For specifications regarding engines other than the 2.8 and 2.9 liter V6, see Part A or C, whichever applies. Part C of Chapter 2 contains the specifications necessary for engine block and cylinder head rebuilding procedures.

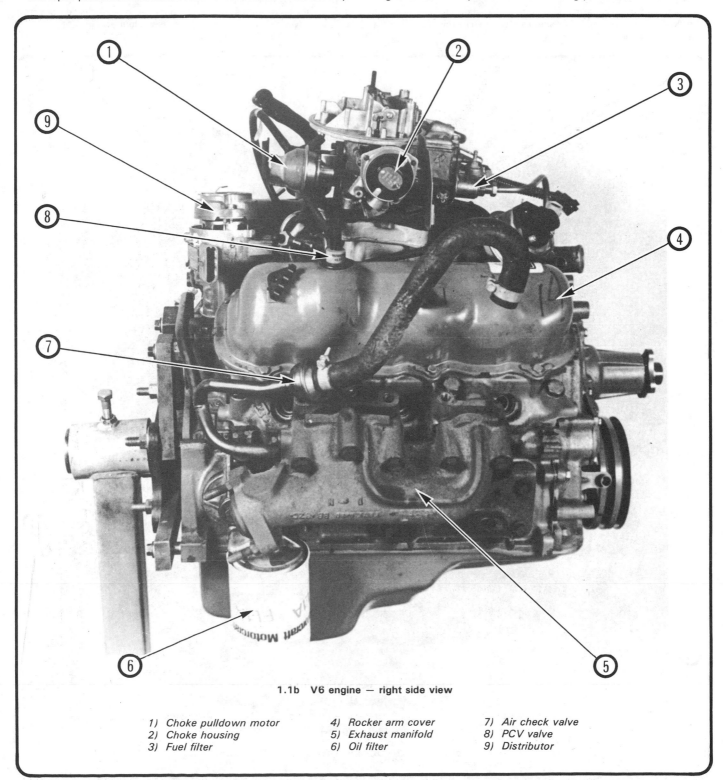

1.1b   V6 engine — right side view

1) Choke pulldown motor	4) Rocker arm cover	7) Air check valve
2) Choke housing	5) Exhaust manifold	8) PCV valve
3) Fuel filter	6) Oil filter	9) Distributor

2   Rocker arm cover — removal and installation

Refer to illustrations 2.4, 2.5, 2.9, 2.10, 2.11, 2.12 and 2.16

Removal

1   Remove the air cleaner, vacuum lines and air duct.
2   Remove the spark plug wires.
3   Remove the PCV valve and hose from the right rocker arm cover.
4   On carburetted models, remove the carburetor choke air deflector plate (see Illustration).
5   Remove the rocker arm cover bolts and load distribution washers (see illustration). Lay out the washers so they can be reinstalled in their original positions.

6   Disconnect the kickdown linkage and carburetor/EFI linkage bracket (automatic transmission only).
7   Position the thermactor air hose and wiring harness away from the right rocker arm cover.
8   Remove the engine oil filler cap.
9   Disconnect the vacuum line at the canister purge solenoid (see illustration) and disconnect the line routed from the canister to the purge solenoid.
10   Disconnect power brake booster hose from dash mounted booster, if so equipped (see illustration).
11   Tap the cover with a light plastic hammer to break the seal or gently pry the cover up with a screwdriver (see illustration).
12   Remove the rocker arm cover (see illustration).

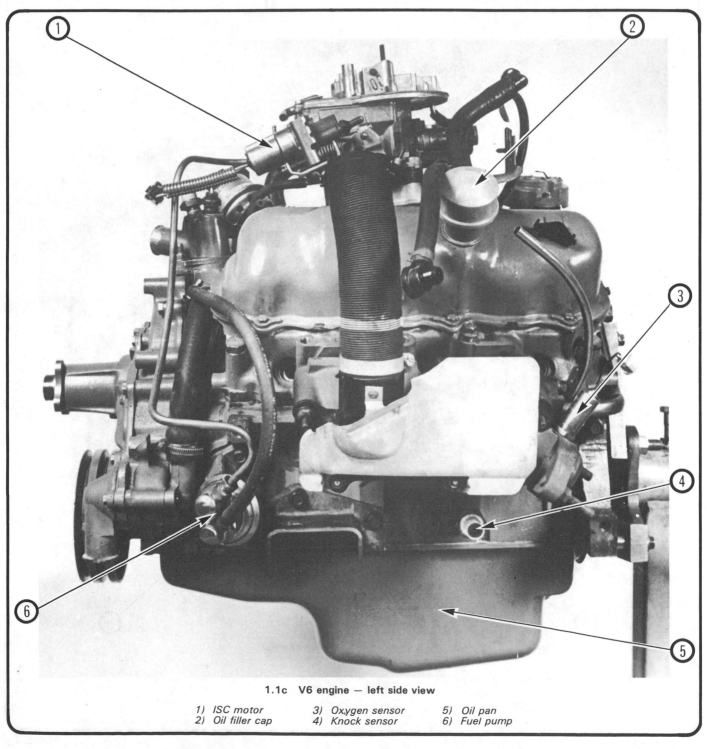

1.1c   V6 engine — left side view

1) ISC motor	3) Oxygen sensor	5) Oil pan
2) Oil filler cap	4) Knock sensor	6) Fuel pump

2.4   Arrow shows the choke air deflector plate

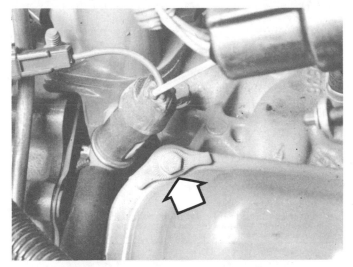

2.5   Be sure the load distribution washers (arrow) are
reinstalled in their original positions on the
rocker arm covers

2.9   Disconnect the vacuum line at the canister purge
solenoid (arrow)

2.10   Disconnect the power brake booster hose,
if so equipped

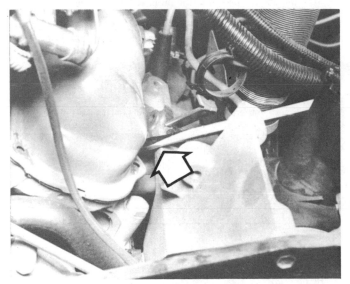

2.11   Gently pry up on the rocker arm cover to
break the seal

2.12   Lift the rocker arm cover out from the rear

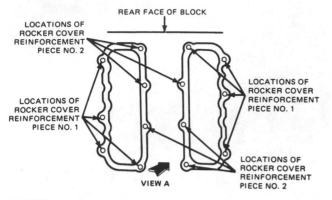

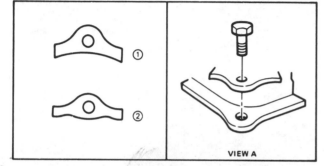

2.16   Reinforcement pieces must be installed in their proper locations to prevent warping the rocker arm cover

Installation

13   Clean all old gasket material and sealer from the cylinder head and rocker arm cover gasket surfaces.
14   Apply a small layer of gasket sealer to the rocker arm cover mating surface and lay the gasket in the cover. Install the rocker arm cover and install the attaching bolts and rocker arm cover reinforcement pieces.
15   Connect the kickdown linkage (automatic transmission only).
16   After ensuring that all rocker arm cover load distribution washers are installed in their original positions (see illustration), tighten the rocker arm cover bolts to specification.
17   Install the spark plug wires.
18   Install the PCV valve and hose.
19   Install the carburetor choke air deflector plate.
20   Reposition the thermactor air hose and wiring harness in their original positions.
21   Install the engine oil filler cap.
22   Connect the vacuum line at canister purge solenoid and connect the line routed from the canister to the purge solenoid.
23   Connect the power brake hose, if so equipped.
24   Install the air cleaner.
25   Start the engine and check for oil leaks.

3   Rocker arm assembly — removal, installation and adjustment

Refer to illustration 3.2

Removal

1   Remove the rocker arm cover (Section 2)
2   Remove the rocker arm shaft stand bolts, loosening the bolts two turns at a time until free (see illustration)
3   Lift off the rocker arm shaft assembly and oil baffle.

Installation

4   Loosen the valve lash adjusting bolts several turns.
5   Thoroughly lubricate all components with engine oil.
6   Install the oil baffle and rocker arm shaft assembly onto the head,

3.2   Remove the three rocker shaft attaching bolts by loosening them two turns at a time

lining up the pushrods and adjusting screws.
7   Starting in the middle and working out, tighten the rocker arm shaft stand bolts two turns at a time to the specified torque.

Adjustment

1983-1985 2.8L
8   Place your finger on the intake valve rocker arm for the number five cylinder.
9   Turn the engine over until the valve just starts to open.
10   Using a feeler gauge to check the clearance, turn the self-locking adjusting bolt until the clearance on the number one intake valve is as specified.
11   Repeat the procedure on the number one exhaust valve. Note that the clearance (valve lash) is *NOT* the same for the intake and exhaust valves.
12   Turn the engine over until the number three cylinder intake valve just starts to open, then adjust the valves for the number *four* cylinder.
13   Turn the engine over until the number six cylinder intake valve just starts to open, then adjust the valves for the number *two* cylinder.
14   Turn the engine over until the number one cylinder intake valve just starts to open, then adjust the valves for the number *five* cylinder.
15   Turn the engine over until the number four cylinder intake valve just starts to open, then adjust the valves for the number *three* cylinder.
16   Turn the engine over until the number two cylinder intake valve just starts to open, then adjust the valves for the number *six* cylinder.

1986 2.9L V6
17   Turn the engine over until both valves for the number one cylinder are closed (lifters on the base circle of the cam).
18   Loosen the adjusting bolts until you can feel a distinct gap between the rocker arm and pushrod.
19   Slowly turn in the adjusting bolt until all lash is just removed (zero clearance).
20   Turn the adjusting bolt in exactly 4-1/2 turns past the zero clearance point.
21   Following the firing order (1-4-2-5-3-6), bring each cylinder to the point where the valves are closed and repeat the adjustment procedure.

4   Oil pan and oil pump — removal and installation

Refer to illustrations 4.1, 4.5, 4.15, 4.16, 4.17 and 4.22

Removal

1   Disconnect negative cable at the battery (see illustration).
2   Remove the air cleaner assembly.
3   Remove the fan shroud and position it over fan.
4   Remove the distributor cap.

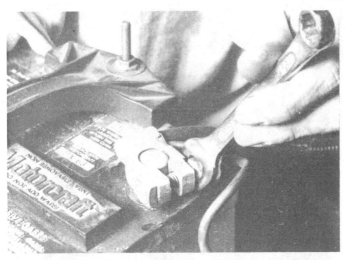

4.1   Before beginning the procedure disconnect the
negative battery cable

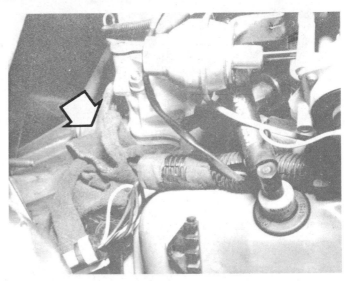

4.5   Stuff a rag in the distributor bore (arrow) to prevent
dirt from entering the engine

4.15   Remove the front stabilizer bar mounting bolts
(arrows)

4.16   Remove the attaching nut (arrow) from the front
motor mount

5   Remove the distributor. Use a rag to protect the opening (see illustration).
6   Remove the engine oil dipstick.
7   Raise the vehicle and support it securely on jackstands.
8   Drain the engine oil (Chapter 1).
9   Remove the oil filter.
10   Disconnect the exhaust pipes from the exhaust manifolds except on 4x2 Ranger vehicles.
11   Disconnect the oil cooler bracket and lower it out of way (if so equipped).
12   Remove the starter cable from the starter.
13   Remove the two attaching bolts and remove the starter motor.
14   Disconnect and position out of way the transmission oil cooler lines (if so equipped).
15   Disconnect the retaining bolts from the front stabilizer bar (see illustration).
16   Disconnect the engine mounts by taking off each of the top nuts (see illustration).
17   Position a jack under the front of the engine oil pan. Place a block of wood between the jack and oil pan so as not to damage the oil pan. Raise engine and install wooden blocks between the front insulator mounts and the crossmember (see illustration).
18   Lower the engine onto the blocks and remove the jack.
19   Remove the oil pan bolts and lower the pan onto the crossmember.
20   Remove the bolts retaining the oil pump and oil pick up tube assembly and lower assembly into the oil pan. On 4x2 Ranger vehicles, remove the oil pump out through the back of the oil pan.

4.17   Install wooden blocks between the front insulator
mounts and the crossmember

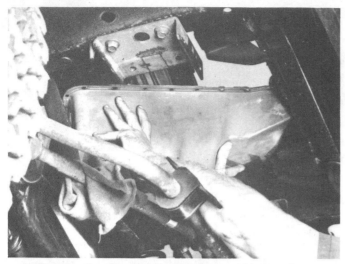

4.22   Drop the oil pump and pick up assembly into the pan and remove the pan from the front

5.6a   Remove the center retaining bolt to remove the pulley

5.6b   A puller may be necessary to remove the pulley

21 Remove the oil pump driveshaft and lower it into the oil pan.
22 Remove the oil pan assembly by sliding it forward over the front axle (see illustration).

Installation
23 Clean the gasket surfaces on the engine and oil pan.
24 Prime the oil pump by filling either the inlet or outlet port with engine oil. Rotate the pump shaft to distribute the oil within the pump body.
25 Insert the oil pump driveshaft into the block with the pointed end facing the block. The pointed end is closest to the pressed on flange.
26 Place the oil pump assembly in position with a new gasket and install the attaching bolts.
27 Apply sealer to the gasket mating surfaces and install the oil pan gaskets.
28 Install the oil pan and tighten the pan bolts to specification.
29 The remainder of the installation procedure is the reverse of removal. Remember to install a new oil filter and fill the engine with oil (Chapter 1).

---

5   Front engine cover — removal and installation

Refer to illustrations 5.6a, 5.6b, 5.8 and 5.14
Note: *Ford recommends that the oil pan be removed before beginning this procedure. However, we found that the cover could be removed for gasket replacement or timing gear inspection without removing the oil pan, as described in the steps which follow. A new pan gasket will be required, however. If removing the cover to replace the timing gears it will be necessary to remove the oil pan.*

1 Drain the coolant and remove the radiator (Chapter 3).
2 Remove the air conditioner compressor and power steering bracket, if so equipped (refer to Chapter 10). **Warning:** *Before removing the p.73*

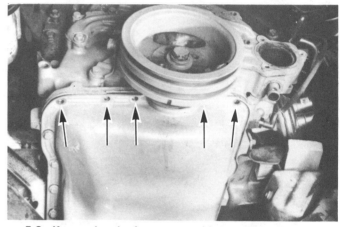

5.8   If removing the front cover without taking off the oil pan, you must remove the front five pan attaching bolts

compressor *the system must be evacuated by an air-conditioning technician.*
3 Loosen the alternator and thermactor pump adjusting bolts and remove the drivebelt. Remove the alternator.
4 Remove the fan (Chapter 3).
5 Remove the heater and radiator hoses connected to the water pump, then remove the water pump (Chapter 3).
6 Remove the drive pulley from the crankshaft by first removing the center retaining bolt (see illustration), then sliding the pulley off. If the pulley will not easily slide off then a puller should be used to remove it (see illustration).
7 Raise the vehicle and support it securely on jackstands.
8 From under the vehicle remove the five front oil pan bolts (see illustration).
9 Remove the seven front cover bolts and carefully remove the cover by prying the top of the cover loose with a screwdriver. Carefully pry the front cover away from the oil pan. If necessary, remove the guide sleeves from cylinder block.

Installation
10 Clean the mating surfaces of all gasket material and apply sealing compound to the gasket surfaces on the block and backside of the cover. Be sure to clean the front section of the oil pan.
11 Cut a section of the new pan gasket to match the removed section, coat with sealant and install.
12 If removed, install the guide sleeves with new seal rings lubricated with engine oil, the chamfered end towards the front cover.

TOOL—T74P 6019-A

5.14   An alignment tool must be used when installing the front cover

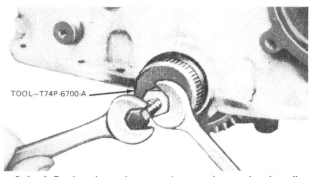

TOOL—T74P-6700-A

6.4   A Ford tool or a large socket can be used to install the new front seal

7.6b   As you tighten down on the bolt the gear slides into place.

13   With sealing compound applied, place the new gasket in position on the front cover.
14   Place the cover on engine and start all the retaining bolts. On 1983-1985 models with 2.8L engines, the cover must be centered by inserting Front Cover Aligner tool T74P-6019-A or equivalent in the oil seal (see illustration).
15   Tighten the attaching bolts to the specified torque.
16   Remove the aligner, install the pulley and tighten the attaching bolt to the specified torque.
17   If removed, install oil pan as described in Section 4.
18   The remainder of the installation is the reverse of the removal procedures.

---

6   Front oil seal — replacement

Refer to illustrations 6.2 and 6.4
1   To replace the front oil seal, drain the coolant and remove the

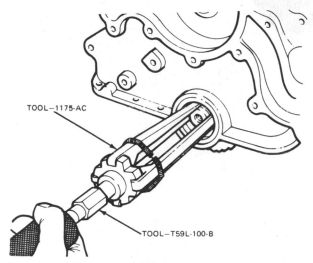

TOOL—1175-AC

TOOL—T59L-100-B

6.2   A special puller and slide hammer are used to remove the front seal

7.6a   We fabricated this installation tool to install the crankshaft timing gear

radiator (Chapter 3). Remove the crankshaft pulley and water pump drivebelt. **Note:** *It is not necessary to remove the front cover.*
2   Remove the front cover seal by using Seal Remover Tool 1175-AC, or its equivalent and Impact Slide Hammer T59L-100-B or its equivalent (see illustration).
3   To replace, coat the new seal with engine oil.
4   Slide the new seal onto the crankshaft and, using a front seal installer T74P-6700-A or a socket the same diameter as the seal, drive the seal in until the tool butts against the front cover (see illustration).
5   Replace crankshaft pulley and bolt and tighten to specification.
6   Install the radiator and drivebelts.
7   Fill the cooling system (Chapter 3).
8   Operate the engine at a fast idle and check for coolant and oil leaks.

---

7   Timing Gears — replacement

Refer to illustrations 7.6a and 7.6b
Note: *Any time a component is to be removed which could effect the timing of the engine, begin the procedure by putting the number one piston at TDC (top dead center) on the compression stroke. Check the alignment of all the timing marks. Remove the distributor cap and see that the rotor is pointing towards the number one cylinder. Do not rotate engine while the timing gears are off.*
1   Remove the oil pan (Section 4).
2   Remove the front cover (Section 5).
3   Remove the radiator.
4   Remove the bolt retaining the camshaft gear to the camshaft and remove the camshaft gear.
5   Using gear puller T71P-19703-B and shaft protector T71P-7137-H or a two prong gear puller, remove the crankshaft gear.
6   To install crankshaft gear, align the keyway in the gear with the Woodruff key, then slide the gear onto the shaft. **Note:** *To install the crankshaft gear we fabricated an installing tool by using a piece of 1-7/8 inch diameter pipe, 3-3/4 inches long and inserted a bolt and washer through the pipe (see illustrations).*

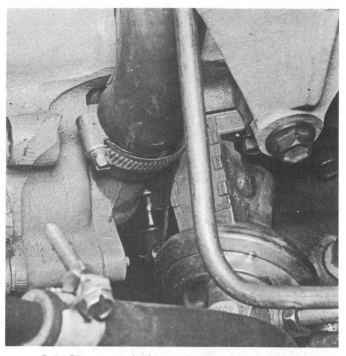

8.4   Disconnect the bypass hose at the rear of the
thermostat housing

8.11   A cardboard box can be used to keep the manifold
bolts in their original locations

8.12   Use a screwdriver wrapped with a rag and carefully
pry up to break the gasket seal

7   With the Woodruff key in the camshaft aligned with the gear
keyway and the timing marks (dot to dot) on both gears aligned, install
the cam gear.
8   Install cam gear retaining bolt and washer and tighten to
specification.
9   Check camshaft end play (Section 12). If not within specifications
replace thrust plate.
10   Install the cylinder front cover, oil pan and radiator.
11   Fill the cooling system and crankcase.
12   Operate the engine at a fast idle and check all hose connections
and gaskets for leaks.

8   Intake manifold — removal and installation

Refer to illustrations 8.4, 8.11, 8.12, 8.13a, 8.13b, 8.15a and 8.15b
1   Disconnect the negative cable at the battery.
2   Remove the air cleaner and attaching vacuum hoses and air ducts.
3   Disconnect the throttle cable.
4   Drain the coolant. Disconnect and remove the hose from water
outlet to radiator (bottom hose). On carburetted engines disconnect
the bypass hose from the intake manifold to the thermostat housing
rear cover (see illustration).
5   Label the spark plug wires (if not already marked by the factory)
and remove distributor cap and plug wires as an assembly. Disconnect
the distributor wiring harness.
6   Observe and mark the location of the distributor rotor and housing
so ignition timing can be maintained at reassembly. Remove distributor
hold down bolt and clamp and lift out distributor.
7   Remove the rocker arm covers (Section 2).
8   On carburetted engines disconnect the fuel line. On EFI engines
remove the fuel lines from the fuel rail. Remove the hoses from the
throttle body then remove the throttle body and plenum.
9   Disconnect and label all wires and hoses that will interfere with
manifold removal.
10   On carburetted models, remove the carburetor and EGR spacer
(Chapters 4 and 6).
11   Remove the intake manifold bolts and nuts by backing off on the
bolts/nuts two turns apiece until loose. Note: *During removal of the
bolts note the length and location of the bolts so they can be installed
in their original location (see illustration).*
12   Tap the manifold lightly with a plastic hammer or wrap a rag around
the tip of a screwdriver and very gently pry up on the manifold to break
the seal (see illustration).
13   Remove all old gasket material and sealing compound from the
manifold and mating surface on the engine block. Place a rag in the
cavity to prevent debris from falling into the ports (see illustrations).

Installation

14   Apply sealing compound to the joining surfaces and place the intake
manifold gasket into position, making sure the tab on the right cylinder
bank fits into the cutout of the manifold gasket.
15   Apply sealing compound to the attaching bolt bosses on the intake
manifold (see illustration) and position the intake manifold. Follow the

8.13a   Scrape all old gasket material from the mating surfaces

8.13b   A rag will help keep pieces of gasket material out of the engine during the cleaning process

8.15a   Apply sealing coumpound to the bolt bosses prior to installation

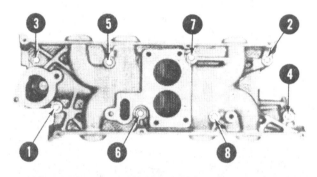

8.15b   Intake manifold bolt tightening sequence

tightening sequence (see illustration) and tighten the bolts to specification.

16   The remainder of the installation is the reverse of the removal procedures.

---

9   Exhaust manifold — removal and installation

Refer to illustrations 9.2, 9.5 and 9.6

1   Remove the air cleaner and attaching vacuum hoses and air duct.

2   Remove the attaching nuts from the exhaust manifold shroud on the left side (see illustration).

9.2   Remove the exhaust heat shield from the manifold

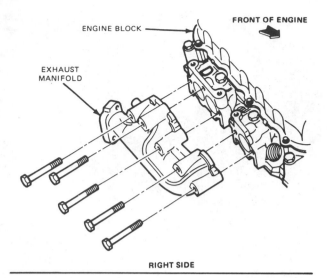

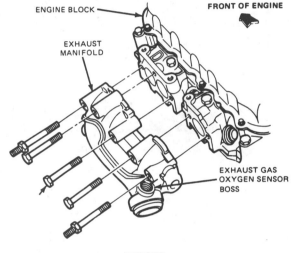

9.6 Exploded view of the exhaust manifolds

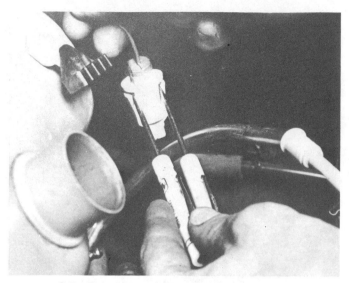

**9.5 Use two screwdrivers to disconnect the
EGO sensor wire**

**10.5 Keep the pushrods in their original order
for installation**

3   Disconnect the attaching nuts from the exhaust pipe at the manifold, then remove the thermactor components (control valves and air injection) by using a screwdriver to back off on the attaching clamp and pulling the valves and hoses out of the way.

4   Unplug the electrical connector from the choke or disconnect choke heat tubes at carburetor.

5   Disconnect the EGO sensor wire on the left side exhaust manifold (see illustration).

6   Remove the manifold attaching bolts and nuts (see illustration).

7   Lift the manifold from the cylinder head.

8   Position the manifold on the studs and install and tighten to specifications the attaching bolts/studs. Tighten the bolts/studs two turns at a time, drawing the manifold to the head evenly.

9   Install a new exhaust pipe gasket, then install the exhaust pipe to the exhaust manifold.

10 Position the exhaust manifold shroud on the manifold (left side) and install and tighten the attaching nuts to specification.

11 Install any thermactor components that were removed.

12 Install the air cleaner and choke heat tube.

13 Connect EGO sensor wire.

10 Cylinder heads — removal and installation

Refer to illustrations 10.5, 10.7, 10.8, 10.9 and 10.12

Removal

1   Disconnect the ground cable at the battery.

2   Drain the coolant (Chapter 3).

3   Refer to Section 8 and remove the intake manifold.

4   Remove the rocker arm covers, rocker arm shafts and oil baffles.

5   Remove the pushrods and keep them in sequence for proper assembly (see illustration).

6   Remove the exhaust manifolds (Section 9).

7   Remove the cylinder head attaching bolts and lift off the cylinder head. Discard the head gasket. It may be necessary to wrap a rag around a screwdriver and carefully pry up on the cylinder to break the seal (see illustration).

8   **Note:** *It may be necessary to remove the cylinder head studs in order to lift up and back on the cylinder head to clear the front cover retainer. To remove the stud run a nut down to the end of the threads and back it up with another nut, then use the first nut to unscrew the stud (see illustration).*

Installation

9   Clean the cylinder heads, intake manifold, rocker arm cover and cylinder block gasket surfaces (see illustration).

10 Place new cylinder head gaskets in position on cylinder block. Gaskets are marked with the words *front* and *top* for correct positioning. Left and right head gaskets are not interchangeable.

10.7   A rag-wrapped screwdriver can be used to break the gasket seal

10.8   A back-up nut and two wrenches can be used to remove the head studs

10.9   Scrape all old gasket material from the head mounting surfaces

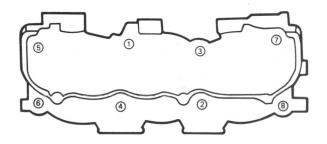

10.12   Tightening sequence for cylinder head bolts

11   A new head gasket set comes with fabricated alignment dowels to make the installation of the head easier. Install fabricated alignment dowels in cylinder block and install cylinder head assemblies on the engine block.

12   Remove the alignment dowels and install cylinder head attaching bolts and studs and tighten in sequence (see illustration) to specifications.

13   Install the intake manifold.

14   Install the exhaust manifolds.

15   Apply engine oil to both ends of the push rods and install them.

16   Install the oil baffles and rocker arm assemblies.

17   The remainder of the installation is the reverse of the removal procedures.

11   Valve lifters — removal, inspection and installation

Refer to illustration 11.2

Removal and installation

1   Remove the cylinder head and related parts.

2   Remove the lifters with a magnet and place them in a rack in sequence so they can be replaced in their original order (see illustration).

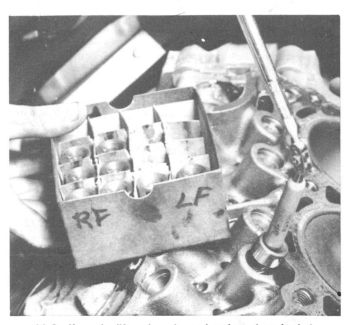

11.2   Keep the lifters in order and replace them in their original locations

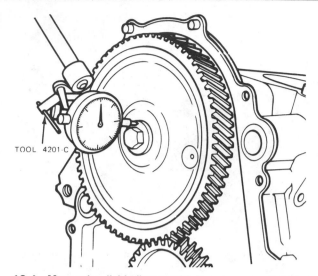

12.4   Mount the dial indicator with the plunger registering on the cam gear

3   If stuck carefully use pliers to remove them by rotating them back and forth to loosen them from gum or varnish deposits.
4   Clean the lifters and apply engine oil to both the lifters and bores before installing. Be sure to install the lifters in their original bores.
5   Install the cylinder head and related parts.

Lifter inspection

6   The faces of the lifters which bear on the camshaft should show no signs of pitting, scoring or other forms of wear. They should also not be a loose fit in the lifter bore. Wear is only normally encountered at very high mileages or in cases of neglected engine lubrication.
7   If the lifters show signs of wear they must be replaced as a complete set and the camshaft must be replaced as well.
8   On 2.9L engines with hydraulic lifters, press down on the plunger to check for freeness of operation. Replace the entire lifter if the plunger is not free in the body.

12   Camshaft end play — check

Refer to illustrations 12.4 and 12.7
Caution: *Prying against the camshaft gear, with the valve train load on the camshaft, can break or damage the gear and camshaft.*
1   Remove the rocker arm cover and timing gear cover.
2   Back off on rocker arm adjusting bolts or loosen the rocker arm shaft stands sufficiently to remove the lifter loading on the camshaft.
3   Push the camshaft toward the rear of the engine.
4   Install a dial indicator so that the indicator point is on the camshaft gear attaching bolt washer (see illustration). Zero the dial indicator.
5   Position a large screwdriver between the camshaft gear and the block.
6   Pull the camshaft forward and release it.
7   Compare the dial indicator reading with specifications. If end play is excessive, replace the thrust plate (see illustration).
8   Remove the dial indicator.
9   After checking the camshaft end play, adjust the valve clearance.
10   Install the rocker arm covers and timing gear cover.

13   Camshaft — removal and installation

Refer to illustrations 13.9 and 13.15
Removal
1   Disconnect the ground cable from the battery.
2   Remove the rocker arm covers (Section 2) and the rocker arm assembly (Section 3).
3   Remove the front engine cover (Section 5).
4   Label and disconnect spark plug wires.

12.7   The camshaft thrust plate

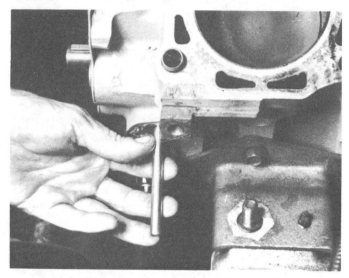

13.9   Remove the fuel pump rod from the block

5   Remove the distributor cap and spark plug wires as an assembly.
6   Disconnect distributor wiring harness connector and remove the distributor.
7   Remove the alternator.
8   Remove the thermactor pump.
9   Disconnect the fuel line at the carburetor and remove the carburetor. Remove the two bolts retaining the fuel pump and set pump out of the way, then remove the fuel pump actuator arm (see illustration).
10   Remove intake manifold (Section 8).
11   Lift out push rods and lifters and place in a marked rack so they can be installed in the same location.
12   Remove the camshaft gear attaching bolt and washer.
13   Slide the gear off the camshaft and remove the Woodruff key from the camshaft.
14   Remove the camshaft thrust plate.
15   Carefully remove the camshaft from the block, avoiding damage to the camshaft bearings (see illustration).

Installation
16   Oil the camshaft journals and cam lobes with engine oil. Install the spacer ring with the chamfered side toward the camshaft and insert the camshaft Woodruff key.
17   Insert the camshaft into the block, carefully avoiding damage to the bearing surfaces.
18   Install the thrust plate so that it covers the main oil gallery and tighten the attaching bolts to specification.
19   Install the camshaft gear and tighten the attaching bolts to specification.
20   Check the camshaft end play (Section 12). The spacer ring and

13.15   Carefully support the camshaft as you remove it from the block

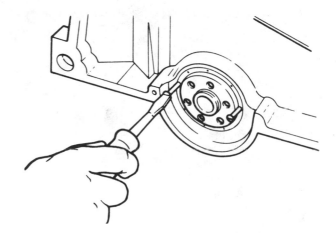

14.6   Sheet metal screws are installed in the rear seal for removal

thrust plate are available in two thicknesses to permit adjusting the end play.

21   The remainder of the installation is the reverse of the removal procedures.

---

14   Rear main oil seal — removal and installation

Refer to illustration 14.6

1   Remove the transmission by following appropriate procedures in Chapter 7.
2   Remove the clutch and pressure plate, if so equipped (Chapter 8).
3   Refer to Chapter 8 and remove the flywheel.
4   Loosen and remove the bolts and spring washers that secure the flywheel housing and rear plate where fitted.
5   Punch two holes in the seal on opposite sides of the crankshaft and just above the bearing cap to cylinder block split line.
6   Install two sheet metal screws into the holes (see illustration) and use two screwdrivers to pry against both screws at the same time to remove the seal. As you move the seal out it may become necessary to use wooden blocks as fulcrum points for the pry bars. **Caution:** *During this operation avoid scratching or otherwise damaging the crank-*

shaft oil seal bore surface.

7   Coat the oil seal to cylinder block surface of the oil seal with sealer.
8   Coat the seal contact surface of the oil seal and crankshaft with engine oil.
9   Start the seal in the recess and install it with tool T72C-6165 or an equivalent such as a hammer and socket. Drive the seal into position until it is firmly seated.
10   The remainder of the installation is the reverse of the removal procedures.

---

15   Front Engine mounts — removal and installation

Refer to illustration 15.4

1   Remove the fan shroud attaching bolts.
2   Support the engine using a wood block and a jack placed under the oil pan.
3   Remove the distributor cap and position it forward where it will not hit the firewall when the engine is lifted.
4   Remove the nuts and washers attaching the insulators to the No. 2 crossmember and lift the engine enough to disengage the insulator stud from the crossmember (see illustration).

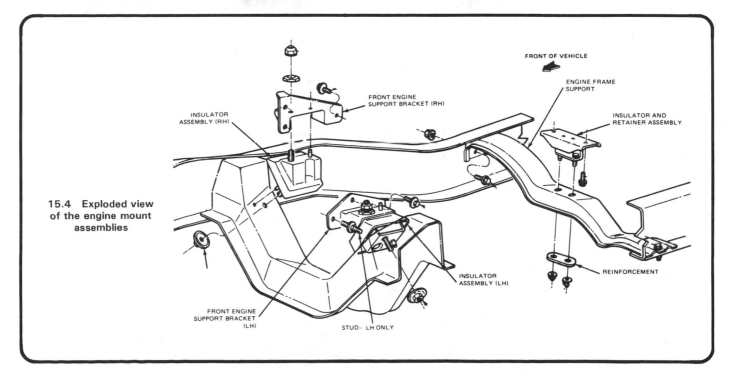

15.4   Exploded view of the engine mount assemblies

16.6   Remove the radiator bracket bolts (arrows)

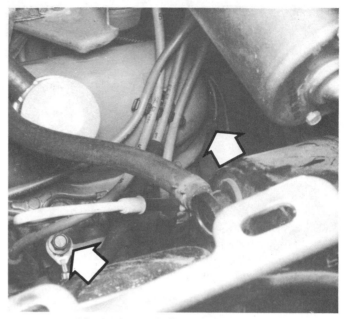

16.11   Arrows indicate ground wires

16.12   Disconnect and plug the fuel line from the tank
(arrow)

16.14   Disconnect the ignition coil wire

5   Remove the bolt attaching the fuel pump shield to the left engine
bracket, if equipped.
6   Remove the engine insulator assembly to cylinder block attaching
bolts and lockwashers and remove the engine mount assembly.
7   To install, position the engine mount assembly to the cylinder block
and install the bracket bolts.
8   Install the bolt attaching the fuel pump shield to the left bracket.
9   Lower the engine until the insulator stud engages and bottoms in
the slot on the No. 2 crossmember pedestal. Tighten the nuts to
specification.
10   Remove the block of wood and jack from the engine oil pan.
11   Install the fan shroud attaching bolts and tighten.

16   Engine — removal and installation

Refer to illustrations 16.6, 16.11, 16.12, 16.14, 16.18, 16.30, 16.33
and 16.36

1   Disconnect the ground cable at the battery.
2   Drain the cooling system (Chapter 3).
3   Remove the air cleaner and intake duct assembly.

4   Disconnect the upper and lower hoses at the radiator.
5   Remove the fan shroud attaching bolts and position the shroud
over the fan.
6   Remove the radiator by removing the radiator attaching brackets
(see illustration).
7   Remove the fan (Chapter 3).
8   Loosen the alternator belt adjusting bolt and remove the drivebelt.
Remove all attaching wires and hoses and remove alternator and thermactor air pump as an assembly by removing the three mounting
bracket bolts.
9   Loosen the belt adjusting bolts and remove the drivebelt, then
remove the air conditioner compressor and power steering unit and
move them out of the way. **Warning:** *Before removing the compressor
the system must be evacuated by an air-conditioning technician.*
10   Disconnect the heater hoses at the top of the block and water
pump.
11   Remove ground wires from left exhaust manifold and left rear of
cylinder head (see illustration).
12   On carburetted engines, disconnect the fuel tank to fuel pump line
and plug the line coming from the tank with a small bolt (see illustration).
On EFI engines disconnect the fuel tank to fuel rail line at the fuel rail.
13   Disconnect the throttle linkage, label all vacuum hoses and wires
attached to carburetor and remove carburetor and EGR spacer (Chapter 4).
14   Disconnect the primary wire (coil wire) from the ignition coil (see
illustration).

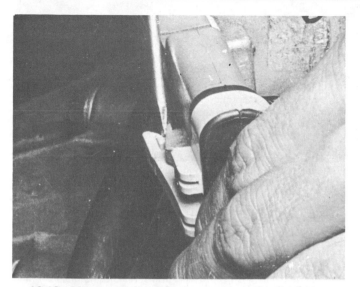

16.18   Disconnect the wiring harness from the distributor

16.30   Attach lifting slings and put rags between chain
and rocker arm covers

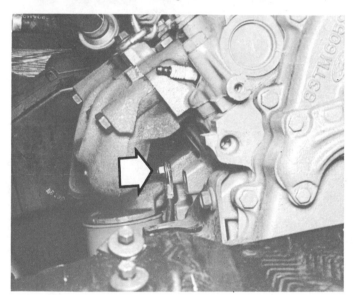

16.33   With the engine raised slightly, remove the ground
cable attached to the block (arrow)

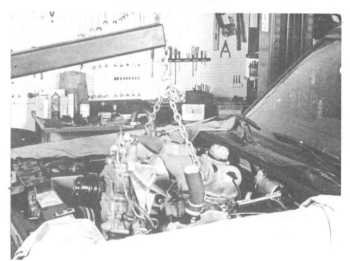

16.36   Carefully lower the engine into the
engine compartment

15 Disconnect the brake booster vacuum hose at the dash mounted booster.
16 Disconnect the wiring from the oil pressure and engine coolant temperature sending units.
17 Pull the plug wires off the spark plugs and label each wire for reinstallation. Remove the distributor cap and plug wires as an assembly.
18 Unplug the wiring harness to the distributor (see illustration).
19 Unplug the electrical connector attached to the EGO sensor.
20 Raise the vehicle and support it securely on jackstands.
21 Disconnect the exhaust pipes at the exhaust manifolds.
22 Remove the starter cable from the starter.
23 Remove the starter.
24 If equipped with a manual transmission, remove the clutch housing attaching bolts.
25 Disconnect the front engine supports (Section 14).
26 If equipped with an automatic transmission, remove the converter inspection cover and disconnect the driveplate from the converter.
27 Disconnect the kickdown rod and transmission linkage bracket.
28 Remove the converter housing to cylinder block bolts and the adapter plate to converter housing bolt.
29 Lower the vehicle.
30 Attach an engine lifting sling and hoist to the lifting brackets at

exhaust manifolds (see illustration).
31 Place a jack and wood block under the transmission.
32 Raise the engine slightly and carefully disengage the engine from the transmission.
33 With the engine raised disconnect the negative ground cable from the block (see illustration).
34 Once clear of the transmission, carefully raise the engine out of the engine compartment.

Installation

35 Attach the engine lifting sling and hoist to the lifting brackets at exhaust manifold.
36 Lower the engine carefully into the engine compartment (see illustration).
37 On a vehicle with a manual transmission, start the transmission main shaft into the clutch disc. It may be necessary to adjust the position of the transmission in relation to the engine with a jack if the input shaft will not enter the clutch disc. If the engine hangs up after the shaft enters, turn the crankshaft slowly with the transmission in gear until the shaft splines mesh with the clutch disc splines. On a vehicle with an automatic transmission, start the converter pilot into the crankshaft.

38 Install the clutch housing or converter housing upper bolts, making sure that the dowels in the cylinder block engage the flywheel housing, then remove the jack under the transmission.

39 On a vehicle with an automatic transmission, position the kickdown rod on the transmission and engine.

40 Raise the vehicle and support it securely on jackstands.

41 On a vehicle with an automatic transmission, position the transmission linkage bracket and install the remaining converter housing bolts. Install the adapter plate to converter housing bolt then install the converter to driveplate nuts.

42 On vehicles with a manual transmission, install the clutch housing attaching bolts.

43 Install the starter and connect the cable.

44 Install new gaskets and connect the exhaust pipes to the exhaust manifolds.

45 Install the engine front support nuts.

46 Lower the vehicle.

47 Connect the ignition coil primary wires.

48 Connect the coolant temperature sending unit and the oil pressure sending unit.

49 Connect the brake booster vacuum hose to the dash mounted brake booster.

50 Install the throttle linkage.

51 Install all vacuum lines and electrical wires to the carburetor or EFI unit.

52 On carburetted engines, connect the fuel tank line at the fuel pump. Engines equipped with EFI should have the line from the fuel tank connected to the fuel rail.

53 Connect the ground cable at the cylinder block.

54 Connect the heater hoses to the water pump and to the connection at the top of the cylinder block.

55 Install the alternator and bracket and connect the alternator wires to the alternator. Install the drivebelt and adjust the tension.

56 Install the ground wires to the left exhaust manifold and left rear of the cylinder head.

57 Install the air conditioner compressor and power steering pump, if so equipped.

58 Install the thermactor pump and adjust the drivebelt.

59 Install the distributor cap and spark plug wires.

60 Install the distributor wiring harness and connect the EGO sensor wire connector.

61 Install the fan.

62 Position the fan shroud over the fan and install the radiator. Connect the radiator upper and lower hoses, then install the fan shroud attaching bolts.

63 Fill the crankcase with the proper grade and quantity of oil.

64 Reconnect the battery ground cable at the battery.

65 Operate the engine at a fast idle until it reaches normal operating temperature and check all gaskets and hoses for leaks.

Chapter 2 Part C
General engine overhaul procedures

Contents

Specifications

2.0L and 2.3L 4-cylinder engines
Valves and related components

Valve face angle	44°
Valve seat angle	45°
Valve head margin	1/32-in
Valve stem diameter	
intake	0.3416 to 0.3423 in
exhaust	0.3411 to 0.3418 in
Stem-to-guide clearance	
intake	0.0010 to 0.0027 in
exhaust	0.0015 to 0.0032 in
Valve seat width	
intake	0.060 to 0.080 in
exhaust	0.070 to 0.090 in
Valve spring free length	1.877 in
Valve spring installed height	1.49 to 1.55 in
Head surface warpage limit	0.006 in over the length of the head

Crankshaft and connecting rods

Crankshaft end play	0.004 to 0.008 in
Connecting rod side clearance	0.0035 to 0.0105 in
Main bearing journal diameter	2.399 to 2.3982 in
Out of round limit	0.0006 in max
Taper limit	0.0006 in per in
Journal runout limit	0.002 in max
Runout service limit	0.005
Main bearing oil clearance	
nominal	0.0008 to 0.0015 in
allowable	0.0008 to 0.0026 in
Rear oil seal installed depth	0.005 in max
Connecting rod bearing journal diameter	2.0462 to 2.0472 in
Connecting rod bearing clearance	
nominal	0.0008 to 0.0015 in
allowable	0.0008 to 0.0026 in
Oil pressure	40 to 60 psi @ 2000 rpm

Engine block
Cylinder bore
  2.0L . . . . 3.5165 to 3.5201 in
  2.3L . . . . 3.7795 to 3.7825 in
Out-of-round limit . . . . 0.0015 in
Taper limit . . . . 0.010 in

Pistons and rings
Compression ring side clearance . . . . 0.0020 to 0.0040 in
Piston diameter
  2.0L . . . . 3.5150 to 3.5156 in
  2.3L . . . . 3.7780 to 3.7786 in
Piston-to-bore clearance (select fit) . . . . 0.0014 to 0.0022 in
Piston ring groove width
  top and bottom compression . . . . 0.080 to 0.081 in
  oil ring . . . . 0.189 to 0.190 in
Piston ring end gap
  compression . . . . 0.010 to 0.020 in
  oil ring . . . . 0.015 to 0.055 in

Camshaft
Lobe lift (intake and exhaust)
  1984-1985
    2.0L . . . . 0.2381 in
    2.3L . . . . 0.2437 in
  1986 (all) . . . . 0.2381 in
Bearing journal diameter . . . . 1.7713 to 1.7720 in
Journal-to-bearing clearance . . . . 0.001 to 0.003 in
Camshaft end play . . . . 0.001 to 0.007 in
Firing order 1-3-4-2

Torque specifications   **Ft-lbs**
Main bearing cap bolts in sequence
  step 1 . . . . 50 to 60
  step 2 . . . . 80 to 90
Connecting rod nuts in sequence
  step 1 . . . . 25 to 30
  step 2 . . . . 30 to 36
Cylinder head bolts in sequence
  step 1 . . . . 50 to 60
  step 2 . . . . 80 to 90
Oil pump to block . . . . 14 to 21

2.8L and 2.9L V6 engine
Valves and related components
Valve face angle . . . . 44°
Valve seat angle . . . . 45°
Valve head margin 1/32-in
Stem-to-guide clearance
  intake . . . . 0.0008 to 0.0025 in
  exhaust . . . . 0.0018 to 0.0035 in
Valve seat width . . . . 0.060 to 0.079 in
Valve spring installed height . . . . 1-37/64 to 1-39/64-in
Valve spring free length . . . . 1.91 in
Head warpage limit . . . . 0.006 in over the length of the head

Crankshaft and connecting rods
Stroke
  1984-1985 2.8L . . . . 2.70 in
  1986 2.9L . . . . 2.83 in
Crankshaft end play . . . . 0.004 to 0.008 in
Connecting rod side clearance . . . . 0.004 to 0.011 in
Main bearing journal
  diameter . . . . 2.2433 to 2.2441 in
  out-of-round limit . . . . 0.0006 in
  taper limit . . . . 0.0006 in
  runout limit . . . . 0.002 in
Main bearing oil clearance
  nominal . . . . 0.0008 to 0.0015 in
  allowable . . . . 0.0005 to 0.0019 in
Connecting rod journal
  diameter . . . . 2.1252 to 2.1260 in
  out-of-round limit . . . . 0.0006 in
  taper limit . . . . 0.0006 in

Connecting rod bearing oil clearance
  nominal . . . .   0.0006 to 0.0016 in
  allowable . . . .   0.0005 to 0.0022 in
Oil pressure . . . .   40 to 60 lbs at 2000 rpm

Engine block
Cylinder bore diameter . . . .   3.6614 to 3.6630 in
Out-of-round
  nominal . . . .   0.0015 in
  service limit . . . .   0.005 in
Taper limit . . . .   0.010 in

Pistons and rings
Compression ring side clearance . . . .   0.0020 to 0.0033 in
Oil ring side clearance . . . .   Snug fit
Piston-to-bore clearance . . . .   0.0011 to 0.0019 in
Piston ring end gap
  compression rings . . . .   0.015 to 0.023 in
  oil ring . . . .   0.015 to 0.055 in

Camshaft
Lobe lift . . . .   0.2555 in
Bearing journal diameter
  #1 . . . .   1.7285 to 1.7293 in
  #2 . . . .   1.7135 to 1.7143 in
  #3 . . . .   1.6985 to 1.6992 in
  #4 . . . .   1.6835 to 1.6842 in
Journal-to-bearing oil clearance
  1984-1985 . . . .   0.001 to 0.0026 in
  1986 . . . .   0.0017 in
Cylinder numbers
  right bank . . . .   1-2-3 (front-to-rear)
  left bank . . . .   4-5-6 (front-to-rear)
Firing order   1-4-2-5-3-6

Torque specifications   **Ft-lbs**
Rocker arm shaft support bolts . . . .   43 to 50
Connecting rod nuts . . . .   19 to 24
Cylinder head bolts in sequence
  1984-1985
    step 1 . . . .   29 to 40
    step 2 . . . .   40 to 51
    step 3 . . . .   70 to 85
  1986
    step 1   22
    step 2 . . . .   51 to 55
    step 3 . . . .   turn an additional 90°
Camshaft gear bolt
  1984-1985 . . . .   30 to 36
  1986 . . . .   19 to 28
Camshaft thrust plate . . . .   13 to 16
Main bearing cap bolt . . . .   65 to 75

1   General information

Included in this portion of Chapter 2 are the general overhaul procedures for the cylinder head and internal engine components. The information ranges from advice concerning preparation for an overhaul and the purchase of replacement parts to detailed, step-by-step procedures covering removal and installation of internal engine components and the inspection of parts.

The following Sections have been written based on the assumption that the engine has been removed from the vehicle. For information concerning in-vehicle engine repair, as well as removal and installation of the external components necessary for the overhaul, see Part A or B of Chapter 2 (depending on engine type) and Section 2 of this Part.

The specifications included here in Part C are only those necessary for the inspection and overhaul procedures which follow. Refer to Part A or B for additional specifications related to the various engines covered in this manual.

2   Repair operations possible with the engine in the vehicle

Many major repair operations can be accomplished without removing the engine from the vehicle.

It is a good idea to clean the engine compartment and the exterior of the engine with some type of pressure washer before any work is begun. A clean engine will make the job easier and will prevent the possibility of getting dirt into internal areas of the engine.

Remove the hood (Chapter 11) and cover the fenders to provide as much working room as possible and to prevent damage to the painted surfaces.

If oil or coolant leaks develop, indicating a need for gasket or seal replacement, the repairs can generally be made with the engine in the vehicle. The oil pan gasket, the cylinder head gasket, intake and exhaust manifold gaskets, timing cover gaskets and the front crankshaft oil seal are accessible with the engine in place.

Exterior engine components, such as the water pump, starter motor, alternator, distributor, fuel pump and carburetor or EFI, as well as the intake and exhaust manifolds, can be removed for repair with the engine in place.

Since the cylinder head(s) can be removed without pulling the engine, valve component servicing can also be accomplished with the engine in the vehicle.

Replacement of, repairs to or inspection of the timing sprockets or chain and the oil pump are all possible with the engine in place.

In extreme cases caused by a lack of necessary equipment, repair or replacement of piston rings, pistons, connecting rods and rod bearings and reconditioning of the cylinder bores is possible with the engine in the vehicle. However, this practice is not recommended because of the cleaning and preparation work that must be done to the components involved.

Detailed removal, inspection, repair and installation procedures for the above mentioned components can be found in the appropriate Part of Chapter 2 or the other Chapters in this manual.

3   Engine overhaul — general information

It is not always easy to determine when, or if, an engine should be completely overhauled, as a number of factors must be considered.

High mileage is not necessarily an indication that an overhaul is needed, while low mileage does not preclude the need for an overhaul. Frequency of servicing is probably the most important consideration. An engine that has had regular and frequent oil and filter changes, as well as other required maintenance, will most likely give many thousands of miles of reliable service. Conversely, a neglected engine may require an overhaul very early in its life.

Excessive oil consumption is an indication that piston rings and/or valve guides are in need of attention. Make sure that oil leaks are not responsible before deciding that the rings and guides are bad. Have a cylinder compression or leak down test performed by an experienced mechanic to determine the extent of the work required.

If the engine is making obvious knocking or rumbling noises, the connecting rod and/or main bearings are probably at fault. Check the oil pressure with a gauge installed in place of the oil pressure sending unit and compare it to the Specifications. If it is extremely low, the bearings and/or oil pump are probably worn.

Loss of power, rough running, excessive valve train noise and high fuel consumption rates may also point to the need for an overhaul, especially if they are all present at the same time. If a complete tune-up does not remedy the situation, major mechanical work is the only solution.

An engine overhaul involves restoring the internal parts to the specifications of a new engine. During an overhaul, the piston rings are replaced and the cylinder walls are reconditioned. If a rebore is done, new pistons are required. The main and connecting rod bearings are replaced with new ones and, if necessary, the crankshaft may be reground to restore the journals. Generally, the valves are serviced as well, since they are usually in less-than-perfect condition at this point. While the engine is being overhauled other components, such as the carburetor, distributor, starter and alternator, can be rebuilt as well. The end result should be a like new engine that will give many trouble free miles.

Before beginning the engine overhaul, read through the entire procedure to familiarize yourself with the scope and requirements of the job. Overhauling an engine is not difficult, but it is time consuming. Plan on the vehicle being tied up for a minimum of two weeks, especially if parts must be taken to an automotive machine shop for repair or reconditioning. Check on availability of parts and make sure that any necessary special tools and equipment are obtained in advance. Most work can be done with typical hand tools, although a number of precision measuring tools are required for inspecting parts to determine if they must be replaced. Often an automotive machine shop will handle the inspection of parts and offer advice concerning reconditioning and replacement. **Note:** *Always wait until the engine has been completely disassembled and all components, especially the engine block, have been inspected before deciding what service and repair operations must be performed by an automotive machine shop.* Since the block's condition will be the major factor to consider when determining whether to overhaul the original engine or buy a rebuilt one, never purchase parts or have machine work done on other components until the block has been thoroughly inspected. As a general rule, time is the primary cost of an overhaul, so it does not pay to install worn or substandard

parts.

As a final note, to ensure maximum life and minimum trouble from a rebuilt engine, everything must be assembled with care in a spotlessly clean environment.

4   Engine rebuilding alternatives

The do-it-yourselfer is faced with a number of options when performing an engine overhaul. The decision to replace the engine block, piston/connecting rod assemblies and crankshaft depends on a number of factors, with the number one consideration being the condition of the block. Other considerations are cost, access to machine shop facilities, parts availability, time required to complete the project and experience.

Some of the rebuilding alternatives include:

Individual parts — If the inspection procedures reveal that the engine block and most engine components are in reusable condition, purchasing individual parts may be the most economical alternative. The block, crankshaft and piston/connecting rod assemblies should all be inspected carefully. Even if the block shows little wear, the cylinder bores should receive a finish hone.

Crankshaft kit — This rebuild package usually consists of a reground crankshaft, main and rod bearings, and a matched set of pistons with rings and connecting rods. The pistons will already be installed on the connecting rods. These kits are commonly available for standard cylinder bores, as well as for engine blocks which have been bored to a regular oversize.

Short block — A short block consists of an engine block with a crankshaft and piston/connecting rod assemblies already installed. All new bearings are incorporated and all clearances will be correct. Depending on where the short block is purchased, a guarantee may be included. The existing camshaft, valve train components, cylinder head and external parts can be bolted to the short block with little or no machine shop work necessary.

Long block — A long block consists of a short block plus an oil pump, oil pan, cylinder head, rocker arm cover, camshaft and valve train components, timing sprockets and chain and timing chain cover. All components are installed with new bearings, seals and gaskets incorporated throughout. The installation of manifolds and external parts is all that is necessary. Some form of guarantee is usually included with the purchase.

Give careful thought to which alternative is best for you and discuss the situation with local automotive machine shops, auto parts dealers or your local dealership before ordering or purchasing replacement parts.

5   Engine removal — methods and precautions

If it has been decided that an engine must be removed for overhaul or major repair work, certain preliminary steps should be taken.

Locating a suitable work area is extremely important. A shop is, of course, the most desirable place to work. Adequate work space, along with storage space for the vehicle, is very important. If a shop or garage is not available, at the very least a flat, level, clean work surface made of concrete or asphalt is required.

Cleaning the engine compartment and engine prior to removal will help keep tools clean and organized.

An engine hoist or A-frame will also be necessary. Make sure that the equipment is rated in excess of the combined weight of the engine and its accessories. Safety is of primary importance, considering the potential hazards involved in lifting the engine out of the vehicle.

If the engine is being removed by a novice, a helper should be available. Advice and aid from someone more experienced would also be helpful. There are many instances when one person cannot simultaneously perform all of the operations required when lifting the engine out of the vehicle.

Plan the operation ahead of time. Arrange for or obtain all of the tools and equipment you will need prior to beginning the job. Some of the equipment necessary to perform engine removal and installation safely and with relative ease are (in addition to an engine hoist) a heavy duty floor jack, complete sets of wrenches and sockets as described in the front of this manual, wooden blocks and plenty of rags and cleaning solvent for mopping up the inevitable spills. If the hoist is to be rented, make sure that you arrange for it in advance and perform beforehand all of the operations possible without it. This will save you money and time.

Plan for the vehicle to be out of use for a considerable amount of time. A machine shop will be required to perform some of the work which the do-it-yourselfer cannot accomplish due to a lack of special equipment. These shops often have a busy schedule, so it would be wise to consult them before removing the engine in order to accurately estimate the amount of time required to rebuild or repair components that may need work.

Always use extreme caution when removing and installing the engine. Serious injury can result from careless actions. Plan ahead. Take your time and a job of this nature, although major, can be accomplished successfully.

6 Engine overhaul — disassembly sequence

1   It is much easier to disassemble and work on the engine if it is mounted on an engine stand. These stands can often be rented for a reasonable fee from an equipment rental yard. Before the engine is mounted on a stand, the flywheel/driveplate should be removed from the engine (refer to Chapter 8).
2   If a stand is not available, it is possible to disassemble the engine with it blocked up on a sturdy workbench or on the floor. Be extra careful not to tip or drop the engine when working without a stand.
3   If you are going to obtain a rebuilt engine, all external components must come off your old engine first in order to be transferred to the replacement engine (just as they will if you are doing a complete engine overhaul yourself). These include:
    Alternator and brackets
    Emissions control components
    Distributor, spark plug wires and spark plugs
    Thermostat and housing
    Water pump
    Carburetor/fuel injection components
    Intake/exhaust manifolds
    Oil filter
    Fuel pump
    Engine mounts
    Flywheel/driveplate

Note: *When removing the external components from the engine, pay close attention to details that may be helpful or important during installation. Note the installed position of gaskets, seals, spacers, pins, washers, bolts and other small items.*

4   If you are obtaining a short block, which consists of the engine block, crankshaft, pistons and connecting rods all assembled, then the cylinder head, oil pan and oil pump will have to be removed as well. See Section 4, *Engine rebuilding alternatives*, for additional information regarding the different possibilities to be considered.
5   If you are planning a complete overhaul, the engine should be dismantled to the basic "short block" stage, which includes the removal of:

2.8L and 2.9L V6
    Carburetor/fuel injection unit
    Rocker arm covers
    Intake and exhaust manifold
    Cylinder heads and pushrods
    Timing chain cover
    Oil pan

2.0 and 2.3L 4-cylinder
    Carburetor/fuel injection unit
    Intake and exhaust manifolds
    Cam cover
    Timing belt/sprocket cover
    Timing belt and sprockets
    Cylinder head
    Oil pan

6   Before beginning the disassembly and overhaul procedures, make sure the following items are available:
    Common hand tools
    Small cardboard boxes or plastic bags for storing parts
    Gasket scraper
    Ridge reamer

    Vibration damper puller
    Micrometers and/or vernier caliper
    Telescoping (snap) gauge
    Dial indicator set
    Valve spring compressor
    Cylinder surfacing hone
    Electric drill motor
    Tap and die set
    Wire brushes
    Cleaning solvent

7 Cylinder head — disassembly

Refer to illustrations 7.3, 7.4 and 7.5
Note: *New and rebuilt cylinder heads are commonly available for most engines at dealerships and auto parts stores. Due to the fact that some specialized tools are necessary for the disassembly and inspection procedures, and replacement parts may not be readily available, it may be more practical and economical for the home mechanic to purchase a replacement head rather than taking the time to disassemble, inspect and recondition the original head.*

2.8L and 2.9L V6
1   Refer to Chapter 2B for the removal procedures for the heads and rocker arm shafts and stands.
2   Remove any deposits from the combustion chambers and valve heads with a scraper and a wire brush before removing the valves. **Caution:** *Be careful not to scratch the gasket surfaces.*
3   Compress the valve springs with a valve spring compressor. Remove the keepers and release the springs (see illustration).
4   Remove the spring retainer, stem seal and valve. Discard the valve stem seals. Keep all the parts for each valve ans spring assembly together and label them so they can be returned to their original positons in the head (see illustration).

7.3   Use a valve spring compressor to compress the springs, then remove the keepers from the valve stem

7.4   Keep all the parts for each valve assembly together and numbered so the valve can be returned to its original position with the original spring and retainer assembly parts

7.5   If the valve won't pull through the guide, use a fine file to deburr the end of the valve stem where the action of the rocker arm or cam follower might have mushroomed it slightly

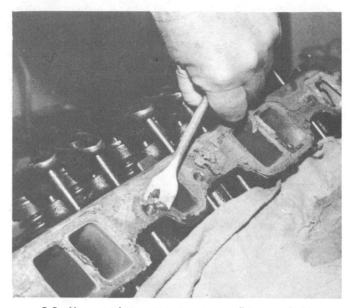

8.2   Use a gasket scraper to remove all traces of old gasket material and sealer from the head

8.5a   Run a tap into all threaded holes to remove old sealer, rust and scale

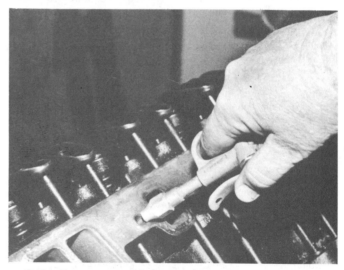

8.5b   Use compressed air to clean out the threaded holes after running the tap through them

5   If the valve stem won't pull through the guide, deburr the top of the valve stem with a fine file (see illustration).

2.0L and 2.3L 4-cylinder
6   Refer to Chapter 2A and remove the cylinder head, camshaft and cam followers. **Note:** *When disassembling mark the cam followers, lash adjusters and valves so that they can be installed in their original positions.*
7   Remove the deposits from the combustion chambers and valve heads with a scraper and a wire brush before removing the valves. **Caution:** *Be careful not to scratch the gasket surfaces.*
8   Compress the valve springs with a valve spring compressor. Remove the keepers and release the springs.
9   Remove the retainer, spring assembly and seal from the valve. The valve can now be removed through the bottom of the head. If the valve binds in the guide (will not pull through), push it back into the head and deburr the area around the head of the stem with a fine file or whetstone.
10   Repeat the procedure for the remaining valves. Remember to keep together all the parts for each valve so they can be reinstalled in the same locations.
11   Once valves have been removed and safely stored, the head should

be thoroughly cleaned and inspected. If a complete engine overhaul is being done, finish the engine disassembly procedures before beginning the cylinder head cleaning and inspection process.

---

8   Cylinder head — cleaning and inspection

Refer to illustrations 8.2, 8.5a, 8.5b, 8.12, 8.14, 8.21 and 8.22
1   Thorough cleaning of the cylinder head and related valve train components, followed by a detailed inspection, will enable you to decide how much valve service work must be done during the engine overhaul.

Cleaning
2   Scrape away all traces of old gasket material and sealing compound from the head gasket, intake manifold and exhaust manifold sealing surfaces (see illustration).
3   Remove any built-up scale around the coolant passages.
4   Run a stiff wire brush through the oil holes to remove any deposits that may have formed in them.
5   It is a good idea to run a tap into each of the threaded holes to remove any corrosion and thread sealant that may be present (see il-

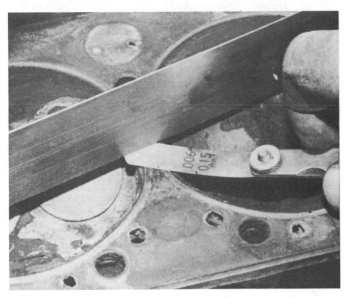

8.12 Use a straightedge and feeler gauge to check for warping of the cylinder head

8.14 Use a dial indicator to check for excessive clearance between the valve stem and valve guide

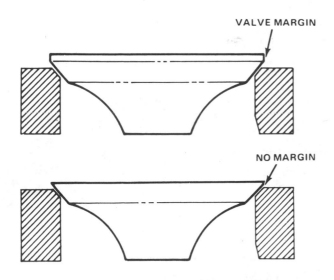

8.21 When grinding has brought the available valve margin to below specifications, the valve must be replaced

lustration). If compressed air is available, use it to clear the holes of debris produced by this operation (see illustration).

6   Clean the exhaust and intake manifold stud threads (V6) in a similar manner with a die. Clean the rocker arm pivot bolt or stud threads, if applicable, with a wire brush.

7   Clean the cylinder head with solvent and dry it thoroughly. Compressed air will speed the drying process and ensure that all holes and recessed areas are clean. **Note:** *Decarbonizing chemicals are available and may prove very useful when cleaning cylinder heads and valve train components. They are very caustic and should be used with caution. Be sure to follow the instructions on the container.*

8   Clean the rocker arms and pushrods (V6) with solvent and dry them thoroughly. Compressed air will speed the drying process and can be used to clean out the oil passages.

9   Clean all the valve springs, keepers, retainers, shields and shims with solvent and dry them thoroughly. Do the components from one valve at a time to avoid mixing up the parts.

10   Scrape off any heavy deposits that may have formed on the valves,

then use a motorized wire brush to remove deposits from the valve heads and stems. Again, make sure the valves do not get mixed up.

Inspection
Cylinder head

11   Inspect the head very carefully for cracks, evidence of coolant leakage or other damage. If cracks are found, a new cylinder head should be obtained.

12   Using a straightedge and feeler gauge, check the head gasket mating surface for warpage (see illustration). If the warpage exceeds 0.006-inch over the length of the head, it can be resurfaced at an automotive machine shop.

13   Examine the valve seats in each of the combustion chambers. If they are pitted, cracked or burned, the head will require valve service that is beyond the scope of the home mechanic.

14   Check the valve stem to valve guide clearance. Use a dial indicator to measure the lateral movement of each valve stem with the valve in the guide and approximately 1/16-inch off the seat (see illustration). If, after this check, there is still some doubt as to the condition of the valve guides, the exact clearance and condition of the guides can be checked by an automotive machine shop, usually for a very small fee.

Rocker arm components — V6 engine

15   Check the rocker arm faces for pits, wear and rough spots. Check the pivot contact areas as well.

16   Inspect the pushrod ends for scuffing and excessive wear. Roll the pushrod on a flat surface, such as a piece of glass, to determine if it is bent.

17   Any damaged or excessively worn parts must be replaced with new ones.

Cam followers — 4-cylinder engine

18   Clean all the parts thoroughly. Make sure that all oil passages are open.

19   Inspect the pad at the valve end of the follower and the camshaft end pad for indications of scuffing or abnormal wear. If the pad is grooved it will be necessary to replace the follower. Do not attempt to true this surface by grinding.

Valves

20   Carefully inspect each valve face for cracks, pits and burned spots. Check the valve stem and neck for cracks. Rotate the valve and check for any obvious indication that it is bent. Check the end of the stem for pits and excessive wear. The presence of any of these conditions indicates the need for valve service by a shop.

21   Measure the width of the valve margin on each valve and compare it to Specifications. Any valve with a margin narrower than specified (see illustration) will have to be replaced with a new one.

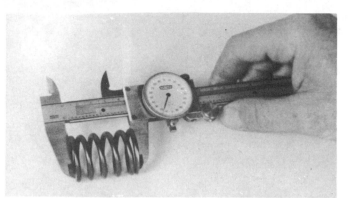

8.22   Measure the free length of each valve spring and replace any which have sagged or collapsed

Valve train components

22   Check each valve spring for wear on the ends and pits. Measure the free length (see illustration) and compare it to the Specifications. Any springs that are shorter than specified have sagged and should not be reused.

23   Check the spring retainers and keepers for obvious wear and cracks. Any questionable parts should be replaced with new ones, as extensive damage will occur in the event of failure during engine operation.

24   If the inspection process indicates that the valve components are in generally poor condition and worn beyond the limits specified, which is usually the case in an engine that is being overhauled, reassemble the valves in the cylinder head and refer to Section 9 for valve servicing recommendations.

25   If the inspection turns up no excessively worn parts, and if the valve faces and seats are in good condition, the valve train components can be reinstalled in the cylinder head without major servicing. Refer to the appropriate Section for cylinder head reassembly procedures.

9   Valves — servicing

1   Because of the complex nature of the job and the special tools and equipment needed, servicing of the valves, the valve seats and the valve guides, commonly known as a valve job, is best left to a shop.

2   The home mechanic can remove and disassemble the head, do the initial cleaning and inspection, then reassemble and deliver the head to a dealer service department or an automotive machine shop for the actual valve servicing.

3   The dealer service department, or automotive machine shop, will remove the valves and springs, recondition or replace the valves and valve seats (4-cylinder engine), recondition the valve guides, check and replace the valve springs, spring retainers and keepers (as necessary), replace the valve seals with new ones (4-cylinder requires using a plastic installation cap), reassemble the valve components and make sure the installed spring height is correct. The cylinder head gasket surface will also be resurfaced if it is warped.

4   After the valve job has been performed by a shop the head will be in like new condition. When the head is returned, be sure to clean it again before installation on the engine to remove any metal particles and abrasive grit that may still be present from the valve service or head resurfacing operations. Use compressed air, if available, to blow out all the oil holes and passages.

10   Cylinder head — reassembly

Refer to illustrations 10.4, 10.7a and 10.7b

1   Regardless of whether or not the head was sent to an automotive repair shop for valve servicing, make sure it is clean before beginning reassembly.

2   If the head was sent out for valve servicing, the valves and related components will already be in place. Begin the reassembly procedure with Step 6.

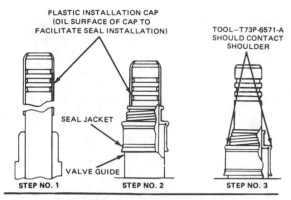

PLASTIC INSTALLATION CAP
(OIL SURFACE OF CAP TO
FACILITATE SEAL INSTALLATION)

TOOL–T73P-6571-A
SHOULD CONTACT
SHOULDER

SEAL JACKET

VALVE GUIDE

STEP NO. 1   STEP NO. 2   STEP NO. 3

STEP NO. 1– WITH VALVES IN HEAD. PLACE PLASTIC INSTALLATION CAP OVER END OF VALVE STEM.
STEP NO. 2– START VALVE STEM SEAL CAREFULLY OVER CAP. PUSH SEAL DOWN UNTIL JACKET TOUCHES TOP OF GUIDE.
STEP NO. 3– REMOVE PLASTIC INSTALLATION CAP. USE INSTALLATION TOOL–T73P-6571-A OR SCREWDRIVERS TO BOTTOM SEAL ON VALVE GUIDE.

10.4   A plastic installation cap covers the valve stem on 4-cylinder engines when installing the new valve seals

10.7a   Valve spring installed height is measured from the floor of the spring pocket to the underside of the retainer

10.7b   Installed height of the valve spring can also be checked with the retainer and keepers installed and the valve pulled up tight against the valve seat, but without the valve spring

11.1   A ridge reamer must be used to completely remove the cylinder wear ridge before attempting to remove the pistons

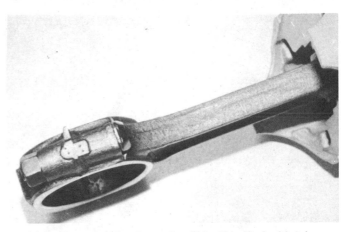

11.2a The rod and rod cap should be identified, either by stamped numbers or dots, to indicate which cylinder the rod and piston came from and to ensure that the rod cap is returned to the proper rod

11.2b   If the rods and caps are not identified, use a hammer and punch to mark them

11.3   Short lengths of rubber hose will protect the crankshaft rod journal and the cylinder walls from the sharp edges on the rod bolts

3   On V6 engines install new seals on each of the valve guides. Using a hammer and a deep socket, gently tap each seal into place until it is properly seated on the guide. Do not twist or cock the seals during installation or they will not seal properly on the valve stems. Install the valves.

4   On 4-cylinder engines install the valves, then install the valve seals. Install the plastic installation cap (see illustration) over the end of the valve stem to allow the seal to pass over the ridges on valve stem. After installation remove the plastic cap and push the seal down until it is fully seated.

5   Install the valve spring shim(s) around the valve guide boss and set the valve spring, cap and retainer in place.

6   Compress the spring with a compressor and install the keepers. Release the compressor, making sure the keepers are seated properly in the valve stem upper groove. If necessary, grease can be used to hold the keepers in place while the compressor is released.

7   Check the installed valve spring height (see illustrations). If it was correct before reassembly it should still be within the specified limits. If it is not, install an additional valve spring seat shims (available from your dealer) to bring the height to within the specified limit.

8   Install the rocker arm shaft (V6) and tighten the nuts to the specified torque. Be sure to lubricate the ball pivots with moly base grease or engine assembly lube.

9   On 4-cylinder engines install the camshaft, lash adjusters and followers.

11   Piston/connecting rod assembly — removal

Refer to illustrations 11.1, 11.2a, 11.2b and 11.3

1   Using a ridge reamer, completely remove the ridge at the top of each cylinder (follow the manufacturer's instructions provided with the ridge reaming tool) (see illustration). Failure to remove the ridge before attempting to remove the piston/connecting rod assemblies will result in piston breakage.

2   Check the connecting rods and connecting rod caps for identification marks (see illustration). If they are not plainly marked, identify each rod and cap, using a small punch to make the appropriate number of indentations to indicate the cylinders they are associated with (see illustration).

3   Loosen each of the connecting rod cap nuts 1/2 turn. Remove the number one connecting rod cap and bearing insert. Do not drop the bearing insert out of the cap. Slip a short length of plastic or rubber hose over each connecting rod cap bolt to protect the crankshaft journal and cylinder wall when the piston is removed (see illustration)) and push the connecting rod/piston assembly out through the top of the engine. Use a wooden tool to push on the upper bearing insert in the connecting rod. If resistance is felt, double-check to make sure that all of the ridge was removed from the cylinder.

12.2   Main bearing caps usually have a cast-in number to indicate position in the block and an arrow which should point to the front of the engine when the cap is installed

12.3   If the main bearing caps aren't numbered, use a punch and hammer to mark them

13.1a   Use a hammer and a large punch to knock the soft plugs into the block

13.1b   Grab the plug with pliers, turn it sideways and pull it out of the block

4   Repeat the procedure for the remaining cylinders. After removal, reassemble the connecting rod caps and bearing inserts in their respective connecting rods and install the cap nuts finger tight. Leaving the old bearing inserts in place until reassembly will help prevent the connecting rod bearing surfaces from being accidentally nicked or gouged.

12   Crankshaft — removal

Refer to illustrations 12.2 and 12.3

1   Loosen each of the main bearing cap bolts 1/4-turn at a time, until they can be removed by hand.
2   Check the main bearing caps to see if they are marked as to their locations. They are usually numbered consecutively (beginning with 1) from the front of the engine to the rear (see illustration).
3   If they are not, mark them with number stamping dies or a center-punch (see illustration).

4   Gently tap the caps with a soft face hammer, then separate them from the engine block. If necessary, use the main bearing cap bolts as levers to remove the caps. Try not to drop the bearing insert if it comes out with the cap.
5   Carefully lift the crankshaft out of the engine. It is a good idea to have an assistant available, since the crankshaft is quite heavy. With the bearing inserts in place in the engine block and in the main bearing caps, return the caps to their respective locations on the engine block and tighten the bolts finger tight.

13   Engine block — cleaning

Refer to illustrations 13.1a, 13.1b and 13.10

1   Remove the soft plugs from the engine block. To do this, knock the plugs into the block (using a hammer and punch), then grasp them with large pliers and pull them back through the holes (see illustrations).

13.10   A large socket and a hammer can be used to install the new soft plugs

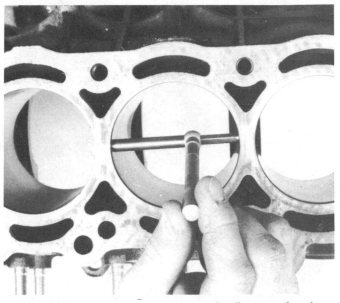

14.4a   Use a snap gauge to measure the diameter of each cylinder

2   Using a gasket scraper, remove all traces of gasket material from the engine block. Be very careful not to nick or gouge the gasket sealing surfaces.

3   Remove the main bearing caps and separate the bearing inserts from the caps and the engine block. Tag the bearings according to which journal they removed from (and whether they were in the cap or the block) and set them aside.

4   Using an Allen wrench, remove the threaded oil gallery plugs from the block.

5   If the engine is extremely dirty it should be taken to an automotive machine shop to be steam cleaned or hot tanked. Any bearings left in the block (such as the camshaft bearings in V6 engines) will be damaged by the cleaning process, so plan on having new ones installed while the block is at the machine shop.

6   After the block is returned, clean all oil holes and oil galleries one more time. Brushes for cleaning oil holes and galleries are available at most auto parts stores. Flush the passages with warm water until the water runs clear, dry the block thoroughly and wipe all machined surfaces with a light, rust preventative oil. If you have access to compressed air, use it to speed the drying process and to blow out all the oil holes and galleries.

7   If the block is not extremely dirty or sludged up, you can do an adequate cleaning job with warm soapy water and a stiff brush. Take plenty of time and do a thorough job. Regardless of the cleaning method used, be sure to thoroughly clean all oil holes and galleries, dry the block completely and coat all machined surfaces with light oil.

8   The threaded holes in the block must be clean to ensure accurate torque readings during reassembly. Run the proper size tap into each of the holes to remove any rust, corrosion, thread sealant or sludge and to restore any damaged threads. If possible, use compressed air to clear the holes of debris produced by this operation. Now is a good time to thoroughly clean the threads on the head bolts and the main bearing cap bolts.

9   Reinstall the main bearing caps and tighten the bolts finger tight.

10   After coating the sealing surfaces of the new soft plugs with a good quality gasket sealer, install them in the engine block (see illustration). Make sure they are driven in straight and seated properly or leakage could result. Special tools are available for this purpose, but good results can be obtained using a large socket (with an outside diameter that will just slip into the soft plug) and a hammer.

11   If the engine is not going to be reassembled right away, cover it with a large plastic trash bag to keep it clean.

14   Engine block — inspection

Refer to illustrations 14.4a, 14.4b, 14.7a, 14.7b and 14.7c

1   Thoroughly clean the engine block as described in Section 13.

2   Visually check the block for cracks, rust and corrosion. Look for

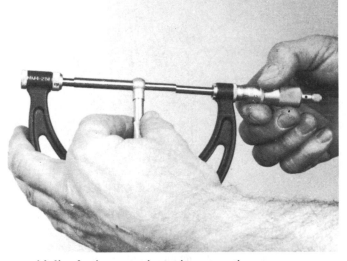

14.4b   A micrometer is used measure the snap gauge, giving the bore size

stripped threads in the threaded holes. It is also a good idea to have the block checked for hidden cracks by an automotive machine shop that has the special equipment to do this type of work. If defects are found, have the block repaired, if possible, or replaced.

3   Check the cylinder bores for scuffing and scoring.

4   Using a cylinder bore gauge, measure each cylinder's diameter at the top (just under the ridge), center and bottom of the cylinder bore, parallel to the crankshaft axis (see illustrations). Next, measure each cylinder's diameter at the same three locations across the crankshaft axis. Compare the results to the Specifications. If the cylinder walls are badly scuffed or scored, or if they are out-of-round or tapered beyond the limits given in the Specifications, have the engine block rebored and honed at an automotive machine shop. If a rebore is done, oversize pistons and rings will be required.

5   If the cylinders are in reasonably good condition and not worn to the outside of the limits, and if the piston-to-cylinder clearances can be maintained properly, then they do not have to be rebored. Honing is all that is necessary.

6   Before honing the cylinders, install the main bearing caps (without the bearings) and tighten the bolts to the specified torque.

14.7a   A fine stone hone is used to prepare the cylinder walls

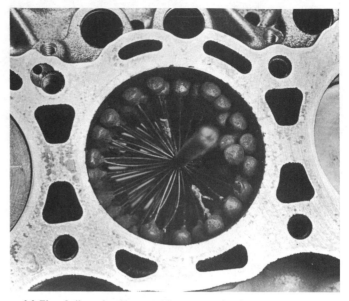

14.7b   A 'bunch-of-grapes' hone can also be used to finish the cylinders

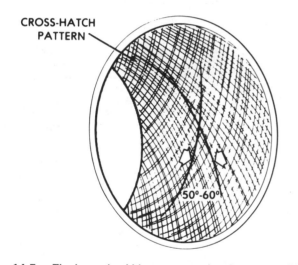

CROSS-HATCH PATTERN

50°-60°

14.7c   The hone should leave a cross-hatch pattern with the lines intersecting at a 60° angle

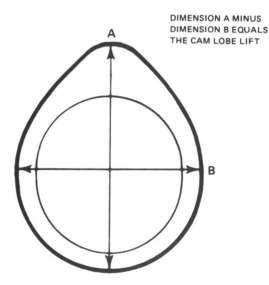

DIMENSION A MINUS DIMENSION B EQUALS THE CAM LOBE LIFT

A

B

15.1   The difference between the base circle measurement (B) and the lobe height (A) is the cam lobe lift

7   To perform the honing operation you will need the proper size flexible hone (with fine stones), plenty of light oil or honing oil, some rags and an electric drill motor. Mount the hone in the drill motor, compress the stones and slip the hone into the first cylinder (see illustrations). Lubricate the cylinder thoroughly, turn on the drill and move the hone up and down in the cylinder at a pace which will produce a fine crosshatch pattern on the cylinder walls with the crosshatch lines intersecting at approximately a 60° angle (see illustration). Be sure to use plenty of lubricant. Wipe the oil out of the cylinder and repeat the procedure on the remaining cylinders. If you do not have the tools or do not desire to perform the honing operation, most automotive machine shops will do it for a reasonable fee.

8   After the honing job is complete, chamfer the top edges of the cylinder bores with a small file so the rings will not catch when the pistons are installed.

9   The entire engine block must be thoroughly washed again with warm, soapy water to remove all traces of the abrasive grit produced during the honing operation. Be sure to run a brush through all oil holes and galleries and flush them with running water. After rinsing, dry the block and apply a coat of light oil to all machined surfaces. Wrap the block in a plastic trash bag to keep it clean and set it aside until reassembly.

15   Camshaft, lifters and bearings — inspection and replacement

Refer to illustrations 15.1, 15.6, 15.12 and 15.15

Camshaft
2.0L and 2.3L 4 cylinder engine

1   Check lobe lift before removing cam or rocker arms. Remove the cam cover and measure the major (A) and minor (B) diameters (see illustration) of each cam lobe with vernier caliper and compare the readings to the Specifications. The difference between the readings on each lobe diameter is the lobe lift.

2   If the readings do not meet specifications, replace the camshaft and all the followers.

3   After the camshaft is removed from the engine, cleaned with solvent and dried, inspect the bearing journals for uneven wear, pitting and evidence of seizure. If the journals are damaged, the bearing inserts are probably damaged as well. Both the camshaft and bearings will have to be replaced with new ones.

15.6   Mount a dial indicator on the rocker arm over the pushrod to measure camshaft lobe lift on V6 engines

15.12   Use a micrometer to check the camshaft journals for wear, taper and out-of-round

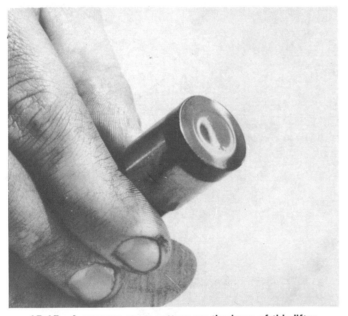

15.15   A concave wear pattern on the base of this lifter indicates the need for a new camshaft and a complete set of lifters

2.8L and 2.9L V6

4   The lobe lift measurement on the V6 can be made with the camshaft still installed in the engine.

5   Remove the rocker arm cover.

6   Beginning with the number one cylinder, mount a dial indicator with the stem resting on the rocker arm directly in line with the pushrod (see illustration).

7   Rotate the crankshaft very slowly in the direction of normal running rotation until the lifter is on the heel of the cam lobe. At this point the pushrod will be at its lowest position.

8   Zero the dial indicator, then very slowly rotate the crankshaft in the direction of rotation until the pushrod is at its highest position. Note and record the reading on the dial indicator, then compare it to the lobe lift specifications.

9   Repeat the procedure for each of the remaining valves.

10 If the lobe lift measurements are not as specified, a new camshaft should be installed.

11 After the camshaft has been removed from the engine, cleaned with solvent and dried, inspect the bearing journals for uneven wear, pitting or evidence of seizure. If the journals are damaged, the bearing inserts are probably damaged as well. Both the camshaft and bearings will have to be replaced with new ones.

12 Measure the camshaft bearing journals with a micrometer (see illustration) to determine if they are excessively worn or out-of-round. If they are more than 0.001-inch out-of-round, the camshaft should be replaced with a new one.

13 Check the camshaft lobes for heat discoloration, score marks, chipped areas, pitting or uneven wear. If the lobes are in good condition and if the lobe lift measurements (Steps 1 through 9) are as specified, the camshaft can be reused.

Lifters

14 Clean the lifters with solvent and dry them thoroughly without mixing them up.

15 Check each lifter wall, pushrod seat and foot for scuffing, score marks or uneven wear. Each lifter foot (the surface that rides on the cam lobe) must be slightly convex — if they are concave (see illustration) the lifters and camshaft must be replaced with new ones. If the lifter walls are damaged or worn (which is not very likely), inspect the lifter bores in the engine block as well.

16 If new lifters are being installed, a new camshaft must also be installed. If a new camshaft is installed, then use new lifters as well. Never install used lifters unless the original camshaft is used and the lifters can be installed in their original locations.

Bearing replacement

17 Camshaft bearing replacement requires special tools and expertise that place it outside the scope of the do-it-yourselfer. Take the block (V6) or head (4-cylinder) to an automotive machine shop to ensure that the job is done correctly.

---

16   Piston/connecting rod assembly — inspection

Refer to illustrations 16.2, 16.4a, 16.4b, 16.5, 16.10 and 16.11

1   Before the inspection process can be carried out, the piston/connecting rod assemblies must be cleaned and the original piston rings removed from the pistons. **Note:** *Always use new piston rings when the engine is reassembled.*

16.2   Use a piston ring tool to remove the old rings
without scratching the pistons

16.4a   A cleaning tool can be used to remove carbon
build-up from the ring grooves in the piston

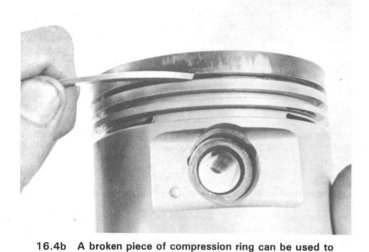

16.4b   A broken piece of compression ring can be used to
clean the piston ring grooves

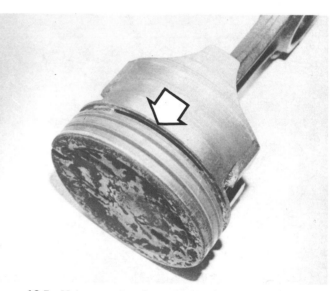

16.5   Make sure the oil return slots (arrow) are clear

2   Using a piston ring installation tool, carefully remove the rings from the pistons (see illustration). Do not nick or gouge the pistons in the process.

3   Scrape all traces of carbon from the top (or crown) of the piston. A hand held wire brush or a piece of fine emery cloth can be used once the majority of the deposits have been scraped away. Do not, under any circumstances, use a wire brush mounted in a drill motor to remove deposits from the pistons. The piston material is soft and will be eroded away by the wire brush.

4   Use a piston ring groove cleaning tool to remove any carbon deposits from the ring grooves (see illustration). If a tool is not available, a piece broken off an old ring will do the job (see illustration). Be very careful to remove only the carbon deposits. Do not remove any metal and do not nick or scratch the sides of the ring grooves.

5   Once the deposits have been removed, clean the piston/rod assemblies with solvent and dry them thoroughly. Make sure that the oil return holes in the back sides of the ring grooves are clear (see illustration).

6   If the pistons are not damaged or worn excessively, and if the engine block is not rebored, new pistons will not be necessary. Nor-

mal piston wear appears as even vertical wear on the piston thrust surfaces and slight looseness of the top ring in its groove. New piston rings should always be used when an engine is rebuilt.

7   Carefully inspect each piston for cracks around the skirt, at the pin bosses and at the ring lands.

8   Look for scoring and scuffing on the thrust faces of the skirt, holes in the piston crown and burned areas at the edge of the crown. If the skirt is scored or scuffed, the engine may have been suffering from overheating and/or abnormal combustion, which caused excessively high operating temperatures. The cooling and lubrication systems should be checked thoroughly. A hole in the piston crown is an indication that abnormal combustion (preignition) was occurring. Burned areas at the edge of the piston crown are usually evidence of spark knock (detonation). If any of the above problems exist, the causes must be corrected or the damage will occur again.

9   Corrosion of the piston (evidenced by pitting) indicates that coolant is leaking into the combustion chamber and/or the crankcase. Again, the cause must be corrected or the problem may persist in the rebuilt engine.

10   Measure the piston ring side clearance by laying a new piston ring

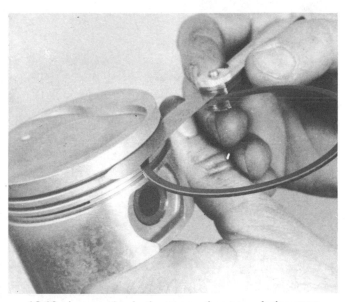

16.10   Insert a ring in the groove then use a feeler gauge
to measure the side clearance

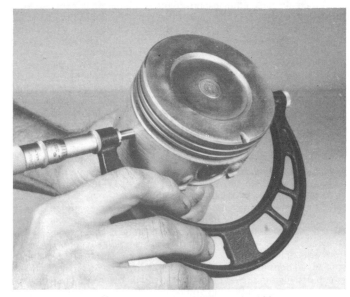

16.11   Measure the piston across the skirt at
90° to the pin

in each ring groove and slipping a feeler gauge in between the ring and the edge of the ring groove (see illustration). Check the clearance at three or four locations around each groove. Be sure to use the correct ring for each groove; they are different. If the side clearance is greater than specified, new pistons will have to be used.

11   Check the piston-to-bore clearance by measuring the bore (see Section 14) and the piston diameter. Make sure that the pistons and bores are correctly matched. Measure the piston across the skirt (see illustration). Subtract the piston diameter from the bore diameter to obtain the clearance. If it is greater than specified, the block will have to be rebored and new pistons and rings installed. Check the piston-to-rod clearance by twisting the piston and rod in opposite directions. Any noticeable play indicates that there is excessive wear, which must be corrected. The piston/connecting rod assemblies should be taken to an automotive machine shop to have new piston pins installed and the pistons and connecting rods rebored.

12   If the pistons must be removed from the connecting rods, such as when new pistons must be installed, or if the piston pins have too much play in them, they should be taken to an automotive machine shop. While they are there have the connecting rods checked for bend and twist, as automotive machine shops have special equipment for this purpose. Unless new pistons or connecting rods must be installed, do not disassemble the pistons from the connecting rods.

13   Check the connecting rods for cracks and other damage. Temporarily remove the rod caps, lift out the old bearing inserts, wipe the rod and cap bearing surfaces clean and inspect them for nicks, gouges or scratches. After checking the rods, replace the old bearings, slip the caps into place and tighten the nuts finger tight.

17   Crankshaft — inspection

Refer to illustration 17.2

1   Clean the crankshaft with solvent and dry it thoroughly. Be sure to clean the oil holes with a stiff brush and flush them with solvent. Check the main and connecting rod bearing journals for uneven wear, scoring, pitting or cracks. Check the crankshaft for cracks and damage.

2   Using a micrometer, measure the diameter of the main and connecting rod journals (see illustration) and compare the results to the Specifications. By measuring the diameter at a number of points around the journal's circumference, you will be able to determine whether or not the journal is out of round. Take the measurement at each end of the journal, near the crank counterweights, to determine whether the journal is tapered.

3   If the crankshaft journals are damaged, tapered, out of round or worn beyond the limits given in the Specifications, have the crankshaft

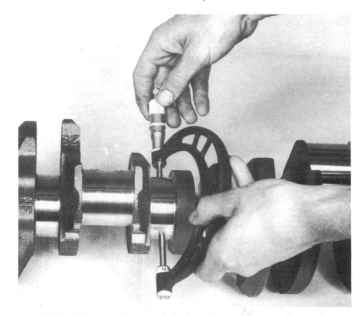

17.2   Measure the crankshaft main and connecting rod
journals with a micrometer

reground by an automotive machine shop. Be sure to use the correct oversize bearing inserts if the crankshaft is reconditioned.

4   Refer to Section 18 and examine the main and rod bearing inserts.

5   New main and connecting rod bearings should be installed whenever the engine is disassembled.

18   Main and connecting rod bearings — inspection

1   Even though the main and connecting rod bearings should be replaced with new ones during the engine overhaul, the old bearings should be retained for close examination, as they may reveal valuable information about the condition of the engine.

2   Bearing failure occurs mainly because of lack of lubrication, the presence of dirt or other foreign particles, overloading the engine and corrosion. Regardless of the cause of bearing failure, it must be corrected before the engine is reassembled to prevent it from happening again.

3   When examining the bearings, remove them from the engine block, the main bearing caps, the connecting rods and the rod caps and lay them out on a clean surface in the same general position as their location in the engine. This will enable you to match any noted bearing problems with the corresponding crankshaft journal.

4   Dirt and other foreign particles get into the engine in a variety of ways. It may be left in the engine during assembly, or it may pass through filters or breathers. It may get into the oil, and from there into the bearings. Metal chips from machining operations and normal engine wear are often present. Abrasives are sometimes left in engine components after reconditioning, especially when parts are not thoroughly cleaned using the proper cleaning methods. Whatever the source, these foreign objects often end up embedded in the soft bearing material and are easily recognized. Large particles will not embed in the bearing and will score or gouge the bearing and shaft. The best prevention for this cause of bearing failure is to clean all parts thoroughly and keep everything spotlessly clean during engine assembly. Frequent and regular engine oil and filter changes are also recommended.

5   Lack of lubrication or lubrication breakdown has a number of interrelated causes. Excessive heat, which thins the oil, overloading, which squeezes the oil from the bearing face, and oil leakage or throw off from excessive bearing clearances, worn oil pump or high engine speeds, all contribute to lubrication breakdown. Blocked oil passages, which usually are the result of misaligned oil holes in a bearing shell, will also oil starve a bearing and destroy it. When lack of lubrication is the cause of bearing failure, the bearing material is wiped or extruded from the steel backing of the bearing. Temperatures may increase to the point where the steel backing turns blue from overheating.

6   Driving habits can have a definite effect on bearing life. Full throttle, low speed operation in too high a gear (or lugging the engine) puts very high loads on bearings, which tends to squeeze out the oil film. These loads cause the bearings to flex, which produces fine cracks in the bearing face (fatigue failure). Eventually the bearing material will loosen in pieces and tear away from the steel backing. Short trip driving leads to corrosion of bearings because insufficient engine heat is produced to drive off the condensed water and corrosive gases. These products collect in the engine oil, forming acid and sludge. As the oil is carried to the engine bearings, the acid attacks and corrodes the bearing material.

7   Incorrect bearing installation during engine assembly will lead to bearing failure as well. Tight fitting bearings leave insufficient bearing oil clearance and will result in oil starvation. Dirt or foreign particles trapped behind a bearing insert result in high spots on the bearing which lead to failure.

---

19   Piston rings — installation

Refer to illustrations 19.3a, 19.3b, 19.9a, 19.9b and 19.12

1   Before installing the new piston rings, the ring end gaps must be checked. It is assumed that the piston ring side clearance has been checked and verified correct (Section 16).

2   Lay out the piston/connecting rod assemblies and the new ring sets so the ring sets will be matched with the same piston and cylinder during the end gap measurement and engine assembly.

3   Insert the top (number one) ring into the first cylinder and square it up with the cylinder walls by pushing it in with the top of the piston (see illustration). To measure the end gap, slip a feeler gauge between the ends of the ring (see illustration). Compare the measurement to the Specifications.

4   If the gap is larger or smaller than specified, double-check to make sure that you have the correct rings before proceeding.

5   If the gap is too small, it must be enlarged or the ring ends may come in contact with each other during engine operation, which can cause serious damage to the engine. The end gap can be increased by filing the ring ends very carefully with a fine file. Mount the file in a vise equipped with soft jaws, slip the ring over the file with the ends contacting the file face and slowly move the ring to remove material from the ends. When performing this operation, file only from the outside in.

6   Excess end gap is not critical unless it is greater than 0.040-inch (1 mm). Again, double-check to make sure you have the correct rings for your engine.

7   Repeat the procedure for each ring that will be installed in the first cylinder and for each ring in the remaining cylinders. Remember to keep

19.3a   Use the crown of a piston to square a ring in the cylinder

19.3b   Using a feeler gauge, measure the ring end gap

rings, pistons and cylinders matched up.

8   Once the ring end gaps have been checked/corrected, the rings can be installed on the pistons.

9   The oil control ring (lowest one on the piston) is installed first. It is composed of three separate components. Slip the spacer/expander into the groove (see illustration), then install the side rails. Do not use a piston ring installation tool on the oil ring side rails, as they may be damaged. Instead, place one end of the side rail into the groove between the spacer/expander and the ring land, hold it firmly in place and slide a finger around the piston while pushing the rail into the groove (see illustration).

10   After the three oil ring components have been installed, check to make sure that both the upper and lower side rails can be turned smoothly in the ring groove.

19.9a Install the oil control ring expander in the bottom piston groove

19.9b Roll the oil ring side rails into place above and below the expander

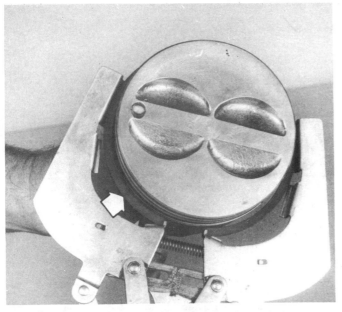

19.12 When installing the compression rings, always use a ring expander tool, don't mix up the top and second rings, and make sure the mark (arrow) is on the top side of the ring when installed

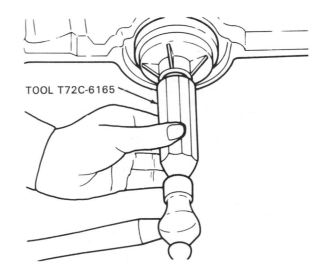

TOOL T72C-6165

20.4 Using a Ford tool and a hammer to install the rear main oil seal on V6 engines

11 The number two (middle) ring is installed next. It should be stamped with a mark so it can be readily distinguished from the top ring. **Note:** *Always follow the instructions printed on the ring package or box — different manufacturers may require different approaches.* Do not mix up the top and middle rings, as they have different cross sections.

12 Use a piston ring installation tool and make sure that the identification mark is facing the top of the piston, then slip the ring into the middle groove on the piston (see illustration). Do not expand the ring any more than is necessary to slide it over the piston.

13 Finally, install the number one (top) ring in the same manner. Make sure the identifying mark is facing up.

14 Repeat the procedure for the remaining pistons and rings.

20 Rear main oil seal — installation

Refer to illustrations 20.4 and 20.6

2.8L and 2.9L V6 engine

1 Make sure the engine block is free of all dirt, lint or foreign matter to ensure a proper fit.

2 To install coat the seal-to-cylinder block surface of the oil seal with engine oil.

3 Coat the seal surface and crankshaft with engine oil.

4 Start the seal in the recess and install it with tool T72C-6165 (see illustration). Alternatively, use a hammer and socket the same diameter as the seal to drive the seal into the seal bore.

5 Drive the seal into position until it is firmly seated.

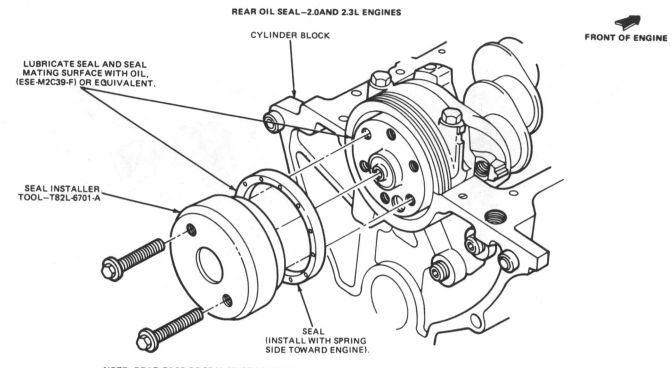

REAR OIL SEAL—2.0AND 2.3L ENGINES

CYLINDER BLOCK

FRONT OF ENGINE

LUBRICATE SEAL AND SEAL
MATING SURFACE WITH OIL,
(ESE-M2C39-F) OR EQUIVALENT.

SEAL INSTALLER
TOOL—T82L-6701-A

SEAL
(INSTALL WITH SPRING
SIDE TOWARD ENGINE).

NOTE: REAR FACE OF SEAL MUST BE WITHIN 0.127mm (0.005-INCH) OF THE REAR FACE OF THE BLOCK.

20.6   Rear main oil seal installation on 4-cylinder engines

2.0L and 2.3L engines

6   Position the seal on Seal Installer Tool no. T82L-6701-A (see illustration) and start the bolts into the crankshaft flange.
7   To seat the seal properly, alternate the tightening of the bolts until the seal is positioned at the proper depth.

21   Crankshaft — installation and main bearing oil clearance check

Refer to illustrations 21.25 and 21.27

1   Crankshaft installation is generally one of the first steps in engine reassembly. It is assumed at this point that the engine block and crankshaft have been cleaned, inspected and repaired or reconditioned.
2   Remove the main bearing cap bolts and lift out the caps. Lay them out in the proper order to help ensure that they are installed correctly.
3   If they are still in place, remove the old bearing inserts from the block and the main bearing caps. Wipe the main bearing surfaces of the block and caps with a clean, lint-free cloth. They must be kept spotlessly clean.
4   Clean the back sides of the new main bearing inserts and lay one bearing half in each main bearing saddle in the block. Lay the other bearing half from each bearing set in the corresponding main bearing cap. Make sure the tab on the bearing insert fits into the recess in the block or cap.
5   The oil hole in the block must line up with the oil hole in the bearing insert. Do not hammer the bearing into place and do not nick or gouge the bearing faces. No lubrication should be used at this time.
6   The flanged thrust bearing must be installed in the number three cap main bearing position on both the 4 and 6 cylinder engines (third position back from front of engine).
7   Clean the faces of the bearings in the block and the crankshaft main bearing journals with a clean, lint-free cloth. Check or clean the oil holes in the crankshaft, as any dirt here can go only one way — straight through the new bearings.
8   Once you are certain that the crankshaft is clean, carefully lay it in position (an assistant would be very helpful here) in the main bearings.

9   Before the crankshaft can be permanently installed, the main bearing oil clearance must be checked.
10   Trim several pieces of the appropriate size of Plastigage (so they are slightly shorter than the width of the main bearings) and place one piece on each crankshaft main bearing journal, parallel with the journal axis.
11   Clean the faces of the bearings in the caps and install the caps in their respective positions (do not mix them up) with the arrows pointing toward the front of the engine. Do not disturb the Plastigage.
12   Starting with the center main and working out toward the ends, tighten the main bearing cap bolts, in three steps, to the specified torque. Do not rotate the crankshaft at any time during this operation.
13   Remove the bolts and carefully lift off the main bearing caps. Keep them in order. Do not disturb the Plastigage or rotate the crankshaft. If any of the main bearing caps are difficult to remove, tap them gently from side-to-side with a soft face hammer to loosen them.
14   Compare the width of the crushed Plastigage on each journal to the scale printed on the Plastigage container to obtain the main bearing oil clearance. Check the Specifications to make sure it is correct.
15   If the clearance is not correct, double-check to make sure you have the right size bearing inserts. Also, make sure that no dirt or oil is between the bearing inserts and the main bearing caps or the block.
16   Carefully scrape all traces of the Plastigage material off the main bearing journals and/or the bearing faces. Do not nick or scratch the bearing faces.
17   Carefully lift the crankshaft out of the engine. Clean the bearing faces in the block, then apply a thin, uniform layer of clean, high quality moly base grease or engine assembly lube to each of the bearing surfaces. Be sure to coat the thrust flange faces as well as the journal face of the thrust bearing.
18   Lubricate the rear main bearing oil seal (where it contacts the crankshaft) with moly base grease or engine assembly lube. Note that on four-cylinder engines the oil seal is installed after the crankshaft is in place.
19   Make sure the crankshaft journals are clean, then lay the crankshaft back in place in the block. Clean the faces of the bearings in the caps, then apply a thin, uniform layer of clean, moly base grease to each of the bearing faces. Install the caps in their respective positions with the arrows pointing toward the front of the engine.

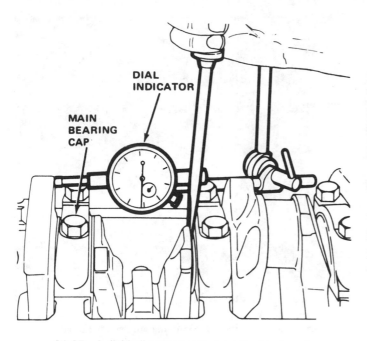

21.25 A dial indicator mounted on the block and registering against a crankshaft counterweight can be used to check crankshaft end play

21.27 A feeler gauge blade inserted between the crankshaft and the thrust bearing can be use to check crankshaft end play

20 Install and tighten all main bearing bolts finger tight. Then tighten all bolts by starting with the middle main and working outwards. Work up to the final torque in three steps.

21 To install a new oil seal see the previous section.

22 Rotate the crankshaft a number of times by hand and check for any obvious binding.

23 The final step is to check the crankshaft end play with a feeler gauge or a dial indicator.

24 To check the end play with a dial indicator, mount the indicator on the block with the plunger parallel to the crankshaft and seated against one of the counterweights.

25 Using a large screwdriver, pry the crankshaft to the rear in the block as far as it will go and zero the dial indicator (see illustration).

26 Pry the crankshaft forward as far as it will go and read the end play off the dial indicator.

27 To check end play with a feeler gauge, pry the crankshaft as far forward in the block as it will go, then insert progessively larger feeler gauge blades between the crankshaft and the face of the thrust bearing until the space is filled (see illustration). The thickness of feeler gauge blades required is the end play.

---

22 Piston/connecting rod assembly — installation and bearing oil clearance check

---

Refer to illustrations 22.5, 22.8a, 22.8b, 22.8c, 22.9, 22.12, 22.13a, 22.13b, 22.14 and 22.20

1 Before installing the piston/connecting rod assemblies the cylinder walls must be perfectly clean, the top edge of each cylinder must be chamfered, and the crankshaft must be in place.

2 Remove the connecting rod cap from the end of the number one connecting rod. Remove the old bearing inserts and wipe the bearing surfaces of the connecting rod and cap with a clean, lint-free cloth. They must be kept spotlessly clean.

3 Clean the back side of the new upper bearing half, then lay it in place in the connecting rod. Make sure that the tab on the bearing fits into the recess in the rod. Do not hammer the bearing insert into place and be very careful not to nick or gouge the bearing face. Do not lubricate the bearing at this time.

4 Clean the back side of the other bearing insert and install it in the rod cap. Again, make sure the tab on the bearing fits into the recess

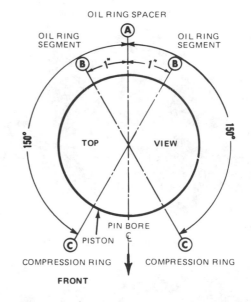

22.5 Compression and oil control ring gap positioning

a) *oil ring spacer butt connection*   b) *oil ring side rail gaps*

c) *compression ring gaps*

in the cap, and do not apply any lubricant. It is critically important that the mating surfaces of the bearing and connecting rod are perfectly clean and oil free when they are assembled.

5 Position the piston ring gaps as shown in the accompanying illustration, then slip a section of plastic or rubber hose over the connecting rod cap bolts.

6 Lubricate the piston and rings with clean engine oil and attach a piston ring compressor to the piston. Leave the skirt protruding about 1/4-inch to guide the piston into the cylinder. The rings must be compressed as far as possible.

7 Rotate the crankshaft until the number one connecting rod journal is as far from the number one cylinder as possible (bottom dead center), and apply a coat of engine oil to the cylinder walls.

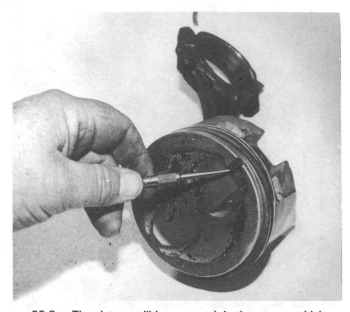

22.8a   The pistons will have a notch in the crown, which should point to the front of the engine after the piston is installed

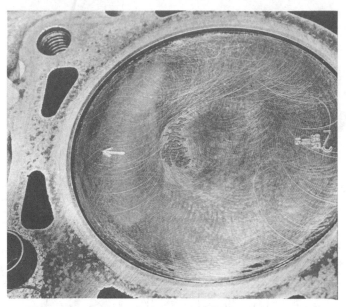

22.8b   Some pistons have an arrow in the crown, rather than a notch on the edge, to indicate installed direction

22.8c   With the ring compressor installed, slide the piston and rod assembly into the cylinder

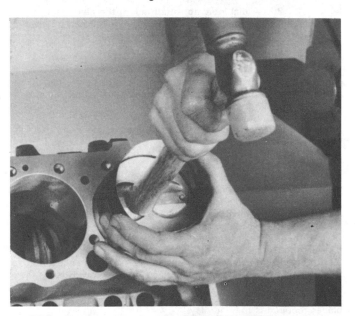

22.9   Gently tap on the top of the piston with a wooden hammer handle to insert the piston into the block

22.12   Cut a piece of Plastigauge and lay it across the crankshaft rod journal

8   With the notch on top of the piston facing to the front of the engine (see illustrations), gently place the piston/connecting rod assembly into the number one cylinder bore and rest the bottom edge of the ring compressor on the engine block (see illustration). Tap the top edge of the ring compressor to make sure it is contacting the block around its entire circumference.

9   Carefully tap on the top of the piston with the end of a wooden hammer handle (see illustration) while guiding the end of the connecting rod into place on the crankshaft journal.

10   The piston rings may try to pop out of the ring compressor just before entering the cylinder bore, so keep some downward pressure on the ring compressor. Work slowly, and if any resistance is felt as the piston enters the cylinder, stop immediately. Find out what is hanging up and fix it before proceeding. Do not, for any reason, force the piston into the cylinder, as you will break a ring and/or the piston.

11   Once the piston/connecting rod assembly is installed, the connecting rod bearing oil clearance must be checked before the rod cap is

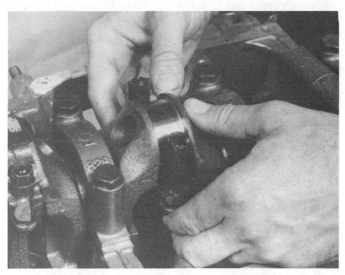

22.13a Pull the connecting rod firmly against the
crankshaft

22.13b Remove the protective hoses from the rod cap
bolts

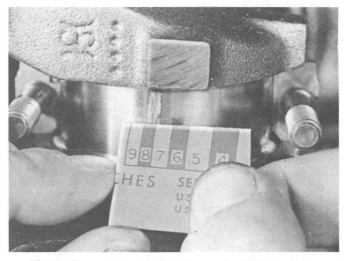

22.14 Compare the width of the crushed Plastigauge to
the scale on the package to determine the oil clearance

22.20 Feeler gauges inserted between the rod cap and
the crankshaft measure the rod side clearance

permanently bolted in place.

12 Cut a piece of the the appropriate size Plastigage slightly shorter than the width of the connecting rod bearing and lay it in place on the number one connecting rod journal, parallel with the journal axis (it must not cross the oil hole in the journal) (see illustration).

13 Pull the connecting rod firmly against the crankshaft (see illustration), remove the protective hoses from the connecting rod bolts (see illustration) and install the rod cap. Make sure the mating mark on the cap is on the same side as the mark on the connecting rod. Install the nuts and tighten them to the specified torque, working up to it in three steps. Do not rotate the crankshaft at any time during this operation.

14 Remove the rod cap, being very careful not to disturb the Plastigage. Compare the width of the crushed Plastigage to the scale printed on the Plastigage container to obtain the oil clearance (see illustration). Compare it to the Specifications to make sure the clearance is correct. If the clearance is not correct, double-check to make sure that you have the correct size bearing inserts. Also, recheck the crankshaft connecting rod journal diameter and make sure that no dirt or oil was between the bearing inserts and the connecting rod or cap when the clearance was measured.

15 Carefully scrape all traces of the Plastigage material off the rod journal and/or bearing face. Be very careful not to scratch the bearing — use your fingernail or a piece of hardwood. Make sure the bearing

faces are perfectly clean, then apply a layer of moly base grease or engine assembly lube to both of them. You will have to push the piston into the cylinder to expose the face of the bearing insert in the connecting rod. Be sure to replace the protective hoses over the rod bolts first.

16 Slide the connecting rod back into place on the journal, remove the protective hoses from the rod cap bolts, install the rod cap and tighten the nuts to the specified torque. Again, work up to the torque in three steps.

17 Repeat the entire procedure for the remaining piston/connecting rod assemblies. Keep the back sides of the bearing inserts and the inside of the connecting rod and cap perfectly clean when assembling them. Make sure you have the correct piston for the cylinder and that the notch on the piston faces to the front of the engine when the piston is installed. Remember, use plenty of oil to lubricate the piston before installing the ring compressor. Also, when installing the rod caps for the final time, be sure to lubricate the bearing faces.

18 After all the piston/connecting rod assemblies have been properly installed, rotate the crankshaft a number of times by hand and check for any obvious binding.

19 As a final step, the connecting rod side clearance must be checked. Compare the measured side clearance to the Specifications to make sure it is correct.

20 Pry the connecting rod (4-cylinder) or rod pair (V6) all the way for-

ward on the journal, then insert progressively thicker feeler gauges between the rod and crankshaft until all the space is taken up (see illustration). The thickness of feeler gauge required is the side clearance.

23   Initial start-up and break-in after overhaul

1   Once the engine has been properly installed in the vehicle, doublecheck the engine oil and coolant levels.
2   With the spark plugs out of the engine and the coil high tension lead grounded to the engine block, crank the engine over until oil pressure registers on the gauge (if so equipped) or until the oil light goes off.
3   Install the spark plugs, hook up the plug wires and the coil high tension lead.
4   Make sure the carburetor choke plate is closed, then start the engine. It may take a few moments for the gasoline to reach the carburetor, but the engine should start without a great deal of effort.
5   As soon as the engine starts it should be set at a fast idle to ensure

proper oil circulation and allowed to warm up to normal operating temperature. While the engine is warming up, make a thorough check for oil and coolant leaks.
6   Shut the engine off and recheck the engine oil and coolant levels. Restart the engine and check the ignition timing and the engine idle speed (refer to Chapter 1). Make any necessary adjustments.
7   Drive the vehicle to an area with minimum traffic, accelerate at full throttle from 30 to 50 mph, then allow the vehicle to slow to 30 mph with the throttle closed. Repeat the procedure 10 or 12 times. This will load the piston rings and cause them to seat properly against the cylinder walls. Check again for oil and coolant leaks.
8   Drive the vehicle gently for the first 500 miles (no sustained high speeds) and keep a constant check on the oil level. It is not unusual for an engine to use oil during the break-in period.
9   At approximately 500 to 600 miles, change the oil and filter and retorque the cylinder head bolts.
10 For the next few hundred miles, drive the vehicle normally. Do not either pamper it or abuse it.
11 After 2000 miles, change the oil and filter again and consider the engine fully broken in.

Chapter 3
Cooling, heating and air conditioning systems

Contents

Specifications

Radiator cap pressure cap rating	13 psi
lower limit	11 psi
upper limit	17 psi
Coolant capacity	See Chapter 1
Coolant type	50/50 mix of water and Ford Long Life Coolant ESE-M97b18-C, or other non-phosphate ethylene glycol antifreeze meeting the above specification.

Thermostat	
Type	Wax pellet
2.0L and 2.3L	
Opening temperature	188° to 195°F
Fully open	212°
2.8L and 2.9L	
Opening temperature	192° to 199°F
Fully open	226°
Water temperature switch	
Lamp on at	249°F

Torque specifications	**Ft-lbs**
Thermostat housing	12 to 15
Radiator to radiator support	14 to 20
Clutch to water pump (4-cylinder)	14 to 20
Fan to clutch	4.5 to 6.0
Clutch to water pump 2.8L and 2.9L	15 to 25
Shroud to radiator	4 to 6
Transmission oil line fitting to radiator	18 to 23
Transmission oil line to fitting on radiator	12 to 18
Temperature sending unit	8 to 18
Water pump to front cover 2.8L and 2.9L	7 to 9
Water pump to front cover 4-cylinder	14 to 21

1 General information

The cooling system consists of a radiator, an engine driven water pump and thermostat controlled coolant flow.

The fan is equipped with a clutch, which allows it to draw air through the radiator at lower speeds. At higher speeds the fan is not needed for cooling, so the clutch automatically lowers the fan speed and reduces the engine power required for fan operation.

The water pump is mounted on the front of the engine and is driven by the timing belt on 4-cylinder engines and by a drivebelt on V6 engines.

The heater utilizes the heated coolant to warm the vehicle interior. The coolant passes through a heater core similar to a small radiator in the passenger compartment. The coolant flow through the core and air which is directed through the heater core to heat the vehicle interior are controlled by the driver or passenger.

Air conditioning is available as an option on these vehicles. The air conditioning compressor is driven from the crankshaft pulley by way of a drivebelt.

2 Antifreeze — general information

Warning: *Do not allow antifreeze to come in contact with your skin or painted surfaces of the vehicle. Flush contacted areas immediately with plenty of water. Antifreeze can be fatal to children and pets. Wipe up any garage floor and drip pan coolant spills immediately. Keep antifreeze containers covered and repair leaks in your cooling system immediately.*

The cooling system should be filled with a water/ethylene glycol based antifreeze solution which will prevent freezing down to at least −20°F. It also provides protection against corrosion and increases the coolant boiling point.

The cooling system should be drained, flushed and refilled at least every other year (see Chapter 1). The use of antifreeze solutions for periods of longer than two years is likely to cause damage and encourage the formation of rust and scale in the system.

Before adding antifreeze to the system, check all hose connections and retorque the cylinder head bolts, because antifreeze tends to search out and leak through very minute openings.

The exact mixture of antifreeze to water which you should use depends on the relative weather conditions. The mixture should contain at least 50 percent antifreeze, but should never contain more than 70 percent antifreeze. Read carefully all instructions printed on the antifreeze container.

3 Thermostat — replacement

Refer to illustrations 3.3, 3.9 and 3.10
Warning: *The engine must be completely cool before beginning this procedure.*

1   Refer to the Warning in Section 2.
2   Drain the cooling system so that the coolant level is below the thermostat.
3   On V6 engines the thermostat is mounted low on the left side of the engine, at the side of the water pump (see illustration).
4   On 4-cylinder engines, disconnect the heater return hose at the thermostat housing, located on the front of the head.
5   Remove the coolant outlet housing retaining bolts. Be prepared for additional coolant to flow from the engine, then pull the housing out sufficiently to provide access to the thermostat.
6   Remove the thermostat by turning counterclockwise and remove the gasket. **Caution:** *Do not pry on the thermostat to remove.*
7   If the thermostat is to be checked for proper operation, see Section 4.
8   Clean the thermostat housing surface and the engine surface thoroughly. All traces of gasket material must be scraped clean before proceeding.
9   Install the thermostat with the bridge section in the outlet casting (see illustration). Turn the thermostat clockwise to lock it in position on the flats cast into the outlet elbow.
10   On 4-cylinder models which have a heater hose connection, make sure that the thermostat is aligned properly to allow full flow to the heater (see illustration).
11   Coat both sides of a new gasket with water resistant gasket sealer and position the gasket on the thermostat housing mating surface.
12   Position the thermostat housing carefully against the block or head, making sure the gasket is not disturbed.
13   Install and tighten the retaining bolts to the specified torque.
14   On 4 cylinder models, connect heater hose to the thermostat housing.
15   Fill the cooling system with the recommended antifreeze and water mixture as described in Chapter 1.
16   Check for leaks and proper heater operation after the engine has reached normal operation temperature. After the engine has completely cooled remove the radiator cap and check for proper coolant level (see Chapter 1).

4 Thermostat — check

1   The best way to check the operation of the thermostat is with it removed from the engine. In most cases, if the thermostat is suspect,

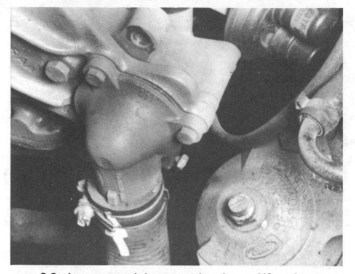

3.3   Low mounted thermostat housing on V6 engine

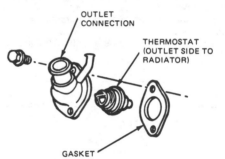

3.9   The thermostat is installed in the housing with the outlet (pointed) side towards the radiator

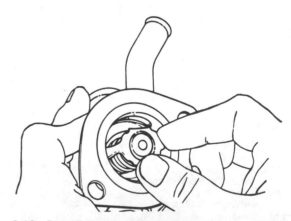

3.10   Port alignment of the thermostat on 4-cylinder engines is required to provide maximum coolant flow to the heater

it is more economical to simply buy and install a replacement thermostat, as they are not very costly.
2   To check, first remove the thermostat as described in Section 3.
3   Inspect the thermostat for corrosion or damage. Replace it with a new one if either of these conditions is noted.
4   Place the thermostat in hot water (25 degrees above the temperature stamped on the thermostat). When submerged in the water (which should be agitated thoroughly), the valve should open all the way.
5   Using a piece of bent wire, remove the thermostat and place it in water which is 10 degrees below the temperature on the thermostat. At this temperature, the thermostat valve should close completely.
6   Reinstall the thermostat if it operates properly. If it does not, purchase a new thermostat of the same temperature rating.

5.4   Use a socket to loosen the hose clamp

5.5   Loosen the clamp (arrow) and remove the upper radiator hose

5.6   Remove the bolts on the radiator retaining brackets to remove the radiator

5   Radiator — removal, servicing and installation

Refer to illustrations 5.4, 5.5, 5.6, 5.7a and 5.7

Warning: *The engine must be completely cool before beginning this procedure. Also, see the Warning in Section 2 pertaining to antifreeze.*

1   Disconnect the ground cable from the battery.

2   Drain the radiator by opening the drain cock, located on the bottom of the radiator.

3   Disconnect the radiator overflow tube, which leads to the reservoir.

4   Disconnect the lower radiator hose. Do this by fully loosening the clamp and then twisting the hose free of the radiator outlet. Be careful not to use excessive force and damage the outlet (see illustration).

5   Loosen the upper hose clamp and disconnect the hose (see illustration).

6   On most models, the radiator is held in place by two brackets (see illustration). Remove the bolts and then lift the brackets away. On late model vehicles with nylon tanks, the radiator is held in place by attaching screws at each upper corner.

7   Remove the screws attaching the fan shroud and place the shroud over the fan, against the engine (see illustrations).

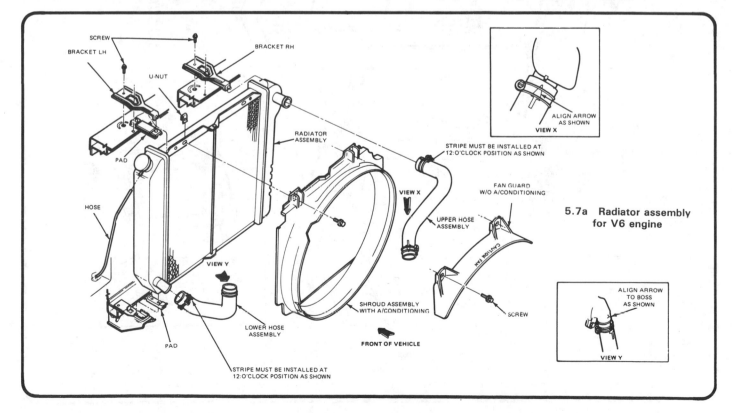

5.7a   Radiator assembly for V6 engine

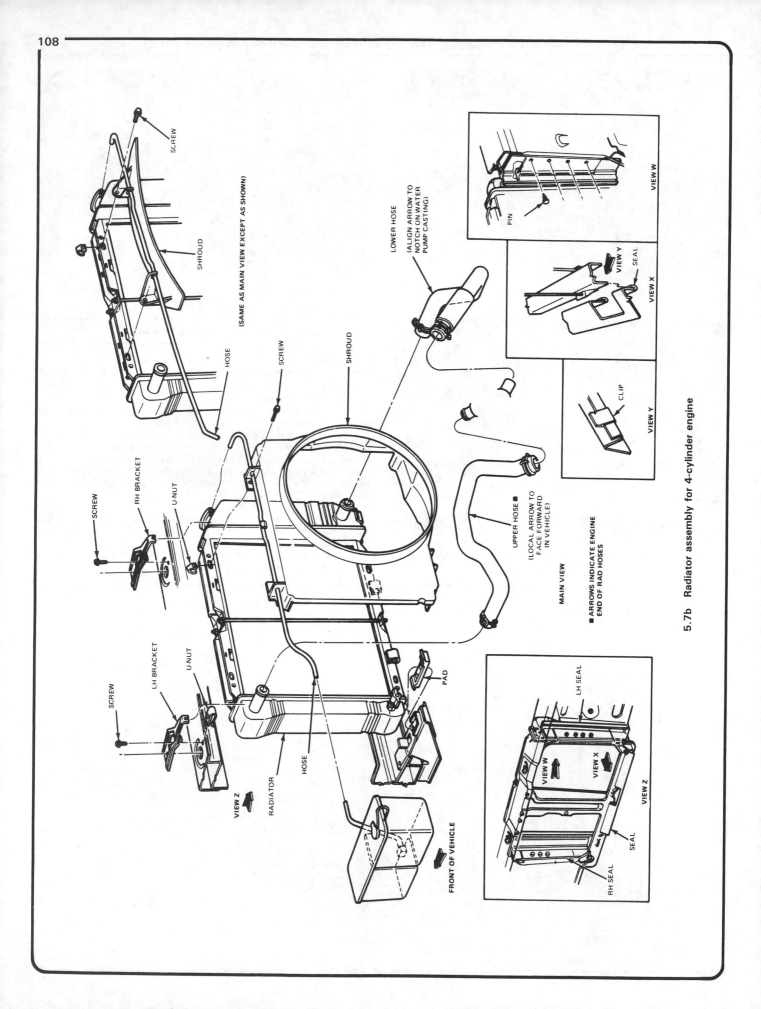

5.7b Radiator assembly for 4-cylinder engine

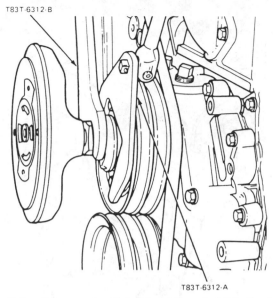

6.2b   Instead of special tools, a strap wrench and large channel locks can be used to remove the fan on a V6

6.2a   A large nut with left-hand threads holds the fan clutch to the water pump

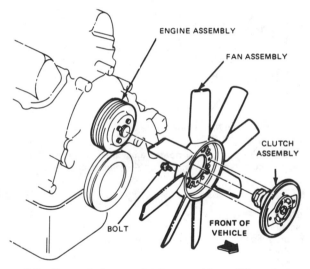

6.3   Fan and viscous clutch assembly on V6 engine

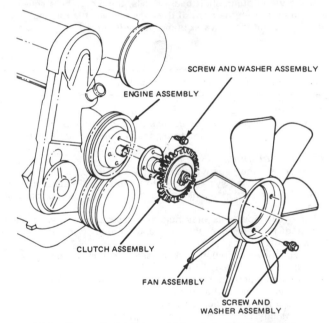

6.11   Fan and clutch assembly on 4-cylinder engine

8   If equipped with an automatic transmission, remove the oil cooler lines attached to the radiator. Put caps over the ends of these lines to prevent contamination while they are disconnected.

9   Lift out the radiator, being very careful not to damage the cooling fins on the fan blades.

10   Installation is essentially the reverse of removal. However, inspect the rubber bracket pads (or round bushings on nylon tank models) and replace if necessary. Make sure the arrows on the hoses are aligned properly.

11   Close the radiator drain cock.

12   Fill the radiator with specified coolant as described in Chapter 1.

13   Connect the ground cable at the battery.

14   Start the engine and check for leaks.

6   Fan and viscous clutch — removal and installation

Refer to illustrations 6.2a, 6.2b, 6.3, and 6.11

Warning: *The engine must be completely cool before beginning this procedure.*

V6 engines

1   Remove the fan shroud. Place the shroud over the fan, against the engine.

2   Remove the large nut which attaches the viscous clutch to the hub of the water pump shaft, using tools T83T-6312-A and T83T-6312-B (see illustration). **Caution:** *This nut has left-hand threads and must be rotated clockwise for removal.* In place of these special tools, we were able to use a strap wrench to hold the assembly stationary and channel lock pliers to loosen the nut (see illustration).

3   On V6 engines remove the fran bolts to the clutch from the inside (see illustration).

4   To install, attach the fan to the clutch (if separated).

5   Install the clutch/fan assembly on the water pump shaft and install the nut using the special tools or strap wrench/channel locks. Remember that these are left-hand threads.

6   Install the fan shroud or finger guard.

4-cylinder engines

7   Disconnect the negative cable from the battery.

8   Remove the fan shroud.

9   Disconnect the overflow tube and lift the shroud off the lower retaining clips.

10   Move the shroud back over the fan in order to get to the fan bolts.

11   Remove the four bolts retaining the clutch and fan assembly to the pulley and remove the assembly from the vehicle (see illustration).

12 If necessary, the fan and clutch can be separated by removing the four bolts which join them.
13 Prior to installation, attach the fan to the clutch with the four bolts (if separated).
14 Position the fan and clutch assembly to the pulley and secure with the four bolts.
15 Install the fan shroud.
16 Connect the battery cable.

7   Water pump — check

1 A failure of the water pump can cause overheating and serious engine damage (the pump will not circulate coolant through the engine).
2 There are three ways to check the operation of the water pump while it is installed on the engine. If the pump is defective, it should be replaced with a new or rebuilt unit.
3 With the engine running and at normal operating temperature, squeeze the upper radiator hose. If the water pump is working properly, a pressure surge will be felt as the hose is released.
4 Water pumps are equipped with a 'weep' or vent hole. If a pump seal failure occurs, small amounts of coolant will leak from the weep hole.
5 If the water pump shaft bearing fails, there may be a squealing sound emitted from the front of the engine while it is running. Shaft wear can be felt if the water pump pulley is forced up and down.

8   Water pump — removal and installation

Refer to illustration 8.11
Warning: *The engine must be completely cool before beginning this procedure. Also, see the Warning in Section 2 pertaining to antifreeze.*

4-cylinder engines
1 Disconnect the negative cable at the battery.
2 Drain the cooling system (refer to Chapter 1, if necessary).
3 Remove the shroud retaining bolts and move the shroud back over the fan.
4 Remove the four bolts retaining the fan assembly to the water pump shaft and then remove the fan and shroud from the engine compartment.
5 Loosen the air conditioner compressor idler pulley and remove the drivebelt (if so equipped).
6 Loosen the alternator and power steering mounting bolts (if so equipped) and remove the alternator and power steering belts.
7 Remove the water pump pulley.
8 Disconnect the heater hose at the water pump.
9 Remove the timing belt cover.
10 Disconnect the lower radiator hose from the water pump.
11 Remove the water pump retaining bolts and remove the water pump (see illustration).
12 Clean all old gasket and sealant from the gasket surfaces.
13 Coat both sides of the new gasket with sealant and place the gasket on the water pump surface.
14 Install the water pump on the cylinder block and install the retaining bolts. Apply D8AZ-19554-A sealer or water resistant sealer to the bolts prior to installing.
15 Install the lower radiator hose.
16 Install the heater hose.
17 Install the timing belt cover and tighten the bolts evenly.
18 Position the water pump pulley on the pump shaft.
19 Position the power steering (if so equipped) and alternator drivebelts to their respective pulleys.
20 Position the air conditioner compressor drivebelt (if so equipped) to its pulley.
21 Put the shroud around the fan assembly and install the fan assembly onto the water pump shaft (Section 6).
22 Position the shroud on the radiator and install the retaining bolts.
23 Adjust all drivebelts (Chapter 1).
24 Fill the cooling system (Chapter 1).
25 Start the engine and check for leaks.

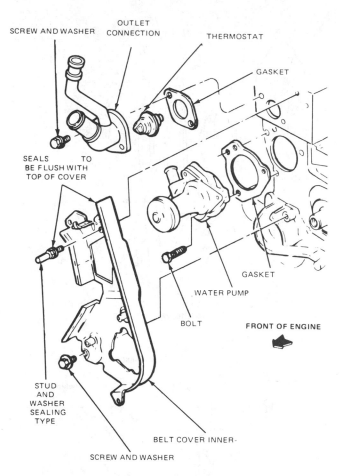

8.11   Water pump, thermostat and inner timing belt cover installation assembly on 4-cylinder engine

V6 engines
26 Disconnect the battery ground cable at the battery.
27 To provide adequate clearance, remove the radiator and radiator hoses (Section 5).
28 Remove the fan and clutch assembly (Section 6).
29 Loosen the alternator mounting bolts and remove the belt. On some models it may be necessary to completely remove the alternator and bracket.
30 Remove the water pump pulley.
31 Remove the water pump assembly attaching bolts making note of the positions of the various length bolts (a hand-drawn diagram will help get the bolts back into their proper positions). Remove the water pump and thermostat housing (with thermostat inside) from the front cover as an assembly.
32 The thermostat and housing can now be separated from the water pump. Remove all gasket material from the sealing surfaces on the front cover and water pump assembly.
33 Install the thermostat and housing on the water pump, using a new gasket (refer to Section 3 if necessary).
34 Install the water pump assembly on the front cover with two bolts. Tighten the bolts only finger-tight.
35 Working around the pump, tighten all the water pump bolts to specification.
36 Install the water pump pulley and the alternator and bracket if removed.
37 Install the radiator and connect all hoses.
38 Install all belts and adjust to the proper tension (Chapter 1).
39 Install the fan and clutch assembly (Section 6).
40 Connect the battery.
41 Fill the cooling system as described in Chapter 1.
42 Start the engine and check for leaks.

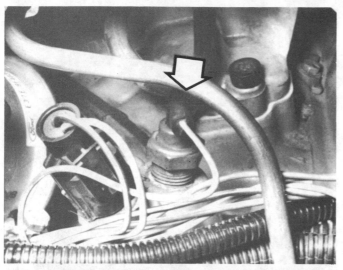

9.2a   The V6 temperature sending unit (arrow) is located next to the MCU temperature sensor

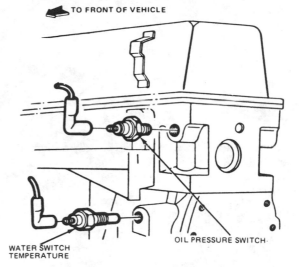

9.2b   Sending units on 4-cylinder engine. Lower unit is coolant temperature sender

10.5   Disconnect the heater hoses where they enter the firewall

9   Coolant temperature sending unit — removal and installation

Refer to illustrations 9.2a and 9.2b

1   With the engine completely cool, remove the cap from the radiator to relieve any pressure and then replace the cap. This reduces coolant loss during sender replacement.
2   Disconnect the temperature sending unit wire at the sending unit (see illustrations).
3   Prepare the new temperature sending unit for installation by applying D8AZ-19554-A or an equivalent sealer to the threads.
4   Remove the temperature sending unit from the intake manifold (V6 engines) or side of the engine block (4-cylinder engines). Immediately install the new sending unit to minimize coolant loss.
5   Connect the temperature sending unit wire.
6   Refill the cooling system to replace lost coolant.
7   Start the engine and check for leaks.

10   Heater core — removal and installation

Refer to illustrations 10.5, 10.6 and 10.7

1   Allow the engine to completely cool before beginning.
2   Using a thick cloth, turn the radiator cap slowly to the first stop.

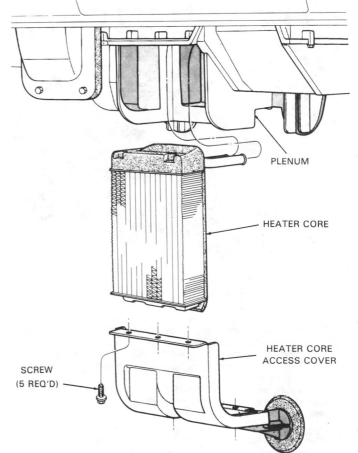

10.6   Exploded view of the heater core assembly

3   Step back and let the pressure release.
4   Once the pressure has been released, tighten the radiator cap.
5   Disconnect the heater hoses at the engine compartment firewall and plug the ends to prevent further draining of the system (see illustration).
6   In the passenger compartment, remove the five screws attaching the heater core access cover to the plenum assembly. Remove the access cover (see illustration).

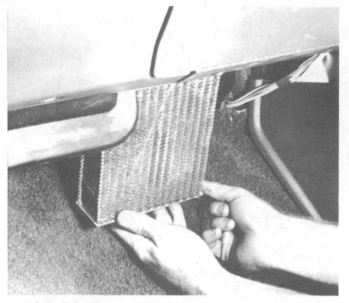

10.7   Pull rearward and down to remove the heater core

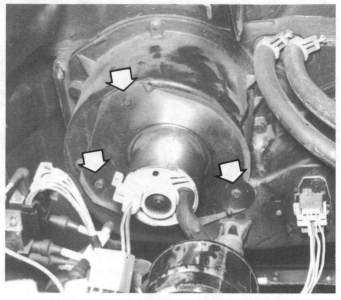

11.5   To remove the blower assembly, disconnect the electrical connections and the three retaining screws (arrows)

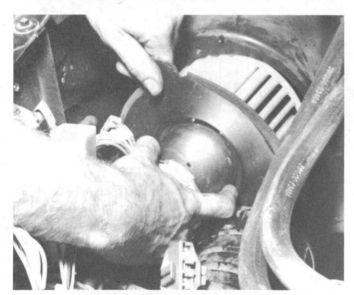

11.6   With the retaining screws removed pull out the blower assembly

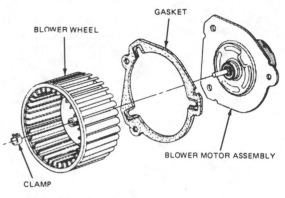

BLOWER WHEEL

GASKET

BLOWER MOTOR ASSEMBLY

CLAMP

11.7   Disassembled blower motor and wheel

7   Pull the heater core rearward and down, removing it from the plenum assembly (see illustration).
8   Position the new heater core and seal in the plenum assembly.
9   Install the heater core access cover to the plenum assembly.
10   Install the heater hoses.
11   Check the coolant level and add coolant as required (see Chapter 1).
12   Check the system for proper operation and for leaks.

11   Heater blower motor — removal and installation

Refer to illustrations 11.5, 11.6 and 11.7

1   Disconnect the ground cable at the battery.
2   The blower motor is located on the right side of the engine compartment firewall. Depending on the engine installed, the air cleaner and/or solenoid cover box may have to be removed for access to the motor.
3   Disconnect the wiring harness at the blower motor. This is done by pushing down on the tab and then pulling the connector away.
4   Disconnect the small rubber cooling tube at the blower motor.
5   Remove the three screws which attach the motor to the heater blower assembly (see illustration).

6   Being very careful not to damage the gasket, pull the blower motor assembly out of the heater (see illustration).
7   At this point the blower wheel can be separated from the motor by removing the clamp on the motor shaft (see illustrtation).
8   Installation is essentially the reverse of removal, however note the following points:
9   The gasket between the blower motor and the heater assembly must be in good condition. If it was damaged on removal, use a new gasket.
10   Make sure the electrical connector is fully seated. Test for proper operation upon completion.

12   Heater control assembly — removal and installation

Refer to illustrations 12.3, 12.10, 12.11 and 12.13

Removal

1   Disconnect the ground cable at the battery.
2   If so equipped, pull the control knobs from the radio shafts.
3   Pry the bottom trim panels from the dash. They are held in place by simple spring type clips (see illustration).
4   Remove the four screws attaching the top cluster finish panel to the upper finish panel pad.
5   Remove the four bolts attaching the bottom of the cluster finish panel.

12.3   The bottom trim panel is held by spring clips

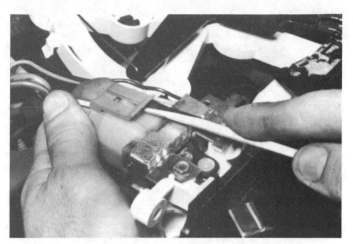

12.10   Spread the clips and pull the electrical connector from the function control

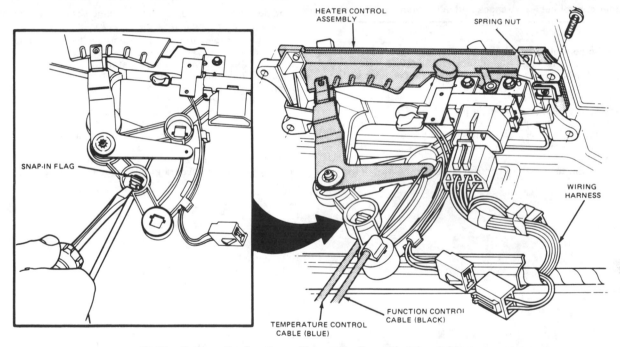

HEATER CONTROL ASSEMBLY

SPRING NUT

SNAP-IN FLAG

WIRING HARNESS

TEMPERATURE CONTROL CABLE (BLUE)

FUNCTION CONTROL CABLE (BLACK)

12.11   Remove the function cable snap-in flag with a screwdriver

6　Remove the cigar lighter.
7　Pull the headlamp switch on and remove the knob to allow the panel to be removed.
8　Remove the cluster finish panel.
9　Remove the four screws attaching the function control assembly to the panel.
10　Pull the control assembly through the instrument panel opening far enough to allow removal of the electrical connectors from the blower switch and control assembly illumination lamp, then remove the connectors (see illustration).
11　Working from the bottom of the control, use a screwdriver or needle-nose pliers to release the function cable (black) snap-in flag from the control bracket (see illustration).
12　Pull enough cable through the instrument panel opening until the function cable (black) can be held vertical to the control, then remove the cable end from the function lever.
13　Working from the top of the control assembly, using needle-nose pliers, release the temperature cable (blue) and the outside air door cable snap-in flags (white) (see illustration).
14　Rotate the control and disconnect the temperature cable wire from the temperature control lever and the air door cable wire from the air door control lever. Remove the control assembly from the dash.

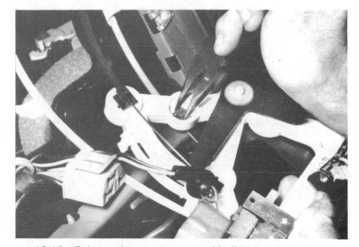

12.13   Release the temperature cable (blue) and air door cable (white) snap-in flags

Installation

15 Pull the control cables approximately eight inches through the opening in the instrument panel.
16 Hold the control assembly up to the instrument panel with control face pointed toward the floor.
17 Attach the temperature cable (blue) and the air door cable (white) to the control levers. Rotate the assembly back to normal position and snap the cable flags into the control assembly bracket. **Note:** *The letters BL on the bottom of control assembly bracket indicate the location for the blue temperature control cable snap-in flag.*
18 Gently bend the function control cable (black) down to the control assembly (end of cable pointing toward the floor) and attach the cable wire to the function control lever. Snap the cable flag into the control assembly bracket. **Note:** *The letters BK on the top of the assembly bracket indicate the location for the black function control snap-in flag.*
19 Install the wire harness connectors.
20 Position the control assembly into the instrument panel and install the four attaching screws.
21 Complete the installation by installing the various trim panels and dashboard items previously removed. Check for proper operation and adjust the cables if necessary by referring to the next Section.

13 Heater control cables — check and adjustment

Check

1 Move the control lever all the way from left to right.
2 If the lever stops before the end or bounces back, the cables should be considered misadjusted and heater output may be substandard.

Adjustment

3 Disengage the glove box door to provide access.
4 Working through the glove box opening, remove the cable jacket from its metal attaching clip on the top of the heater assembly. The cable ends should remain attached to the door cams and/or crank arms at this time.
5 To adjust the temperature control, set the temperature lever to cool and hold it in this position.
6 Push gently on the cable jacket (blue) to seat the blend door (push until you feel resistance).
7 Reinstall the cable to the clip by pushing the jacket into the clip from the top until it snaps in.
8 To adjust the function control cable, set the function lever to defrost and hold.
9 Pull on the cam jacket until cam travel stops.
10 Reinstall the cable to the clip by pushing the jacket into the clip from the top until it snaps in.
11 To adjust the outside air cable, set the lever to the off position and hold.
12 Set the outside air door crank arm (white) in the down position (door closed to shut off air flow).
13 Reinstall the cable to the clip by pushing the jacket into the clip from the top until it snaps in.
14 Run the system on high and actuate the levers, checking for proper adjustment.
15 Install the glove box door.

14 Air conditioning system — servicing

Warning: *Before servicing, the air conditioning system must be evacuated by an air conditioning technician.*

1 Regularly inspect the condenser fins (located ahead of the radiator) and brush away leaves and bugs.
2 Clean the dirt from the evaporator drain tubes.
3 Check the condition of the system hoses. If there is any sign of deterioration or hardening, have them replaced by a dealer or air conditioning repair facility.
4 At the recommended intervals, check and adjust the compressor drive belt as described in Chapter 1.
5 Because of the special tools, equipment and skills required to service air conditioning systems, and the differences between the various systems that may be installed, major air conditioning servicing procedures cannot be covered in this manual.

Chapter 4   Fuel and exhaust systems

Contents

Specifications

Fuel tank
Capacity
  Ranger
SWB, center-mounted tank	15.2 gallons
LWB, center-mounted tank	17.0 gallons
Supercab, center-mounted tank	14.5 gallons
rear-mounted tank	13.0 gallons
Bronco II	23.0 gallons

Torque specifications   **Ft-lbs**
Center-mounted tank
front strap nut	18 to 25
rear strap nut	22 to 30
skid plate bolts	22 to 30

Rear-mounted tank
front strap nut (4x2)	12 to 18
front strap nut (4x4)	12 to 18
rear strap nut (4x4)	27 to 36

Mechanical fuel pump
Minimum volume flow
2.8L V6	1 pint in 30 seconds
2.0L and 2.3L 4-cylinder	1 pint in 25 seconds

Pressure
2.8L V6	4.5 to 6.5 psi
2.0L and 2.3L 4-cylinder	5 to 7 psi

Torque specifications   **Ft-lbs**
Fuel pump to engine	14 to 21
Fuel line to fuel pump outlet fitting	15 to 18

Electric fuel pump
Torque specifications   **Ft-lbs**
Fuel line fittings	10 to 15
High pressure pump to frame rail	11 to 16

YFA-1V carburetor

Torque specifications	In-lbs
Air horn to main body screws	27 to 37
Main body to throttle body screws	50 to 55
Accelerator pump housing screws	6 to 11
Choke pulldown diaphragm housing screws	32 to 36
Fast idle cam retaining screw	50 to 55
Choke plate to choke shaft screws	9 to 11
Throttle plate to throttle shaft screws	4 to 5
Main metering jet	20 to 22
Choke cap retaining screws	17 to 20
Carburetor to intake manifold	13 to 14 Ft-lbs
ISC motor bracket retaining screw	60
Throttle control bracket retaining nut	30
Feedback or altitude solenoid screws	45 to 50

2150-2V carburetor

Torque specifications	In-lbs
Air horn to main body	27 to 37
Fuel inlet valve seat	45
Accelerator pump diaphragm cover	13 to 20
Choke pulldown diaphragm	20 to 30
Fast idle lever retaining nut	20 to 28
Enrichment valve	100 to 120
Enrichment valve cover	13 to 20
Accelerator pump discharge screw	65 to 85
Main jets	28
Choke housing retaining screw	13 to 20
Choke plate screws	4 to 9
Carburetor body flange to intake manifold	14 to 16 Ft-lbs
Air cleaner anchor screw	5 to 7 Ft-lbs
Air cleaner wing nut (steel)	15 to 25
Air cleaner wing nut (plastic)	25 to 35
Temperature compensated pump valve cover	19 to 24
Integral attitude compensator	20 to 30
Feedback duty cycle solenoid	20 to 30
Throttle position sensor	11 to 16
Feedback booster venturi screw	65 to 85
Temperature compensated pump	19 to 24
Aneroid assembly to main body	20 to 30

2.9L V6 fuel injection

Torque specifications	Ft-lbs
Lower intake manifold to block	11 to 15
EGR valve	11 to 15
Upper intake manifold to lower intake manifold	11 to 15
Throttle body to upper intake manifold	6 to 8
Air bypass valve to upper intake manifold	6 to 8
Throttle position sensor to throttle body	10 to 16 in-lbs
Fuel pressure regulator to manifold	6 to 8
Fuel injector manifold to fuel charging assembly	6 to 8
Throttle cable bracket to manifold	11 to 15

2.3L 4-cylinder fuel injection

Torque specifications	Ft-lbs
Lower intake manifold to head	12 to 15
EGR tube	6 to 8.5
Air supply tube clamps	15 to 23 in-lbs
Upper intake manifold to lower intake manifold	14 to 21
Throttle body to upper intake manifold	12 to 15
Air bypass valve to air cleaner	6 to 8.5
Throttle position sensor to throttle body	14 to 15 in-lbs
Fuel pressure relief valve	4 to 7
Fuel pressure regulator to manifold	2 to 3
Fuel injector manifold to fuel charging assembly	15 to 22
Water bypass line	12 to 20
Fuel pressure relief cap	4.4 to 6.2 in-lbs
Fuel pressure relief valve	4 to 7
Throttle position sensor connector to throttle body	14 to 16 in-lbs

Exhaust system

Torque specifications	Ft-lbs
Exhaust pipe to exhaust manifold	25 to 34
Managed thermactor air U-bolt	5 to 8
Converter pipe assembly to muffler assembly	
1983-1984	19 to 25
1985	18 to 26
1986	20 to 30
Muffler shield	12 to 17
Muffler shield band strap	16 to 20 in-lbs
Y-pipe to converter pipe	20 to 30

1 General information

The fuel system consists of a rear mounted fuel tank on the Bronco II and a standard center mounted tank on the Ranger (an auxiliary tank is optional), a mechanically operated fuel pump (carburetor-equipped engines) or an electrically operated fuel pump (electronic fuel injection models), a carburetor or fuel injection assembly and an air cleaner.

The exhaust system includes a catalytic converter, muffler, emissions equipment and associated pipes and hardware. Because a catalytic converter is fitted, only unleaded gasoline is to be used.

2 Mechanical fuel pump — check

Warning: *Gasoline is extremely flammable, so extra precautions must be taken when working on any part of the fuel system. Do not smoke or allow open flames or bare light bulbs near the work area. Also, do not work in a garage if a natural gas appliance with a pilot light is present.*

1 On carburetor-equipped engines the fuel pump is located on the left side of the engine.
2 The fuel pump is sealed and no repairs are possible other than component replacement. However, the fuel pump can be inspected and tested on the vehicle as follows.
3 Make sure there is fuel in the fuel tank.
4 With the engine running, check for leaks at all fuel line connections between the fuel tank and the carburetor.
5 Tighten any loose connections and inspect all lines for flat spots and kinks which could restrict fuel flow. Air leaks or restrictions on the suction side of the fuel pump will greatly affect pump output.
6 Check for leaks at the fuel pump diaphragm flange.
7 Disconnect the coil wire from the distributor and the fuel inlet line from the carburetor. Direct the fuel line from the pump into a metal container.
8 Crank the engine several revolutions and make sure that well defined spurts of fuel are ejected from the line. If not, the fuel line is clogged or the fuel pump is defective.
9 Disconnect the fuel line at both ends of the line and blow through it with compressed air to determine if the fuel line is clogged.

3 Mechanical fuel pump — removal and installation

Refer to illustrations 3.2 and 3.7
Warning: *Gasoline is extremely flammable, so extra precautions must be taken when working on any part of the fuel system. Do not smoke or allow open flames or bare light bulbs near the work area. Also, do not work in a garage if a natural gas appliance with a pilot light is present.*

1 Loosen the mounting bolts two turns. Wiggle the fuel pump to break the gasket seal.
2 Turn the engine over until the cam lobe is down, reducing the tension on the fuel pump (see illustration).
3 Disconnect the fuel pump inlet and outlet lines.
4 Remove the fuel pump attaching bolts and remove the pump and gasket. On V6 engines remove the pushrod from the block.
5 Remove all old fuel pump gasket material from the engine and fuel pump.
6 Insert the bolts into the fuel pump and install a new gasket on the bolts.

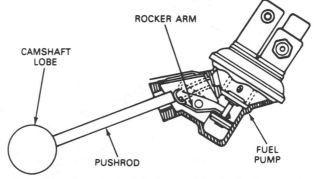

3.2 **Bring the camshaft fuel pump lobe to the low point before removing the fuel pump**

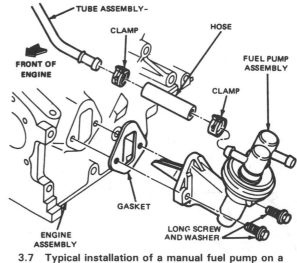

3.7 **Typical installation of a manual fuel pump on a 4-cylinder engine**

7 Position the pump to the mounting pad (on V6 engines first install the pushrod) (see illustration).
8 Turn the bolts alternately and evenly to tighten.
9 Install the inlet and outlet fuel lines and tighten the connecting nuts.
Note: *Check for hardened, cracked or frayed rubber hoses and replace if necessary.*
10 Start the engine and check for fuel leaks.
11 Stop the engine and check all fuel pump line connections for fuel leaks by running a finger under the connections.
12 Check for oil leaks at the fuel pump mounting pad.

4 Fuel lines — replacement

Refer to illustrations 4.1, 4.8, 4.12, 4.13, and 4.22
Warning: *Fuel supply lines on vehicles with fuel injected engines will remain pressurized for long periods of time after the engine is shut down. The pressure must be relieved before servicing the fuel system. See the Section on fuel pressure relief.*

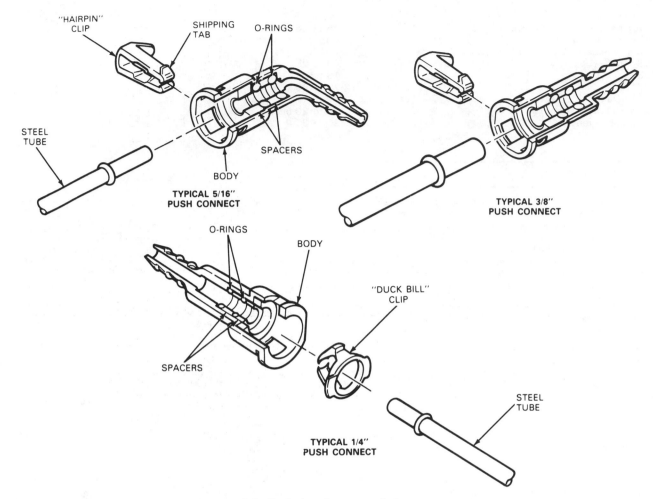

4.1 Typical push connect fittings

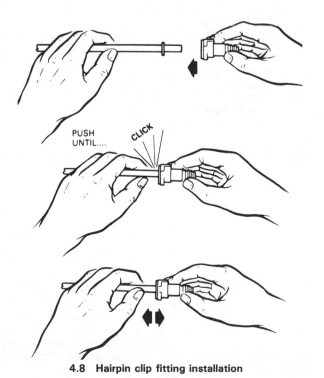

4.8 Hairpin clip fitting installation

Push Connect fittings

1   Two different type of push connect fittings are used. The *hairpin* is used on 3/8-inch and 5/16-inch lines, and the *duck bill* clip is used on 1/4-inch lines (see illustration). Each type of fitting requires different procedures for service. Clips should be replaced whenever a connector is removed. The push connect fittings to connect the flexible fuel lines to the fuel tank sender cannot be disconnected until the tank is partially lowered.

Hairpin clip

2   Inspect the visible portion of fitting for dirt accumulation. Clean the fitting before disassembly.
3   Due to adhesion, separate by twisting the fitting on the tube, then push and pull the fitting until it moves freely on the tube.
4   Remove the hairpin clip by first bending the shipping tab downward so that it will clear the body. Spread the two clip legs about 3.2 mm (1/8-inch) each to disengage the body and push the legs into the fitting. Complete the removal by lightly pulling from the triangular end of the clip and working it clear of the tube and fitting.
5   **Note:** *It is recommended that the original clip not be reused.*
6   To install the new clip, insert the clip with the triangular portion pointing away from the fitting opening. Fully engage the body so the legs of the clip lock on the outside of the body.
7   Before reinstalling the fitting, wipe the tube end clean and inspect inside to ensure it is free of dirt and/or obstructions.
8   Reinstall the fitting onto the tube by aligning the fitting and tube and pushing the fitting onto the tube end until a definite click is heard (see illustration).
9   Pull on the fitting to ensure that it is fully engaged.

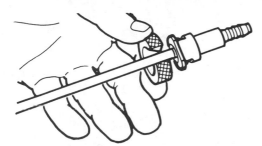

4.12 Disconnect tool used to remove push connect fittings

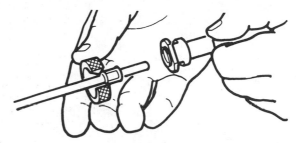

4.13 Removing the push connect fitting

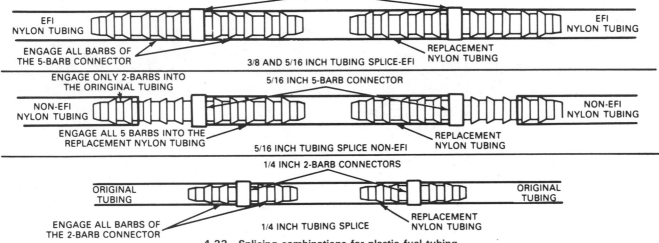

4.22 Splicing combinations for plastic fuel tubing

Duck bill clip

Note: *The fitting consists of a body, spacers, O-rings and a duck bill retaining clip.*

10 Inspect the visible portion of fitting for dirt accumulation. Clean the fitting before disassembly.

11 Due to adhesion, separate by twisting the fitting on the tube, then push and pull the fitting until it moves freely on the tube. **Note:** *Two methods for disconnecting the fitting are available.*

12 The preferred method is to disengage the tube from the fitting by aligning the slot on push connect disassembly tool T82L-9500-AH or its equivalent with either tab on the clip (90 degrees from the slots on side of fitting) and inserting the tool (see illustration). This will disengage the fitting from the tube.

13 Holding the tube and tool with one hand, pull away from the tube (see illustration). **Note:** *Only moderate effort is required if the tube has been properly disengaged.*

14 An acceptable method for disassembly disengages the retaining clip from the fitting body by using a pair of narrow pliers (6-inch channel-lock pliers are ideal). Pliers must have a jaw width of 5 mm (0.2 inch).

15 Align the jaws of the pliers with the openings in the side of the fitting case. Compress the portion of the retaining clip that engages the fitting case. This disengages the retaining clip from the case. Often one side of the clip will disengage before the other. It is necessary to disengage the clip from both openings.

16 Pull the fitting off the tube. **Note:** *Only moderate effort is required if the retaining clip has been disengaged properly.*

17 The retaining clip will remain on the tube. Disengage the clip from the tube bead and remove.

18 Use a new replacement clip only. Install the new clip into the body by inserting one of the retaining clip serrated edges on the duck bill portion into one of the window openings, then push on the other side until the clip snaps into place.

19 Before reinstalling the fitting, wipe the tube end clean and inspect inside to ensure it is free of dirt and/or obstructions.

20 Reinstall the fitting onto tube by aligning the fitting and tube and pushing the fitting onto the tube end until a definite click is heard.

21 Pull on the fitting to ensure it is fully engaged.

Fuel lines — plastic

Warning: *Avoid using alternate tubing materials with nylon fuel tubing. Use of nonapproved tubing could pose a hazard in service.*

22 Plastic fuel tubing must not be repaired using hose and hose clamps (see illustration). Push connect fittings cannot be repaired except to replace the retaining clips. Should the plastic tubing, push connect fittings or steel tubing ends become damaged, approved service parts must be used to service the fuel lines.

23 The plastic fuel lines can be damaged by torches, welding sparks, grinding and other operations which involve heat. If any repairs or service operations will be performed which involve heat relocate all fuel system components, especially the plastic fuel lines, to be certain they will not be damaged. It is recommended that the plastic fuel lines be removed from the vehicle if a torch or high heat producing equipment is to be used for service.

Steel fuel lines

24 If a section of metal fuel line must be replaced, only seamless steel tubing should be used, since copper or aluminum does not have enough durability to withstand normal operating vibration.

25 If only one section of a metal line is damaged, it can be cut out and replaced with rubber hose. Be sure to use only reinforced fuel resistant hose, identified by the word ''fluroelastomer'' on the hose. The inside diameter of the hose should match the outside diameter of the tubing. The rubber hose should be cut four inches longer than the section it's replacing, so there is two inches of overlap between the rubber and metal line at either end of the section. Hose clamps should be used to secure both ends of the repaired section.

26 If a section of metal line longer than six inches is being removed, use a combination of metal tubing and rubber hose so the hose lengths will be no longer than ten inches.

27 Never use rubber hose within four inches of any part of the exhaust system or within ten inches of the catalytic converter.

28 When replacing clamps, make sure the replacement clamp is identical to the one being replaced, as different clamps are used depending on location.

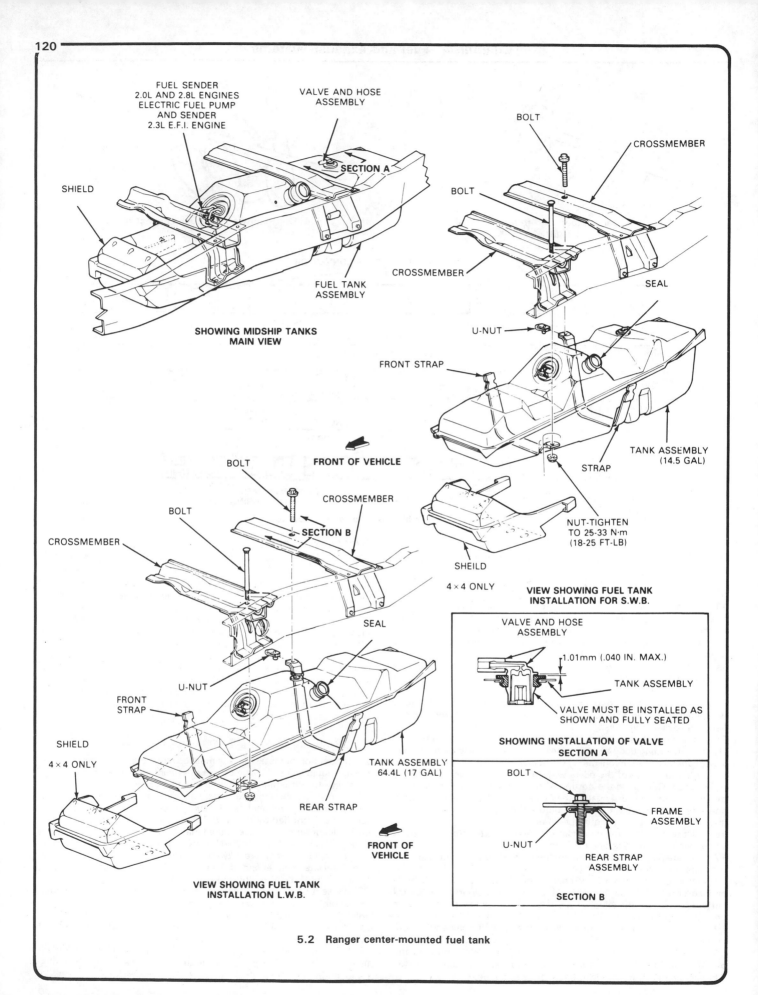

FUEL SENDER
2.0L AND 2.8L ENGINES
ELECTRIC FUEL PUMP
AND SENDER
2.3L E.F.I. ENGINE

VALVE AND HOSE
ASSEMBLY

SECTION A

SHIELD

FUEL TANK
ASSEMBLY

**SHOWING MIDSHIP TANKS
MAIN VIEW**

BOLT

CROSSMEMBER

BOLT

CROSSMEMBER

SEAL

U-NUT

FRONT STRAP

TANK ASSEMBLY
(14.5 GAL)

STRAP

NUT-TIGHTEN
TO 25-33 N·m
(18-25 FT-LB)

SHEILD

4 × 4 ONLY

**VIEW SHOWING FUEL TANK
INSTALLATION FOR S.W.B.**

FRONT OF VEHICLE

BOLT

CROSSMEMBER

BOLT

SECTION B

CROSSMEMBER

SEAL

U-NUT

FRONT
STRAP

SHIELD

4 × 4 ONLY

TANK ASSEMBLY
64.4L (17 GAL)

REAR STRAP

**FRONT OF
VEHICLE**

**VIEW SHOWING FUEL TANK
INSTALLATION L.W.B.**

VALVE AND HOSE
ASSEMBLY

1.01mm (.040 IN. MAX.)

TANK ASSEMBLY

VALVE MUST BE INSTALLED AS
SHOWN AND FULLY SEATED

**SHOWING INSTALLATION OF VALVE
SECTION A**

BOLT

FRAME
ASSEMBLY

U-NUT

REAR STRAP
ASSEMBLY

SECTION B

5.2 Ranger center-mounted fuel tank

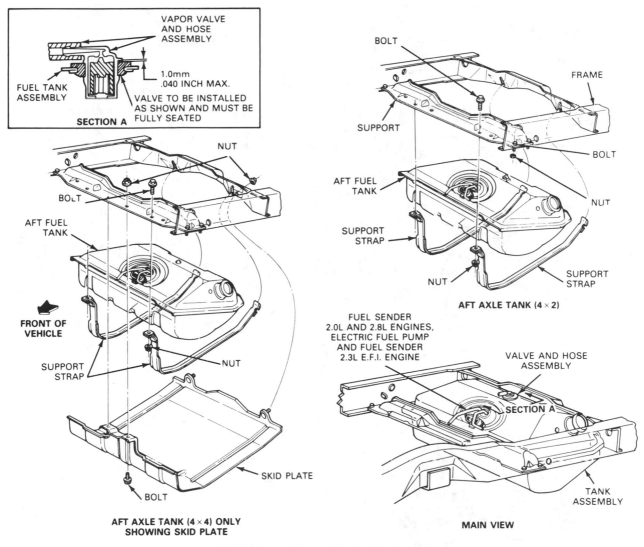

5.24 Bronco II rear-mounted fuel tank

5 Fuel tank — removal and installation

Refer to illustrations 5.2 and 5.24
Warning: *Fuel supply lines on vehicles with fuel injection will remain pressurized for long periods after the engine is shut down. The pressure must be relieved before servicing the fuel system. See the Section on fuel pressure relief.*

Warning: *Gasoline is extremely flammable, so extra precautions must be taken when working on any part of the fuel system. Do not smoke or allow open flames or bare light bulbs near the work area. Also, do not work in a garage if a natural gas appliance with a pilot light is present.*

Ranger center-mounted fuel tank

1   Drain the fuel from the fuel tank.
2   Loosen the filler pipe clamp (see illustration).
3   Remove the bolts securing the skid plate bracket to the frame, if so equipped. Remove the skid plate and brackets as an assembly.
4   Remove the bolt and nut from the rear strap and remove the rear strap.
5   Remove the nut and bolt from the front strap and remove the strap.
6   Remove the feed hose at the sender unit push connector.
7   Remove the fuel hose from the sender unit push connector.
8   Remove the fuel vapor hose from the vapor valve.
9   Lower the tank from the vehicle.
10 Remove the shield from the tank

11 Remove the front mounting bolt from the vehicle by drilling a hole in the cab floor over the bolt hole.
12 Install the front mounting bolt to the vehicle.
13 Attach the rear strap to the vehicle.
14 Install the shield on the tank.
15 Position the tank to the vehicle and attach the front strap to the vehicle.
16 Attach the fuel vapor hose to the vapor valve.
17 Attach the fuel hose to the sender unit push connector.
18 Install the feed and return hoses at the sender push connector unit.
19 Install the filler pipe and tighten the filler pipe clamp.
20 Install the nut to the front mounting bolt and tighten.
21 Install the bolt to the rear strap and tighten.
22 Install the skid plate and bracket assembly, if so equipped.

Rear-mounted fuel tank

23 Drain the fuel from the tank.
24 Remove the skid plate, if so equipped (see illustration).
25 Remove the two bolts from the fuel tank support and straps.
26 Loosen the screw clamp from the filler pipe.
27 Lower the fuel tank.
28 Remove the sender unit, vapor valve tubes and push connectors.
29 Raise the fuel tank and attach the sender unit, vapor valve tubes, and push connectors.
30 Install the fuel filler pipe on the tank and tighten the clamp.
31 Attach the two bolts to the fuel tank support and straps and tighten.
32 Install the skid plate and tighten the mounting bolts and nuts.

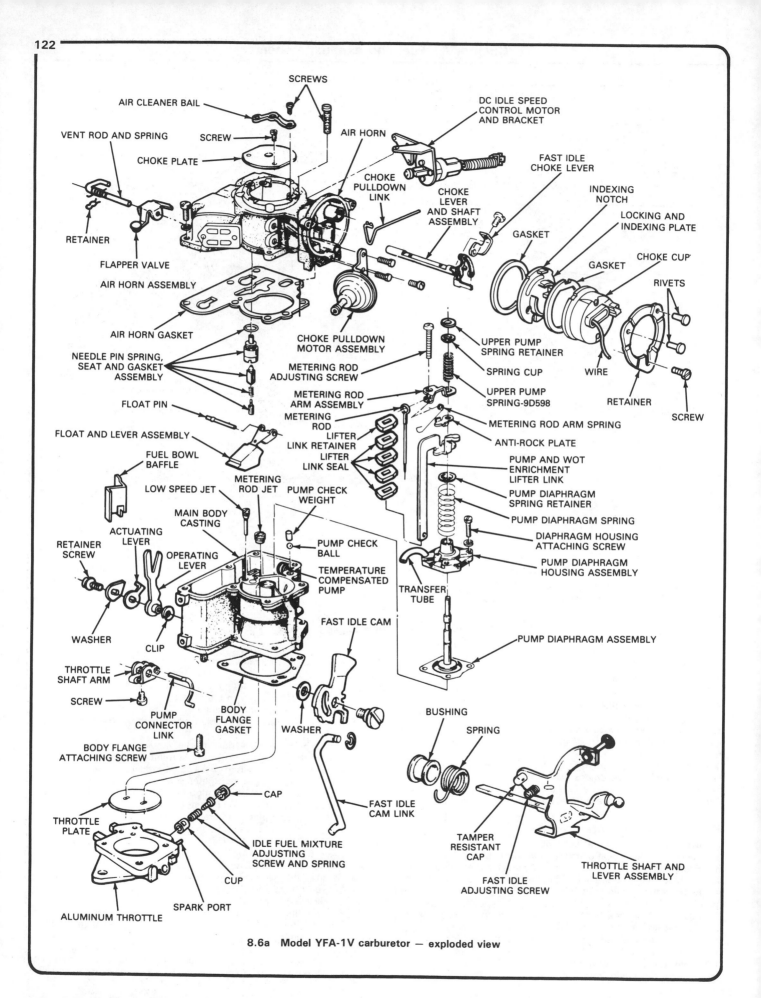

8.6a Model YFA-1V carburetor — exploded view

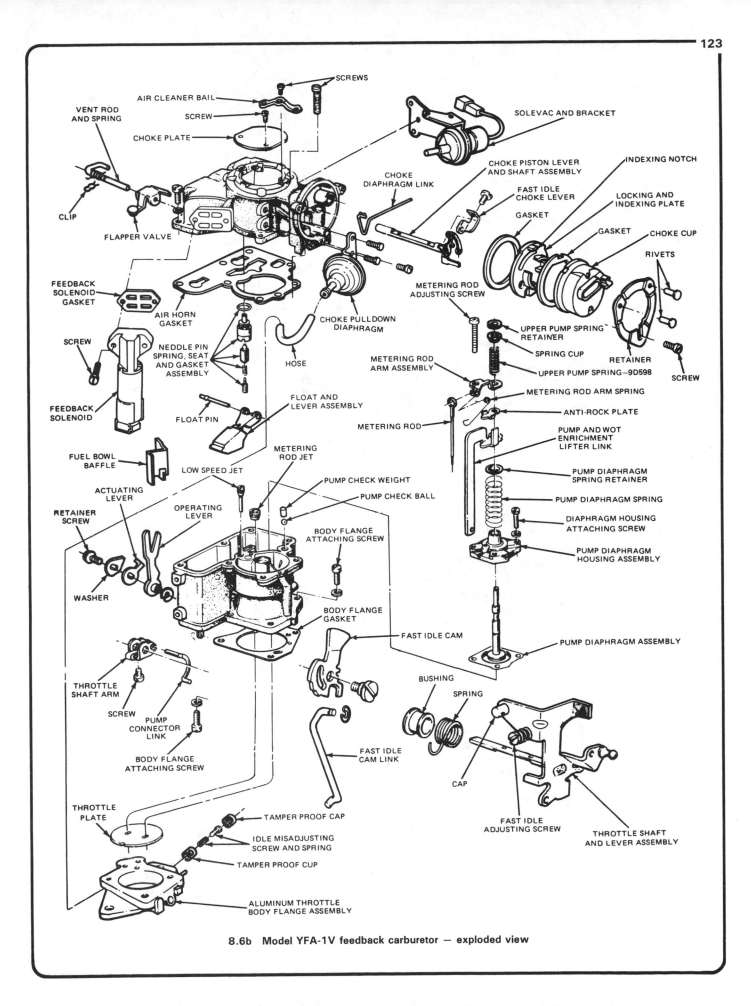

8.6b Model YFA-1V feedback carburetor — exploded view

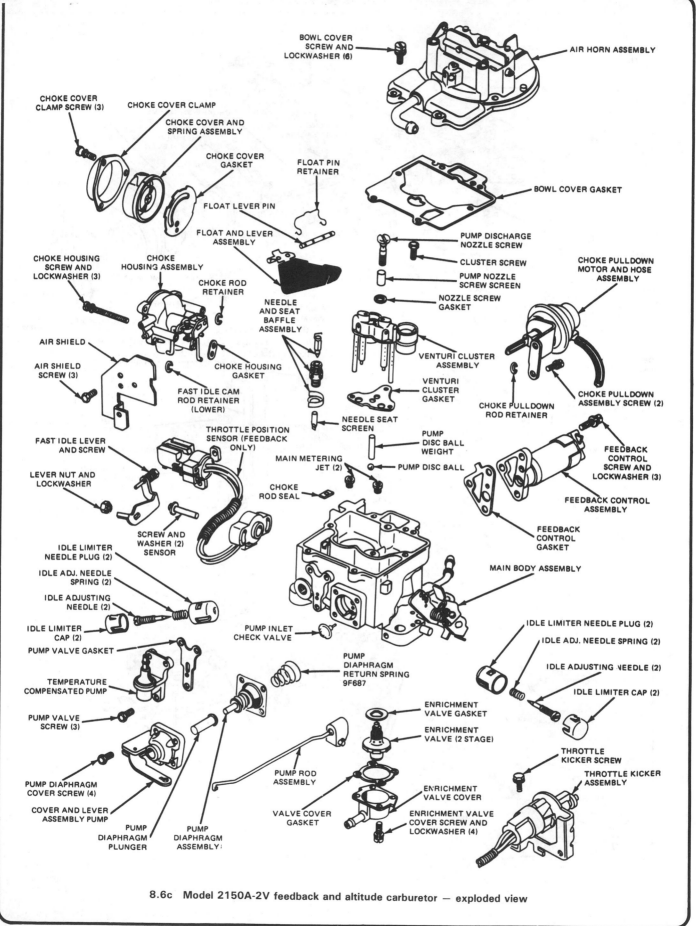

8.6c Model 2150A-2V feedback and altitude carburetor — exploded view

6 Fuel tank — repair

1   Any repairs to the fuel tank or filler neck should be carried out by a professional who has experience in this critical and potentially dangerous work. Even after cleaning and flushing of the fuel system, explosive fumes can remain and ignite during repair of the tank.

2   If the fuel tank is removed from the vehicle, it should not be placed in an area where sparks or open flames could ignite the fumes coming out of the tank. Be especially careful inside garages where a natural gas appliance is located, because the pilot light could cause an explosion.

7 Carburetor — removal and installation

Warning: *Gasoline is extremely flammable, so extra precautions must be taken when working on any part of the fuel system. Do not smoke or allow open flames or bare light bulbs near the work area. Also, do not work in a garage if a natural gas appliance with a pilot light is present.*

Note: *Flooding, stumble on acceleration and other performance complaints are, in many instances, caused by the presence of dirt, water or other foreign matter in the carburetor. To aid in diagnosing problems remove the carburetor without removing the fuel from the bowl. The contents may then be examined for contamination as the carburetor is disassembled.*

1   Remove the air cleaner.

2   Remove the throttle cable and remove the transmission kickdown linkage (if equipped) from the throttle lever.

3   Disconnect all vacuum lines.

4   Disconnect the emission hoses.

5   Disconnect the fuel line.

6   Disconnect the electrical connections.

7   Remove the four attaching nuts and remove the carburetor and spacer.

8   Clean the gasket mounting surfaces of the spacer and carburetor.

9   Position a new gasket on the spacer and install the carburetor.

10   Secure the carburetor with the attaching nuts. **Note:** *To prevent leakage, distortion or damage to the carburetor body flange, snug the nuts, then alternately tighten each nut in a crisscross pattern.*

11   Connect the fuel line, throttle cable, transmission linkage and all emission lines, electrical connections, and any vacuum lines removed. Be sure to observe color coded vacuum line connections on the carburetor.

8 Carburetor — adjustment and overhaul

Refer to illustrations 8.6a, 8.6b and 8.6c

Warning: *Gasoline is extremely flammable, so extra precautions must be taken when working on any part of the fuel system. Do not smoke or allow open flames or bare light bulbs near the work area. Also, do not work in a garage if a natural gas appliance with a pilot light is present.*

1   A thorough road test and check of carburetor adjustments should be done before any major carburetor service. Specifications for some adjustments are listed on the Vehicle Emissions Control Information label found in the engine compartment.

2   Some performance complaints directed at the carburetor are actually a result of loose, misadjusted or malfunctioning engine or electrical components. Others develop when vacuum hoses leak, are disconnected or are incorrectly routed. The proper approach to analyzing carburetor problems should include a routine check as follows.

a)   Inspect all vacuum hoses and actuators for leaks and proper installation (see Chapter 5, *Emissions control systems).*

b)   Tighten the intake manifold nuts and carburetor mounting nuts evenly and securely.

c)   Perform a cylinder compression test.

d)   Clean or replace the spark plugs as necessary.

e)   Test the electrical resistance of the spark plug wires.

f)   Inspect the ignition primary wires and check the vacuum advance operation. Replace any defective parts.

g)   Check the ignition timing according to the instructions listed on the Emissions Control Information label.

h)   Check the fuel pump pressure.

i)   Inspect the heat control valve in the air cleaner for proper operation.

j)   Remove the carburetor air filter element and blow out any dirt with compressed air. If the filter is extremely dirty replace it.

k)   Inspect the crankcase ventilation system.

3   Carburetor problems usually show up as flooding, hard starting, stalling, severe backfiring, poor acceleration and lack of response to idle mixture screw adjustments. A carburetor that is leaking fuel and/or covered with wet looking deposits needs attention.

4   Diagnosing carburetor problems may require that the engine be started and run with the air cleaner removed. While running the engine without the air cleaner backfires are possible. This situation is likely to occur if the carburetor is malfunctioning, but just the removal of the air cleaner can lean the air/fuel mixture enough to produce an engine backfire. Perform tests without the air cleaner for as short a time as possible. Do not position your face or any portions of your body directly over the carburetor during inspection or servicing procedures.

5   Once it is determined that the carburetor is in need of work or an overhaul, several alternatives should be considered. If you are going to attempt to overhaul the carburetor yourself, first obtain a good quality carburetor rebuild kit which will include all necessary gaskets, internal parts, instructions and a parts list. You will also need carburetor cleaning solvent and some means of blowing out the internal passages of the carburetor with air.

6   Due to the many configurations and variations of carburetors offered on the range of engines covered in this book, it is not feasible for us to do a step-by-step overhaul of each type. You will find a good, detailed instruction list with any quality carburetor overhaul kit and it will apply in a more specific manner to the carburetor you have. In addition, exploded views of typical Ranger/Bronco II carburetors are included here (see illustrations).

7   An alternative to rebuilding is to obtain a new or rebuilt carburetor. These are readily available from dealers and auto parts stores for all engines covered in this manual. Make sure the exchange carburetor is identical to the original. Often a tag is attached to the top plate of the carburetor which will aid in determining the exact type of carburetor you have. When obtaining a rebuilt carburetor or a rebuild kit, take time to ascertain that the kit or carburetor matches your application exactly. Seemingly insignificant differences can make a considerable difference in the overall performance of your engine.

8   If you choose to overhaul your own carburetor, allow enough time to disassemble the carburetor carefully, soak the necessary parts in the cleaning solvent (usually for at least one-half day or according to the instructions listed on the carburetor cleaner) and reassemble it, which will usually take you much longer than disassembly. When you are disassembling a carburetor, take care to match each part with the illustration in your carburetor kit and lay the parts out in order on a clean work surface to help you reassemble the carburetor. Overhauls by amateurs sometimes result in a vehicle which runs poorly or not at all. To avoid this use care and patience when disassembling your carburetor so you can reassemble it correctly.

9 Electronic fuel injection (EFI) — general information

On the EFI system an air-only throttle body assembly controls air flow to the engine through a single butterfly valve. The body is a single piece die casting made of aluminum. It has a single bore with an air bypass channel around the throttle plate. The valve assembly is an electo-mechanical device controlled by the EEC computer.

The air throttle body includes an adjustment screw to set the throttle plate at minimum idle air flow, a preset stop to locate the WOT position and a throttle position sensor.

The fuel supply manifold assembly is the component that delivers high pressure fuel to the fuel injectors. The assembly consists of two preformed tubes or stampings, one for fuel supply and one for fuel return. The manifold is equipped with a fuel pressure relief valve on the fuel supply tube.

Fuel pressure is governed by a regulator attached to the fuel supply manifold downstream of the fuel injectors. It regulates the fuel pressure supplied to the injectors. The regulator is a diaphragm operated relief valve in which one side of the diaphragm senses fuel pressure and the other side is subjected to intake manifold vacuum. Fuel in excess of that used by the engine is bypassed through the regulator and returned to the fuel tank.

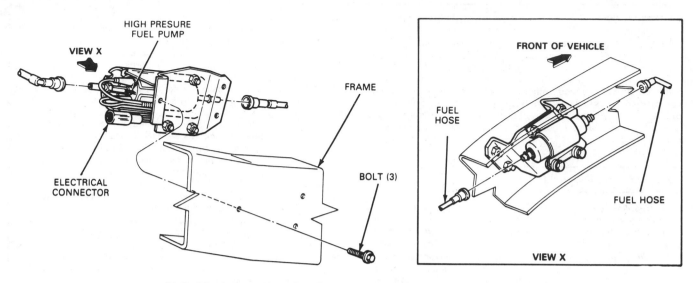

11.3 The frame-mounted high pressure fuel pump used on EFI engines

The system receives air from a two piece intake manifold (upper and lower) made of aluminum. Runner lengths are tuned to optimize engine torque and power output.

10 EFI fuel system — pressure relief

Caution: *Fuel supply lines on vehicles with fuel injection will remain pressurized for long periods after the engine is shut down. The pressure must be relieved before servicing the fuel system.*

2.3L engine
1   A valve is provided on the throttle body for relieving the pressure. The valve can be located by removing the air cleaner. Before opening the fuel system on EFI engines, relieve fuel pressure as follows:
2   Remove the fuel tank cap.
3   Disconnect the vacuum hose from the fuel pressure regulator, located on the engine fuel rail.
4   Using a hand vacuum pump, apply about 84.2 kPa (25 in. Hg) pressure to the pressure regulator. Fuel pressure will be released into the fuel tank through the fuel return hose.

2.9L engine
5   Disconnect the electrical connector to the fuel pump on the frame rail.
6   Disconnect the coil wire from the distributor cap and ground it to the engine.
7   Turn the engine over with the starter for a minimum of 20 seconds.

11 Electric fuel pump — removal and installation

Refer to illustrations 11.3 and 11.10

The EFI system consists of two fuel pumps. The high pressure pump is frame mounted and is accessible from under the vehicle. The low pressure pump is located in the fuel tank and requires removal of the tank for replacement. **Warning:** *Gasoline is extremely flammable, so extra precautions must be taken when working on any part of the fuel system. Do not smoke or allow open flames or bare light bulbs near the work area. Also, do not work in a garage if a natural gas appliance with a pilot light is present.*

High pressure pump
1   Relieve the fuel pressure.
2   Remove the push connectors on the fuel lines and the electrical connector.

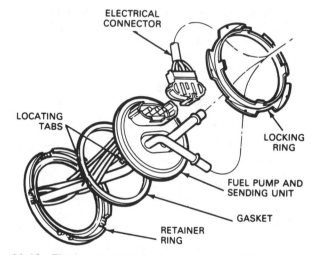

11.10 The low pressure fuel pump used on EFI engines is mounted inside the fuel tank

3   With the lines disconnected, remove the three screws attaching the high pressure fuel pump to the frame (see illustration).
4   Install the new pump in the reverse sequence.

Low pressure pump
5   Relieve the fuel pressure.
6   Remove the fuel from the fuel tank until the fuel level is below fuel sender mounting hole.
7   Disconnect the wiring connector from the fuel system sender.
8   Remove any dirt that has accumulated around the sender/pump so that it will not enter the tank or lines.
9   Remove the push connectors on the fuel lines and remove the fuel tank line at the sender.
10 Turn the locking ring counterclockwise with tool D84P-9275-A or its equivalent and remove the locking ring, sender/pump and sealer gasket (see illustration).
11 Clean the fuel sender mounting surface on the fuel tank.
12 Place a new sealing gasket in the groove of the fuel tank.
13 Install the new sender/pump into the fuel tank so that the tabs of the sender are positioned into slots of the fuel tank. Keep the gasket in place during installation.
14 Holding the fuel sender/pump in place, install and rotate the locking ring clockwise until the stop is against the retainer ring tab.
15 Connect the fuel sender wire and the fuel tank line.
16 Refill the tank and check for leaks and proper gauge operation.

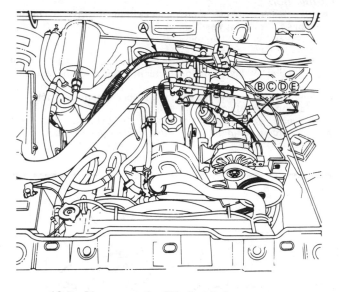

12.5 Disconnect the EFI electrical connectors

A) Throttle position sensor
B) Injector wiring harness
C) Knock sensor
D) Air charge temperature sensor
E) Engine coolant temperature sensor

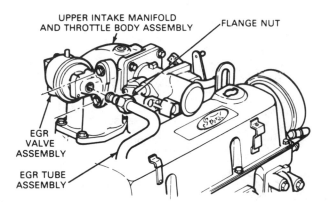

12.12 Disconnect the EGR tube from the EGR valve

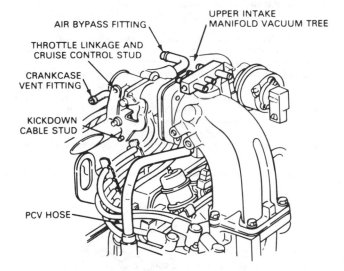

12.6 Disconnect the upper intake manifold vacuum fittings and the throttle linkage

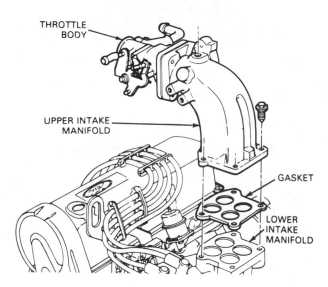

12.14 Disconnect and remove the throttle body and upper intake manifold from the lower intake manifold

12 Electronic fuel injection (2.3L engines) — removal and installation

Refer to illustrations 12.5, 12.6, 12.12, 12.14, 12.16, 12.18, 12.19, 12.23, 12.28, 12.29, 12.30, 12.32 and 12.35
Warning: *Gasoline is extremely flammable, so extra precautions must be taken when working on any part of the fuel system. Do not smoke or allow open flames or bare light bulbs near the work area. Also, do not work in a garage if a natural gas appliance with a pilot light is present.*

Removal
1　Drain the coolant from the radiator (Chapter 3).
2　Disconnect the negative cable at the battery.
3　Remove the fuel cap to relieve fuel tank pressure.
4　Release the pressure from fuel system at the fuel pressure relief valve using tool T80L-9974-A or equivalent.
5　Disconnect the electrical connectors at the throttle position sensor, injector harness, knock sensor, air charge temperature sensor and engine coolant temperature sensor (see illustration).

6　Disconnect the upper intake manifold vacuum fitting connections by disconnecting the following components (see illustration):
　　a)　Vacuum lines at the upper intake manifold vacuum tree. Label the hose locations with tape to aid reinstallation.
　　b)　Vacuum line to the EGR.
　　c)　Vacuum line to the fuel pressure regulator.
7　Remove the throttle linkage shield and disconnect throttle linkage, cruise control, and kickdown cable.
8　Unbolt the accelerator cable from the bracket and position it out of the way.
9　Disconnect the air intake hose, air bypass hose and crankcase vent hose.
10　Disconnect the PCV system by disconnecting the hose from the fitting on the underside of the upper intake manifold.
11　Loosen the hose clamp on the water bypass line at the lower intake manifold and disconnect the hose.
12　Disconnect the EGR tube from the EGR valve by removing the flange nut (see illustration).
13　Remove the four upper intake manifold retaining nuts.
14　Remove the upper intake manifold and air throttle body assembly (see illustration).
15　Disconnect the push connect fitting at the fuel supply manifold

fuel supply and fuel return lines.

16 Disconnect the fuel return line from the fuel supply manifold (see illustration).

17 Remove the engine oil dipstick bracket retaining bolt.

18 Disconnect the electrical connectors from all four fuel injectors and move the harness aside (see illustration).

19 Remove the two fuel supply manifold retaining bolts and carefully remove the fuel supply manifold and injectors (see illustration).

20 **Note:** *The injectors can be removed from the fuel supply manifold at this time by exerting a slight twisting/pulling motion.*

21 Remove the four bottom retaining bolts from the lower manifold.

22 Remove the four upper retaining bolts from the lower manifold.

23 Remove the lower intake manifold assembly (see illustration).

Installation

24 Clean and inspect the mounting faces of the fuel charging manifold assembly and cylinder head.

25 Clean and oil the manifold bolt threads.

26 Install a new gasket.

27 Position the lower manifold assembly to the head and install the engine lift bracket. Install the four upper manifold retaining bolts finger tight.

28 Install the four remaining manifold bolts and torque all bolts in sequence (see illustration).

29 Lubricate new O-rings with motor oil and install two on each injector (see illustration). **Caution:** *Do not use silicone grease, as it will clog the injector.*

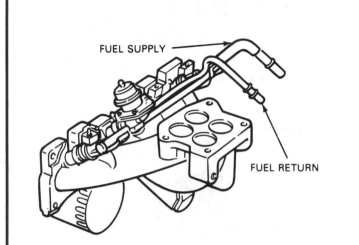

12.16   The larger line is for fuel supply and the smaller line is for fuel return

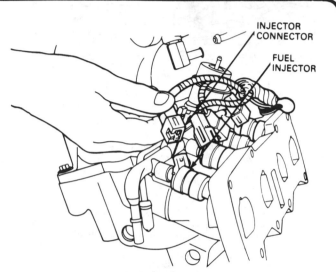

12.18   Unplug the electrical connectors from the fuel injectors

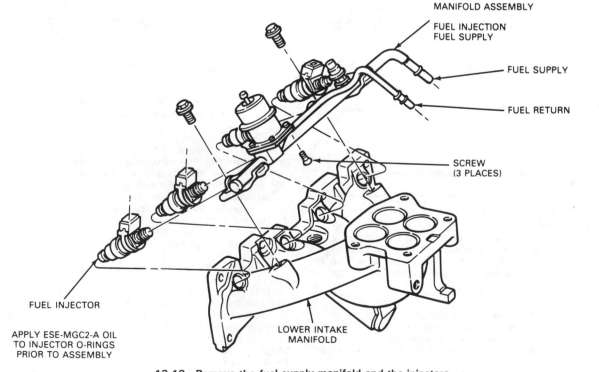

12.19   Remove the fuel supply manifold and the injectors

30 Using a twisting and pushing motion, install the injectors on the fuel supply manifold (see illustration).
31 Install the fuel supply manifold and injectors with the two retaining bolts and tighten.
32 Connect the four electrical connectors to the injectors.
33 Clean the gasket surfaces of the upper and lower intake manifolds.
34 Place a new gasket on the lower intake manifold assembly and place the upper manifold in position.
35 Install the four retaining bolts and tighten in sequence (see illustration).
36 Install the engine oil dipstick.
37 Connect the fuel supply and fuel return lines to the fuel supply manifold.
38 Connect the EGR tube to the EGR valve and tighten.
39 Connect and tighten the water bypass line.
40 Connect the PCV system hose to the fitting on the underside of the upper intake manifold.
41 Using teflon tape on the threads, install the upper intake manifold vacuum tree.
42 Connect the upper intake manifold vacuum connections.
43 Hold the accelerator cable bracket in position on the upper manifold and install the retaining bolt.

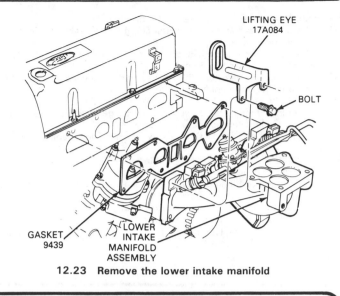

12.23 Remove the lower intake manifold

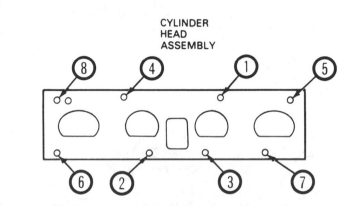

12.28 Intake manifold to head bolt tightening sequence

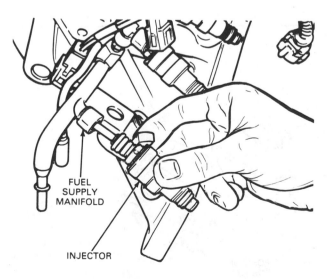

12.30 To install the injector grasp the injector body and push it on while twisting it

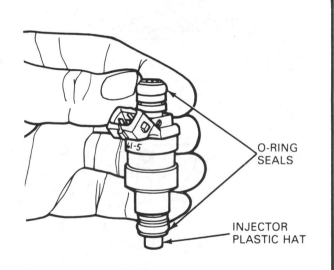

12.29 Coat the O-rings with engine oil before installing them on the injectors

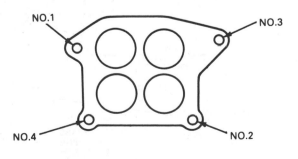

12.35 Tighten the upper to lower intake manifold bolts in sequence

44 Install the accelerator cable to the bracket.
45 Position a new gasket on the fuel charging assembly air throttle body mounting flange.
46 Install the air throttle body to the fuel charging assembly and install the two retaining nuts and bolts.
47 Connect the accelerator cable, cruise control, and kickdown cable and install the throttle linkage shield.
48 Connect the electrical connectors to the throttle position sensor, injector wiring harness, knock sensor, air charge temperature sensor and engine coolant temperature sensor.
49 Reconnect the air intake hose, air bypass hose and crankcase vent hose.
50 Connect the negative battery cable.
51 Refill the cooling system.
52 Replace fuel pressure relief cap, then build up fuel pressure. Without starting the engine, turn key back and forth at least six times between the ''on'' and ''off'' positions, leaving the key ''on'' for 15 seconds each time. Check the fuel system for leaks.
53 Start the engine and let it run until the engine temperature stabilizes and check for cooling leaks.
54 Verify correct engine idle.

13 Electronic fuel injection (2.9L engines) — removal and installation

Refer to illustrations 13.5, 13.13, 13.15, 13.17 and 13.18

Warning: *Gasoline is extremely flammable, so extra precautions must be taken when working on any part of the fuel system. Do not smoke or allow open flames or bare light bulbs near the work area. Also, do not work in a garage if a natural gas appliance with a pilot light is present.*

Removal

1 Disconnect the negative cable at the battery.
2 Remove the air inlet tube from the air cleaner to the throttle body.
3 Remove the fuel filler cap to relieve tank pressure.
4 Relieve the fuel system pressure as described in Section 10.
5 Disconnect the air bypass valve, throttle position sensor, EGR sensor and air charge temperature sensor electrical sensors (see illustration).
6 Remove the throttle linkage shield and disconnect the throttle cable.

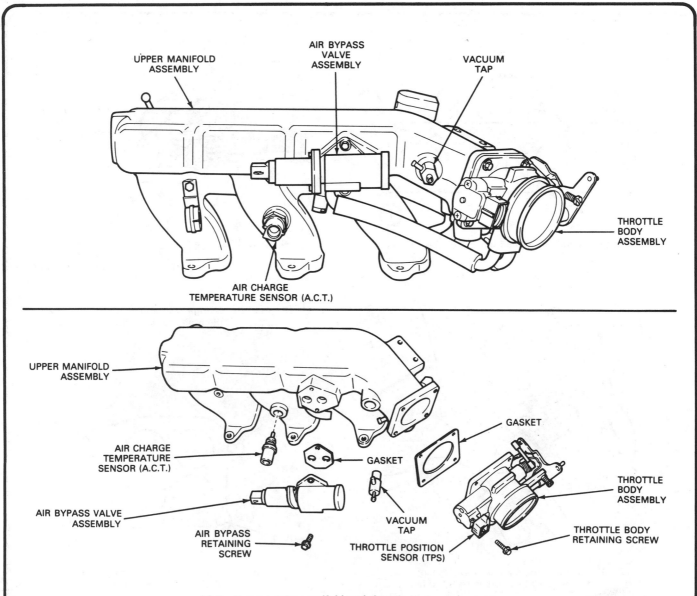

13.5 Upper intake manifold and throttle body components

7   Disconnect the front and rear vacuum fittings including the EGR valve and the vacuum line to the fuel pressure regulator.
8   Disconnect the PCV tube from under the throttle body.
9   Disconnect the PCV vacuum tube from under the the manifold.
10   Remove the canister purge line from the fitting near the power steering pump.
11   Disconnect the EGR tube from the EGR valve.
12   Remove the upper intake manifold retaining bolts and remove the upper intake manifold and throttle body as a unit.
13   Use spring lock coupling tool T81-19623-G or G1 to disconnect the crossover fuel line from the fuel supply manifold (see illustration).
14   Disconnect the fuel supply and return lines from the fuel supply manifold.
15   Remove the fuel supply manifold retaining bolts and lift the fuel supply manifold from the lower intake manifold (see illustration).
16   Remove the retainer clips to release the fuel injectors.

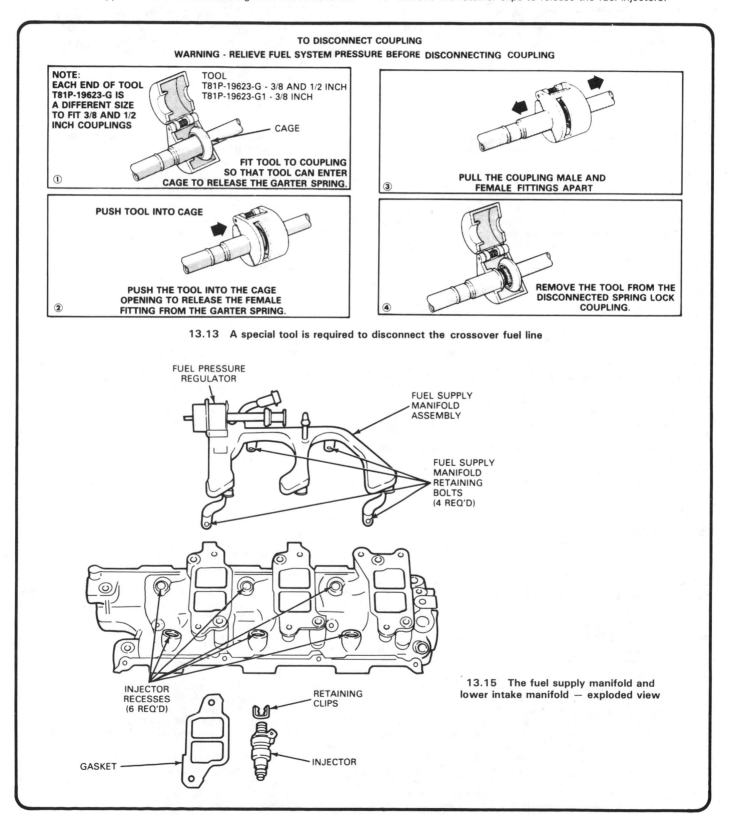

TO DISCONNECT COUPLING

WARNING - RELIEVE FUEL SYSTEM PRESSURE BEFORE DISCONNECTING COUPLING

NOTE:
EACH END OF TOOL T81P-19623-G IS A DIFFERENT SIZE TO FIT 3/8 AND 1/2 INCH COUPLINGS

TOOL
T81P-19623-G - 3/8 AND 1/2 INCH
T81P-19623-G1 - 3/8 INCH

CAGE

① FIT TOOL TO COUPLING SO THAT TOOL CAN ENTER CAGE TO RELEASE THE GARTER SPRING.

③ PULL THE COUPLING MALE AND FEMALE FITTINGS APART

PUSH TOOL INTO CAGE

② PUSH THE TOOL INTO THE CAGE OPENING TO RELEASE THE FEMALE FITTING FROM THE GARTER SPRING.

④ REMOVE THE TOOL FROM THE DISCONNECTED SPRING LOCK COUPLING.

13.13   A special tool is required to disconnect the crossover fuel line

FUEL PRESSURE REGULATOR

FUEL SUPPLY MANIFOLD ASSEMBLY

FUEL SUPPLY MANIFOLD RETAINING BOLTS (4 REQ'D)

INJECTOR RECESSES (6 REQ'D)

RETAINING CLIPS

GASKET

INJECTOR

13.15   The fuel supply manifold and lower intake manifold — exploded view

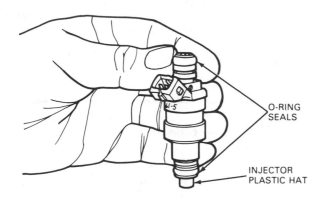

13.17   Check the condition of the plastic hat and lubricate the O-rings before installing the injectors

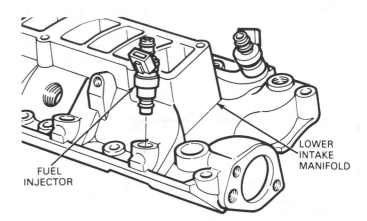

13.18   The injectors are installed in the lower intake manifold with a twisting motion

Installation

17   Lubricate new O-rings with engine oil and install two on each injector (see illustration). Check to make sure the plastic hat is in place and in good condition. If it is not there, check inside the lower intake manifold. **Caution:** *Do not use silicone grease on the injector O-rings, as it will clog the injector.*
18   Push the injectors into the lower intake manifold with a twisting motion (see illustration).
19   Replace the retainer clips.
20   Line up the injectors with the recesses in the fuel supply manifold and press the manifold down, lining up the bolt holes.
21   Install the fuel supply manifold retaining bolts.
22   Install the electrical connectors on the fuel injectors.
23   Carefully clean the mounting faces of the upper and lower intake manifolds.
24   Install a new gasket on the lower intake manifold and install the upper intake manifold on the lower manifold.
25   Align the EGR tube in the EGR valve.
26   Install and tighten the upper intake manifold bolts.
27   Tighten the EGR tube flare fitting.
28   Install the canister purge line.
29   Connect the PCV vacuum hose to the bottom of the upper manifold.
30   Connect the PCV closure hose to the throttle body.
31   Connect all the previously removed vacuum lines.
32   Connect the throttle cable and shield.
33   Connect all the previously removed electrical connectors.
34   Refill the cooling system.
35   Connect the battery ground cable.
36   Start the engine and check for fuel and coolant leaks.

14   Exhaust system — removal and installation

Refer to illustrations 14.9 and 14.19
Warning: *The vehicle's exhaust system generates very high temperatures and should be allowed to cool down completely before any of the components are touched. Be especially careful around the catalytic converter, where the highest temperatures are generated.*

Due to the high temperatures and exposed locations of the exhaust system components, rust and corrosion can freeze parts together. Liquid penetrating oils are available to help loosen frozen fasteners. However, in some cases it may be necessary to cut the pieces apart with a hacksaw or cutting torch. The latter method should be employed only by persons experienced in this work.

Inspect the exhaust pipes and mufflers for cracked joints, broken welds and corrosion damage that could result in a leaking exhaust system. **Note:** *It is normal for a certain amount of moisture and staining to be present around the muffler seams. The presence of soot, light surface rust or moisture does not indicate a faulty muffler.*

Muffler and outlet pipe assembly

1   Remove the two nuts and bolts at the muffler flange.
2   Apply a soap solution to the surface at the support insulators and rod ends of the metal supports.
3   Force the support rods out of the rubber insulators.
4   Remove the muffler and outlet pipe assembly by sliding it out over the axle housing.
5   Position the muffler and outlet assembly (by sliding it in over the axle housing) to the converter/inlet pipe assembly.
6   Apply soap solution to the metal support rods.
7   Force the metal support rods through the rubber insulators.
8   Install the nuts and bolts to the muffler flange.

Convertor and/or pipe assembly

4-cylinder engines

9   Remove the nuts and bolts attaching the converter pipe assembly to the muffler and outlet pipe (see illustration).
10   Remove the nuts attaching the converter pipe assembly to the exhaust manifold.
11   Loosen the clamp holding the manifold brace to the exhaust pipe.
12   Remove the converter pipe assembly.
13   Install the converter onto the exhaust manifold studs and loosely secure it in place.
14   Install a new gasket between the converter pipe and muffler and outlet pipe assembly and loosely secure the flanges, gasket and steady rest bracket with two bolts and nuts.
15   Loosely position the clamp on the converter inlet pipe over the manifold brace.
16   Alternately tighten the exhaust manifold connection nuts until secure.
17   Tighten the manifold brace clamp.
18   Tighten the converter to muffler flange.

V6 engine

19   Remove the two nuts and bolts attaching the converter pipe assembly to the muffler and outlet pipe (see illustration). On vehicles equipped with managed thermactor air, remove the clamp securing the MTA tube to the catalytic converter.
20   Remove the screw and washer assembly supporting the MTA tube to inlet pipe and separate the MTA tube from the connector.
21   Disconnect the hose from top of the MTA tube and check valve.
22   Remove the MTA tube and check valve by rotating the assembly as it is lowered.
23   Loosen and remove the nuts and bolts connecting the converter to the ''Y'' pipe assembly, swing the muffler and outlet pipe to the rear and then remove the converter and gaskets.
24   Loosen and remove the exhaust manifold stud nuts.
25   Move the ''Y'' pipe rearward and rotate it to clear the studs, then remove.
26   Install the ''Y'' pipe onto the exhaust manifold studs and loosely secure it in place with the retaining nuts.
27   Install a new gasket between the converter and the muffler/outlet pipe assemblies and secure the flange gasket and steady rest bracket.
28   Install a new gasket between the converter and ''Y'' pipe and

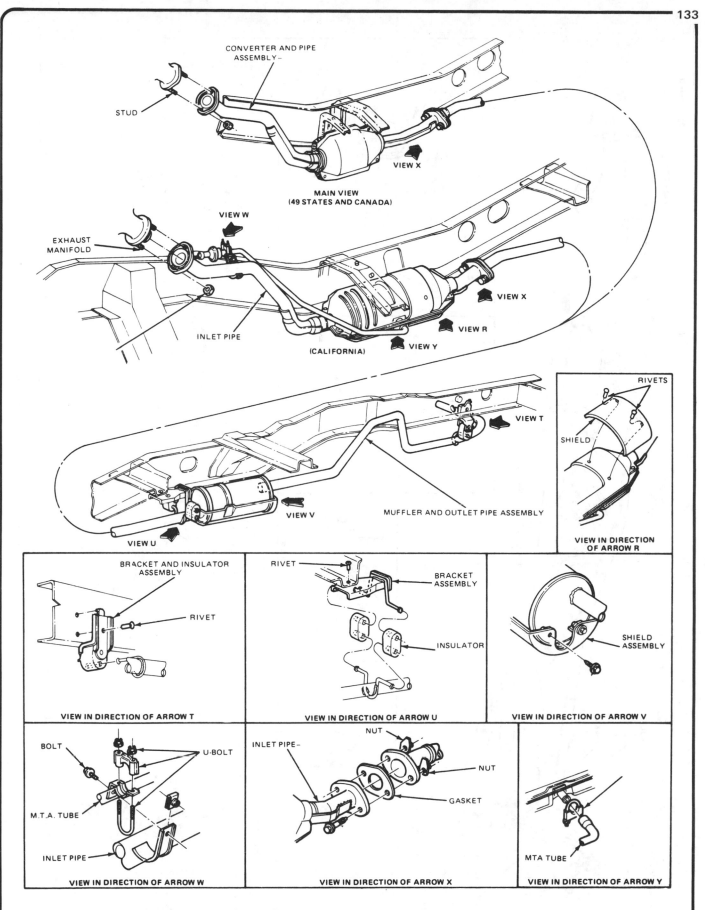

CONVERTER AND PIPE
ASSEMBLY –

STUD

VIEW X

**MAIN VIEW
(49 STATES AND CANADA)**

VIEW W

EXHAUST
MANIFOLD

VIEW X

VIEW R

INLET PIPE

VIEW Y

(CALIFORNIA)

VIEW T

RIVETS

SHIELD

**VIEW IN DIRECTION
OF ARROW R**

VIEW V

MUFFLER AND OUTLET PIPE ASSEMBLY

VIEW U

BRACKET AND INSULATOR
ASSEMBLY

RIVET

VIEW IN DIRECTION OF ARROW T

RIVET

BRACKET
ASSEMBLY

INSULATOR

VIEW IN DIRECTION OF ARROW U

SHIELD
ASSEMBLY

VIEW IN DIRECTION OF ARROW V

BOLT

U-BOLT

M.T.A. TUBE

INLET PIPE

VIEW IN DIRECTION OF ARROW W

NUT

INLET PIPE–

NUT

GASKET

VIEW IN DIRECTION OF ARROW X

MTA TUBE

VIEW IN DIRECTION OF ARROW Y

14.9 Exhaust system used with 4-cylinder engines

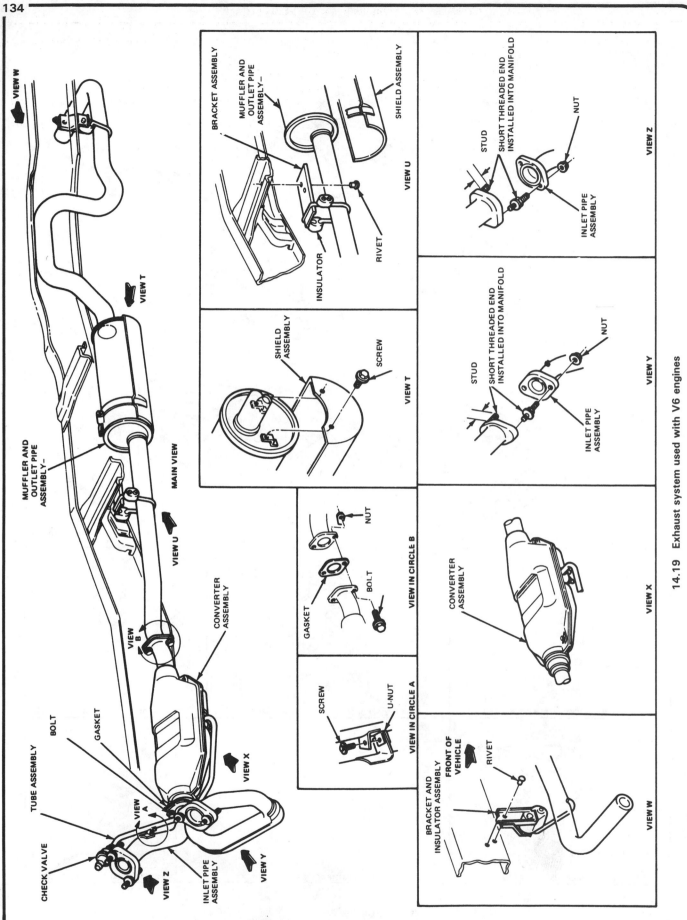

14.19 Exhaust system used with V6 engines

secure with the attaching bolts.
29 Tighten the exhaust manifold connections.
30 Install the MTA tube and check valve.
31 Tighten the MTA tube to the catalytic converter clamp.
32 Attach the MTA tube to the "Y" pipe and tighten.
33 Attach and tighten the rubber hose to the check valve.

Hanger brackets

34 Remove the muffler outlet pipe assembly from the brackets.
35 Remove the rivets which hold the bracket to the frame. Reinstall
by positioning the brackets on the frame and attaching the nuts and
bolts.

Muffler grass shield

36 Remove the band strap from the worm gear.
37 Remove the two screws and washer assembly holding the shield
to the rear of the muffler.
38 Position the shield under the muffler body and secure the screws
to the rear of muffler.
39 Start the band strap in the worm gear and tighten.

Chapter 5 Engine electrical systems

Contents

Specifications

Alternator brush length
  new . . . . 0.48 in
  minimum . . . . 0.25 in
Starter brush length
  new . . . . 0.50 in
  minimum . . . . 0.25 in

Torque specifications	Ft-lbs
Alternator adjustment bolt	24 to 40
Alternator pivot bolt	40 to 50
Distributor clamp bolt	17 to 25
Starter housing bolts	15 to 20
Solenoid mounting screws	5 to 7
TFI rotor attaching screws	2.1 to 2.9
TFI distributor cap adapter attaching screws	2.1 to 2.9
TFI distributor rotor to mounting plate	2.1 to 2.9

Torque specifications	In-lbs
Alternator brush holder to housing	17 to 25
Diaphragm assembly to distributor base	15 minimum
Distributor cap to base	18 to 23
Electrical leads to alternator	25 to 35
Relay-to-starter cable	70 to 100
Stator assembly to distributor	15 minimum
TFI module mounting screws	
1983-1984 2.8L	9 to 16
1985-1986	15 to 35
Starter through bolts	55 to 75

1 Ignition system — general information and precautions

All models are fitted with an electronic (breakerless) type distributor.

Mechanically, the system is similar to the contact breaker type with the exception that the distributor cam and contact breaker are replaced by an armature and magnetic pickup unit. The coil primary circuit is controlled by an amplifier module.

When the ignition is switched on, the ignition primary circuit is energized. When the distributor armature "teeth" or "spokes" approach the magnetic coil assembly, a voltage is induced which signals the amplifier to turn off the coil primary current. A timing circuit in the amplifier module turns the coil current back on after the coil field has collapsed.

When on, current flows from the battery through the ignition switch, the coil primary winding, the amplifier module and then to ground. When the current is off, the magnetic field in the ignition coil collapses, inducing a high voltage in the coil secondary winding. This is conducted to the distributor where the rotor directs it to the appropriate spark plug. This process is repeated for each power stoke of the engine.

The distributor is fitted with devices to control the actual point of ignition according to the engine speed and load. As the engine speed increases two weights move outwards and alter the position of the armature in relation to the distributor shaft to advance the spark. As engine load increases (for example when climbing hills or accelerating), a reduction in intake manifold depression causes the base plate assembly to move slightly in the opposite direction (clockwise) under the action of the spring in the vacuum unit, thus retarding the spark and counteracting the centrifugal advance. Under light loading conditions (for example at moderate steady speeds), the comparatively high intake manifold depression on the vacuum advance diaphragm causes the base plate assembly to move in a counterclockwise direction to give a larger amount of spark advance.

Checking the ignition timing is carried out as with conventional ignitions. However, there is also a monolithic timing system with a timing receptacle for use with an electronic probe. This latter system can only be used with special electronic equipment, and checks using it are beyond the scope of this manual.

Two different ignition modules are used, depending on the engine calibration. One module is the standard Duraspark module and the other is a Universal Ignition Module (UIM). The UIM is capable of providing spark timing retard through signals received from the MCU unit.

Beginning in 1985 all all-models except the 2.0L engine come equipped with a Thick Film Integrated (TFI) ignition system which is part of the EEC-IV (Electronic Engine Control System IV). The ignition system uses a universal distributor that has no centrifugal or vacuum advance. The distributor has a die cast base which incorporates an integrally mounted TFI-IV ignition module, a Hall Effect vane switch stator assembly, and a rod for octane adjustment. No distributor calibration is required and initial timing is not a normal adjustment.

The TFI-IV module features a *push start* mode. This allows push starting of the vehicle should it be necessary (manual transmission only).

Fault finding on the breakerless ignition system which cannot be rectified by substitution of parts or cleaning/tightening connectors, etc. should be entrusted to a Ford dealer, since special test procedures and equipment are required.

2 Battery — removal and installation

1 The battery is located at the front of the engine compartment. It is held in place by a hold-down clamp at the top of the battery case.

2 **Warning:** *Hydrogen gas is produced by the battery, so keep open flames and lighted cigarettes away from it at all times.*

3 Always keep the battery in an upright position. Spilled electrolyte should be rinsed off immediately with large quantities of water. Always wear eye protection when working around a battery.

4 Always disconnect the negative battery cable first, followed by the positive cable.

5 After the cables are disconnected from the battery, remove the hold down clamp.

6 Carefully lift the battery out of the engine compartment.

7 Installation is the reverse of removal. The cable clamps should be

tight, but do not overtighten them as damage to the battery case could occur. The battery posts and cable ends should be cleaned prior to connection (see Chapter 1).

3 Battery — emergency jump starting

Refer to the Booster battery (jump) starting procedure at the front of this manual.

4 Battery cables — checking and replacement

1 Periodically inspect the entire length of each battery cable for damage, cracked or burned insulation and corrosion. Poor battery cable connections can cause starting problems and decreased engine performance.

2 Check the cable to terminal connections at the ends of the cables for cracks, loose wire strands and corrosion. The presence of white or green fluffy deposits under the insulation at the cable terminal connection is a sign the cable is corroded and should be replaced. Check the terminals for distortion, missing mounting bolts or nuts and corrosion.

3 If only the positive cable is to be replaced, be sure to disconnect the negative cable from the battery first.

4 Disconnect and remove the cable from the vehicle. Make sure the replacement cable is the same length and diameter.

5 Clean the threads of the starter, solenoid or ground connection with a wire brush to remove rust and corrosion. Apply a light coat of petroleum jelly to the threads to ease installation and prevent future corrosion. Inspect the connections frequently to make sure they are clean and tight.

6 Attach the cable to the starter, solenoid or ground connection and tighten the mounting nut or bolt securely.

7 Before connecting the new cable to the battery, make sure it reaches the terminal without having to be stretched.

8 Connect the positive cable first, followed by the negative cable. Tighten the nuts and apply a thin coat of petroleum jelly to the terminal and cable connection.

5 Dura-Spark II distributor — removal and installation

Refer to illustrations 5.3 and 5.6

Removal

1 Disconnect the spring clips retaining the distributor cap to the adapter and position the cap and wires to one side.

2 Disconnect and plug the diaphragm assembly hose(s), if so equipped.

3 Disconnect the distributor connector from the wiring harness (see illustration).

4 Rotate the engine to align the stator assembly pole and the armature pole.

5 Scribe marks on the distributor body and engine to indicate the position of the distributor in the engine and the position of the rotor in the distributor.

6 Remove the distributor hold-down bolt and clamp (see illustration).

7 Remove the distributor from the engine. **Caution:** *The engine should not be rotated while the distributor is out of the engine. If the engine is rotated refer to the installation procedure below.*

Installation if engine was rotated while distributor was removed

8 Rotate the engine until the number one piston is on the compression stroke (refer to Chapter 1).

9 Align the timing marks for the correct initial timing, determined by referring to the Emissions Control Information label in the engine compartment.

10 Install the distributor in the engine with the rotor pointing at the

number one cylinder terminal position on the cap and with the armature and stator assembly poles aligned.

11 Make sure the oil pump intermediate shaft properly engages the distributor shaft.

12 If the distributor will not seat properly in the engine it may be necessary to crank the engine after the distributor gear is partially engaged in order to properly mesh the distributor shaft with the oil pump intermediate shaft.

13 If it was necessary to crank the engine, again rotate the engine until the number one piston is on the compression stroke and align the timing marks for correct initial timing.

14 Rotate the distributor in the engine to align the armature and stator assembly poles and verify that the rotor is pointing at the number one cylinder cap terminal.

15 Install the distributor hold-down clamp and bolt, but do not tighten the bolt.

Installation if engine was not rotated while distributor was removed and original distributor is being reinstalled

16 Install the distributor in the engine with the rotor and distributor aligned with the previously scribed marks. The armature and stator assembly poles should also align when the distributor is fully seated in the engine.

17 If the distributor will not properly seat in the engine, crank the engine until the distributor shaft and oil pump intermediate shaft are properly meshed and the distributor is properly seated.

18 Install the distributor hold-down clamp and bolt, but do not tighten the bolt.

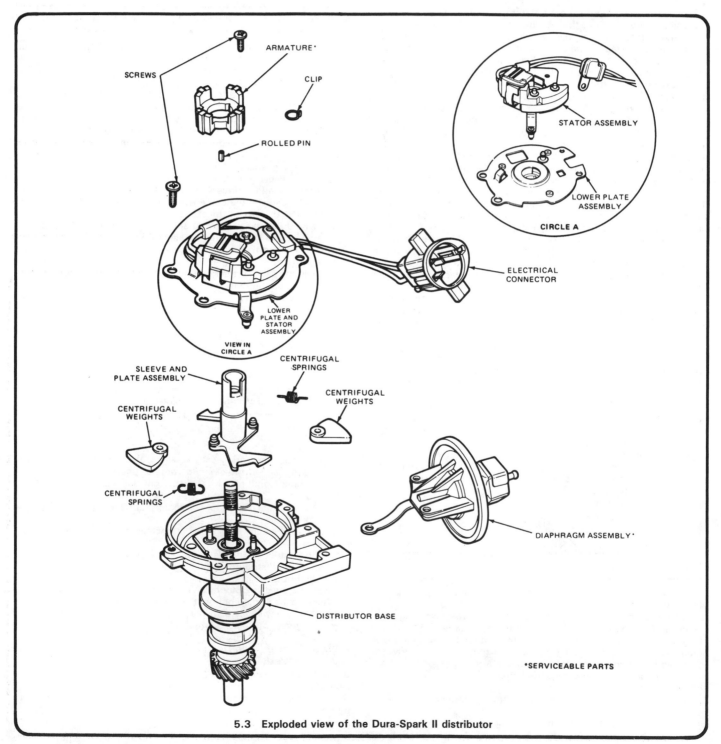

5.3 Exploded view of the Dura-Spark II distributor

Installation if the engine was not rotated while the distributor was removed and a new distributor is being installed

19 Install the distributor in the engine with the rotor aligned with the previously scribed mark on the block/manifold.
20 If necessary, crank the engine to seat the distributor.
21 Rotate the engine until the timing marks for the correct initial timing (determined by referring to the Emissions Control Information label in

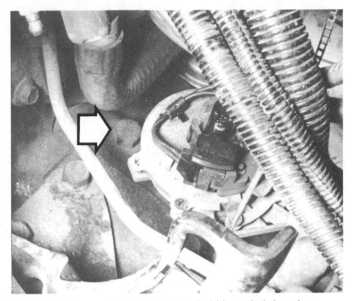

5.6 Arrow shows distributor holddown bolt location (2.3L)

the engine compartment) are aligned and the rotor is pointing at the number one cylinder cap terminal.
22 Rotate the distributor to align the armature and stator assembly poles.
23 Install the distributor hold-down clamp and bolt, but do not tighten the bolt.

Installation (all)

24 If, in Steps 10, 14, 16, or 22 above, the armature and stator assembly poles cannot be aligned by rotating the distributor, pull the distributor out of the engine enough to disengage the distributor gear and rotate the distributor shaft to engage a different gear tooth, then reinstall the distributor and repeat the steps in the appropriate installation procedure as necessary.
25 Connect the distributor connector to the wiring harness.
26 Install the distributor cap and ignition wires, making sure that the wires are securely connected to the distributor cap and spark plugs.
27 Set the initial timing according to the Emissions Control Information label located in the engine compartment.
28 Tighten the distributor hold-down bolt to the specified torque.
29 Recheck the initial timing and adjust as necessary.
30 Connect the diaphragm assembly hose(s), if so equipped.

---

6 Stator — removal and installation (2.0L engine)

Refer to illustration 6.4

Removal

1 Disconnect the cable from the negative battery terminal.
2 Disconnect the spring clips retaining the distributor cap and place the cap and wires aside.
3 Remove the rotor from the distributor shaft.
4 Disconnect the distributor connector from the wiring harness (see illustration).

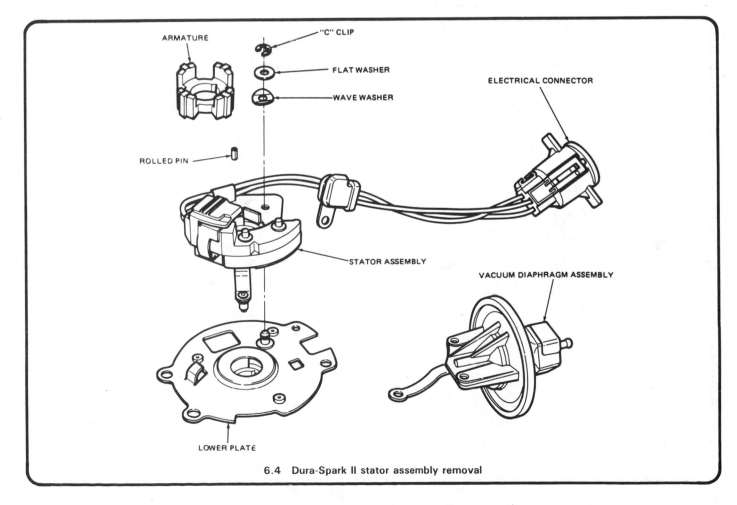

6.4 Dura-Spark II stator assembly removal

5   Using a small gear puller or two screwdrivers as levers, remove the armature.

6   Remove the two screws retaining the lower plate assembly and stator assembly to the distributor base, noting that there are two different size screws employed.

7   Remove the lower plate assembly and stator assembly from the distributor.

8   Remove the E-clip, flat washer and wave washer securing the stator assembly to the lower plate assembly, then separate the stator assembly from the lower plate assembly. Note the installation of the wave washer.

Installation

9   Before installing the stator remove any accumulated dirt or grease from parts that are to be reused.

10   Place the stator assembly on the lower plate assembly and install the wave washer (outer edges up), flat washer and E-clip.

11   Install the stator assembly/lower plate assembly on the distributor base, making sure to engage the pin on the stator assembly in the diaphragm rod.

12   Attach the lower plate assembly and stator assembly to the distributor base, making sure to install the different size screws in their proper locations.

13   When installing the armature, note that there are two notches in it. Install the armature on the sleeve and plate assembly employing the unused notch and a new roll pin.

14   Connect the distributor connector to the wiring harness.

15   Reinstall the rotor and distributor cap, making sure that the ignition wires are securely connected to the cap and spark plugs.

16   Connect the cable to the negative battery terminal.

17   Check the initial timing (refer to Chapter 1).

7   EEC IV electronic ignition system — general information

Refer to illustration 7.1

The EEC IV Thick Film Integrated (TFI) ignition system (see illustration) features a universal distributor design which is driven from the camshaft gear and uses no centrifugal or vacuum advance. The distributor is mounted on the engine in a die cast base incorporating an integrally mounted TFI IV ignition module. No distributor calibration is required and initial timing is not a normal adjustment. The high voltage distribution is accomplished through a conventional rotor, cap and ignition wires. These conventional distributor components can be cleaned, inspected and serviced in the same manner as the distributors described in other Sections of this Chapter.

8   EEC IV distributor and TFI module — removal and installation

Refer to illustrations 8.3a, 8.3b and 8.14

Distributor assembly

Note: *Service procedures other than those applied to conventional distributors must be done by a professional service department. However, it may be financially advantageous to remove and install the distributor assembly yourself.*

1   Disconnect the primary wiring connector from the distributor.

2   Using a screwdriver, remove the distributor cap and position it and the attached wires aside so they won't interfere with removal of the distributor.

3   Detach the distributor rotor by removing the two hold-down screws. Note the position of the polarizing square and circle in the shaft

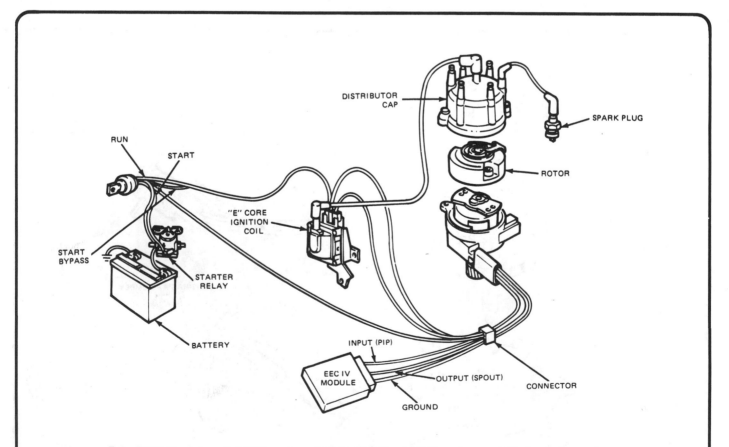

7.1   Thick film Integrated (TFI) system used on all 2.8L and 2.9L and some 2.3L 4-cylinder engines

plate. This should be used as a reference during reinstallation. Some engines may be equipped with a security type distributor hold-down bolt (see illustration). If this is the case, a special tool is required (Ford tool no. T82L-12270-A). Other distributors use a conventional hold-down bolt and clamp (see illustration). Remove the hold-down bolt and separate the distributor from the engine.

4 Before installing the distributor, rotate the shaft by hand to make sure it turns freely.

5 Position the polarizing square and circle in the shaft plate in the same location as they were when the distributor was removed. Install the distributor in the engine maintaining the same orientation of the TFI-IV module to the engine as when removed.

6 Install the distributor hold-down bolt and clamp and tighten the bolt so that the distributor can barely be rotated.

7 Install the distributor rotor.

8 Reconnect the vehicle wiring harness connector to the distributor and install the distributor cap with the attached wires. Check all spark plug wires to ensure that they are completely seated in the cap and on the plugs.

9 Check the ignition timing with a timing light (Chapter 1) and adjust it if necessary. Refer to the vehicle Emission Control Information label for specific timing information for your vehicle.

10 With the initial timing verified, tighten the distributor hold-down bolt to specification.

TFI IV ignition module

11 To remove the ignition module, first detach the distributor cap and position it and the attached wires aside.

12 Remove the TFI harness connector.

13 Remove the distributor from the engine.

14 Place the distributor on a workbench and remove the two TFI module mounting screws (see illustration).

15 Slide the right side of the module down the distributor mounting flange and then back up the flange. Slide the left side of the module down the distributor mounting flange and then back up the flange. Continue alternating side-to-side until the module terminals are disengaged from the connector in the distributor base. With the terminals completely disengaged, slide the module down and pull it gently away from the mounting surface. **Caution:** *Do not attempt to lift the module from the mounting surface prior to moving the entire TFI module toward the distributor flange, as you will break the pins at the distributor module connector.*

16 Place the TFI module on the distributor base mounting flange and carefully position it on the distributor connector pins.

17 Install the two TFI module mounting screws.

18 Install the distributor in the engine.

19 Install the distributor cap and tighten the cap mounting screws.

20 Install the TFI harness connector.

21 Using a timing light, verify the engine timing according to the specific recommendations on the vehicle Emission Control Information label.

9 Starting system — general information

The starting system consists of an electric starter motor with an integral positive engagement drive, the battery, a starter switch, a neutral start switch (automatic transmission equipped vehicles only), a clutch interlock switch (manual transmissions), a starter solenoid and wiring looms connecting these components.

When the ignition switch is turned to the Start position, the starter solenoid is energized through the starter control circuit. The solenoid then connects battery voltage to the starter motor.

Vehicles with automatic transmissions have a neutral start switch in the starter control circuit which prevents operation of the starter if the selector lever is not in the N or P position.

Vehicles with manual transmissions use a clutch interlock switch which prevents operation of the starter unless the clutch pedal is depressed.

When the starter is energized by the battery, current flows to the grounded field coil and operates the magnetic switch. This switch drives the starter drive plunger forward to engage the flywheel ring gear. When the drive plunger reaches full travel, the field coil grounding contacts open and the starter motor contacts engage, turning the starter. A

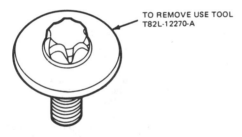

TO REMOVE USE TOOL
T82L-12270-A

8.3a   Security-type hold down clamp bolt requires a special tool to remove distributor

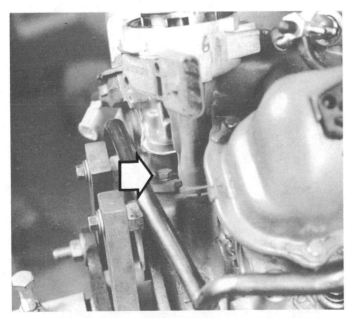

8.3b   Remove the distributor hold down bolt and clamp

8.14   Note inset TFI module attachment screws (arrows)

holding coil is used to keep the starter drive shoe in the fully seated position while the starter is turning the engine.

When the battery voltage is released from the starter, a retracting spring withdraws the starter drive pinion from the flywheel and the motor contact is broken.

10   Starter motor — testing in vehicle

1   If the starter motor does not turn when the switch is operated, make sure that the shift lever is in Neutral or Park (automatic transmission) or that the clutch pedal is depressed (manual transmission).
2   Make sure that the battery is charged and that all cables, both at the battery and starter solenoid terminals, are secure.
3   If the motor spins but the engine is not cranked, the overrunning clutch in the starter motor is slipping and the starter motor must be removed from the engine and disassembled.
4   If, when the switch is actuated, the starter motor does not operate at all but the solenoid clicks (with the battery fully charged), then the problem is in the main solenoid contacts or the starter motor itself.
5   If the solenoid plunger cannot be heard when the switch is actuated, the solenoid is defective or the solenoid circuit is open.
6   To check the solenoid, connect a jumper lead between the battery positive terminal and the terminal on the solenoid. If the starter motor now operates, the solenoid is OK and the problem is in the ignition or neutral start switches or in the wiring.
7   If the starter motor still does not operate, remove the starter for disassembly, testing and repair.
8   If the starter motor cranks the engine at an abnormally slow speed, first make sure that the battery is charged and that all terminal connections are tight.
9   Start the engine and run it until normal operating temperature is reached, then stop the engine and disconnect the coil wire from the distributor cap. Ground the coil wire to the engine.
10 Connect a voltmeter positive lead to the starter motor terminal of the solenoid and then connect the negative lead to ground.
11 Actuate the ignition switch and take the voltmeter readings as soon as a steady figure is indicated. Do not allow the starter motor to turn for more than 30 seconds at a time. A reading of 9-volts or more, with the starter motor turning at normal cranking speed, is normal. If the reading is 9-volts or more but the cranking speed is slow, the motor is faulty. If the reading is less than 9-volts and the cranking speed is slow, the solenoid contacts are probably burned.

11   Starter motor — removal and installation

1   Disconnect the negative cable from the battery.
2   Disconnect the cable connecting the starter solenoid to the starter motor.
3   Remove the retaining bolts securing the starter to the bellhousing.
4   Pull the starter out of the bellhousing and lower it from the vehicle.
5   Installation is the reverse of removal. When inserting the starter into its opening of the bellhousing, make sure it fits squarely and the mating faces are flush. Tighten the retaining bolts to the proper torque.

12   Starter brushes — replacement

Note: *The starter must be removed from the vehicle before the brushes can be replaced. Before attempting to replace the brushes in the starter, make sure the problem you are having is related to the brushes. Often, loose connections, poor battery condition or wiring problems are a more likely cause of no start or poor starting conditions. Check on the availability of internal replacement parts before proceeding.*
1   Remove the starter from the vehicle (Section 14).
2   Remove the two through bolts from the starter frame.
3   Pull the brush endplate, along with the brush springs and brushes, from the case.
4   Remove the ground brush retaining screws from the frame. Remove the brushes from the frame.

5   Cut the insulated brush leads from the field coils as close to the field connection point as possible.
6   Inspect the plastic brush holder for any signs of cracks or broken mounting pads. If these conditions exist, replace the plastic brush holder.
7   Place the new insulated field brush lead onto the field coil connection.
8   Crimp the clip provided with the brushes to hold the brush lead to the connection.
9   Using a low heat soldering gun (300 watts), solder the lead, the clip and the connection together using rosin core solder.
10 Install the ground brush leads to the frame with the retaining screws.
11 Install the brush holder and insert the brushes into the holder.
12 Install the brush springs. Make sure that the positive brush leads are positioned in their respective slots in the brush holder to prevent any chance of grounding the brushes.
13 Install the brush endplate. Make sure the endplate insulator is positioned correctly on the endplate.
14 Install the through bolts in the starter frame and tighten to the specified torque.
15 A battery can be used to check the starter by connecting heavy cables, such as jumper cables, to the positive and negative battery posts.
16 Connect the ground lead to the starter.
17 Secure the starter in a vise or other similar clamping device.
18 Momentarily contact the starter connection with the positive cable from the battery.
19 The starter should spin and the solenoid drive should engage the gear in a forward position when this connection is completed.
20 If the starter operates correctly, install the starter in the vehicle as described in the previous Section.

13   Starter solenoid — removal and installation

Refer to illustrations 13.1 and 13.5
1   The starter solenoid is located in the engine compartment on the fender well inside a black plastic box (see illustration).
2   Disconnect the negative cable from the battery, followed by the positive cable.
3   Disconnect the positive battery cable and feed cable from the terminal on the starter solenoid. Mark them to prevent mix-ups during installation.

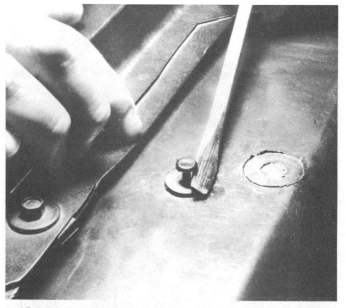

13.1   Pry up on the tab retaining the black box top to gain access to the solenoid on V6 Bronco II then loosen the attaching bolt to remove the unit

4   Disconnect the starter feed wire from the opposite terminal on the starter solenoid. Mark the feed wire as above.
5   Disconnect the starter solenoid triggering wire from the post on the solenoid (see illustration).
6   Remove the starter solenoid.
7   Before installing the new or replacement solenoid, use a wire brush to carefully clean the mounting surface on the fender well for better grounding.
8   Attach the starter solenoid to the fender. **Caution:** *Use care when tightening these bolts as they are self-threading and can easily be stripped.*
9   Reconnect all wires to their original positions.

14   Charging system — general information

The charging system consists of the alternator, voltage regulator and battery. These components work together to supply electrical power

13.5   Remove the triggering wire (arrow) from the solenoid

for the ignition, lights, radio, etc.
    The alternator is turned by a drivebelt at the front of the engine. When the engine is operating, voltage is generated by the internal components of the alternator to be sent to the battery for storage.
    The purpose of the voltage regulator is to limit the alternator voltage to a preset value. This prevents power surges, circuit overloads, etc., during peak voltage output.
    The charging system does not ordinarily require periodic maintenance. The drivebelts, electrical wiring and connections should, however, be inspected at the intervals suggested in Chapter 1.
    Take extreme care when making circuit connections to a vehicle equipped with an alternator and note the following:
    When making connections to the alternator from a battery, always match correct polarity. Before using electric arc welding equipment to repair any part of the vehicle, disconnect the wires from the alternator and the battery terminals. Never start the engine with a battery charger connected. Always disconnect both battery leads before using a battery charger.

15   Charging system — check

Refer to illustrations 15.2 and 15.3
1   If a malfunction occurs in the charging circuit, do not immediately assume that the alternator is causing the problem. First check the following items:
    a)   The battery cables where they connect to the battery. Make sure the connections are clean and tight.
    b)   The battery electrolyte specific gravity. If it is low, charge the battery.
    c)   Check the external alternator wiring and connections.
    d)   Check the drivebelt condition and tension (see Chapter 1).
    e)   Check the alternator mounting bolts for tightness.
    f)   Run the engine and check the alternator for abnormal noise.
2   Using a voltmeter, check the battery voltage with the engine off. It should be approximately 12-volts (see illustration).
3   Start the engine and check the battery voltage again. It should now be approximately 14 to 15-volts (see illustration).
4   Due to the special equipment necessary to test or service the alternator, is recommended that if a fault is suspected the vehicle be taken to a dealer or a shop with the proper equipment. Because of this the home mechanic should limit maintenance to checking connections and the inspection and replacement of the brushes.
5   The ammeter (ALT) gauge or alternator warning lamp on the instrument panel indicates charge or discharge — current passing into or

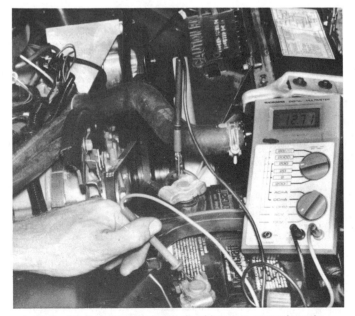

15.2   Static battery voltage should test at approximately 12 volts

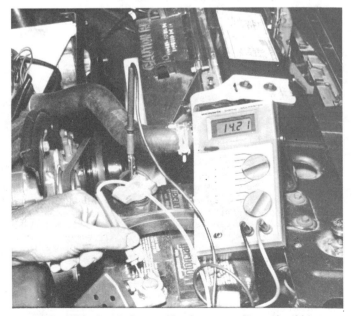

15.3   With the engine running battery voltage should be between 14 and 15 volts

out of the battery. With the electrical equipment switched on and the engine idling the gauge needle may show a discharge condition. At fast idle or at normal driving speeds the needle should stay on the charge side of the gauge, with the charged state of the battery determining just how far over.

6   If the gauge does not show a change or (if equipped) the alternator lamp remains on, there is a fault in the system. Before inspecting the brushes or replacing the alternator, the battery condition, belt tension and electrical cable connections should be checked.

16 Alternator — removal and installation

1   Disconnect the negative battery cable.
2   Carefully note the terminal connections at the rear or side of the alternator and disconnect them. Most connections will have a retaining nut and washer, however some connections may have a plastic snap-fit connector with a retaining clip. If a terminal is covered by a slip-on plastic cover, be careful when pulling the cover back so as not to damage the terminal or connector.
3   Loosen the alternator adjustment arm bolt.
4   Loosen the alternator pivot bolt.
5   Pivot the alternator to allow the drivebelt to be removed from the pulleys.
6   Remove the belt from the pulley.
7   Remove the adjustment arm bolt and pivot the arm out of the way.
8   Remove the pivot bolt and spacer and carefully lift the alternator up and out of the engine compartment. Be careful not to drop or jar the alternator as it can be damaged. **Note:** *If purchasing a new or rebuilt alternator, take the original one with you to the dealer or parts store so the two can be compared side by side.*
9   Installation is the reverse of removal. Be careful when connecting all terminals at the rear or side of the alternator. Make sure they are clean and tight and that all terminal ends are tight on the wires. If you find any loose terminal ends, make sure you install new ones, as any arcing or shorting at the wires or terminals can damage the alternator.

17 Alternator brushes — replacement

Refer to illustrations 17.2, 17.3a, 17.3b, 17.4, 17.5a, 17.5b, 17.7a, 17.7b, 17.7 c and 17.18
Note: *Internal replacement parts for alternators may not be readily available in your area. Check into availability before proceeding.*

Rear terminal alternator
1   Remove the alternator as described in Section 19.
2   Scribe a line across the length of the alternator housing to ensure correct reassembly (see illustration).

3   Remove the housing through bolts (see illustration) and the nuts and insulators from the rear housing. Make a careful note of all insulator locations (see illustration).
4   Withdraw the rear housing section from the stator, rotor and front housing assembly (see illustration).
5   Remove the brushes and springs from the brush holder assembly, which is located inside the rear housing (see illustrations).
6   Check the length of the brushes against the wear dimensions given in the specifications and replace the brushes with new ones if necessary.
7   Install the springs and brushes in the holder assembly (see illustrations) and retain them in place by inserting a piece of stiff wire through the rear housing and brush terminal insulator (see illustration). Make sure enough wire protrudes through the rear housing so it can be withdrawn at a later stage.

17.2   Scribe a line across the housings for alignment reference

17.3a   Remove the three through bolts (arrows) to separate the housings

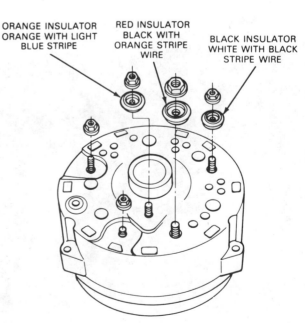

17.3b   Note which insulators go where on the alternator

17.4   Separate the front housing rotor assembly from the rear housing

17.5a   Remove the attaching bolts and remove the brush holder and one brush in holder

17.5b   Remove the rear field housing nut (orange) to remove the remaining brush

17.7a   Install the bottom brush in the rear field housing

17.7b   Use a screwdriver to hold the brush in place

17.7c   Insert a paper clip through the hole in the back to retain the bottom brush

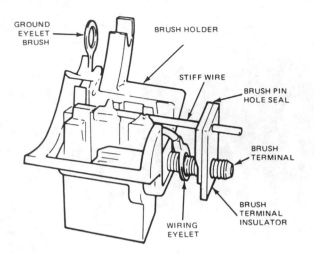

GROUND
EYELET
BRUSH

BRUSH HOLDER

STIFF WIRE

BRUSH PIN
HOLE SEAL

BRUSH
TERMINAL

BRUSH
TERMINAL
INSULATOR

WIRING
EYELET

**17.18 A piece of stiff wire is used to hold the brushes
in place on a side terminal alternator**

8   Attach the rear housing rotor and front housing assembly to the
stator, making sure the scribed marks are aligned.
9   Install the housing through bolts and rear end insulators and nuts
but do not tighten the nuts at this time.
10 Carefully extract the piece of wire from the rear housing and make
sure that the brushes are seated on the slip ring. Tighten the through
bolts and rear housing nuts.
11 Install the alternator as described in Section 19.

Side terminal alternator

12 Remove the alternator as described in Section 19 and scribe a mark
on both end housings and the stator for ease of reassembly.
13 Remove the through bolts and separate the front housing and rotor
from the rear housing and stator. Be careful that you do not separate
the rear housing and stator.
14 Use a soldering iron to unsolder and disengage the brush holder
from the rear housing. Remove the brushes and springs from the brush
holders.
15 Remove the two brush holder attaching screws and lift the brush
holder from the rear housing.
16 Remove any sealing compound from the brush holder and rear
housing.
17 Inspect the brushes for damage and check their dimensions against
the specifications. If they are worn, replace them with new ones.
18 To reassemble, install the springs and brushes in the brush holders,
inserting a piece of stiff wire to hold them in place (see illustration).

19 Place the brush holder in position in the rear housing, using the
wire to retract the brushes through the hole in the rear housing.
20 Install the brush holder attaching screws and push the holder
toward the shaft opening as you tighten the screws. **Caution:** *The rectifier can be overheated and damaged if the soldering is not done quickly.
Press the brush holder lead onto the rectifier lead and solder them in
place.*
21 Place the rotor and front housing in position in the stator and rear
housing. After aligning the scribe marks, install the through bolts.
22 Turn the fan and pulley to check for binding in the alternator.
23 Withdraw the wire which is retracting the brushes and seal the
hole with waterproof cement. **Caution:** *Do not use RTV-type sealer
on the hole.*

18 Regulator — removal and installation

1   Remove the negative cable from the battery.
2   Locate the voltage regulator. It will usually be positioned near the
front of the vehicle.
3   Push the two tabs on either side of the quick release clip retaining
the wiring loom to the regulator. Pull the quick release clip straight out
from the side of the regulator.
4   Remove the two regulator retaining screws. Notice that one screw
will locate the ground wire terminal.
5   Remove the regulator.
6   Installation is the reverse of removal. Make sure you get the wiring
clip positioned firmly onto the regulator terminals and that both clips
click into place.

19 Ignition coil — checking and replacement

Checking

1   The ignition coil cannot be satisfactorily tested without the proper
electronic diagnostic equipment. If a fault is suspected in the coil, have
it checked by a dealer or repair shop specializing in electrical repairs.
The coil can be replaced with a new one using the following procedure.

Replacement

2   Disconnect the negative cable from the battery.
3   Using coded strips of tape, mark each of the wires at the coil to
help return the wires to their original positions during reinstallation.
4   Remove the coil to distributor high tension lead.
5   Remove the connections at the coil. These connections may be
of the push-lock connector type. Separate them from the coil by releasing the tab at the bottom of the connector.
6   Remove the retaining bolts holding the coil bracket to the engine.
7   Remove the coil from the coil bracket by loosening the clamp bolt.
8   Installation is the reverse of removal.

Chapter 6   Emissions control systems

Contents

Specifications

Torque specifications	Ft-lbs
EGR valve	10 to 20
EFE heater relay	3
AIR pump pulley	24
AIR pump through-bolt	23
AIR management valve bolt	12
Oxygen sensor	30

1   General information

In order to meet U.S. anti-pollution laws, vehicles are equipped with a variety of emissions control systems, depending on the model and the states in which they are sold.

The information in this Chapter describes the subsystems within the overall emissions control system and the maintenance operations for these subsystems that are within the reach of the home mechanic. The Emissions Control Information label, located in the engine compartment, contains information required to properly maintain the emissions control, ignition and fuel systems and for keeping the vehicle correctly tuned.

Due to the complexity of the subsystems, especially those governed by Electronic Engine Control (EEC), it is suggested that professional assistance be sought when you run into an emissions problem that cannot be readily diagnosed and/or repaired.

2   Electronic Control Assembly (ECA)

Refer to illustrations 2.2, 2.5 and 2.6

1   The ECA is a microprocessor module. As the heart of the EEC-IV system, it is programmed to interface with various types of sensors, switches and actuators to perform engine control functions. The ECA contains a specific calibration for optimizing emissions, fuel economy, and driveabliity. Based on information received and programmed into its memory, the ECA generates output signals to control various relays, solenoids and other actuators.

2   The ECA is a microprocessor like other EEC systems, but differs in that it has the calibration module located inside the ECA assembly (see illustration).

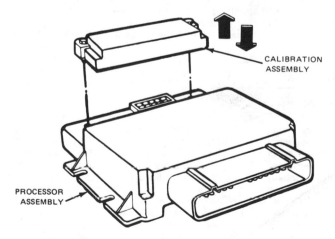

2.2   The Electronic Control Assembly (ECA) is made up of a processor assembly and a calibration assembly

3   The ECA unit is located under the instrument panel and the right kick panel.

Component removal

4   Remove the attaching screw on the right hand kick panel in the passenger compartment and remove kick panel. It may be necessary to loosen the chrome carpet hold down strip to remove the kick panel.

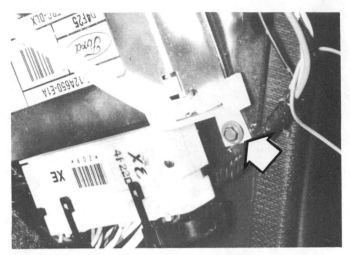

2.5   Remove the hold down bracket bolt

3.1   Loosen the retaining bolt (arrow) to unplug the MCU unit

5   Remove the bolt retaining ECA bracket (see illustration).
6   Loosen bolt attaching the ECA plug connector to the ECA unit and unplug the unit (see illustration).
7   Installation is the reverse of the removal procedure.

---

3   Microprocessor Control Unit (MCU)

Refer to illustration 3.1

The MCU is the heart of the electronic engine fuel control system used on most pre-1985 models. Its function is to keep the air/fuel ratio at a proper balance to obtain maximum catalyst efficiency. The MCU is the master of the fuel control "loop" which consists of the microprocessor, exhaust gas oxygen (EGO) sensor and a carburetor with feedback carburetor actuator (FBCA).

The EGO sensor senses whether the mixture is rich or lean, and a signal is sent to the MCU module, which sends a signal to the FBCA to alter the air/fuel ratio. This operation is called "closed loop" operation. During the "open loop" operation, the input from the EGO sensor is ignored. During this mode the MCU sends out a fixed signal to the FBCA.

The determining factor when the system goes into open loop is based upon information from the switch inputs, which senses parameters such as coolant temperature, manifold vacuum and rpm. Generally, the vehicle will be in closed loop when the vehicle is at operating temperature and at a steady part-throttle cruise.

Other functions controlled by the MCU are Canister Purge (CANP), Thermactor Air Diverter (TAD), Thermactor Air Bypass (TAB), Throttle Kicker (TK), and Spark Retard System, or spark retard through the knock sensor.

The MCU is located inside the black box on the right side of the engine compartment.

2.6   Remove the bolt (arrow) and unplug the connector from the ECA unit

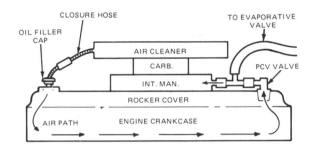

4.2   Typical positive crankcase ventilation system (PCV)

Component replacement

1   Replacement is a straightforward procedure. Pry up on the plastic black box top, which houses several electrical connections. Once inside loosen the attaching bolt holding the MCU plug, then pull the plug from the unit (see illustration).
2   Under the fender, inside the fender well, remove the two attaching screws retaining the black box and MCU unit then lift out the MCU unit.
3   Installation is the reverse of removal procedure.

---

4   Positive Crankcase Ventilation (PCV) system

Refer to illustration 4.2

General description

1   The positive crankcase ventilation system is a closed recirculating system which is designed to prevent engine crankcase fumes from escaping into the atmosphere through the engine oil filler cap. The crankcase control system regulates these blowby vapors by circulating them back into the intake manifold where they are burned with the incoming fuel and air mixture.
2   The system consists of a replaceable PCV valve, a crankcase ventilation filter in the air cleaner and connecting hoses and gaskets (see illustration).
3   The air source for the crankcase ventilation system is in the air cleaner. Air passes through a filter located in the air cleaner to a hose connecting the air cleaner to the oil filler cap. The oil filler cap is sealed at the opening to prevent the entrance of outside air. From the oil filler cap the air flows into the rocker arm chamber and into the crankcase. The air then circulates from the crankcase up into another section of the rocker arm chamber. The air and crankcase gasses then enter a spring loaded regulator valve (PCV valve) that controls the amount of flow as operating conditions vary. Some engines have a fixed orifice PCV valve that meters a steady flow regardless of the extent of engine blowby gasses. In either case, the mixture is routed to the intake manifold through the crankcase vent hose tube and fittings. This process goes on continuously while the engine is running.

Checking

4   Checking and replacement procedures for the PCV system are described in Chapter 1.

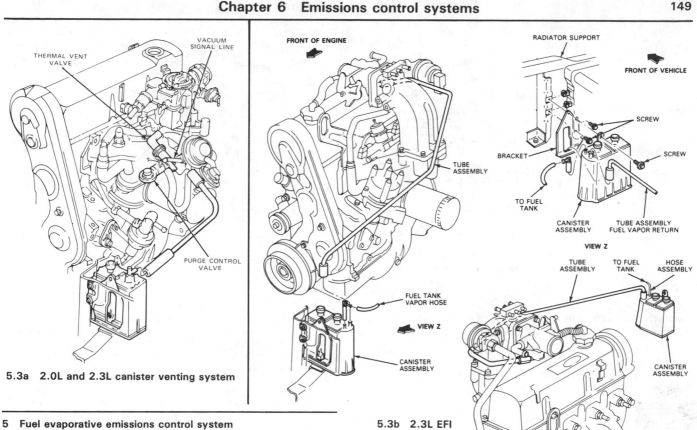

5.3a   2.0L and 2.3L canister venting system

5.3b   2.3L EFI canister venting system

5   Fuel evaporative emissions control system

Refer to illustrations 5.3a, 5.3b and 5.3c

General description

1   This system is designed to limit fuel vapors released to the atmosphere by trapping and storing fuel that evaporates from the fuel tank which would normally enter the atmosphere, contributing to hydrocarbon emissions.

2   The serviceable parts of the system include a charcoal filled canister, connection lines to the fuel tank and carburetor and the fuel tank filler cap.

3   Fuel vapors are vented from the fuel tank for temporary storage in the canister, which is mounted in the engine compartment, near the radiator. The canister outlet is connected to the carburetor air cleaner so the stored vapors will be drawn into the engine and burned (see illustrations). The fuel tank filler cap is of a special design that vents air into the tank to replace the fuel being used, but does not vent fuel

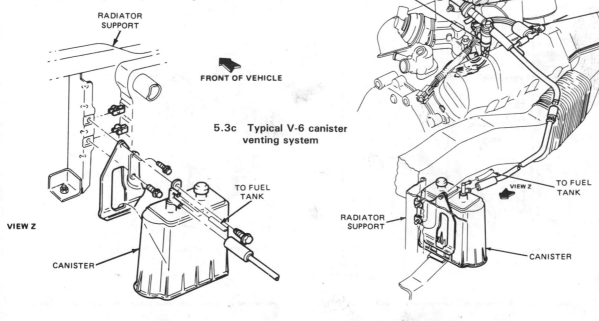

5.3c   Typical V-6 canister venting system

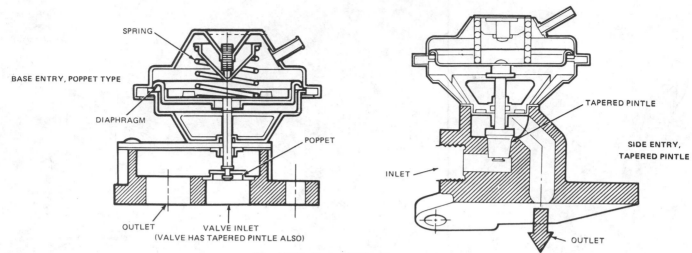

SPRING

BASE ENTRY, POPPET TYPE

DIAPHRAGM

POPPET

OUTLET   VALVE INLET
(VALVE HAS TAPERED PINTLE ALSO)

TAPERED PINTLE

SIDE ENTRY,
TAPERED PINTLE

INLET

OUTLET

6.3 Ported EGR valve

vapors to the outside air under normal conditions (unless tank pressure builds up to more than approximately two psi above normal atmospheric pressure).

Checking

4   The checking procedures for the fuel evaporative emissions control system are described in Chapter 1.

---

6 Exhaust Gas Recirculation (EGR) system

Refer to illustrations 6.3, 6.5, 6.14, 6.16, 6.17, 6.18 and 6.19

General description

1   The EGR system is designed to reintroduce small amounts of exhaust gas into the combustion cycle, thus reducing the generation of nitrous oxide emissions. The amount of exhaust gas reintroduced and the timing of the cycle is controlled by various factors such as engine speed, altitude, engine vacuum, exhaust system backpressure, coolant temperature and throttle angle. All EGR valves are vacuum actuated and the vacuum diagram for your particular vehicle is shown on the Emissions Control Information label in the engine compartment.

2   For the vehicles covered by this manual, there are four basic types of EGR valves: the ported valve, the integral backpressure valve, the electronic sonic valve and the valve and transducer type EGR valve.

Ported valve

3   Two passages in the base connecting the exhaust system with the intake manifold are blocked by the ported EGR valve, which is opened by vacuum and closed by spring pressure. The valve may be of the poppet or tapered stem design and may have a base entry or side entry, the function being the same (see illustration).

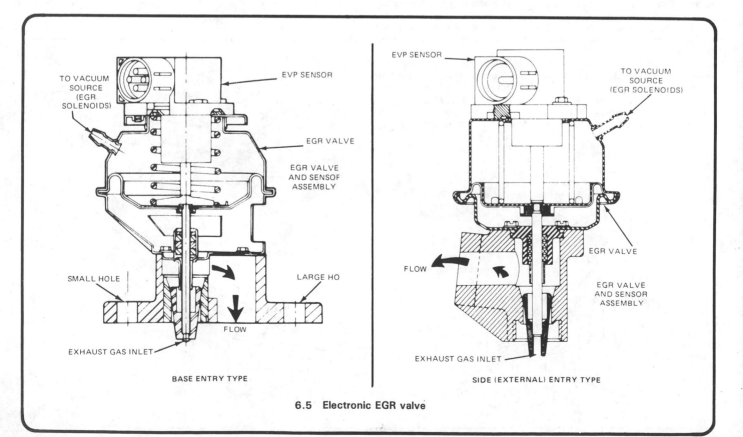

TO VACUUM
SOURCE
(EGR
SOLENOIDS)

EVP SENSOR

EGR VALVE

EGR VALVE
AND SENSOR
ASSEMBLY

SMALL HOLE

LARGE HO

FLOW

EXHAUST GAS INLET

BASE ENTRY TYPE

EVP SENSOR

TO VACUUM
SOURCE
(EGR SOLENOIDS)

EGR VALVE

EGR VALVE
AND SENSOR
ASSEMBLY

FLOW

EXHAUST GAS INLET

SIDE (EXTERNAL) ENTRY TYPE

6.5 Electronic EGR valve

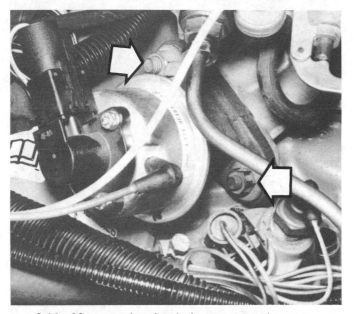

**6.14   After removing electrical connector and vacuum
hose remove two attaching nuts (arrows) to remove
EGR unit**

**6.16   Disconnect the throttle cable by prying off
with a screwdriver**

**6.17   Disconnect the power brake vacuum line,
if equipped**

Integral backpressure valve

4   This poppet or tapered (pintle) valve cannot be opened by vacuum until the bleed hole is closed by exhaust backpressure. Once the valve opens, it seeks a level dependent upon the exhaust backpressure flowing through the orifice, and in so doing oscillates at that level. The higher the signal vacuum and exhaust backpressure, the more the valve opens. The valve body may be base entry or side entry. Electronic sonic valve assembly

5   On vehicles equipped with an Electronic Engine Control (EEC) system, exhaust gas recirculation is controlled by the EEC through a system of engine sensors. The EGR valve in this system resembles and is operated in the same manner as a conventional ported design valve. However, it uses a tapered pintle valve for more exact control of the flow rate, which is very closely proportional to the valve stem position. A sensor on top of the valve tells how far the EGR valve is open, sends an electrical signal to the EEC, which is also receiving several other signals, such as temperature, rpm and throttle opening. The EEC then

signals the EGR control solenoids to maintain or alter the flow as required by the engine operating conditions. Source vacuum from the manifold is then either bled off or applied to the diaphragm, depending on what the EEC commands (see illustration). A cooler is used to reduce the temperature of the exhaust gasses, helping the gasses to flow better, reducing the tendency of the engine to detonate and making the valve more durable.

6   The EGR valve operates only in the part throttle mode. It remains closed in cranking mode, closed throttle mode and wide open throttle mode.

Valve and transducer EGR valve

7   This valve consists of a modified EGR valve with a remote transducer. It operates similarly to the integral backpressure valve.

Checking

Ported valve and integral backpressure valve

8   Check that all vacuum lines are properly routed, all connections are secure and that the hoses are not crimped, cracked or broken. If deteriorated hoses are encountered, replace them with new ones.

9   Visually inspect the valve for rust or corrosion. If rust or corrosion is encountered, clean the valve or replace it with a new one.

10   Using finger pressure, press in on the diaphragm on the bottom of the valve. If the valve sticks open or closed or does not operate smoothly, clean the valve or replace it with a new one.

Electronic sonic valve assembly

11   If a malfunction is suspected in the electronic sonic valve or the EVP sensor to which it is attached, have the system checked at a Ford dealer service department

Component replacement

12   When replacing any vacuum hoses, remove only one hose at a time and make sure that the replacement hose is of the same quality and size as the hose being replaced.

13   When replacing the EGR valve, label each hose as it is disconnected from the valve to ensure proper connection to the replacement valve.

14   The valve is easily removed from the intake manifold after disconnecting and labeling the attached hoses and electrical connection. Remove the two attaching nuts retaining the unit at the base (see illustration). Use a new gasket when installing the valve and check for leaks when the job is complete.

15   Disconnect the valve lines at the manifold vacuum fitting.

16   Disconnect the throttle cable (see illustration) and disconnect the automatic throttle valve line.

17   If equipped, disconnect the power brake vacuum line (see illustration).

6.18   The EGR spacer is retained with five bolts (arrows)

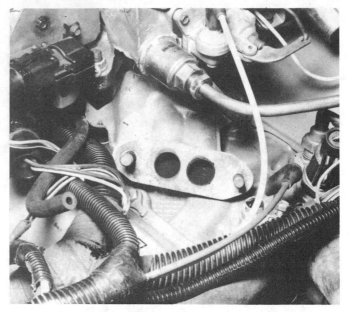

6.19   Clean the EGR intake ports before installation

18 Remove the EGR spacer bolts and lift off the spacer (see illustration).
19 Clean the mating surfaces before installing the new gasket and make sure the intake ports are clear of obstructions (see illustration).
20 Install the new gasket, EGR spacer, carburetor gasket and carburetor.
21 Installation is the reverse of the removal procedure.

7   Inlet air temperature control system

Refer to illustrations 7.3, 7.8 and 7.9
General description
1   The air cleaner temperature control system is used to keep the air

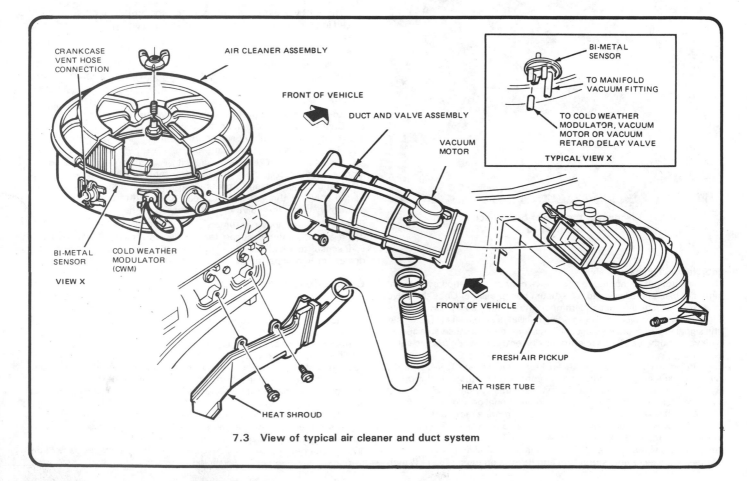

7.3   View of typical air cleaner and duct system

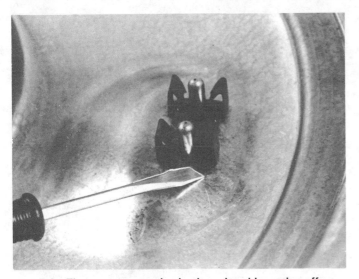

7.8 Thermactor control valve is replaced by prying off retaining clip

7.9 Door vacuum diaphram is replaced by drilling out the rivet and securing the new unit with a sheet metal screw or new rivet

entering the carburetor or EFI unit at a consistent temperature. The carburetor can then be calibrated leaner for emissions reduction, improved warm-up and better driveability.

2　Two air flow circuits are used. They are controlled by intake manifold vacuum and temperature sensing valves. A vacuum motor, which operates a heat duct valve in the air cleaner, is activated by these two circuits.

3　When the under hood temperature is cold, air is drawn through the shroud which fits over the exhaust manifold, up through the heat riser tube and into the air cleaner (see illustration). This provides warm air for the carburetor, resulting in better driveability and faster warm-up. As the under hood temperature rises, the duct valve will be closed by the vacuum motor and the air that enters the air cleaner will be drawn through the cold air snorkel or duct. This provides a consistent intake air temperature.

Checking

4　Checking of this system should be done while the engine is cold.

5　Remove the clamp retaining the air hose to the rear of the metal duct and valve assembly. Start the engine and, looking through the rear of the duct and valve assembly, observe that the duct valve (heat control door) rotates to allow hot air from the heat riser tube to enter the air cleaner. As the engine warms up, the vacuum motor should pull the valve open, closing off the heat riser tube and allowing ambient air to enter the duct.

6　If the duct valve does not perform as indicated, check that it is not rusted in an open or closed position by attempting to move it by hand. If it is rusted, it can usually be freed by cleaning and oiling it. Otherwise replace it with a new unit.

7　If the vacuum motor fails to perform as indicated, check carefully for a leak in the hose leading to it. If no leak is found, replace the vacuum motor with a new one.

Component replacement

8　To replace the air cleaner temperature sensor turn the cleaner housing over and pry retaining clip off with screwdriver (see illustration).

9　To remove the air cleaner vacuum motor it will be necessary to drill out the retaining rivet and slide the unit out of the slot retainer (see illustration).

10　Install the new unit and secure it with a rivet or sheet metal screw.

8　Thermactor systems

Refer to illustrations 8.20 and 8.26

General description

1　Thermactor systems are employed to reduce carbon monoxide and hydrocarbon emissions. Two types are found on vehicles covered by this manual, a conventional thermactor air injection system and a managed air thermactor system.

2　The conventional thermactor air injection system consists of an air supply pump, an air bypass valve, a check valve, an air manifold and connecting hoses. The managed air thermactor system adds a second check valve and an air control valve to the system. The air control valve may be incorporated with the air bypass valve into a single air bypass/air control valve in some applications.

3　The thermactor air injection system functions by continuing combustion of unburned gasses after they leave the combustion chamber by injecting fresh air into the hot exhaust system leaving the exhaust ports. At this point, the fresh air mixes with hot exhaust gas to promote further oxidation of both hydrocarbons and carbon monoxide, thereby reducing their concentration and converting some of them into harmless carbon dioxide and water. During some modes of operation, such as the extended idle, the thermactor air is dumped into the atmosphere by the bypass valve to prevent overheating of the exhaust system.

4　The managed air thermactor system serves the same function as the thermactor air injection system, but, through the addition of the air control valve, diverts thermactor air either upstream to the exhaust manifold check valve, or downstream to the added, rear section check valve and on to the dual catalytic converter. The air is utilized in the converter to maintain feed gas oxygen contents at a high level. This system is configured in both electronic and non-electronic controlled versions.

Checking

Air supply pump

5　Check and adjust the drivebelt tension (refer to Chapter 1).

6　Disconnect the air supply hose at the air bypass valve inlet.

7　The pump is operating satisfactorily if air flow is felt at the pump outlet with the engine running at idle, increasing as the engine speed is increased.

8　If the air pump does not successfully pass the above tests, replace it with a new or rebuilt unit.

Air bypass valve

9　With the engine running at idle, disconnect the hose from the outlet valve.

10　Remove the vacuum line from the vacuum nipple and remove or bypass any restrictors or delay valves in the vacuum line.

11　Verify that vacuum is present in the vacuum line by putting your finger over its end.

12　Reconnect the vacuum line to the vacuum nipple.

13　With the engine running at 1500 rpm, the air pump supply air should be felt or heard at the air bypass valve outlet.

14　With the engine running at 1500 rpm, disconnect the vacuum line. Air at the valve outlet should be decreased or shut off and air pump

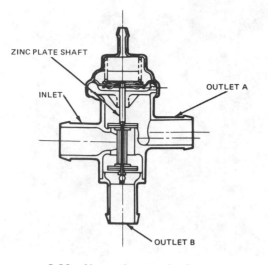

8.20   Air supply control valve

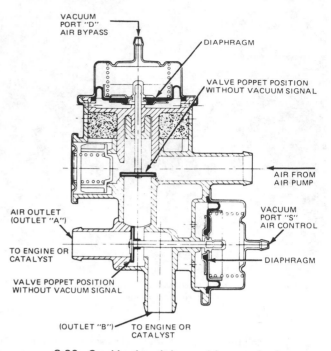

8.26   Combination air bypass/air control valve

supply air should be felt or heard at the silencer ports.
15 Reconnect all disconnected hoses.
16 If the normally closed air bypass valve does not successfully pass the above tests, check the air pump (refer to Steps 5 through 7).
17 If the air pump is operating satisfactorily, replace the air bypass valve with a new one.

Air supply control valve
18 With the engine running at 1500 rpm, disconnect the hose at the air supply control valve inlet and verify the presence of air flow through the hose.
19 Reconnect the hose to the valve inlet.
20 Disconnect the hoses at the vacuum nipple and at outlets A and B (see illustration).
21 With the engine running at 1500 rpm, air flow should be felt at outlet B with little or no air flow at outlet A.
22 With the engine running at 1500 rpm, connect a line from any manifold vacuum fitting to the vacuum nipple.
23 Air flow should be present at outlet A with little or no air flow at outlet B.
24 Restore all connections
25 If all conditions above are not met, replace the air control valve with a new one.

Combination air bypass/air control valve
26 Disconnect the hoses from outlets A and B (see illustration).
27 Disconnect the vacuum line at port D and plug the line.
28 With the engine running at 1500 rpm, verify that air flows from the bypass vents.
29 Unplug and reconnect the vacuum line to port D, then disconnect and plug the line attached to port S.
30 Verify that vacuum is present in the line to vacuum port D by momentarily disconnecting it.
31 Reconnect the vacuum line to port D.
32 With the engine running at 1500 rpm, verify that air is flowing out of outlet B with no air flow present at outlet A.
33 Attach a length of hose to port S.
34 With the engine running at 1500 rpm, apply vacuum by mouth to the hose and verify that air is flowing out of outlet A.
35 Reconnect all hoses. Be sure to unplug the line to Port S before reconnecting it.
36 If all conditions above are not met, replace the combination valve with a new one.

Check valve
37 Disconnect the hoses from both ends of the check valve.
38 Blow through both ends of the check valve, verifying that air flows in one direction only.
39 If air flows in both directions or not at all, replace the check valve with a new one.
40 When reconnecting the valve, make sure it is installed in the proper direction.

Component replacement
41 The air bypass valve, air supply control valve, check valve and combination air bypass/air control valve may be replaced by disconnecting the hoses leading to them (be sure to label the hoses as they are disconnected to facilitate reconnection), replacing the faulty element with a new one and reconnecting the hoses to the proper ports. Make sure that the hoses are in good condition. If not, replace them with new ones.
42 To replace the air supply pump, first loosen the appropriate engine drivebelts, then remove the faulty pump from its bracket mounting, labeling all wires and hoses as they are removed to facilitate installation of the new unit.
43 After the new pump is installed, adjust the drivebelts to the specified tension (refer to Chapter 1).

9   Catalytic converter

Refer to illustration 9.2

General description
1   The catalytic converter is designed to reduce hydrocarbon and carbon monoxide pollutants in the exhaust. The converter oxidizes these components and converts them to water and carbon dioxide.
2   The converter is located in the exhaust system and closely resembles a muffler (see illustration). Some models have two converters, a light-off catalyst type, mounted just past the exhaust manifold pipe, and a conventional oxidation catalyst or three-way catalyst type mounted farther downstream.
3   **Note:** *If large amounts of unburned gasoline enter the converter, it may overheat and cause a fire. Always observe the following precautions:*
    a) Use only unleaded gasoline
    b) Avoid prolonged idling
    c) Do not run the engine with a nearly empty fuel tank
    d) Avoid coasting with the ignition turned Off

Checking
4   The catalytic converter requires little if any maintenance and servicing. However, the system should be inspected whenever the vehicle is raised on a lift or if the exhaust system is checked or serviced.
5   Check all connections in the exhaust pipe assembly for looseness or damage. Also check all the clamps for damage, cracks or missing

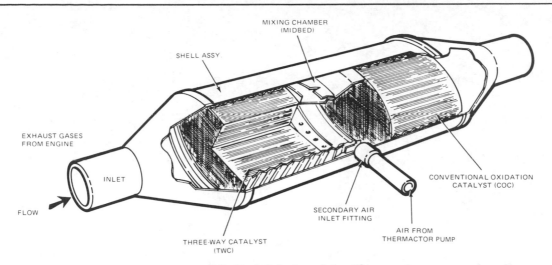

9.2 Typical dual catalytic converter

fasteners. Check the rubber hangers for cracks.

6   The converter itself should be checked for damage or dents (maximum 3/4-in deep) which could affect its performance. At the same time the converter is inspected, check the metal protector plate under it as well as the heat insulator above it for damage or loose fasteners.

Component replacement

7   Do not attempt to remove the catalytic converter until the complete exhaust system is cool. Raise the vehicle and support it securely on jackstands. Apply penetrating oil to the clamp bolts and allow it to soak in.

8   Remove the bolts and the rubber hangers, then separate the converter from the exhaust pipes. Remove the old gaskets if they are stuck to the pipes.

9   Installation of the converter is the reverse of removal. Use new exhaust pipe gaskets. Replace the rubber hangers with new ones if the originals are deteriorated. Start the engine and check carefully for exhaust leaks.

---

10 Spark control system

Note: *The information in this Section is applicable only to vehicles equipped with the Dura-Spark II ignition system. Because spark advance and retard functions on vehicles equipped with EEC-IV ignition systems are controlled by the Electronic Engine Control (EEC) microprocessor, checks and tests involving the spark control system on these vehicles must be performed by a Ford dealer service department.*

General description

1   The spark control system is designed to reduce hydrocarbon and oxides of nitrogen emissions by advancing the ignition timing when the engine is cold.

2   These systems are fairly complex and have many valves, relays, amplifiers and other components built into them. Each vehicle will have a system peculiar to the model year, geographic region and gross vehicle weight rating. A schematic diagram located near the radiator side under the hood will detail the exact components and vacuum line routing of the particular system on your vehicle.

3   Various vacuum switches are used in the emissions system for modifying spark timing and engine idle. These vacuum switches have anywhere from two to four ports, depending on their function.

Ported Vacuum Switches (PVS)

4   A ported vacuum switch is situated in the cooling system to increase idle rpm when the engine overheats. When the coolant is at normal temperature, the vacuum goes through the top and center ports of the PVS, providing the distributor with vacuum advance suitable for normal driving. When hot, the PVS center and bottom ports are connected so that the engine manifold vacuum allows the distributor to advance and increase idle.

Distributor vacuum vent valve

5   Some engines use a distributor vacuum vent valve both to prevent fuel from migrating into the distributor advance diaphragm and to act as a spark advance delay valve. During light acceleration, deceleration and idle, the vent valve dumps vacuum through a check valve. This keeps the distributor from advancing excessively for the load and evacuates the fuel in the spark port line.

Cold Start Spark Advance (CSSA)

6   The CSSA system is located in the distributor spark control system. When coolant temperature is below 128 °F (53 °C), it momentarily traps the spark port vacuum at the distributor advance diaphragm. The vacuum follows a path through the carburetor vacuum tap, the Distributor Retard Control Valve (DRCV), the CSSA ported vacuum switch and then the cooling vacuum switch to the distributor. At coolant temperatures above 128 °F, the CSSA PVS operates and the vacuum follows a path from the carburetor spark port through the cooling PVS to the distributor.

Cold Start Spark Hold (CSSH)

7   When the engine is cold, the CSSH momentarily provides spark advance for improved cold engine acceleration. Below 128 °F, the CSSH ported vacuum switch is closed and the distributor vacuum is routed through a restrictor. Under cold starting conditions, the high vacuum present advances the distributor. During cold acceleration, the vacuum is slowly bled off through the restrictor, slowing the vacuum advance during initial acceleration.

Spark Delay Valve (SDV)

8   SDVs are designed to slow the air flow in one direction while a check valve allows free flow in the opposite direction. This allows closer control of vacuum operated emission devices.

Checking

9   Visually check all vacuum hoses for cracks, splits or hardening. Remove the distributor cap and rotor and apply a vacuum to the distributor advance port (and retard port, if so equipped) to see if the breaker or relay plate inside of the distributor moves. The plate should move opposite the distributor direction of rotation when vacuum is applied to the advance port and should move in the direction of rotation if vacuum is applied to the retard port (if so equipped).

10   Checking of the temperature relays, delay valves or other modifiers of the spark timing system is beyond the scope of the home mechanic. Consult an expert if you suspect that you have other problems within the spark advance system.

Component replacement

11   When replacing any vacuum hoses, remove only one hose at a time and make sure that the replacement hose is of the same quality and size as the hose being replaced.

12   If it is determined that a malfunction in the spark control system is due to a faulty distributor, refer to Chapter 5 for the replacement procedure.

Chapter 7 Part A   Manual transmissions

Contents

Specifications

Transmission types	4 speed synchromesh and 5-speed synchromesh
Oil capacity	
Mazda 4 speed and 5 speed	3 US pints
Mitsubishi 5 speed	4.8 US pints
Oil type	D8DZ-19C547-A or equivelant (SAE 80W)

Torque specifications	Ft-lbs
Access cover-to-case screw (Mazda)	23 to 34
Drain plug	
Mazda	29 to 43
Mitsubishi	25 to 32
Filler plug	
Mazda	18 to 29
Mitsubishi	22 to 25
Backup light switch	22 to 29
Gearshift lever to case bolts (Mitsubishi)	6 to 10
Transmission to clutch housing	30 to 40
Damper to insulator on crossmember	71 to 94
Insulator to transmission	60 to 80
Crossmember to frame bracket	65 to 85

1   General information

Refer to illustrations 1.1a and 1.1b

The manual transmissions covered in this section are four and five speed models, with fifth gear being an overdrive. Earlier Rangers came with four speed transmissions made by Mazda. Mazda and Mitsubishi supply the five speed overdrive transmissions now found in the Rangers and Bronco II's (see illustrations). Application of the transmissions depends on the year, engine and model of the vehicle in which it is installed. If you are in doubt as to which transmission is in your particular vehicle, check with your local Ford dealer or automotive transmission facility.

The five speed manual transmissions are very similar to the four speed transmissions used in Rangers. Both transmissions are fully synchronized on all gears except reverse. Reverse gear uses an idler gear which is in constant mesh with the countershaft gear. All forward speed gears are helical cut for quiet running. The reverse gear and reverse idler gear are spur cut.

The top mounted shifter operates shift rails through a set of shift forks. Shift forks mounted on the rails operate the synchronizer sleeves that control shifts of the forward gears. A shift interlock system located in the side of the transmission case prevents the shift rails from engaging two gears at the same time.

Due to the complexity of transmissions and because of the special tools and expertise required to perform an overhaul, it is not advised that it be undertaken by the home mechanic. Therefore, the procedures in this Chapter are limited to routine adjustments and removal and installation procedures.

Depending on the expense involved in having a faulty transmission overhauled, it may be of advantage to consider replacing the unit with either a new or rebuilt one. Your local dealer or transmission shop should be able to supply you with information concerning cost, availability and exchange policy. Regardless of how you decide to remedy a faulty transmission problem, however, you can still save considerable expense by removing and installing the unit yourself.

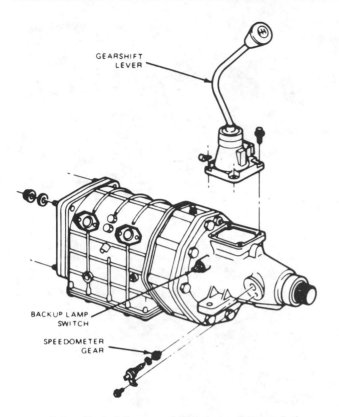

GEARSHIFT
LEVER

BACKUP LAMP
SWITCH

SPEEDOMETER
GEAR

1.1a   Typical five speed (Mazda type) transmission

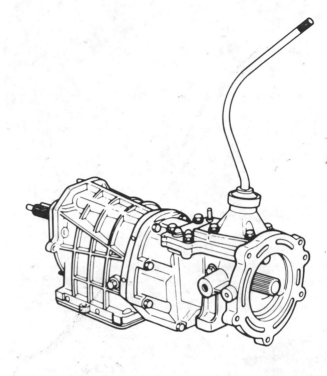

1.1b   Typical five speed (Mitsubishi type)
manual transmission

2.2   Pry up on the transmission mount and check for
excessive looseness

2.3   Remove the two bolts attaching the insulator to the
crossmember and the two bolts attaching the insulator to
the transmission

2   Transmission mounts — check and replacement

Refer to illustrations 2.2 and 2.3

1   Insert a large screwdriver or pry bar into the space between the
transmission tailshaft and the crossmember and pry up.

2   The transmission should not spread excessively away from the
insulator (see illustration).
3   To replace, remove the two nuts attaching the insulator to the
crossmember and the two bolts attaching the insulator to the transmission (see illustration).
4   Raise the transmission with a jack and remove the insulator.
5   Installation is the reverse of the removal procedure.

3.2a Hold back the carpet to get at the shifter boot
retaining bolts

3.2b With the shifter boot removed, remove the four
retaining bolts and lift the gearshift lever assembly
straight up and out

3.4 Cover the opening to keep dirt out of the transmission

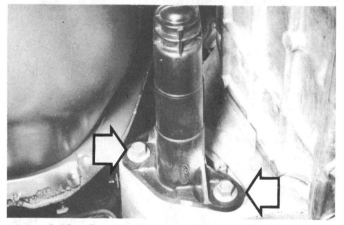

3.10a Remove the slave cylinder bolts (arrows)

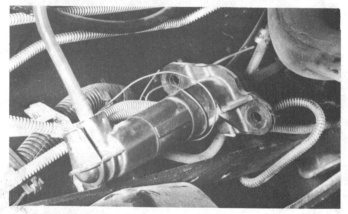

3.10b Once the slave cylinder is removed, wire the unit
to the frame rail out of your way

3   Manual transmission — removal and installation

Refer to illustrations 3.2a, 3.2b, 3.4, 3.10a, 3.10b, 3.11 and 3.19

Removal

1   Place the gearshift selector in the neutral position.
2   Carefully fold back the carpet and remove the shifter boot retainer bolts (see illustration). Remove the bolts attaching the retainer cover to the gearshift lever retainer (see illustration).
3   Pull the gearshift lever assembly, shim and bushing straight up and

away from the gearshift lever retainer.
4   Cover the shift tower opening in the extension housing with a rag to avoid dropping dirt into the transmission (see illustration).
5   From inside the cab disconnect the clutch master cylinder pushrod from the clutch pedal.
6   Open the hood and disconnect the negative battery cable from the battery terminal.
7   From under the hood, remove the top two transmission housing bolts.
8   Raise the vehicle and support it securely on jackstands.
9   Remove the driveshaft(s) (refer to Chapter 8) and install a plug in the rear extension housing or transfer case adapter, if so equipped, to prevent leakage.
10 On vehicles with an internal slave cylinder, disconnect the hydraulic fluid line from the clutch slave cylinder and plug the line to prevent spillage. On external type slave cylinders, remove the two attaching bolts (see illustration). Wire the unit out of the way (see illustration).
11 Disconnect the speedometer cable (see illustration).
12 Unbolt and remove the starter motor. Wire the starter out of the way.
13 Disconnect the backup lamp switch and shift indicator switch wire.
14 Place a jack under the engine, protecting the oil pan with a wood block.
15 On four-wheel drive vehicles, remove the transfer case (refer to Part C of this chapter).
16 Disconnect the catalytic converter, then disconnect the exhaust crossover pipe (if equipped).
17 Place a transmission jack under the transmission.
18 Remove the remaining transmission bolts.
19 Remove the nuts and bolts attaching the transmission mount to the crossmember (see illustration).
20 Remove the nuts attaching the crossmember to the frame side rails.

3.11   Remove the retaining bolt and retainer to disconnect the speedometer cable

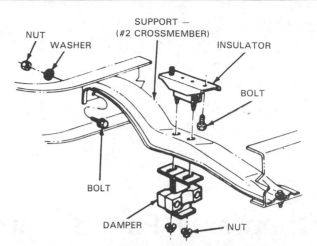

3.19   Transmission mount — exploded view

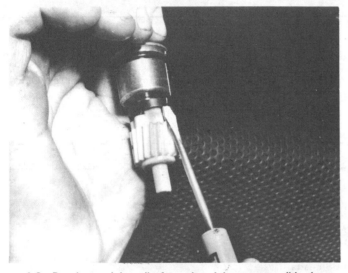

4.3   Pry the retaining clip from the pinion gear to slide the gear off the cable

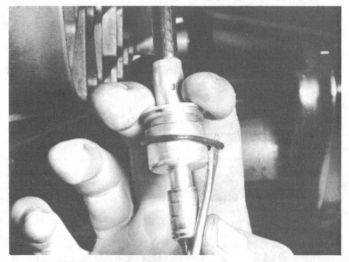

4.4   To replace the oil O-ring pry off the O-ring with a small screwdriver

If you did not remove the transmission insulator from the transmission it will be necessary to raise the transmission enough to clear the insulator retaining bolts, then slide crossmember rearward.
21   Lower the engine jack and work the transmission housing off the locating dowels and slide the transmission rearward until the input shaft clears the clutch disc, allowing transmission removal.

Installation
22   Mount the transmission on a transmission jack and position it under the vehicle.
23   Start the input shaft into the clutch disc. Align the splines on the input shaft with the splines in the clutch disc and move the transmission forward.
24   Installation is the reverse of the removal procedure.

---

4   Speedometer pinion gear and seal — removal and installation

Refer to illustrations 4.3 and 4.4
1   Remove the bolt on the speedometer cable retaining bracket and remove the bracket and bolt as an assembly.
2   Pull the pinion gear assembly straight out of the transfer case or extension housing.
3   Use a small screwdriver to remove the retaining clip from the pinion gear and slide the gear off the cable (see illustration).
4   To replace the O-ring use a screwdriver to remove the O-ring from the retaining groove (see illustration).

5   Lubricate the new O-ring and slide it onto the pinion shaft until it seats in the retaining groove.
6   Install the new gear and secure with the retaining clip.
7   Install the pinion gear assembly and secure it with the retaining bracket and bolt.

---

5   Extension housing oil seal — replacement

1   Raise the vehicle and support it securely on jackstands.
2   Remove the driveshaft (Chapter 8). Scribe marks on the driveshaft and yoke and the rear axle companion flange to assure proper positioning of the driveshaft during assembly.
3   Remove the oil seal from the end of the extension housing with a seal removing tool or a special Ford tool T71P-7657-A. If there is access, a thin blade screwdriver or chisel may also be used to remove the seal and the extension housing bushing, which is behind the seal.
4   Before installing the new seal inspect the sealing surface of the universal joint yoke for scoring. If scoring is found, replace the yoke.
5   Inspect the counterbore of the housing for burrs. Remove burrs with emery cloth or medium grit wet-and-dry sandpaper.
6   Install the new extension housing bushing and oil seal after coating the inside diameter of the seal with silicone sealant and the end of the rubber boot portion with grease.
7   Install the driveshaft using the scribe mark as a guide to assure correct balance. Lower the vehicle and check the oil level in the transmission. Add oil if necessary.

Chapter 7 Part B Automatic transmission

Contents

Specifications

Transmission types	C3, C5 and A4LD
Fluid capacity	
1986 2.3L and 2.9L A4LD (2x4)	9.5 US quarts
1986 2.9L A4LD (4x4)	10.3 US quarts
1985 A4LD (all)	9.0 US quarts
1983-1984 C3 (Ranger 4x2)	8.0 US quarts
1983-1984 C5 (Ranger 4x2)	7.5 US quarts
1983-1984 C5 (Ranger 4x4 and Bronco II)	7.9 US quarts
Ranger C3 (4x2)	8 US quarts
Ranger C5 (4x2)	7.5 US quarts
Ranger/Bronco II (4x4)	7.9 US quarts
Fluid type	See recommendation on transmission oil dipstick
C3 front (intermediate band) adjustment	Remove and discard locknut. Install new locknut. Tighten adjusting screw to 10 ft-lbs. Back off 2 turns. Hold screw and tighten locknut to 35 to 45 ft-lbs.
C5 intermediate band adjustment	Remove and discard locknut then install new locknut. Torque bolt to 10 ft-lbs then back off 4-1/4 turns. Hold screw and tighten lock nut to 40 ft-lbs.
C5 low reverse band adjustment	Remove and discard locknut then install new locknut. Torque bolt to 10 ft-lbs then back off 3 turns. Hold screw and tighten lock nut to 40 ft-lbs.

C3 transmission

Torque specifications	Ft-lbs
Shifter trunnion bolt	13 to 23
Bellcrank bracket bolts	20 to 30
Shifter bezel screws	2 to 3
Insulator to crossmember nuts	71 to 94
Insulator to transmission bolts	60 to 80
Driveplate to converter	27 to 49
Oil pan	12 to 17
Converter housing to engine	28 to 38
Outer downshift lever nut	7 to 11
Inner manual lever nut	30 to 40
Neutral switch to case	7 to 10
Oil cooler line to connetor	7 to 10
Connector to case	10 to 15
Converter drain plug	20 to 30
Filler tube to engine clip	28 to 38

C5 transmission

Torque specifications	Ft-lbs
Shifter trunnion bolt	13 to 23
Bellcrank bracket bolts	20 to 30
Shifter bezel screws	2 to 3
Insulator to crossmember nuts	71 to 94
Insulator to transmission bolts	60 to 80
Torque converter to driveplate nuts	20 to 34
Converter housing to engine rear cover plate	2 to 3
Oil pan to case	12 to 16
Engine to transmission	28 to 38
Drain plug to converter cover	15 to 28
Oil cooler line to transmission case	18 to 23
Neutral switch to case	55 to 75 in-lb
Cooler line tube nut	12 to 18

A4LD transmission

Torque specifications	Ft-lbs
Shifter trunnion bolt	13 to 23
Bellcrank bracket bolts	20 to 30
Shifter bezel screws	2 to 3
Insulator bracket to insulator bolts	60 to 80
1986 Insulator bracket to crossmember nuts	
2.3L 4x2 only	65 to 80
all others	71 to 94
1985 insulator to crossmember nuts	71 to 94
1985 insulator to transmission bolts	60 to 80
Transmission to engine	28 to 38
Converter housing cover to converter housing	12 to 16
Oil pan to case	5 to 10
Manual lever nut	30 to 40
Converter to driveplate attaching nut	20 to 34
Cooler line to case connector	18 to 23
Push connect cooler line fitting to case	18 to 23
Cooler line to connector tube nut	12 to 18
Neutral start switch to case	84 to 120 in-lbs

1 General information

Due to the complexity of the automatic transmissions covered in this manual and to the specialized equipment necessary to perform most service operations, this Chapter addresses only those procedures concerning routine maintenance and adjustment. Except for removal and installation of the transmission assembly, major repair operations should be undertaken by a professional mechanic with the proper facilities.

Models covered in this manual may be equipped with any one of three automatic transmissions. They are, the C3, C5 and A4LD, which are of the same fundamental design but with varying power handling capabilities. The A4LD automatic is the first Ford Motor Company production automatic transmission to use electronic controls integrated into the on-board EEC-IV system. These controls operate a piston/plate clutch in the torque converter that eliminates converter slip when applied.

Components of the A4LD are similar to the C3 automatic transmission from the intermediate brake drum rearward to the output shaft and extension housing.

Ford specifies a different grade transmission fluid than other manufacturers, and this must be used when refilling or adding fluid. The fluid specification for your vehicle can be found embossed on the transmission fluid dipstick or on the certification label on the left front door post.

2 General diagnosis

Automatic transmission malfunctions may be caused by four general conditions: poor engine performance, improper adjustments, hydraulic malfunctions and mechanical malfunctions. Diagnosis of these problems should always begin with the easily checked items such as fluid level and condition, band adjustment and shift linkage adjustment. Perform a road test to determine if the problem has been corrected or if more diagnosis is necessary. If the problem persists after the preliminary tests and corrections are completed, additional diagnosis should be undertaken by a dealer or repair shop.

3 Automatic transmission — fluid level check

See Chapter 1 for transmission fluid level and condition checking procedures.

4 Automatic transmission — removal and installation

Refer to illustrations 4.3, 4.18 and 4.19
Note: *If the transmission is being removed for a major overhaul it is important to completely clean all components, including the converter, cooler, cooler lines and control valve body. Contaminants are a major cause for recurring transmission troubles and must be removed from the system before the transmission is put back into service.*

1 If possible, raise the vehicle on a hoist or place it over an inspection pit. Alternatively, raise the vehicle to obtain the maximum possible amount of working room underneath. Support it securely on jackstands (refer to *Jacking and Towing* at the front of the book).

2 Place a large drain pan beneath the transmission oil pan. Working from the rear, loosen the oil pan bolts and allow the fluid to drain. Remove all the bolts except the two front ones to drain as much fluid as possible, then temporarily install two bolts at the rear to hold the pan in place.

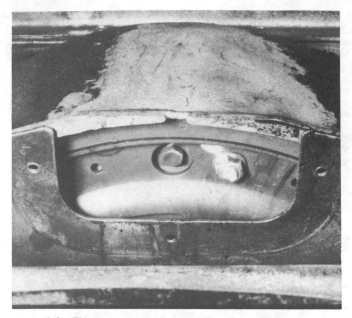

4.3   The converter drain plug (arrow) must be at the bottom center before removing it to drain the fluid from the converter

4.18   The oil cooler lines should be removed with the aid of a flare-nut wrench

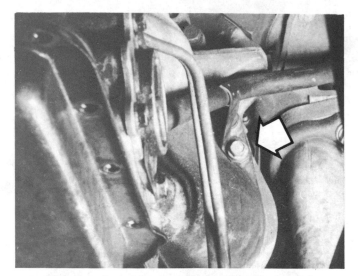

4.19   Location of the transmission filler tube (arrow) (C5 transmission shown)

10 Disconnect the neutral safety switch leads or wire connector.

11 Remove the vacuum line from the transmission vacuum modulator.

12 Position a transmission jack beneath the transmission and raise the jack so that it just begins to lift the transmission weight.

13 Remove the nuts and bolts securing the rear mount and insulator to the crossmember.

14 Remove the crossmember-to-frame side support attaching bolts and remove the crossmember insulator and support and damper.

15 Remove the nuts and bolts securing the crossmember to the frame rails, raise the transmission slightly and remove the crossmember.

16 Support the rear of the engine using a jack and a block of wood.

17 Lower the jack under transmission and allow the transmission to hang.

18 Disconnect the oil cooler lines at the transmission and plug them to prevent dirt from entering. Use a flare nut wrench to avoid rounding off the nuts (see illustration).

19 Remove the lower converter housing to engine bolts and the transmission filler tube (see illustration).

20 Place the transmission jack under the transmission.

21 Make sure that the transmission is securely mounted on the jack, then remove the two upper converter housing to engine bolts.

22 Carefully move the transmission to the rear and down and away from the vehicle.

23 Remove the transmission from the jack and remove the oil pan.

24 Clean all gasket material from the transmission oil pan.

25 Install a new oil pan gasket and tighten the pan bolts to specification.

26 Installing the transmission is essentially the reverse of the removal procedure, but the following points should be noted:

   a) Position the converter to the transmission, making sure the converter hub is fully engaged in the pump gear.

   b) Rotate the converter to align the bolt drive lugs and drain plug with their holes in the driveplate.

   c) When inserting the transmission, do not allow the transmission to take a nose-down attitude as the converter will move forward and disengage from the pump gear.

   d) When installing the driveplate to converter bolts, position the driveplate so the pilot hole is in the six o'clock position. First, install one bolt through the pilot hole and tighten it, followed by the remaining bolts. Do not attempt to install it in any other way.

   e) Adjust the kickdown rod and selector linkage as necessary.

   f) When the vehicle has been lowered to the ground, follow the fluid change procedures in Chapter 1 to refill the transmission.

   g) Start the engine and check transmission, converter assembly and oil cooler lines for leaks.

3   If the torque converter is equipped with a drain plug, remove the torque converter drain plug access cover and adapter plate bolts from the lower end of the converter housing. Remove the plug (see illustration) and drain the converter. Once the converter is drained replace and tighten the drain plug.

4   Remove the driveplate to converter attaching nuts, turning the engine as necessary to gain access by means of a socket on the crankshaft pulley bolt. **Caution:** *Do not rotate the engine backward.*

5   If equipped with a transfer case (four-wheel drive), refer to Part C of this Chapter for transfer case removal procedures.

6   Remove the driveshaft by referring to Chapter 8. Place a polyethylene bag over the end of the transmission to prevent dirt from entering.

7   Detach the speedometer cable from the extension housing by removing the hold-down bolt and withdrawing the cable and gear.

8   Disconnect the shift rod at the transmission manual lever and the kickdown rod at the transmission downshift lever. Remove the two bolts securing the bellcrank bracket to the converter housing.

9   Remove the three bolts retaining the starter to the engine and position the starter out of the way (refer to Chapter 5).

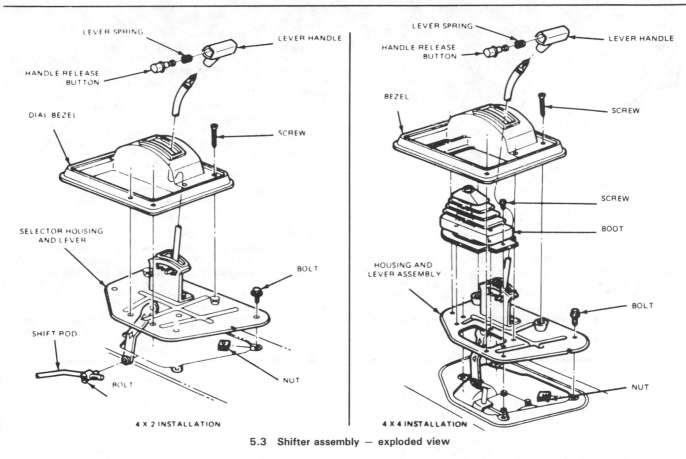

5.3 Shifter assembly — exploded view

5 Selector lever housing assembly — removal and installation

Refer to illustration 5.3

1 Loosen the trunnion bolt and remove the trunnion from the shift control arm grommet. **Caution:** *Use caution when removing the trunnion so as not to damage the shifter lower arm.*
2 Remove the shifter handle by grasping the handle firmly with the shifter in the Drive (D) position and pulling straight up.
3 Remove the attaching screws, disconnect the wiring connector and remove the bezel assembly (see illustration). On four wheel drive vehicles, remove the bolts retaining the transfer case shift boot to housing.
4 Remove the four (six on four wheel drive) fasteners attaching the selector housing to the floor pan and remove the selector housing from the vehicle.
5 To install, position the shifter in the floor pan opening and install and tighten the attaching bolts. On four wheel drive vehicles, install the transfer case shift boot.
6 Connect the shifter rod and trunnion to the lever and adjust the linkage. Apply grease to the trunnion prior to installation into the grommet.
7 Connect the bezel wiring to the body wiring connector and install the bezel assembly.
8 Position the lever in Drive (D).
9 Place the handle/button on the shift lever. Using a rubber mallet, strike a sharp blow to the center of the shift handle. **Note:** *If the handle chrome ring is not lined up with the shift lever lower character groove, the handle is not completely seated onto the shift lever. Remove and repeat the above procedure.*

6 Neutral start switch — removal and installation

Refer to illustrations 6.4 and 6.10

C5 transmission

1 Jack up the vehicle and support it securely on jackstands.

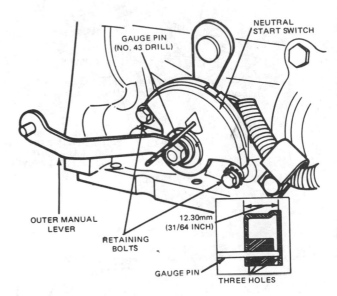

6.4 To remove the C5 neutral start switch remove the two retaining bolts.

2 Disconnect the downshift linkage rod from the transmission downshift lever.
3 Apply penetrating oil to the downshift lever shaft and nut and allow it to soak for a few minutes. Remove the transmission downshift lever retaining nut and lift away the lever.
4 Remove the two neutral start switch securing bolts (see illustration).
5 Disconnect the wire connector from the switch. Remove the switch.

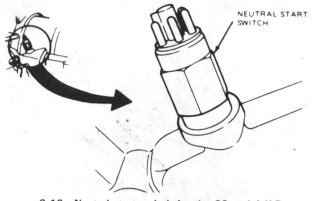

6.10   Neutral start switch for the C3 and A4LD transmission

6   To install, place the switch on the transmission and install the bolts finger tight. Move the selector lever to Neutral position. Rotate the switch and fit a No. 43 drill bit into the gauge pin hole. The bit must be inserted a full 1/2 inch (12.3 mm). Tighten the switch securing bolts fully and remove the drill.

7   Check that the engine starts only when the selector is in the Neutral and Park positions.

C3 and A4LD transmissions

8   Disconnect the ground cable at the battery.

9   Disconnect the electrical connector from the neutral start switch.

10   Use tool T74P-77247-A to remove the switch (see illustration). **Caution:** *Use of other tools could crush or puncture the walls of the switch.*

11   Install the switch and tighten to the specified torque.

12   Install the electrical connector.

13   Connect the negative battery cable.

14   Check that the engine starts only when the selector is in the Neutral and Park positions.

---

7   Shift linkage — check and adjustment

Refer to illustrations 7.2a, 7.2b and 7.2c

Floor shift linkage (all models)

1   Raise the vehicle and support it securely on jackstands.

2   Have an assistant position the shift selector in the Drive position and hold it in place during adjustment (see illustrations). On A4LD transmissions do not use Overdrive. **Note:** *Make sure the shift lever detent pawl is held against the rearward Drive (D) detent stop during adjustment (see illustration).*

3   Position the transmission manual shift lever in the Drive position by moving the lever all the way rearward, then forward the specified

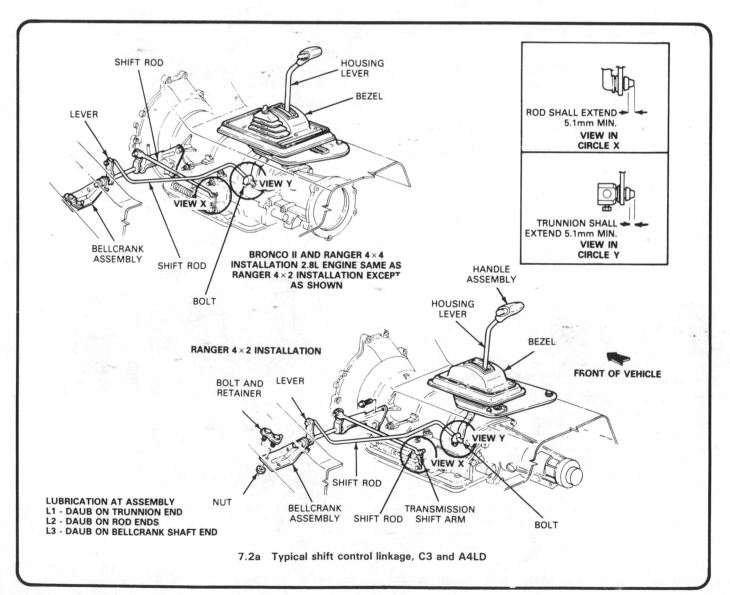

7.2a   Typical shift control linkage, C3 and A4LD

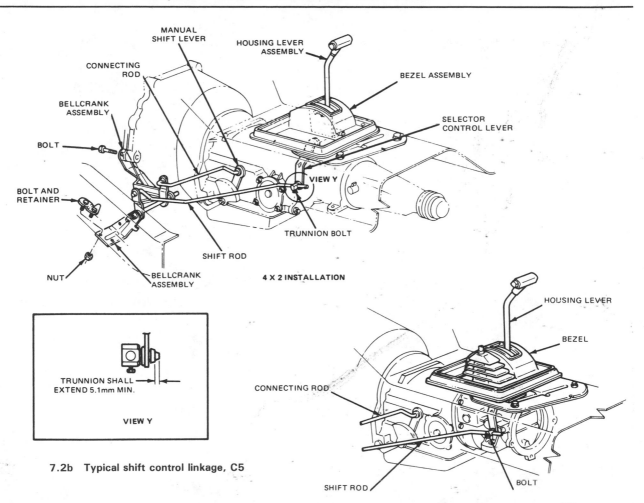

MANUAL SHIFT LEVER
HOUSING LEVER ASSEMBLY
CONNECTING ROD
BELLCRANK ASSEMBLY
BOLT
BOLT AND RETAINER
NUT
BELLCRANK ASSEMBLY
SHIFT ROD
BEZEL ASSEMBLY
SELECTOR CONTROL LEVER
VIEW Y
TRUNNION BOLT

4 X 2 INSTALLATION

HOUSING LEVER
BEZEL
CONNECTING ROD
SHIFT ROD
BOLT

4 X 4 INSTALLATION

TRUNNION SHALL EXTEND 5.1mm MIN.

VIEW Y

7.2b Typical shift control linkage, C5

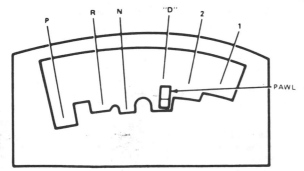

P   R   N   "D"   2   1
PAWL

PAWL TO BE AGAINST REARWARD "D" (DRIVE) DETENT STOP

7.2c Shifter pawl to be against the Drive 'D' position for proper adjustment

number of detents (three detent positions on C3, C5 models and four detents on A4LD).
4   With the levers in the Drive (D) position, apply light forward pressure to the shifter control lower arm while tightening the trunnion bolt. The forward pressure will ensure correct positioning within the drive detent.
5   After adjustment, check for Park (P) engagement. The control lever must move to right when engaged in Park (P). Check the control lever in all detent positions with the engine running to ensure correct detent/transmission action and readjust if necessary.
6   Remove the safety stands and lower the vehicle.

8 Bellcrank assembly — removal and installation

1   Raise the vehicle and support it securely on jackstands.
2   Disconnect the two shift rod ends from the bellcrank assembly levers.
3   Remove the two bolts attaching the bellcrank bracket assembly to the bellhousing. Remove the bolt and retainer assembly attaching the bellcrank assembly to the frame rail.
4   Remove the bellcrank assembly from the vehicle.
5   Installation is the reverse of the removal procedure with these noted exceptions. Apply multi-purpose grease to the bellcrank assembly shaft prior to insertion and grease the rod ends before inserting the rod into the assembly. **Note:** *New grommets are required in the bellcrank lever arms prior to rod installation.*
6   Refer to the Section on linkage adjustment and adjust the shift linkage.
7   Remove the jackstands and lower the vehicle.

9 Kickdown rod — adjustment

Refer to illustration 9.3
Note: *Whenever possible engine should be at operating temperature when kickdown rod adjustments are made.*

1   Place a six pound weight on the kickdown lever or have an assistant hold the throttle wide open.
2   From under the hood, check that throttle is in the wide open position.

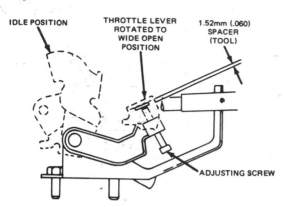

9.3 With throttle wide open insert the spacer tool and adjust the screw until contact is made

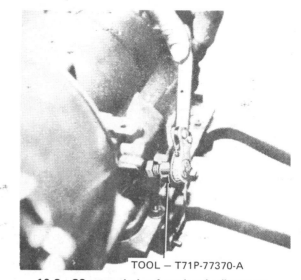

TOOL — T71P-77370-A

10.3 C3 transmission front band adjustment

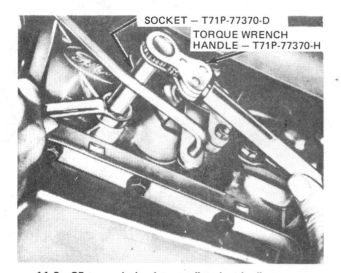

SOCKET — T71P-77370-D
TORQUE WRENCH
HANDLE — T71P-77370-H

11.3 C5 transmission intermediate band adjustment

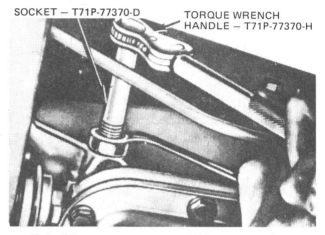

SOCKET — T71P-77370-D   TORQUE WRENCH
                               HANDLE — T71P-77370-H

12.3 C5 transmission low reverse band adjustment

3   Insert a 1.52 mm (.06 inch) spacer between the throttle lever and the adjusting screw (see illustration).
4   Rotate the adjusting screw until contact is made between the screw and spacer.
5   Remove the spacer.
6   Remove the weight from kickdown lever or have assistant release accelerator pedal. **Warning:** *After adjustment, check to insure the accelerator returns to idle on slow release of foot pressure without binding or dragging.*

10   Front band (1983-1984 C3) — adjustment

Refer to illustration 10.3

1   Remove the downshift rod from the transmission downshift lever.
2   Clean all dirt from the band adjusting screw area located on the left side of the transmission. Remove and discard the locknut.
3   Install a new locknut on the adjusting screw. Using tool T71P-77370-A or a preset-type torque wrench and socket as an equivalent, tighten the adjusting screw until the tool handle clicks (see illustration). The tool is preset and breaks loose when the torque reaches 10 ft-lbs.
4   Back off the adjusting screw exactly two turns.
5   Hold the adjusting screw to keep it from turning and tighten the locknut.
6   Install the downshift rod on the transmission downshift lever.

11   Intermediate band (1983-1984 C5) — adjustment

Refer to illustration 11.3

1   Clean all dirt from the band adjusting screw area located on the left side of the transmission next to the shift linkage. Remove and discard the locknut.
2   Install a new locknut on the adjusting screw.
3   Tighten the adjusting screw using tool T71P-77370-H and socket T71P-77370-D which is a preset torque wrench that releases when the torque reaches 10 ft-lbs, or a preset type torque wrench and socket as an equivalent (see illustration).
4   Back off the adjusting screw exactly 4-1/4 turns.
5   Hold the adjusting screw to keep it from turning and tighten the locknut.

12   Low reverse band (1983-1984 C5) — adjustment

Refer to illustration 12.3

1   Clean all dirt from the band adjusting screw. Remove and discard the locknut.
2   Install a new locknut on the adjusting screw.
3   Tighting the adjusting screw using tool T71P-77370-H and socket T71P-77370-D, which is a preset torque wrench that releases when

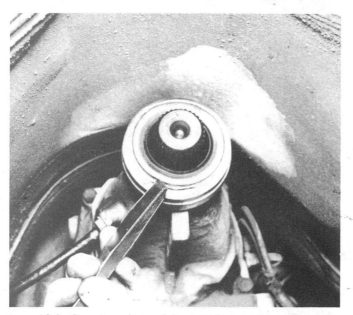

13.3 Be extremely careful not to damage the sealing surface on the housing when prying out the rear seal

13.6 The outside perimeter of the new seal should receive a generous bead of silicone sealant

the torque reaches 10 ft-lbs., or use a preset-type torque wrench and a socket as an equivalent (see illustration).
4   Back off the adjusting screw exactly 3 turns.
5   Hold the adjusting screw to keep it from turning and tighten the locknut.

---

13   Extension housing oil seal — replacement

Refer to illustrations 13.3, 13.6 and 13.7
1   Raise the vehicle and support it securely on jackstands.
2   Remove the driveshaft (Chapter 8). Scribe marks on the driveshaft and yoke and the rear axle companion flange to assure proper positioning of the driveshaft during assembly.
3   Remove the oil seal from the end of the extension housing with a seal removing tool or a special Ford tool T71P-7657-A. If there is access, a thin blade screwdriver or chisel may also be used to remove the seal (see illustration).
4   Before installing the new seal inspect the sealing surface of the universal joint yoke for scoring. If scoring is found, replace the yoke.
5   Inspect the counterbore of the housing for burrs. Remove any burrs with emery cloth or medium grit wet-and-dry sandpaper.

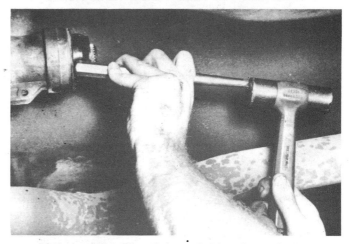

13.7 Installing the new extension housing seal with a punch and hammer. A large socket or length of pipe of the proper diameter may also be helpful as installation tools

6   Coat the outside (case) diameter of the seal with RTV sealant (see illustration).
7   Install the new seal into the extension housing (see illustration).
8   The remainder of the installation is the reverse of the removal procedures.

Chapter 7 Part C   Transfer case

Contents

Specifications

Lubricant capacity	3 US pints of Dexron-II automatic transmission fluid, XT-2-QDX or equivalent

Torque Specifications	Ft-lbs
Breather vent	6 to 14
Drain and filler plugs	14 to 22
Front driveshaft yoke bolts (1986 electronic)	12 to 15
Rear driveshaft flange bolts (1986 electronic)	61 to 87
Front and rear driveshaft bolts (1983-1986 manual control)	12 to 15
Shift control bolts — large	70 to 90
Shift control bolts — small	31 to 42
Shift lever nut	19 to 26
Skid plate to frame bolt	22 to 30
Transfer case to transmission adapter	
1983 to 1986 manual control	25 to 35
1986 electronic control	25 to 43
Upper shift control lever and heat shield bolts	27 to 37
Yoke nut	
1983 to 1985	120 to 150
1986	150 to 180
Wire connector bracket	5 to 7

1   General information — Borg-Warner 13-50 transfer case

Refer to illustrations 1.1, 1.5 and 1.6

Manual control

The Borg-Warner 13-50 is a three piece part-time transfer case (see illustration). The unit transfers power from the transmission to the rear axle and, when actuated, also to the front driveaxle. The unit is lubricated by a positive displacement oil pump that channels oil flow through drilled holes in the rear output shaft. The pump turns with the rear output shaft and allows towing of the vehicle at maximum legal road speeds for extended distances without disconnecting the front or rear driveshaft.

Due to the time and expense in rebuilding a transfer case, we recommend replacing a faulty unit with either a new or rebuilt unit. Your dealer or local transmission shop should be able to supply you with information as to the cost, availability and exchange policy concerning these units.

One of the biggest problems a beginner will face when working on the external and mounting components of a transfer case is trying to remember exactly where each part came from. To help alleviate this problem, it may be helpful to draw your own simple diagram or take instant photos during the disassembly process. Laying each part out in the order in which it was removed and tagging parts may also be useful.

Cleanliness is extremely important when working on a precision piece of equipment such as a transfer case. The work area should be kept as clean and free of dirt and dust as possible. Also, adequate space should be available to lay out the various parts as they are removed.

Electronic shift control

Mechanically, the electronically controlled transfer case is similar to the manual unit (see illustration).

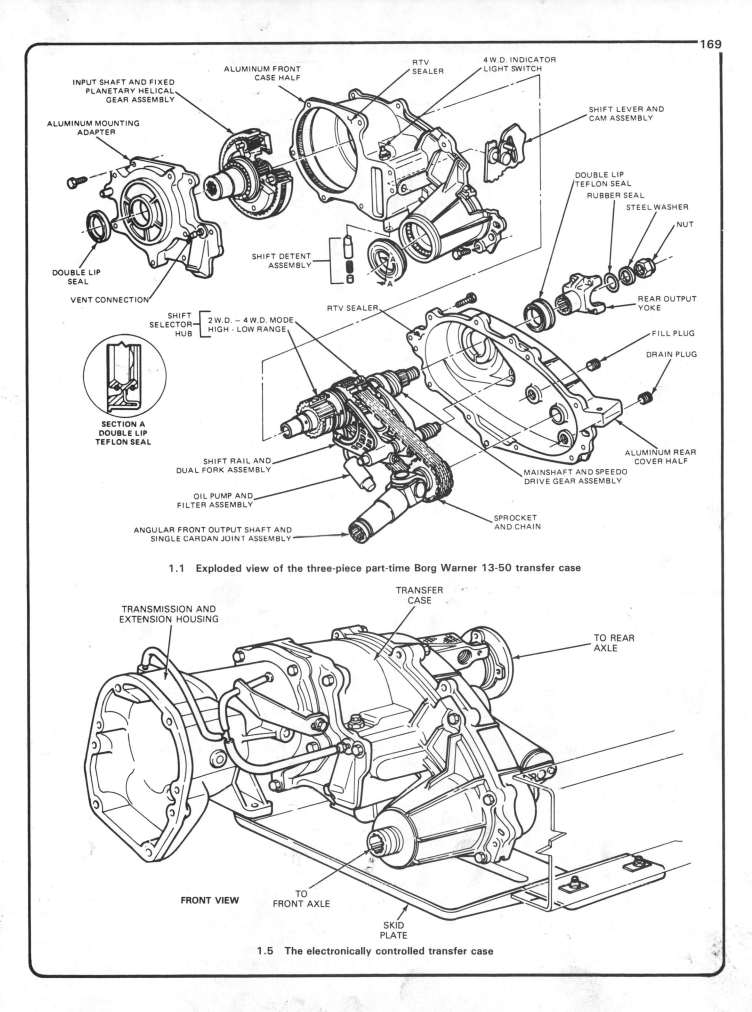

INPUT SHAFT AND FIXED PLANETARY HELICAL GEAR ASSEMBLY

ALUMINUM FRONT CASE HALF

RTV SEALER

4 W.D. INDICATOR LIGHT SWITCH

SHIFT LEVER AND CAM ASSEMBLY

ALUMINUM MOUNTING ADAPTER

DOUBLE LIP TEFLON SEAL

RUBBER SEAL

STEEL WASHER

NUT

DOUBLE LIP SEAL

VENT CONNECTION

SHIFT DETENT ASSEMBLY

REAR OUTPUT YOKE

SHIFT SELECTOR HUB

2 W.D. – 4 W.D. MODE
HIGH · LOW RANGE

RTV SEALER

FILL PLUG

DRAIN PLUG

SECTION A
DOUBLE LIP
TEFLON SEAL

SHIFT RAIL AND DUAL FORK ASSEMBLY

OIL PUMP AND FILTER ASSEMBLY

ANGULAR FRONT OUTPUT SHAFT AND SINGLE CARDAN JOINT ASSEMBLY

MAINSHAFT AND SPEEDO DRIVE GEAR ASSEMBLY

ALUMINUM REAR COVER HALF

SPROCKET AND CHAIN

1.1   Exploded view of the three-piece part-time Borg Warner 13-50 transfer case

TRANSMISSION AND EXTENSION HOUSING

TRANSFER CASE

TO REAR AXLE

TO FRONT AXLE

SKID PLATE

FRONT VIEW

1.5   The electronically controlled transfer case

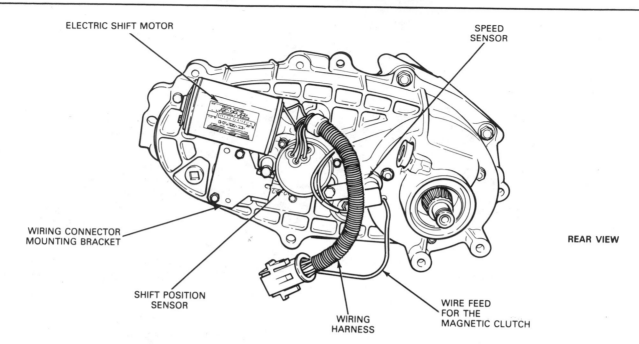

ELECTRIC SHIFT MOTOR

SPEED
SENSOR

WIRING CONNECTOR
MOUNTING BRACKET

REAR VIEW

SHIFT POSITION
SENSOR

WIRE FEED
FOR THE
MAGNETIC CLUTCH

WIRING
HARNESS

1.6   An electric motor controls the transfer case operation on the electronic shift model

**2.2   Remove the four retaining bolts to remove the
transfer case skid plate (if equipped)**

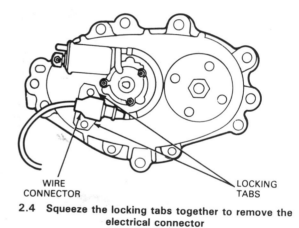

WIRE
CONNECTOR

LOCKING
TABS

**2.4   Squeeze the locking tabs together to remove the
electrical connector**

An electronic control unit (module) is located in the instrument panel. The unit accepts signals from the overhead console, the speed sensor and the shift position sensor (both located in the transfer case), and interprets the signals to control the operation of the transfer case.

At the rear of the transfer case an electric motor drives a worm gear and a rotary helical cam to shift the transfer case.

Inside the transfer case is a magnetic clutch, used to synchronize the rear and front output shafts, allowing shifts between two-wheel drive high and four-wheel drive high at any speed. The shift from four-wheel drive high to four-wheel drive low, however, cannot be made at speeds greater than 3 mph.

2   Transfer case — removal and installation

Refer to illustrations 2.2, 2.4. 2.5, 2.8, 2.9, 2.10, 2.11, 2.12a. 2.12b, 2.12c and 2.15

Removal

1   Raise the vehicle and support it securely on jackstands.
2   If so equipped, remove the skid plate from the frame (see illustration).
3   Place a drain pan under the transfer case, remove the drain plug and drain the fluid.
4   Remove the wire connector from the rear of the transfer case by squeezing the locking tabs together then pulling the connectors apart (see illustration).

2.5   Arrow points to four-wheel drive indicator plug

This system consists of a pushbutton shifter control mounted in an overhead console, a graphics display, an electronic control unit and an electric shift motor mounted on the transfer case (see illustration).

The graphics display indicates whether the vehicle is in two-wheel drive high, four-wheel drive high or four-wheel drive low mode.

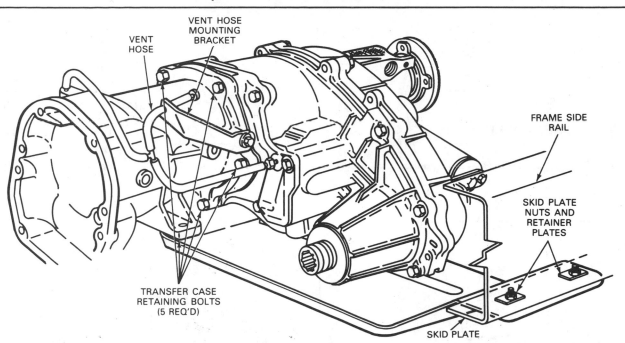

2.8   Disconnect the vent hose from the mounting bracket on electronically controlled models

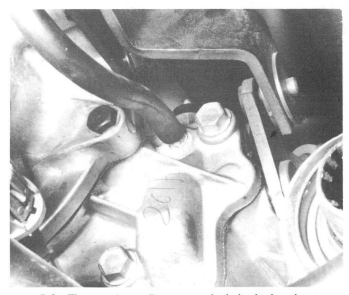

2.9   The vent hose slips over a nipple in the housing

2.10   Disconnect the large bolt retaining the shifter to the extension housing

2.11   Two bolts retain the heat shield to the transfer case

5   Disconnect the four wheel drive indicator switch wire connector at the transfer case (see illustration).
6   Disconnect the driveshafts (see Chapter 8).
7   Disconnect the speedometer driven gear from the transfer case rear cover.
8   On electronically controlled models, disconnect the vent hose from the mounting bracket (see illustration).
9   On mechanically controlled models, disconnect the vent hose from the control lever (see illustration).
10   On manually controlled models, remove the large bolt and the small bolt retaining the shifter to the extension housing (see illustration). Pull on the control lever unit until the bushing slides off the transfer case shift lever pin. If necessary, unscrew the shift lever from the control lever.
11   Remove the heat shield (if equipped) from the transfer case (see illustration). **Caution:** *The catalytic converter is located beside the heat shield. Be careful when working around the catalytic converter because of the extremely high temperatures generated by the converter. It is advisable to let the catalytic converter cool for several hours before beginning work.*

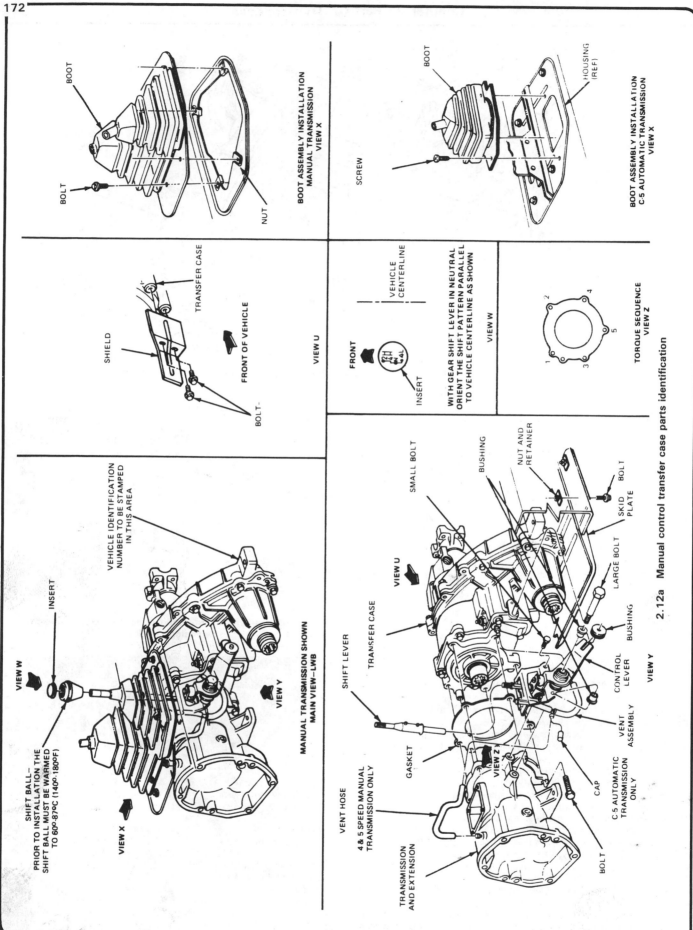

BOOT ASSEMBLY INSTALLATION
MANUAL TRANSMISSION
VIEW X

BOOT
BOLT
NUT

BOOT ASSEMBLY INSTALLATION
C-5 AUTOMATIC TRANSMISSION
VIEW X

BOOT
HOUSING
(REF)
SCREW

TRANSFER CASE
SHIELD
FRONT OF VEHICLE
BOLT
VIEW U

VEHICLE CENTERLINE
FRONT
INSERT
WITH GEAR SHIFT LEVER IN NEUTRAL
ORIENT THE SHIFT PATTERN PARALLEL
TO VEHICLE CENTERLINE AS SHOWN
VIEW W

TORQUE SEQUENCE
VIEW Z

SHIFT BALL—
PRIOR TO INSTALLATION THE
SHIFT BALL MUST BE WARMED
TO 60°-82°C (140°-180°F)

INSERT
VIEW W
VIEW X

VEHICLE IDENTIFICATION
NUMBER TO BE STAMPED
IN THIS AREA

MANUAL TRANSMISSION SHOWN
MAIN VIEW—LWB

VIEW Y

VENT HOSE
4 & 5 SPEED MANUAL
TRANSMISSION ONLY
TRANSMISSION
AND EXTENSION

SHIFT LEVER
TRANSFER CASE
VIEW U
SMALL BOLT
BUSHING
NUT AND RETAINER
SKID
PLATE
BOLT
LARGE BOLT
BUSHING
CONTROL
LEVER
VENT
ASSEMBLY
GASKET
C-5 AUTOMATIC
TRANSMISSION
ONLY
VIEW Z
CAP
BOLT
VIEW Y

2.12a Manual control transfer case parts identification

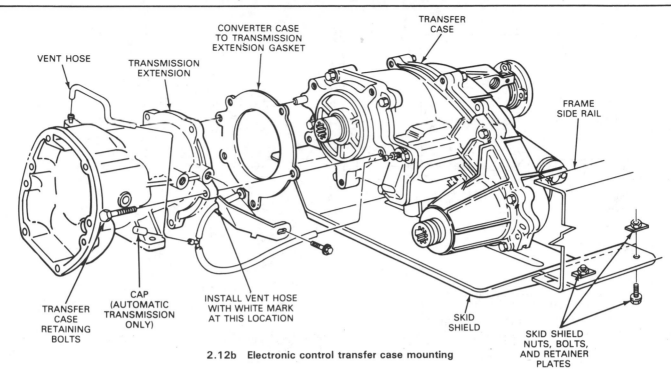

VENT HOSE

TRANSMISSION
EXTENSION

CONVERTER CASE
TO TRANSMISSION
EXTENSION GASKET

TRANSFER
CASE

FRAME
SIDE RAIL

TRANSFER
CASE
RETAINING
BOLTS

CAP
(AUTOMATIC
TRANSMISSION
ONLY)

INSTALL VENT HOSE
WITH WHITE MARK
AT THIS LOCATION

SKID
SHIELD

SKID SHIELD
NUTS, BOLTS,
AND RETAINER
PLATES

2.12b   Electronic control transfer case mounting

**2.12c   Use a block of wood between the jack and transfer
case when supporting the transfer case**

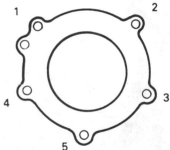

TIGHTEN
CASE-TO-EXTENSION
BOLTS IN THIS SEQUENCE

2.15   Retaining bolt tightening sequence

16 If applicable, install the vent assembly so the white marking on the hose is in position in the notch in the shifter or the mounting bracket (electronically controlled models). **Note:** *The upper end of the vent hose should be two inches above the top of the shifter on manually controlled models.*
17 Push the driveshaft boot to engage the external groove on the transfer case front output shaft and secure.
18 After installing the drain plug, remove the fill plug and fill the case.

12 Remove the five bolts retaining the transfer case to the transmission and the extension housing (see illustrations). Support the transfer case with a jack and a block of wood (see illustration).
13 Slide the transfer case rearward off the transmission output shaft and lower the transfer case from the vehicle. Remove the gasket from between the transfer case and extension housing.

Installation
14 Installation is the reverse of the removal procedure with these noted exceptions.
15 With the transfer case on a transmission jack, align the output shaft with the splines on the transfer case input shaft. Slide the transfer case forward onto the transmission output shaft and onto the dowel pin. Install the five retaining bolts and tighten in the sequence shown (see illustration). **Note:** *On manually controlled models, always tighten the large bolt retaining the shifter to the extension housing before tightening the small bolt.*

3   Shift lever — removal and installation

Refer to illustration 3.6
Note: *Remove only the shift ball if the shift ball, boot or lever is to be replaced. If the ball, boot or lever are not being replaced, remove the ball, boot and lever as an assembly.*

Removal
1 Remove the plastic insert from the shift ball. Warm the ball with a heat gun to 60°-87°C (140°-180°F) and knock the ball off the lever with a block of wood and a hammer. Be careful not to damage the finish on the shift lever.
2 Remove the rubber boot and floor pan cover.
3 Disconnect the vent hose from the control lever.
4 Unscrew the shift lever from the control lever.
5 Remove the large and small housing bolts retaining the shifter to the extension housing. Remove the control lever and bushings.

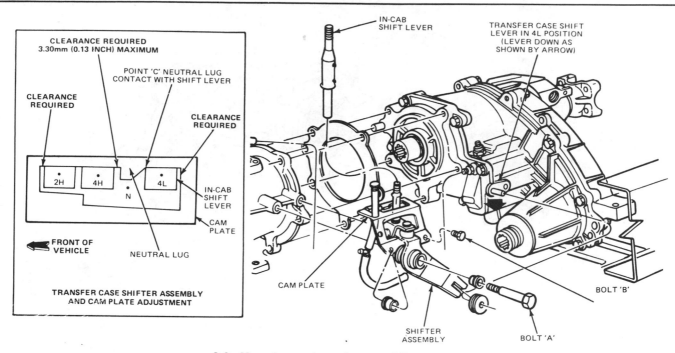

3.6 **Manual control transfer case shifter assembly**

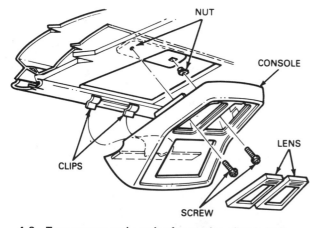

4.2 **Two screws and a pair of mounting clips hold the overhead console in place**

Installation

6   Prior to installing the shifter assembly, move the transfer case lever to the ''4L'' position (lever down) (see illustration).

7   Install the large and small bolts finger tight and move the cam plate rearward until the bottom chamfered corner of the neutral lug just contacts the forward right edge of the shift lever. Refer to accompanying illustrations.

8   Hold the cam plate in position and tighten the large bolt first, then tighten the smaller retainer.

9   Attach the shift lever to the control lever and move the in-cab shift lever to all positions to check for positive engagement. There should be clearance between the shift lever and the cam plate in the ''2H'' front, ''4H'' rear (clearance not to exceed 3.30 mm or 0.13-inch) and ''4L'' shift positions.

10   Tighten the shift lever to control lever bolts.

11   Install the vent assembly so the white marking on the house is in position in the notch in the shifter, if applicable. **Note:** *The upper end of the vent hose should be two inches above the top of the shifter and positioned inside of the shift lever boot.*

12   Install the rubber boot and floor pan cover.

13   Warm the ball with a heat gun to 140° to 180°F and tap the ball onto the lever with a socket and mallet. Install the plastic shift pattern insert. **Note:** *The end of the shift ball should be to the end of the knurl on the upper portion of the shift lever.*

14   Check the transfer case for proper operation.

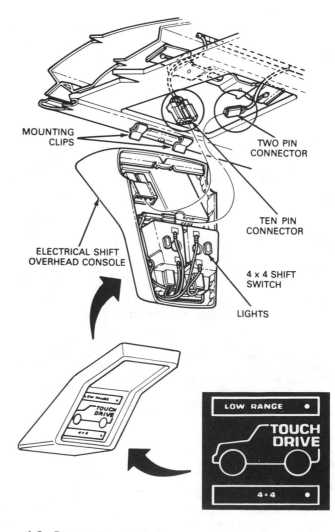

4.3 **Remove the electrical connectors to free the console**

4 Electronic shift overhead console — removal and installation

Refer to illustrations 4.2 and 4.3

1   Remove the two light lenses by prying in the notch at the top of each lens with a small screwdriver.
2   Remove the two mounting screws and pull down on the rear of the console, then push it forward to disengage it from the front mounting clips (see illustration).
3   Disconnect the electrical connectors (see illustration) and remove the console.
4   Installation is the reverse of the removal procedure.

5 Front output shaft oil seal — removal and installation

Removal

1   Raise the vehicle and support it securely on jackstands.
2   Remove the front driveshaft from the axle input yoke. Loosen the clamp retaining the driveshaft boot to the transfer case. Pull the driveshaft and boot assembly out of the transfer case front output shaft.
3   Place a drain pan under the transfer case, remove the drain plug and drain the fluid.
4   Remove the front seal from the output housing bore with Seal Remover Tool-1175-AC and impact slide hammer T50T-100-A, or their equivalents.

Installation

5   Make sure the housing face and bore are free of burrs and nicks. Coat the seal with multi-purpose grease and position the seal into the front output shaft housing bore, making sure the oil seal is not cocked in the bore. Drive the oil seal into the bore with output shaft seal installer T83T-7065-B and driver handle T80T-4000-W or carefully drive the seal into the bore with a hammer and a large socket as an equivalent.
6   Clean the transfer case front output female splines and apply multipurpose grease, then insert the front driveshaft splined shaft into the female splines.
7   Connect the front driveshaft to the axle input yoke and tighten the bolts.
8   Install the driveshaft boot over the external groove on the transfer case front output shaft and secure the boot with a clamp.
9   Install the drain plug and remove the filler plug and fill transfer case.
10   Replace and tighten the filler plug.
11   Remove the jackstands and lower the vehicle.

6 Rear output shaft oil seal — removal and installation

Removal

1   Raise the vehicle and support it securely on jackstands.
2   Remove the rear driveshaft from the transfer case output shaft yoke and wire the driveshaft out of the way (Chapter 8).
3   Remove the output shaft yoke by removing the nut, steel washer and rubber seal from the rear of the output shaft.
4   Remove the oil seal from the rear output housing bore with seal remover tool-1175-AC and impact slide hammer T50T-100-A, or carefully pry out the seal with a large screwdriver.

Installation

5   Installation is the reverse of the removal procedure with these noted exceptions:
6   Be sure the housing is free of burrs and that the seal is not cocked in the bore.
7   Drive the oil seal into the bore with output shaft seal installer T83T-7065-B and drive handle T80T-4000-W, or carefully drive the seal in with a hammer and socket matching the diameter of the seal.

Chapter 8   Clutch and drivetrain

Contents

Specifications

Clutch

Type	Single dry plate, diaphragm spring
Actuation	Hydraulic
Driveshaft type	One or two-piece with single or double cardan universal joints

Rear axle

Type	Integral carrier
Ring gear size	6.75 in, 7.5 in or 8.8 in. See identification tag
Rear axle oil capacity	
6.75 inch	3.3 US pints
7.5 inch	
1983-1984	4.0 US pints
1985-1986	
Ranger	5.0 US pints
Bronco II	5.5 US pints
8.8 in	5.5 US pints
Oil type	Ford EOAZ-19580-A (ESP-M2C154-A) or equivalent plus 4 ounces of Friction Modifier C8AZ-19B546-A or equivalent

Front driveaxle

Type	Dana Model 28
Hubs	Manual or optional automatic locking hubs
Oil capacity	17 ounces
Oil type	Hypoid gear lubricant C6AZ-19580-E or equivalent plus one-half ounce of Friction Modifier C8AZ-19B546-A or equivalent

Torque specifications	**Ft-lbs**
Clutch housing to engine block bolt	28 to 38
Clutch housing to transmission bolt	30 to 40
Pressure plate to flywheel bolt	15 to 24
Crossmember to right frame nut	110 to 140
Crossmember to left frame nut	
all except 2.3L Ranger 4x4	110 to 140
2.3L Ranger 4x4 only	75 to 95
Insulator to crossmember	71 to 94
Insulator to transmission	60 to 80
Clutch reservoir to firewall	1.5 to 2
Clutch master cylinder to firewall	15 to 20
Dust cover to clutch housing	5 to 10
Slave cylinder to clutch housing	15 to 20

CV-type driveshaft	
transfer case flange bolts	61 to 87
axle flange bolts	61 to 87
Single Cardan-type driveshaft	
circular flange bolts	
1983-1984	70 to 95
1985-1986	61 to 87
U-bolt nuts (Ranger 4x4 w/8.8 inch axle)	8 to 15
Double Cardan-type driveshaft	
transfer case bolts	
1983-1984	12 to 15
1985	12 to 16
1986	61 to 87
rear axle bolts	
1983-1984	12 to 15
1985-1986	61 to 87
Driveshaft to companion flange......................	70 to 95
Front driveshaft U-bolt nuts	8 to 15
Front driveshaft to front yoke bolts	10 to 15
Rear axle	
cover bolts (all except ratio tag bolt)	25 to 35
cover bolt (ratio tag only)	15 to 25
oil filler plug	15 to 30
pinion shaft lock bolt............................	15 to 30
Brake backing plate nuts/bolts	20 to 40
Leaf spring U-bolt nuts	55 to 75
Rear shock absorber to axle bracket	40 to 60
Front axle	
pivot bolt	120 to 150
pivot bracket to frame nut........................	70 to 92
axle stud	155 to 205
lower balljoint nut	
1983-1985	80
1986..	95 to 110
upper balljoint nut	
1983-1985	110
1986..	85 to 100
bearing cap bolts	35 to 40
carrier to axle arm bolts	40 to 50
carrier shear bolt	75 to 95
Front shock absorber to radius arm nut	42 to 72
Front spring seat nut	70 to 100
Front radius arm bracket bolt	
front...	27 to 37
lower	160 to 220

1 Clutch — general information

The single dry disc diaphragm-type clutch, consisting of the clutch disc, pressure plate and clutch release bearing, is actuated by a pedal operated linkage.

When the clutch pedal is in the up (released) position, the clutch disc is clamped between flywheel and the face of the pressure plate, thus transmitting the drive of the engine through the disc, which is splined to the transmission. Friction lining material is riveted to the clutch disc and the splined hub is spring cushioned to absorb transmission shocks.

When the clutch pedal is depressed, the clutch release lever (early models) moves the release bearing against the pressure plate diaphragm, which moves the pressure plate away from the clutch disc, disengaging the clutch and disconnecting the drive to the transmission. On newer models (1985-1986) a clutch sleeve is mounted over the input shaft of the transmission which eliminates the clutch release lever. The hydraulic system operates in the same manner as the earlier model by disengaging the clutch and disconnecting the drive to the transmission, only it achieves it without the use of the release lever. Clutch pedal free play is adjusted automatically by a hydraulic clutch control system which consists of a fluid reservoir, a master cylinder, a slave cylinder and connecting tubing.

The clutch reservoir is mounted directly in front of the driver under the hood. The clutch master cylinder is located on the lower firewall, below and outboard of the brake master cylinder. It is connected to the clutch pedal by a push rod. The master cylinder converts mechanical clutch pedal movement into hydraulic fluid movement. The slave cylinder is mounted on the bellhousing and converts the hydraulic fluid movement into mechanical movement to activate the clutch release lever.

2 Clutch — diagnosis and testing

Before removal of the clutch hydraulic system, verify the malfunction by removing the clutch housing dust shield and measuring the travel of the clutch slave cylinder push rod. Press the clutch pedal to the floor, and the slave cylinder push rod should extend 13.5 mm (0.53 inch) minimum against the clutch release lever. Do not replace the hydraulic system if push rod travel exceeds this distance.

If the slave cylinder travel does not meet this requirement, check the reservoir fluid level. Proper level is indicated by a molded-in step on the reservoir. Fill to the specified level with Ford Heavy Duty Brake Fluid C6AZ-19542-A or -B or equivalent. Be careful not to overfill the system. The upper portion of the reservoir must accept fluid that is displaced from the slave cylinder as the clutch wears. **Caution:** *Carefully clean the top and sides of the reservoir before opening to prevent contamination of the system with dirt, water or other foreign matter.* Remove the reservoir diaphragm before adding fluid. Carefully replace the diaphragm, cover gasket and cover after filling.

If the reservoir requires fluid, check the system components for leakage. Remove the rubber boots from the cylinder and check for leakage past the pistons. A slight wetting of the surfaces is acceptable. Replace the system if excessive leakage is evident.

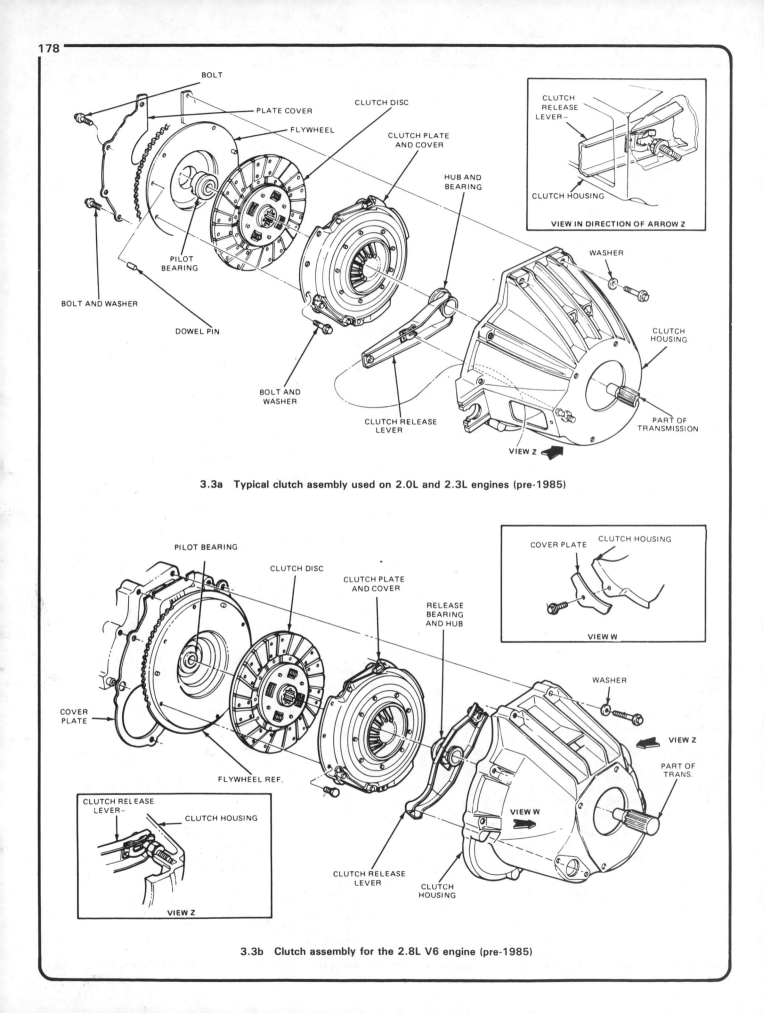

BOLT

PLATE COVER

CLUTCH DISC

FLYWHEEL

CLUTCH PLATE AND COVER

HUB AND BEARING

PILOT BEARING

BOLT AND WASHER

DOWEL PIN

BOLT AND WASHER

CLUTCH RELEASE LEVER

CLUTCH RELEASE LEVER

CLUTCH HOUSING

VIEW IN DIRECTION OF ARROW Z

WASHER

CLUTCH HOUSING

PART OF TRANSMISSION

VIEW Z

3.3a Typical clutch asembly used on 2.0L and 2.3L engines (pre-1985)

PILOT BEARING

CLUTCH DISC

CLUTCH PLATE AND COVER

RELEASE BEARING AND HUB

COVER PLATE

CLUTCH HOUSING

VIEW W

COVER PLATE

FLYWHEEL REF.

WASHER

VIEW Z

PART OF TRANS.

CLUTCH RELEASE LEVER

CLUTCH HOUSING

VIEW W

CLUTCH RELEASE LEVER

CLUTCH HOUSING

VIEW Z

3.3b Clutch assembly for the 2.8L V6 engine (pre-1985)

3 Clutch assembly — removal, installation and inspection

Refer to illustrations 3.3a, 3.3b, 3.3c, 3.3d, 3.7, 3.8, and 3.14

In 1985 a new hydraulic clutch system was introduced which eliminates the clutch release lever. Note the differences in the following procedures.

Removal

1   Raise the vehicle and support it securely on jackstands.
2   Disconnect the negative cable at the battery.
3   Remove the clutch hydraulic system on 1985-1986 models (Section 7). On earlier models disconnect the clutch master cylinder from the clutch pedal (see illustrations).
4   Remove the shifter (Chapter 7).

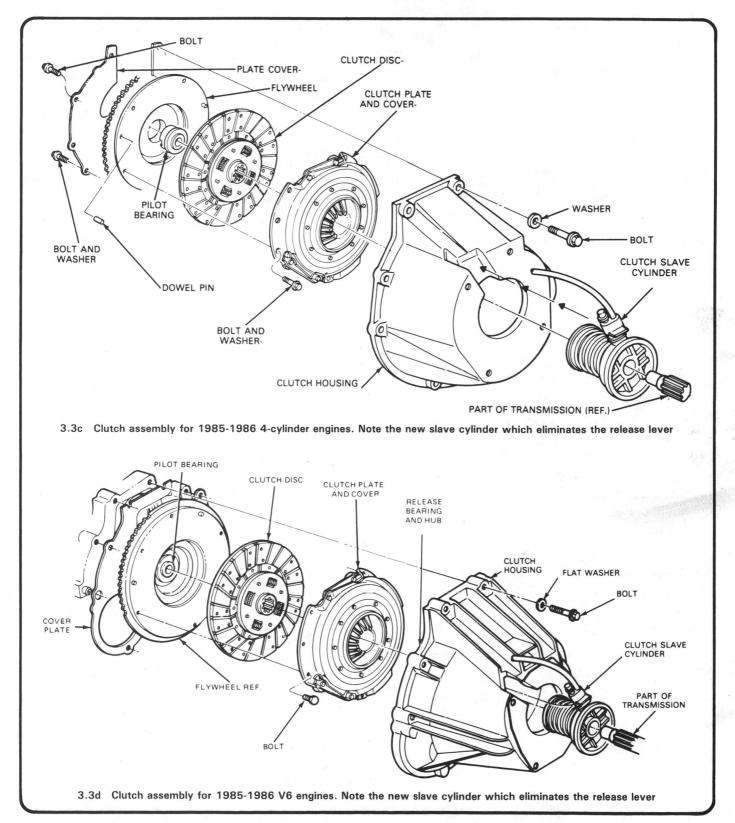

3.3c   Clutch assembly for 1985-1986 4-cylinder engines. Note the new slave cylinder which eliminates the release lever

3.3d   Clutch assembly for 1985-1986 V6 engines. Note the new slave cylinder which eliminates the release lever

5   Remove the starter (Chapter 5).
6   On early models, remove the dust cover from the clutch housing. Disconnect the hydraulic clutch linkage from the housing and release lever.
7   Index (paint or scratch a mark) the driveshaft to the companion

3.7   Make an alignment mark on the U-joint flange to align the shaft for reassembly

flange, to assure proper installation, then remove the driveshaft (see illustration).
8   Remove the nuts attaching the transmission and insulator to the #2 crossmember support (see illustration).
9   If equipped, remove the transfer case (Chapter 7).
10   Remove the bolts attaching the clutch housing to the engine and note the size and location of the bolts.
11   Raise the transmission with a transmission jack and remove the crossmember.
12   Lower the transmission and clutch housing.
13   Mark the assembled position of the pressure plate to flywheel for reassembly.
14   Loosen the pressure plate attaching bolts evenly until the pressure plate springs are expanded, then remove the bolts (see illustration).
15   Remove the pressure plate and clutch disc from the flywheel.

Inspection

16   Inspect the machined surfaces of the flywheel and pressure plate for scoring, ridges and burned marks. Minor defects can be removed by machining, but if any components are badly scored or burned they should be replaced with new ones.
17   Check the wear on the clutch fingers. If there is considerable difference in wear between the fingers, the excessively worn finger is binding, which means that the pressure plate assembly must be replaced with a new one.
18   Check the pressure plate for warpage, using a steel rule.
19   Examine the clutch disc for worn or loose lining, distortion, loose

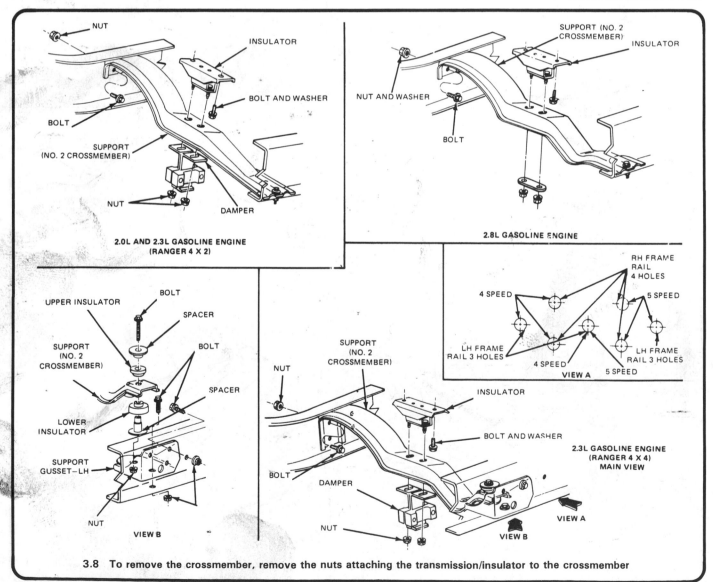

3.8   To remove the crossmember, remove the nuts attaching the transmission/insulator to the crossmember

nuts at the hub and broken springs. If any of these defects are found, replace the disc with a new or rebuilt unit.

20 Wipe all oil and dirt off the release bearing but do not clean it in solvent, as it is prelubricated. Inspect the bearing retainer for loose spring clips and rivets. Hold the bearing inner race and rotate the outer race. If it is noisy or rough, replace the bearing with a new one. Because of the nominal cost involved, it is a good practice to install a new release bearing every time the clutch is replaced.

Installation

21 To install, position the clutch disc on the flywheel so that the clutch alignment tool T74P-7137-K or an equivalent alignment tool can enter the clutch pilot bearing to align the disc.

22 When reinstalling the original pressure plate assembly, align the assembly and flywheel according to the marks made during removal. Position the pressure plate on the flywheel, then install the retaining bolts and tighten in sequence to the specified torque.

23 Remove the alignment tool.

24 On early models, position the clutch release bearing and the bearing hub on the release lever. Install the release lever on the release lever seat in the flywheel housing. Apply a light film of lithium base grease to the release lever fingers and to the lever pivot ball. Fill the annular groove of the release bearing with multi-purpose grease.

25 With the transmission on a transmission jack, raise the transmission and clutch housing into position. Install the #2 crossmember support to the frame. Install the connecting nuts, bolts and washers and tighten to specification.

26 Lower the transmission and insulator onto the support and install and tighten nuts then remove transmission jack.

27 If equipped, install the transfer case.

28 Install the driveshaft, making sure the index marks align on the companion flange.

29 Install and tighten the bolts attaching the housing to the engine block in the correct position as removed. Install the dust cover.

30 Lower the vehicle, connect and bleed the hydraulic system.

31 Install the shifter linkage.

32 Install the battery ground cable.

33 Check the clutch for proper operation.

---

4 Flywheel — inspection

1 Inspection of the flywheel is indicated when vehicle suffers from excessive transmission gear wear, transmission jumping out of gear, driveline vibration, clutch pedal vibration, pilot bearing noise or release bearing noise. Common complaint areas or obvious misadjustment should always be checked and corrected prior to checking alignment, to be sure the basic system is in working order.

2 Prior to inspecting the flywheel and pilot bearing, the transfer case (if 4x4), transmission, clutch housing and clutch assembly must be removed.

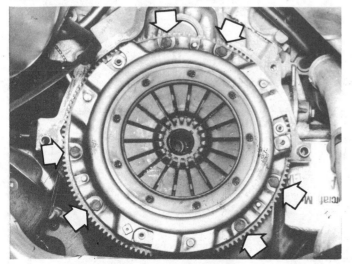

3.14 **Loosen the pressure plate bolts (arrows) one turn at a time in rotation until they are free**

3 Visually inspect the flywheel for any signs of cracking, warpage, scoring or heat checking. If any of these conditions exist, the flywheel must be removed and resurfaced at an automotive machine shop.

---

5 Flywheel — replacement

1 Refer to the sections pertaining to removal and installation of the transmission and clutch assembly and remove them.

2 If the flywheel is to be replaced, remove the retaining bolts connecting the flywheel to the crankshaft and lift off the flywheel.

3 Installation of the flywheel is the reverse of the removal procedure.

---

6 Clutch pilot bearing — removal and installation

Refer to illustration 6.1

1 A needle roller bearing is used as a clutch pilot bearing on all vehicles (see illustration). The bearing is inserted directly into the crankshaft. The bearing can be installed only with the seal end of the bearing facing the transmission. The bearing is pregreased and does not require additional lubrication. A new bearing should be installed whenever bearing is removed.

2 Remove the transmission, clutch and pressure plate (Section 3).

3 Pull the bearing from the crankshaft using a slide hammer or Ford tool T50T-100A or T59L-100B with puller attachment T58L-101-A.

4 To install the new bearing, coat the opening on the crankshaft with lithium grease. Apply only a small amount of grease, as the excess can find its way to the clutch, causing slippage.

5 With the bearing in position, tap it into the crankshaft. A socket and extension can be used to carefully tap the bearing squarely into place. Care must be taken when installing the bearing because it is easily damaged, which can lead to early failure.

6 Reinstall the clutch, pressure plate and transmission.

---

7 Clutch hydraulic system — removal and installation

Note: *The hydraulic system on 1985-1986 models is serviced as a complete unit. Individual components of the system are not available separately. The system does have a bleed procedure, but cannot be overhauled. Pre-1985 models can be serviced and individual components can be purchased.*

Caution: *Prior to any vehicle service that requires removal of the slave cylinder (i.e. transmission and clutch housing removal), the master cylinder push rod must be disconnected, permanent damage to the slave cylinder will occur if the clutch pedal is depressed while the slave cylinder is disconnected.*

1 Remove the lock pin and disconnect the master cylinder push rod from the clutch pedal.

2 On 4-cylinder models remove the bolt attaching the dust cover to the clutch housing and remove the cover. Push the slave cylinder rearward to disengage from the recess in the housing lugs, then slide outward to remove. For V6 models remove the bolts attaching the slave cylinder to the clutch housing and remove the slave cylinder. Disengage the push rod from release lever as cylinder is removed. Retain the push rod to release lever plastic bearing inserts.

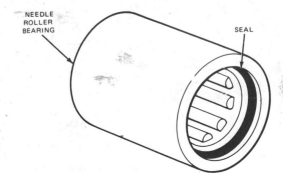

6.1 **The re-lubricated pilot bearing is a roller bearing type**

3   Remove the two bolts attaching the clutch master cylinder to the firewall.

4   Remove the two bolts attaching the fluid reservoir to the cowl access cover.

5   Remove the clutch master cylinder from the opening in the firewall and remove the hydraulic system assembly upward from the engine compartment.

6   To install, position the hydraulic system downward into the engine compartment. The slave to master cylinder tube routing is to be above the brake tubes and below the steering column shaft. **Note:** *On V6 engines the tube must lay on top of the clutch housing.*

7   Insert the master cylinder push rod through the opening in the firewall and install the attaching bolts.

8   Position the fluid reservoir on the cowl opening cover and install the attaching bolts.

9   Install the slave cylinder by pushing the push rod into the cylinder, engage the push rod and plastic bearing inserts into the release lever, and attach the cylinder to the clutch housing. **Note:** *With a new system, the slave cylinder contains a shipping strap that pre-positions the push rod for installation. Following installation of the slave cylinder, the first actuation of the clutch pedal will break the shipping strap and give normal system operation.*

10   For 4-cylinder models snap the dust shield into position and install the retaining bolts.

11   For V6 models install the bolts attaching the slave cylinder to the clutch housing and tighten.

12   Clean and apply a thin film of oil to the master cylinder push rod bushing and install the bushing and rod into the clutch pedal. Retain with the lock pin.

13   Depress the clutch pedal at least 10 times to verify smooth operation and proper clutch release.

8 Clutch hydraulic system — bleeding procedure

1   Clean any dirt and grease from around the cap.

2   Remove the cap and diaphragm and fill the reservoir to the top with brake fluid. **Note:** *To keep brake fluid from entering the clutch housing, route a rubber tube of appropriate inside diameter from the bleed screw to a container.*

3   Loosen the bleed screw, located in the slave cylinder body next to the inlet connection.

4   Fluid will now begin to flow from the master cylinder, down the red tube that feeds the slave cylinder. **Caution:** *The reservoir must be kept full at all times to ensure that no additional introduction of air gets into the system.*

5   Note that bubbles appear at the outlet. This means that air is being expelled. When the slave cylinder is full, a steady stream of fluid will come from the slave cylinder outlet. Tighten the bleed screw.

6   Place the diaphragm and cap on the reservoir. The fluid in the reservoir should be level with the step.

7   Exert a light load on the clutch pedal and loosen the bleed screw. Maintain pressure until the pedal touches the floor. Tighten the bleed screw. Do not allow the clutch pedal to return until the bleed screw has been tightened.

8   Refill the reservoir to the step. Install the diaphragm and cap.

9   Have an assistant actuate the clutch pedal slowly. Check for air in the red tube. If air is found, tap on the tube to encourage it to flow to the master cylinder. After the air has reached the master cylinder it will flow into the reservoir.

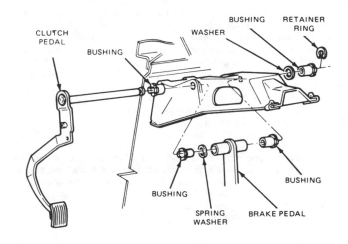

9.6 Clutch pedal — exploded view

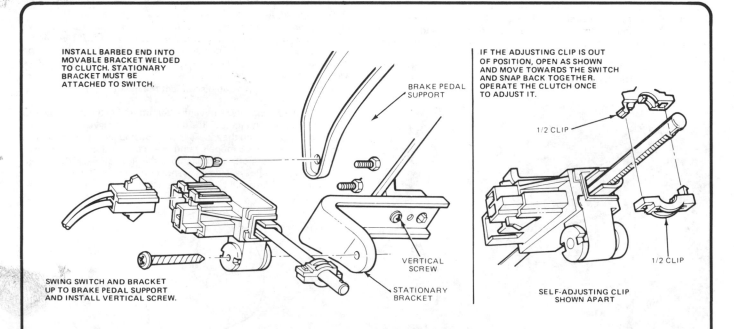

10.3 To adjust the clutch/starter interlock switch, press the pedal to the floor and position the half-clips on the rod closer to the switch

9 Clutch pedal — removal and installation

Refer to illustration 9.6

1 Disconnect the negative cable from the battery.
2 Disconnect the the barbed end of the clutch/starter interlock switch rod from the clutch pedal. Remove the lock pin and remove the master cylinder push rod from the clutch pedal. Remove the plastic bushing.
3 If the clutch pedal shaft is to be removed, remove the brake pedal as described in Chapter 9.
4 Remove the relay nut and lever.
5 Slide the pedal assembly from the pedal support bracket, then remove the entire assembly.
6 Inspect the pedal assembly, paying particular attention to the pedal pivot bushings (see illustration). If they are cracked or galled, replace them.
7 Prior to installation, lightly coat the clutch pedal pivot with oil.
8 Slide the clutch pedal shaft through the pedal support bracket.
9 Hold the pedal against the stop and install the master cylinder push rod.
10 Attach the retaining clip.
11 Pump and release the pedal several times to insure adequate hydraulic pressure.
12 Reconnect the negative battery cable.

10 Clutch/starter interlock switch — check and adjustment

Refer to illustration 10.3

1 Disconnect the electrical connector (located under the dash on the clutch pedal) at the switch.
2 Using a test light or voltmeter, check the continuity of the switch. The light should come on or the meter should read battery voltage. The switch contacts should be open with the clutch pedal up (clutch engaged) and the contacts should be closed when the clutch is depressed to the floor (disengaged).
3 If the switch does not work, remove the clip and reposition the clip closer to the switch (see illustration).
4 Depress the clutch pedal to the floor to reset the switch.
5 Replace the switch if it still doesn't work.

11 Driveshafts — removal and installation

Refer to illustrations 11.2, 11.3a, 11.3b and 11.3c
Note: *Where two piece driveshafts are involved, the rear shaft must be removed before the front shaft.*

1 Raise the vehicle and support it securely on jackstands.
2 Use chalk or a scribe to index the relationship of the driveshaft to the mating flange (see illustration). This will ensure correct alignment when the driveshaft is reinstalled.
3 Remove the nuts and bolts securing the universal joint clamps to the flange. If the driveshaft has a spline on one end be sure and scribe an index mark for installation (see illustrations).

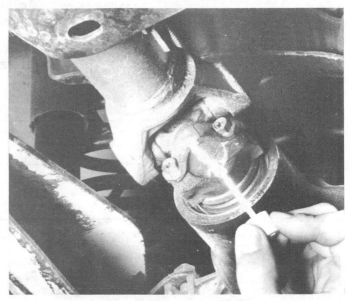

11.2 Index the driveshaft U-joint assembly for reinstallation

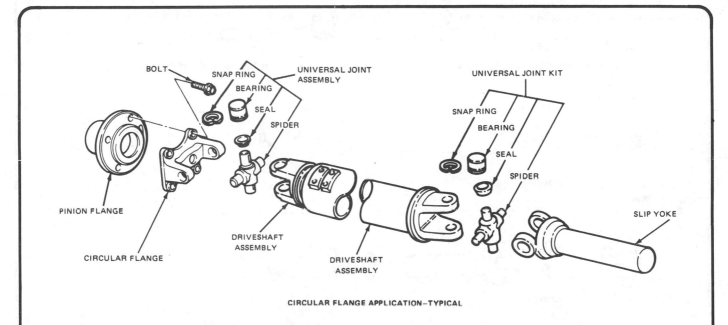

11.3a Exploded driveshaft and U-joint assembly for Ranger 4x2

4   Remove the nuts or bolts retaining the straps or universal joint to the flange on the opposite end of the driveshaft, if so equipped.

5   Pry the universal joint away from mating flange and remove the shaft from the flange. Be careful not to let the caps fall off the universal joints. **Caution:** *Do not allow driveshaft to hang free. support the driveshaft during removal procedures.*

6   Repeat the process for the opposite end if it is equipped with a universal joint coupled to a flange.

7   If the opposite end is equipped with a sliding joint (spline), simply slide the yoke off the splined shaft.

8   If the shaft being removed is the front shaft of a two piece unit, the rear is released by unbolting the two bolts securing the center bearing assembly. Again, make sure both ends of the shaft have been marked for installation purposes.

9   Installation is the reverse of removal. If the shaft cannot be lined up due to the components of the differential or transmission having been rotated, put the vehicle in neutral or rotate one wheel to allow the original alignment to be achieved. Always tighten the retaining nuts or bolts to the correct torque and make sure the universal joint caps are properly placed in the flange seat.

Front shaft — 4x4

Note: *This procedure requires a number 30 Torx bit to remove the attaching bolts securing the front driveshaft U-joint.*

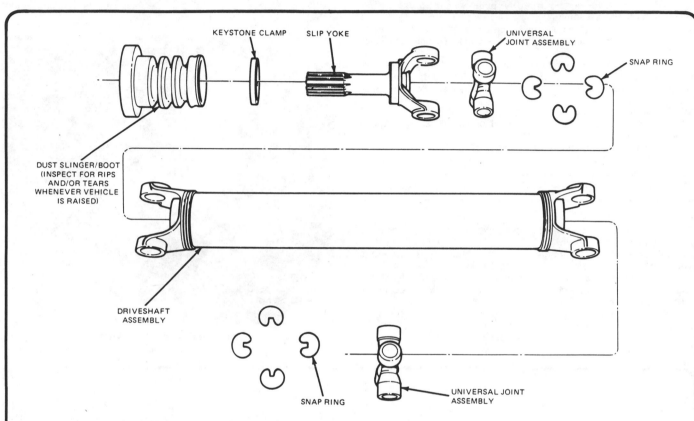

11.3b   Disassembled view of the front driveshaft and U-joints for Ranger 4x4 and Bronco II

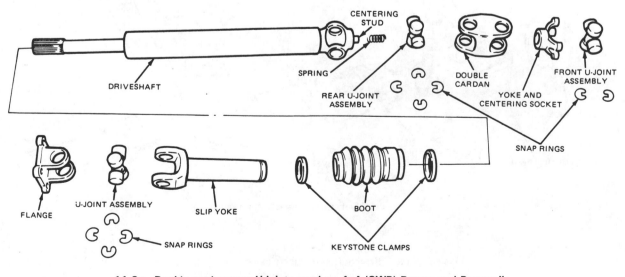

11.3c   Double cardan type U-joints used on 4x4 (SWB) Ranger and Bronco II

10 Scribe a reference line on the driveshaft to U-joint flange for in-stallation purposes.
11 Remove the bolts retaining the driveshaft to the front axle.
12 Remove the U-joint assembly from the front axle yoke.
13 Pry back the protective boot from the transfer case.
14 Slide the splined yoke out of the transfer case and remove the driveshaft assembly.
15 Installation is the reverse of the removal procedure, making sure to align previously scribed marks.

Constant Velocity (CV) driveshaft on Bronco II with A4LD automatic transmission

16 Removal is basically the same as on regular U-joint driveshafts except the driveshaft is attached to the transfer case and rear axle flange by the flanges on the outer bearing retainers.

12.2 The universal joint snap rings can be removed with pliers

17 Be sure to index the flanges when removing for proper balance on installation. **Note:** *The CV joint components are matched during manufacture and cannot be interchanged with components from another CV joint.*

12 Single Cardan type U-joint — overhaul

Refer to illustrations 12.2, 12.3a and 12.3b
1 Remove the driveshaft.
2 Position the driveshaft assembly in a sturdy vise and remove the snap-rings retaining the bearings in the slip yoke and in the driveshaft (see illustration).
3 Using a large punch or press, drive one of the bearing cups toward the center of the joint. This will force the opposite bearing out (see illustration). Grasp each bearing cup with pliers and pull it from the driveshaft yoke as it is being pressed out of the universal joint assembly. Drive or press the spider in the opposite direction so that the opposite bearing cup is accessible to be removed with pliers (see illustration). Use this procedure to remove all the bearings from the universal joints.
4 When the bearings have been removed, lift the spider from the yoke and thoroughly clean all dirt and debris from the yokes on both ends of the driveshaft.
5 We recommend the use of a vise when installing new bearings in the universal joint yokes. However, if a vise is not available, the bearings can be driven into position, with extreme care taken to prevent damage or misalignment.
6 Start a new bearing into the yoke at the rear of the driveshaft, posi-tion a new spider in the rear of the yoke and press or drive in the new bearing about 1/4-inch below the outer surface of the yoke. Install a new snap-ring.
7 Repeat the procedure on the opposite side of the yoke. Press or drive the bearing until the opposite cap, which has just been installed, contacts the inner surface of the snap-ring.
8 Install a new snap-ring on the second bearing.
9 Reposition the driveshaft so that the opposite end is accessible for bearing replacement. Install the new bearings, spider and snap-rings in the same manner as described previously.
10 Position the slip yoke on the spider and install new bearings and snap-rings.
11 Check both reassembled joints for freedom of movement. If any part has been misaligned and binds, this can sometimes be remedied by tapping sharply on the side of the yoke with a brass hammer. This should firmly seat the needle bearings and provide the desired freedom

12.3a The universal joint bearing cups can be pressed out with a vise and sockets

12.3b The bearing cup can be extracted with locking pliers

of movement. Exercise care to firmly support the shaft during this operation and under no circumstances apply direct blows to the bearings themselves. Do not install the driveshaft into the vehicle if there is any binding in the universal joints.

12　Install the driveshaft.

13　Double Cardan type U-joint — overhaul

Note: *The Double Cardan type U-joint is similar to the Single Cardan type, so refer to the Single Cardan procedure for photos showing U-joint removal.*

1　Remove the driveshaft.

2　Place the driveshaft in a vise, being careful not to dent the driveshaft.

3　Use paint or a small punch and hammer to mark the positions of the spiders, the center yoke, and the centering socket as related to the stud yoke which is welded to the front of the driveshaft tube. The spiders must be assembled with the bosses in their original position to provide proper clearance.

4　Use a small screwdriver to pry out the snap rings that attach the bearings in the front of the center yoke.

5　Using a large punch or press, drive one of the bearing cups toward the center of the joint. This will force the opposite bearing out. Grasp each bearing cup with pliers and pull it from the driveshaft yoke as it is being pressed out of the universal joint assembly. Drive or press the spider in the opposite direction so that the opposite bearing cup is accessible to be removed with pliers. Use this procedure to remove all the bearings from the universal joints.

6　With the front bearing cups removed, remove the spider from the center yoke.

7　Pull the centering socket yoke off the center stud and remove the rubber seal from the centering ball stud.

8　Remove the snap rings from the center yoke and from the driveshaft yoke.

9　Press or drive the bearing out as described previously.

10　With the bearing cups removed, remove the center yoke from the spider.

11　Remove the spider from the driveshaft yoke.

12　Clean all serviceable parts in solvent. If using a repair kit, install all of the parts supplied.

13　Remove the clamps on the driveshaft boot seal and discard the clamps.

14　Note the orientation of the slip yoke to the driveshaft tube for installation during assembly. Mark the relation of the slip yoke to the driveshaft tube.

15　Carefully pull the slip yoke from the driveshaft, taking care not to damage the boot seal.

16　Inspect the spline area and clean all foreign matter from the splines.

17　Lubricate the driveshaft slip splines with multi-purpose grease.

18　With the boot loosely installed on the driveshaft tube, install the slip yoke into the driveshaft splines in their original position.

19　Install new clamps on the driveshaft boot.

20　To assemble the Double Cardan joints, position the spider in the driveshaft yoke. Make sure the spider bosses (or lubrication plugs) will be in the same position as originally installed.

21　Use of a vise when installing new bearings will again be of assistance. However, if a vise is not available, the bearings can be driven into position, with extreme care taken to prevent damage or misalignment.

22　Start a new bearing into the yoke at the rear of the driveshaft, position a new spider in the rear of the yoke and press or drive in the new bearing about 1/4-inch below the outer surface of the yoke. Install a new snap-ring.

23　Repeat the procedure on the remaining bearings. Press or drive the bearing until the opposite cap, which has just been installed, contacts the inner surface of the snap-ring.

24　Pack the socket relief and the ball with multi-purpose grease, then position the center yoke over the spider ends and press in the bearing.

25　Install the snap rings.

26　Install a new seal on the centering ball stud and position the centering socket yoke on the stud.

27　Place the front spider in the center yoke and make sure the spider bosses (or lubrication plugs) are properly positioned.

28　With the spider loosely positioned on the center stop, proceed to seat the first pair of bearings into the centering socket yoke, then press the second pair into the centering yoke and install the snap rings.

29　Lubricate the U-joints through the grease fitting using multi-purpose grease.

14　Constant Velocity (CV) U-joint — removal and installation

Removal

1　Remove the clamp retaining the shroud to the outer bearing race and flange assembly. **Caution:** *The CV joint components are matched during manufacture and should not be interchanged with components from another CV joint. Do not mix or substitute components between CV joints.*

2　Remove the shroud, being careful not to tear it, and remove the rubber boot or outer bearing race and flange assembly. Remove the shroud from the dust boot by carefully tapping with a blunt tool.

3　Peel the rubber boot up and away from the outer bearing race and flange assembly.

4　Remove the wire ring retaining the inner race to the outer race.

5　Remove the inner race and shaft assembly from the outer race and flange assembly.

6　Remove the cap and spring from inside the outer retainer.

7　Use snap ring pliers to remove the clip that retains the inner race assembly to the shaft. Discard the circlip and remove the inner race assembly.

8　If necessary, remove the boot by removing the clamp which retains the boot to the shaft.

9　Pry the ball bearings from the cage with a small screwdriver. Make sure you do not scratch or damage the cage, race or ball bearings. **Caution:** *Remove any sharp edges on the screwdriver to insure against harming the finished edges.*

10　Rotate the inner race to align with the cage windows and remove the inner race through the wider end of the bearing cage.

Installation

11　Install the inner bearing race in the bearing cage. Install the race through the large end of the cage with the circlip counterbore facing the large end of the cage.

12　Push the race to the top of the cage and rotate the race until all the ball slots are aligned with the windows. This will lock the race to the top of the cage.

13　Once aligned, install the ball bearings. Press the bearings through the bearing cage with the heel of your hand. Repeat this procedure until all the bearings are replaced.

14　If removed, install a new dust boot on the shaft and secure it with a new clamp. Make sure the boot is seated in its groove. **Note:** *The clamp is actually a fixed diameter push-on metal ring.*

15　Install the inner bearing assembly on the shaft, making sure the circlip groove is exposed.

16　Install a new circlip on the shaft, being careful not to bend or twist the circlip during installation.

17　Install the spring and cap in the outer bearing retainer and flange.

18　Fill the outer bearing retainer with Constant Velocity Joint Grease, D8RZ-19590-A or an equivalent multi-purpose bearing grease.

19　Insert the inner race and shaft assembly in the outer bearing retainer flange.

20　Push the inner race down until the wire spring groove is installed and install the wire ring.

21　Fill the top of the outer bearing retainer with constant velocity joint grease D8RZ-19590-A or an equivalent multi-purpose bearing grease. Clean all excess grease from the outside of the bearing retainer.

22　Pull the rubber dust boot over the retainer and make sure the boot is fully seated in its groove.

23　Insert a dulled screwdriver blade between the boot and outer bearing retainer and allow the trapped air to escape from the boot.

24　Install the shroud over the boot and retainer and install the clamp.

15　Rear axle — general information

Refer to illustration 15.1

The 7.5 inch ring gear axle is standard. The 8.8 inch ring gear axle is optional. Either of these units may be equipped with a limited slip

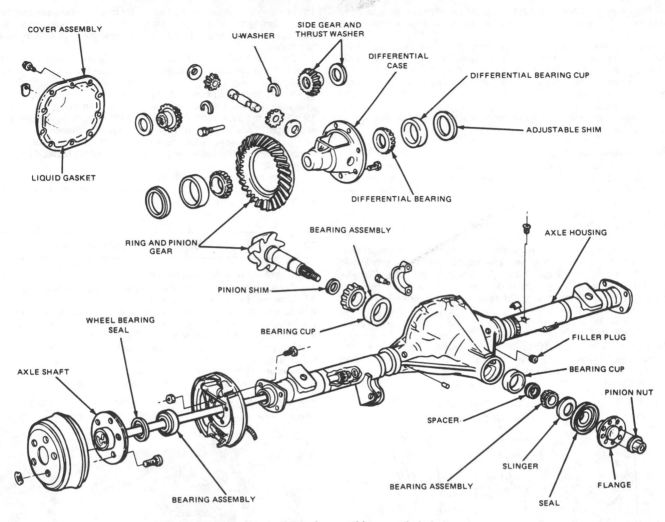

15.1 Rear axle 7.5 inch assembly — exploded view

differential. Earlier models (pre-1985) came with a 6.75 inch ring gear differential, which is similar in construction to the 7.5 inch axle assembly (see illustration). **Note:** *The 7.5 inch and 8.8 inch ring gear axle has 10 cover bolts. The smaller 6.75 inch ring gear axle has 8 cover bolts.*

On models covered in this manual, two basic types of rear differentials are used: the standard integral carrier type and the Traction-Lok limited slip differential, which is also an integral carrier. Integral carrier axles use C-locks on the inside end of the axle shafts to retain them. The Auburn type of limited slip carrier uses a unique type of C-lock, but is basically the same as the standard type. The two types of C-locks cannot be interchanged. The axle type and ratio are stamped on a plate attached to a rear housing cover bolt. Always refer to this plate code and ratio when ordering parts.

Certain rear axle and driveline trouble symptoms are also common to the engine, transmission, wheel bearings, tires and other parts of the vehicle. For this reason, be sure the cause of the trouble is actually the rear axle before adjusting, repairing or replacing any of the axle parts.

If replacing any rear axle components, carefully inspect the damage and determine the cause before disassembly. The inspection can help find the actual cause of the trouble and determine the action to be taken to correct the problem.

16 Rear axle assembly — removal and installation

1   Raise the vehicle and support it securely on jackstands.
2   Remove the wheels.

3   Disconnect the hydraulic brake lines from the rear axle housing and wheel cylinders.
4   Disconnect the emergency brake cable by removing the brake drums and disconnecting the cable from each side. Refer to Chapter 9 if necessary.
5   Disconnect the rear axle housing vent tube from the frame rail.
6   Position a jack under the rear axle and raise it.
7   Remove the U-bolt nuts retaining the leaf springs.
8   Lower and remove the rear axle housing from under the vehicle.
9   Installation is basically the reverse of the removal procedure.
10 Refer to the Section on adjusting the emergency brake and adjust the cable tension (Chapter 9).
11 Bleed the brake system.
12 Remove the jackstands and lower the vehicle after replacing the wheels.

17 Axleshafts, bearings and oil seals — removal and installation

Refer to illustration 17.9

Axleshaft

1   Raise the vehicle and support it securely on jackstands.
2   Remove the rear wheels and tires.
3   Remove the brake drums (Chapter 9).
4   Clean all dirt from the area of carrier cover with a wire brush.
5   Drain the rear axle lubricant by removing the housing cover.
6   On all axles except 3.73:1 and 4.10:1 skip to Step 8.

7   For axles 3.73:1 and 4.10:1 the pinion shaft must be rotated to
face the side gear to provide clearance for C-lock removal and
installation.
8   Remove the differential shaft lock bolt and differential pinion shaft.
Note: *The pinion gears may be left in place. Once the axleshafts are
removed, reinstall the pinion shaft and lock bolt.*
9   Push the flanged end of the axleshafts toward the center of the
vehicle and remove the C-locks from the button end of the axleshafts
(see illustration).
10   Remove the axleshaft from the housing, being careful not to
damage the oil seal.

Oil seal and bearing

11   Insert rear axle bearing remover tool T77F-1102-A, and slide hammer tool T50T-0100-A, or an equivalent axle bearing remover with
slide hammer, into the bore and position it behind the bearing outer
race. Remove the bearing and seal as a unit.
12   Lubricate the new bearing with rear axle lubricant and install the
bearing into the housing bore using axle tube bearing replacer tool
T78P-1225-A or a large socket to drive in the new bearing.
13   Apply multi-purpose grease between the lips of the axleshaft seal.
14   Install the new axleshaft seal using axle tube seal replacer tool
Y4T78P-1177-A or a large socket to drive in the seal. **Caution:**
*Installation of the bearing or seal assembly without the proper tools
may result in component failure if the seal becomes cocked in the bore
during installation.*

Axleshaft assembly

15   Except 3.73:1 and 4.10:1 ratio axles, carefully insert the axle into
the housing and install the C-lock on the button end of the axleshaft
splines, then push the shaft outboard until the shaft splines engage
and the C-lock seats in the counterbore of the differential side gear.

16   Position the differential pinion shaft through the case and pinion
gears, aligning the hole in the shaft with the lock bolt hole. Apply thread
locking compound to the lock bolt and install the lock bolt in the lock
bolt hole.
17   On 3.73:1 and 4.10:1 ratio axles rotate the pinion shaft so the
relief in the shaft faces the side gear and install the C-lock on the axleshaft button end.
18   Rotate the pinion shaft 180° so the relief faces the opposite side
gear and install the C-lock on the axleshaft button end.
19   Rotate the pinion shaft 90° to align the hole in the case and shaft
and install the lock bolt and tighten to specifications.
20   Clean the gasket mounting surface on the rear axle housing and
cover. Apply a continuous bead of silicone sealant D6AZ-19562-B or
equivalent.
21   Install and tighten the cover bolts.
22   Add lubricant until it is 1/2-inch below the bottom of the filler hole.
23   Install and tighten the filler plug.

18   Manual locking hubs — removal and installation

Refer to illustrations 18.4 and 18.5
1   Raise the front of the vehicle and support it securely on jackstands.
2   Remove the front wheels and tires.
3   Remove the retainer washers from the lug nut studs and remove
the manual locking hub assembly.
4   To remove the internal hub lock assembly from the outer body
assembly, remove the outer lock ring seated in the hub body groove.
Insert a small screwdriver behind the ring inside one of the splined
grooves and work the ring gently out of its groove (see illustration).
5   The internal assembly, spring and clutch gear will now slide out

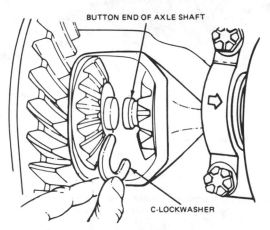

**17.9   With the axleshafts pushed inwards the C-locks can
be removed**

**18.4 Insert a small screwdriver behind the ring, inside one
of the splined grooves inside the manual locking hub, and
work the retaining ring gently out of its groove**

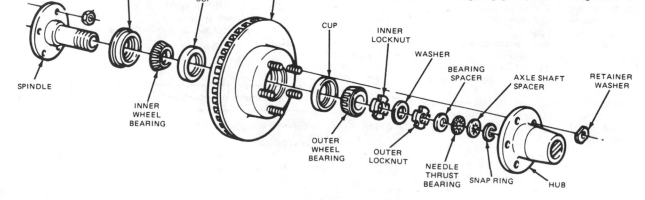

18.5   Manual locking hubs — exploded view

of hub body (see illustration). **Caution:** *Do not remove the screw from the plastic dial.*

6   Rebuild the hub assembly in the reverse order of disassembly. Apply multi-purpose grease to all internal parts before reassembly.

7   Install the manual locking hub assembly over the spindle and place the retainer washers on the lug nut studs.

8   Install the wheel and tire assembly.

9   Refer to the manual locking hub adjustment Section.

---

19   Manual locking hubs — adjustment

Refer to illustrations 19.5 and 19.6

1   Raise the vehicle and support it securely on jackstands.

2   Remove the front wheels.

3   Remove the retainer washers from lug nut studs and remove the manual locking hub assembly from the spindle.

4   Remove the snap ring from the end of the spindle shaft.

5   Remove the axleshaft spacer, needle thrust bearing and bearing spacer (see illustration).

6   Remove the outer wheel bearing locknut from the spindle using Four-Prong Spindle Nut Spanner Wrench, T83T-1197-A (see illustration). Check that the tabs on the tool engage the slots in locknut.

7   Remove the locknut washer from spindle.

8   Loosen the inner wheel bearing locknut using spanner wrench and make sure tabs on tool engages slots in locknut and that slot in tool is over the pin on the locknut.

9   Tighten the inner locknut to specification to seat the bearings.

10   Spin the rotor and back off the inner locknut 1/4-turn. Install the lockwasher on spindle. If necessary, turn the inner locknut slightly so pin on locknut aligns with the closest hole in the lockwasher.

11   Install the outer wheel bearing locknut using the four pronged wrench.

12   Install the bearing thrust spacer, needle thrust bearing and axleshaft spacer.

13   Clip the snap ring onto the end of the spindle.

14   Install the manual hub assembly over the spindle and install the retainer washers.

15   Install the wheels and tires.

---

20   Automatic locking hubs — removal and adjustment

Refer to illustrations 20.3, 20.6 and 20.14

1   Raise the vehicle and support it securely on jackstands.

2   Remove the front wheels and tires.

3   Remove the retainer washers from lug nut studs and remove the locking hub assembly from the spindle (see illustration).

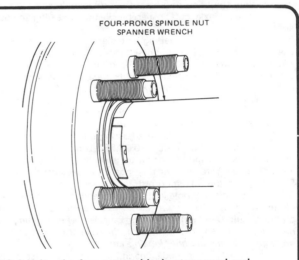

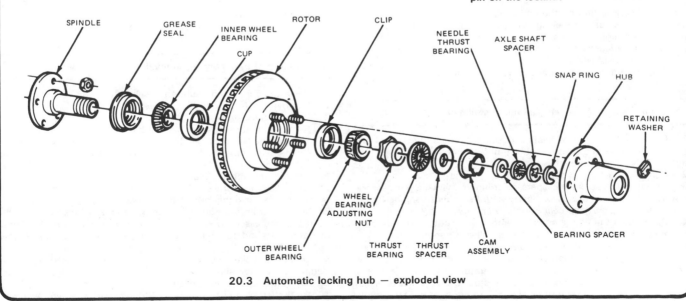

19.5   After the snap ring has been removed, lift off the axleshaft spacer, needle thrust bearing and bearing spacer

19.6 Using the four-pronged locknut removal and installation tool, loosen the inner locknut from the spindle, making sure the small slot (center) is over the pin on the locknut

20.3   Automatic locking hub — exploded view

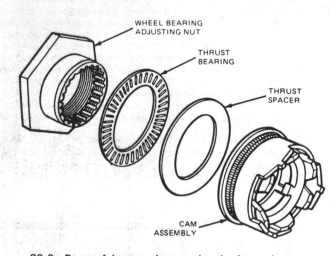

20.6 Be careful not to damage the plastic moving cam when removing the cam assembly from the wheel bearing adjusting nut

4   Remove the snap ring from the end spindle shaft.
5   Remove the axleshaft spacer, needle thrust bearing and the bearing spacer.
6   Being careful not to damage the plastic moving cam, pull the cam assembly, thrust spacer and needle thrust bearing from the adjusting nut (see illustration). **Caution:** *To prevent damage to the spindle threads, look into the spindle keyway under the adjusting nut hole and remove any portion of the locking key that has been separated from the cam assembly before removing the adjusting nut. If this condition exists, discard the entire cam assembly and replace with service kit 1A053 or equivalent aftermarket kit.*
7   Loosen the wheel bearing adjusting nut from the spindle using a 2-3/8 inch hex socket tool, T70T-4252-B or an equivalent socket.
8   While the rotating hub and rotor assembly, tighten the wheel bearing adjusting nut to seat the bearings, then back off the nut 1/4-turn.
9   Retighten the adjusting nut.
10 Align the closest hole in the wheel bearing adjusting nut with the center of the spindle keyway slot. Advance the nut to next hole if required. **Caution:** *Extreme care must be taken when aligning the spindle nut adjusting hole with the center of the spindle keyway slot to prevent damage to cam assembly locking key.*
11 Install the locknut needle bearing and thrust washer in the reverse order of removal and push or press the cam assembly onto the locknut by lining up the key.
12 Install the bearing thrust washer, needle thrust bearing and axleshaft spacer.
13 Clip the snap ring on the end of spindle.
14 Install the automatic locking hub assembly over the spindle by lining up the three legs in hub assembly with three pockets in the cam assembly (see illustration) and install the retainer washers.
15 Install wheels and tires.
16 Remove the jackstands and lower the vehicle.

---

21   Front axle (4x4) — removal and installation

1   Raise the vehicle and install jackstands under the radius arm brackets. Disconnect the driveshaft from the front axle yoke (see Section on driveshaft removal).
2   Remove the front wheels and tires.
3   Remove the disc brake calipers, referring to Chapter 9 if necessary. **Caution:** *Do not let the caliper hang with its weight hanging on the brake lines. Support the caliper on a frame rail.*
4   Disconnect the tie rod ends by removing the cotter pins and nuts retaining the steering linkage to the spindles (Chapter 10).
5   Position a jack under the axle arm assembly and slightly compress the coil spring. Once compressed, remove the nut retaining the lower portion of the spring to the axle arm. Carefully lower the jack, and remove the coil spring, spacer, seat and stud. **Caution:** *The axle arm assembly must be supported on the jack throughout spring removal*

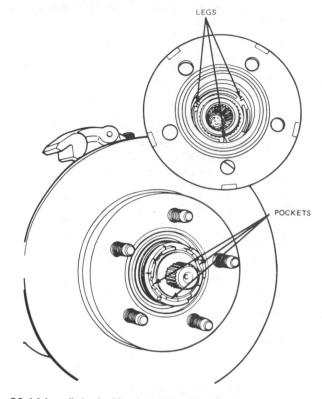

20.14 Install the locking hub assembly over the spindle by lining up the three legs in the hub assembly with the three pockets in the cam assembly and installing the retaining washers

and installation. Do not let the arm assembly hang suspended by the brake hose. These precautions must be taken to prevent serious damage to the tube portion of the caliper hose assembly.
6   Remove the shock absorber from the radius arm bracket.
7   Remove the stud and bolts that connect the radius arm bracket and radius arm to the axle arm. Remove the bracket and radius arm.
8   Remove the pivot bolt securing the right axle arm assembly to the crossmember. Remove the clamps securing the axleshaft boot from the axleshaft slip yoke and axleshaft and then slide the rubber boot over the stub shaft. Once the right driveshaft is disconnected from the slip yoke, lower the jack and remove the right axle arm assembly.
9   Position another jack under the differential housing and remove the bolt connecting the left axle to the crossmember. Lower and remove the left axle arm assembly.
10 Installation is the reverse of the removal procedure.

---

22   Shaft joint assembly — removal and installation

1   Raise the vehicle and support it securely on jackstands.
2   Remove the front wheels and tires.
3   Remove the calipers.
4   Remove the locking hubs, wheel bearings and lock nuts.
5   Remove the nuts retaining the spindle to the steering knuckle. Tap the spindle with a plastic or soft hammer to jar the spindle free and remove the spindle.
6   Remove the splash shield.
7   On the right side of the vehicle, remove the shaft and joint assembly by pulling the assembly out of the carrier.
8   Working from the right side, remove the metal clamps from the shaft and joint assembly and the stub shaft. Slide the rubber boot onto the stub shaft and pull the shaft and joint assembly from the splines of the stub shaft.
9   On the right side of carrier, install the rubber boot and new metal clamps on the stub shaft slip yoke. The spline will fit only one way. Be sure it is fully seated and crimp the metal clamp.
10 On the left side of the carrier, slide the shaft and joint assembly

through the knuckle and engage the splines on the shaft in the carrier.
11 Install the splash shield and spindle on the steering knuckle and install and tighten the spindle nuts.
12 Using bearing cup replacer T73T-4222-B and driver handle T80T-4000-W or their equivalents, drive the bearing cups into the rotor.
13 Pack the inner liner and outer wheel bearings with multi-purpose grease.
14 Place the inner wheel bearing into the inner cup and drive the grease seal into the bore with the previously mentioned seal replacer. Coat the bearing seal lip with multi-purpose grease.
15 Install the rotor on the spindle and install the outer wheel bearing into the cup.
16 Install the locknut, thrust bearing, snap ring and locking hubs.
17 Install the brake calipers.
18 Replace the wheels and tires.
19 Remove the jackstands and lower the vehicle.

23 Right slip yoke and stub shaft assembly, carrier, carrier oil seal, and bearing — removal and installation

1   Raise the vehicle and support it securely on jackstands.
2   Remove the front wheels and tires.
3   Remove the nuts and U-bolts connecting the driveshaft to the yoke.
4   Refer to Section 22 and remove both spindles and the left and right shaft and U-joint assemblies.
5   Support the carrier with a transmission jack and remove both bolts retaining the carrier to the support arm. Separate the carrier from the support arm and drain the lubricant from the carrier. Remove the carrier.
6   Rotate the slip yoke and shaft assembly so the open side of the snap ring is exposed. Remove the snap ring.
7   Remove the slip yoke and shaft assembly from the carrier.
8   Remove the oil seal and caged needle bearings.
9   Clean and inspect the bearing bore for nicks and burrs before installing a new caged needle bearing. Drive the bearing in until it is fully seated in the bore.

10 Coat the seal with multi-purpose lubricant and drive it into the carrier housing.
11 Install the slip yoke and shaft assembly into the carrier so the groove in the shaft is visible.
12 Install the snap ring in the groove.
13 Clean all traces of gasket sealant from the mating surfaces. Apply RTV sealant in a bead 1/4 inch wide. The bead should be continuous and should not pass through or outside the holes.
14 Position the carrier on a transmission jack and install it in position on the support arm, using the guide pins to align it. Install and tighten the bolts in a clockwise pattern.
15 Install the shear bolt retaining the carrier to the axle arm and tighten.
16 Install both spindles and the left and right shaft and joint assemblies.
17 Connect the driveshaft to the yoke.
18 Fill the carrier with lubricant.
19 Install the wheels and tires, remove the jackstands and lower the vehicle.

24 Universal joints — check

1   Wear in the universal joints is characterized by vibration in the driveline, clunking noises when starting from a standstill and metallic squeaking and grating sounds. Another symptom of universal joint or driveline bearing problems is a harmonic rumbling at highway cruising speeds.
2   To make a check of universal joint condition, park the vehicle on a level surface with the transmission in gear (manual transmission) or Park. Block the wheels and engage the parking brake.
3   From underneath the car, hold the axle pinion flange with one hand while moving the driveshaft with the other. If there is noticeable looseness in the universal joint, the joint is worn and should be replaced with a new one.
4   Repeat this check at the front of the driveshaft, paying particular attention to the universal joint condition and wear or looseness in the sliding spline section of the yoke.

Chapter 9 Brakes

Contents

Specifications

General
Brake fluid type	DOT type 3
Brake fluid level	1/4-inch from top of reservoir

Drum brakes
Drum wear limit	Specified on drum
Brake lining wear limit	1/8-inch above rivet heads

Disc brakes
Pad lining service limit	1/8-in from shoe surface
Lining to disc clearance	0.010 in max
Disc thickness	
standard	0.870 in
service limit	0.810 in
maximum runout	0.003 in

Torque specifications	Ft-lbs
Drum brake wheel cylinder to backing plate	10 to 20
Drum brake backing plate to axle housing	20 to 40
Drum brake wheel cylinder bleeder screw	8 to 15
Disc brake caliper bleeder screw	6 to 15
Brake booster to firewall	13 to 25
Master cylinder to firewall	13 to 25
Master cylinder to booster	13 to 25
Pressure differential to frame	13 to 16
Rear disc brake anchor plate to axle	90 to 120
Rear caliper end retainer	75 to 95
Caliper key retaining screws	12 to 16
Rear disc parking brake retainer screw	16 to 22
Brake hose to caliper	10 to 15
Parking brake control mounting screws	12 to 24
Splash shield on spindle (4x2)	13 to 19
Splash shield on spindle (4x4)	5 to 8

1 General information

Refer to illustrations 1.3a and 1.3b

Warning: *Dust and dirt present on brake and clutch assemblies may contain asbestos fibers that are hazardous to your health. When wheel assemblies must be cleaned use a vacuum cleaner and take care not to breathe in any dust particles.*

All front brakes are disk-type while the rear brake systems are drum type brakes. The rear drum brakes are of the single anchor type, actuated by one wheel cylinder.

The hydraulic system consists of a dual master cylinder and a two-way brake control valve assembly (see illustration). The hydraulic master cylinder has two supply reservoirs (see illustration). The reservoir that is the smallest of the two supplies the rear drums and the larger supplies the front discs. If unequal hydraulic pressure occurs between the front and rear brakes, the pressure differential valve will

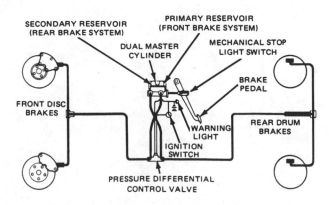

1.3a Typical dual master cylinder brake system

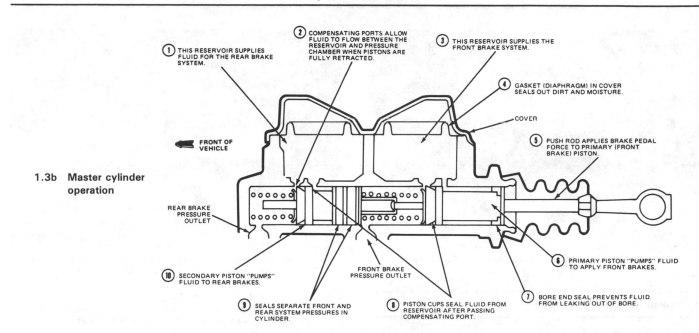

① THIS RESERVOIR SUPPLIES FLUID FOR THE REAR BRAKE SYSTEM.

② COMPENSATING PORTS ALLOW FLUID TO FLOW BETWEEN THE RESERVOIR AND PRESSURE CHAMBER WHEN PISTONS ARE FULLY RETRACTED.

③ THIS RESERVOIR SUPPLIES THE FRONT BRAKE SYSTEM.

④ GASKET (DIAPHRAGM) IN COVER SEALS OUT DIRT AND MOISTURE.

COVER

⑤ PUSH ROD APPLIES BRAKE PEDAL FORCE TO PRIMARY (FRONT BRAKE) PISTON.

FRONT OF VEHICLE

1.3b Master cylinder operation

REAR BRAKE PRESSURE OUTLET

⑩ SECONDARY PISTON "PUMPS" FLUID TO REAR BRAKES.

⑨ SEALS SEPARATE FRONT AND REAR SYSTEM PRESSURES IN CYLINDER.

FRONT BRAKE PRESSURE OUTLET

⑧ PISTON CUPS SEAL FLUID FROM RESERVOIR AFTER PASSING COMPENSATING PORT.

⑥ PRIMARY PISTON "PUMPS" FLUID TO APPLY FRONT BRAKES.

⑦ BORE END SEAL PREVENTS FLUID FROM LEAKING OUT OF BORE.

sense the condition and activate the brake warning lamp switch, which is displayed on the instrument panel. The pressure to the rear brakes is controlled by the proportioning valve, which is one of the two functions of the two-way brake control valve assembly.

On some vehicles the hydraulic brake system may be assisted by a vacuum booster. The single diaphragm vacuum booster is a self contained unit that uses engine vacuum and atmospheric pressure for its power. Vacuum is supplied through a fitting in the intake manifold.

After completing any operation involving the disassembly of any part of the brake system, always test drive the vehicle to check for proper braking performance before resuming normal driving. When testing the brakes, perform the tests on a clean, dry, flat surface. Conditions other than these can lead to inaccurate test results. Test the brakes at various speeds with both light and heavy pedal pressure. The vehicle should stop evenly without pulling to either side. Avoid locking the brakes because this slides the tires and diminishes braking efficiency and control.

Tires, vehicle load and front end alignment are factors which also affect braking performance.

The torque values given in the Specifications are for dry, unlubricated fasteners.

2 Hydraulic brake hoses and lines — inspection and replacement

Refer to illustration 2.10

1   Every six months, with the vehicle raised and placed securely on jackstands, the flexible hoses which connect the steel brake lines with front and rear brake assemblies should be inspected for cracks, chafing of the outer cover, leaks, blisters and other damage. These are important and vulnerable parts of the brake system and inspection should be complete.

2   If a section of the brake tubing becomes damaged, the entire section should be replaced with tubing of the same type, size, shape and length. Copper tubing should never be used in a brake hydraulic system. When bending brake tubing to fit under body or rear axle contours, be careful not to kink or crack the tubing.

Steel hydraulic brake lines

3   When it becomes necessary to replace steel lines use only double wall steel tubing. The outside diameter of the tubing is used for sizing.

4   Auto parts stores and brake supply houses carry various lengths of prefabricated brake line. Depending upon the type of tubing used, these sections can either be bent by hand to the desired shape or can be bent with a tubing bender.

5   If prefabricated lines are not available, obtain the recommended steel tubing and fittings to match the line to be replaced. Determine the correct length by measuring the old brake line, then cutting the

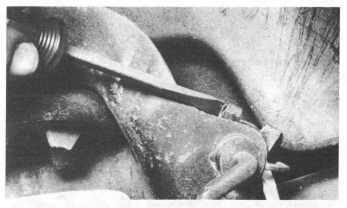

2.10 Lift up on the retainer spring clip while spreading the outer half of the spring clip enough to clear the hose flange

new tubing to length, leaving about 1/2 inch extra for flaring the ends. All brake tubing should be double flared to provide leak proof connections. Clean the brake tubing by flushing with clean brake fluid before installation. Install the fittings onto the cut tubing and flare the ends using an ISO flaring tool.

6   Tube flaring and bending can usually be performed by a local auto parts store if the proper equipment is not available.

7   When installing the brake line, leave at least 3/4 inch clearance between the line and any moving parts.

Flexible brake hose

8   Disconnect the brake line hose at union.

9   Tap the retaining spring clip down and stick a screwdriver between the two halves of the spring clip. Spread the outer half enough to clear the hose flange.

10   Using another screwdriver, pry up on the spring clip while spreading the outer half of the spring clip (see illustration).

11   When installing a new front brake hose, position the hose to avoid contact with other chassis parts. Install the hose on the caliper. Engage the other end of the hose in the bracket on the frame.

12   Install the retaining clip by spreading the outer part of the retaining spring clip so the clip will slide down and seat on the hose.

13   Connect the steel brake line tube to the hose.

14   A rear brake hose should be installed so that it does not touch adjacent chassis parts or body. Position the hose junction block on the axle and attach it with a bolt and lockwasher. Connect the hose to the wheel cylinder, then engage the other end in the bracket. Install the retaining clips. Install the steel lines to the junction block, thread them into the hose fitting and tighten them with a tubing wrench.

3.3   Check the brake line connections for leaks

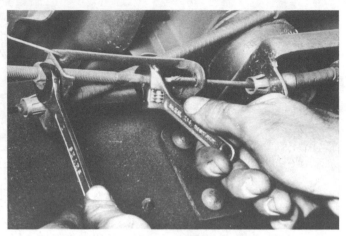

**4.2   Hold the tension limiter and tighten the equalizer nut
up the rod to adjust the parking brake**

3   Hydraulic system — bleeding

Refer to illustration 3.3

1   Removal of all the air from the braking system is essential for the
correct operation of the system. Before undertaking this task check
the level of fluid in the reservoir and top up if necessary.
2   Check all brake line unions and connections for possible leakage,
and at the same time check the condition of the rubber hoses, which
may be cracked or worn.
3   If the condition of a caliper or wheel cylinder is in doubt, check
for signs of fluid leakage (see illustration).
4   If there is any possibility that incorrect fluid has been used in the
system, drain all the fluid and flush with methylated spirits. Replace
all piston seals and cups, as they will be affected and could possibly
fail under pressure.
5   You will need a clean jar, a 12-inch length of rubber tubing which
fits tightly over the bleed valve and the correct grade of brake fluid.
6   Bleed the master cylinder first by loosening the master cylinder
to hydraulic line nut.
7   Wrap a rag around the tubing union to absorb the escaping fluid.
8   Have an assistant push the brake pedal slowly to the floor, which
will force any air in the master cylinder to escape at the fitting.
9   With pedal held to the floor tighten the fitting. Release the brake
pedal. **Caution:** *Do not release the brake pedal until the fitting is tightened or air will enter the master cylinder.*
10   Repeat this procedure until air ceases to escape from the fitting.
11   The primary (front) and secondary (rear) hydraulic brake systems
are bled separately. Always bleed the longest line first.
12   To bleed the secondary system (rear), clean the area around the
bleed valves and start at the right rear wheel cylinder. Remove the rubber cap over the bleed valve and fit the rubber tube over the bleed
nipple.
13   Place the end of the rubber tube in the jar, which should contain
sufficient brake fluid to keep the end of the tube submerged during
the operation.
14   Open the bleed valve approximately 3/4-turn and have an assistant
depress the brake pedal slowly through its full travel. Hold the brake
pedal fully depressed.
15   Close the bleed valve and allow the pedal to return to the released
position.
16   Continue this sequence until no more air bubbles issue from the
bleed tube.
17   At regular intervals during the bleeding sequence make sure that
the reservoir is kept topped up, otherwise air will enter again at this
point. Do not reuse fluid bled from the system.
18   Repeat the procedure on the left rear brake line.
19   To bleed the primary system (front), start with the right front side
and finish with the left front. The procedure is identical to that previously described.
20   Top up the master cylinder to within 1/4-inch of the top of the
reservoir, check that the gasket is correctly located in the cover and
install the cover.

Centralizing the pressure differential valve

21   After bleeding the system the brake warning light will likely stay
lit. Centralize the pressure differential control valve as follows.
22   Turn ignition to ACC or ON position.
23   Make sure master cylinder reservoir is filled to 1/4-inch from the
top.
24   Push the brake pedal down firmly, and the piston will center itself,
causing the brake warning light to go off.

4   Parking brake — adjustment

Refer to illustration 4.2

Note: *Adjust the rear brakes before adjusting the parking brake cables.*

     Parking brakes employ a cable system that incorporates a tension
limiter. If the parking brake system is in normal operating condition,
depressing the parking brake pedal to the floor will automatically set
the proper tension.

Initial adjustment procedure

1   Apply the parking brake.
2   Grip the tension limiter bracket to prevent it from turning and
tighten the equalizer nut 2-1/2 inches up the rod (see illustration).
3   Check to make sure cinch strap has slipped (less than 1-3/8 inch
remaining).
4   Position the parking brake pedal to the fully depressed position.
5   Scribe a mark on the threaded rod at the equalizer nut to note the
original position.
6   Grip threaded rod to prevent it from turning and tighten the
equalizer nut six full turns past its original position.
7   Release the parking brake and check for rear wheel drag. The cables
should be tight enough to provide full application of the rear brake shoes
with the pedal fully applied. The cable should be loose enough to ensure
complete release of the brake shoes when the lever is in the released
position.

5   Stop light switch — removal and installation

Refer to illustration 5.2

1   The stop light switch is located on a flange or a bracket protruding
from the brake pedal support. If the brake lights are inoperative, and
it has been determined that the bulbs are not burned out, replace the
switch as follows:
2   Disconnect the electrical connector from the switch (see
illustration).
3   Remove the cotter pin and spacer. Slide the stop light switch
pushrod and the nylon washers and bushing away from the pedal and
remove the switch.
4   Position the new switch, pushrod, bushing and washers on the
brake pedal pin and install the retaining cotter pin.
5   Assemble the lead connector to the switch and install the wires
in the retaining clip.

5.2 Pull off the electrical connector to disconnect the brake light switch

6 Brake pedal — removal and installation

Refer to illustrations 6.4 and 6.5

1   Disconnect the negative cable at the battery.
2   Disconnect the stoplight switch wire from the switch.
3   Disconnect the cotter pin and spacer connecting the brake pedal assembly, stop lamp switch assembly and master cylinder push rod together and remove.
4   On vehicles with manual transmissions you will have to disconnect the hydraulic clutch control by removing the nut on the clutch rod lever and then remove the lever and bushing (see illustration). Push the clutch pedal assembly to the side, allowing the brake pedal assembly to come off the shaft. Remove the bushings and spring washer.
5   On vehicles equipped with an automatic transmission, remove the spring retainer and bushing from the brake pedal shaft. From the other end, pull out the shaft and remove pedal assembly, including bushings and washer spring from the brake pedal (see illustration).

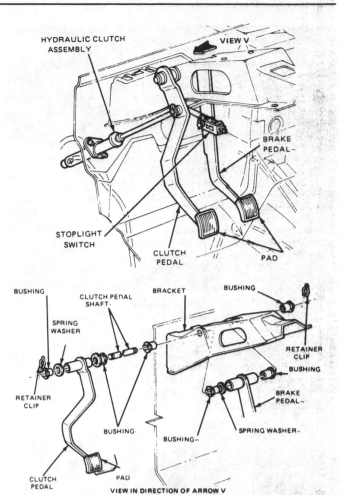

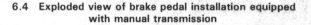

6.4 Exploded view of brake pedal installation equipped with manual transmission

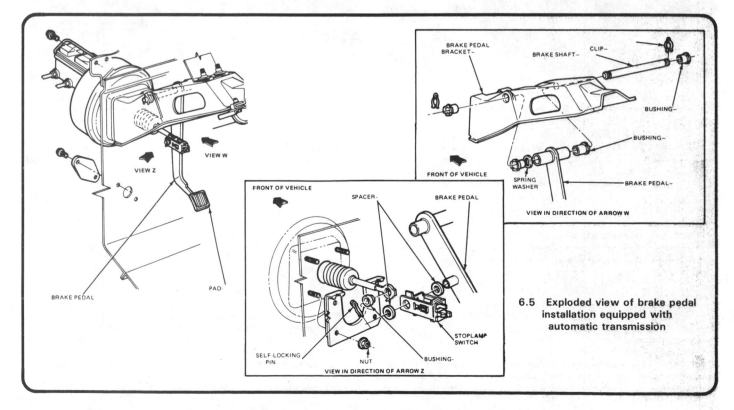

6.5 Exploded view of brake pedal installation equipped with automatic transmission

7.6   Use pliers to squeeze the caliper retainer pin while prying on the other end until the tabs on the pin enter the spindle groove

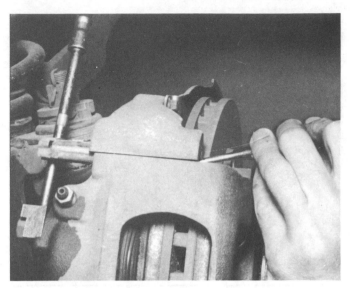

7.7   Drive out the pin with a punch and hammer

7.9   If the caliper is not to be serviced remove it and wire it out of the way. Do not let the caliper hang by the brake hose

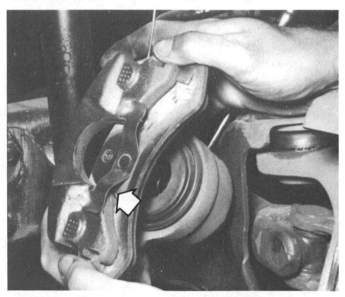

7.10   This spring clip (arrow) holds the outside brake pad to the caliper. Push down and slide out to remove

6   Remove the stop lamp switch from the brake pedal.
7   Installation is the reverse of removal. During installation, coat the pivot points with motor oil to prolong bearing life and ease of operation.
8   Check for proper operation before driving.

7   Front disc brake caliper and pad — removal and installation

Refer to illustrations 7.6, 7.7, 7.9, 7.10, 7.13, 7.14, 7.15, 7.16, 7.19, 7.20, 7.21a, 7.21b, 7.22, 7.23 and 7.26
Note: *Replace pads when the lining is worn to a minimum thickness of 1/8-inch above the rivets.*
1   Raise the vehicle and support it securely on jackstands.
2   Remove the front wheels.

Caliper removal
Note: *There are several types of caliper retaining pins used. The pin removal process is dependent upon how the pin is installed. To remove the retaining pins, squeeze the outside of the pin until the tabs (stops)*

enter the pin groove and knock the pin through the groove. The bolt head type is different and requires a different procedure (described below). Always remove the upper pin first.
3   Clean dirt away from area around the pin tabs.
4   Tap upper caliper retaining pin towards inboard side until the pin tabs touch the spindle face.
5   If applicable, insert a screwdriver into the slot behind the pin tabs on the inboard side of the pin.
6   Use needle nose pliers to compress the outboard end of the pin and pry at the same time with the screwdriver, until tabs enter spindle groove (see illustration).
7   Place a 7/16-inch punch against the end of the caliper pin and drive the pin out of the groove (see illustration).
8   Repeat the procedure for lower pin.
9   If the caliper is to be removed for service, remove the brake hose from the caliper. Otherwise remove the caliper from the rotor and wire the caliper out of your way (see illustration). Do not let the caliper hang by the hose.
10   To remove the outer pad press down on the pad, releasing the locking tabs and slide pad from the caliper (see illustration).
11   Remove the inner pad and the anti-rattle clips.

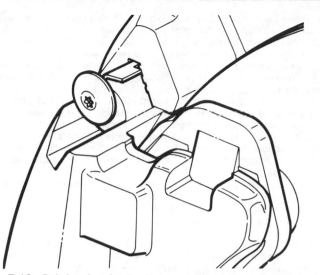

7.13 Bolt head style pin sticks outside of the caliper and must be cut off for removal

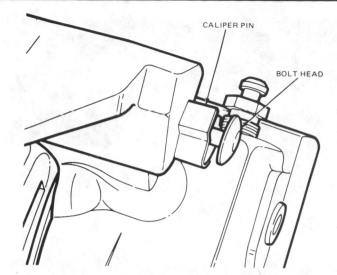

7.14 Separate the bolt head from the caliper by tapping on the pin from inside with a hammer

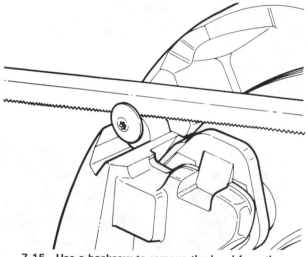

7.15 Use a hacksaw to remove the head from the retaining pin

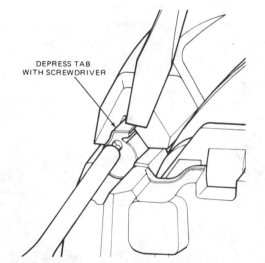

7.16 A punch will asist in removing the pin from the caliper

Threaded bolt and nut type pin

12 On some applications (early models) the pin may be retained by a nut and Torx-head bolt.

13 If the bolt head is on the outside of the caliper, as shown in the accompanying illustration, use the following procedure.

14 From the inboard side of the caliper, tap the bolt within the caliper pin until the bolt head on the outer side shows a separation between the bolt head and the caliper pin (see illustration).

15 Use a hacksaw to remove the bolt head from the bolt (see illustration).

16 Depress the retaining tab on the bolt head end with a screwdriver while tapping on the pin with a hammer until the tab is depressed by the V-slot (see illustration).

17 Place one end of a 7/16-inch punch against the end of the caliper pin and drive the pin out of the groove. Do not use a screwdriver to drive out the caliper pin, as the V-grooves may be damaged.

Pad replacement

Caution: *Never reuse the caliper pins. Always install new pins whenever a caliper is removed.*

18 Clean the caliper, anchor plate and disc and inspect them for wear, damage, corrosion and leakage.

19 Using a large C-clamp on the caliper, tighten the clamp to bottom the caliper piston in the cylinder bore (see illustration) **Note:** *Remove some of the brake fluid in the reservoir so back pressure doesn't cause the master cylinder to overflow. Place the master cylinder top back*

7.19 Squeeze the piston into the caliper with C-clamp to bottom the piston

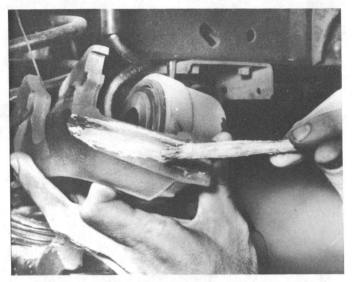

7.20   Lightly lubricate the V-grooves with white grease before assembly

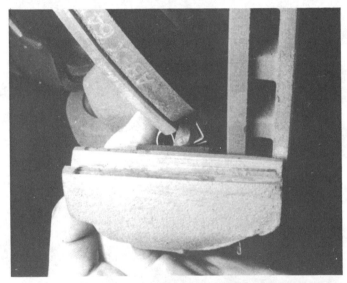

7.21a   Be sure the tabs on the spring clips are positioned properly and fully seated (arrow)

7.22   Compress the anti-rattle clip and slide the upper end of the pad into position

on the unit but do not clamp the top down. Place a rag under the master cylinder to catch any fluid that might escape.

20 Prior to installing the caliper, lightly lubricate the V grooves where the caliper slides into the anchor plate (see illustration).

21 Insert a new anti-rattle clip on the lower end of the inner shoe, being sure tabs on clip are positioned properly and the clip is fully seated (see illustrations).

22 Position the inner pad and anti-rattle clip in the shoe abutment with the anti-rattle clip tab against the shoe abutment and the loop side of the spring clip away from the rotor. Compress the anti-rattle clip and slide the upper end of the pad in position (see illustration).

23 Make sure the torque buttons on the pad spring clip are seated in the matching holes in the caliper when installing the outer pad (see illustration).

24 Install the caliper on the rotor, making sure the mounting surfaces are free of dirt.

25 Install the new pin with the pin retention tabs oriented adjacent to the spindle groove. **Note:** *Do not use an old bolt and nut with the new pin.*

26 Using a hammer, tap the pin inward until the retention tabs on the sides of the pin contact the spindle face. Repeat the procedure for the lower pin (see illustration). **Note:** *During installation do not allow the tabs of the caliper pin to be tapped too far into the spindle groove. If this happens it will be necessary to tap the other end of the caliper pin until the tabs snap into place. The tabs on each end of the caliper pin must be free to catch on the spindle flanks.*

27 If removed, install the brake hose to the caliper.

28 Bleed the brake system if the brake hose was removed or air is suspected in the lines.

29 Install the wheel assembly.

30 Lower the vehicle and check the brake fluid level.

31 Check the brakes for proper operation before returning the vehicle to normal use.

7.21b   The anti-rattle spring clip properly installed on the brake pad

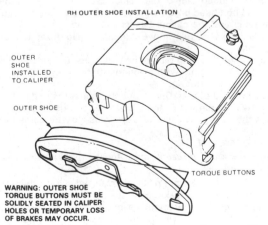

RH OUTER SHOE INSTALLATION

OUTER SHOE INSTALLED TO CALIPER

OUTER SHOE

TORQUE BUTTONS

WARNING: OUTER SHOE TORQUE BUTTONS MUST BE SOLIDLY SEATED IN CALIPER HOLES OR TEMPORARY LOSS OF BRAKES MAY OCCUR.

7.23   The outer shoe torque buttons must be seated in the caliper holes

8 Rear drum brake shoes — adjustment

Automatic adjusters are fitted to the rear drum brakes and these operate when the vehicle is backed up and stopped. Should the vehicle use be such that it is not backed up very often and the pedal movement has increased, it will be necessary to adjust the brakes as follows:

1   Drive the vehicle backwards and apply the brake pedal firmly. Now drive it forwards, and again apply the brake pedal firmly.

7.26   Tap the pin inward until the retention tabs contact the spindle groove

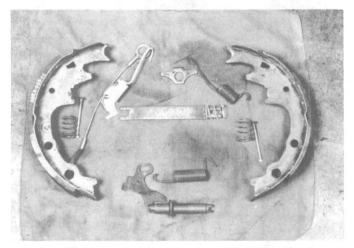

9.1   During removal lay the parts out in their order of removal to keep from getting confused

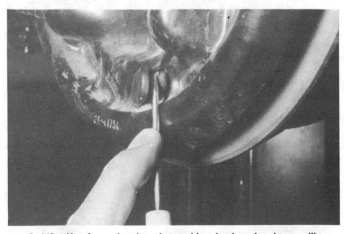

9.4/2   If, after releasing the parking brake, the drum will not slide off the shoes, remove the rubber plug from the backing plate

2   Repeat the cycle until a desirable pedal movement is obtained. Should this not happen it will be necessary to remove the drum and hub assembly and inspect the adjuster mechanism as described in Section 11.

9 Rear drum brake shoes — replacement

Refer to illustrations 9.1 and 9.4/1 thru 9.4/25

Warning: *Whenever you are working on the brake system, be aware that asbestos dust is present. It has been proven to be harmful to your health, so be careful not to inhale any of it. Use an asbestos approved type vacuum cleaner or a liquid brake cleaner to get dirt from brake parts.*

1   To help on the installation of the brake assembly, during the removal procedures lay out all parts in an assembled order on a rag near the work area (see illustration).

2   Raise the vehicle and place it securely on jackstands.

3   Remove the wheel and tire assembly. **Note:** *All four rear shoes should be replaced at the same time, but to avoid mixing up parts, work on only one brake assembly at a time.*

4   Refer to the accompanying illustrations and perform the brake shoe replacement procedures.

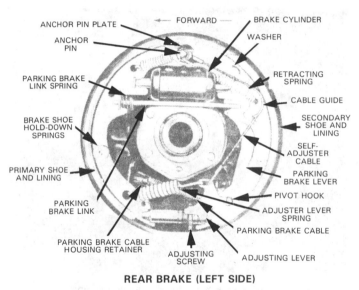

REAR BRAKE (LEFT SIDE)

9.4/1   Components of a typical rear brake assembly

9.4/3   Use a screwdriver or brake tool to retract the adjuster, moving the shoes away from the drum

9.4/4   Slide the drum off the shoes

9.4/5   Use a spring removal tool to remove the primary and secondary shoe anchor springs

9.4/6   Pull up on the adjusting cable and disconnect the cable eye from the anchor pin

9.4/7   Remove the shoe guide

9.4/8   Remove the shoe retaining springs and pins (one on each shoe)

9.4/9   Pull the shoes apart and remove the adjusting screw

9.4/10 Remove the primary shoe then slide out the parking brake strut and spring

9.4/11 Remove the adjuster pawl

9.4/12 Pull the secondary shoe away from the backing plate

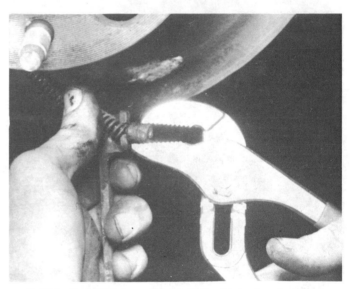

9.4/13 Separate the parking brake cable and spring from the actuating lever

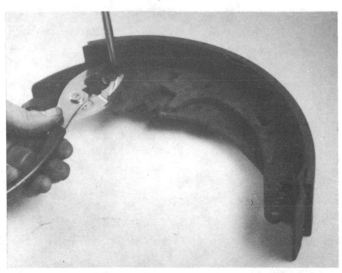

9.4/14 Remove the E-clip which holds the parking brake actuating lever to the brake shoe

9.4/15 Install the parking brake actuator lever on the new brake shoe and install the E-clip

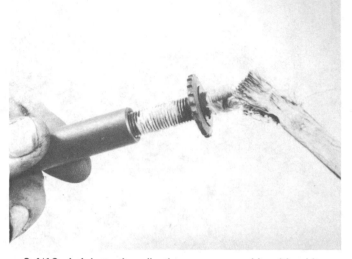

9.4/16   Lubricate the adjusting screw assembly with white grease

9.4/17   Lightly coat the shoe guide pads on the backing plate with white grease

9.4/18   Insert the retaining pins through the backing plate and shoes and put the springs over them

9.4/19   Install the retaining spring caps

9.4/20   Make sure the slots in the wheel cylinder plungers and the parking brake strut properly engage the brake shoes

9.4/21   Install the adjusting screw with the long end pointing towards the front of the vehicle

9.4/22 **Install the adjusting pawl**

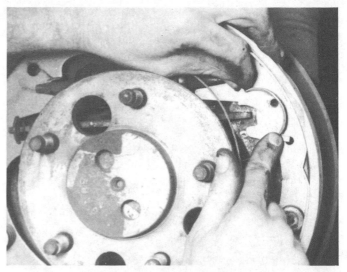

9.4/23 **Install the cable guide and cable**

9.4/24 **Connect the cable and spring to the pawl**

9.4/25 **Install the shoe guide and adjusting cable eye to the anchor pin, then install the primary and secondary springs. Replace and drum and adjust the brake shoe to drum clearance**

5   Before reinstalling the drum it should be checked for cracks, score marks, deep scratches and hard spots, which will appear as small discolored areas. If the hard spots cannot be removed with fine emery cloth or if any of the other conditions listed exist, the drum must be taken to an automotive machine shop to have it turned. If the drum will not clean up before the maximum drum diameter is reached in the machining operation, the drum will have to be replaced with a new one. **Note:** *The maximum diameter is indicated on each brake drum.*

---

10   Rear wheel cylinder — removal and installation

Refer to illustrations 10.2 and 10.3
Note: *Due to the wide availability of reconditioned and aftermarket brake components, it has become easier and comparable in cost to replace a damaged or worn wheel cylinder than it is to rebuild it yourself. Therefore, overhaul of wheel cylinders is not covered in this manual. Be sure to take your old wheel cylinder with you to the parts dealer for positive identification.*

1   Remove the brake shoes.
2   On the back side of the brake backing plate, loosen the brake line fitting at the wheel cylinder (see illustration). Do not try to pull the brake tube from the wheel cylinder as this could bend it, making installation difficult.

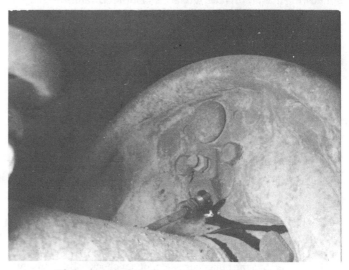

10.2 **Loosen but do not remove the brake line**

10.3   Remove the bolts from the backing plate and remove the wheel cylinder

3   Remove the two bolts securing the wheel cylinder to the brake backing plate and remove the cylinder (see illustration).
4   Plug the brake line to stop hydraulic fluid leakage.
5   Installation is the reverse of removal. After reinstallation it will be necessary to bleed the hydraulic line that serves the wheel cylinder.

11   Master cylinder — removal, installation and overhaul

Refer to illustrations 11.8 and 11.32

Removal and installation

1   On non-power brake systems begin inside the cab below the instrument panel. Disconnect the wires from the stop lamp switch. On power assisted units push the brake pedal down several times to expel vacuum from the brake booster.
2   On non-power units remove the retaining clip, shoulder bolt and spacers securing the master cylinder push rod to the brake pedal assembly. Remove the stop lamp switch from the pedal.
3   Unscrew the brake lines from the primary and secondary outlet ports of the master cylinder. Plug the ends of the lines to prevent contamination. Take suitable precautions to catch the hydraulic fluid as the unions are detached from the master cylinder body.
4   Remove the two bolts securing the master cylinder to the firewall or servo unit.
5   Pull the master cylinder forward and lift it upward from the car. Do not allow brake fluid to spill on the paint, as it acts as a solvent.
6   If equipped, remove the boot from the master cylinder push rod.

Overhaul

Note: *It should be noted that new and rebuilt master cylinders are commonly available for these vehicles. If one of these is purchased, skip to the installation instructions. If it is decided to overhaul the original unit, obtain an overhaul kit, which will contain all necessary parts, and then proceed as follows.*

7   Clean the exterior of the master cylinder and wipe dry with a lint free rag. Remove the filler cover and gasket from the top of the reservoir and pour out any remaining hydraulic fluid.
8   Depress the primary piston and remove snap ring from retaining groove at the rear of the master cylinder (see illustration).
9   Remove the primary piston assembly from the master cylinder and inspect for seal damage. Take note of the installed direction for installation.
10   Do not remove the screw that retains the primary return spring retainer, return spring, primary cup and protector on the primary piston. This is factory set and must not be disturbed.
11   Remove the secondary piston. Inspect the seal for damage.
12   Do not remove the outlet line seats, outlet check valves and outlet check valve springs from the master cylinder body.

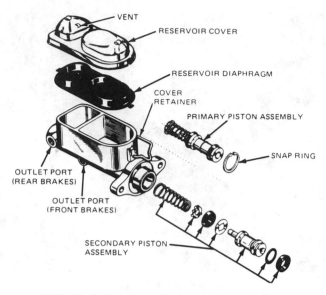

11.8   Typical master cylinder — exploded view

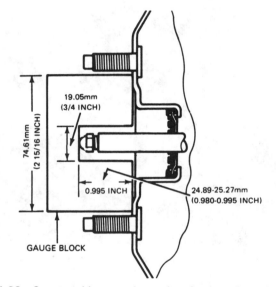

11.32   On assembly, note the push rod gauge dimensions and adjustment for the brake booster

13   Inspect the master cylinder bore for etching, pitting, scoring or other damage.
14   If the master cylinder bore is damaged or worn, replace the master cylinder with a new one — **DO NOT** hone the master cylinder bore.
15   If the rubber seals are swollen or very loose on the pistons, suspect oil contamination in the system. Oil will swell these rubber seals and if one is found to be swollen it is reasonable to assume that all seals in the brake system need attention.
16   Thoroughly clean all parts in clean hydraulic fluid or isopropyl alcohol to remove any contamination.
17   All components should be assembled wet after dipping them in fresh heavy duty brake fluid C6AZ-19542-A or B or equivalent Dot 3 brake fluid.
18   Carefully insert the complete secondary piston and return spring assembly into the master cylinder bore, easing the seals into the bore, taking care that they do not roll over. Push the assembly all the way in.
19   Insert the primary piston assembly into the master cylinder bore.
20   Push in the primary piston and tighten the secondary piston stop screw in the bottom of the cylinder.
21   Depress the piston again and install the snap-ring.
22   If a replacement master cylinder is to be fitted, it will be necessary to lubricate the seals before fitting to the car, as they have a protective

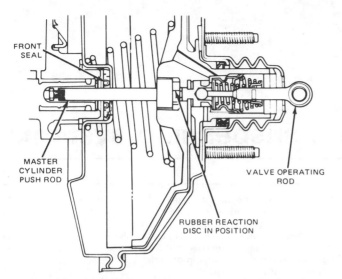

FRONT
SEAL

MASTER
CYLINDER
PUSH ROD

VALVE OPERATING
ROD

RUBBER REACTION
DISC IN POSITION

12.7 The reaction disc may become dislodged when the master cylinder push rod is removed or accidentally pulled out

coating when originally assembled.

23 Remove the blanking plugs from the hydraulic line union seats. Inject some clean hydraulic fluid into the master cylinder and operate the pushrod several times so that the fluid spreads over all the internal working surfaces.

24 Before installing the master cylinder it should be bench-bled to remove air from the unit. Because it will be necessary to apply pressure to the master cylinder piston and, at the same time, control flow from the brake line outlets, it is recommended that the master cylinder be mounted in a vice. Use caution not to clamp the vice too tightly, or the master cylinder body might be cracked.

25 Insert threaded plugs into the brake line outlet holes and snug them down so that there will be no air leakage past them, but not so tight that they cannot be easily loosened.

26 Fill the reservoirs with brake fluid of the recommended type (see *Recommended fluids and lubricants*).

27 Remove one plug and push the piston assembly into the master cylinder bore to expell the air from the master cylinder. A large Phillips screwdriver can be used to push on the piston assembly.

28 To prevent air from being drawn back into the master cylinder, the plug must be replaced and snugged down before releasing the pressure on the piston assembly.

29 Repeat the procedure until only brake fluid is expelled from the brake line outlet hole. When only brake fluid is expelled, repeat the procedure with the other outlet hole and plug. Be sure to keep the master cylinder reservoir filled with brake fluid to prevent the introduction of air into the system.

30 Since high pressure is not involved in the bench bleeding procedure, an alternative to the removal and replacement of the plugs with each stroke of the piston assembly is available. Before pushing in on the piston assembly, remove the plug as described in Step 4. Before releasing the piston, however, instead of replacing the plug, simply put your finger tightly over the hole to keep air from being drawn back into the master cylinder. Wait several seconds for brake fluid to be drawn from the reservior into the piston bore, then depress the piston again, removing your finger as brake fluid is expelled. Be sure to put your finger back over the hole each time before releasing the piston, and when the bleeding procedure is complete for that outlet, replace the plug and snug it before going on to the other port.

Installation

31 On non-power assisted models installation is the reverse of the removal procedure. Bleed the system, referring the Section concerning bleeding the hydraulic system if necessary. Centralize the differential valve by turning the ignition switch to the ON position and pushing the brake pedal down firmly. The piston will center itself, causing the warning light to go off.

32 Before installing the power assisted unit, check the distance from the outer end of the booster assembly push rod to the front face of

the brake booster assembly (see illustration). Turn the push rod adjusting screw in or out as required to obtain the correct length.

33 Position the master cylinder assembly over the booster push rod and onto the two studs on the booster assembly. Install the attaching nuts and tighten to specification.

34 Install the hydraulic lines to the master cylinder.

35 Bleed the hydraulic system.

36 Centralize the differential valve by turning the ignition switch to the ON position and pushing the brake pedal down firmly. The piston will center itself, causing the warning light to go off.

37 Check that the reservoir is full and replace the gasket and reservoir cover.

12 Power brake booster — removal and installation

Refer to illustrations 12.7

A vacuum booster is part of the power brake circuit. It provides assistance to the driver when the brake pedal is depressed. This reduces the effort required by the driver to operate the brakes under all braking conditions. The unit utilizes a vacuum obtained from the intake manifold and is comprised of a booster diaphragm and check valve.

Under normal operating conditions the vacuum booster will give trouble free service for a very long time. If, however, it is suspected that the unit is faulty it must be exchanged for a new unit. No attempt should be made to repair the old unit, as it is not a serviceable item.

1 From inside under the dash, disconnect the stop lamp switch.

2 Remove the master cylinder-to-booster retaining nuts.

3 Loosen the clamp that secures the manifold vacuum hose to the booster check valve and remove the hose. Remove the booster check valve.

4 Pull the master cylinder off the booster and support it far enough away to allow removal of the booster assembly.

5 Work inside the cab under the dash and disconnect the retaining pin. Slide the stop lamp switch, push rod, spacers and bushing off the brake pedal arm.

6 From inside the engine compartment, remove the bolts that attach the booster to the dash panel.

7 Installation is the reverse of the removal procedure. **Caution:** *Make sure that the booster rubber reaction disc is properly installed if the master cylinder push rod is removed or accidentally pulled out (see illustration). A dislodged disc may cause excessive pedal travel and extreme operation sensitivity. The disc is black, compared to the silver colored valve plunger that will be exposed after the push rod and front seal is removed. The booster is serviced as a unit and the entire unit must be replaced if the disc cannot be properly installed and aligned, or if the disc cannot be located within the unit itself.*

13 Pressure differential valve assembly — removal and installation

The pressure differential valve senses an unbalanced hydraulic pressure condition existing between the front and rear brake systems. When there is a pressure loss in either system during brake application, the piston will move off center, causing the brake warning lamp to light. The warning lamp will shut off when the brake system is serviced, properly bled and the brakes are applied to center the piston. The brake warning lamp switch is mounted on top of the control valve body.

1 Disconnect the brake warning light connector from the warning light switch.

2 Disconnect the unions from the valve assembly. Plug the ends of the lines to prevent loss of hydraulic fluid.

3 Remove the two nuts and bolts securing the valve bracket to the underside of the fender apron. Remove the assembly from the vehicle.

4 To install the assembly, position the brake control valve assembly at the fender apron holes and install the two assembly mount nuts and bolts.

5 Reconnect all brake lines to the control valve assembly.

6 Connect the brake warning lamp switch wiring harness connector to the brake warning lamp switch. Verify this connection by turning the ignition switch to the Start Position. The lamp should come on.

7 Bleed the brake system and centralize the pressure differential valve.

Chapter 10   Steering and suspension systems

Contents

Specifications

Front suspension	twin I-beam with coil springs
Rear suspension	leaf spring
Steering	Ford integral power steering or manual steering
Power steering pump	Ford Model CII
Manual steering gear	
Gear ratio	
SMK-A	24:1 (constant)
SMK-B	20-24:1 (variable)
Lubricant capacity	10.2 ounces
Power steering gear	
gear ratio	17:1
fluid capacity (reservoir included)	1.6 pints
fluid type	Motorcraft Type F automatic transmission fluid (XT-1-QF) or equivalent

Torque specifications

	Ft-lbs
Front suspension	
Axle arm to bracket nut	120 to 150
Axle arm pivot bracket to frame nut	70 to 92
Axle pivot bolt	120 to 150
Bumper to spring seat bolt	13 to 18
Front shock absorber to radius arm nut	42 to 72
Front shock absorber to spring nut	25 to 35
Pitman arm to drag link nut	51 to 75
Jounce bumper bolt	11 to 19
Radius arm to frame nut	81 to 120
Radius arm bracket to frame bolt	77 to 110
Radius arm bracket connecting bolts	35 to 50
Radius arm to rear bracket nut	80 to 120
Radius arm front bracket and axle stud	160 to 220
Radius arm front bracket front bolts	27 to 37
Radius arm front bracket lower bolts	160 to 220
Shock absorber to upper seat	25 to 35
Spring retainer nut	70 to 100
Stabilizer bar retainer bolts	77 to 110
Stabilizer bar U-bolt nuts	48 to 68
Stabilizer bar to mounting bracket bolt	35 to 50
Stabilizer to radius arm nut	48 to 64
Tie rod adjusting sleeve	30 to 42
Tie rod to spindle nut	51 to 75
Lower balljoint stud nut	104 to 146
Upper balljoint stud nut	85 to 110
Axle to radius arm	160 to 220

Rear suspension
  Rear leaf spring U-bolt nut . . . .   65 to 75
  Shock to lower bracket nut . . . .   40 to 60
  Shock to upper bracket . . . .   41 to 63
  Shackle to spring nut . . . .   74 to 115
  Spring to frame nut . . . .   74 to 115
  Spring to front bracket nut . . . .   74 to 115
  Spring shackle to rear bracket bolt . . . .   74 to 115
  Stabilizer to mounting bracket . . . .   30 to 42
  Stabilizer to bar and frame . . . .   40 to 60
Steering system
  Flex coupling to steering gear box . . . .   25 to 34
  Drag link to connecting rod ball stud nut . . . .   50 to 75
  Drag link to Pitman arm ball stud nut . . . .   50 to 75
  Pitman arm to steering gear nut . . . .   170 to 230
  Tie rod to spindle ball stud nut . . . .   50 to 75
  Manual steering coupling to input shaft bolt . . . .   25 to 35
  Power steering gear to flex coupling bolt . . . .   26 to 34
  Power steering hose clamps . . . .   1 to 2
  Power steering steering gear to frame bolt . . . .   50 to 62
  Power steering pressure hose to gear . . . .   16 to 25
  Power steering return hose to gear . . . .   25 to 34
  Power steering Pitman arm to sector shaft . . . .   170 to 228
  4-cyl steering pump to bracket . . . .   30 to 45
  4-cyl steering pump bracket to engine . . . .   30 to 45
  V6 steering pump slider bolts . . . .   35 to 47
  V6 front and rear support bracket bolts . . . .   35 to 47
  V6 steering pump to bracket . . . .   35 to 47
  V6 steering pump outlet to valve cover . . . .   25 to 34
  V6 steering pump quick connect fitting . . . .   10 to 20

1 General information

The front suspension on models covered in this manual is a coil spring, twin I-beam type, which is composed of coil springs, I-beam axle arms, radius arms, upper and lower balljoints and spindles, tie rods,

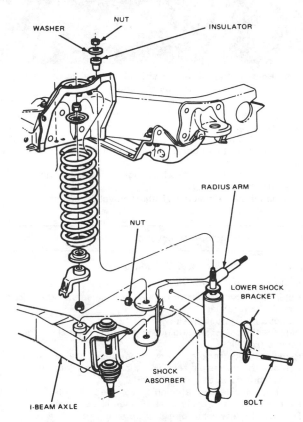

2.1 Front shock absorber mounting — exploded view

shock absorbers and optional stabilizer bar. The four-wheel drive model is basically the same except the Independent Front Suspension (IFS) system is composed of a two piece driveaxle assembly.

The front suspension consists of two independent axle arm assemblies. One end of each axle arm assembly is anchored to the frame and the other is supported by the coil spring and radius arm. The spindle is connected to the axle by upper and lower balljoints. The balljoints are constructed of a lubricated for life special bearing material. Lubrication points can be found on the tie rods, steering linkage and U-joints on earlier 4x4 models. Movement of the spindles is controlled by tie rods and the steering linkage.

Two adjustments can be performed on the axle assembly. Camber is adjusted by removing and replacing an adapter between the upper balljoint stud and the spindle on two-wheel drive models. Four-wheel drive models require replacing the camber adapter on the upper balljoint stud. Adapters are available in 0°, 1/2°, 1° and 1-1/2° increments. Toe-in adjustment is accomplished on both models by turning the tie rod adjusting sleeve.

The hydraulic shock absorbers are of the direct, double acting type, with later models having low pressure gas shocks. Both shock absorbers are of the telescopic design and come equipped with rubber grommets at the mounting points for quiet operation. The low pressure gas shock absorbers are sealed and charged with nitrogen gas to reduce shock absorber fade and improve ride. The shock absorbers are nonadjustable. The shock absorbers are not rebuildable and must be replaced as complete assemblies.

The rear suspension consists of semi-elliptical leaf springs. The forward end of each spring is attached to a bracket on the frame side member. The rear of each spring is shackled to a bracket on the frame rail. The rear shock absorbers are direct, double acting units with staggered mounting positions. The right shock is mounted forward of the axle and the left mounted to the rear.

2 Front shock absorber — removal and installation

Refer to illustration 2.1, 2.2 and 2.3
Caution: *The low pressure gas shock absorbers are charged to 135 PSI with nitrogen gas. Do not attempt to open, puncture or apply heat to the shock absorbers.*

1   The shock absorbers are mounted next to the coil springs (see illustration).

2.2   Hold the shock absorber shaft while removing the top
retaining nut

2.3   Lower mounting bracket for the front shock absorber
is attached to the radius arm

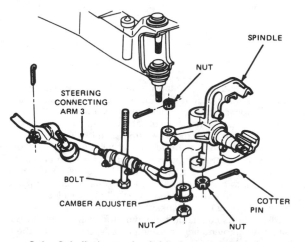

SPINDLE

NUT

STEERING
CONNECTING
ARM 3

BOLT

CAMBER ADJUSTER

NUT   NUT

COTTER
PIN

3.1   Spindle (two-wheel drive) — exploded view

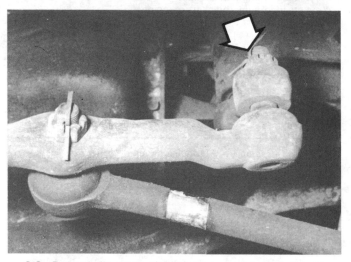

3.3   Remove the cotter pin and nut (arrow) to disconnect
the tie rod end

2   Remove the top shock mount by removing the nut with a deep
socket while holding the shaft with an open end wrench, and lift off
washer (see illustration).
3   Remove the nut and bolt that retain the shock to the radius arm
(see illustration).
4   To remove the shock absorber, slightly compress the shock and
remove it from its bracket.
5   Installation is the reverse of the removal procedure.

3   Front wheel spindle — removal and installation

Refer to illustration 3.1, 3.3, 3.7 and 3.17

Two-wheel drive models

1   Refer to Chapter 1 on front wheel bearing servicing and remove
the wheel and rotor (see illustration).
2   Remove brake dust shield.
3   Remove the cotter pin and nut to disconnect the tie rod end from
the spindle (see illustration).
4   Remove the cotter pin and nut from upper balljoint stud.
5   Remove the cotter pin retaining the lower balljoint stud nut.
6   Loosen but do not remove the nut.
7   Strike the inside of the spindle near the balljoints to break the
spindle loose from the balljoint studs (see illustration).
8   Remove the lower balljoint stud retaining nut, then remove the
spindle.

3.7   Strike the inside of the spindle (arrows) with a
hammer to break the spindle loose from the balljoint studs

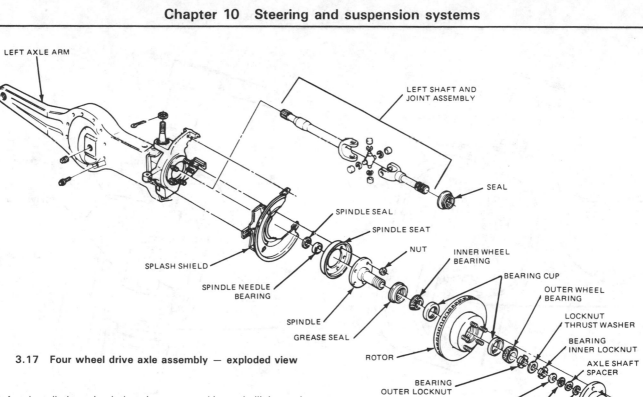

3.17 Four wheel drive axle assembly — exploded view

9   Before installation, check that the upper and lower balljoint seals were not damaged during spindle removal and are in place.
10 Apply thread locking compound to the upper and lower balljoint stud threads.
11 Position the spindle over the balljoints.
12 Install and partially tighten the lower balljoint stud nut.
13 Install and tighten the upper balljoint stud nut to specifications.
Caution: *A three step sequence for tightening balljoint nuts must be followed to avoid excessive turning force of the spindle about the axle. Refer to the specifications and divide the final torque specification into thirds for the proper sequence.*
14 Tighten the lower balljoint stud nut to specification and advance the nut to the next castellation to install the cotter pin.
15 Install the dust shield.
16 Refer to Chapter 1, *Front wheel bearing servicing*, to install the hub components.

Four-wheel drive

17 Refer to Chapter 8 for spindle and axleshaft removal procedures (see illustration).

---

4   Camber adapter — adjustment

Camber can be adjusted by replacing a camber adjuster in the upper balljoint socket, but due to the adjustment tools required it is considered beyond the scope of the home mechanic. Have this work done by a Ford dealer or a front end alignment specialist.

---

5   Upper and lower balljoints — removal and installation

Refer to illustration 5.3, 5.4, 5.5 and 5.8
Caution: *Do not heat axle or balljoint to aid removal.*

Two-wheel drive

1   Remove the spindle as described in Section 3.
2   Remove the snap ring from the balljoints. **Note:** *Remove the upper balljoint first.*
3   Install C-frame assembly tool T74P-4635-C and receiving cup D81T-3010-A on the upper balljoint or make a substitute tool out of a C-clamp and a piece of thick walled pipe (see illustration). **Note:** *If the C-frame assembly and receiver tool are not available or will not remove the balljoints it may be necessary to remove the axle and take the assembly to have the balljoints pressed out.*

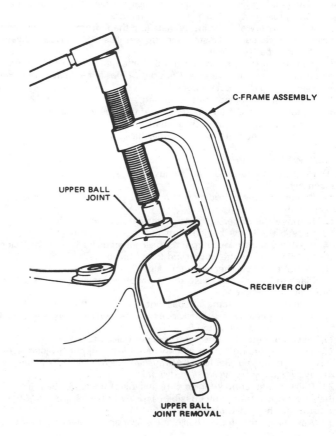

5.3 Use a Ford tool or a C-clamp and piece of tubing to remove the balljoints

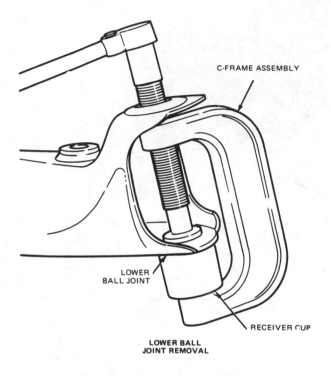

5.4   Removing the lower balljoint

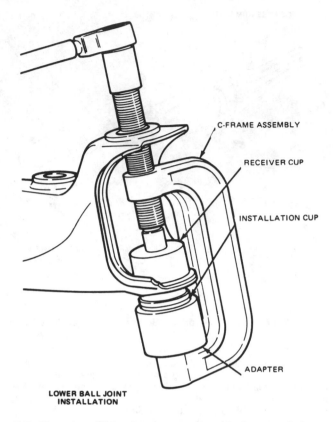

LOWER BALL JOINT INSTALLATION

5.5   Note the additional reciever cup required to install the lower balljoint. Install the lower balljoint first

4   Install the C-frame assembly and receiving cup onto the lower balljoint and press out the balljoint (see illustration).

5   Install the lower balljoint by installing the C-frame assembly and balljoint receiver cup and installation cup (see illustration). **Note:** *Always install lower balljoint first.*

6   Turn the forcing screw on the C-frame clockwise until the balljoint is seated against the axle. **Caution:** *Do not apply heat to the axle or balljoint to aid in installation.*

7   Install the lower balljoint snap ring.

8   Assemble the C-frame and receiver cup assembly and press the upper balljoint until seated (see illustration).

9   Install the snap ring on the upper balljoint.

Four-wheel drive

10   Refer to Chapter 8 and remove the spindle, shaft and joint assembly.

11   Disconnect the tie rod by removing the cotter pin and nut and tapping on the stud to free it.

12   Remove the upper balljoint cotter pin and nut.

13   Loosen the lower balljoint nut to the end of stud.

14   Break the spindle loose from the balljoint studs by striking the inside of the spindle near the upper and lower balljoints.

15   Remove the camber adjuster sleeve.

16   Place the knuckle in a vise and remove the snap ring from the bottom balljoint socket.

17   Assemble the C-frame and balljoint remover on the lower balljoint.

18   Turn the forcing screw clockwise until the lower balljoint is removed from the steering knuckle.

19   Assemble the C-frame on the upper balljoint.

20   Turn the forcing screw clockwise until the upper balljoint is removed from the knuckle. **Note:** *Always remove the lower balljoint first. Always install the lower balljoint first.*

21   Clean the steering knuckle bore and insert the lower balljoint into the knuckle as straight as possible. The lower balljoint doesn't have a cotter pin hole in the stud.

22   Assemble the C-frame, balljoint installer and receiver cup to install the lower balljoint.

23   Turn the forcing screw clockwise until the lower balljoint is firmly seated. Install the snap ring on the lower balljoint. **Note:** *If the ball-*

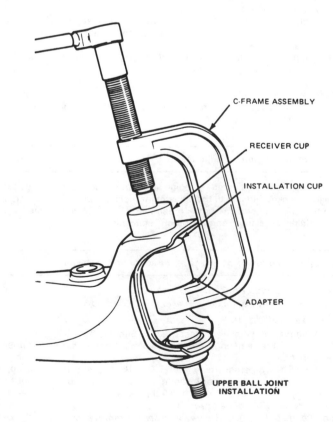

UPPER BALL JOINT INSTALLATION

5.8   Installing the upper balljoint

6.1   With the vehicle supported by jackstands, use a jack to raise and lower the axle

6.5a   Remove the lower spring retainer nut

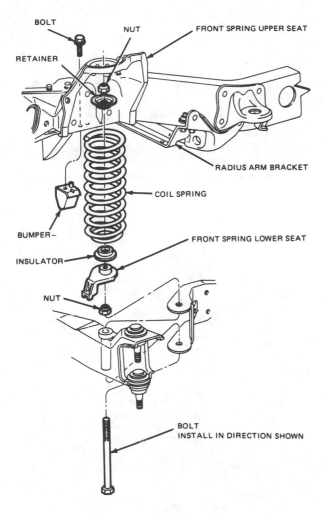

6.5b   Two-wheel drive front spring assembly — exploded view

joint cannot be installed to the proper depth, realignment of the receiver cup and installer will be necessary.

24   Install the upper balljoint with the C-frame.

25   Assemble the knuckle to the axle arm assembly and install the camber adjuster on the top balljoint stud with the arrow pointing outboard for positive camber and the arrow pointing inboard for negative camber. Zero camber bushings will not have an arrow and may be rotated in either direction as long as the lugs on the yoke engage the slots in the bushing. **Caution:** *The following tightening sequence must be followed exactly when securing the spindle. Excessive spindle turning effort may result in reduced steering returnability.*

26   Install and tighten the nut on the bottom balljoint to half the specified torque. Refer to the specifications for the proper torque value.

27   Install a new nut on the top ball stud and tighten to specification, then advance the nut until the castellation aligns with the cotter pin hole. Install the cotter pin.

28   Finish tightening the lower balljoint nut to specifications. **Note:** *The camber adjuster will seat itself into the spindle at a predetermined position during the tightening sequence. Do not attempt to adjust this position.*

29   For proper alignment take the vehicle to your dealer or an alignment specialist.

6   Coil spring — removal and installation

Refer to illustration 6.1, 6.5a, 6.5b, 6.9 and 6.10

1   Raise the vehicle and place jackstands under the frame and a jack under the the axle (see illustration).

2   Remove the wheel.

3   Disconnect the shock absorber at the lower shock bracket.

4   Refer to Chapter 9 and remove the brake caliper and wire the caliper out of your work area, making sure the brake hose has no strain on it.

5   Remove the lower spring retainer by removing the nut (inside the spring) securing the lower retainer to the spring slot (see illustration). **Note:** *The nut is attached to a stud on four-wheel drive models and a bolt runs through the I-beam axle on two-wheel drive models (see illustration).*

6   If equipped, remove the through bolt attaching the sway bar.

7   The axle should now be free, allowing spring removal. **Note:** *If the axle doesn't drop down far enough to allow spring removal, remove the pivot bolt securing the left axle to the frame.*

8   If necessary, use a pry bar to lift the spring over the bolt that passes through the lower spring seat. Rotate the spring so the built-in retainer on the upper spring seat is cleared, allowing spring removal.

9   Install the axle pivot bolt in the axle arm (if removed) and tighten the nut to specification. Install the spring lower seat and lower insulator (see illustration).

10   Push the axle down to allow installation of the spring by installing the top of the spring into the upper seat and rotating spring into place (see illustration).

11   A pry bar may be used to lift the lower end of the spring over the bolt if necessary.

12   Use the jack to lift the axle until the spring is seated.

13   Install the lower retainer and nut.

14   Connect the lower shock mount to its bracket.

15   Install the wheel, remove the jack and safety stands and lower the vehicle.

7   Radius arm — removal and installation

Refer to illustration 7.2a, 7.2b, 7.3 and 7.4

1   Refer to Section 6 and remove the spring assembly.

2   Remove the spring lower seat, stud and washer from the left radius arm only, then remove the bolts that attach the radius arm to the axle and front bracket (see illustrations) on four-wheel drive models. On two-wheel drive models remove the spring lower seat from the radius arm, then remove the bolt and nut that attaches the radius arm to the axle and front bracket.

3   From the rear side of the radius arm rear bracket, remove the nut, rear washer and insulator (see illustration).

6.9   Before assembly make sure the lower spring seat and insulator are in position

6.10   Push down on the axle to allow spring installation

7.2a   Remove the bolts (arrows) attaching the radius arm to the front bracket

7.2b   On four-wheel drive models remove the stud and bolt (arrows) attaching the radius arm to the axle. On two-wheel drive models a throughbolt is used instead of the stud and bolt

4   Remove the radius arm and remove the inner insulator and retainer from the radius arm stud (see illustration).
5   Install the front end of the radius arm to the axle. From underneath the axle install the attaching bolt and install the nut finger tight on two-wheel drive models. On four-wheel drive models, position the front end of the radius arm from bracket to the axle and install the attaching bolts and stud (and washer on the left axle only) in the bracket. Install the bolts and stud finger tight.
6   Before inserting the stud through the radius arm rear bracket, install the retainer and inner insulator on the radius arm stud.
7   Install the rear washer, insulator and nut on the stud at the rear side of the arm rear bracket and tighten the nut to specifications.
8   Tighten the stud and axle bolts to specification.
9   Position the spring lower seat and spring insulator on the radius arm so the hole in the seat goes over the arm to axle bolt and tighten axle pivot bolt (if removed during spring removal) to specifications.
10 Refer to Section 6 for spring installation.

---

8   Radius arm insulators — removal and installation

---

1   Remove the coil spring (refer to Section 6).
2   Loosen the axle pivot bolt.
3   Remove the nut and washer retaining the radius arm to the radius arm bracket and remove the outer insulator and spacer.
4   On four-wheel drive models disconnect the front driveshaft (refer to Chapter 8).
5   Loosen the front radius arm retaining bolts on four-wheel drive models or the through bolt on two-wheel drive models.
6   Place a jack under the radius arm and raise the axle until the radius arm is level.
7   Pull the axle arm assembly forward until the radius arm is free of the radius arm bracket.
8   Remove the radius arm insulators.
9   Installation is the reverse of the removal procedure.

7.3   Remove the nut, washer and insulator to remove the rear radius arm support

---

9   Axle pivot bracket — removal and installation

Refer to illustration 9.4, 9.5, 9.9, 9.10 and 9.13

Two-wheel drive models
1   Raise the vehicle and support it securely on jackstands.
2   Remove the tires and wheels.
3   Remove the front spring and radius arm.

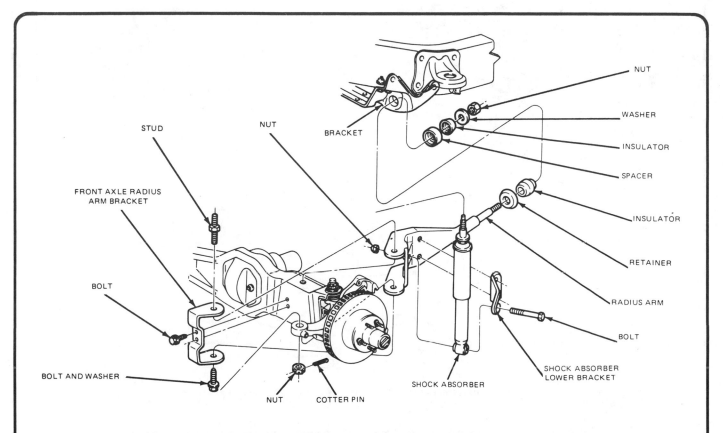

7.4   Four-wheel drive radius arm — exploded view

9.4   Remove the retaining bolt to remove the I-beam axle

4   Remove the axle pivot retaining bolt (see illustration) to remove the I-beam axle.

5   Unbolt the four attaching nuts and two bolts retaining the the axle pivot bracket and remove the bracket (see illustration).

6   Position the axle bracket against the frame and install the bolts and retainer assemblies from the inside of the axle pivot bracket out through the crossmember. Do not tighten any of the nuts until all four of them have been installed, then tighten them to the specified torque value. **Note:** *Special nuts are used to attach the axle pivot bracket to the crossmember. These nuts are undercut to provide clearance. If the undercut nuts must be replaced with standard nuts it will be necessary to install a 0.20 inch thick washer under each nut.*

7   Install the I-beam axle, spring, radius arm spindle, wheels and tires. Remove the jackstands and lower the vehicle.

Four-wheel drive models

8   Raise the vehicle, support it securely on jackstands, and remove the wheels and tires, front spring and radius arm. Refer to Chapter 8 for the front driveaxle removal procedures. Remove the front axle.

9   Remove the attaching nuts on the right pivot bracket. Remove the upper and side bolts and retainers and discard the side bolt and retainer. Remove the pivot bracket from the crossmember (see illustration).

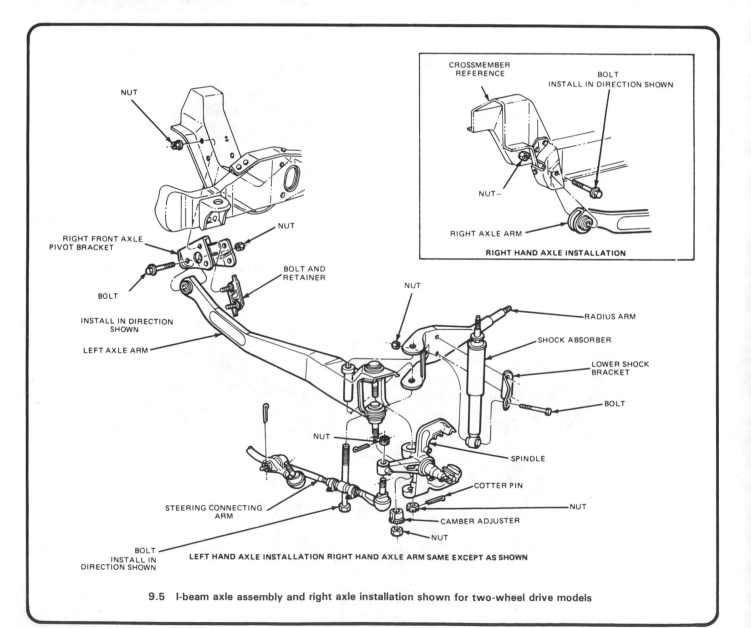

9.5   I-beam axle assembly and right axle installation shown for two-wheel drive models

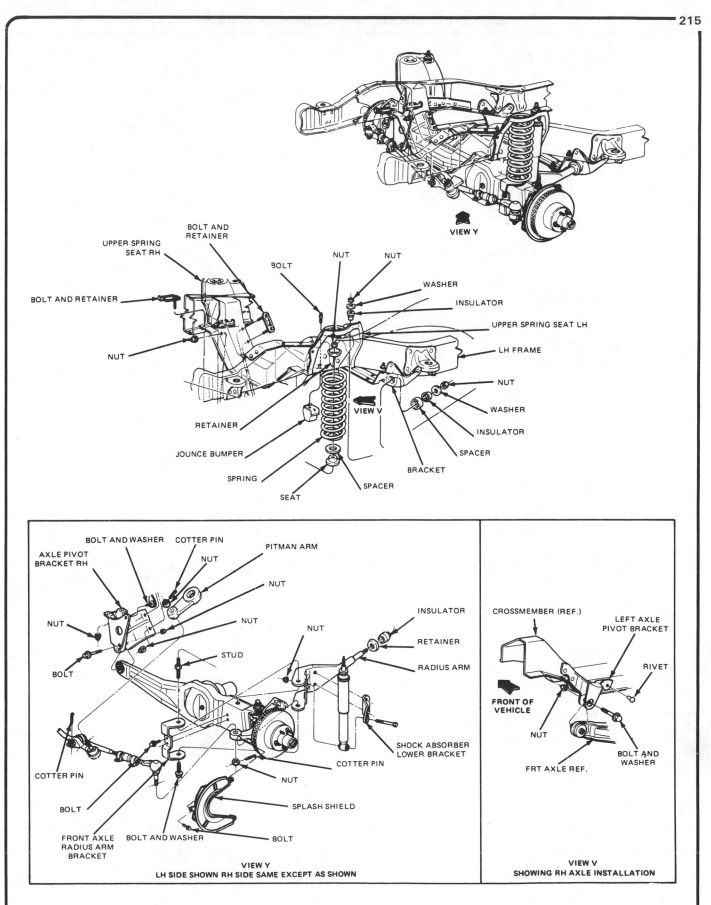

BOLT AND RETAINER

UPPER SPRING SEAT RH

BOLT AND RETAINER

NUT

BOLT

NUT

NUT

WASHER

INSULATOR

UPPER SPRING SEAT LH

LH FRAME

NUT

WASHER

INSULATOR

SPACER

BRACKET

RETAINER

JOUNCE BUMPER

SPRING

SEAT

SPACER

VIEW V

VIEW Y

AXLE PIVOT BRACKET RH

BOLT AND WASHER

COTTER PIN

NUT

PITMAN ARM

NUT

NUT

NUT

STUD

INSULATOR

RETAINER

RADIUS ARM

NUT

BOLT

SHOCK ABSORBER LOWER BRACKET

COTTER PIN

CROSSMEMBER (REF.)

LEFT AXLE PIVOT BRACKET

RIVET

FRONT OF VEHICLE

NUT

BOLT AND WASHER

FRT AXLE REF.

COTTER PIN

BOLT

FRONT AXLE RADIUS ARM BRACKET

BOLT AND WASHER

NUT

SPLASH SHIELD

BOLT

VIEW Y
LH SIDE SHOWN RH SIDE SAME EXCEPT AS SHOWN

VIEW V
SHOWING RH AXLE INSTALLATION

9.9 Axle assembly for four-wheel drive

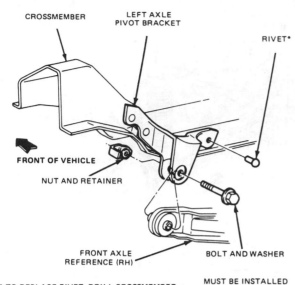

CROSSMEMBER   LEFT AXLE PIVOT BRACKET   RIVET*

FRONT OF VEHICLE

NUT AND RETAINER

FRONT AXLE REFERENCE (RH)   BOLT AND WASHER

MUST BE INSTALLED IN DIRECTION SHOWN

* TO REPLACE RIVET, DRILL CROSSMEMBER AND BRACKET HOLES TO 9/16-INCH. REPLACE RIVET WITH GRADE 8 FASTENERS: BOLT—58697 (9/16-12 x 1-1/2), WASHERS—44880 (2), AND NUT—34990, TIGHTEN TO 210 N·m (150 FT-LB)

VIEW SHOWING RIGHT AXLE ARM
INSTALLATION IN LEFT PIVOT BRACKET

9.10   Remove the axle pivot bracket by drilling the rivets
out with a 9/16-inch drill bit and install the bracket by
using a Grade 8 9/16-12x1-1/2 inch long bolt with nuts
and washers

10   Drill out the rivets on the left pivot bracket with a 9/16-inch drill
bit and remove the bracket (see illustration).
11   Position the left pivot bracket on the crossmember and align the
9/16-inch holes and install 9/16-12x1-1/2 inch Grade 8 bolts.
12   Install the washers and retaining nuts on the pivot bolts and tighten
to specifications.
13   Position the right axle pivot bracket to the crossmember (see illustration). Install the bolts and retainers in the direction shown so the
bolt heads face the engine oil pan giving maximum clearance. Install
and tighten the retaining nuts to specifications.
14   Drill out the lower mounting hole, bracket and crossmember to a
9/16-inch diameter and install a Grade 8 replacement bolt with two
flat washers and retaining nut. Tighten the pivot bracket bolts to
specification.
15   Refer to Chapter 8 and install the front driveaxle.
16   Install the radius arm and front spring.
17   Install the brake caliper if removed.
18   Install the wheels and tires and lower the vehicle.

10   Axle pivot bushing — removal and installation

Two-wheel drive

1   Raise the vehicle and support it securely on jackstands.
2   If removing the left axle pivot bushing, remove the retaining bolt
and nut then pull the pivot end of the axle down until the bushing is
exposed.
3   If removing the right axle pivot bushing the entire right I-beam axle
must be removed to get at the bushing. If removing the axle pivot
bushing on four-wheel drive models refer to Chapter 8 and follow the
procedure to remove the right front axle. If removing the axle pivot
bushing on a two-wheel drive model you should refer to the sections
on removing the coil spring and radius arm from the axle before disconnecting the axle pivot bolt.
4   Install forcing tool T78P-5638-A1, bushing remover
T80T-5638-A2, spacer T82T-3006-A4 and receiver cup
T78P-5638-A3 or equivalent bushing removing tools onto the bushing.
With the spacer between the walls of the axle, turn the forcing screw
and remove the pivot bushing.

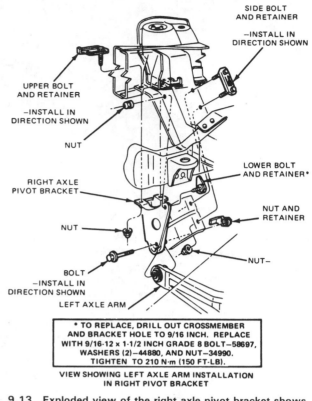

SIDE BOLT AND RETAINER
—INSTALL IN DIRECTION SHOWN

UPPER BOLT AND RETAINER
—INSTALL IN DIRECTION SHOWN

NUT

RIGHT AXLE PIVOT BRACKET

NUT

BOLT —INSTALL IN DIRECTION SHOWN

LEFT AXLE ARM

LOWER BOLT AND RETAINER*

NUT AND RETAINER

NUT—

* TO REPLACE, DRILL OUT CROSSMEMBER AND BRACKET HOLE TO 9/16 INCH. REPLACE WITH 9/16-12 x 1-1/2 INCH GRADE 8 BOLT—58697, WASHERS (2)—44880, AND NUT—34990. TIGHTEN TO 210 N·m (150 FT-LB).

VIEW SHOWING LEFT AXLE ARM INSTALLATION
IN RIGHT PIVOT BRACKET

9.13   Exploded view of the right axle pivot bracket shows
bracket installation

Four-wheel drive

5   Remove the axle.
6   Install forcing tool T78P-5638-A1, bushing remover
T80T-5638-A2, and receiver cup T78P-5638-A4 or their equivalent
onto the pivot bushing. Turn the forcing screw to remove the pivot
bushing.
7   Insert the pivot bushing in the axle housing and install receiver cup
T78P-5638-A4, forcing screw T78P-5638-A1, and bushing replacer
T82T-3006-A1 into the housing and turn the forcing screw to install
the bushing.
8   After installing, the bushing lip must be flared to prevent movement. To flare the lip install forcing screw T78P-5638-A, flaring tool,
T82T-3006-A1 or their equivalents and turn the forcing screw to flare
the lip.

11   Tie rod ends — removal and installation

Refer to illustrations 11.4a and 11.4b

1   Raise the vehicle and support it securely on jackstands with the
wheels pointed straight ahead.
2   Remove the drag link and steering connecting rod.
3   Loosen the nuts on the adjusting sleeve and count the number of
turns it takes to back the sleeve off the tie rod end.
4   Remove the tie rod end from the spindle using Tool 3290-C, Tie
Rod Remover, or a pickle fork removal tool. **Note:** *On four-wheel drive
models the tie rod end is inserted in the top of the spindle and on two-
wheel drive models it is inserted from the bottom of the spindle (see
illustrations).*
5   Install the new tie rod end in the spindle arm. Make sure the steering
wheel and tires are in the straight ahead position. Make sure the tie
rod stud is seated in the taper to prevent it from rotating while turning.
6   Install the tie rod end nut and tighten to specifications. Install a
new cotter pin.
7   Install the adjusting sleeve on the tie rod the same number of turns
it took to remove the old one. Tighten the adjusting sleeve nuts and
make sure the tie rod is installed in the same position as when it was
taken off.

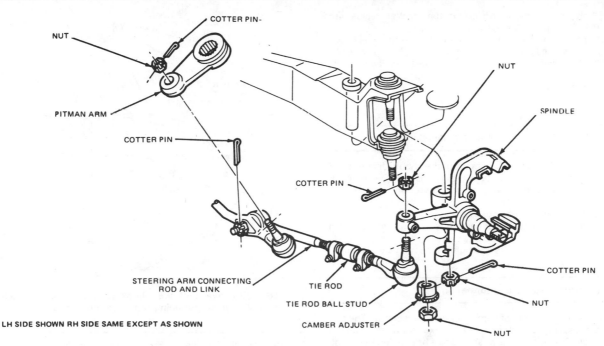

11.4a Exploded view shows that the tie rod end inserts from the bottom on two-wheel drive models

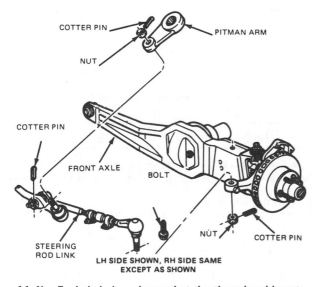

11.4b Exploded view shows that the tie rod end inserts from the top on four-wheel drive models

8   Install the drag link and connecting rod.
9   Remove the jackstands and lower the vehicle.
10   For proper toe-in adjustment take the vehicle to a front end specialist.

12 Drag Link — removal and installation

1   Raise and support the vehicle on jackstands with the wheels in the straight ahead position.
2   Remove the cotter pin and nut from the ball stud at the Pitman arm steering connecting rod.
3   Loosen the bolts on the tie rod adjusting sleeve and count the number of turns it takes to remove the sleeve from the drag link.
4   Install the drag link the same number of turns it took to remove it from the tie rod and tighten the clamp bolts to specification.
5   Position the drag link ball end into the Pitman arm. Position the steering connecting arm ball end in the drag link. Check that the wheels are still pointed straight ahead and that the steering wheel is in the

straight ahead position. Make sure the ball ends are seated in the taper to prevent rotation while turning. Install and tighten the nuts.
6   Install new cotter pins.
7   Remove the jackstands and lower the vehicle.
8   For proper toe-in adjustment take the vehicle to a front end specialist.

13 Steering connecting rod — removal and installation

1   Raise the vehicle and support on jackstands with the wheels pointed straight ahead.
2   Remove the cotter pin and nut from the ball end of the connecting rod. Remove the ball end from the drag link using Tool 3290-C or a pickle fork removal tool.
3   Loosen the bolts on the tie rod and remove the connecting rod by counting the number of turns it takes to remove the connecting rod from the tie rod.
4   Install the connecting rod in the tie rod sleeve the same number of turns it took to remove it. Tighten the tie rod end nuts to specification.
5   Insert the connecting arm ball end in the drag link. Make sure tires and steering wheel are still pointed straight ahead. Make sure the ball end is seated in the taper to prevent rotation while tightening. Install and tighten the ball end retaining nut.
6   Install new cotter pins.
7   Remove the jackstands and lower the vehicle.
8   For proper toe-in adjustment take the vehicle to a front end specialist.

14 Front I-beam axle — removal and installation

Note: For four-wheel drive axle removal refer to Chapter 8.

1   Raise the vehicle and support it securely on jackstands. Remove the front wheel.
2   Remove the spindle and spring.
3   Remove the spring lower seat from the radius arm and remove the bolt and nut attaching the radius arm to the front axle.
4   Remove the axle to frame pivot bracket bolt and nut and remove the axle.
5   Position the axle to the frame pivot bracket and install the bolt and tighten the nut finger tight.
6   Position the opposite end of the axle to the radius arm and install

the attaching bolt from underneath through the bracket, radius arm and axle. Install and tighten the nut.

7   Install the spring lower seat on the radius arm so the hole in the seat indexes over the arm to axle bolt. **Note:** *Before tightening the axle pivot bolt and nut, lower the vehicle onto its wheels or support the front springs.*

8   Install the spindle and wheel/tire assembly.

9   Tighten the axle to frame pivot bracket bolt.

15   Front stabilizer bar — removal and installation

1   Remove the retaining nuts attaching both the U-bolts in the lower shock bracket and the stabilizer bar bushing to radius arm. On Bronco II, first remove the bolts and retainers from the center and right end of the stabilizer bar.

2   Disconnect the stabilizer bar bushings.

3   To install, first place the stabilizer bar in position against the radius arm and bracket.

4   Install the retainers and U-bolts and tighten the nuts and retainers.

16   Rear suspension — general information

The rear suspension consists of semi-elliptical leaf springs. The forward end of each spring is attached to a bracket on the frame side member. The rear of each spring is shackled to a bracket on the frame rail. The hydraulic shock absorbers are direct, double acting units with staggered mounting positions from the rear axle. The right shock is mounted forward of the axle and the left mounted to the rear. The shock absorbers are sealed, nonadjustable units and must be replaced as complete assemblies.

17   Shock absorbers — inspection

1   The most common test of the shock damping is simply to bounce the corners of the vehicle several times and observe whether or not the vehicle stops bouncing once the input is stopped. A slight rebound and settling indicates good damping, but if the vehicle continues to bounce several times, the shock absorbers must be replaced.

2   If your shock absorbers stand up to the bounce test, visually inspect the shock body for signs of fluid leakage, punctures or deep dents in the metal of the body. Replace any shock absorber which is leaking or damaged, in spite of proper damping indicated in the bounce test.

3   When you have removed a shock absorber, pull the piston rod out and push it back in several times to check for smooth operation throughout the travel of the piston rod. Replace the shock absorber if it gives any signs of hard or soft spots in the piston travel.

4   When you install a new shock absorber, pump the piston rod fully in and out several times to lubricate the seals and fill the hydraulic sections of the unit.

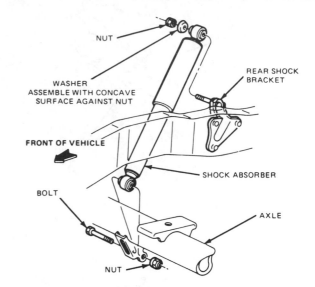

18.2   Remove the lower shock absorber retainers then remove the top retaining nut to remove the rear shock

18   Rear shock absorber — removal and installation

Refer to illustration 18.2

1   Place a jack under the the axle to take the load off the shock absorber.

2   Remove the nuts and bolts from the lower end of the shock absorber attached to the spring plate (see illustration).

3   Remove the nut retaining the top end of the shock to the upper mounting bracket. Compress the shock absorber and remove it.

4   Install the shock in the reverse order of removal.

19   Rear leaf spring — removal and installation

Refer to illustration 19.5

1   Raise the vehicle and support it securely under the frame rails with jackstands.

2   Remove the rear wheels.

3   Place a jack under the axle housing and raise it sufficiently to remove the weight from the springs.

4   Disconnect the lower end of the shock absorber and compress it upward and out of the way.

5   Remove the nuts from the U-bolts and remove the U-bolts and spring plate. If applicable, remove the spacer on four-wheel drive models (see illustration).

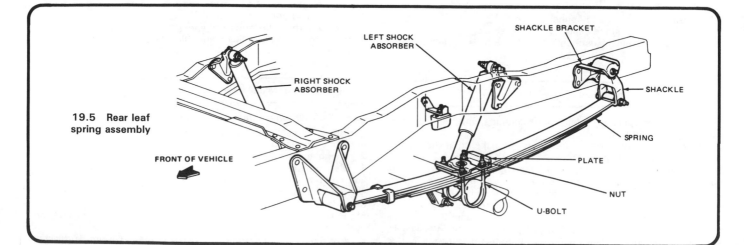

19.5   Rear leaf spring assembly

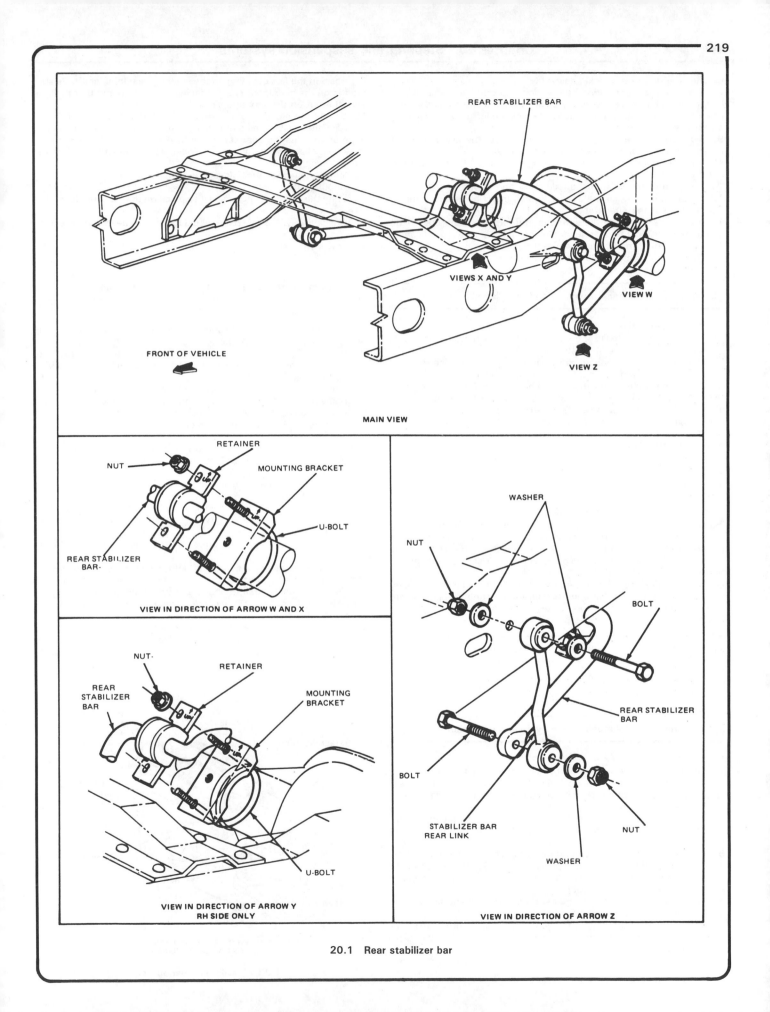

REAR STABILIZER BAR

VIEWS X AND Y

VIEW W

VIEW Z

FRONT OF VEHICLE

MAIN VIEW

NUT

RETAINER

MOUNTING BRACKET

U-BOLT

REAR STABILIZER BAR·

VIEW IN DIRECTION OF ARROW W AND X

NUT·

RETAINER

REAR STABILIZER BAR

MOUNTING BRACKET

U-BOLT

**VIEW IN DIRECTION OF ARROW Y
RH SIDE ONLY**

WASHER

NUT

BOLT

REAR STABILIZER BAR

BOLT

STABILIZER BAR REAR LINK

NUT

WASHER

VIEW IN DIRECTION OF ARROW Z

20.1   Rear stabilizer bar

6   Remove the rear shackle assembly.
7   Remove the front spring hanger bolt and remove the spring.
8   If the bushings in the spring eyes are distorted or worn and in need of replacement, it is recommended that this be left to your dealer or a properly equipped shop.
9   To install, place the spring in position under the axle and install the shackle assembly, with the nuts finger tight.
10   Place the spring front eye in the hanger and insert the bolt, tightening the nut finger tight.
11   Lower the jack so that the axle rests on the spring.
12   If applicable, install the spacer. Install the U-bolts and plate.
13   Reconnect the shock absorber lower end.
14   Lower the axle until the spring is at its approximate ride height and tighten the front hanger nut and rear shackle bolts to specification.
15   Replace the wheels and remove the jackstands.
16   Remove the jack and lower the vehicle.

20   Rear stabilizer bar — removal and installation

Refer to illustration 20.1

1   Disconnect the stabilizer bar from the links by removing the nuts, bolts and washers (see illustration).
2   Disconnect the U-bolt from the mounting bracket and retainer. Remove the mounting bracket, retainer and stabilizer bar.
3   To mount the unit, position the U-bolt and mounting bracket on the axle with the bracket having the *UP* marking facing up.
4   Install the stabilizer bar and retainer on the mounting bracket. Be sure retainer marked *UP* is facing up.
5   Connect the stabilizer bar to the rear link and tighten the retainer.
6   Secure the mounting bracket U-bolt nuts.

21   Steering system — general information

The steering linkage is composed of a Pitman arm, drag link, steering connecting rod and tie rods. The Pitman arm transfers the steering gear movements through the drag link and steering connecting rod to the tie rods. The tie rods move the spindles to the desired steering movement. The tie rods are equipped with an adjusting sleeve for setting the toe-in.
The vehicle will come equipped with either the Ford Integral Power Steering Gear or a manual unit. The power steering pump is a Ford model C-11.

22   Steering wheel — removal and installation

Steering wheel removal and installation is covered in Chapter 12, Section 23.

23   Steering gear (Manual) — removal and installation

Refer to illustration 23.2

1   Raise the vehicle and support it securely on jackstands.
2   Disengage the plastic flex coupling shield from the steering gear input shaft shield by prying it rearward and sliding it up the intermediate shaft (see illustration).
3   Remove the bolt retaining the flex coupling to the steering gear.
4   Disconnect the steering gear input shaft shield from the steering gear.
5   Remove the large nut securing the Pitman arm to the sector shaft and remove the Pitman arm using puller T64P-3590-F or an equivalent puller. **Caution:** *Damage to the steering gear can occur if a hammer is used on the end of the puller.*
6   Remove the steering box retainer nuts and bolts and remove the box.
7   Center the gear by rotating the gear input shaft (wormshaft) from stop to stop, counting the total number of turns. Turn the gear back exactly half way.
8   Install the steering gear input shaft shield on the steering gear input shield.

9   Position the flex coupling on the steering gear input shaft. Be sure the flat on the gear input shaft is facing straight up and that it aligns with the flat on the flex coupling.
10   Secure the steering box to the side rail with the retainer bolts.
11   Align the two blocked teeth on the Pitman arm with the four missing teeth on the steering gear sector shaft. Assemble the Pitman arm on the sector shaft and install the attaching washer and nut. Tighten the nut to specifications.
12   Install and tighten the bolt securing the flex coupling to the steering gear input shaft.
13   Snap the flex coupling shield into place on the steering gear input shield.
14   Check the system to ensure equal turns from dead center to each side.
15   Lower the vehicle.

24   Steering gear (power assist) — removal and installation

Refer to illustration 24.2

1   Disconnect both the pressure and return lines from the steering box and plug the lines and ports to prevent contamination.
2   Remove the steering gear shaft U-joint shields from the flex coupling and disconnect the flex coupling at the steering box by removing the bolt (see illustration).
3   Raise the vehicle and support it securely on jackstands.
4   Remove the Pitman arm attaching nut and washer.
5   Using tool T64P-3590-F or an equivalent puller, remove the Pitman arm from the sector shaft. Be careful not to damage the sector shaft seals.
6   Support the steering gear before removing the retaining bolts.
7   Remove the steering gear from the vehicle by working the unit free of the flex coupling.
8   Begin installation by installing the lower U-joint shield onto the back of the steering gear.
9   Install the upper U-joint shield into place on the steering shaft assembly by turning the steering wheel so the spokes are in the horizontal position.
10   Center the steering gear input shaft with the indexing flat facing down.
11   Slide the steering gear input shaft into the flex coupling and secure the steering gear to the frame rail with the attaching bolts.
12   Turn the wheels straight ahead and install the Pitman arm on the sector shaft. Install the Pitman arm attaching washer and nut and tighten to specification.
13   Install the power steering hydraulic lines.
14   Check that the fluid reservoir is full. Disconnect the coil wire and turn the steering wheel from side to side while cranking the engine

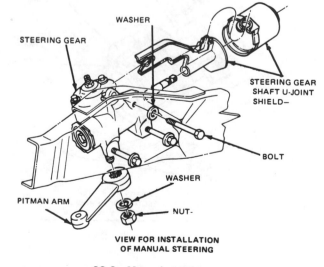

23.2 Manual steering gear

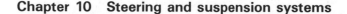

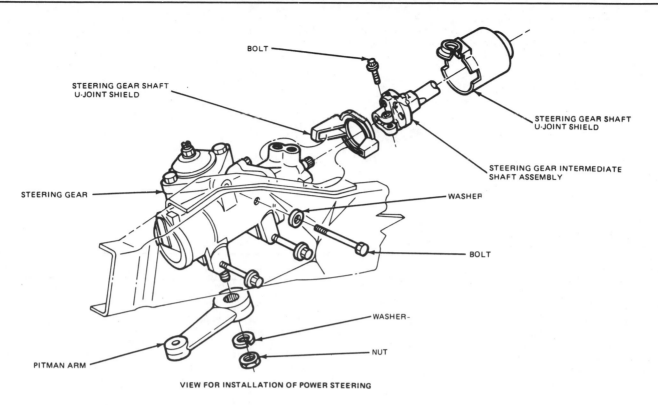

VIEW FOR INSTALLATION OF POWER STEERING

24.2 Power steering gear

with the starter (not more than 30 seconds) to distribute the fluid.
15 Recheck the fluid level.
16 Connect the coil wire, start the engine and check for leaks.
17 Lower the vehicle.

25 Power steering pump — removal and installation

1 Disconnect the return hose at the reservoir and drain the fluid into a container. Raise the vehicle and support it securely on jackstands.
2 Disconnect the pressure hose from the pump.
3 On 4-cylinder engines, loosen the alternator pivot bolt and the adjusting bolt to slacken the belt tension. On V6 engines, loosen the adjustment nut and the slider bolts on the pump support and push in the pump to slacken the belt tension.
4 Remove the drivebelt pulley.

5 Install the pump pulley removal and installation tool T69L-10300-B or an equivalent puller onto the pulley.
6 While holding the pump, rotate the tool nut counterclockwise to remove the pulley. Be careful not to apply excessive pressure to the pump shaft resulting in damage to the internal parts.
7 Remove the pump retaining bolts and remove the pump.
8 Install the pump on the bracket and secure the attaching bolts.
9 Install the pump pulley removal/installation tool T65P-3A733-C or an equivalent installation tool to install the pulley.
10 Install the pulley belt.
11 On 4-cylinder engines, move the alternator to tighten the belt to specification. Tighten the slider bolt. On V6 engines tighten the adjustment nut and adjust the belt tension.
12 Install the hoses to their proper fittings.
13 Fill the reservoir with the specified power steering fluid and start the engine. With the engine running turn the wheel from stop to stop to remove all air in the system.
14 Check for leaks and recheck the fluid level.

Chapter 11   Body

Contents

Specifications

Torque specifications	Ft-lbs
Door latch to door bolt	3 to 6
Door latch attaching bolt	7 to 10
Hood hinge bolts	5 to 8
Hood latch bolts......................................	7 to 10
Front bumper air deflector	5 to 8
Front bumper guard attaching bolts...................	17 to 23
Liftgate hinge to liftgate bolts	5 to 8
Liftgate hinge to body nut	12 to 19
Liftgate latch to liftgate bolts	7 to 10
Rear bumper bracket to frame bolts	92 to 136
Rear bumper bracket to frame nut....................	92 to 136
Rear bumper to bracket bolts	26 to 40
Rear bumper extension assembly bolt (XLS)	6 to 8
Rear bumper bracket to frame bolts (Bronco II)	74 to 100
Rear bumper to bracket bolts (Bronco II)	17 to 22
Rear bumper extension (Bronco II).....................	5 to 8
Rear stone deflector bolts (Bronco II)	8 to 14
Tailgate latch to bed..................................	7 to 10
Tailgate anchor post to bed	33 to 51
Tailgate latch release to tailgate	7 to 10
Tailgate latch assembly to tailgate	16 to 25
Tailgate hinge to bed	20 to 29

1   General information

As with other parts of the vehicle, proper maintenance of body components plays an important part in retention of the vehicle's market value. It is far less costly to handle small problems before they grow into larger ones. Information in this Chapter will tell you all you need to know to keep seals sealing, body panels aligned and general appearance up to par.

The vehicle body is of welded construction. Major body components which are particularly vulnerable in accidents are removable. It is often cheaper and less time consuming to replace an entire panel than it is to attempt a restoration of the old one. However, this must be decided on a case by case basis.

2 Body — maintenance

1   The condition of your vehicle's body is very important, because it is on this that the second hand value will mainly depend. It is much more difficult to repair a neglected or damaged body than it is to repair mechanical components. The hidden areas of the body, such as the fender wells, the frame, and the engine compartment, are equally important, although obviously do not require as frequent attention as the rest of the body.

2   Once a year, or every 12,000 miles, it is a good idea to have the underside of the body and the frame steam cleaned. All traces of dirt and oil will be removed and the underside can then be inspected carefully for rust, damaged brake lines, frayed electrical wiring, damaged cables, and other problems. The front suspension components should be greased after completion of this job.

3   At the same time, clean the engine and the engine compartment using either a steam cleaner or a water soluble degreaser.

4   The fender wells should be given particular attention, as undercoating can peel away and stones and dirt thrown up by the tires can cause the paint to chip and flake, allowing rust to set in. If rust is found, clean down to the bare metal and apply an anti-rust paint.

5   The body should be washed once a week (or when dirty). Wet the vehicle thoroughly to soften the dirt, then wash it down with a soft sponge and plenty of clean soapy water. If the surplus dirt is not washed off very carefully, it will in time wear down the paint.

6   Spots of tar or asphalt coating thrown up from the road should be removed with a cloth soaked in solvent.

7   Once every six months, give the body and chrome trim a thorough waxing. If a chrome cleaner is used to remove rust from any of the vehicle's plated parts, remember that the cleaner also removes part of the chrome, so use it sparingly.

3 Roof covering and vinyl trim — maintenance

Under no circumstances try to clean any external vinyl trim or roof covering with detergents, caustic soap or petroleum based cleaners. Plain soap and water is all that is required, with a soft brush to clean dirt that may be ingrained. Wash the covering as frequently as the rest of the vehicle.

After cleaning, application of a high quality rubber and vinyl protectant will help prevent oxidation and cracking. This protectant can also be applied to all interior and exterior vinyl components, as well as to vacuum lines and rubber hoses, which often fail as a result of chemical degradation.

4 Upholstery and carpets — maintenance

1   Every three months remove the carpets or mats and clean the interior of the vehicle (more frequently if necessary). Vacuum the upholstery and carpets to remove loose dirt and dust.

2   If the upholstery is soiled, apply upholstery cleaner with a damp sponge and wipe it off with a clean, dry cloth.

5 Body repair — minor damage

See color photo sequence ''Repair of minor scratches''

1   If the scratch is superficial and does not penetrate to the metal of the body, repair is very simple. Lightly rub the scratched area with a fine rubbing compound to remove loose paint and built up wax. Rinse the area with clean water.

2   Apply touch-up paint to the scratch, using a small brush. Continue to apply thin layers of paint until the surface of the paint in the scratch is level with the surrounding paint. Allow the new paint at least two weeks to harden, then blend it into the surrounding paint by rubbing with a very fine rubbing compound. Finally, apply a coat of wax to the scratch area.

3   If the scratch has penetrated the paint and exposed the metal of the body, causing the metal to rust, a different repair technique is required. Remove all loose rust from the bottom of the scratch with a

pocket knife, then apply rust inhibiting paint to prevent the formation of rust in the future. Using a rubber or nylon applicator, coat the scratched area with glaze-type filler. If required, the filler can be mixed with thinner to provide a very thin paste, which is ideal for filling narrow scratches. Before the glaze filler in the scratch hardens, wrap a piece of smooth cotton cloth around the tip of a finger. Dip the cloth in thinner and then quickly wipe it along the surface of the scratch. This will ensure that the surface of the filler is slightly hollow. The scratch can now be painted over as described earlier in this section.

Repair of dents

4   When repairing dents, the first job is to pull the dent out until the affected area is as close as possible to its original shape. There is no point in trying to restore the original shape completely as the metal in the damaged area will have stretched on impact and cannot be restored to its original contours. It is better to bring the level of the dent up to a point which is about 1/8-inch below the level of the surrounding metal. In cases where the dent is very shallow, it is not worth trying to pull it out at all.

5   If the back side of the dent is accessible, it can be hammered out gently from behind using a soft-face hammer. While doing this, hold a block of wood firmly against the opposite side of the metal to absorb the hammer blows and prevent the metal from being stretched.

6   If the dent is in a section of the body which has double layers, or some other factor makes it inaccessible from behind, a different technique is required. Drill several small holes through the metal inside the damaged area, particularly in the deeper sections. Screw long, self tapping screws into the holes just enough for them to get a good grip in the metal. Now the dent can be pulled out by pulling on the protruding heads of the screws with locking pliers.

7   The next stage of repair is the removal of paint from the damaged area and from an inch or so of the surrounding metal. This is easily done with a wire brush or sanding disk in a drill motor, although it can be done just as effectively by hand with sandpaper. To complete the preparation for filling, score the surface of the bare metal with a screwdriver or the tang of a file or drill small holes in the affected area. This will provide a good grip for the filler material. To complete the repair, see the Section on filling and painting.

Repair of rust holes or gashes

8   Remove all paint from the affected area and from an inch or so of the surrounding metal using a sanding disk or wire brush mounted in a drill motor. If these are not available, a few sheets of sandpaper will do the job just as effectively.

9   With the paint removed, you will be able to determine the severity of the corrosion and decide whether to replace the whole panel, if possible, or repair the affected area. New body panels are not as expensive as most people think and it is often quicker to install a new panel than to repair large areas of rust.

10   Remove all trim pieces from the affected area except those which will act as a guide to the original shape of the damaged body, such as headlight shells, etc. Using metal snips or a hacksaw blade, remove all loose metal and any other metal that is badly affected by rust. Hammer the edges of the hole inward to create a slight depression for the filler material.

11   Wire brush the affected area to remove the powdery rust from the surface of the metal. If the back of the rusted area is accessible, treat it with rust-inhibiting paint.

12   Before filling is done, block the hole in some way. This can be done with sheet metal riveted or screwed into place, or by stuffing the hole with wire mesh.

13   Once the hole is blocked off, the affected area can be filled and painted. See the following sub-section on filling and painting.

Filling and painting

14   Many types of body fillers are available, but generally speaking, body repair kits which contain filler paste and a tube of resin hardener are best for this type of repair work. A wide, flexible plastic or nylon applicator will be necessary for imparting a smooth and contoured finish to the surface of the filler material. Mix up a small amount of filler on a clean piece of wood or cardboard (use the hardener sparingly). Follow the manufacturer's instructions on the package, otherwise the filler will set incorrectly.

15   Using the applicator, apply the filler paste to the prepared area. Draw the applicator across the surface of the filler to achieve the desired

contour and to level the filler surface. As soon as a contour that approximates the original one is achieved, stop working the paste. If you continue, the paste will begin to stick to the applicator. Continue to add thin layers of paste at 20-minute intervals until the level of the filler is just above the surrounding metal.

16 Once the filler has hardened, the excess can be removed with a body file. From then on, progressively finer grades of sandpaper should be used, starting with a 180-grit paper and finishing with 600-grit wet-or-dry paper. Always wrap the sandpaper around a flat rubber or wooden block, otherwise the surface of the filler will not be completely flat. During the sanding of the filler surface, the wet-or-dry paper should be periodically rinsed in water. This will ensure that a very smooth finish is produced in the final stage.

17 At this point, the repair area should be surrounded by a ring of bare metal, which in turn should be encircled by the finely feathered edge of good paint. Rinse the repair area with clean water until all of the dust produced by the sanding operation is gone.

18 Spray the entire area with a light coat of primer. This will reveal any imperfections in the surface of the filler. Repair the imperfections with fresh filler paste or glaze filler and once more smooth the surface with sandpaper. Repeat this spray-and-repair procedure until you are satisfied that the surface of the filler and the feathered edge of the paint are perfect. Rinse the area with clean water and allow it to dry completely.

19 The repair area is now ready for painting. Spray painting must be carried out in a warm, dry, windless and dust free atmosphere. These conditions can be created if you have access to a large indoor work area, but if you are forced to work in the open, you will have to pick the day very carefully. If you are working indoors, dousing the floor in the work area with water will help settle the dust which would otherwise be in the air. If the repair area is confined to one body panel, mask off the surrounding panels. This will help minimize the effects of a slight mismatch in paint color. Trim pieces such as chrome strips, door handles, etc., will also need to be masked off or removed. Use masking tape and several thicknesses of newspaper for the masking operations.

20 Before spraying, shake the paint can thoroughly, then spray a test area until the spray painting technique is mastered. Cover the repair area with a thick coat of primer. The thickness should be built up using several thin layers of primer rather than one thick one. Using 600-grit wet-or-dry sandpaper, rub down the surface of the primer until it is very smooth. While doing this, the work area should be thoroughly rinsed with water and the wet-or-dry sandpaper periodically rinsed as well. Allow the primer to dry before spraying additional coats.

21 Spray on the top coat, again building up the thickness by using several thin layers of paint. Begin spraying in the center of the repair area and then, using a circular motion, work out until the whole repair area and about two inches of the surrounding original paint is covered. Remove all masking material 10 to 15 minutes after spraying on the final coat of paint. Allow the new paint at least two weeks to harden, then use a very fine rubbing compound to blend the edges of the new paint into the existing paint. Finally, apply a coat of wax.

6 Body repair — major damage

1   Major damage must be repaired by an auto body shop specifically equipped to perform unibody repairs. These shops have available the specialized equipment required to do the job properly.

2   If the damage is extensive, the underbody must be checked for proper alignment or the vehicle's handling characteristics may be adversely affected and other components may wear at an accelerated rate.

3   Due to the fact that all of the major body components (hood, fenders, etc.) are separate and replaceable units, any seriously damaged components should be replaced rather than repaired. Sometimes these components can be found in a wrecking yard that specializes in used vehicle components, often at considerable savings over the cost of new parts.

8.3   **Paint or scribe alignment marks on the hood to assure proper alignment during installation**

9.1   **Index the hood latch location for proper installation**

9.3   **Pry the plastic retainer off the anchor post to remove the cable**

7 Hinges and locks — maintenance

Every 3000 miles or three months, the door, hood and rear hatch hinges and locks should be lubricated with a few drops of oil. The door and rear hatch striker plates should also be given a thin coat of white lithium base grease to reduce wear and ensure free movement.

8 Hood — removal and installation

Refer to illustration 8.3
1   Raise the hood.
2   Place protective pads along the edges of the engine compartment to prevent damage to the painted surfaces.
3   Scribe or paint lines around the mounting brackets so the hood can be installed in the same position (see illustration).
4   With an assistant supporting the weight of the hood, remove the bracket bolts and detach the hood from the vehicle.
5   Installation is the reverse of removal. Be sure to align the brackets with the marks made prior to removal.

9 Hood latch cable — removal and installation

Refer to illustrations 9.1, 9.3, 9.4, 9.5 and 9.7
1   Index the location of the the hood latch with paint for proper alignment during installation (see illustration).
2   Remove the two retaining screws to remove the hood latch.
3   Turn the latch over and use a small screwdriver to pry the plastic cable retainer off the anchor post (see illustration).
4   Use pliers to lift the cable out of the retaining slot cut into the hood latch (see illustration).
5   With the cable loose lift the eye of the cable off the anchor post (see illustration).
6   Remove the fuse cover to allow room for removing the hood latch cable handle.
7   Remove the two retaining screws attaching the hood release handle to the dash (see illustration).
8   Work the cable through the firewall into the passenger compartment by first releasing any plastic cable routing retainers.
9   Installation is the reversal of the removal procedure.

10 Door latch striker — removal, installation and adjustment

1   Use a pair of locking pliers to unscrew the door latch striker stud.
2   The striker stud may be adjusted vertically and laterally as well as fore-and-aft.
3   The latch striker must not be used to compensate for door misalignment.
4   The door latch striker can be shimmed to obtain the correct clearance between the latch and striker.
5   The clearance can be checked by cleaning the latch jams and striker area and applying a thin layer of dark grease to the striker. Close and open the door, noting the pattern of the grease.
6   Move the striker assembly laterally to provide a flush fit at the door and pillar or quarter panel.
7   Tighten the striker stud after adjustment.

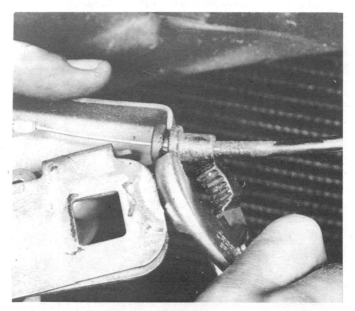

9.4   Use pliers to remove the rubber cable anchor from
the latch

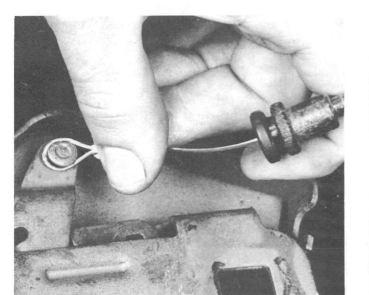

9.5   Lift the eye of the hood release cable off the
anchor post

9.7   With the fuse cover removed, remove the two screws
that attach the hood release handle to the dash

This photo sequence illustrates the repair of a dent and damaged paintwork. The procedure for the repair of a hole is similar. Refer to the text for more complete instructions

After removing any adjacent body trim, hammer the dent out. The damaged area should then be made slightly concave

Use coarse sandpaper or a sanding disc on a drill motor to remove all paint from the damaged area. Feather the sanded area into the edges of the surrounding paint, using progressively finer grades of sandpaper

The damaged area should be treated with rust remover prior to application of the body filler. In the case of a rust hole, all rusted sheet metal should be cut away

Carefully follow manufacturer's instructions when mixing the body filler so as to have the longest possible working time during application. Rust holes should be covered with fiberglass screen held in place with dabs of body filler prior to repair

Apply the filler with a flexible applicator in thin layers at 20 minute intervals. Use an applicator such as a wood spatula for confined areas. The filler should protrude slightly above the surrounding area

Shape the filler with a surform-type plane. Then, use water and progressively finer grades of sandpaper and a sanding block to wet-sand the area until it is smooth. Feather the edges of the repair area into the surrounding paint.

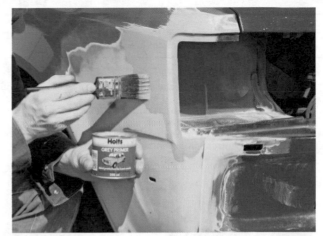

Use spray or brush applied primer to cover the entire repair area so that slight imperfections in the surface will be filled in. Prime at least one inch into the area surrounding the repair. Be careful of over-spray when using spray-type primer

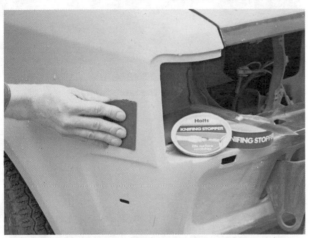

Wet-sand the primer with fine (approximately 400 grade) sandpaper until the area is smooth to the touch and blended into the surrounding paint. Use filler paste on minor imperfections

After the filler paste has dried, use rubbing compound to ensure that the surface of the primer is smooth. Prior to painting, the surface should be wiped down with a tack rag or lint-free cloth soaked in lacquer thinner

Choose a dry, warm, breeze-free area in which to paint and make sure that adjacent areas are protected from over-spray. Shake the spray paint can thoroughly and apply the top coat to the repair area, building it up by applying several coats, working from the center

After allowing at least two weeks for the paint to harden, use fine rubbing compound to blend the area into the original paint. Wax can now be applied

11 Inner door handle latch — removal and installation

Refer to illustrations 11.1, 11.2 and 11.3

1   Remove the screws retaining the inner door latch assembly to the door (see illustration).
2   Insert a screwdriver in the notch on the aft end of the latch and pry the assembly out (see illustration).
3   Rotate the inner door latch assembly up 90° to release it from the door latch remote control link assembly (see illustration).
4   Installation is the reversal of the removal procedure.

11.1   Remove the retaining screw attaching the latch to the door

11.3   Twist the latch up to release it from the remote actuator rod

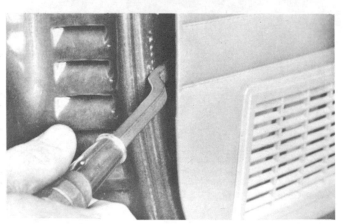

12.5   Wedge a flat screwdriver under the panel and pry near the plastic retainers to remove the panel. Do not pull on the panel or the retainers could pull out of the panel

12 Door trim panel and door vent valve — removal and installation

Refer to illustrations 12.1, 12.5, 12.6 and 12.12

1   Remove the three screws attaching the arm rest to the door panel (see illustration).
2   Remove the screws retaining the door inside door handle cup and remove the handle cup.
3   Remove the screw attaching the window crank and remove crank and washer.

11.2   Pry the latch forward

12.1   Remove the three screws retaining the arm-rest to the door

12.6   Pull the weather cover off gently so as not to tear it

4   If equipped, remove the door lock control.
5   Using a screwdriver, carefully pry the door inner panel away from
the door at each of the clip locations (see illustration). **Caution:** *Never
pull on the panel to release the plastic clips.*
6   Pull back the protective weather cover from the door (see
illustration).
7   Before installation replace any broken or missing clips on the panel.
8   Position the trim on the door with all the plastic clips aligned with
their respective holes.
9   Firmly press on the panel at each of the clip locations until it is
seated.
10   The rest of the installation is the reverse of removal.

Door vent valve

11   Remove the door panel.
12   Remove the four retaining screws attaching the door vent valve
and lift the valve out (see illustration).
13   Reverse the the proceeding removal steps for installation.

---

13   Door latch assembly — removal and installation

Refer to illustrations 13.2 and 13.4

1   Roll up the window then remove the door trim and water shield.
2   Disconnect the rod ends from the latch and disconnect the remote
control assembly (see illustration).

**12.12   To remove the door vent valve, remove the four
retaining screws**

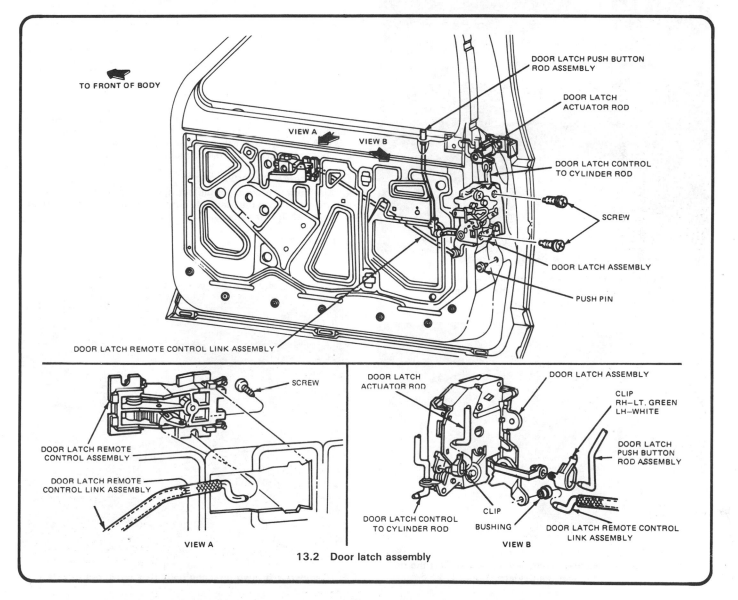

13.2   Door latch assembly

3   Disconnect the handle rod and pushbutton rod from the latch.
4   Remove the screws attaching the latch assembly to the door and remove the latch (see illustration).
5   Install the rod retaining clips in the new latch assembly.
6   Attach the control rod and lock cylinder rod to the latch before installation of the latch.
7   Install the latch in the door and attach with the retaining screws.
8   Reassemble the rods to the handle, lock cylinder and remote control.
9   Install the handle rod and pushbutton rod to the latch and check latch operation.
10 Install the water shield and trim panel.

14   Door lock cylinder — removal and installation

1   Roll up the window.
2   Remove the door panel.
3   Disconnect the door latch control to cylinder rod from the retainer clip.
4   Use a pair of pliers to slide the cylinder retainer away from the lock cylinder.
5   Pull the lock cylinder from the door.
6   Installation is the reverse of the removal procedure.

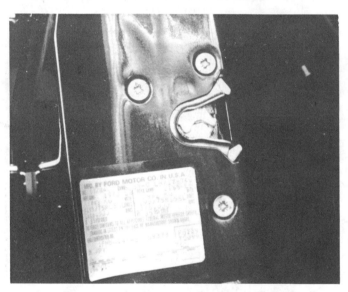

13.4   Once the control rods are disconnected, remove the three retaining screws and lift the door latch out of the door

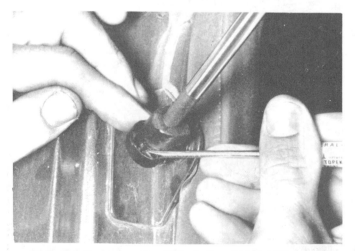

15.2   Pry the spring clip off the ball socket and lift the rod from the tailgate

15   Liftgate — removal and installation

Refer to illustrations 15.2 and 15.7

Liftgate gas cylinder assist rod
1   Open the liftgate and secure it in the open position.
2   Use a screwdriver to pry out the spring clip from the ball socket at both ends (see illustration).
3   The lift rod can now be removed.
4   Installation is the reversal of the removal procedure.

Liftgate removal
5   Follow the procedure to remove the liftgate gas cylinder assist rod.
6   Paint index markings around the hinge and retaining bolts.
7   Remove the retaining bolts attaching the liftgate to the hinge (see illustration) and remove the liftgate.
8   Installation is the reverse of the removal procedure.

Liftgate hinge removal
9   Remove the liftgate.
10 Remove the interior upper rear garnish molding to get at the retaining nut attaching the hinge to the body.
11 Paint alignment marks around the hinge for proper installation.
12 Remove the attaching nut.
13 Remove the liftgate hinge.
14 Installation is the reverse of the removal procedure.

16   Liftgate latches

Refer to illustrations 16.6 and 16.12

Liftgate panel
1   Remove the six retaining screws attaching the panel to the rear liftgate.
2   Use a flat screwdriver to pry out the plastic retainers holding the panel to the liftgate. **Caution:** *Be careful not to pull on the panel as this will rip the plastic retainers out of the panel.*
3   Installation is the reverse of the removal procedure.

Outside lock cylinder latch
4   Use a pair of pliers to pull the lock cylinder retainer from the cylinder assembly and bring the assembly out through the hole in the liftgate.
5   Installation is the reverse of the removal procedure.

Liftgate latches
6   Use a screwdriver to pry up on the actuator rod retainers and slide

15.7   Index the hinge for proper installation before removing the two retaining bolts that retain the liftgate

the rod off the latch assembly (see illustration).

7   Remove the bolts attaching the latch to the liftgate and pull the rod and latch out as an assembly.

8   Installation is the reverse of the removal procedure.

Liftgate latch control assembly

9   Remove the panel.

10 Remove the outside lock cylinder latch.

11 Remove the latch actuator arms.

12 Remove the three retaining bolts attaching the control assembly to the liftgate (see illustration).

13 Remove the control assembly.

14 Reverse the removal procedure for installation.

17   Liftgate flipper window glass and hinge (Bronco II) — removal and installation

Refer to illustration 17.5

1   Open and secure the flipper window.

2   Pry off both gas cylinder assist rods.

3   Remove the retaining nut and washer attaching the hinge to the glass assembly.

4   Remove the flipper glass assembly.

5   If necessary, remove the attaching screws retaining the window hinge to the liftgate and remove the hinge (see illustration).

6   Reverse the removal procedure for installation.

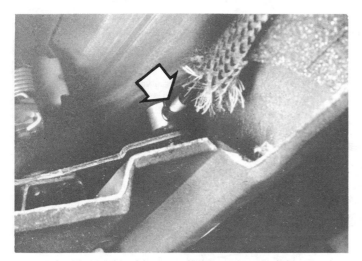

16.6   Pry the metal keeper off the actuator rod then pry the rod off the latch

16.12   Disconnect the actuator rods and remove the two bolts attaching the latch to the door

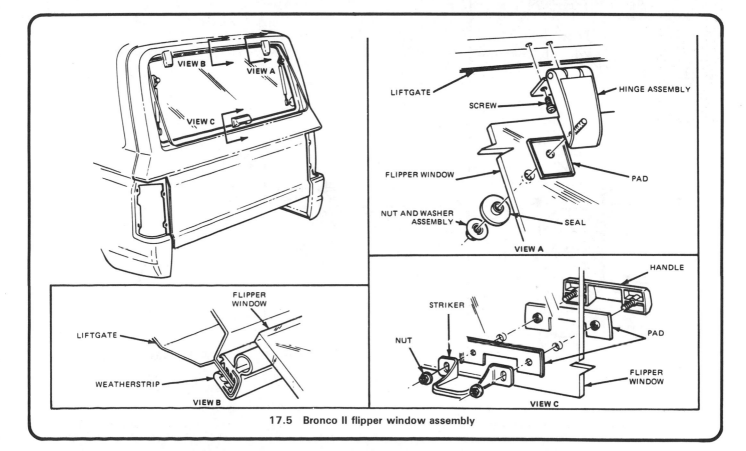

17.5   Bronco II flipper window assembly

18   Tailgate — removal and installation

Refer to illustration 18.2

Tailgate removal
1   Open the tailgate.
2   Lift up on the spring retainer keeping the cable support on the support pin and lift off the cable support (see illustration).
3   Raise the tailgate right side and lift the gate off of the left hinge.
4   Installation is the reversal of the removal procedure.

Tailgate on body latch
5   Open the tailgate.
6   Remove the two latch retaining screws and remove the latch.

7   Install the latch to the body and loosely install the two attaching screws.
8   Adjust the latch and tighten the screws.

Tailgate support, handle and latch support
9   With the tailgate open disconnect the upper support by prying out on the spring retainer and lift the support off the pin. If the pin is to be removed use a Torx screwdriver or socket to unscrew the pin from the body.
10 To remove the handle assembly, remove the three tailgate handle screws and disconnect the handle release links.
11 Remove the latch bracket assembly by removing the two latch bracket to tailgate attaching screws and remove the latch bracket.
12 Reverse the removal procedures for installation.

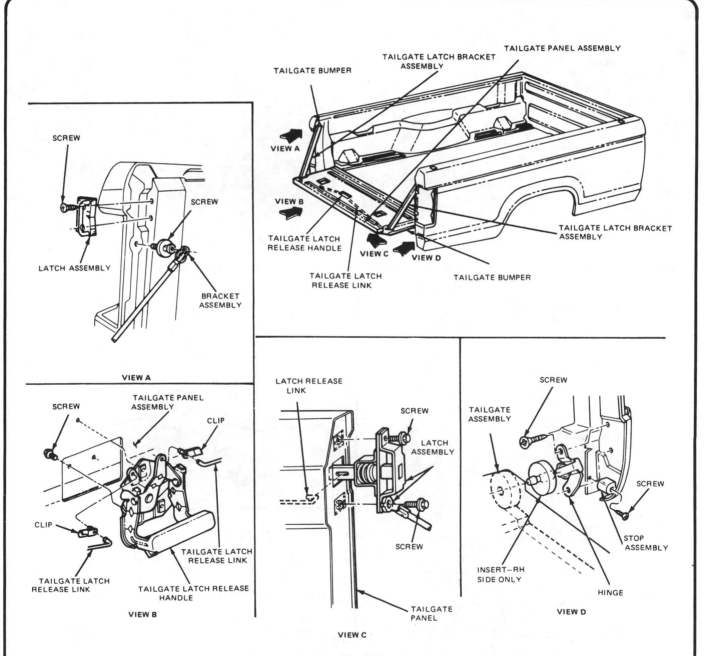

18.2   The Ranger tailgate is designed to lift off. Latch assemblies are shown removed

19 Front bumper and air deflector — removal and installation

Refer to illustration 19.4

Air deflector

1   Remove the nine air deflector attaching bolts.
2   Push the deflector aft and remove it from the vehicle.
3   Reverse the removal procedure for installation.

Front bumper

4   Remove the four attaching bolts (two on each side), that attach the bumper to the frame rail (see illustration).
5   If equipped with bumper guards, remove the upper attaching bolts from the bumper guards, then remove the nuts retaining the bumper guards to the bumper.
6   Remove the bumper. If equipped with bumper guards, remove the guards first, then the bumper.
7   Reverse the removal procedure for installation.

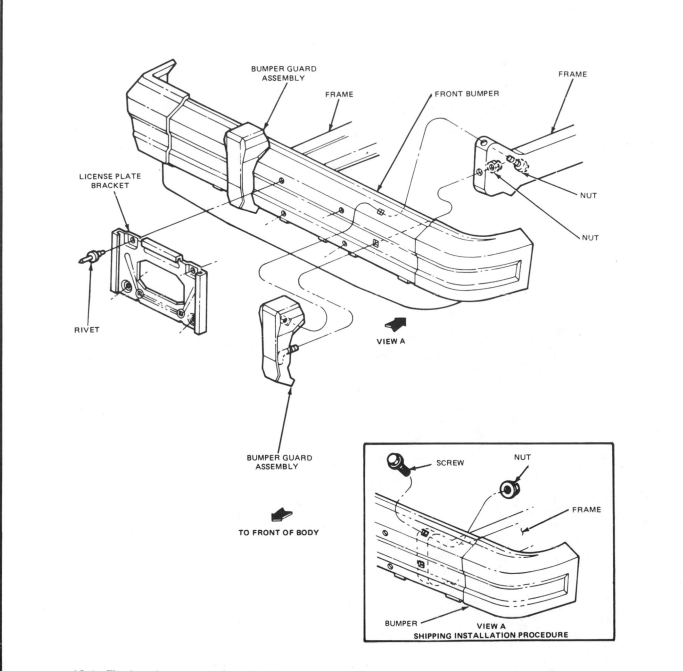

19.4   The front bumper attaches directly to the frame. If equipped with bumper guards, the bolts are located under the guard

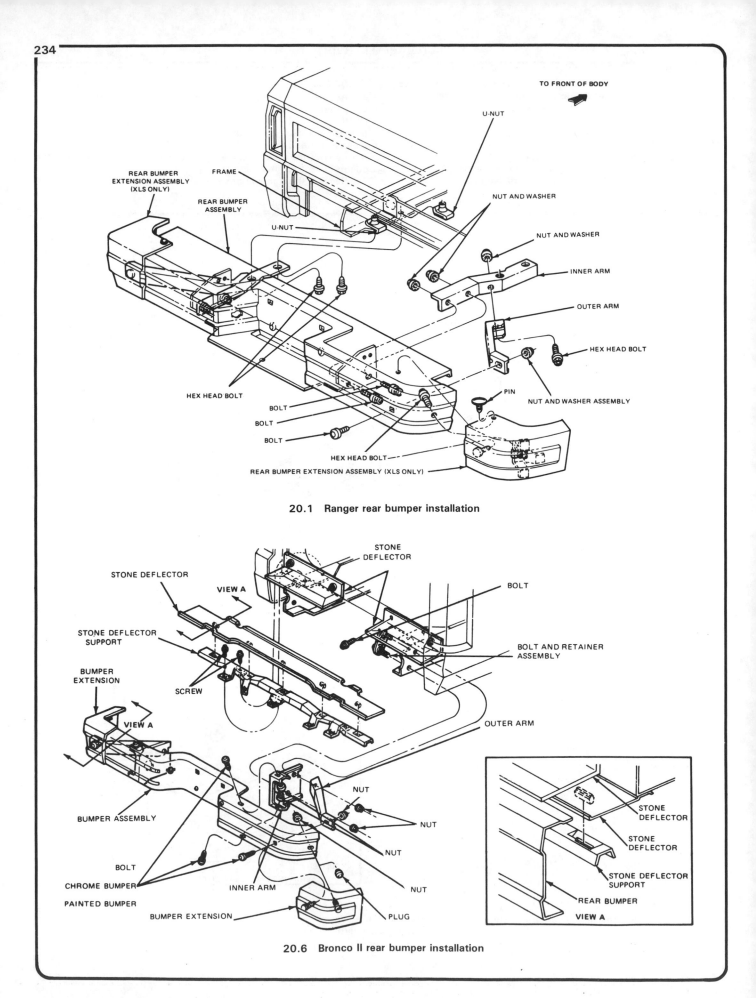

TO FRONT OF BODY

U-NUT

REAR BUMPER
EXTENSION ASSEMBLY
(XLS ONLY)

FRAME

REAR BUMPER
ASSEMBLY

NUT AND WASHER

U-NUT

NUT AND WASHER

INNER ARM

OUTER ARM

HEX HEAD BOLT

HEX HEAD BOLT

BOLT

BOLT

BOLT

PIN

NUT AND WASHER ASSEMBLY

HEX HEAD BOLT

REAR BUMPER EXTENSION ASSEMBLY (XLS ONLY)

20.1   Ranger rear bumper installation

STONE
DEFLECTOR

STONE DEFLECTOR

VIEW A

BOLT

STONE DEFLECTOR
SUPPORT

BOLT AND RETAINER
ASSEMBLY

BUMPER
EXTENSION

VIEW A

SCREW

OUTER ARM

NUT

STONE
DEFLECTOR

BUMPER ASSEMBLY

NUT

STONE
DEFLECTOR

NUT

BOLT

NUT

STONE DEFLECTOR
SUPPORT

CHROME BUMPER

INNER ARM

PAINTED BUMPER

REAR BUMPER

BUMPER EXTENSION

PLUG

VIEW A

20.6   Bronco II rear bumper installation

20 Rear bumper — removal and installation

Refer to illustrations 20.1 and 20.6

Ranger

1   Remove the two attaching bolts on each side of the bumper attaching the bumper to the inner arm (see illustration).
2   Disconnect the license lights at their electrical connectors.
3   Get the help of an assistant or support the bumper and remove the outside attaching bolts (one on each side).
4   Remove the bumper.
5   Reverse the removal procedure to install.

Bronco II

6   Disconnect the four bumper to bracket bolts (two on each side). It will be necessary to use a U-joint (knuckle type) socket to remove the top retainer (see illustration).
7   Get the help of an assistant or support the bumper and remove the outside attaching bolts (one on each side).
8   Remove the bumper.
9   Reverse the removal procedure to install.

21 Sliding Rear Window (Ranger) — removal and installation

Refer to illustrations 21.1 and 21.14

1   From inside the cab, pull down the weatherstrip lip along the window opening and push out the window frame and weatherstrip (see illustration).
2   Place the moveable windows in the open position then remove the weatherstrip from the window frame.
3   Working from the top of the window frame, locate and remove the screw retaining each division bar. Remove the anchor plate by removing the two screws retaining the plate to the frame.
4   Work the movable window from its track by spreading the frame, if necessary.
5   If replacing the stationary glass, remove the division bar lower retaining screw and remove the division bar.
6   Spread the frame enough to allow removal of the stationary glass.
7   If the stationary glass was replaced, apply lubricant (COAZ-19553-A) or an equivalent weatherstrip lubricant to the window weatherstrip and track. Spread the frame slightly to allow installation of the stationary glass. Do not allow the weatherstrip to bunch up.

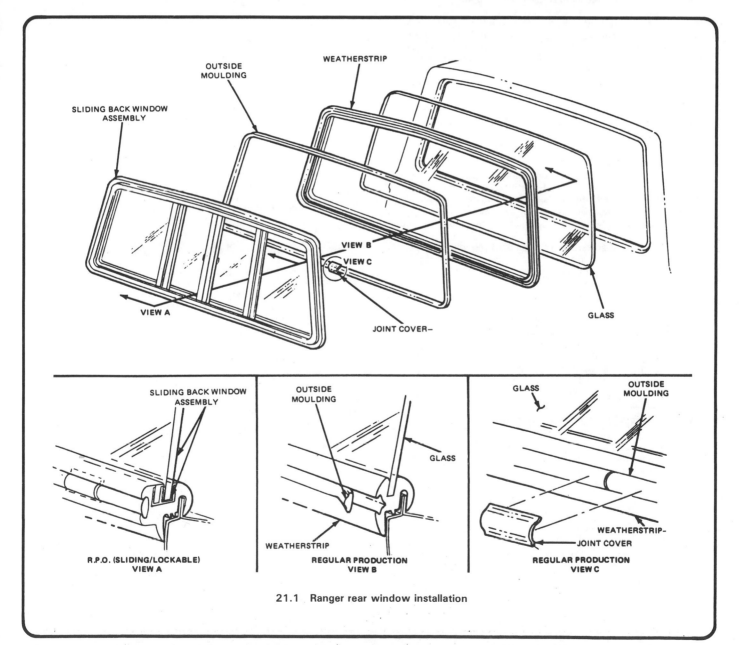

21.1 Ranger rear window installation

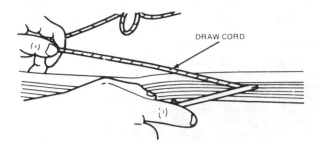

21.14 Use a draw cord to install the weatherstrip in the rear window

8   Install and secure the division bar with its lower attaching screw.
9   Install the moveable glass in its track by slightly spreading the frame.
10 Position and secure with attaching screws the anchor plate in the window track.
11 Secure the division bar with its top retaining screw.
12 Place the weatherstrip in the window frame.
13 Install a new draw cord all around the weatherstrip in the flange crevice and allow the cord to overlap at the bottom center of the glass.
14 Position the window into the window opening. With an assistant applying hand pressure from outside the cab, pull the weatherstrip over the lower flange while pulling one end of the cord (see illustration). Next pull the seal over the side flanges and upper flange.

22 Stationary back window (Bronco II liftgate) — removal and installation

Refer to illustration 22.2
1   From inside the cab, pull down the weatherstrip and push the back window glass and weatherstrip out of the window opening.
2   If equipped, install the outside molding and position the weatherstrip to the back window glass (see illustration).
3   If reusing the weatherstrip or glass, clean all sealer off before reusing.
4   Clean all traces of sealer from the back of the window opening.
5   Install a draw cord around the weatherstrip in the flange crevice, letting the cord to overlap at the bottom center of the glass. Use rubber lubricant to coat the weatherstrip mounting surface. **Note:** *Green Soap (ESB-M1B9-A) or its equivalent diluted to 10 to 1 with water may be used to facilitate installation of the mouldings and weatherstrip.*
6   Position the window into the window opening. With an assistant applying hand pressure from outside the cab, pull the weatherstrip (from inside cab) over the lower flange while pulling one end of the cord at a time. Next pull the seal over the side flanges and upper flange.
7   Clean the glass and surrounding area of excess sealer.
8   Test for water leaks with a hose.

23 Weatherstripping — removal and installation

1   Remove the old weatherstripping by pulling it away from the door to break it loose from the adhesive.
2   Clean out the old adhesive.

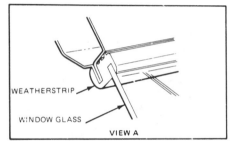

22.2 Installation of weatherstrip and glass in the liftgate of the Bronco II

3   Apply new adhesive.
4   Press the new weatherstripping into position until it is secure.
5   Note that the new weatherstripping should be cut longer than necessary and then compressed to insure a proper seal.

24 Windshield glass — removal and installation

The windshield glass on all models are sealed in place with a special butyl compound. Removal of the existing sealant requires the use of an electric knife specially made for the operation, and glass replacement is a complex operation.
In view of this, it is not recommended that stationary glass removal be attempted by the home mechanic. If replacement is necessary due to breakage or leakage, the work should be referred to your dealer or a qualified glass or body shop.

Chapter 12   Chassis electrical system

Contents

Specifications

Fusible links and circuit breakers

#38 circuit alternator	16 gauge fusible link
#37 circuit trailer lamps	16 gauge fusible link at starter relay
#22 circuit electric brakes........................	16 gauge fusible link
Headlights and high beam indicator	22 amp circuit breaker integral with headlamp switch
Liftgate wiper...................................	4.5 amp circuit breaker located in instrument panel above glove box
Premium bucket seat power lumbar support	30 amp circuit breaker in fuse panel

Bulb application .... Type/trade number

Headlight	H6054 type 2B rectangular headlamps
Air conditioning illumination (optional)	161
Air conditioning control pushbutton....................	8605
Charge indicator light	194
Radio dial illumination	1893
Ashtry light	1892
Back up light	1156
Brake warning light	194
Cargo light (optional)	906
Dome light	912
Engine coolant warning light	194
Fasten seat belt	194
Front turn signal/parking light	1157
Front side marker	194
Glove compartment	1891
Headlight switch illumination	1815
Heater control illumination	161
High beam indicator	194
Instrument panel lights	194
Instrument panel courtesy light	89
License plate light	194
Transfer case lock indicator	Ford part E27B-10C915-B
Oil pressure indicator light	194
Rear tail/stop light	1157
Turn signal indicator light	194

---

1   General information

This Chapter covers service and repair procedures for electrical components not included in Chapter 5, *Engine Electrical System*. Look in this Chapter for information concerning wiring, lighting and electrically driven accessories.

Electrical systems on vehicles covered in this manual are of the 12-volt negative ground type. The vehicle's electrical components draw power from a lead/acid battery, the charge of which is maintained by the alternator. **Caution:** *When servicing any electrical component or performing major non-electrical procedures, disconnect the negative cable at the battery to prevent electrical short-circuiting and fires.*

2   Electrical troubleshooting — general information

A typical electrical circuit consists of the component, any switches, relays, motors, etc. related to that component and the wiring and connectors that connect the component to both the battery and the chassis. To aid in locating a problem in any electrical circuit, representative wiring diagrams are included at the end of this manual.

Before tackling any troublesome electrical circuit, first study the appropriate diagrams to get a complete understanding of what makes up that individual circuit. Trouble spots can often be narrowed down by noting if other components related to that circuit are operating properly or not. If several components or circuits fail at one time, chances are the problem lies in the fuse or ground connection, as several circuits often are routed through the same fuse and ground connections.

Electrical problems often stem from simple causes, such as loose or corroded connections, a blown fuse or a melted fusible link. Prior to any electrical troubleshooting always visually check the condition of the fuses, wires and connections in the problem circuit.

If testing instruments are going to be utilized, use the diagrams to plan ahead of time where you will make the necessary connections in order to accurately pinpoint the trouble spot.

The basic tools needed for electrical troubleshooting include a circuit tester or voltmeter (a 12-volt bulb with a set of test leads can also be used), a continuity tester (which includes a bulb, battery and set of test leads) and a jumper wire, preferably with a circuit breaker incorporated, which can be used to bypass electrical components.

Voltage checks should be performed if a circuit is not functioning properly. Connect one lead of a circuit tester to either the negative battery terminal or a known good ground. Connect the other lead to the circuit being tested, preferably near to the battery or fuse. If the bulb of the tester goes on, voltage is reaching that point, which means the part of the circuit between that point and the battery is problem free. Continue checking along the entire circuit in the same fashion. When you reach a point where no voltage is present, the problem lies between there and the last good test point. Most of the time the prob-

lem is due to a loose connection. Keep in mind that some circuits receive voltage only when the ignition key is in the Accessory or Run position.

A method of finding shorts in a circuit is to remove the fuse and connect a test light or voltmeter in its place. With the component being energized by that circuit shut off, there should be no load in the circuit. Move the wiring harness from side-to-side while watching the test light. If the bulb goes on, there is a short to ground somewhere in that area, probably where insulation has rubbed off a wire. The same test can be performed on other components of the circuit, including the switch.

A ground check should be done to see if a component is grounded properly. Disconnect the battery and connect one lead of a self powered test light, such as a continuity tester, to a known good ground. Connect the other lead to the wire or ground connection being tested. If the bulb goes on, the ground is good. If the bulb does not go on, the ground is not good.

A continuity check is performed to see if a circuit, section of circuit or individual component is passing electricity properly. Disconnect the battery and connect one lead of a self powered test light to the battery side of the circuit. Connect the other lead of the test light to a good ground. If the bulb goes on, there is continuity, which means the circuit is passing electricity properly. Switches can be checked in the same way.

Remember that all electrical circuits are composed of electricity running from the battery, through the wires, switches, relays, etc. to the electrical component (light bulb, motor, etc.). From there it is run to the body or frame (ground) where it is passed back to the battery. Any electrical problem is an interruption in the flow of electricity to and from the battery.

3   Fuses — general information

Refer to illustration 3.1

The electrical circuits of the vehicle are protected by a combination of fuses, circuit breakers and fusible links. The fuse block is located

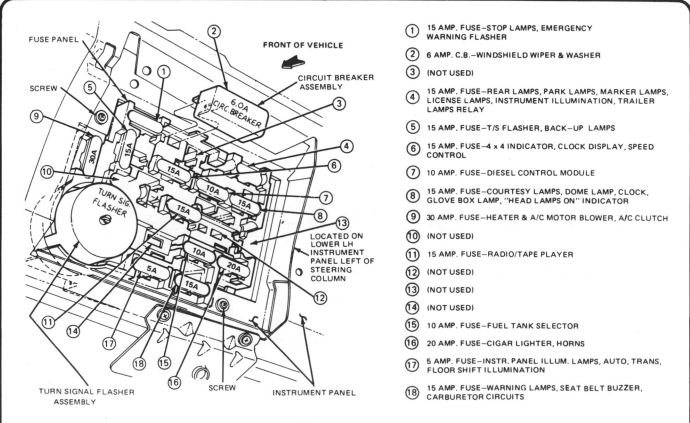

1. 15 AMP. FUSE—STOP LAMPS, EMERGENCY WARNING FLASHER
2. 6 AMP. C.B.—WINDSHIELD WIPER & WASHER
3. (NOT USED)
4. 15 AMP. FUSE—REAR LAMPS, PARK LAMPS, MARKER LAMPS, LICENSE LAMPS, INSTRUMENT ILLUMINATION, TRAILER LAMPS RELAY
5. 15 AMP. FUSE—T/S FLASHER, BACK—UP LAMPS
6. 15 AMP. FUSE—4 x 4 INDICATOR, CLOCK DISPLAY, SPEED CONTROL
7. 10 AMP. FUSE—DIESEL CONTROL MODULE
8. 15 AMP. FUSE—COURTESY LAMPS, DOME LAMP, CLOCK, GLOVE BOX LAMP, "HEAD LAMPS ON" INDICATOR
9. 30 AMP. FUSE—HEATER & A/C MOTOR BLOWER, A/C CLUTCH
10. (NOT USED)
11. 15 AMP. FUSE—RADIO/TAPE PLAYER
12. (NOT USED)
13. (NOT USED)
14. (NOT USED)
15. 10 AMP. FUSE—FUEL TANK SELECTOR
16. 20 AMP. FUSE—CIGAR LIGHTER, HORNS
17. 5 AMP. FUSE—INSTR. PANEL ILLUM. LAMPS, AUTO. TRANS, FLOOR SHIFT ILLUMINATION
18. 15 AMP. FUSE—WARNING LAMPS, SEAT BELT BUZZER, CARBURETOR CIRCUITS

3.1   Fuse panel identification

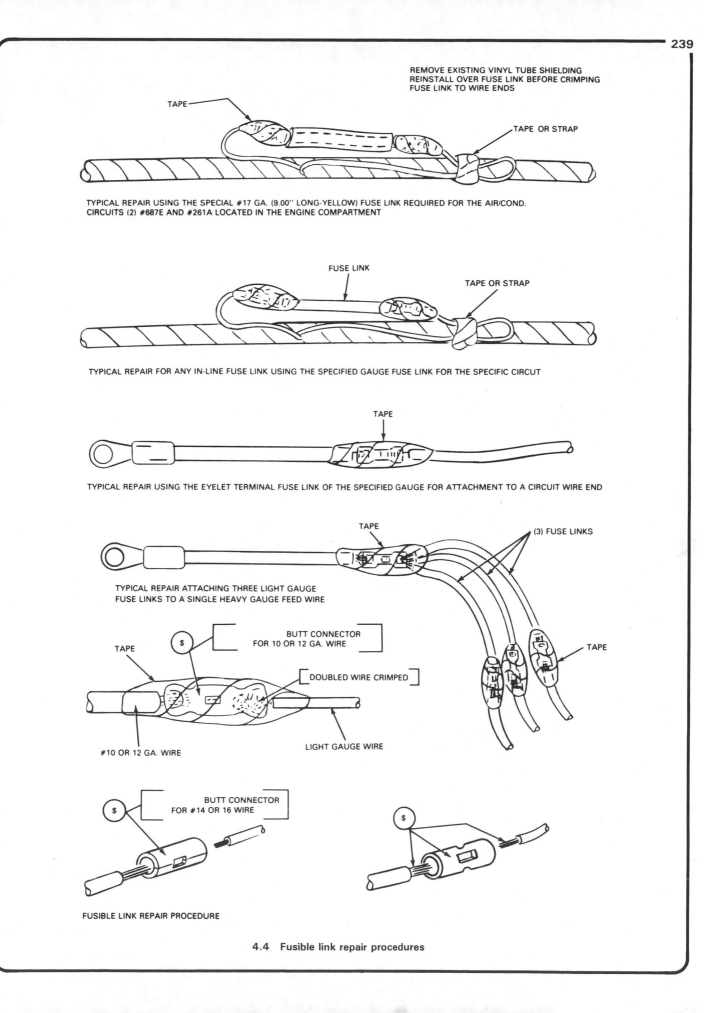

REMOVE EXISTING VINYL TUBE SHIELDING
REINSTALL OVER FUSE LINK BEFORE CRIMPING
FUSE LINK TO WIRE ENDS

TAPE

TAPE OR STRAP

TYPICAL REPAIR USING THE SPECIAL #17 GA. (9.00'' LONG-YELLOW) FUSE LINK REQUIRED FOR THE AIR/COND.
CIRCUITS (2) #687E AND #261A LOCATED IN THE ENGINE COMPARTMENT

FUSE LINK

TAPE OR STRAP

TYPICAL REPAIR FOR ANY IN-LINE FUSE LINK USING THE SPECIFIED GAUGE FUSE LINK FOR THE SPECIFIC CIRCUT

TAPE

TYPICAL REPAIR USING THE EYELET TERMINAL FUSE LINK OF THE SPECIFIED GAUGE FOR ATTACHMENT TO A CIRCUIT WIRE END

TAPE

(3) FUSE LINKS

TYPICAL REPAIR ATTACHING THREE LIGHT GAUGE
FUSE LINKS TO A SINGLE HEAVY GAUGE FEED WIRE

TAPE

TAPE

$

BUTT CONNECTOR
FOR 10 OR 12 GA. WIRE

DOUBLED WIRE CRIMPED

#10 OR 12 GA. WIRE

LIGHT GAUGE WIRE

$

BUTT CONNECTOR
FOR #14 OR 16 WIRE

$

FUSIBLE LINK REPAIR PROCEDURE

4.4   Fusible link repair procedures

on the underside of the instrument panel on the driver's side. Each of the fuses is designed to protect a specific circuit, and the various circuits are identified on the fuse panel (see illustration).

Miniaturized fuses are employed in the fuse block. These compact fuses, with blade terminal design, allow fingertip removal and replacement.

If an electrical component has failed, your first check should be the fuse. A fuse which has *blown* is easily identified by inspecting the element inside the plastic body. Also, the blade terminal tips are exposed in the fuse body, allowing for continuity checks.

It is important that the correct fuse be installed. The different electrical circuits need varying amounts of protection, indicated by the amperage rating on the fuse body.

At no time should the fuse be bypassed with pieces of metal or foil. Serious damage to the electrical system could result.

If the replacement fuse immediately fails, do not replace it again until the cause of the problem is isolated and corrected. In most cases, this will be a short circuit in the wiring caused by a broken or deteriorated wire.

4   Fusible links — general information

Refer to illustration 4.4

In addition to fuses, the wiring is protected by fusible links. These links are used in circuits which are not ordinarily fused, such as the ignition circuit.

Although the fusible links appear larger than the wire they are protecting, the appearance is deceiving due to the special, Hypalon (high temperature resistance) insulation used. All fusible links are four wire gauges smaller than the wire they are designed to protect. Under no circumstances should a fusible link replacement be made using standard wire cut from bulk stock or from another wiring harness.

The location of the fusible links may be determined by referring to the wiring diagrams at the end of this manual.

The fusible links cannot be repaired, but a new link of the same size wire can be put in its place (see illustration). The procedure is as follows:
  a) Disconnect the battery ground cable.
  b) Cut the damaged fusible link out of the wiring.
  c) Strip the insulation approximately 1/2-inch.
  d) Position the wire from the harness on the new fusible link and crimp it into place.
  e) Use rosin core solder at each end of the new link to obtain a good solder joint.
  f) Use plenty of electrical tape around the soldered joints. No wires should be exposed.
  g) Connect the battery ground cable. Test the circuit for proper operation.

Production fusible links have color coded flags moulded on the wire for identification. The blue flag is 20 gauge wire, red-18 gauge wire, yellow-17 gauge wire, orange-16 gauge wire, and green-14 gauge wire.

5   Circuit breakers — general information

Circuit breakers are sometimes used with accessories such as power windows, power door locks and the rear window defogger.

The circuit breakers may be found by referring to the wiring diagrams at the end of this manual.

A circuit breaker is used to protect the windshield wiper/washer wiring and is located on the fuse panel. An electrical overload in the system will cause the wipers or washer to go on and off, or in some cases to remain off. If this happens, check the entire circuit immediately. Once the overload condition is corrected, the circuit breaker will function normally.

6   Battery — removal and installation

1   The battery is located at the front of the engine compartment. It is held in place by a hold down bracket across the top of the battery.
2   Since hydrogen gas is produced by the battery, keep open flames or lighted cigarettes away from the battery at all times.
3   Avoid spilling any of the electrolyte on the vehicle or yourself. Always keep the battery in an upright position. Any spilled electrolyte should be immediately flushed with large amounts of water. Wear eye protection when working with a battery to prevent eye damage from splashed fluid.
4   Always disconnect the negative battery cable first, followed by the positive cable.
5   After the cables are disconnected from the battery, remove the hold down assembly.
6   Carefully lift the battery from the tray and out of the engine compartment.
7   Installation is the reverse of the removal procedure. Make sure that the hold down assembly is securely tightened. Do not overtighten, as this may damage the battery. The battery posts and cable ends should be cleaned prior to connection.

7   Battery charging

1   In winter, when heavy demand is placed upon the battery, such as when starting from cold, and most of the electrical equipment is continually in use, it is a good idea to occasionally have the battery fully charged from an external source at the rate of 3.5 to 4 amps.
2   Continue to charge the battery at this rate until no further rise in specific gravity is noted over a four hour period.
3   Alternatively, a trickle charging at the rate of 1.5 amps can be safely used overnight.
4   Special rapid boost charges which are claimed to restore the power of the battery in one to two hours are most dangerous, as they can cause serious damage to the battery plates. This type of charge should be used only in an emergency.

8   Turn signal and hazard flashers — check and replace

1   Small canister shaped flasher units are incorporated into the electrical circuits for the directional signals and hazard warning lights.
2   When the units are functioning properly, an audible click can be heard with the circuit in operation. If the turn signals fail on one side only and the flasher unit cannot be heard, a faulty bulb is indicated. If the flasher can be heard a fault in the wiring is indicated.
3   If the turn signals fail on both sides, the problem may be due to a blown fuse, faulty flasher unit or switch, or a broken or loose connection. If the fuse has blown, check the wiring for a short before installing a new fuse.
4   The hazard warning lights are checked as described in Step 3 above.
5   The hazard warning flasher and turn signal flasher are mounted in the fuse box, located under the dash on the drivers side.
6   When replacing either of the flasher units, be sure to buy a replacement of the same capacity. Compare the new flasher to the old one before installing it.

9   Headlight sealed beam unit — removal and installation

Refer to illustrations 9.2, 9.3 and 9.4
Note: *Due to the stiffness of the rubber around the headlight rim we found it necessary to first remove the grill to replace the headlight.*
1   Remove the ten visible attaching screws retaining the grille.
2   The grill will now tilt forward, revealing two hidden retaining screws located under the headlights. Remove the screws and lift off the grill (see illustration).
3   Remove the headlamp screws, door and retaining ring. Make sure that the retaining screws and not the adjusting screws are removed (see illustration).
4   Pull the headlight forward and support it as you disconnect the wiring plug (see illustration).
5   Install the plug to the new headlamp and position it by locating the glass tabs at the back in the slots in the receptacle.
4   Install the headlight retaining ring, screws and door.
5   Check the headlight alignment.

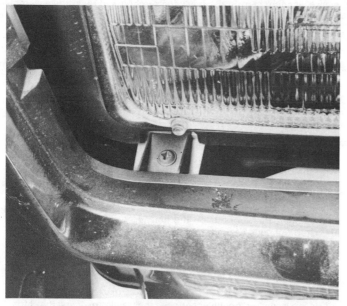

9.2 These grille screws are hidden under the headlights

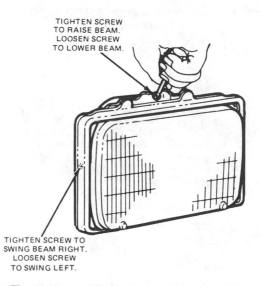

9.3 Don't confuse the headlight ring screws with the two adjusting screws (arrows)

9.4 Support the headlight while you pull the connector off

TIGHTEN SCREW TO RAISE BEAM. LOOSEN SCREW TO LOWER BEAM.

TIGHTEN SCREW TO SWING BEAM RIGHT. LOOSEN SCREW TO SWING LEFT.

10.5 The top screw adjusts the headlight up and down, while the screw on the side adjusts the light left or right

10 Headlights — adjustment

Refer to illustration 10.5

It is important that the headlights be aimed correctly. If adjusted incorrectly they could blind an oncoming car and cause a serious accident or seriously reduce your ability to see the road.

Headlights have two spring loaded adjusting screws, one on the top affecting up and down movement and one on the side affecting left and right movement.

There are several methods of adjusting the headlights. The simplest method uses a screen or empty wall 10 feet in front of the vehicle.

Preparation

1   Park the vehicle on a known level floor 10 feet from the screen or light colored wall.
2   Position masking tape vertically on the screen in reference to the vehicle center line and the center lines of both head lights. **Note:** *If* the vehicle has a four headlight system then four vertical lines plus the vehicle center line will be used.
3   Position a horizontal tape line in reference to the center line of the headlights. **Note:** *It may be easier to position the tape on the screen with the vehicle parked only a few inches away.*

Adjustment

4   Adjustment should be made with the vehicle sitting level, the gas tank half full and someone sitting in the driver's seat.
5   Starting with the low beam adjustment, position the high-intensity zone so it is two inches below the horizontal line and two inches to the right of the headlight vertical line. Adjustment is made by turning the adjusting screws (see illustration).
6   With the high beams on, the high-intensity zone should be vertically centered with the center just below the horizontal line. **Note:** *It may not be possible to position the headlight aim exactly for both high and low beams. If a compromise must be used, keep in mind that the low beams are the most used and have the greatest effect on driver safety.*

11   Running lights — removal and installation

Refer to illustrations 11.1, 11.2, 11.5, 11.7, 11.8, 11.9, 11.11 and 11.12

Turn signal

1   Remove two retaining screws (see illustration).
2   Pull the turn signal assembly out (see illustration) and grab the bulb

11.1   Arrows point to the screws attaching the turn signal assembly to the vehicle

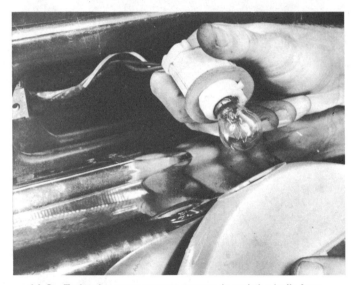

11.2   Twist the connector to remove it and the bulb from the turn signal housing

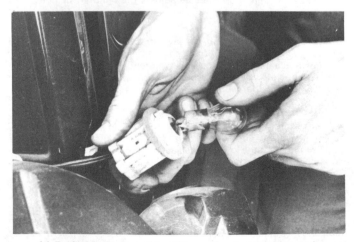

11.7   Hold the assembly with one hand and insert and turn to lock the bulb

electrical connector (in the rear of assembly) and twist the assembly while holding the connector firmly.
3   Grab the bulb with one hand and the connector with the other and push in and twist the bulb to release the retaining tabs from the connector.
4   Installation of bulb and signal assembly is the reverse of the removal procedure.

Backup/stop/turn signal bulb

5   Remove the four retaining screws that attach the tail light lens (see illustration).
6   To remove the light bulb grab the connector with one hand and turn it to remove it from the assembly.
7   To replace the bulb hold the bulb with one hand and the connector with the other and push in while twisting the bulb (see illustration).

License plate light — replacement

8   Insert a small screwdriver between the license plate light housing and bumper, then pry out on the housing (see illustration).
9   Grab the back of the light bulb connector and twist it to remove it from the housing (see illustration).
10   For installation, position the light housing to the bumper and press in until seated.

Dome light — removal and installation

11   Insert a small screwdriver between the plastic cover and the chrome

11.5   Remove the four screws and pull the tailight assembly out

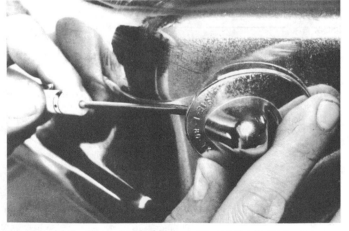

11.8   Use a screwdriver to pry out the license light assembly

body of the dome light and pry the plastic cover off (see illustration).
12 Pull the bulb straight out of its connector (see illustration).
13 Insert a new bulb and replace the plastic cover.

Side marker lamps

14 Remove the one screw securing the lamp assembly to the vehicle.
15 Remove the lamp assembly by pulling out on the top and lifting the bottom of the lens.
16 Pull the light socket out of the lamp assembly.
17 The bulb pulls straight out.
18 Install the bulb by pushing it into the socket.
19 Push the socket into the lamp assembly.
20 Position the tab on the bottom of the lamp assembly in first, then push the top of the assembly into place.
21 Secure the assembly to the body with the retaining screw.

---

12   Radio — removal and installation

Refer to illustration 12.3

1 Disconnect the battery ground cable.
2 Refer to the Section on cluster panel instruments and remove the dash panels.
3 Remove the four screws attaching the mounting brackets to the instrument panel and remove the radio with the brackets attached as an assembly (see illustration).

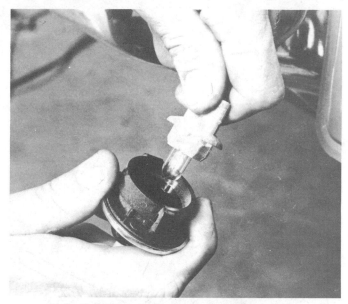

11.9   Twist the electrical connector to remove it from the housing

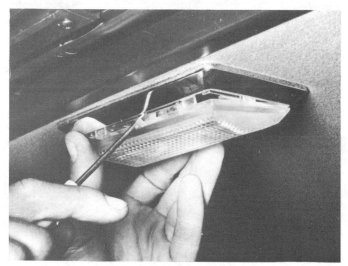

11.11   Carefully pry the plastic lens from the dome light to get at the light bulb

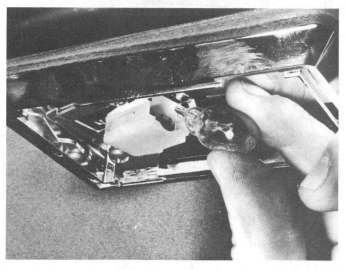

11.12   The dome light bulb pulls straight out to remove

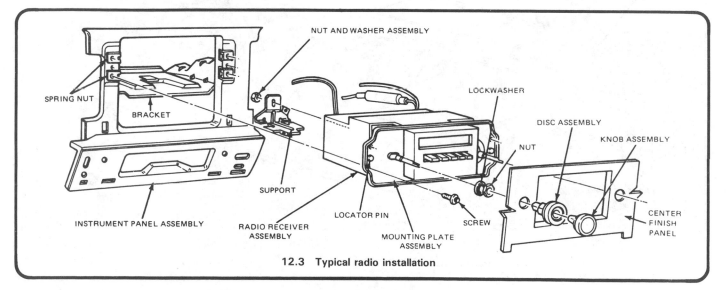

12.3   Typical radio installation

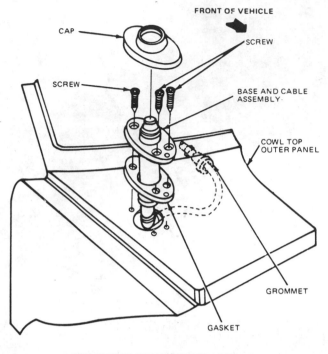

VIEW SHOWING INSTALLATION OF ANTENNA
ON COWL TOP OUTER PANEL (RH SIDE)

13.3   Radio antenna removal

4   With the radio pulled from dash, remove the antenna wire by pulling straight out on the wire.
5   Disconnect the speaker wires and electrical plug.
6   Remove the screws attaching the mounting brackets to the radio.
7   Installation is the reverse of the removal procedure.

13   Radio antenna — removal and installation

Refer to illustration 13.3
1   Reach under the dash and disconnect the radio antenna from the radio by pulling straight out on the cable.
2   Disconnect the cable from the plastic retainers located along the top of the defroster nozzle.
3   Carefully use a small screwdriver to pry up the cap from the antenna base and remove the cap (see illustration).
4   Remove the four attaching screws and lift out the antenna.
5   Reverse the removal procedure for installation.

14   Speakers — removal and installation

Refer to illustration 14.2
Note: *Your particular model may vary from the following procedure due to size and configuration of aftermarket speakers installed in some models.*
1   Remove the screws retaining the speaker cover and remove the cover.
2   Remove the three screws that attach the speaker to the instrument panel (see illustration).
3   Lift out the speaker and disconnect the wiring connector at the speaker. **Note:** *Do not operate the radio with speakers disconnected.*
4   Reverse the removal procedure for installation.

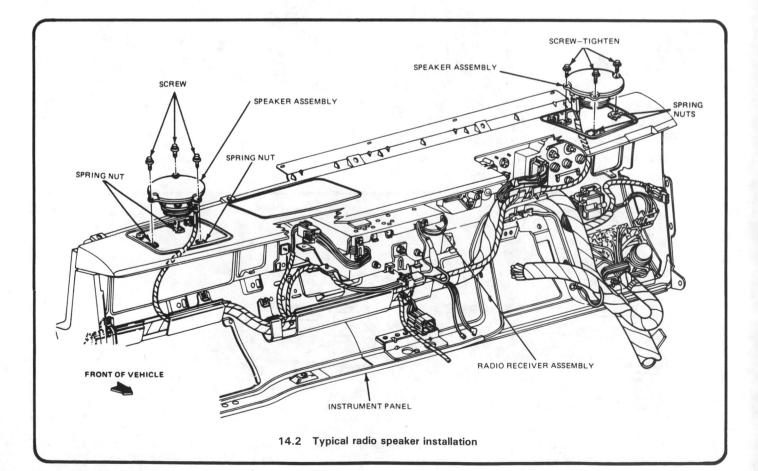

14.2   Typical radio speaker installation

15 Instrument panel — removal and installation

Refer to illustrations 15.2, 15.3, 15.4a and 15.4

1   Disconnect the negative cable from the battery.
2   Pry off the three face panels by inserting a small screwdriver behind the panel and prying the panel from the dash (see illustration).
3   The left panel with the headlight switch requires inserting a small screwdriver into the slot on the light switch knob and pushing in on the retaining clip (inside knob) while pulling the knob from the light switch shaft (see illustration).
4   Remove the retaining screws (top and bottom) attaching the instrument panel to the dash (photos).
5   Carefully lift off the panel.
6   Remove the four retaining screws located at each corner of the cluster.
7   Reach behind the instrument cluster and squeeze the speedometer cable quick disconnect union (tang) and pull the cable from the speedometer.
8   Disconnect the electrical connector by squeezing the two prongs on the connector while pulling the connector from the cluster.
9   Grab the 4x4 indicator connector and turn the connector to disconnect from the cluster, if equipped.
10 Installation is the reverse of the removal procedure.

16 Instrument cluster lights — removal and installation

Refer to illustration 16.2

1   Refer to the appropriate section and remove the instrument panel.
2   To replace the warning bulbs and illumination bulbs, grab the bulb from the backside and turn to release (see illustration).

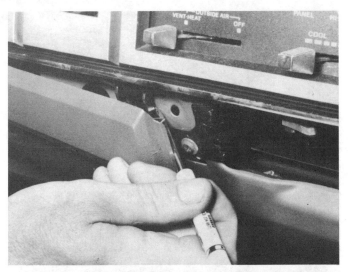

15.2 The bottom dash panels are secured with spring clips

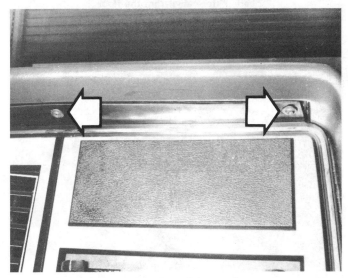

15.4a Note the location of the top instrument panel screws

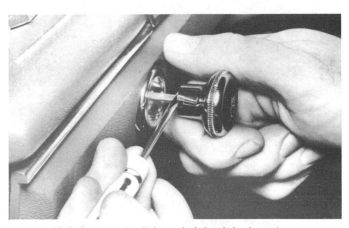

15.3 Remove the light switch knob by inserting a screwdriver into the slot and pressing in on the retaining clip while pulling the knob off the switch shaft

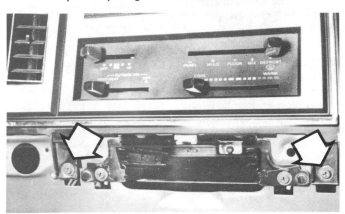

15.4b Note the location of the bottom instrument panel screws

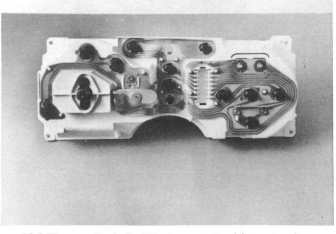

16.2 The warning bulbs (black connectors) have no wires connected to them. To replace the bulb, simply twist and remove it from the cluster panel

17.3   Remove the hold down screw to free the speedometer cable from the floor

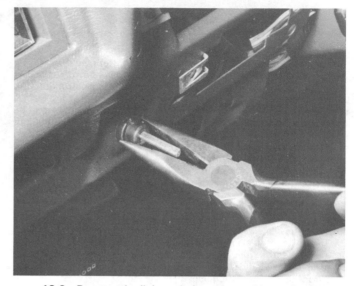

18.2   Remove the light switch retainer with a pair of needle nose pliers

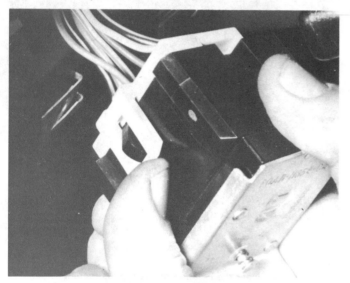

18.4   Pry up on the tangs to disconnect the light switch connector

18.5   Align the light switch tab (arrow) in the groove when installing

17   Speedometer — removal and installation

Refer to illustration 17.3

Speedometer cable

1   Refer to the appropriate Section and remove the instrument cluster and panel.
2   Squeeze the cable at the speedometer connection and pull the cable from the speedometer.
3   Remove the retaining screw attaching the cable to the floor (see illustration).
4   Disconnect the speedometer cable from the transmission by unscrewing the retaining ring and pulling the cable and driven gear from the transmission.
5   Pull the cable through the floor opening.
6   Installation is the reverse of the removal procedure.

Speedometer head

Note: *U.S. Federal law requires that the odometer in any replacement speedometer must register the same mileage as that registered in the removed speedometer.*

7   Follow Steps 1 and 2.

8   Remove the lens and mask from the cluster and remove the two screws attaching the speedometer to the cluster.
9   Lift out the speedometer.
10   Reverse the removal procedure for installation with the noted exception of lubricating the square drive hole with speedometer cable lubricant.

18   Headlight switch — removal and installation

Refer to illustrations 18.2, 18.4 and 18.5

1   Refer to the appropriate Section and remove the instrument cluster for access to the light switch.
2   With a pair of pliers, unscrew the retaining nut attaching the light switch shaft to the dash (see illustration).
3   Pull the light switch through the panel opening and pull the electrical connector through the dash for accessibility.
4   Lift the tangs and pull the connector from the switch (see illustration).
5   On installation align the tab of the light switch shaft into the groove in the dash (see illustration).
6   Installation is the reverse of the removal procedure.

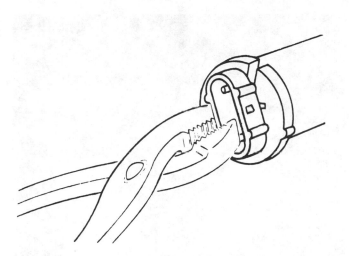

19.4 Grip the wall around the electrical terminal to pull the motor/pump assembly from the servior

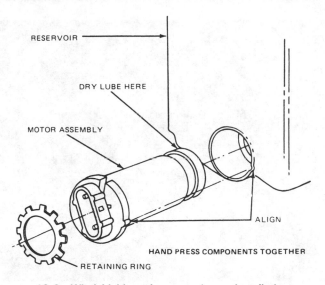

RESERVOIR

DRY LUBE HERE

MOTOR ASSEMBLY

ALIGN

HAND PRESS COMPONENTS TOGETHER

RETAINING RING

19.6 Windshield washer motor/pump installation

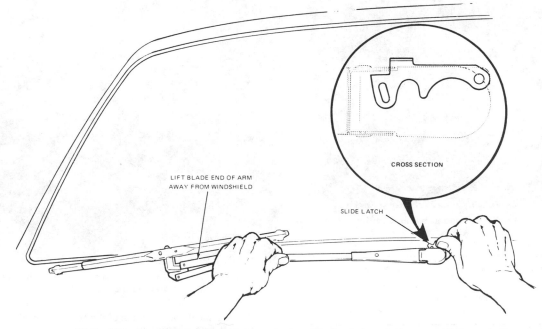

LIFT BLADE END OF ARM
AWAY FROM WINDSHIELD

CROSS SECTION

SLIDE LATCH

20.2 Lift up on the arm and push up on the slide latch to pull the arm off the spindle

19 Windshield washer motor, seal and pump — removal and installation

Refer to illustrations 19.4 and 19.6

1   Disconnect the electrical plug and hose from the reservoir.
2   Disconnect the two screws attaching the reservoir to the fender well and remove and drain the reservoir.
3   Use a small screwdriver and pry out the retaining ring.
4   Use pliers to grip the wall around the electrical terminal and pull the motor, seal and impeller assembly from the reservoir (see illustration).
5   Clean all foreign material from the pump chamber before installing the pump assembly into the reservoir.
6   Lubricate the outside diameter of the seal with a powdered graphite to prevent the seal from sticking to the reservoir (see illustration).
7   Align the small projection on the motor end with the slot in the reservoir and assemble so seal seats against the bottom of the motor cavity.
8   Use a 1 inch (12 point preferably) socket to hand press the retaining ring securely against the motor. **Caution:** *Do not operate the pump until the reservoir has been filled with fluid.*
9   Replace the reservoir. Plug in the electrical connector and insert the hose.
10 Fill the reservoir.
11 Check for leaks.

20 Windshield wiper arm — removal and replacement

Refer to illustration 20.2

1   Before removing a wiper arm, turn the windshield wiper switch on and off to ensure that the arms are in their normal parked position parallel with the bottom of the windshield.
2   To remove the arm, swing the arm away from the windshield, slide out the latch in the wiper arm boss and pull the arm off the spindle (see illustration).
3   When replacing the arm, position it in the parked position and push the boss onto the spindle.

23.1   Pop off the cover over the steering wheel retainer nut (Bronco II shown)

23.2   Index mark to align the steering wheel during installation

23.4   A wheel puller is needed to remove the steering wheel

21   Windshield wiper blade element — removal and installation

Refer to Chapter 1, Routine maintenance.

22   Cruise control — general information

The cruise control switches are located in the steering wheel horn pad. The system consists of the ON-OFF switch and the SET/ACCEL, COAST and RESUME switches, a clutch switch (manual transmissions), an amplifier assembly vacuum dump valve and the necessary wires and vacuum hoses to connect the components.

To operate the cruise control system the vehicle has to be in operation at over 30 mph. To decrease the speed setting depress the brake or clutch pedal then reset to desired speed. To increase the speed setting depress the accelerator until the desired speed is reached then push the SET/ACCL switch. The RESUME switch will resume the desired speed after braking if the speed did not fall below the 30 mph minimum limit.

23   Steering wheel — removal and installation

Refer to illustrations 23.1, 23.2 and 23.4

1   Pry off the steering wheel cover plate with a small screwdriver (see illustration).

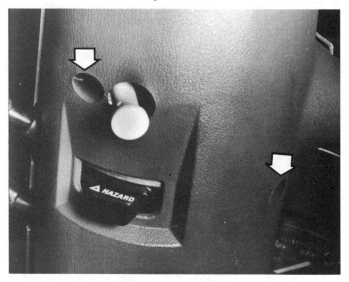

24.2   Arrows show the screws to remove the steering column plastic cover

2   Index with paint the alignment of the steering wheel to the steering column shaft (see illustration).
3   Remove the nut retaining the steering wheel to the steering column.
4   Install a steering wheel puller and pull the wheel from the column (see illustration).
5   To install, align the index marks made at removal and install and tighten the retaining nut.

24   Steering column switches — removal and installation

Refer to illustrations 24.2, 24.4, 24.5 and 24.7

1   Refer to the appropriate Section and remove the steering wheel.
2   Remove the two retaining screws that attach the plastic column covers to the column (see illustration).
3   Peel off the foam covering the column switches.
4   To remove the turn signal/high beam and horn switch assembly, remove the two retaining screws attaching the switch assembly to the column (see illustration).
5   Lift the tangs with a small screwdriver and pull the electrical connector from the turn signal/high beam assembly (see illustration).
6   To remove the windshield washer switch, remove the two retaining screws that attach the switch to the column.

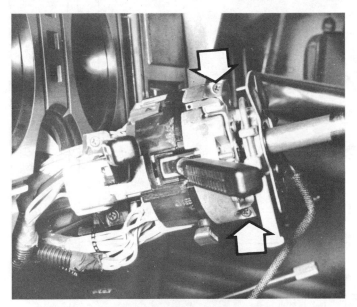

24.4   Two screws (arrows) attach the combination turn signal/high beam switches to the column

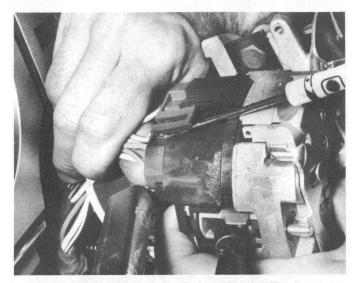

24.5   Lift the tangs allowing connector removal

24.7   Pry up on the tang (arrow) to release the switch

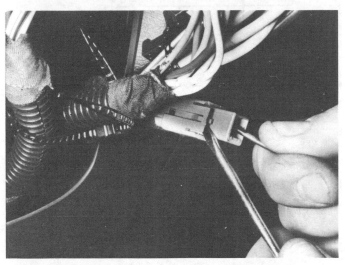

25.5   Pry up on the tang and pull to disconnect the electrical connector

7   Pry up on the electrical connector tang to release it and then pull on the connector to separate it from the switch (see illustration).
8   Installation is the reverse of the removal procedure.

---

25   Ignition switch — removal and installation

Refer to illustrations 25.5 and 25.6

1   Disconnect the negative cable from the battery.
2   Insert the key and turn to the first position (*RUN*) forward.
3   If equipped with tilt control, remove the upper extension shroud by squeezing at the six and twelve o'clock positions and popping it free of the retaining plate.
4   Remove the steering column plastic trim shroud (stationary column) by removing the two retaining screws.
5   Pull the electrical switch connector to disconnect (see illustration).
6   Insert a small screwdriver into the ignition switch housing and release the actuator pin while pulling out on the switch (see illustration).
7   To install, push in the new switch and reverse the remainder of the removal procedure.

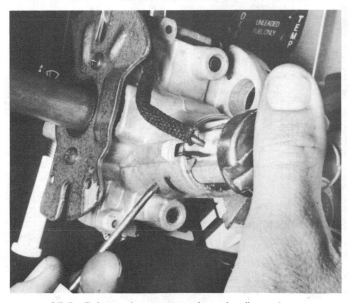

25.6   Release the actuator pin and pull out the ignition switch

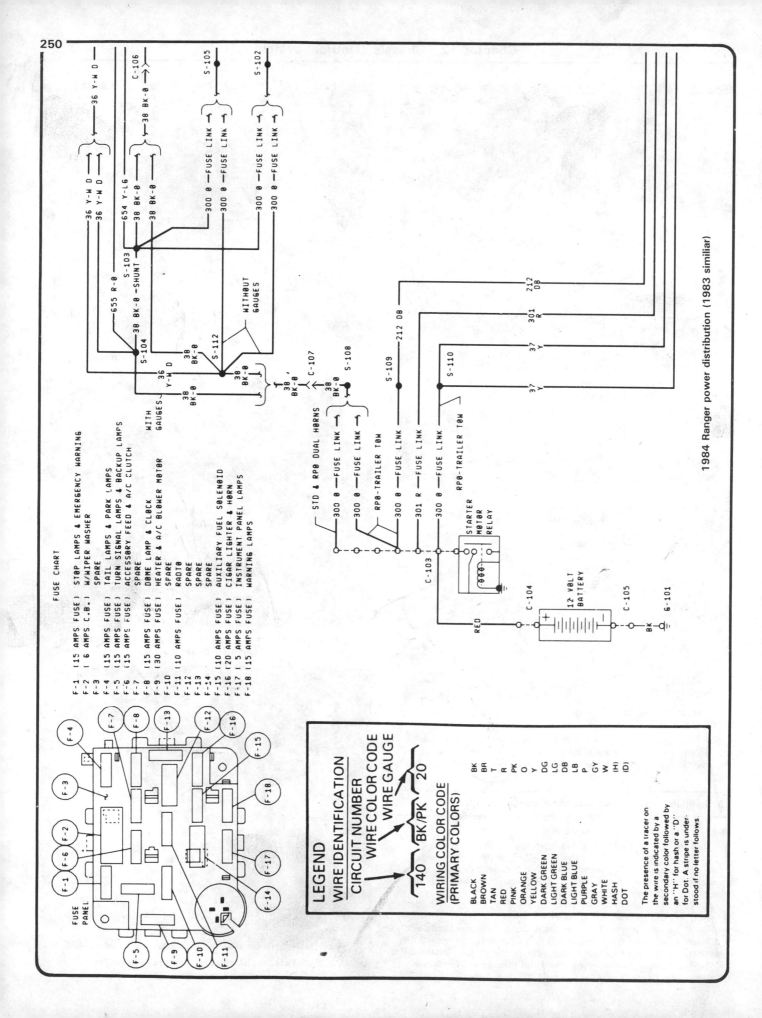

1984 Ranger power distribution (1983 similiar)

FUSE CHART

Fuse	Amps	Circuit
F-1	(15 AMPS FUSE)	STOP LAMPS & EMERGENCY WARNING
F-2	(6 AMPS C.B.)	W/WIPER WASHER
F-3		SPARE
F-4	(15 AMPS FUSE)	TAIL LAMPS & PARK LAMPS
F-5	(15 AMPS FUSE)	TURN SIGNAL LAMPS & BACKUP LAMPS
F-6	(15 AMPS FUSE)	ACCESSORY FEED & A/C CLUTCH
F-7		SPARE
F-8	(15 AMPS FUSE)	DOME LAMP & CLOCK
F-9	(30 AMPS FUSE)	HEATER & A/C BLOWER MOTOR
F-10		SPARE
F-11	(10 AMPS FUSE)	RADIO
F-12		SPARE
F-13		SPARE
F-14		SPARE
F-15	(10 AMPS FUSE)	AUXILIARY FUEL SOLENOID
F-16	(20 AMPS FUSE)	CIGAR LIGHTER & HORN
F-17	(5 AMPS FUSE)	INSTRUMENT PANEL LAMPS
F-18	(15 AMPS FUSE)	WARNING LAMPS

FUSE PANEL

LEGEND

WIRE IDENTIFICATION

CIRCUIT NUMBER
WIRE COLOR CODE
WIRE GAUGE

140 — BK/PK — 20

WIRING COLOR CODE
(PRIMARY COLORS)

BLACK	BK
BROWN	BR
TAN	T
RED	R
PINK	PK
ORANGE	O
YELLOW	Y
DARK GREEN	DG
LIGHT GREEN	LG
DARK BLUE	DB
LIGHT BLUE	LB
PURPLE	P
GRAY	GY
WHITE	W
HASH	(H)
DOT	(D)

The presence of a tracer on the wire is indicated by a secondary color followed by an "H" for hash or a "D" for Dot. A stripe is understood if no letter follows.

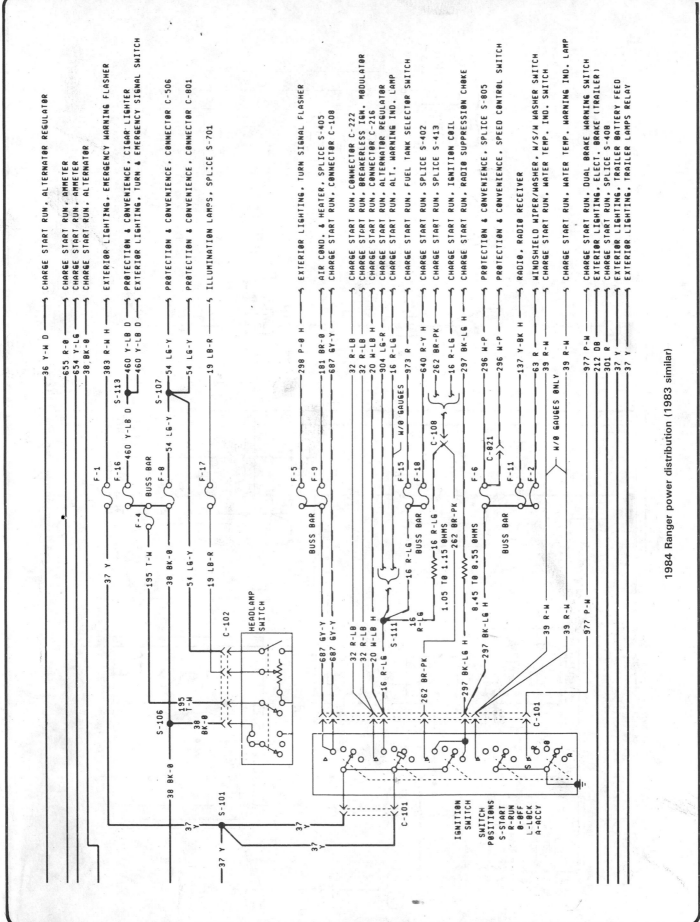

1984 Ranger power distribution (1983 similar)

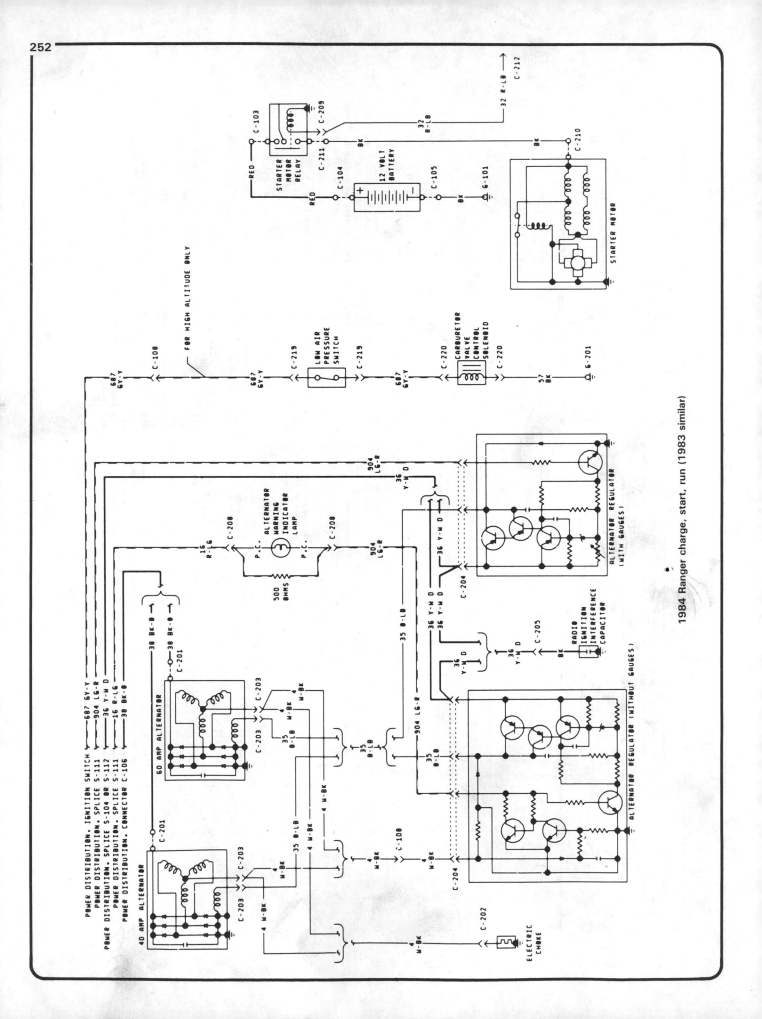

1984 Ranger charge, start, run (1983 similar)

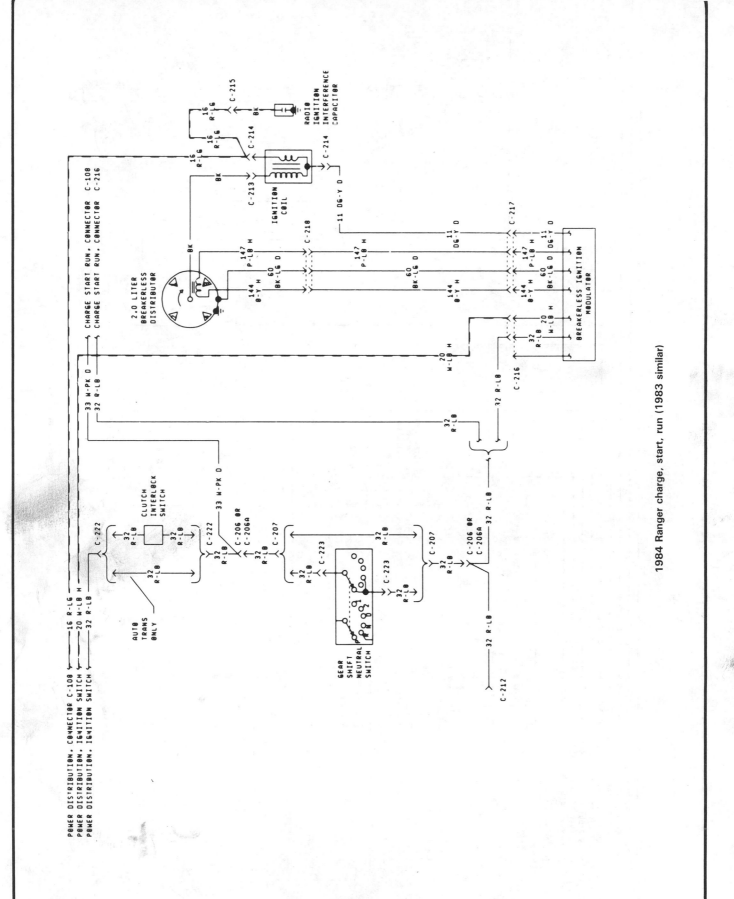

1984 Ranger charge, start, run (1983 similar)

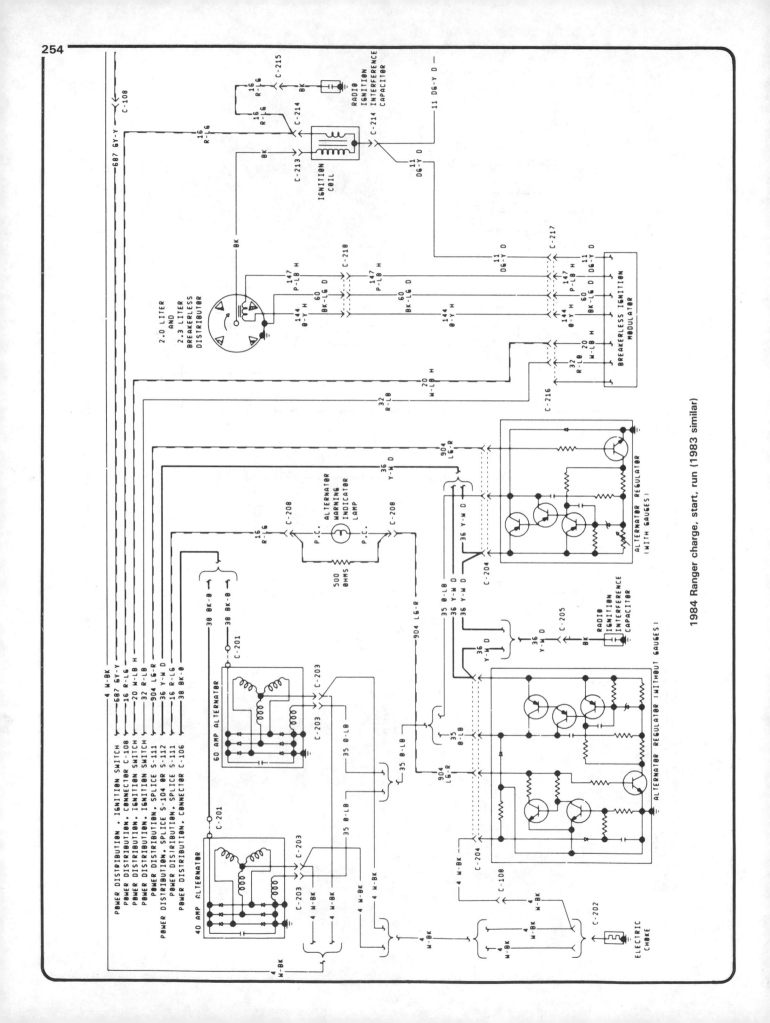

1984 Ranger charge, start, run (1983 similar)

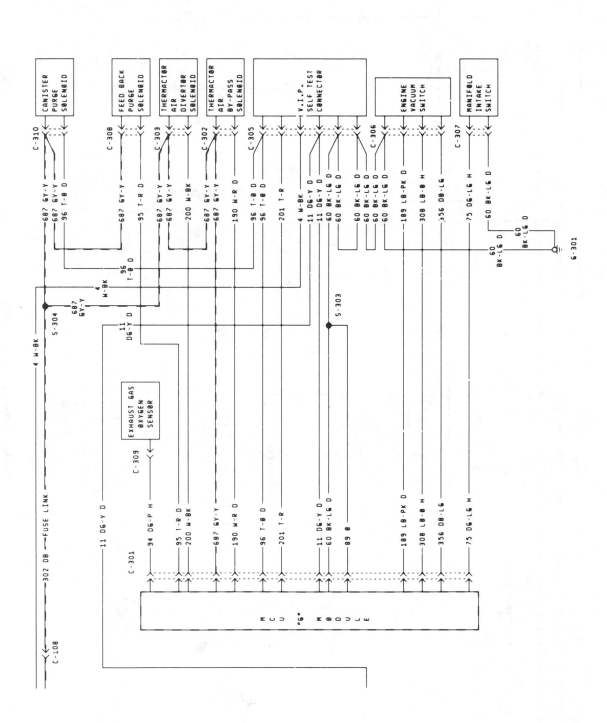

1984 Ranger charge, start, run (1983 similar)

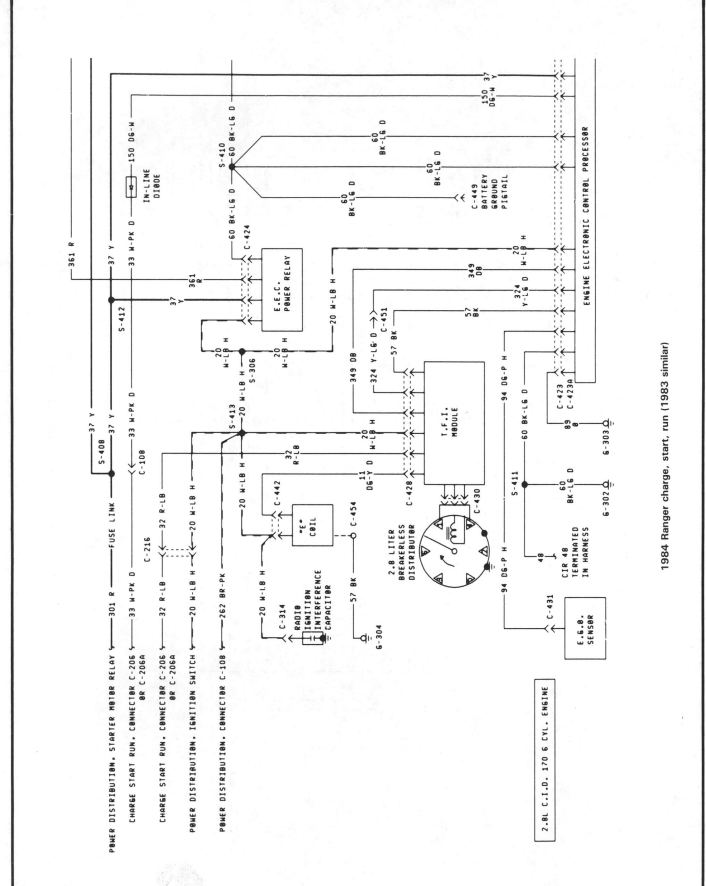

1984 Ranger charge, start, run (1983 similar)

2.8L C.I.D. 170 6 CYL. ENGINE

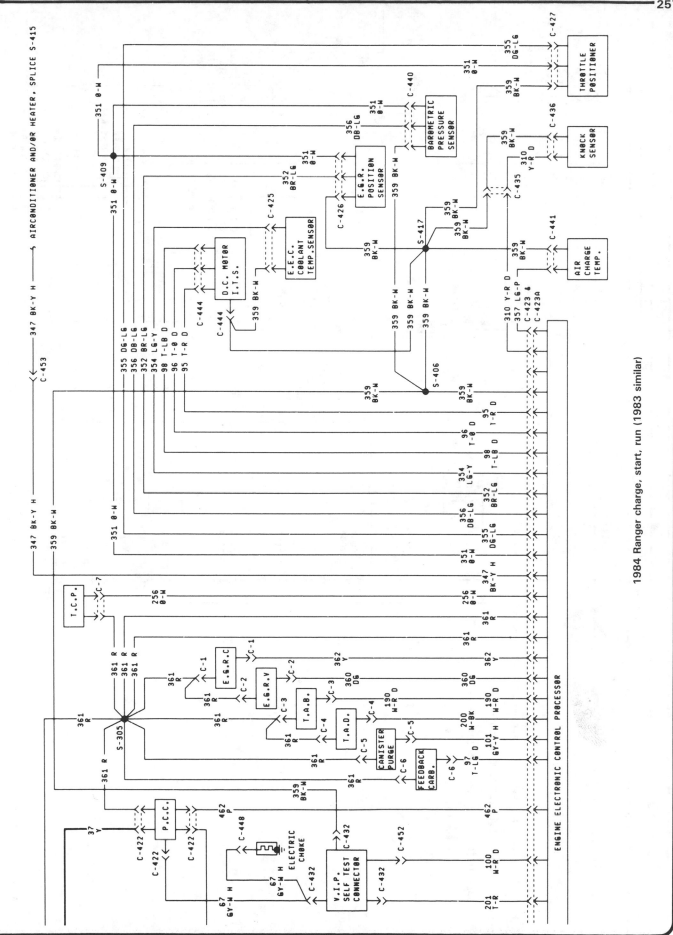

1984 Ranger charge, start, run (1983 similar)

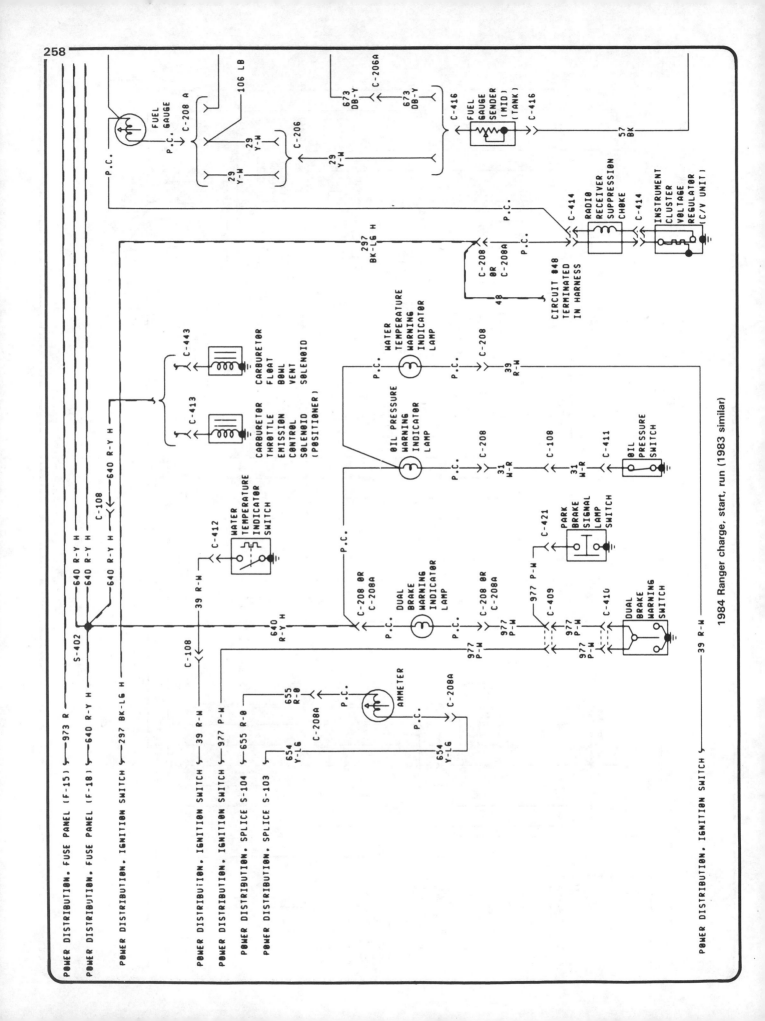

258

1984 Ranger charge, start, run (1983 similar)

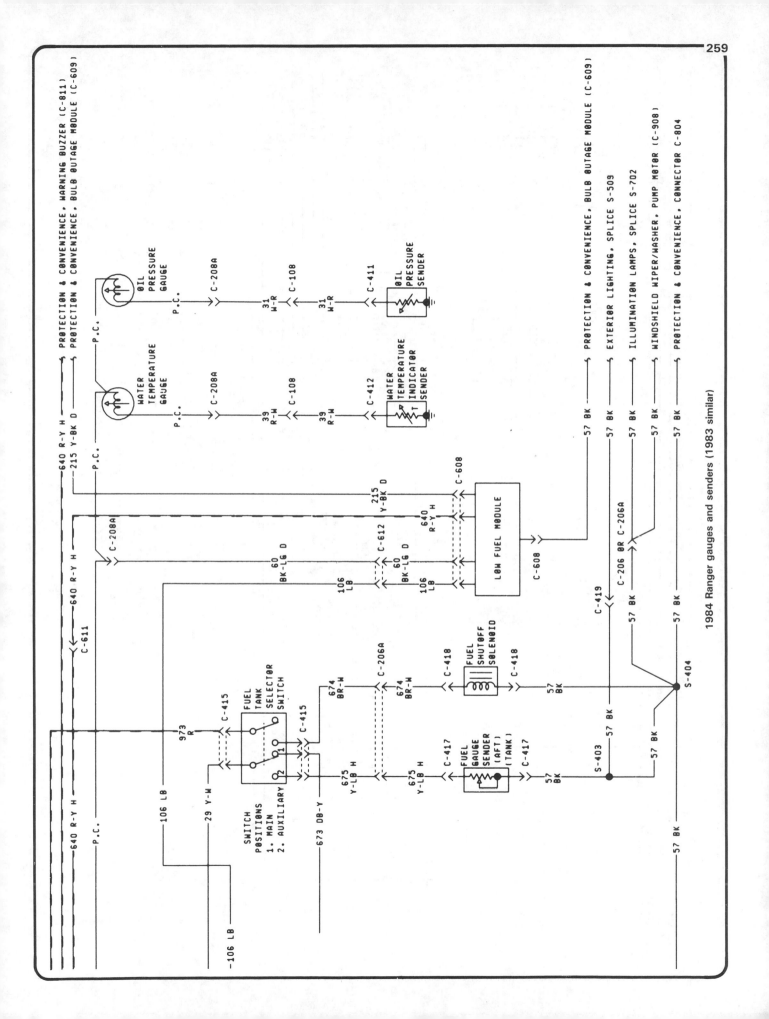

1984 Ranger gauges and senders (1983 similar)

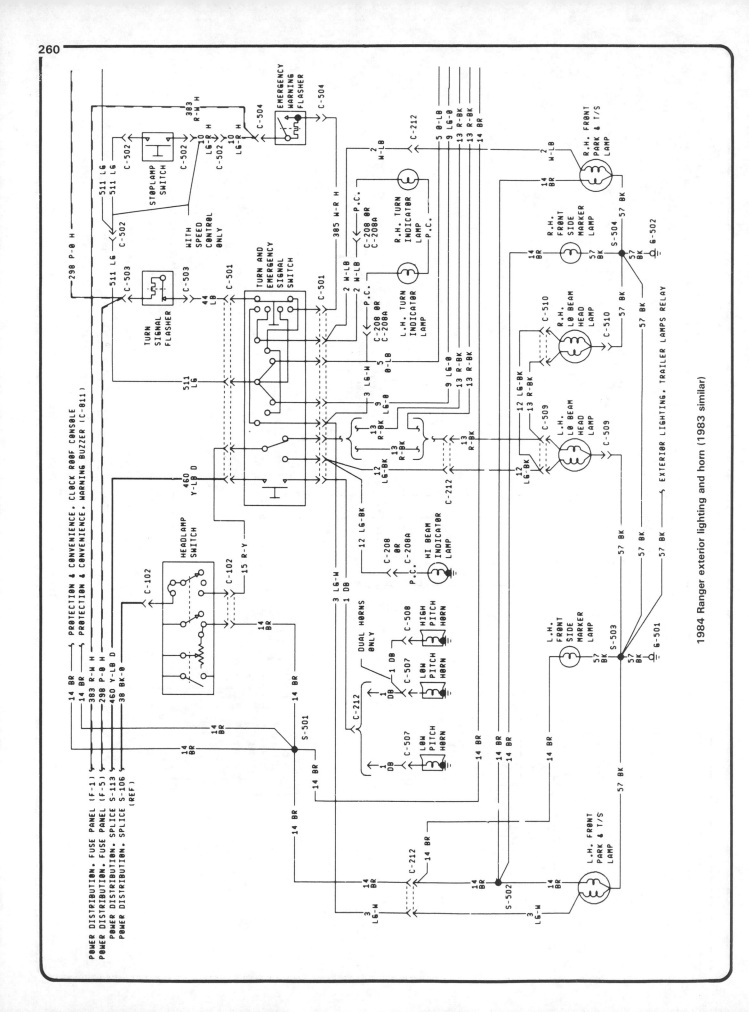

1984 Ranger exterior lighting and horn (1983 similar)

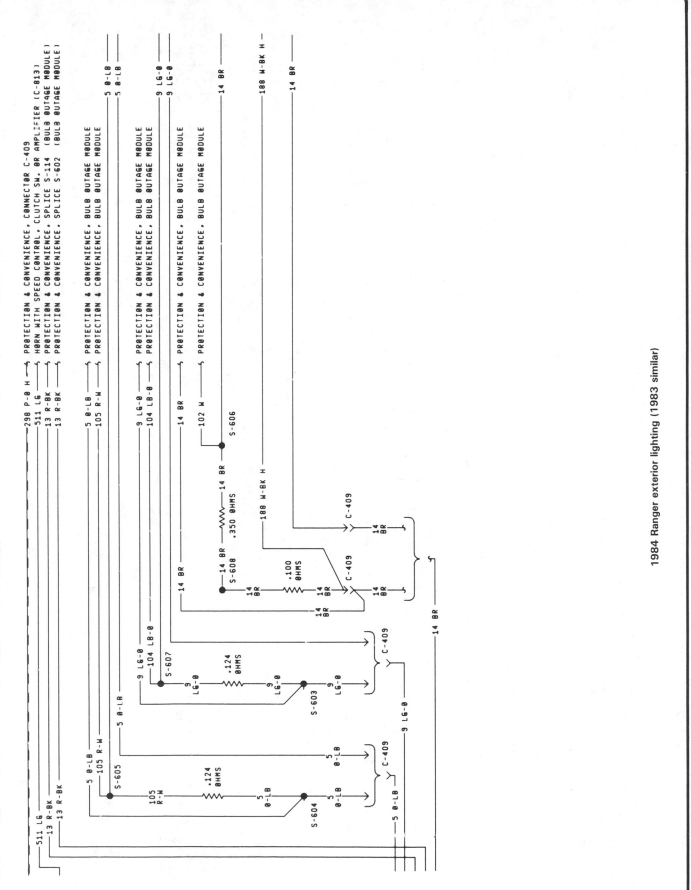

261

1984 Ranger exterior lighting (1983 similar)

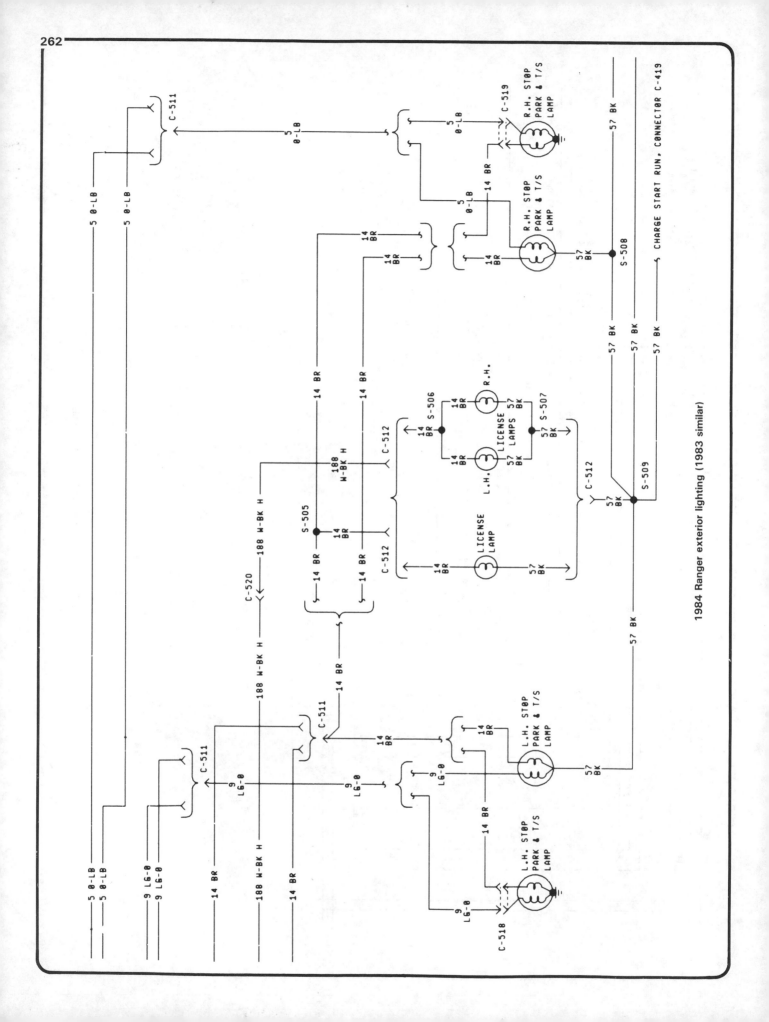

1984 Ranger exterior lighting (1983 similar)

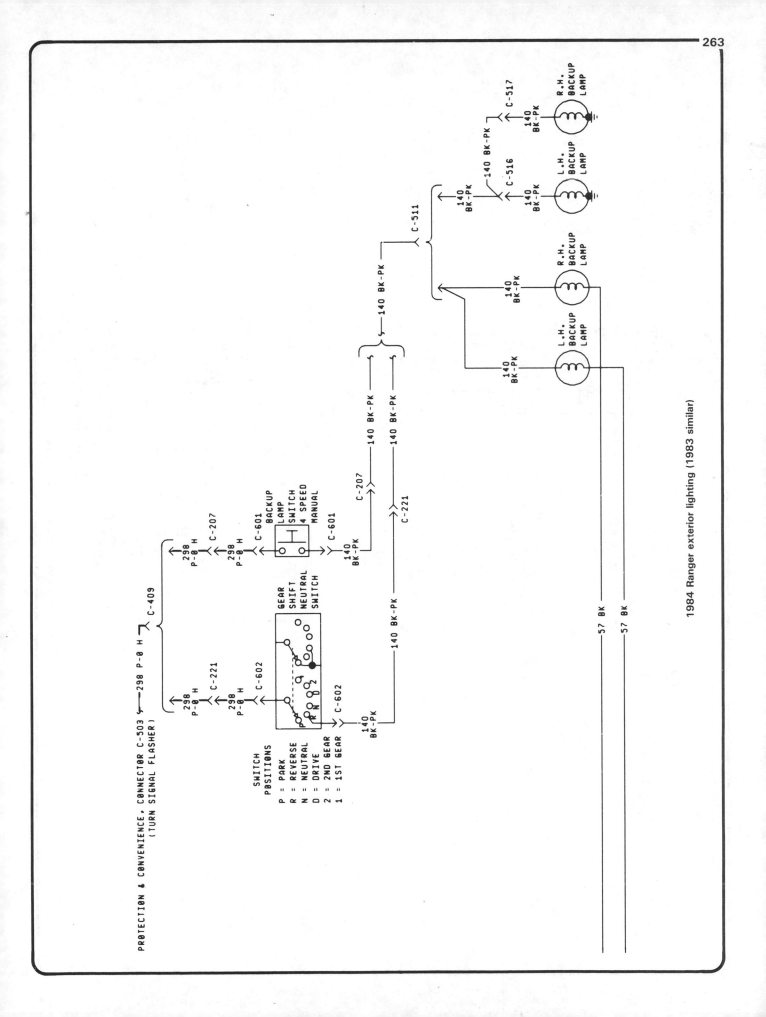

1984 Ranger exterior lighting (1983 similar)

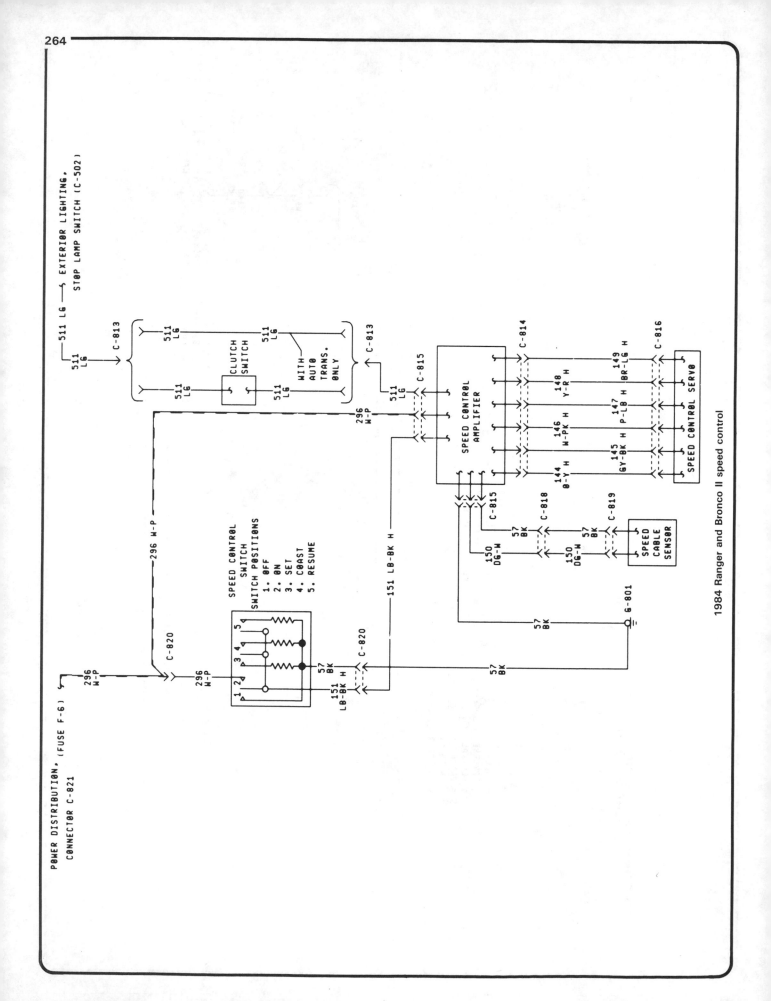

1984 Ranger and Bronco II speed control

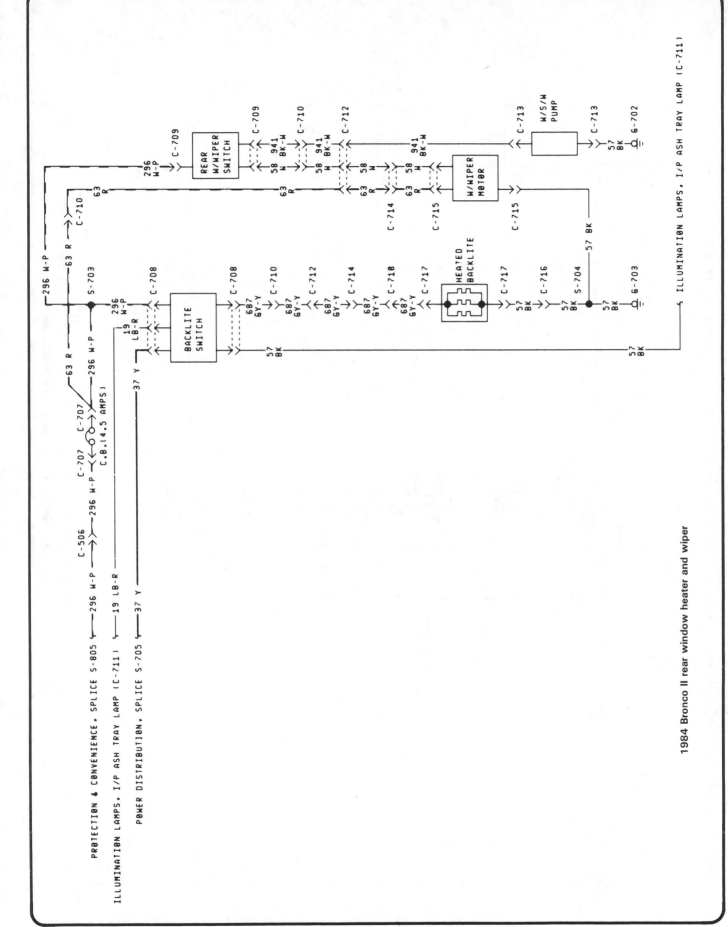

1984 Bronco II rear window heater and wiper

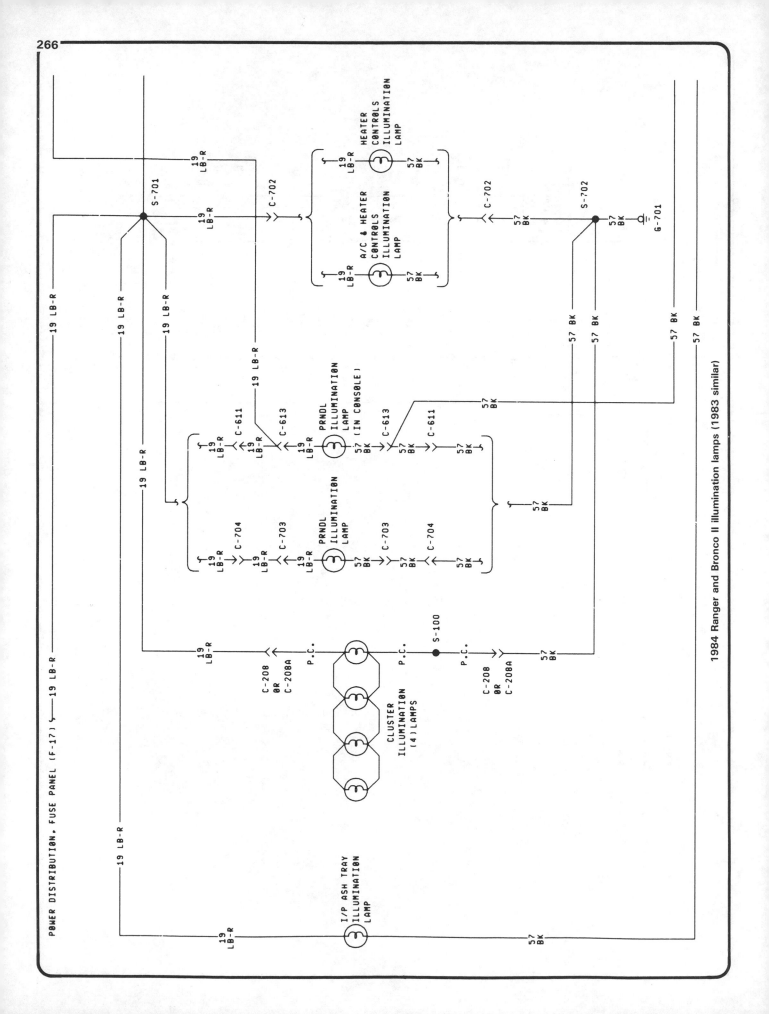

266

POWER DISTRIBUTION, FUSE PANEL (F-17)

1984 Ranger and Bronco II illumination lamps (1983 similar)

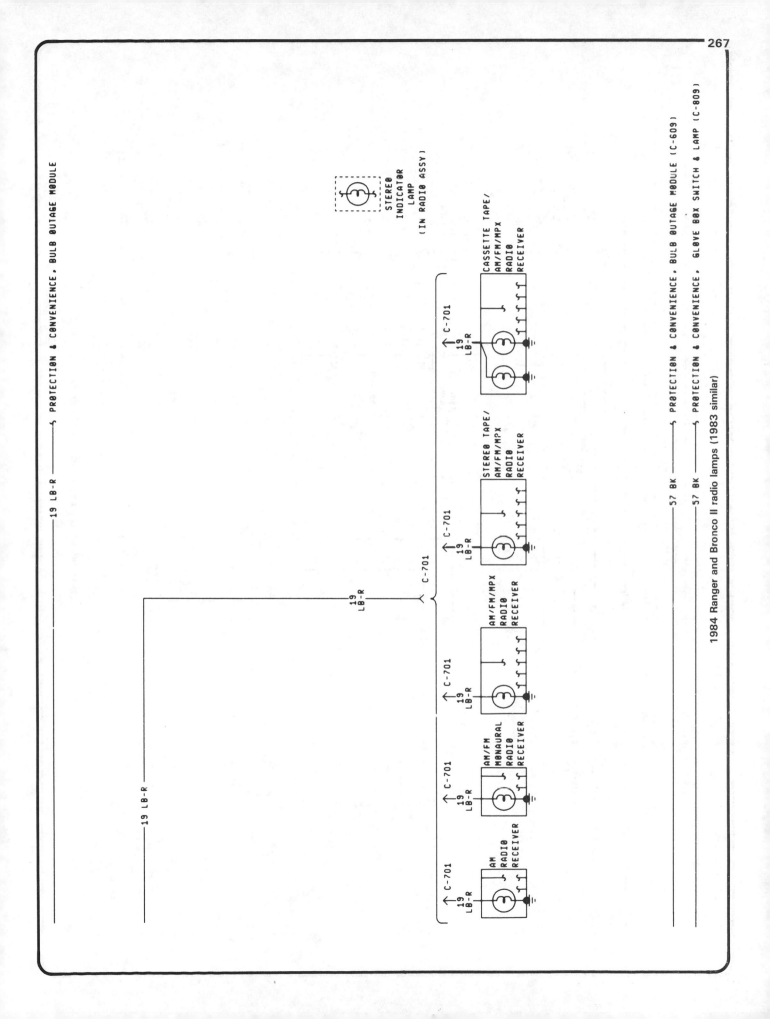

1984 Ranger and Bronco II radio lamps (1983 similar)

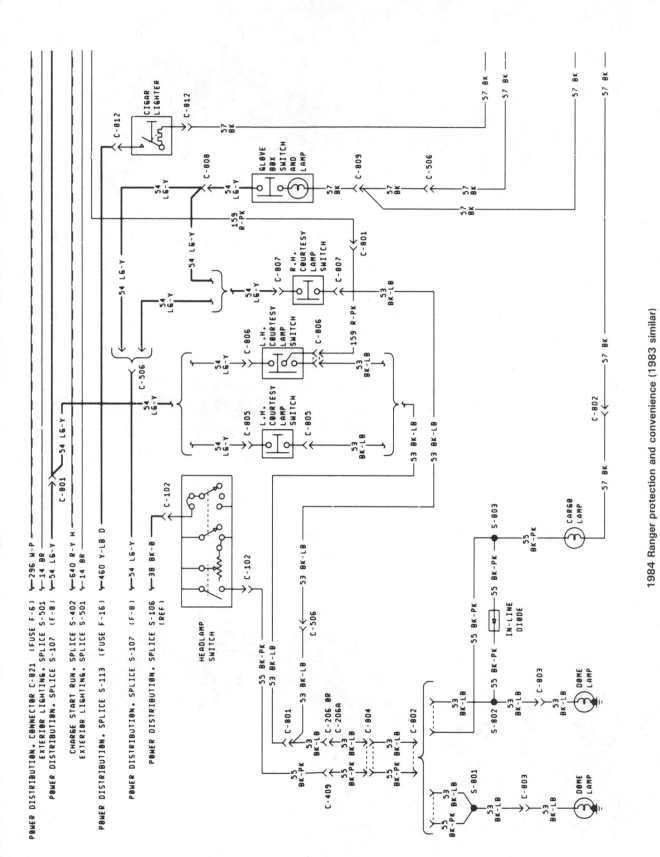

1984 Ranger protection and convenience (1983 similar)

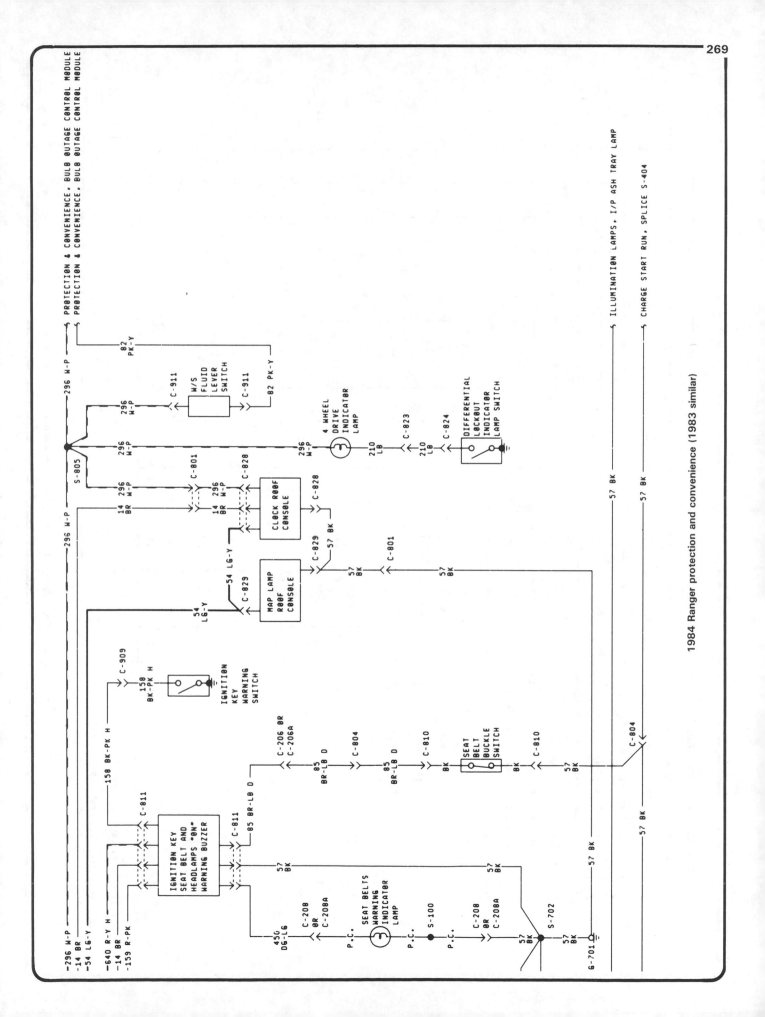

1984 Ranger protection and convenience (1983 similar)

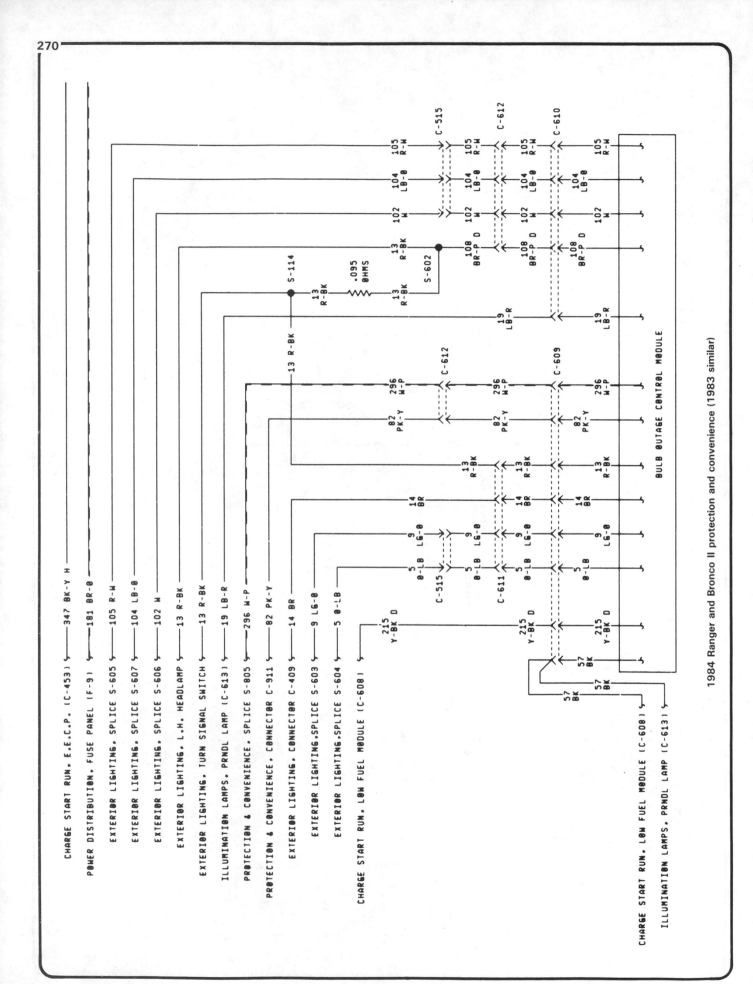

1984 Ranger and Bronco II protection and convenience (1983 similar)

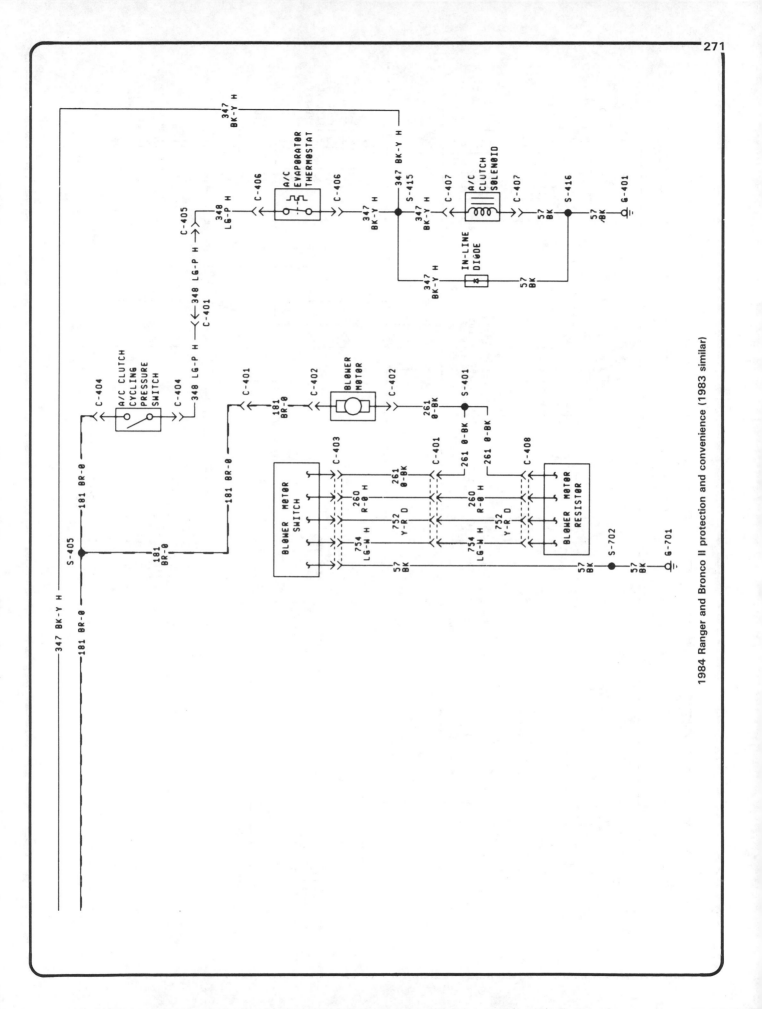

1984 Ranger and Bronco II protection and convenience (1983 similar)

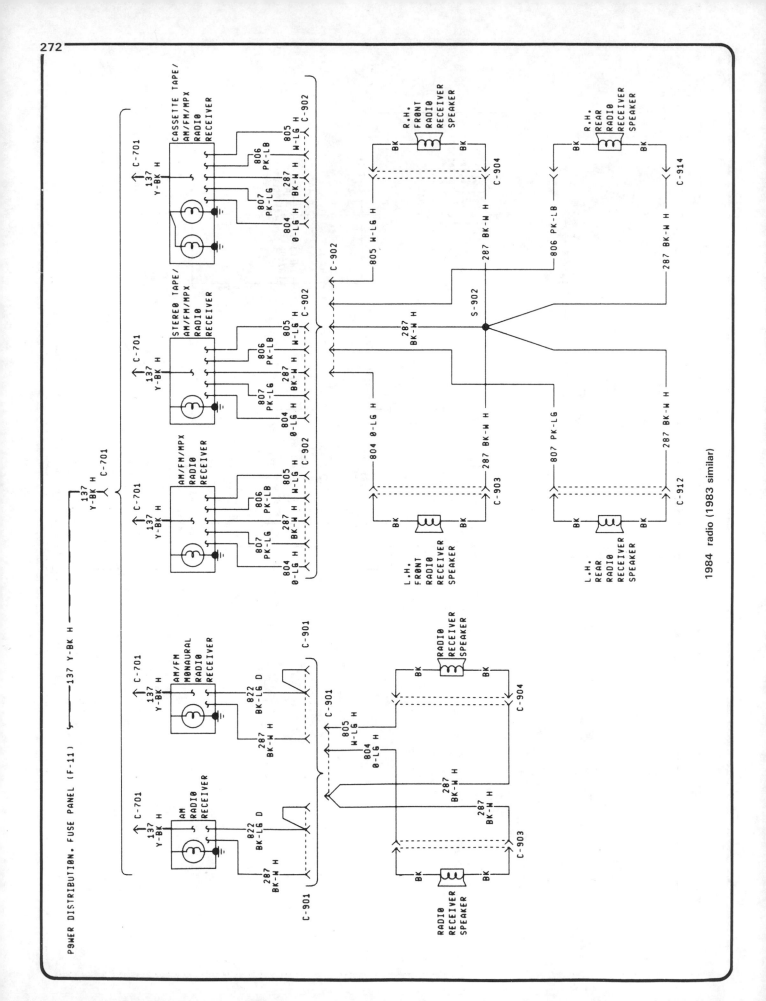

POWER DISTRIBUTION, FUSE PANEL (F-11)

1984 radio (1983 similar)

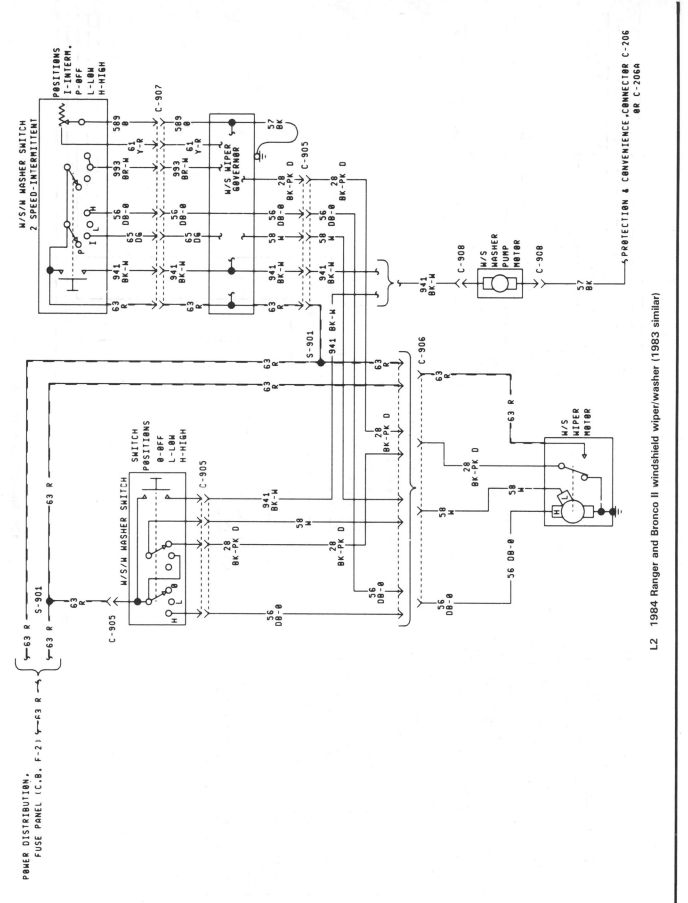

L2 1984 Ranger and Bronco II windshield wiper/washer (1983 similar)

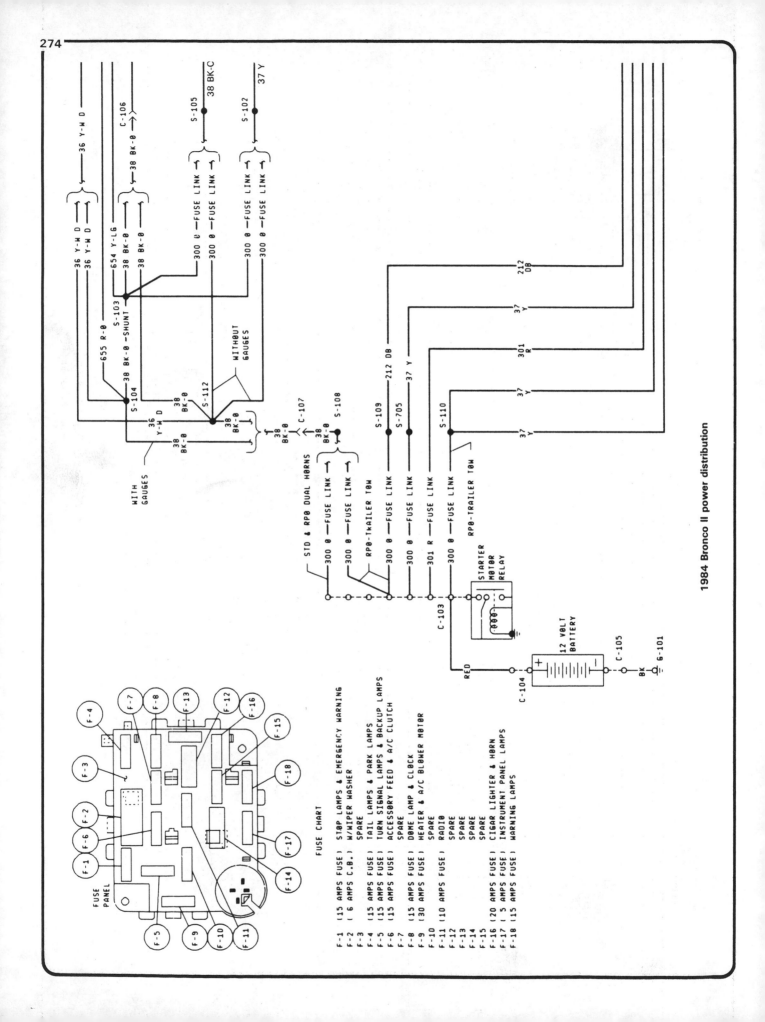

1984 Bronco II power distribution

FUSE CHART

F-1 (15 AMPS FUSE) STOP LAMPS & EMERGENCY WARNING
F-2 (6 AMPS C.B.) W/WIPER WASHER
F-3 SPARE
F-4 (15 AMPS FUSE) TAIL LAMPS & PARK LAMPS
F-5 (15 AMPS FUSE) TURN SIGNAL LAMPS & BACKUP LAMPS
F-6 (15 AMPS FUSE) ACCESSORY FEED & A/C CLUTCH
F-7 SPARE
F-8 (15 AMPS FUSE) DOME LAMP & CLOCK
F-9 (30 AMPS FUSE) HEATER & A/C BLOWER MOTOR
F-10 SPARE
F-11 (10 AMPS FUSE) RADIO
F-12 SPARE
F-13 SPARE
F-14 SPARE
F-15 SPARE
F-16 (20 AMPS FUSE) CIGAR LIGHTER & HORN
F-17 (5 AMPS FUSE) INSTRUMENT PANEL LAMPS
F-18 (15 AMPS FUSE) WARNING LAMPS

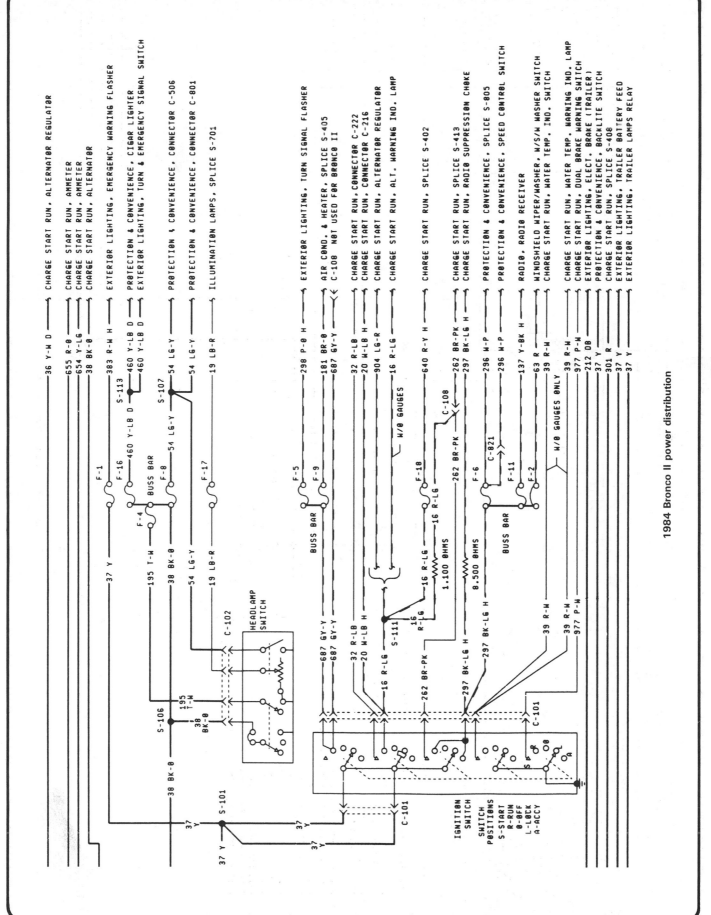

1984 Bronco II power distribution

275

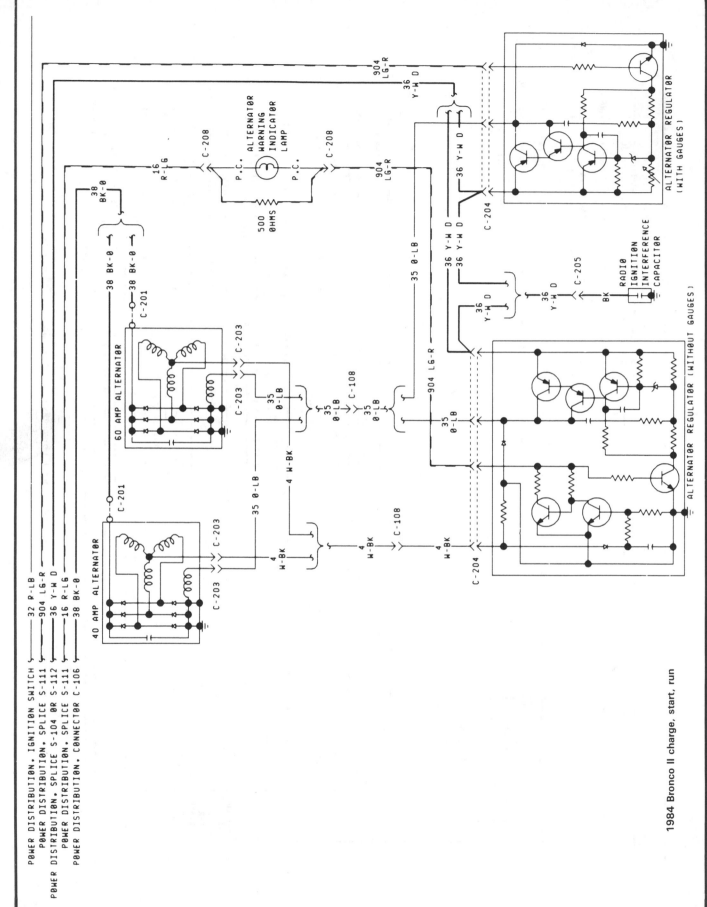

POWER DISTRIBUTION. IGNITION SWITCH ⌐ 32 R-LB
POWER DISTRIBUTION. SPLICE S-111 ⌐ 904 LG-R
POWER DISTRIBUTION. SPLICE S-104 OR S-112 ⌐ 36 Y-W D
POWER DISTRIBUTION. SPLICE S-111 ⌐ 16 R-LG
POWER DISTRIBUTION. CONNECTOR C-106 ⌐ 38 BK-O

ALTERNATOR REGULATOR (WITH GAUGES)

ALTERNATOR REGULATOR (WITHOUT GAUGES)

RADIO IGNITION INTERFERENCE CAPACITOR

ALTERNATOR WARNING INDICATOR LAMP

500 OHMS

60 AMP ALTERNATOR

40 AMP ALTERNATOR

1984 Bronco II charge, start, run

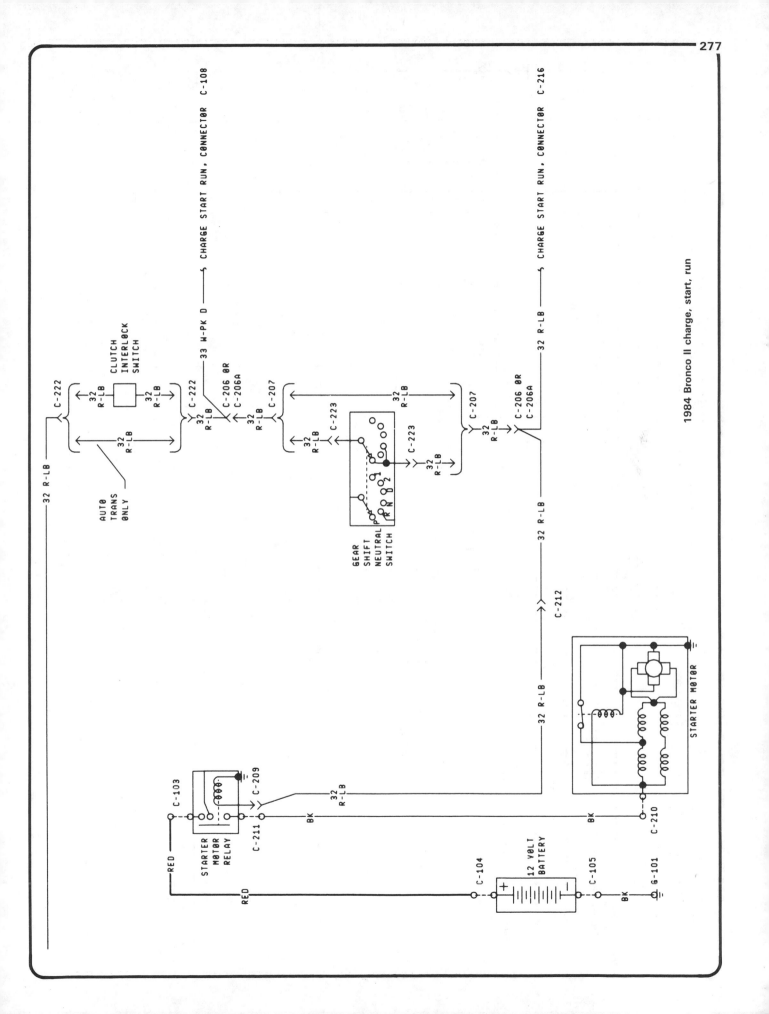

1984 Bronco II charge, start, run

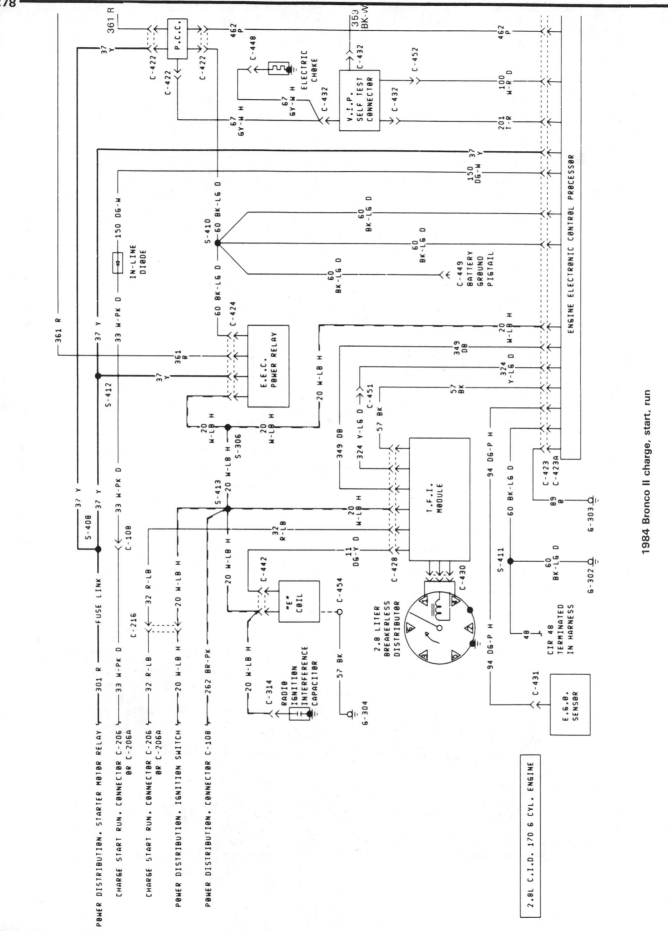

1984 Bronco II charge, start, run

2.8L C.I.D. 170 6 CYL. ENGINE

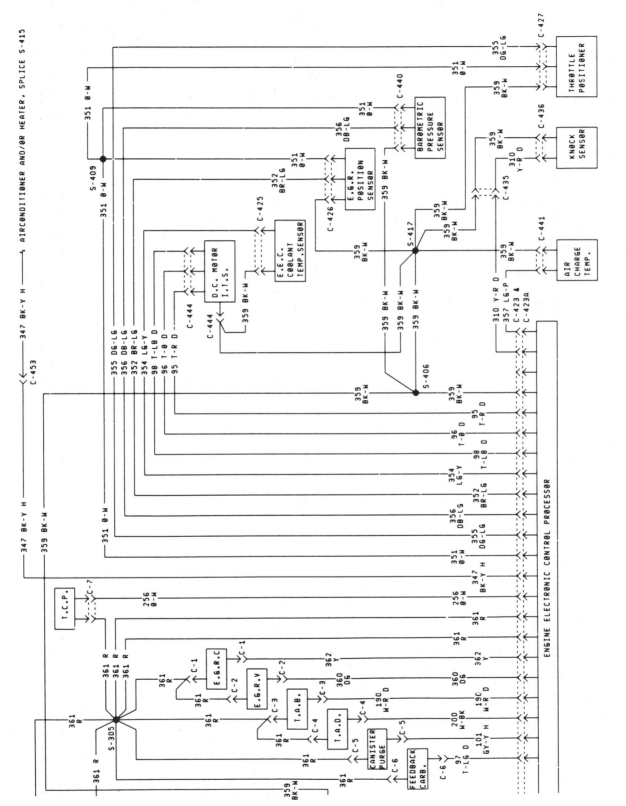

1984 Bronco II charge, start, run

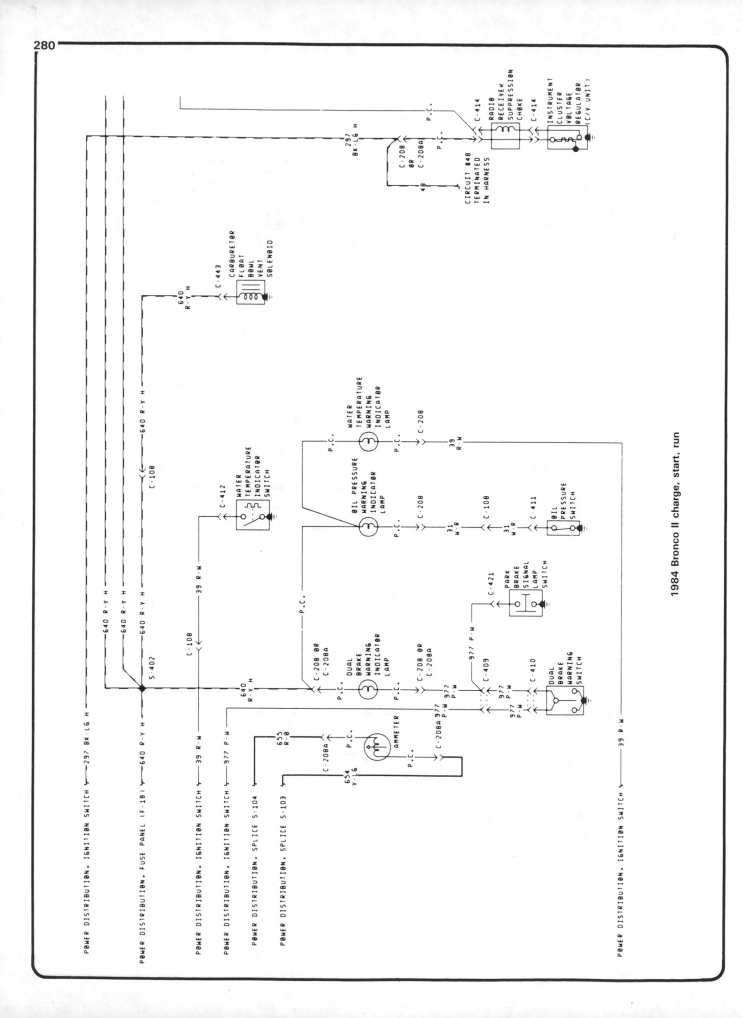

1984 Bronco II charge, start, run

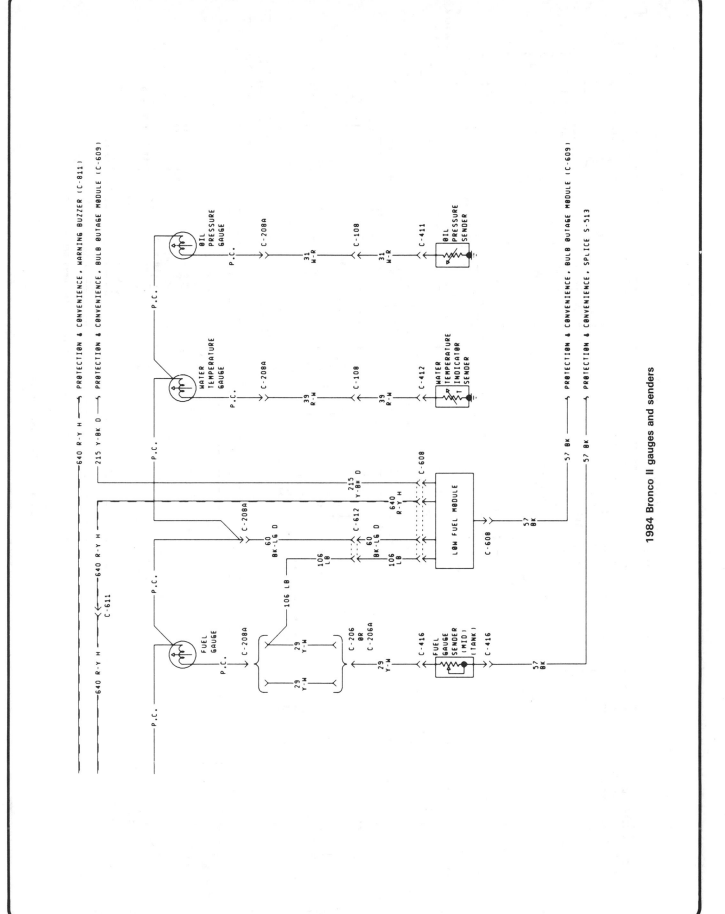

1984 Bronco II gauges and senders

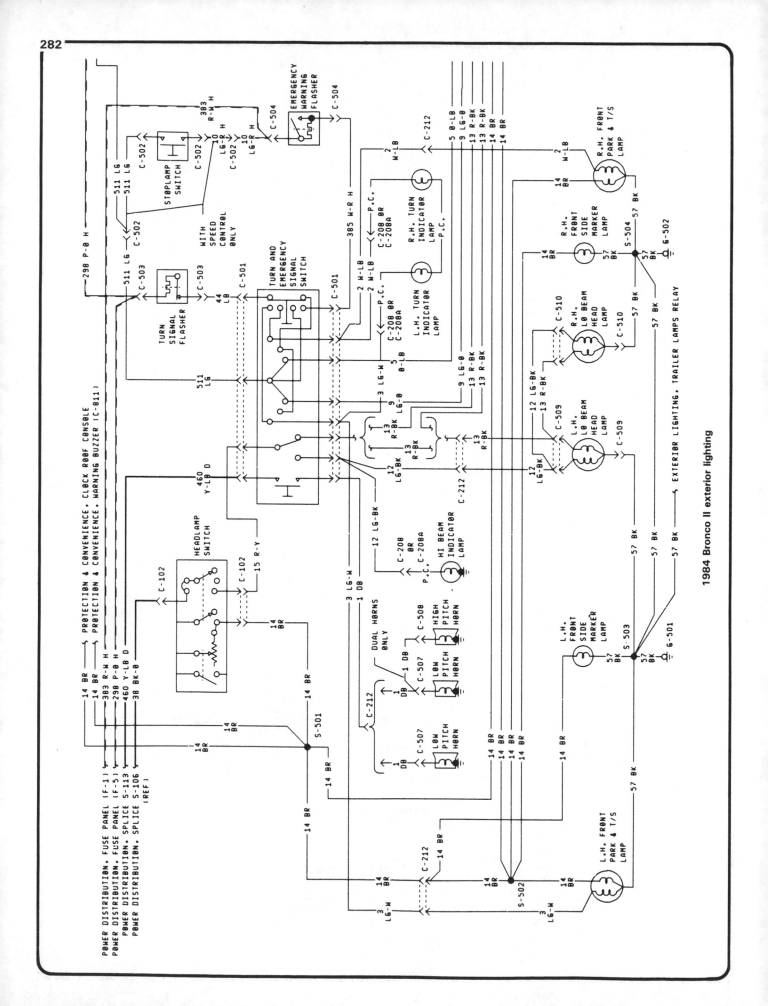

1984 Bronco II exterior lighting

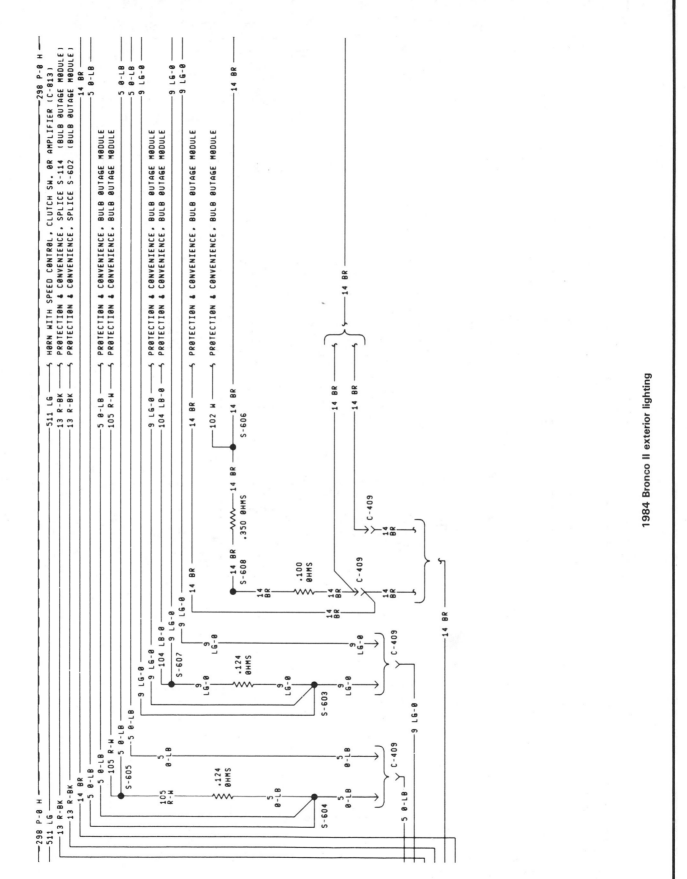

1984 Bronco II exterior lighting

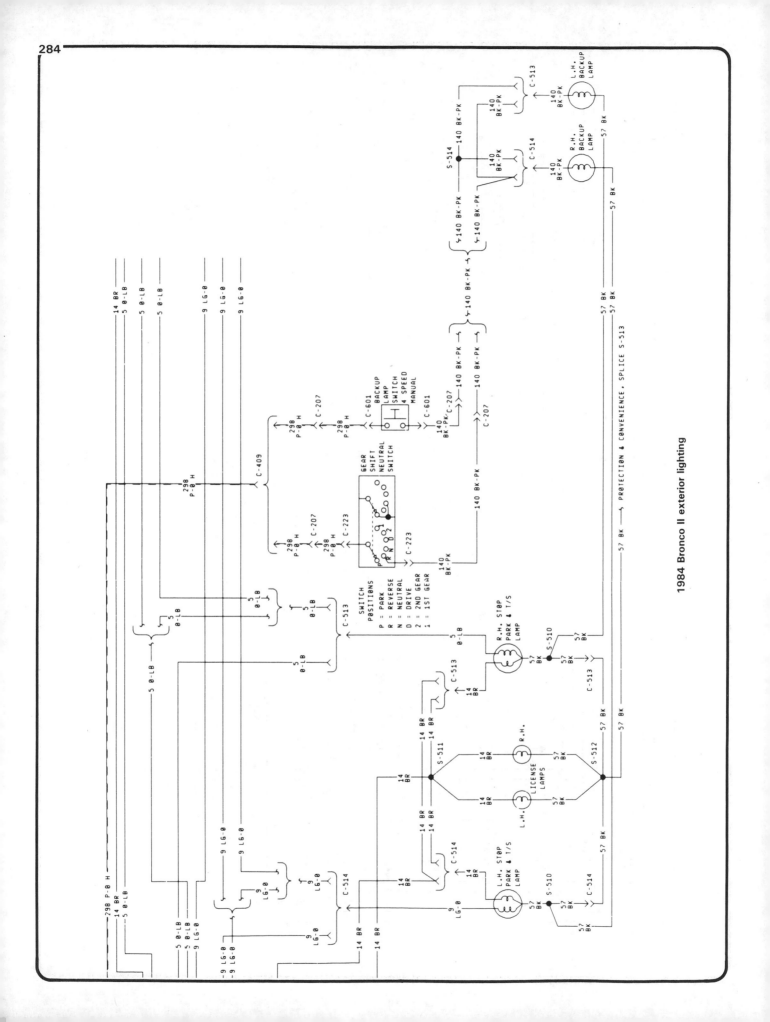

1984 Bronco II exterior lighting

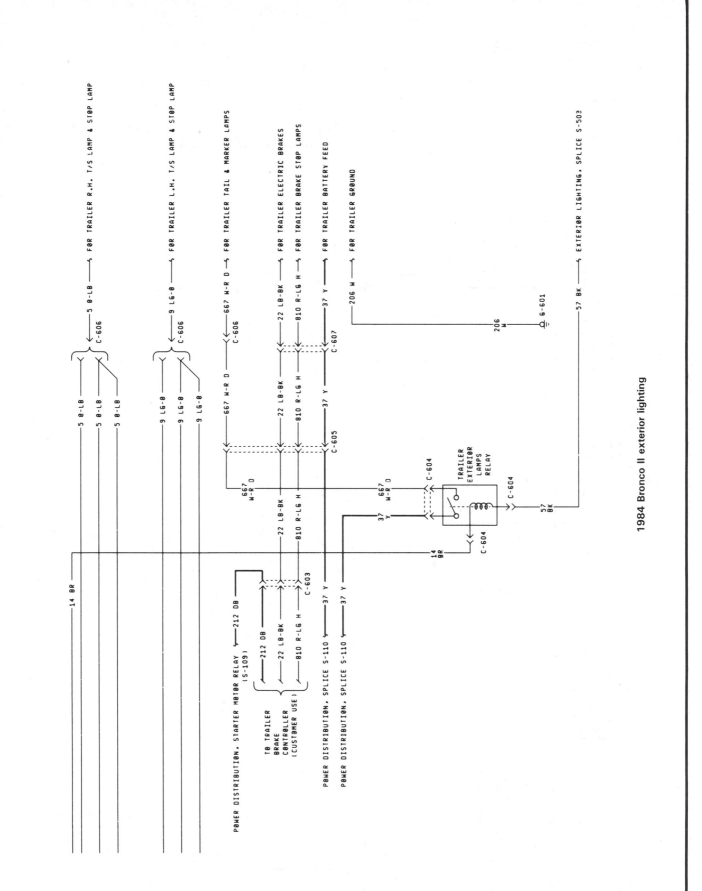

1984 Bronco II exterior lighting

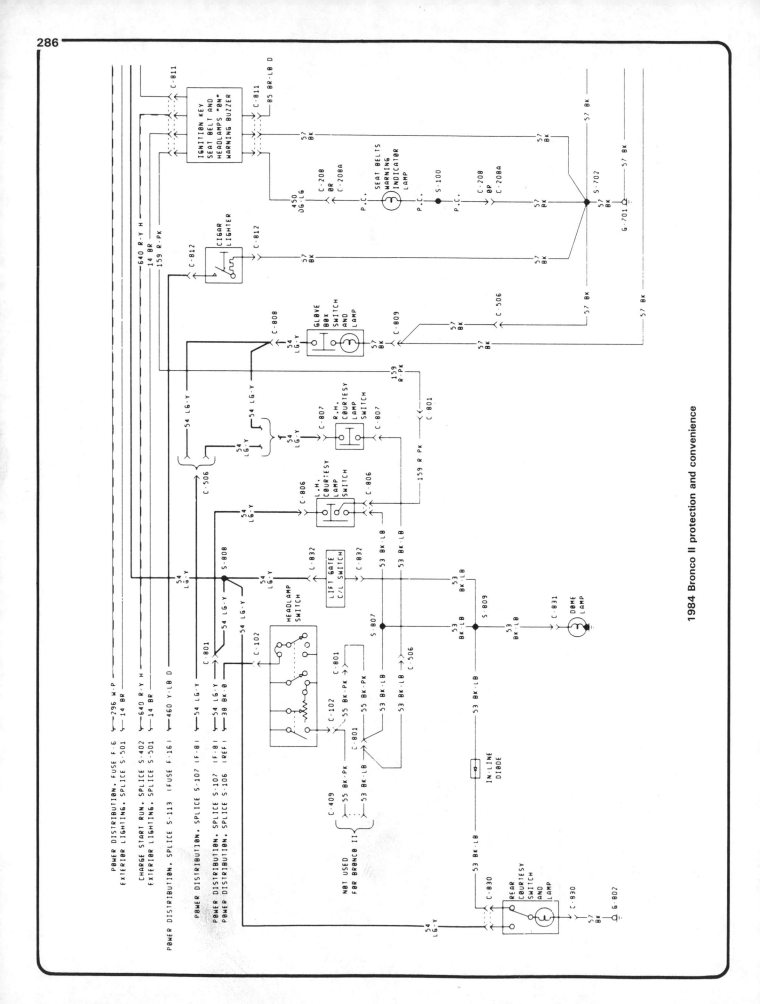

1984 Bronco II protection and convenience

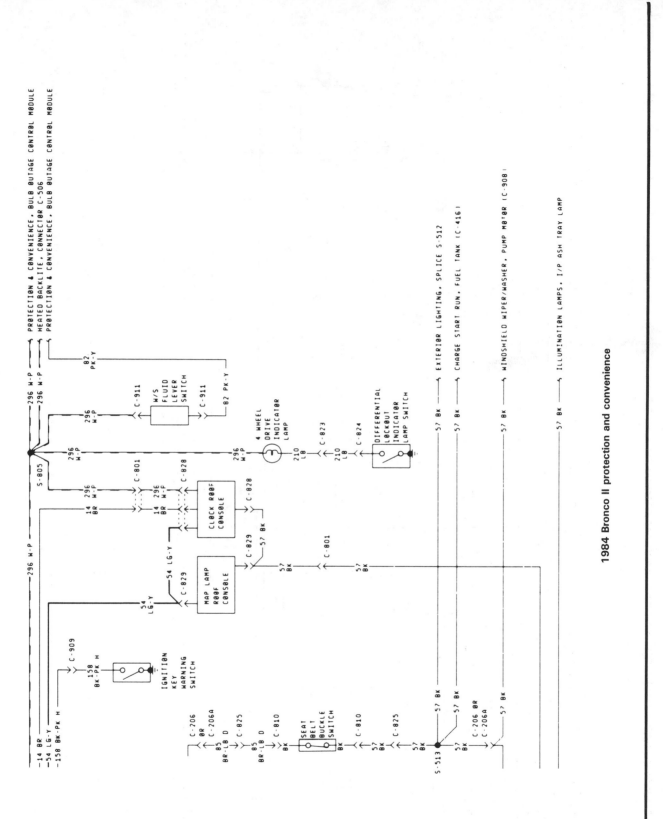

1984 Bronco II protection and convenience

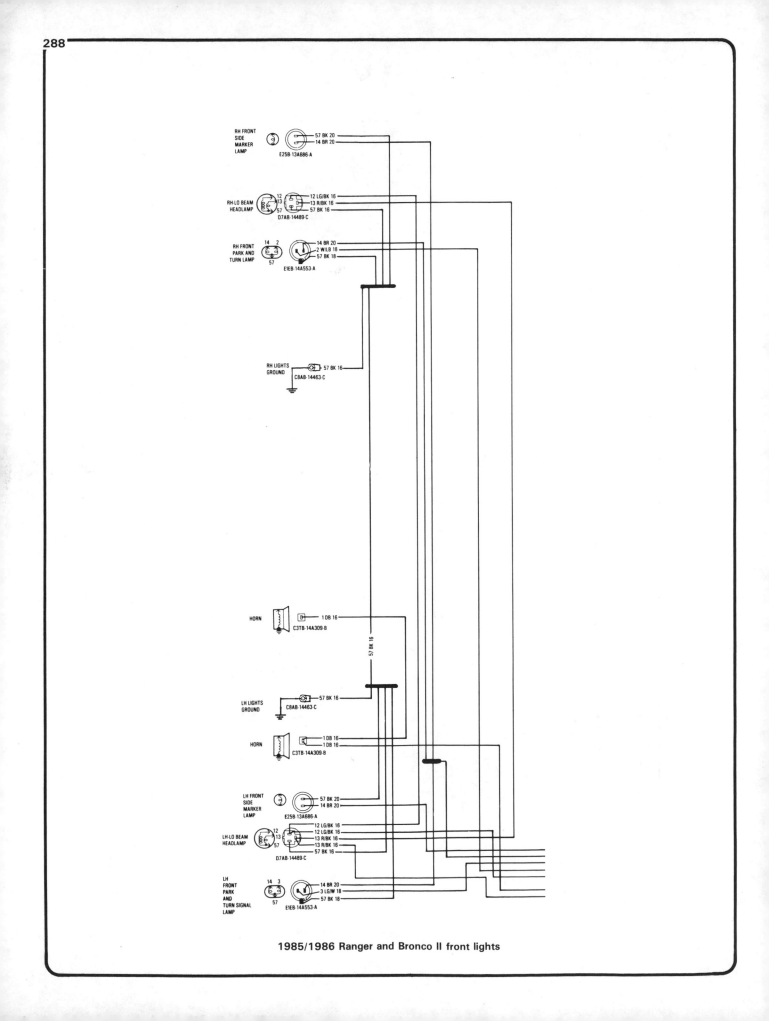

RH FRONT
SIDE
MARKER
LAMP

57 BK 20
14 BR 20

E25B-13A686-A

RH-LO BEAM
HEADLAMP

12
13
57

12 LG/BK 16
13 R/BK 16
57 BK 16

D7AB-14489-C

RH FRONT
PARK AND
TURN LAMP

14   2

57

14 BR 20
2 W/LB 18
57 BK 18

E1EB-14A553-A

RH LIGHTS
GROUND

57 BK 16

C8AB-14463-C

HORN

1 DB 16

C3TB-14A309-B

57 BK 16

LH LIGHTS
GROUND

57 BK 16

C8AB-14463-C

HORN

1 DB 16
1 DB 16

C3TB-14A309-B

LH FRONT
SIDE
MARKER
LAMP

57 BK 20
14 BR 20

E25B-13A686-A

LH-LO BEAM
HEADLAMP

12
13
57

12 LG/BK 16
12 LG/BK 16
13 R/BK 16
13 R/BK 16
57 BK 16

D7AB-14489-C

LH
FRONT
PARK
AND
TURN SIGNAL
LAMP

14   3

57

14 BR 20
3 LG/W 18
57 BK 18

E1EB-14A553-A

1985/1986 Ranger and Bronco II front lights

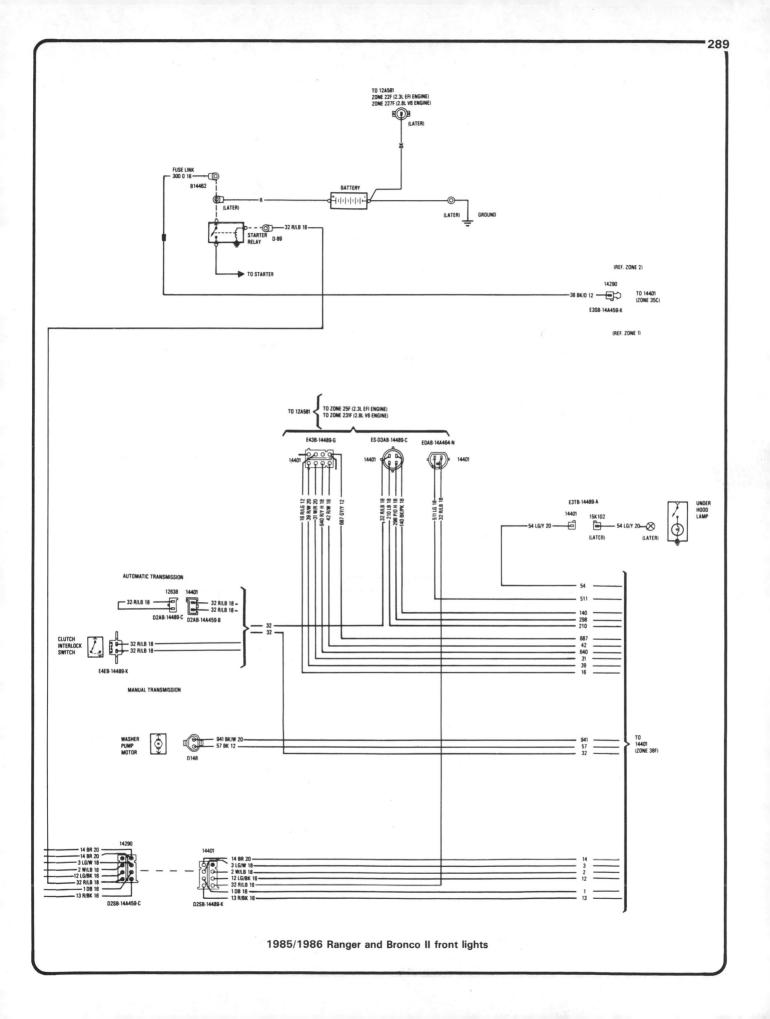

1985/1986 Ranger and Bronco II front lights

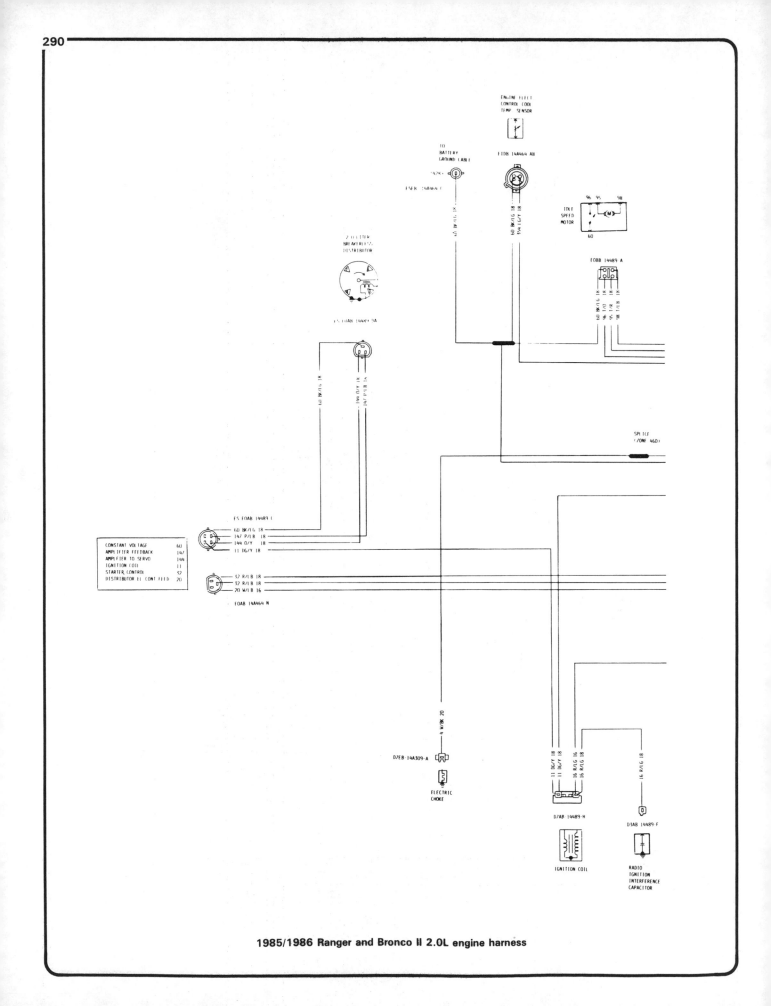

1985/1986 Ranger and Bronco II 2.0L engine harness

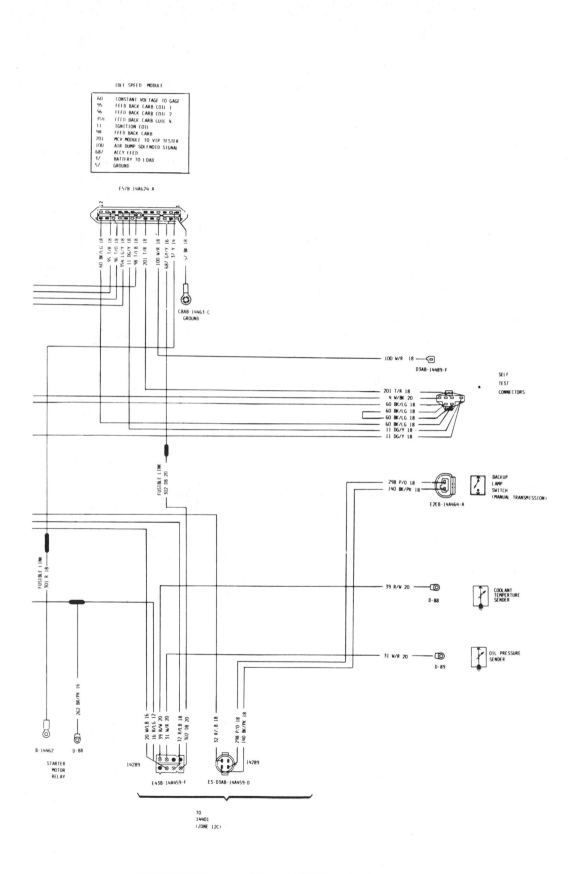

1985/1986 Ranger and Bronco II 2.0L engine harness

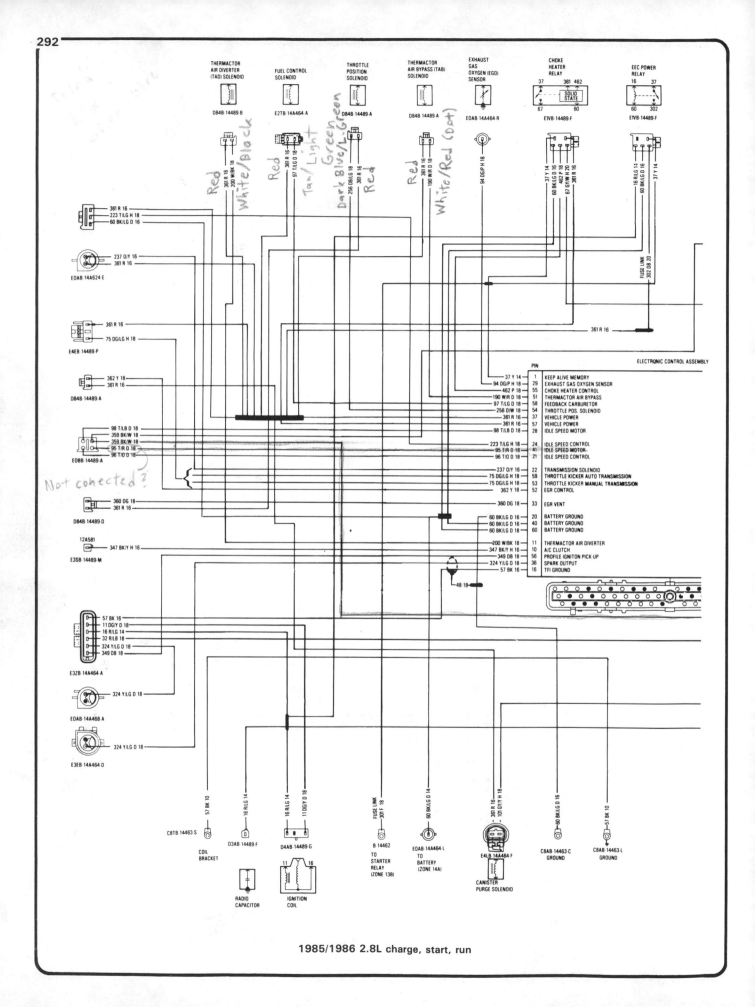

1985/1986 2.8L charge, start, run

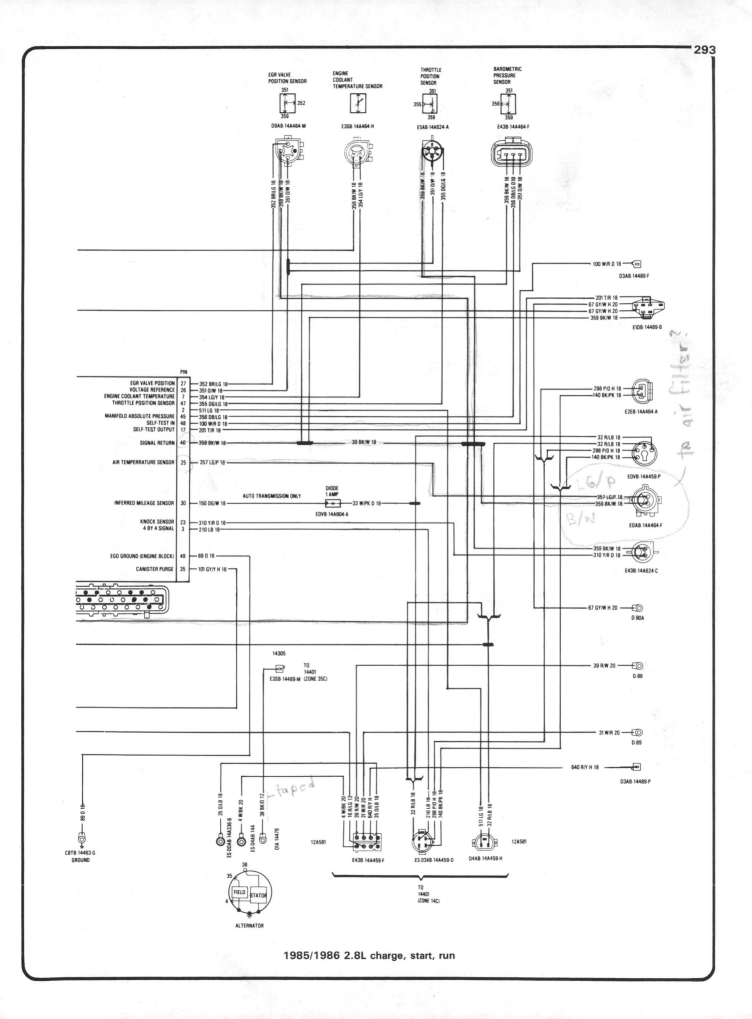

1985/1986 2.8L charge, start, run

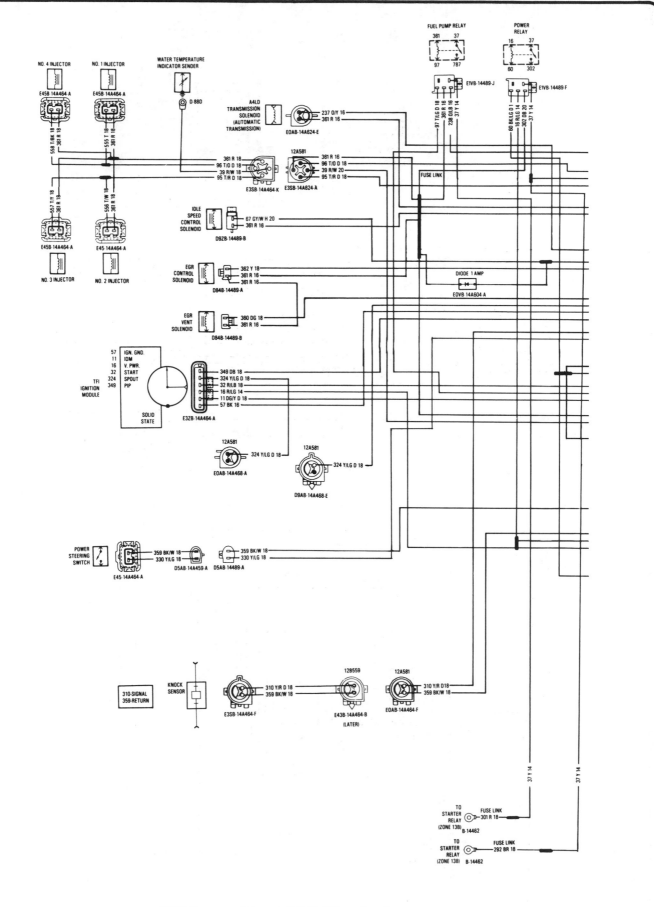

1985 Ranger and Bronco II 2.3L EFI engine charge, start, run

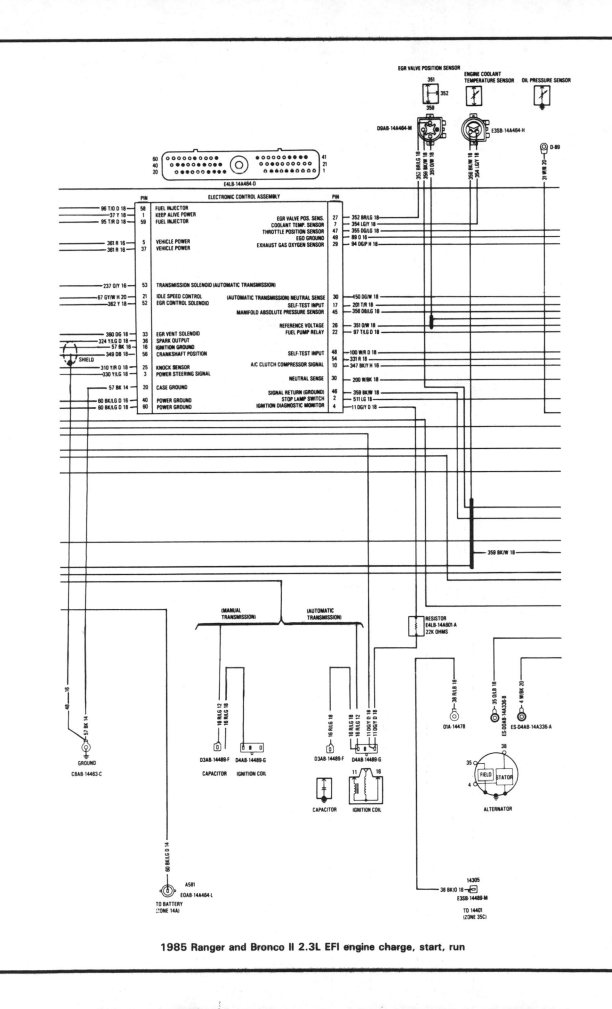

1985 Ranger and Bronco II 2.3L EFI engine charge, start, run

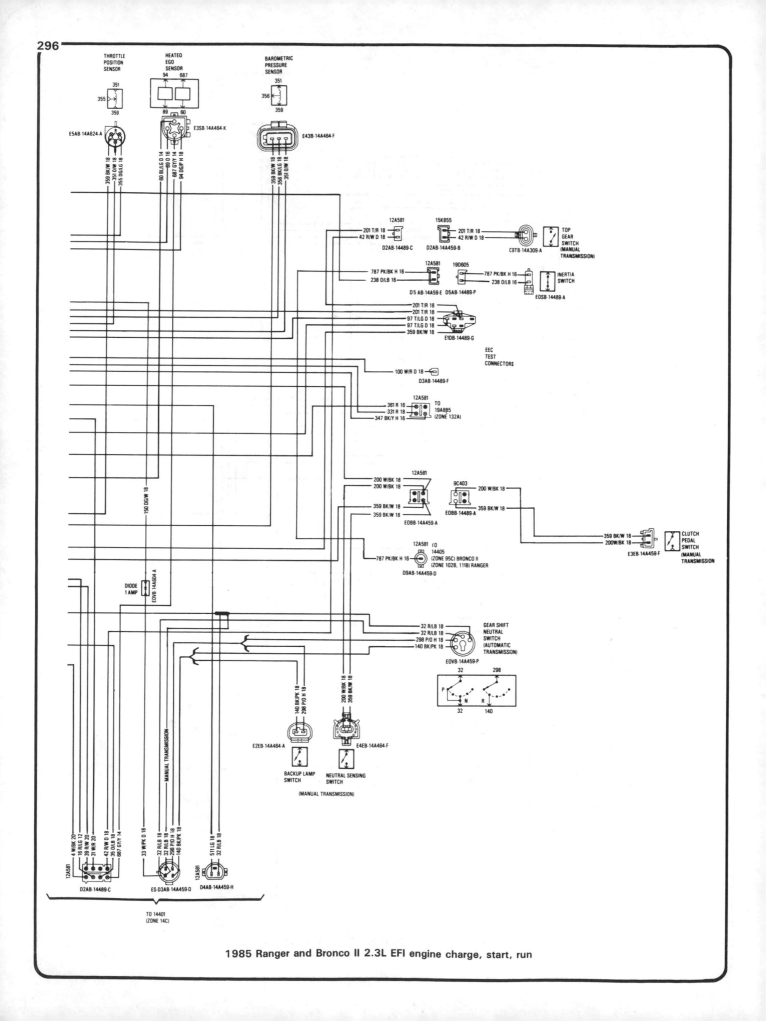

1985 Ranger and Bronco II 2.3L EFI engine charge, start, run

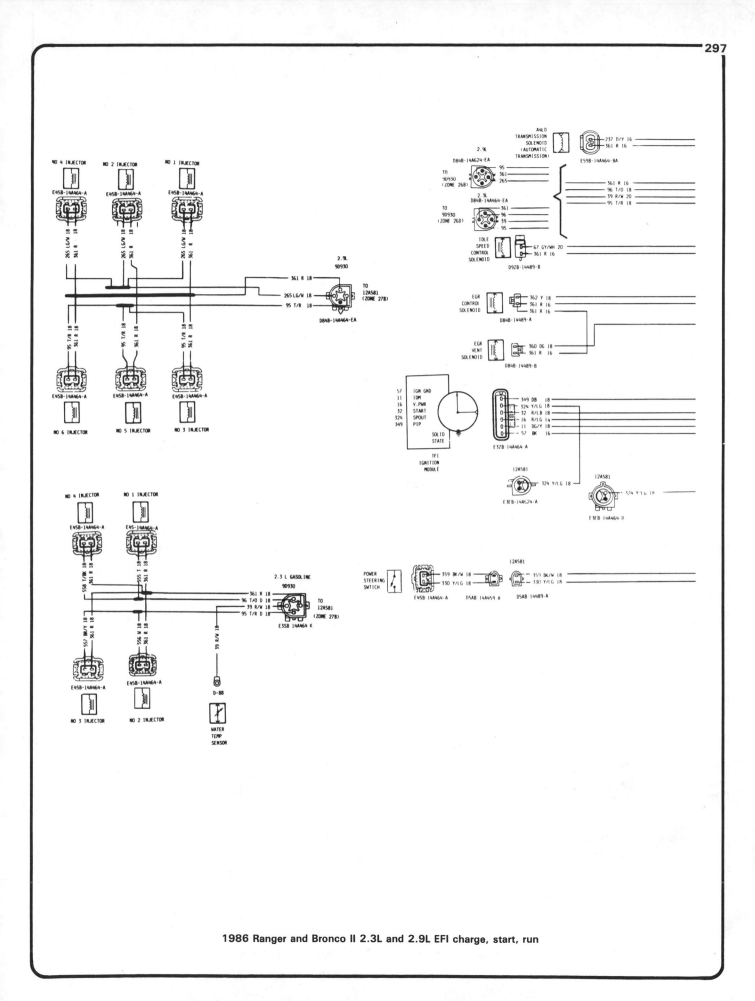

1986 Ranger and Bronco II 2.3L and 2.9L EFI charge, start, run

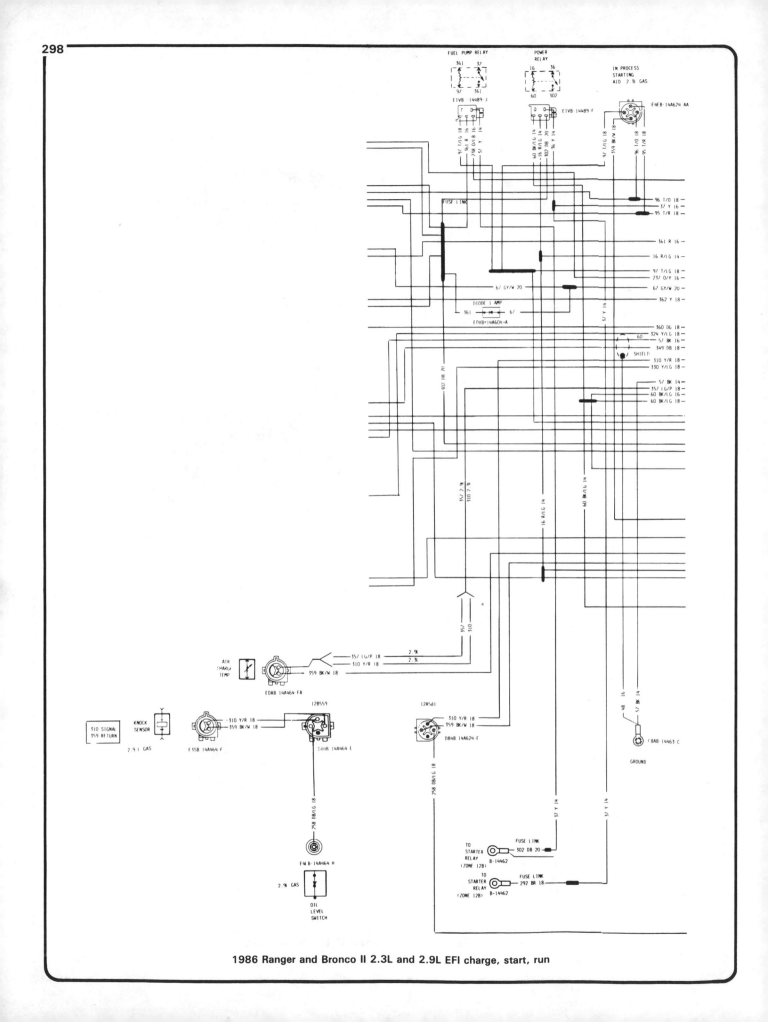

298

1986 Ranger and Bronco II 2.3L and 2.9L EFI charge, start, run

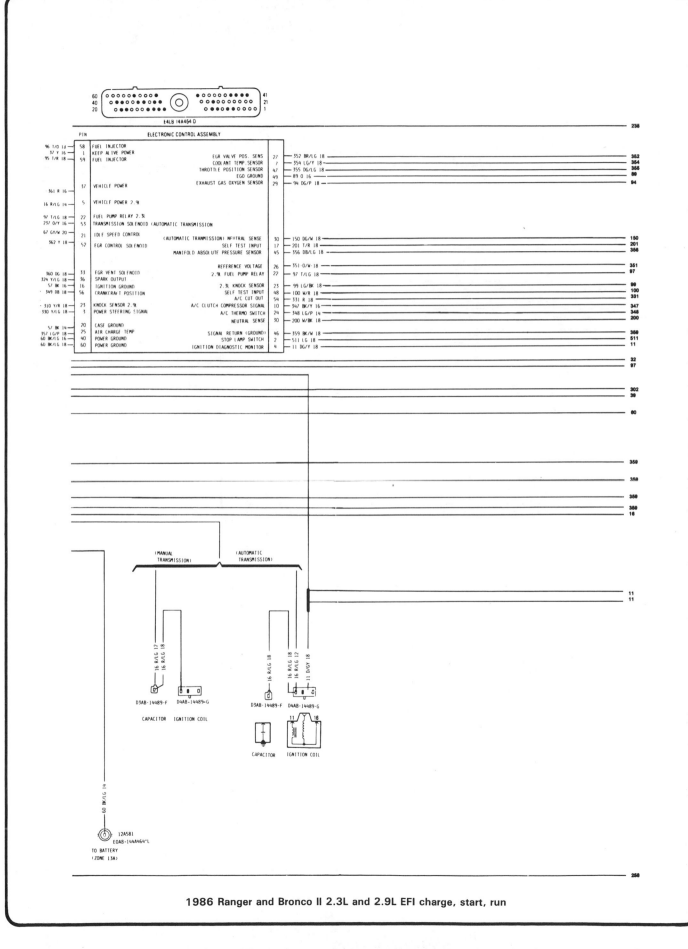

1986 Ranger and Bronco II 2.3L and 2.9L EFI charge, start, run

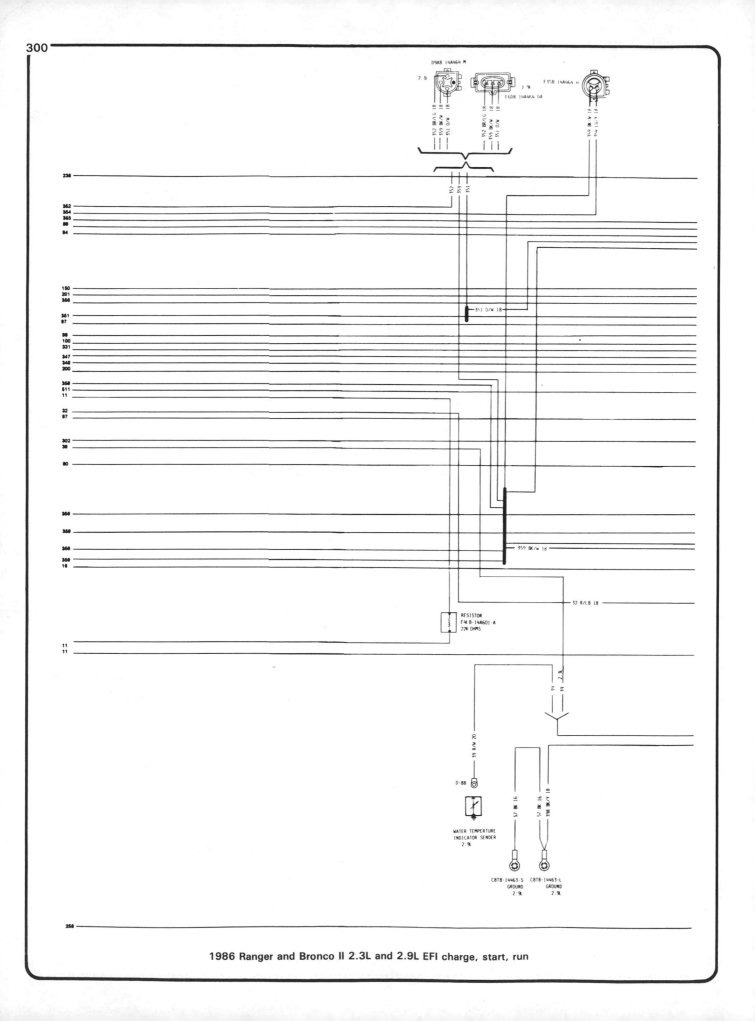

1986 Ranger and Bronco II 2.3L and 2.9L EFI charge, start, run

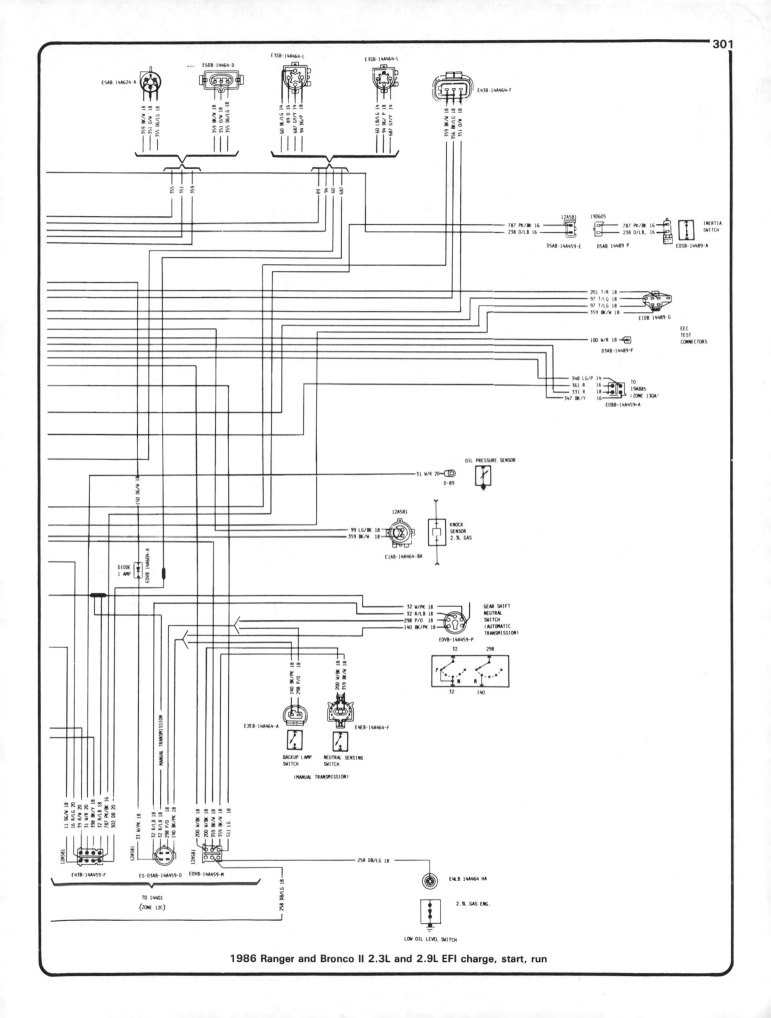

1986 Ranger and Bronco II 2.3L and 2.9L EFI charge, start, run

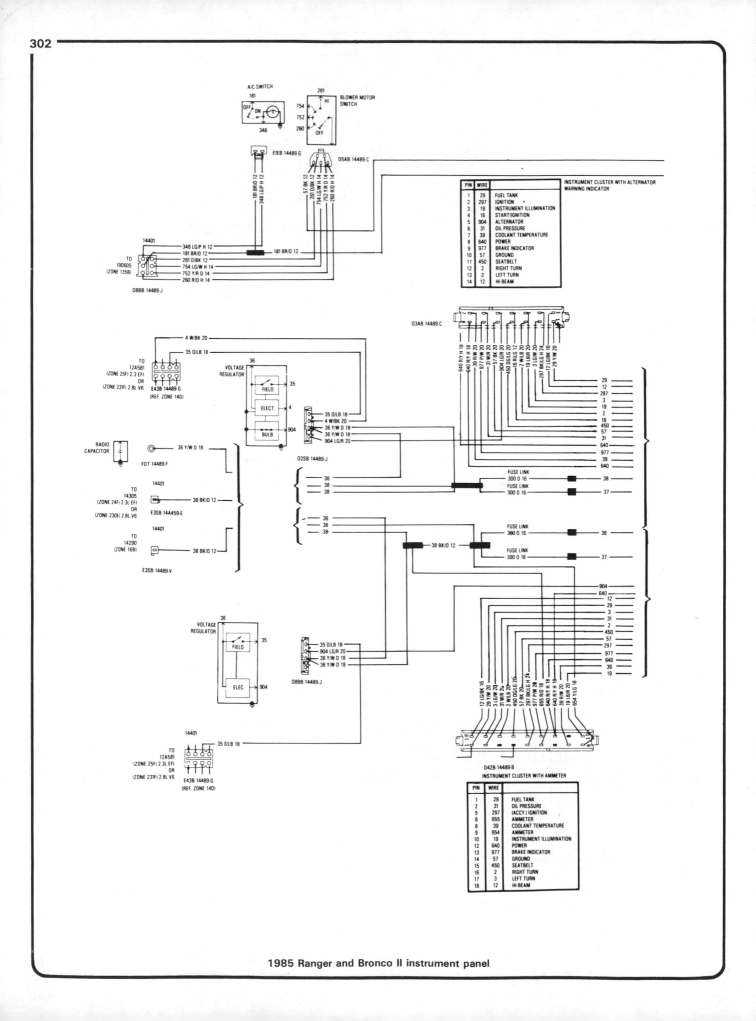

A/C SWITCH

181

OFF ON

348

BLOWER MOTOR SWITCH

261

HI

754
752
260

OFF

E1EB-14489-G

D5AB-14489-C

PIN	WIRE	
1	29	FUEL TANK
2	297	IGNITION
3	19	INSTRUMENT ILLUMINATION
4	16	START/IGNITION
5	904	ALTERNATOR
6	31	OIL PRESSURE
7	39	COOLANT TEMPERATURE
8	640	POWER
9	977	BRAKE INDICATOR
10	57	GROUND
11	450	SEATBELT
12	2	RIGHT TURN
13	3	LEFT TURN
14	12	HI-BEAM

INSTRUMENT CLUSTER WITH ALTERNATOR WARNING INDICATOR

14401

348 LG/P H 12
181 BR/O 12
261 O/BK 12
754 LG/W H 14
752 Y/R D 14
260 R/O H 14

TO
19D605
(ZONE 135B)

D8BB-14489-J

181 BR/O 12

57 BK 12
261 O/BK 14
754 LG/W H 14
752 Y/R D 14
260 R/O H 14

D3AB-14489-C

640 R/Y H 18
640 R/Y H 18
977 P/W 20
39 R/W 20
31 W/R 20
57 BK 20
904 LG/R 20
16 W/LB 20
450 DG/LG 20
2 W/LB 20
19 LB/R 20
297 BK/LG H 24
3 LG/W 20
12 LG/BK 16
29 YLG 20

VOLTAGE REGULATOR

36

FIELD 35

ELECT. 4

BULB 904

4 W/BK 20
35 O/LB 18

TO
12A581
(ZONE 25F) 2.3 EFI
OR
(ZONE 231F) 2.8L V6

E43B-14489-G
(REF. ZONE 14D)

35 O/LB 18
4 W/BK 20
36 Y/W D 18
36 Y/W D 18
904 LG/R 20

D2SB-14489-J

RADIO CAPACITOR

36 Y/W D 18

FDT-14489-F

14401

TO
14305
(ZONE 24F) 2.3L EFI
OR
(ZONE 230E) 2.8L V6

38 BK/O 12

E3SB-14A459-E

14401

TO
14290
(ZONE 16B)

38 BK/O 12

E3SB-14489-V

36
38
38

36
38
38

FUSE LINK
300 0 16

FUSE LINK
300 0 16

38
37

38 BK/O 12

FUSE LINK
300 0 16

FUSE LINK
300 0 16

38
37

29
12
297
3
19
2
16
450
57
31
640
977
39
640

904
640
12
29
3
31
2
450
57
297
977
640
39
19

VOLTAGE REGULATOR

36

FIELD 35

ELEC. 904

35 O/LB 18
904 LG/R 20
36 Y/W D 18
36 Y/W D 18

D8BB-14489-J

14401

35 O/LB 18

TO
12A581
(ZONE 25F) 2.3L EFI
OR
(ZONE 231F) 2.8L V6

E43B-14489-G
(REF. ZONE 14D)

12 LG/BK 16
29 Y/W 20
3 LG/W 20
31 W/R 20
2 W/LB 20
450 DG/LG 20
57 BK 20
297 BK/LG H 24
977 P/W 20
655 R/O 18
640 R/Y H 18
640 R/Y H 18
39 R/W 20
19 LB/R 20
654 Y/LG 18

1 18

D4ZB-14489-B
INSTRUMENT CLUSTER WITH AMMETER

PIN	WIRE	
1	29	FUEL TANK
2	31	OIL PRESSURE
5	297	(ACCY.) IGNITION
6	655	AMMETER
8	39	COOLANT TEMPERATURE
9	654	AMMETER
10	19	INSTRUMENT ILLUMINATION
12	640	POWER
13	977	BRAKE INDICATOR
14	57	GROUND
15	450	SEATBELT
16	2	RIGHT TURN
17	3	LEFT TURN
18	12	HI-BEAM

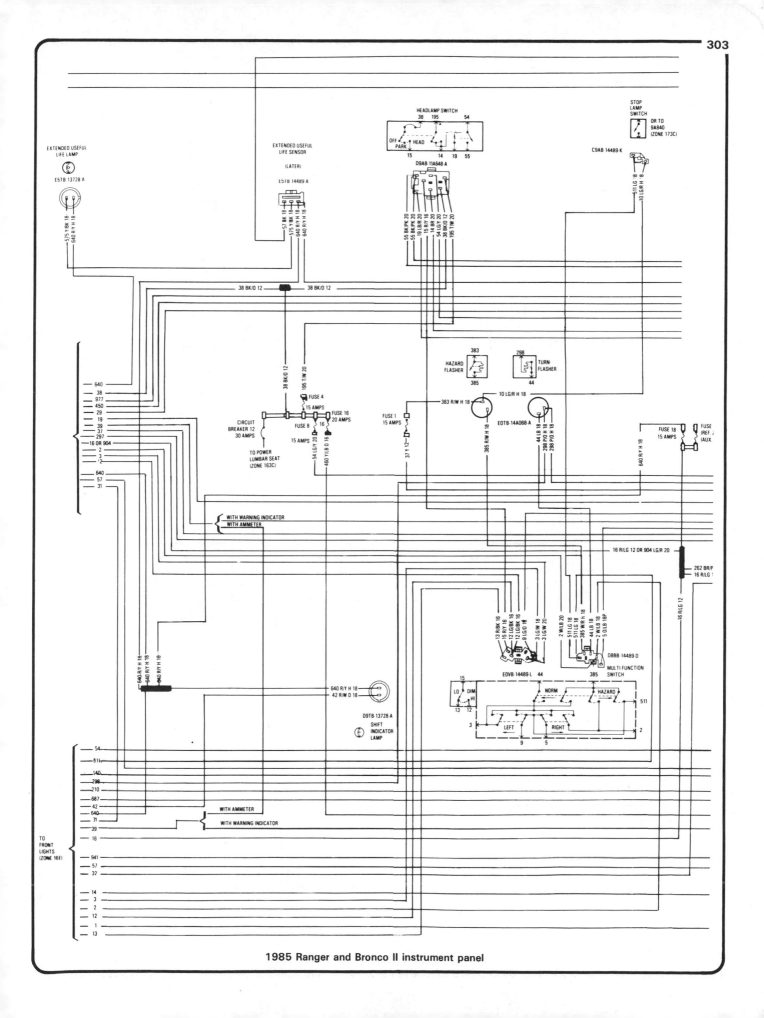

1985 Ranger and Bronco II instrument panel

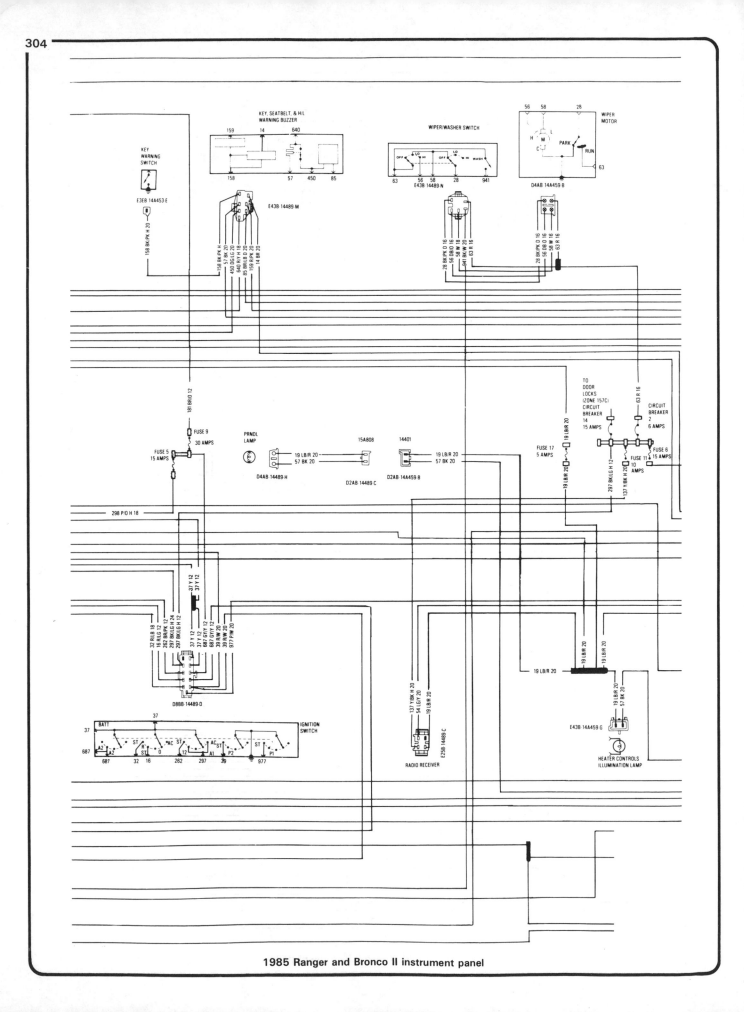

1985 Ranger and Bronco II instrument panel

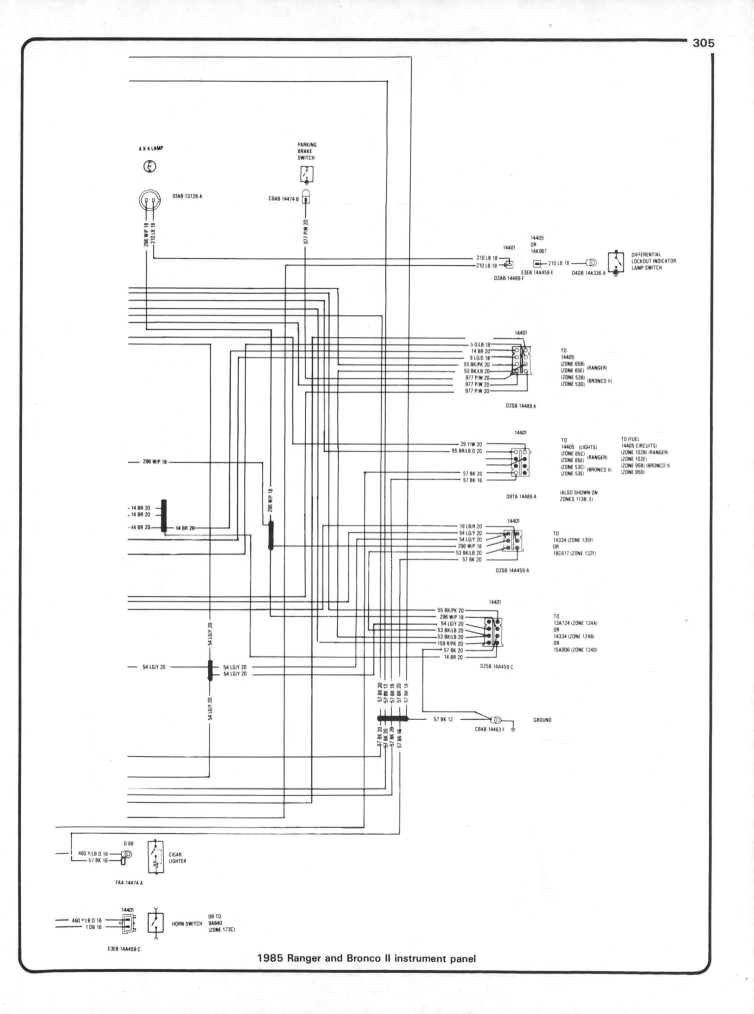

1985 Ranger and Bronco II instrument panel

306

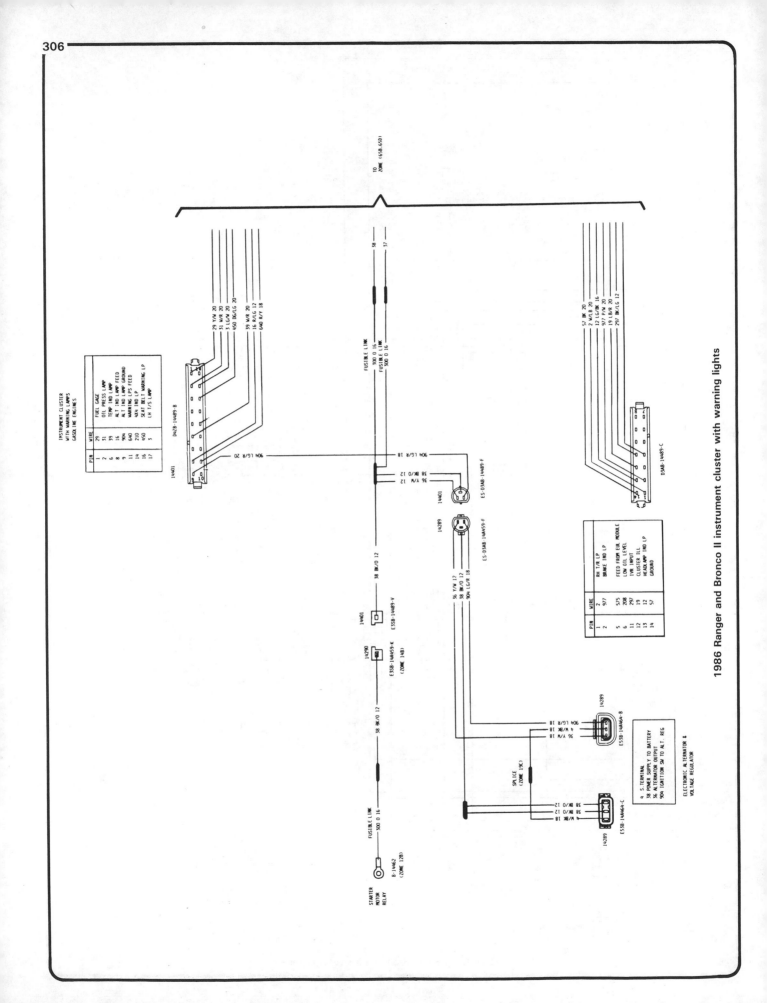

1986 Ranger and Bronco II instrument cluster with warning lights

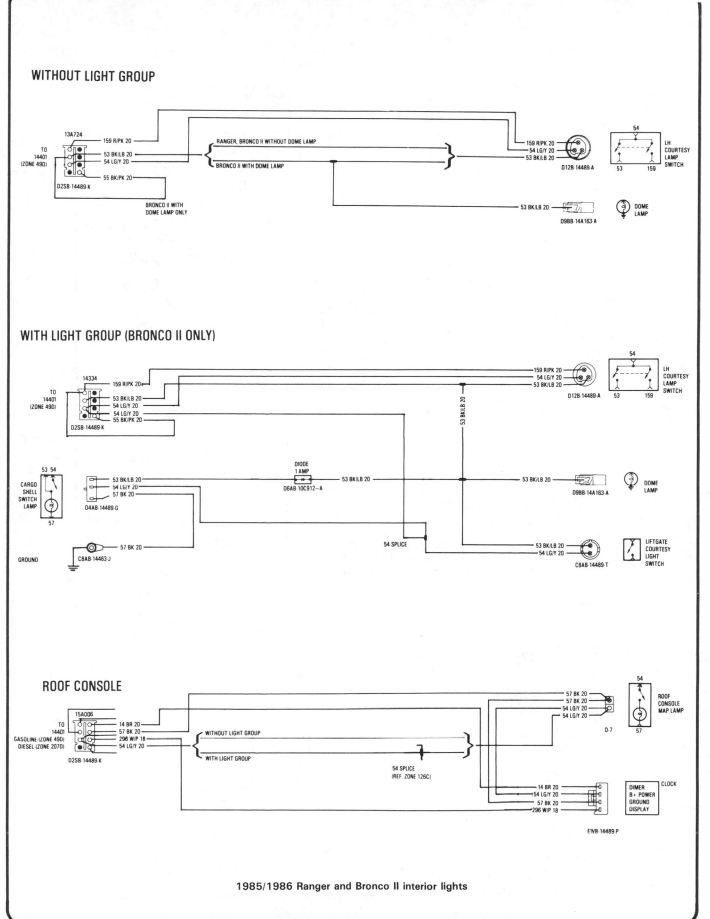

1985/1986 Ranger and Bronco II interior lights

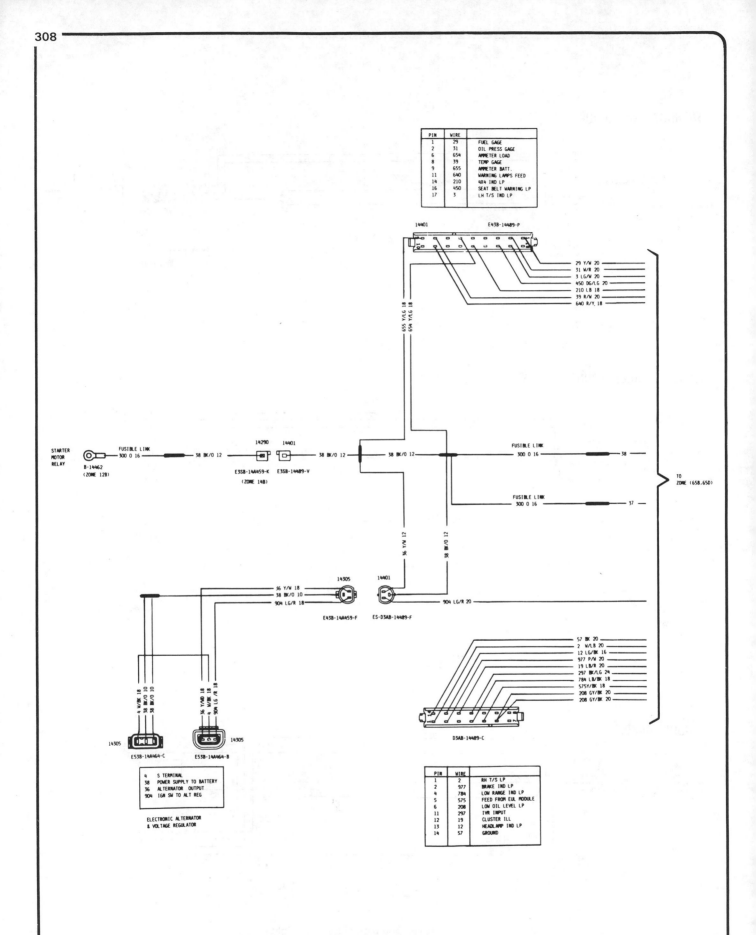

PIN	WIRE	
1	29	FUEL GAGE
2	31	OIL PRESS GAGE
6	654	AMMETER LOAD
8	39	TEMP GAGE
9	655	AMMETER BATT.
11	640	WARNING LAMPS FEED
14	210	4X4 IND LP
16	450	SEAT BELT WARNING LP
17	3	LH T/S IND LP

14401   E43B-14489-P

29 Y/W 20
31 W/R 20
3 LG/W 20
450 DG/LG 20
210 LB 18
39 R/W 20
640 R/Y, 18

655 Y/LG 18
654 Y/LG 18

STARTER
MOTOR
RELAY

FUSIBLE LINK
300 0 16   38 BK/O 12   14290   14401   38 BK/O 12   38 BK/O 12   FUSIBLE LINK   38

B-14462
(ZONE 12B)   E3SB-14A459-K   E3SB-14489-V   300 0 16

(ZONE 14B)

TO
ZONE (65B.65D)

FUSIBLE LINK
300 0 16   37

56 Y/W 12
38 BK/O 12

56 Y/W 18   14305   14401
38 BK/O 10
904 LG/R 18   904 LG/R 20

E43B-14A459-F   ES-D3AB-14489-F

57 BK 20
2 W/LB 20
12 LG/W 16
977 P/W 20
19 LB/R 20
297 BK 24
784 LB/BK 18
575Y/BK 18
208 GY/BK 20
208 GY/BK 20

4 W/BK 18
38 BK/O 10
38 BK/O 10

56 Y/WO 18
4 W/BK 18
90A LG /R 18

14305   14305

E53B-14A464-C   E53B-14A464-B

D3AB-14489-C

4	S TERMINAL
38	POWER SUPPLY TO BATTERY
36	ALTERNATOR OUTPUT
904	IGN SW TO ALT REG

ELECTRONIC ALTERNATOR
& VOLTAGE REGULATOR

PIN	WIRE	
1	2	RH T/S LP
2	977	BRAKE IND LP
4	784	LOW RANGE IND LP
5	575	FEED FROM EUL MODULE
6	208	LOW OIL LEVEL LP
11	297	IVR INPUT
12	19	CLUSTER ILL
13	12	HEADLAMP IND LP
14	57	GROUND

1986 Ranger and Bronco II instrument cluster with gauges

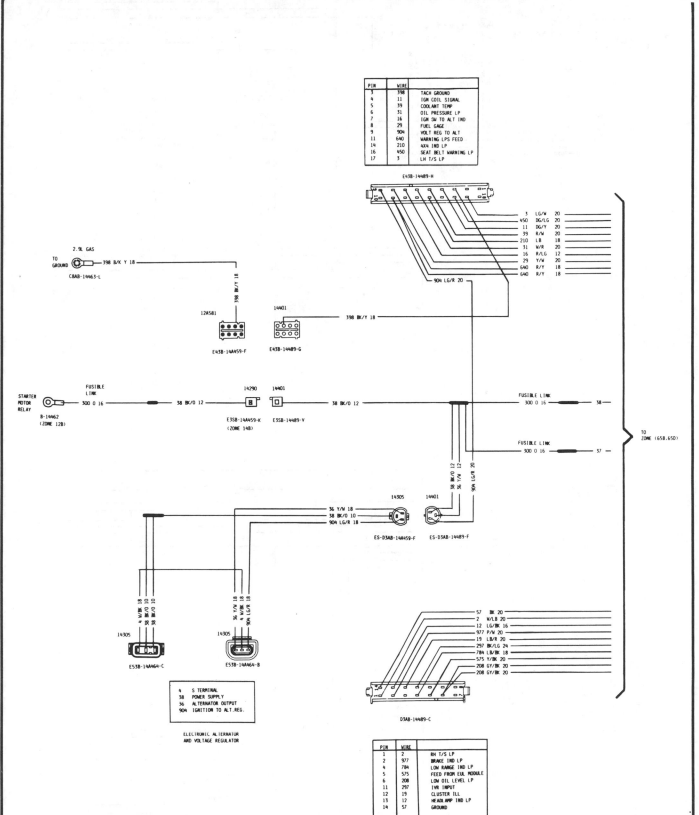

PIN	WIRE	
3	398	TACH GROUND
4	11	IGN COIL SIGNAL
5	39	COOLANT TEMP
6	31	OIL PRESSURE LP
7	16	IGN SW TO ALT IND
8	29	FUEL GAGE
9	904	VOLT REG TO ALT
11	640	WARNING LPS FEED
14	210	4X4 IND LP
16	450	SEAT BELT WARNING LP
17	3	LH T/S LP

E43B-14489-H

3	LG/W	20
450	DG/LG	20
11	DG/Y	20
39	R/W	20
210	LB	18
31	W/R	20
16	R/LG	12
29	Y/W	20
640	R/Y	18
640	R/Y	18

904 LG/R 20

2.9L GAS
TO GROUND
398 B/K Y 18
C8AB-14463-L
398 BK/Y 18

12A581
E43B-14A459-F

14401
398 BK/Y 18
E43B-14489-G

STARTER MOTOR RELAY
300 0 16
B-14462 (ZONE 12B)

FUSIBLE LINK
38 BK/O 12

14290
E3SB-14A459-K (ZONE 14B)

14401
38 BK/O 12
E3SB-14489-V

FUSIBLE LINK
300 0 16
38

FUSIBLE LINK
300 0 16
37

TO ZONE (65B,65D)

38 BK/O 12
36 Y/W 12
904 LG/R 20

36 Y/W 18
38 BK/O 10
904 LG/R 18

14305
ES-D3AB-14A459-F

14401
ES-D3AB-14489-F

4 W/BK 18
38 BK/O 10
38 BK/O 10

36 Y/W 18
4 W/BK 18
904 LG/R 18

14305
E53B-14A464-C

14305
E53B-14A464-B

4	S TERMINAL
38	POWER SUPPLY
36	ALTERNATOR OUTPUT
904	IGNITION TO ALT.REG.

ELECTRONIC ALTERNATOR AND VOLTAGE REGULATOR

57	BK	20
2	W/LB	20
12	LG/BK	16
977	P/W	20
19	LB/R	20
297	BK/LG	24
784	LB/BK	18
575	Y/BK	20
208	GY/BK	20
208	GY/BK	20

D3AB-14489-C

PIN	WIRE	
1	2	RH T/S LP
2	977	BRAKE IND LP
4	784	LOW RANGE IND LP
5	575	FEED FROM EUL MODULE
6	208	LOW OIL LEVEL LP
11	297	IVR INPUT
12	19	CLUSTER ILL
13	12	HEADLAMP IND LP
14	57	GROUND

1986 Ranger and Bronco II instrument cluster with tachometer

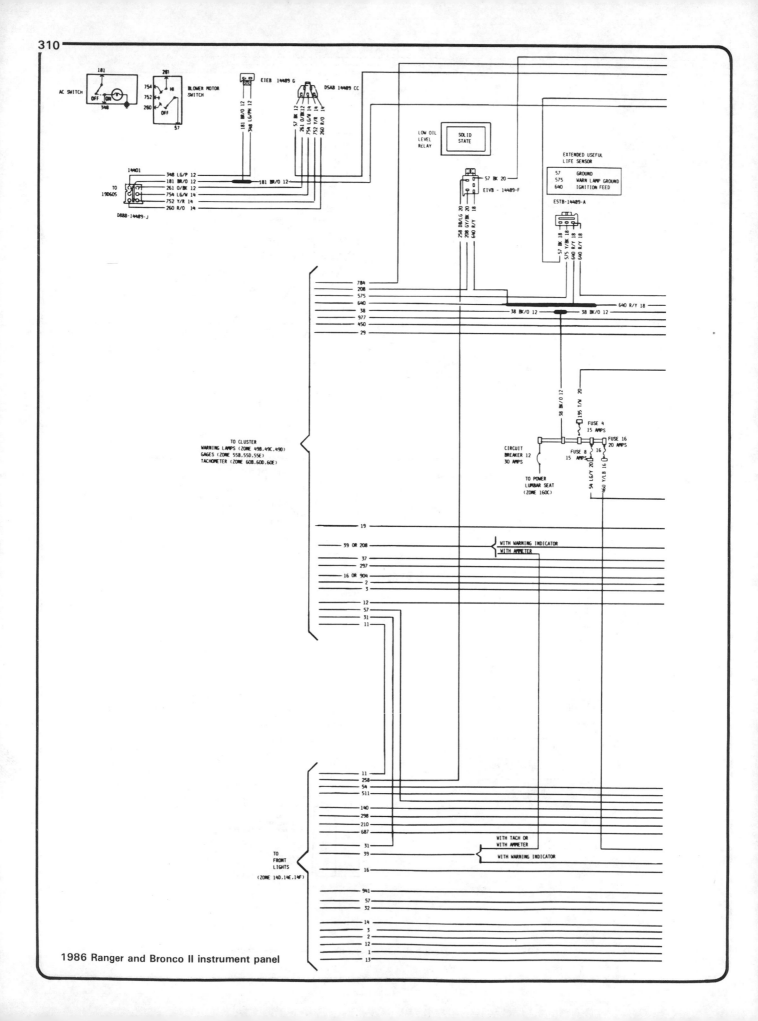

310

1986 Ranger and Bronco II instrument panel

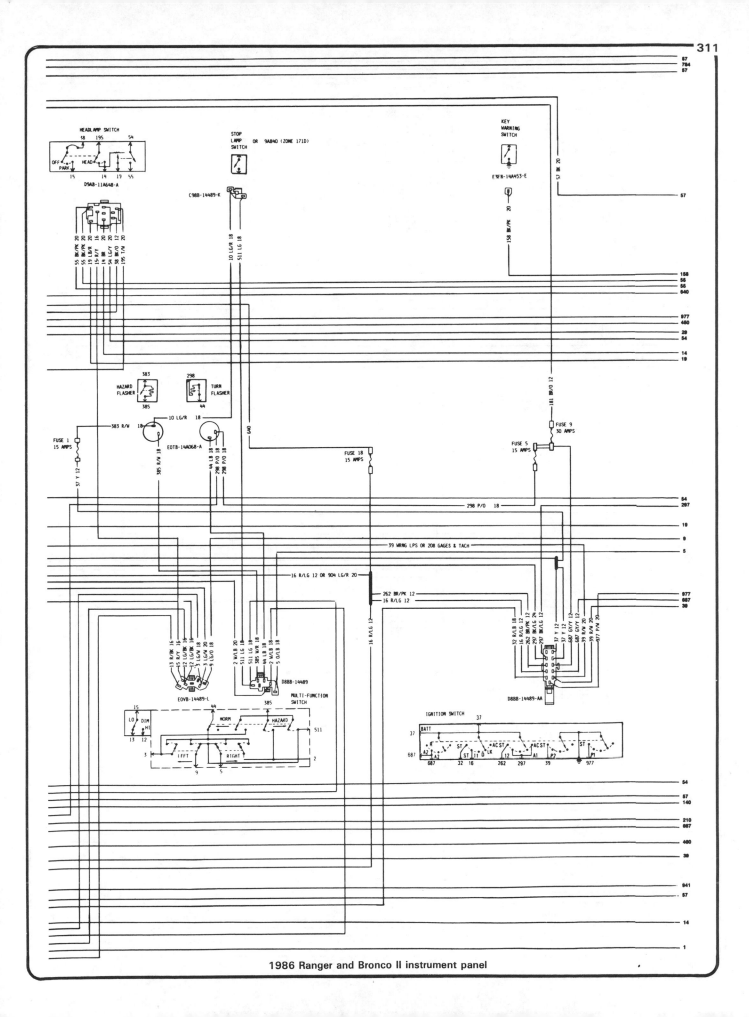

1986 Ranger and Bronco II instrument panel

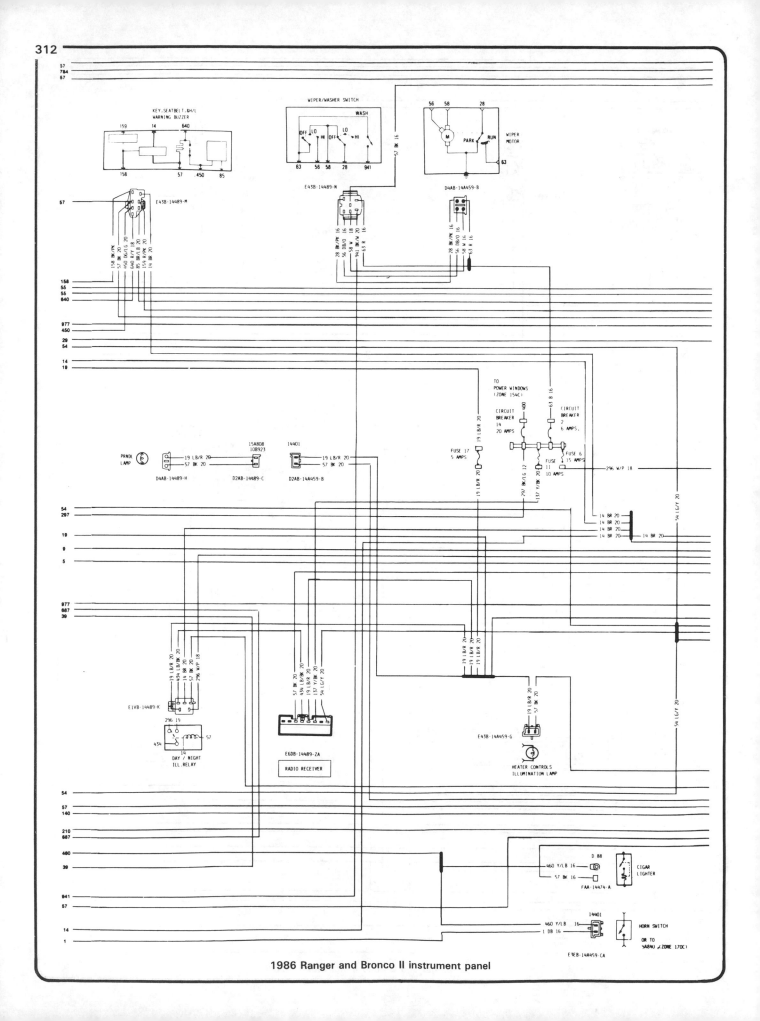

1986 Ranger and Bronco II instrument panel

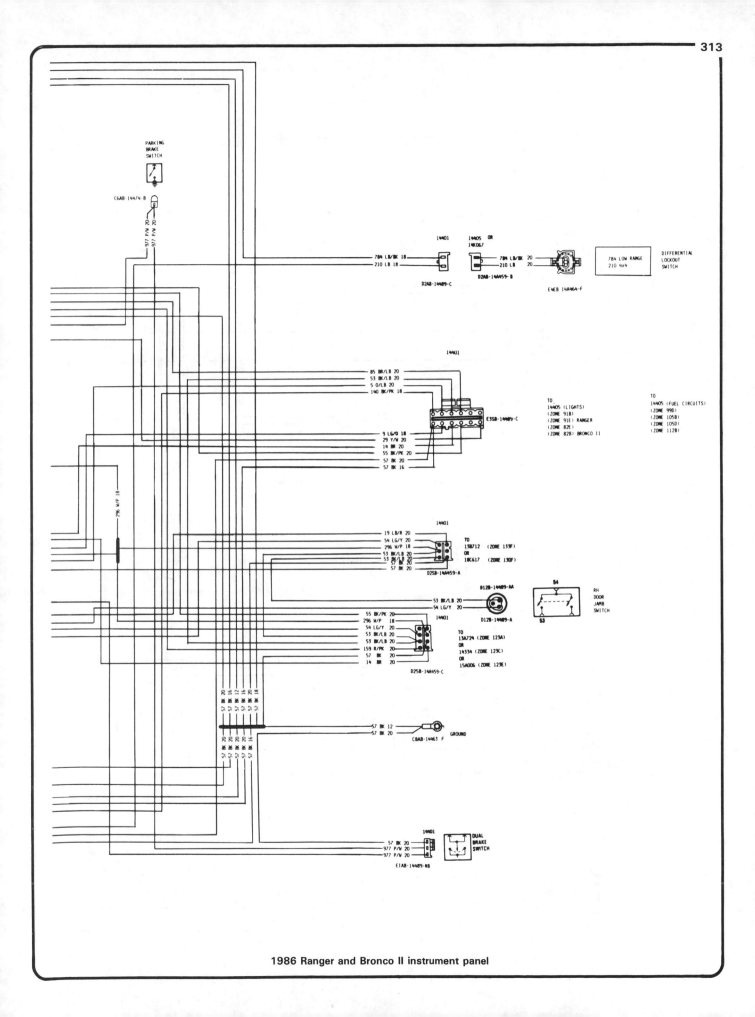

1986 Ranger and Bronco II instrument panel

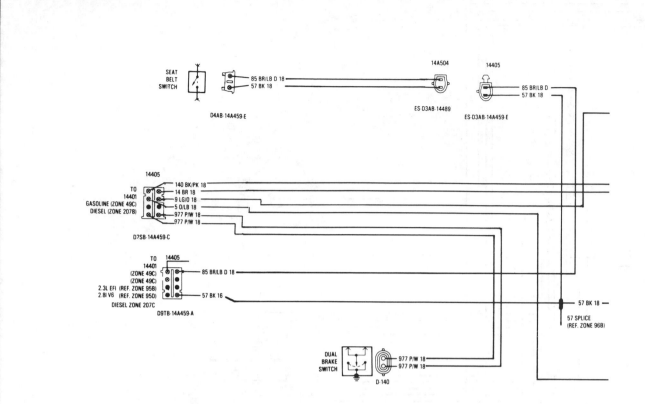

1985/1986 Bronco II rear lights without console

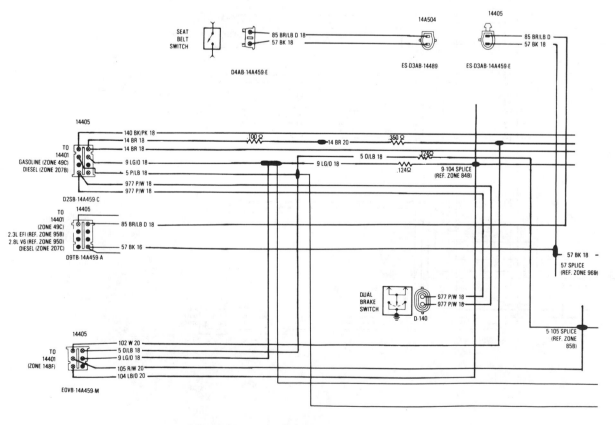

1985/1986 Bronco rear lights with console

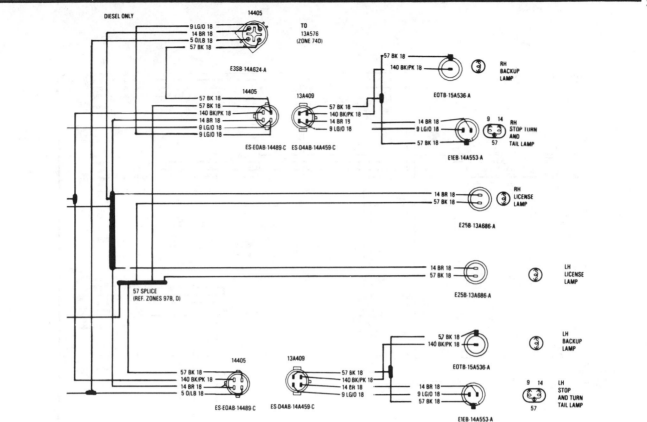

1985/1986 Bronco II rear lights without console

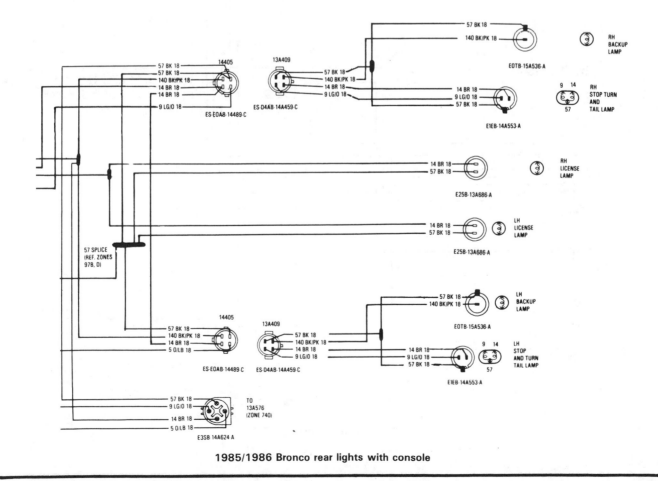

1985/1986 Bronco rear lights with console

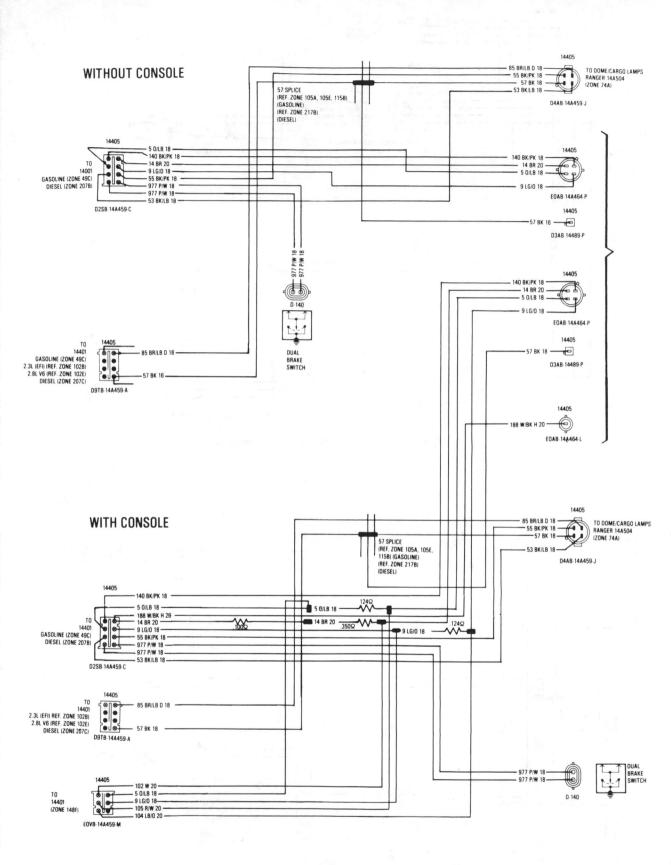

WITHOUT CONSOLE

WITH CONSOLE

1985/1986 Ranger rear-lights

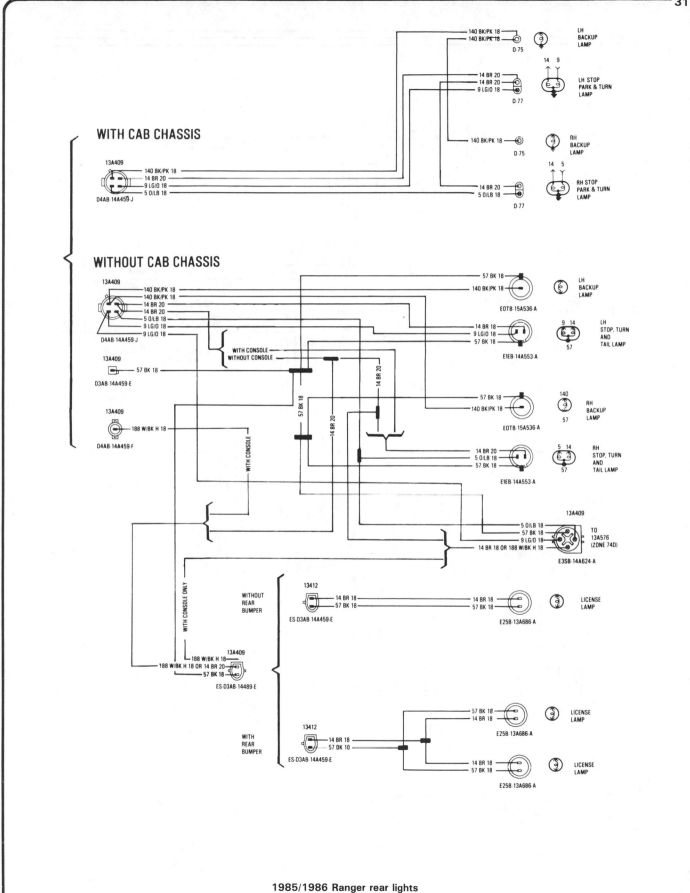

1985/1986 Ranger rear lights

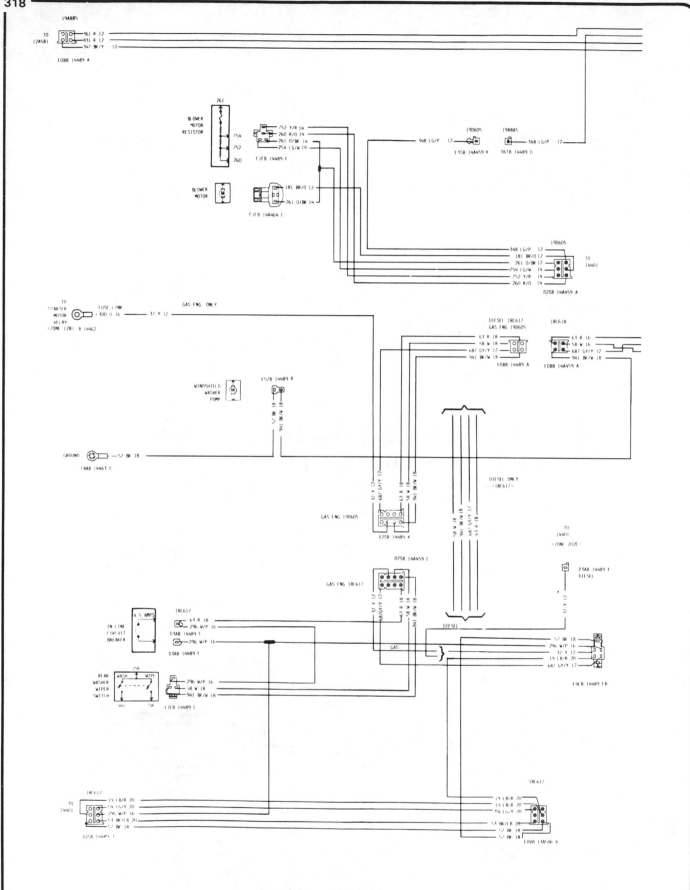

1985/1986 Ranger and Bronco II air conditioning, rear window heater and rear wiper/washer

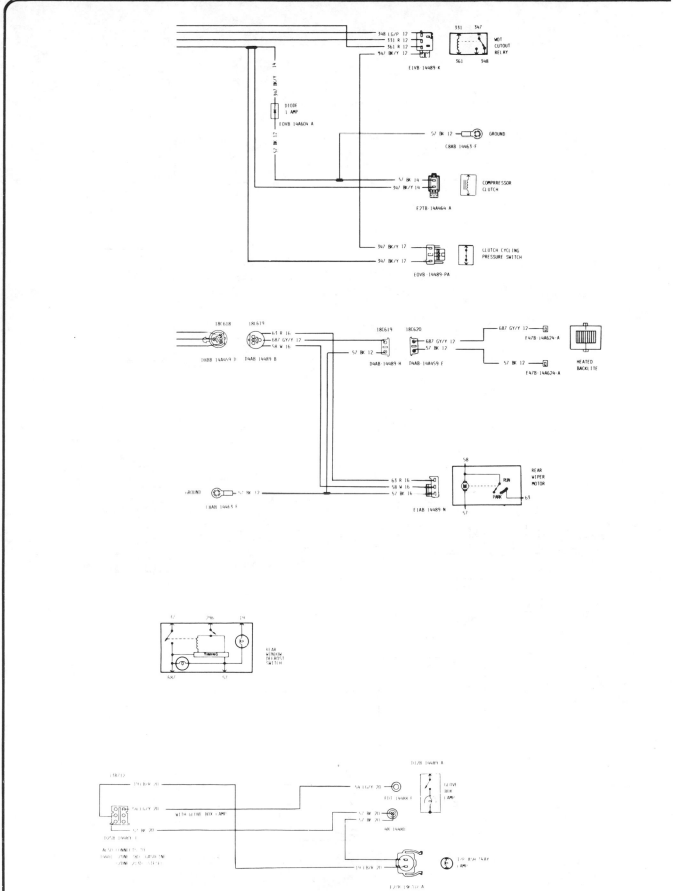

1985/1986 Ranger and Bronco II air conditioning, rear window heater and rear wiper/washer

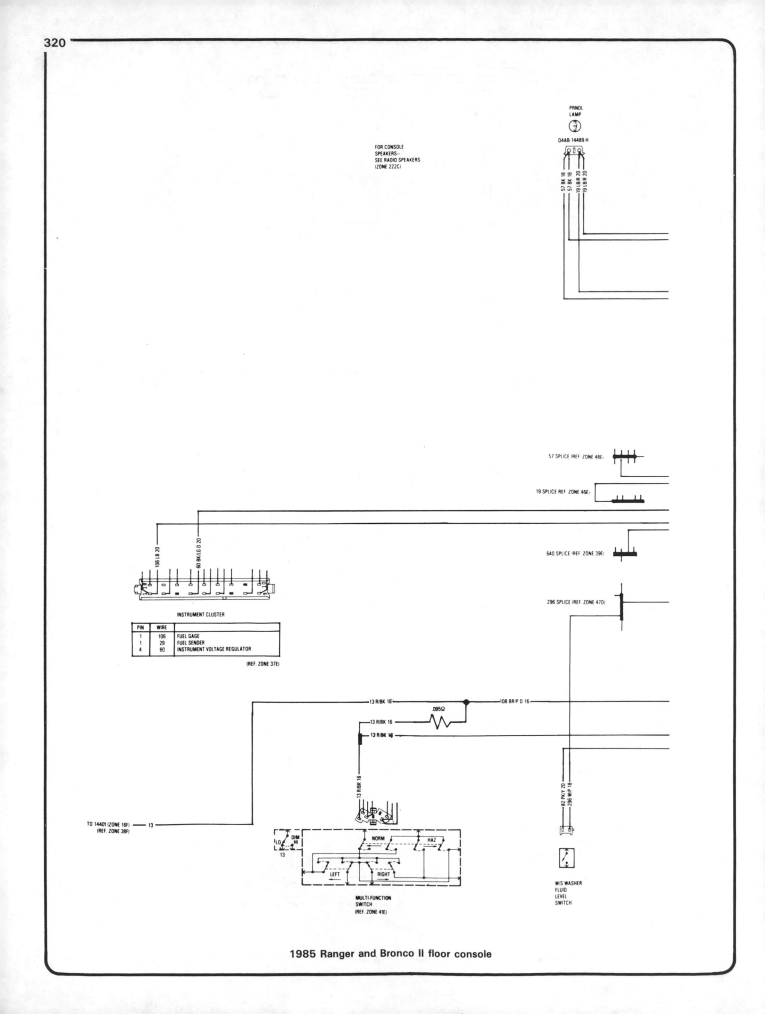

FOR CONSOLE
SPEAKERS—
SEE RADIO SPEAKERS
(ZONE 222C)

PRNDL
LAMP

D4AB-14489-H

57 BK 18
57 BK 18
19 LB/R 20
19 LB/R 20

57 SPLICE (REF. ZONE 48E)

19 SPLICE REF. ZONE 46E)

640 SPLICE (REF. ZONE 39E)

296 SPLICE (REF. ZONE 47D)

106 LB 20
60 BK/LG D 20

INSTRUMENT CLUSTER

PIN	WIRE	
1	106	FUEL GAGE
1	29	FUEL SENDER
4	60	INSTRUMENT VOLTAGE REGULATOR

(REF. ZONE 37E)

13 R/BK 16   .095Ω   108 BR/P D 16

13 R/BK 16

13 R/BK 16

13 R/BK 16

TO 14401 (ZONE 16F) — 13
(REF. ZONE 38F)

13

DIM
LO   HI

NORM   HAZ

LEFT   RIGHT

MULTI-FUNCTION
SWITCH
(REF. ZONE 41E)

82 PK/Y 20
296 W/P 18

W/S WASHER
FLUID
LEVEL
SWITCH

1985 Ranger and Bronco II floor console

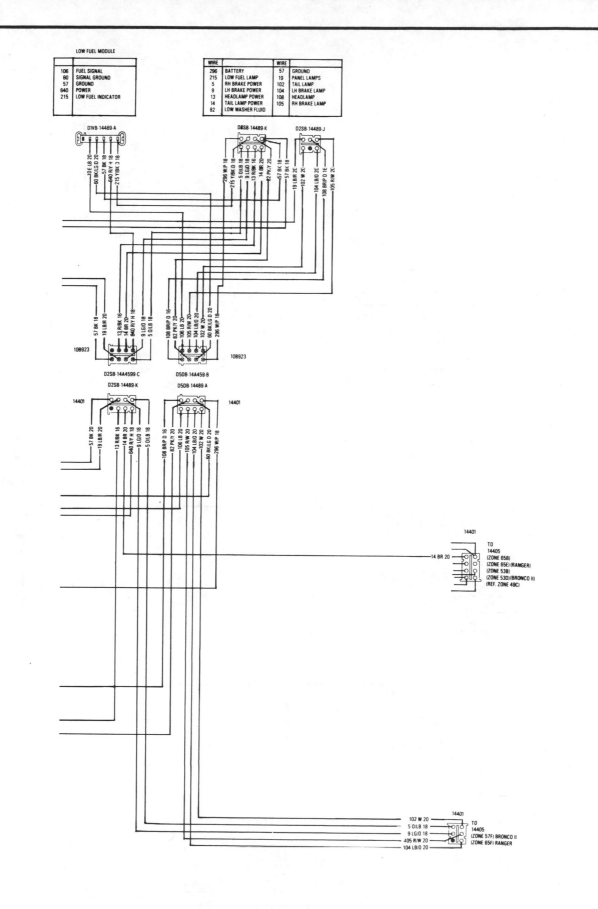

LOW FUEL MODULE

106	FUEL SIGNAL
60	SIGNAL GROUND
57	GROUND
640	POWER
215	LOW FUEL INDICATOR

WIRE		WIRE	
296	BATTERY	57	GROUND
215	LOW FUEL LAMP	19	PANEL LAMPS
5	RH BRAKE POWER	102	TAIL LAMP
9	LH BRAKE POWER	104	LH BRAKE LAMP
13	HEADLAMP POWER	108	HEADLAMP
14	TAIL LAMP POWER	105	RH BRAKE LAMP
82	LOW WASHER FLUID		

1985 Ranger and Bronco II floor console

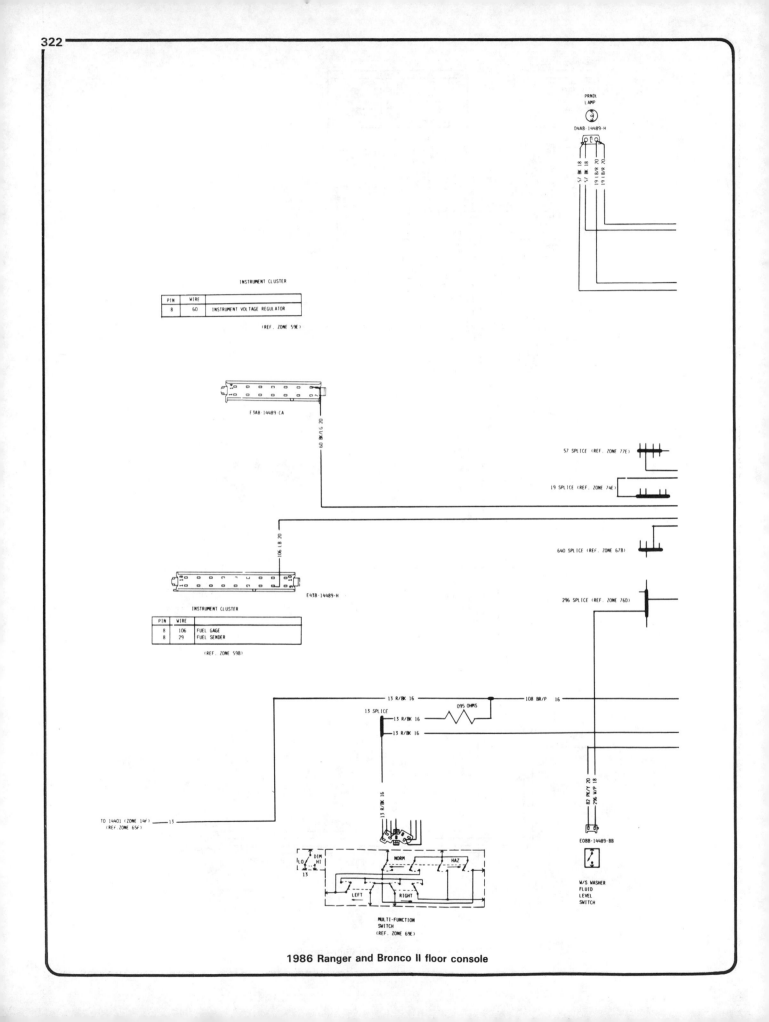

1986 Ranger and Bronco II floor console

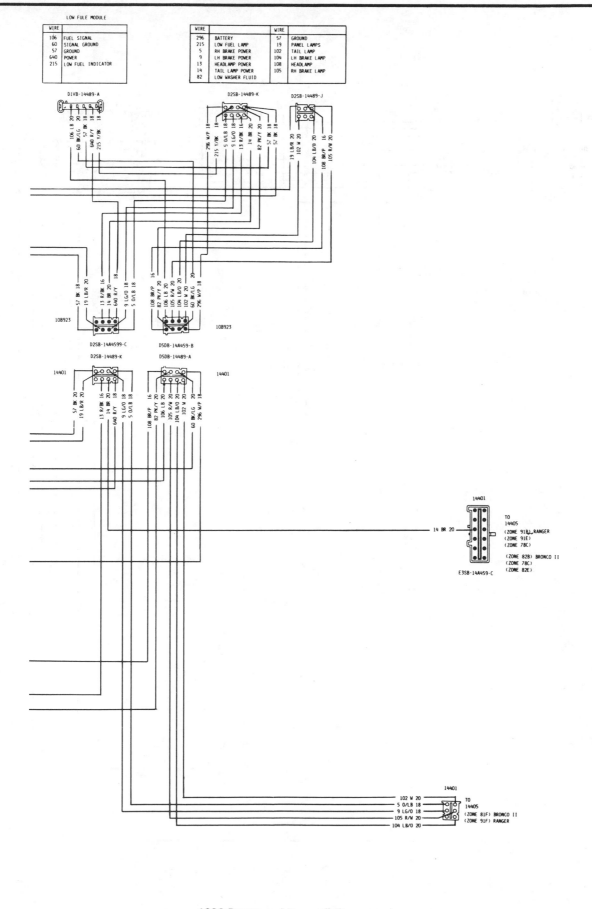

1986 Ranger and Bronco II floor console

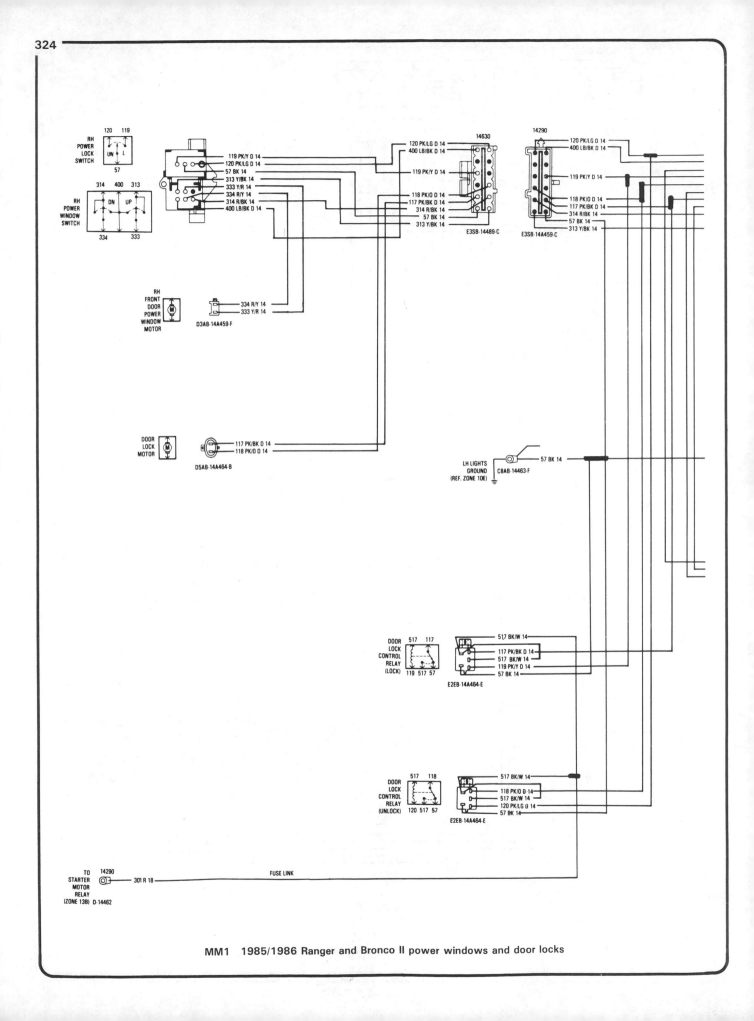

MM1   1985/1986 Ranger and Bronco II power windows and door locks

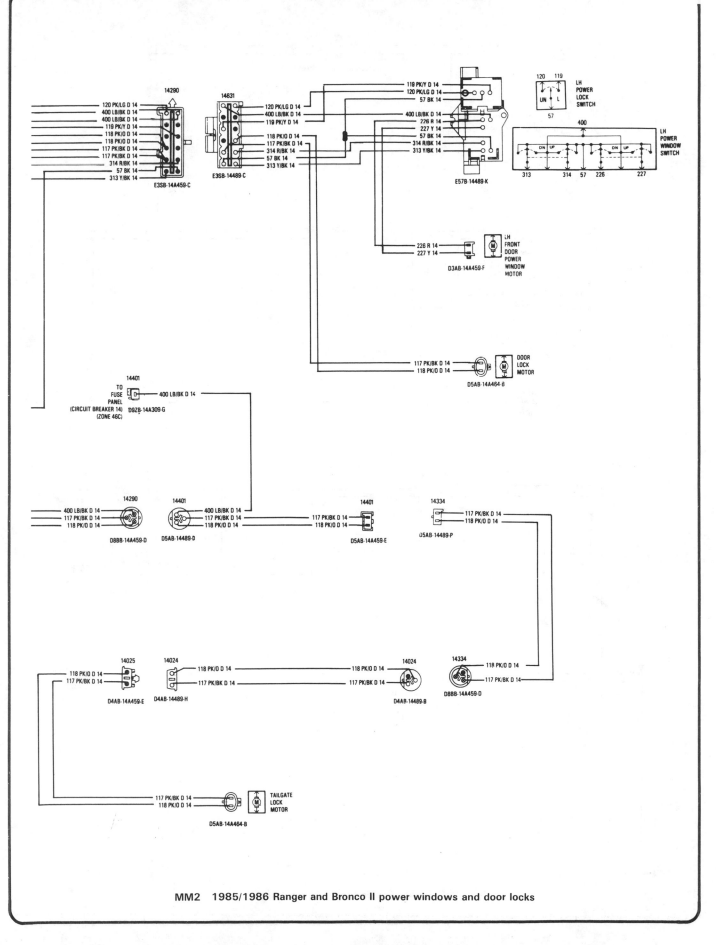

MM2 1985/1986 Ranger and Bronco II power windows and door locks

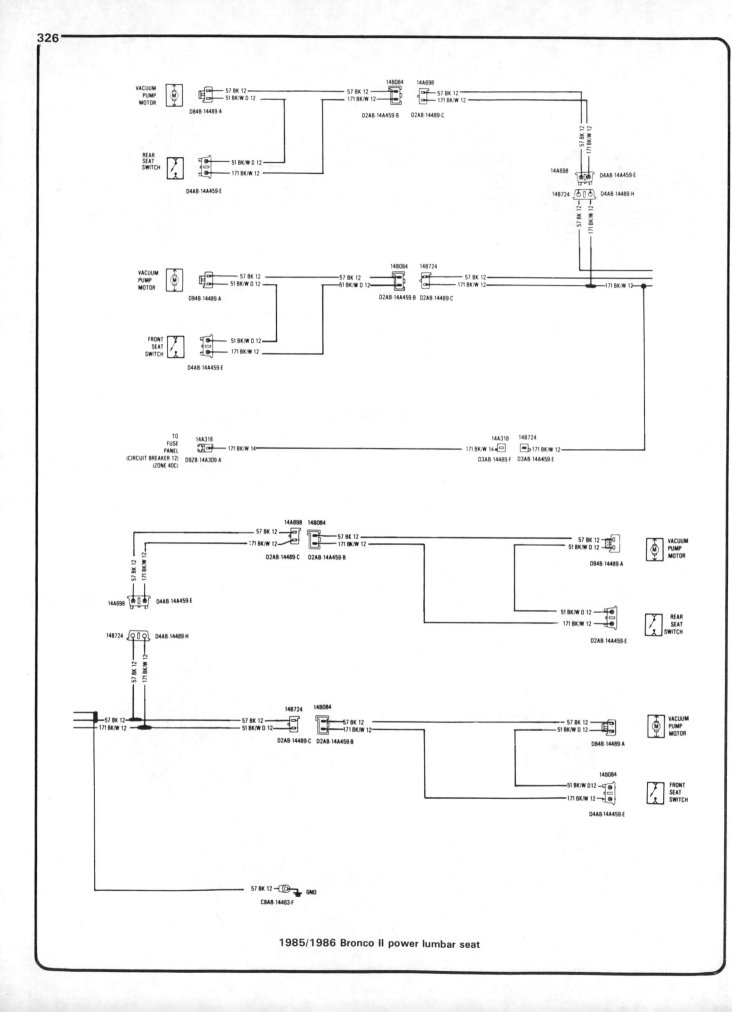

1985/1986 Bronco II power lumbar seat

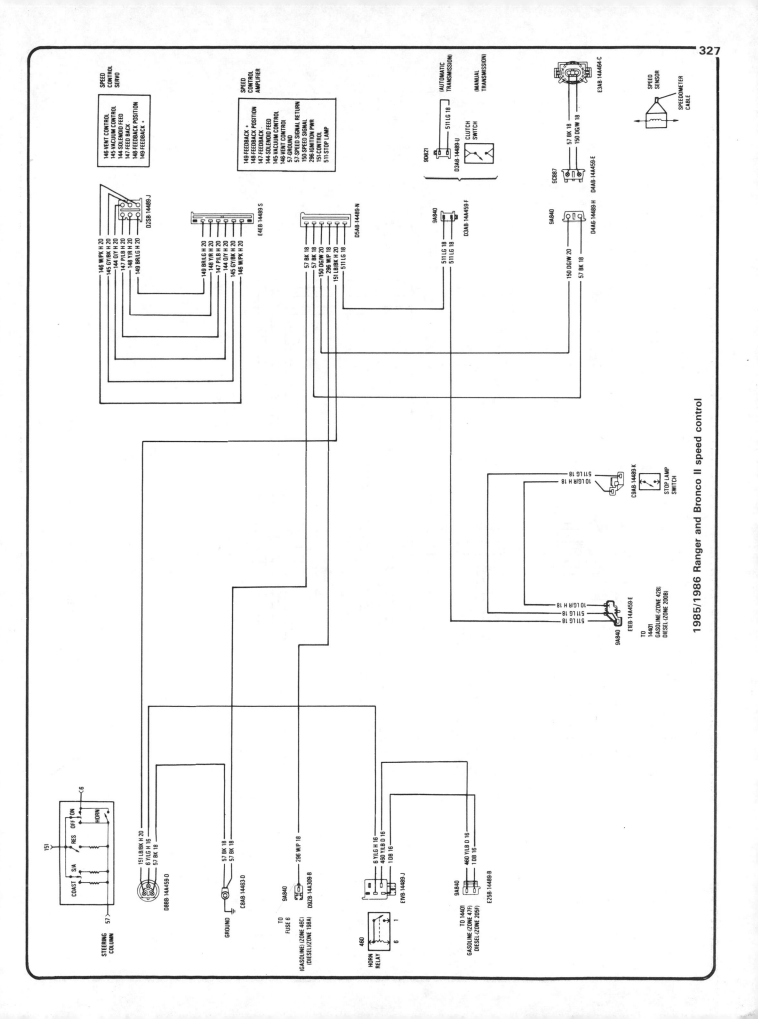

1985/1986 Ranger and Bronco II speed control

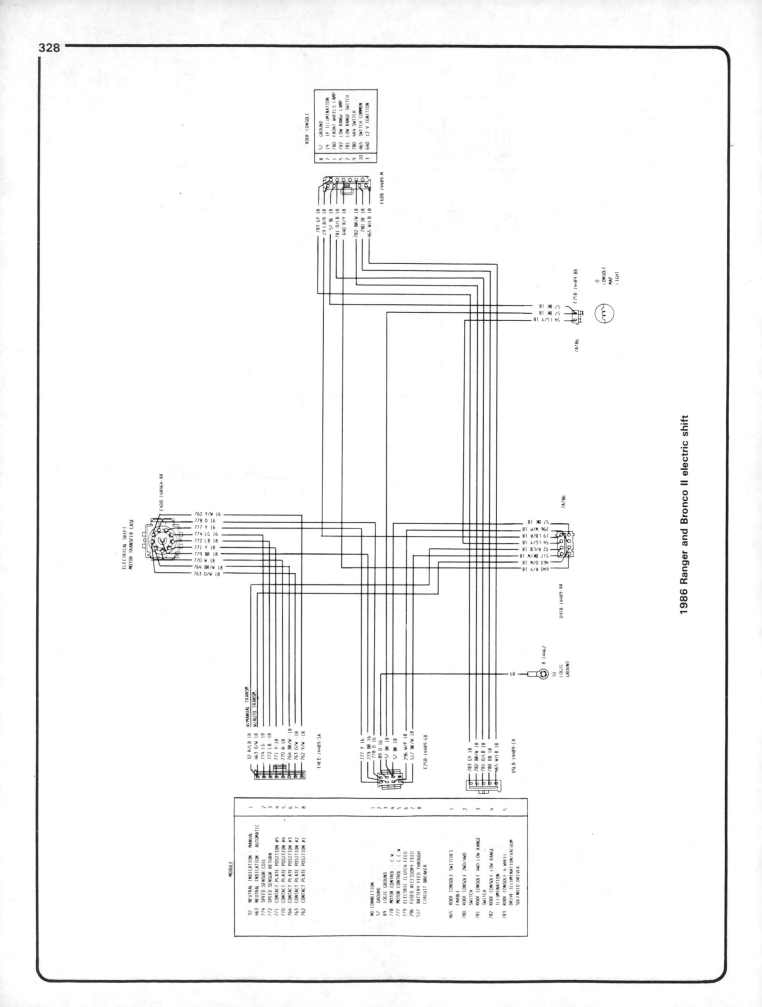

1986 Ranger and Bronco II electric shift

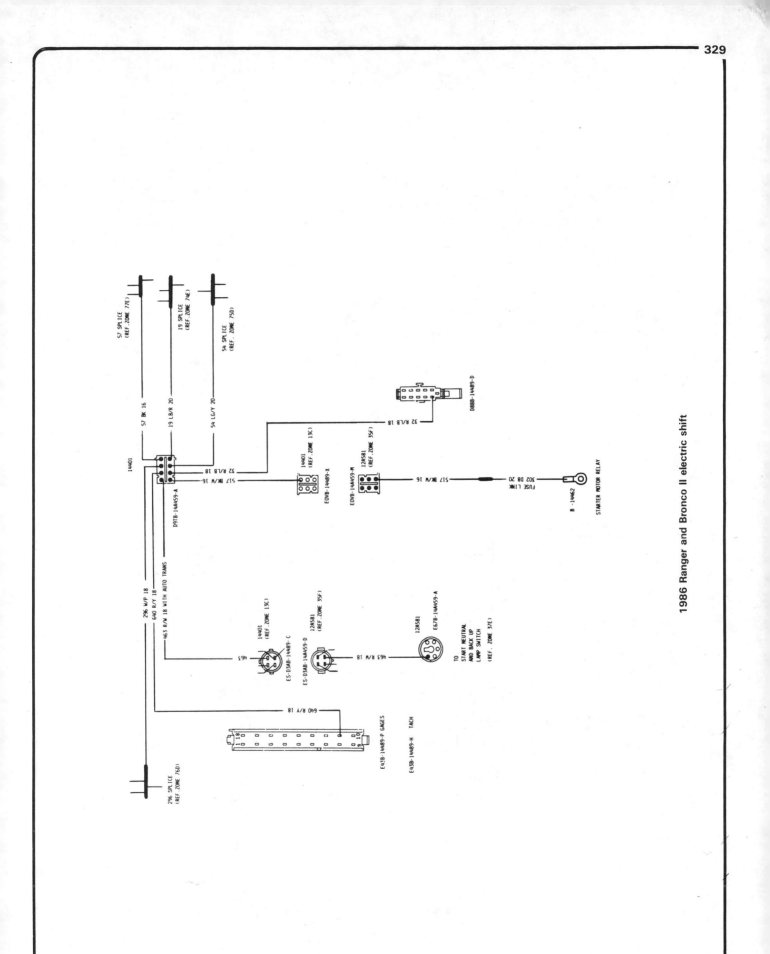

1986 Ranger and Bronco II electric shift

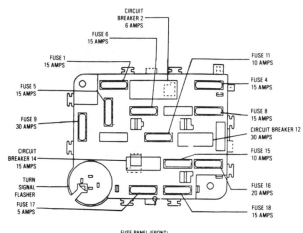

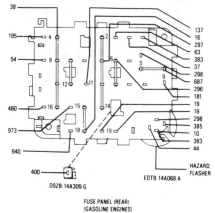

FUSE PANEL (FRONT)
(GASOLINE ENGINES)

FUSE PANEL (REAR)
(GASOLINE ENGINES)

1985 Ranger and Bronco II fuse panel

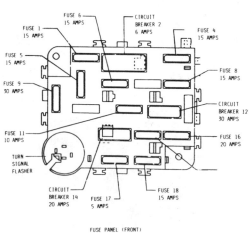

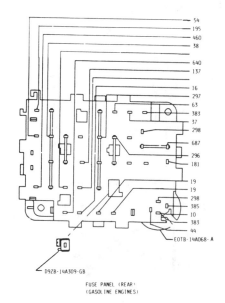

FUSE PANEL (FRONT)
(GASOLINE ENGINES)

FUSE PANEL (REAR)
(GASOLINE ENGINES)

1986 Ranger and Bronco II fuse panel

Index